THE HALT PERSPECTIVE 2

Colonel Charles Irwin Halt
USAF Retired

in collaboration with

Retired UK West Midlands Police Detective
John Hanson

THE HALT PERSPECTIVE 2

Copyright © 2021 Charles Halt and John Hanson. All rights reserved.

A catalogue record for this book is available from the British Library.

ISBN 978-0-9956428-8-1

No part of this book shall be reproduced or transmitted in any form or by any means, electronic or mechanical, including photocopying, recording, or by any information retrieval system without written permission of the publisher.

Published by *Haunted Skies Publishing*

Copies of this book will be available on Amazon.com

For any comments please email: john.hanson.ee@gmail.com or johndawn1@sky.com
Telephone: UK mobile 07983766958 – UK landline 01214066824

Designed and typeset by Bob Tibbitts

Although every precaution has been taken in the preparation of this book, the publisher and author assume no responsibility for errors or omissions. Neither is any liability assumed for damages resulting from the use of this information contained within.

THE HALT PERSPECTIVE 2

This volume celebrates the commitment taken by retired USAF Colonel Charles Irwin Halt, now in his 80th year – often in the face of adversity and media ignorance – to create awareness of the existence of a phenomenon that continues to haunt the skies of the world, on what is now the 40th Anniversary of the UFO incident that took place in Rendlesham Forest, Suffolk, England at the end of December 1980.

"It is simply that, in the long run, the sheer weight of observational evidence finally broke down the barriers of disbelief."

(Source: 'Other Worlds Than Ours' *C. Maxwell Cade*)

THE HALT PERSPECTIVE 2

THE HALT PERSPECTIVE 2

CONTENTS

COLONEL CHARLES IRWIN HALT will comment on many inexplicable UFO sightings brought to his attention by John Hanson, during 25 years of research from the mid to late 20th Century, both in the US and UK. He agrees that the events which took place in Rendlesham Forest, Suffolk, just outside the American Air Base – now over 40 years ago – which have excited the imagination of the public, should not be judged in its singularity. Surely common sense dictates that any judgement as to what happened in December 1980 cannot be reached without taking into consideration the enormous number of sightings of UFO activity, including many which took place in the East Anglia region. Never mind elsewhere! These include important interviews with pilots and senior RAF officers. Followed by respects paid to the work and life of the late Washington-based UFO researcher, Richard 'Dick' 'H' Hall who was a friend of Colonel Halt. *Our journey begins…*

1943: A look at the early years of the phenomenon. **Alien being** seen near RAF Ludham Norfolk. **1945**: RAF pilot opens fire on UFO. **1947**: Lt Colonel's 'death bed' confession; meets 'alien' being from Roswell crash! Did **'aliens' land in Herefordshire? 1948: US pilot dies** while attempting to intercept UFO – up-to-date investigation. **1950**: RAF Wartling tracks UFOs on radar. **Did a UFO cause airliner to crash?** RAF pilot sights **'Flying Discus'**. UFO seen over RAF Farnborough. **Landed UFO Philadelphia! 1951**: 'Diamond'-shaped UFO sighted over RAF Church Lawford, Northants. **1952**: Huge 'wave' of sightings reported. **US pilots sight eight UFOs over Virginia – Later tracked on radar!** UFOs seen over the **White House, Washington.** Five 'lights' seen – tracked on radar by US navy pilots. RAF pilots sight UFO over RAF Topcliffe Yorkshire. RAF personnel at Neatishead track six plots! Questions raised in the **House of Commons** seven years later! **1953: RAF pilots sight three UFOs over Gloucestershire.** Five 'saucers' over Dorset. 'Flying Saucer' over Essex. 'Flying Saucer' sighted over East Anglia. RAF pilot sights **UFO with 'stabilising fins'** over Wiltshire. **1954**: A brief look at early Australian/New Zealand UFO sightings – includes, Flying 'Mushroom' over Melbourne. **UFO sighted by schoolboys – Prince Philip takes an interest!** Formation of UFOs seen over Coventry. **Mysterious black sphere** seen over RAF Church Lawford. **Australia:** UFO sighted over railway train. **Three UFOs** over Eastern Taranaki. BOAC pilots sight UFOs. UFO photographed at Oyster Cove, Queensland. RAAF pilot sights **saucer-shaped objects, tracked on radar**. RAF pilot Lt. James Salandin M.B.E. encounters, **three UFOs over Essex**. RAF pilot sights UFO over Biggleswade. **1955: Claims that UFO snatched up jet aircraft!** Meteor or UFO? RAF scrambled! Flying Saucer lands in London. Mysterious event at Kentucky USA, alien or ghostly spectres? New York, UFOs seen over Titicus Reservoir. Strange craft sighted over London. **1956: RAF Bentwaters tracks UFOs on radar, US jet scrambled. Radar stations put on alert. 1957:** 'Saucer'-shaped object seen over Esso refinery, England. Pilot reports UFO over Lincolnshire. **USAF pilot ordered to fire on UFO!** UFO tracked on radar. UFOs tracked on Scottish radar. **RAF scrambled over Hampshire, UFOs tracked on Radar.** Questions asked in the House of Commons. Pilot reports UFO over Lincolnshire. USAF pilot ordered to open fire! 'Flying Saucers', cigar-shaped, cylindrical, hexagonal objects and glowing lights seen, moving through the sky during this year. **1966**: Cheshire Police Constable's encounter with UFO. Wiltshire man encounters UFO, marks to chest. London man photographs 'Flying Saucer.' Selected UFO reports from **1967/1968/1969/1970/1971/1972/1973/1974/1975/1976/1977.**

Part 2 – Spotlight on 1980 – Pages 159 to 205 (125 sightings recorded for this year). Colonel Charles Irwin Halt a man of impeccable character: A look at his awards and his career.

Part 3 – Pages 207 to 274 December in Suffolk. Colonel Halt comments on reports brought to his attention, from the late 1970's outlined previously, including sightings near the Airbase, and the East Anglia area. Then describes what he witnessed during the eventful nights running over the end of December 1980, and of the roles

THE HALT PERSPECTIVE 2

played by others, including Adrian Bustinza, Jim Penniston and Michael Stacy Smith. Other points of interest include the passing of **Colonel Alan Brown, a close friend of General Gordon Williams**, and putting the record straight with regard to a host of fanciful allegations, and then his personal reflections of what he witnessed.

Part 4 – **Pages 275 to 320 UK spotlight on 1981-2008.** UFO sighted above the Forest during January 1981, by a serviceman. **A strange incident at Orford Ness**, lighthouse keeper tells his tale! **Close Encounters involving injury and other ailments. Mysterious occurrence on the flight line at RAF Bentwaters,** and so much more . . . including Vehicular Unidentifiable Flying Objects – Celebrating the work of Mr T. R. Dutton. **UFO caught on film over Rendlesham Forest**, **Lord Hill Norton asks questions in Parliament!** Meeting Georgina Bruni – a treasured conversation. Larry Warren puts some questions to Georgina Bruni – Her answers!

Part 5 – **2009-2013 Pages 321 to 340** The Colonel brings the reader's attention to several misleading comments made in various British newspapers about what occurred, odd nobody ever bothered to contact him! Photos are shown of celebrations held in the Forest in 2012. **2014** The Colonel comments on the Book *'Encounter In Rendlesham Forest'*, Nick Pope, Jim Penniston & John Burroughs, and an article published in *Phenomena Magazine*, and film *Hanger 10*.

Part 6 – **2015 Pages 345 to 358** *'The Woodbridge Conference'*. **The Colonel fights back.** A rebuttal of some of the British newspapers' articles published following inaccuracies and personal attacks on both of our characters. His comments about Larry Warren precipitated an avalanche of hatred after the Colonel appeared at Woodbridge Community Hall in 2015. Further vicious attacks via Facebook, then in September the release of a publication by Peter Robbins, in response to comments made by Colonel Halt. Followed by misleading comments made in *Phenomena Magazine*.

Part 7 – **Page 359 Astronauts and other worlds!** – A fascinating look at what the astronauts told David Bryant, followed by an amazing anomaly found in a meteorite. The implications could be life changing for mankind!

Part 8 – **2016 Page 367** Colonel Halt comments on yet another attack on his character by, of all people, Captain Robert Salas, in Peter Robbins book. **May 2016** – UFO expert Gary Heseltine claims RAF Bentwaters encounter was aliens searching for nuclear weapons! Threats made by Larry Warren in a podcast hosted by Ben Emlyn Jones.

Part 9 – **2016/2017 Page 379** Retired USA Police Officer Steven Longero comes forward!

Part 10 – **Page 389** Gary Heseltine posts up a lengthy post on Facebook, criticising Colonel Halt for his comments made in 2015.

Part 11 – **2017 Page 397** Re Josh Gates *Expedition Unknown* – visit to Suffolk. A visit to see retired Squadron leader Donald Moreland. Larry Warren posts up on Facebook about the A10 photos showing a UFO – faked according to the Colonel, who has the original photos!

Part 12 – **Page 403 Book:** *The Rendlesham File, Britain's Roswell* written by Andrew Pike is discussed by the Colonel.

Part 13 – **2018 Page 407** The 'never-ending stories' merits further discussion with putting the record straight, about further explanations, offered by all and sundry, for what took place under Colonels Halt's watch! Media interest in the forthcoming *Capel Green* film – *Indigo Transmit Films Ltd* (still waiting) which boasts of new witnesses. The Colonel makes his position clear and bans Dion Johnson from using the 'Memo'. A meet up in the Forest with Tim Acheson and Colonel Halt takes place and a trip to Hull in the same year where the Colonel lectures.

Part 14 – **2019 Page 429** In July the book *The Rendelsham Enigma* published. Vicious attacks on the integrity of Colonel Halt by Monroe Nevels . . . Followed by another book, in December 2020 – *Weaponisation Of An Unidentified Aerial Phenomenon, The Rendlesham Forest UAP Incident 40 Years Later*. Further comments required.

Part 15 – **2020 Page 461** Handshake with a Martian! Budd Hopkins, Leslie Kean and more.

Part 16 – **Page 479 Royalty, about Prince Philip, Lord Louis Mountbatten** and the Media's celebration of the 40th Anniversary.

Special Feature on GENERAL GORDON WILLIAMS

In an explosive revelation which initially began with contact from the General's family, we were told that the General had 'something to get off his chest' as he approached his demise . . . What that means is anybody's guess! The Colonel was invited to the funeral by the family and makes some interesting comments. He was asked to sign a five-page disclaimer! RIP.

FOREWORD

By IRENA McCAMMON SCOTT PhD MSc BSc

JOHN Hanson has sent me some un-proofed PDFs about the *Halt Perspective 2* book he has been working on for some years with Colonel Charles Halt following the publication of the first *Halt Perspective* in 2016, which reflects on the depth of his investigation as a retired Police Detective.

John and Charles tell me that they decided to write this book for a number of reasons.

(1) To set the record straight, regarding the way in which the media still get their facts wrong! The incident that took place at Rendlesham Forest, Suffolk, England still continues, like its Roswell counterpart, to have worldwide interest, but unfortunately it has spawned a superabundance of all manner of explanations that are based on individual flawed, belied systems which often denigrate the UFO incidents that occurred over some nights running.

(2) Its facts, based on common sense evidence, personal interviews by both men with a host of witnesses, and 'gut instinct,' are presented to the readers, so that they may make up their own minds.

(3) As the authors point out, you cannot ignore the evidence of other incidents involving allegations of UFO activity, both in the UK and the USA. They show examples from the early 1940s to today and cover some up-to-date investigation of classic cases.

(4) Sadly, Colonel Halt, after 40 years of interest by the media, now finds himself the target of malicious, unfounded attacks on his integrity by his own colleagues, following the release of recent books. It is only right and proper that the Colonel has the opportunity to defend himself.

Over here in the States, the biggest development has been the revelation that the Pentagon had a UFO program generally referred to in the media as the **Advanced Aerospace Threat Identification Program (AATIP)** – though the precise name is disputed. On the 16th of December 2017, *The New York Times* broke the story followed by articles in the *Washington Post* and by TV news coverage on all the major networks. Central to the story was the release of a number of declassified videos of US Navy jets apparently chasing UFOs.

THE HALT PERSPECTIVE 2

The declassified MoD intelligence assessment of the UFO phenomenon is known as **Project Condign**. Its final report contains the following sentence: *"The well-reported Rendlesham Forest/Bentwaters event is an example where it might be postulated that several observers were probably exposed to UAP [Unidentified Aerial Phenomenon] radiation for longer than normal UAP sighting periods."*

People continually ask me what do I think these things are and where do they come from?

Like John and Charles Halt I reply, I don't know. All I can say is that whatever this phenomenon is, it may have existed for hundreds, if not thousands, of years and the history of humankind may have had manifestations that perhaps changed the story of the world, both good and bad.

From a personal perspective, as a young child I experienced, along with my sister, a terrifying incident one night when we were in the attic. A *'Thing'* like a piece of hot metal appeared, and flew around the room without striking anything – as if it were guided. Whether that indicates a form of intelligence, who knows? But whatever it was it began to circle the chandelier before finally disappearing. We ran down the stairs and told our parents, who didn't believe us. We have experienced over the years, sightings of other inexplicable objects as adults.

Irena McCammon Scott PhD, MS, BS

This lady has a BSc from Ohio State University, an MSc from the University of Nevada, and a PhD from the University of Missouri in the Department of Veterinary Medicine. Her post-doctoral studies took place at Cornell University. She has been employed as an Assistant Professor (Department of Biology) at St. Bonaventure University, and has done research and teaching at the Ohio State University, the University of Missouri, the University of Nevada, and at Battelle Memorial Institute. Irena worked in related fields and for many years studied many species of animals including bonobos (apes) and their behaviour. She was a correspondent for *Popular Mechanics* magazine.

Irena has also worked as a volunteer astronomer at the Ohio State University Radio Observatory, in *photogrammetry at the Defense Intelligence Agency, and has participated in UFO investigations for the Center for UFO Studies. She is the author of six books, including several on UFOs, (a photo on the previous page shows Charles Halt holding one of Irena's books, **UFOs Today: 70 Years of Lies, Misinformation and Government Cover-Up** published by *Flying Disk Press*) and has contributed chapters and articles to scientific journals, magazines, and newspapers. Her listings include *Who's Who in the World, World Who's Who of Women, Who's Who in the Midwest, Dictionary of International Biography,* and *Who's Who in Frontier Science and Technology*. Her 2008 book, *Uncle: My Journey with John Purdue,* is a biography of John Purdue, founder of Purdue University and of the Purdue Block in Lafayette, Indiana. The book is the first of the Founders Series, published by the Purdue University Press.

*Photogrammetry is the science and technology of obtaining reliable information about physical objects and the environment through the process of recording, measuring and interpreting photographic images and patterns of electromagnetic radiant imagery and other phenomena.

THE HALT PERSPECTIVE 2

* * *

Track 12 in Rendlesham Forest in the 1980s

WELCOME FROM COLONEL CHARLES IRWIN HALT 2020

A warm welcome to those people who have supported us following the publication of our first book, *The Halt Perspective*, and to those that have turned out to see me during my many visits to Britain; the last one being at Woodbridge in 2019. The UFO incident I was involved in near enough 40 years ago, changed my life completely, and despite time passing still attracts so much attention from folks who just want to hear what happened from my perspective, rather than relying on so many other dubious sources! John Hanson, a retired Police Officer, and I have corresponded at great length and personally met on several occasions, both in the UK and at my homes in Washington and West Virginia. He is dedicated to getting to the real truth out there with the *Haunted Skies* books. A photo is shown with me and John talking at a MUFON lunchtime venue in May 2018 hosted by Director Susan Swiatek.

Susan and Rob Swiatek

Johns' work has not always seen the success it merits, despite that it clearly lays out the facts requiring further official investigation. Is it the case that nobody in a position of authority wants to face the truth, or could it be that the truth is known to a few? I leave that for the reader to decide.

If you wish to know more about the events that took place in Rendlesham including my own assessment of what I and others saw during the end of December 1980, then please read *The Halt Perspective,* available on Kindle or hardback on Amazon. In addition to this, there are many updates and several rebuttals which I will answer to counter continuing wild claims made over the last few years.

John has invited me to comment on UFO reports from the 1940's onwards, that are in the main, now mostly forgotten, apart from the 'classic cases' if only to show the reader that while the events that occurred at Rendlesham are of importance, and still the subject of controversy to this present day, we were not the only ones, despite the media's attempts to singularize the event.

We've worked together both in the UK and the US. I've invited John and his friends to my house in Washington. They've met the family and the family dog, *Caesar* **...so I'm looking forward to this follow up book which will once again rebut the ever-continuing wild allegations made by those that weren't there, not forgetting 'new witnesses ' who have come forward nearly 40 years later to claim that they were there!**

People often ask me what life was like at RAF Bentwaters?

Here is how I saw it then…It was really like a small American city with a total base population of nearly 14,000. Although there was little crime there was always something going on. Drink and drugs – little rock and roll! Most problem issues revolved around young airmen with drug or drink issues. Some things I distinctly remember including the time the contract barber shop was found to be skimming money and was closed while the contract was being re-advertised. That meant the males had a choice of driving into Ipswich (10 miles) or going to the beauty shop. Due to being busy I went to the shop. What an experience! The gossip was beyond belief and I was constantly peppered with very personal questions that I would never consider asking a person. That was the first and last time I did that.

One of my duties was to oversee the base high school. Every time there was a disciplinary problem of note it ended up in my office. Everything from a runaway to a hardened former member of a major stateside gang, who proudly showed off bullet and knife wound scars, came before me. He had gotten into a fight that took five police officers to subdue him. When placed in the police car in cuffs and leg restraints, he kicked the rear door off the car. Needless to say, he was heavily escorted to the airport and put on a plane back to the States. I remarked to the school principal: "within 6 months he'll be dead or in prison." We heard a few months later he was on trial for murder.

Base under attack by outlaw motorcycle gang & drugs busts by the police!

On another occasion, an outlaw motorcycle gang attempted to breach the base gate. I just happened to be in the area and found a lone policeman facing them. I quickly told him *"do not touch your gun".* We managed to convince them there was nothing on the base worth a confrontation. One night whilst I was riding with the police, they conducted a suspected drug bust. They entered the barracks with a drug dog and breached the suspect's door only to find him tossing the drugs out the window. He was caught red-handed as the police had someone outside expecting him to try and escape. The look on his face was priceless as the policeman outside caught his drugs. I ran into his father several years later and found out he straightened up and was now a state cop in North Carolina, to this day I'm careful driving through that State as I'm sure he'll remember me! Some things there hit closer to home.

Teenagers!

One Saturday morning my teenage son came running into the house screaming: *"where's the fire extinguisher."* Apparently, when he went to start the lawnmower it caught fire while sitting next to the car. I quickly ran out using a towel to beat out the flames. Needless to say, he had to borrow the neighbour's mower. On another occasion I went looking for the gas can only to be told it was at school. I inquired *"how did it get there?"* He replied, *"Oh, I took it to school on the school bus, the driver never noticed. Don't worry, I told all the kids not to smoke."* I later found out he had built a go-cart in the school metal shop. This I discovered when he was apprehended for driving it on the base roads.

Major Guenon

One evening I was having dinner in the Officer's Club when I noticed my college room-mate who was heading up a visiting inspection team was sitting at a table across the room. In that he was always playing pranks on me while in school, so I decided to give him one. I quietly called the on-duty police flight chief and explained who he was and asked him to help me. I had him page and then arrest *Major Guenon and take him to our holding cell. I finished dinner and went to the police station only to find him quite upset and demanding an attorney. Needless to say, he calmed down and forgave me. We then had a good visit and reminisced over old times.

Major Guenon

William Guenon was born on April 1, 1940, in Pennsylvania. He entered Officer Training School with the U.S. Air Force on November 9, 1962, and was commissioned a 2d Lt at Lackland AFB, Texas, on February 5, 1963. Lt Guenon completed Undergraduate Pilot Training and was awarded his pilot wings at Craig AFB, Alabama, in June 1964, and he then served as a C-130 Hercules and MC-130E Combat Talon I pilot with the 779th Troop Carrier Squadron at Pope AFB, North Carolina, from July 1964 to September 1966. His next assignment was as an MC-130E pilot with Detachment 1 of the 314th Tactical Airlift Wing at Nha Trang AB, South Vietnam, from September 1966 to March 1968, followed by service as an MC-130E pilot and flight examiner with the 7th Special Operations Squadron and the 322nd Tactical Airlift Wing at Ramstein AB and Rhein-Main AB, West Germany, from April 1968 to January 1975. During this time, Capt Guenon served as the Pilot of the MC-130E "Cherry One" during the Son Tay Raid, a clandestine mission to rescue American Prisoners of War 21 miles West of Hanoi, North Vietnam, on November 21, 1970. Bill Guenon's mission was amazing but unfortunately the POW's had been moved a week prior. More info is available in the book Secret and Dangerous. Major Guenon then cross-trained as an Air Traffic Control Officer, serving as Chief of Air Traffic Control Operations with the 2069th Communications Squadron at Nellis AFB, Nevada, from June 1976 to June 1978. His next assignment was as Director of Air Traffic Control Operations and Chief of the Air Traffic Control Analysis Division with Air Traffic Services, Southern Communications Area, at Oklahoma City AFS, Oklahoma, from August 1978 to April 1981, followed by service at Ramstein AB, and Kapaun Barracks, West Germany, with the European Communications Division as U.S. Air Force ATC Analysis Team Chief for bases in Europe and South-west Asia through May 1984. He then returned to McGuire AFB, New Jersey, where he retired from the Air Force on June 1, 1984. He completed service as an Air Force Command Pilot, Senior Air Traffic Controller, and air commando pilot. Awarded the Silver Star: Captain William A. Guenon, Jr., distinguished himself by gallantry in connection with military operations against an opposing armed force during the Prisoner of War Search and Rescue Operation at Son Tay, North Vietnam, on 21 November 1970. [Colonel Hait: Bill Gunenon's mission was amazing but the POW's had been moved a week prior. More info is available in the book Secret and Dangerous.] On that date, Captain Guenon performed as Pilot on the lead aircraft of a force penetrating deep into enemy territory to rescue United States Prisoners of War interned at Son Tay. Completely aware of the enemy anti-aircraft and surface-to-air missile threats en route and in the objective area, Captain Guenon totally disregarded his personal safety and skilfully and accurately performed his pilot duties, thereby enabling the crew to lead the force precisely to the target. As a result of Captain Guenon's heroic efforts, the force arrived at Son Tay as planned, the enemy forces were completely surprised, and the mission was successfully completed. By his gallantry and devotion to duty, Captain Guenon has reflected great credit upon himself and the United States Air Force. (Source: Wikipedia)

THE HALT PERSPECTIVE 2

Invaded by the '*Sky Crash* crowd'

In 1982 I returned briefly to the States to clear up an issue and left my son in the care of the then Base Commander. Unknown to me he made contact with the authors of "*Sky Crash*" and they were plying him for information.

He and several friends were enjoying the attention and free drinks at a local pub. I came home and went jogging. I no sooner got back to the house when the "*Sky Crash*" people came to the front door demanding to come in for a meeting with my son. I was tired, sweaty and still wearing my jogging clothes. They kept trying to push their way in. I finally went to the red phone and called the police and asked that they be removed. Somehow the police thought I was under duress and sent a force to be reckoned with. The next thing I knew there were armed cops everywhere. I heard the bullhorn announcement: *"Come out with your hands up."* I ran out trying to explain there was no threat and I just wanted them to leave. The British Police arrived and removed them. The "red phone" was a direct line that a few top officers had that allowed immediate access worldwide.

The times I spent with the Territorial Army celebrating their Remembrance Day and numerous other social events. I especially remember all the good times and fond memories I spent with the Anglo-American Friendship Council. All in all, it was a fantastic tour. As you can see from the following photographs I forgave them for their antics, and am shown with Dot Street and Brenda Butler at the 2016 Woodbridge Conference.

Wild unsubstantiated claims as to the answer!

In the past years there have been claims of fertilizer trucks catching fire, flying lighthouses, misidentified planets, cop cars with their blue lights, wandering over the runway, satellites down, space capsules crashing into the forest, wild tales of machine-gun posts, foxholes in the forest, you name it they've come up with it over the years. Fortunately, at least one story has been finally put to rest, that of Airmen Larry Warren whose book *Left At East Gate* has been taken off sale, unfortunately, there are a few 'die-hards' that won't relinquish their support or accept that his version of events can't be trusted!

The 33 ARRS Commander was Col. Charlie Wicker, he was my racquet-ball partner. Charlie was the Air Rescue (Helicopter) Commander. We talked about the incident the next day. His comment was *"we were down for the holiday, if it happens again call me and I'll get a crew airborne."*

Both the Air Traffic Controllers as well as their British counterparts both picked up the objects as well as numerous civilians and the whole WSA crew. I would like to meet this so-called SAS Officer and put him in his place. He's a disgrace to his organization! Sadly, there is a wide gulf between stories like this – which are often accepted as having some feasibility by those that will not accept the possibility of something or someone which breaches our cultural conception of another life form, which exists alongside us on Planet Earth. This doesn't deter people from coming up with the most amazing theories based on individual belief systems to explain what lies behind this phenomena!

Aliens – abductions – and mysterious marks and scars!

Most of them are adamant that the human race is controlled by various aliens and that their agenda is utilising us as a resource for their own means. Stories of aliens abducting women and having sex – producing hybrid offspring attracts the attention of the media and TV documentaries who love to portray the role of the alleged abductees – often 'tongue in cheek', with no intention of treating such people seriously – usually accompanied by men of science, who dismiss such 'interludes' as the product of overactive imaginations if only it was that easy!

People often ask me what I think of people who claim they have been abducted by Aliens and whether such experiences can be treated seriously in our modern society. I tell them I am not qualified to judge the validity of the information, obtained by way of hypnotic regression (often pointed out now as an unreliable means of extraction) or cast any judgement on the abduction experience itself. Having said that I remain puzzled as to the cause of the physical marks and scars sometimes discovered on people who have been involved in a close encounter with a UFO. At the end of the day, I was out there in the forest in December 1980 and I, with others, saw something I (we) have never been able to explain. Many people will spend time looking on the internet for information about UFOs and what happened at Rendlesham Forest forty years ago.

DISINFORMATION

Some will think of trying Wikipedia… This is what they will see!

Wikipedia 2019: Charles I Halt – In the late hours of December 27, and early December 28, 1980, then Lieutenant Colonel Halt led a patrol to investigate an alleged UFO landing site near the eastern edge of Rendlesham Forest. During this investigation they witnessed several unidentified lights, most prominent of them being a bright flashing light in the direction of Orford Ness. In January 1981 Halt composed an official Air Force memorandum listing details of the events. The memo was then dispatched to the Ministry of Defence. Halt also made an audiotape recording of the incident. Halt stated afterwards he was given sodium pentothal and a "cover story." which may have affected his memory of the night's events. One theory is that Holt was seeing the Orfordness Lighthouse. Notably, Holt sees a flashing light every 5 seconds, which is the rotation rate of the lighthouse.

> The problem is that very few people take the subjects seriously, what we need to do is expand the collective consciousness of those people who believe the spoon-fed tripe handed out by the media in the main that such things cannot be treated seriously. In essence, we need to move on and raise the bar on the reality rather than the ridiculous assertions continually made to denigrate the subject. I was never given SODIUM PENTOTHAL-what a cover story! Orford Ness Lighthouse is another inference no doubt calculated to give any reader who looks at this entry, on the internet an erroneous /misleading impression of what went on, never mind the misspelling of my name!

THE HALT PERSPECTIVE 2

Now let's look at what's published on 2018 – *Wikipedia* on Rendlesham/UFO sightings Rendlesham' on *Wikipedia* in 2018 contains approx 44 reference entries: 20 from Ian Ridpath, 5 from Dr Clarke, a reference to *Sky Crash*, a reference to sceptical comments made by Brian Dunning *'Skeptoid'*, who comments, from his 6th January 2009 *Skeptoid* podcast episode titled "The Rendlesham Forest UFO". It is also reported on the same page that in 2010 Jenny Randles quotes "emphasized her previously expressed doubts that the incident was caused by extraterrestrial visitors". While suggesting that a UAP, an unidentified atmospheric phenomena of unknown origin, might have caused parts of the case she noted, *"Whilst some puzzles remain we can probably say that no unearthly craft were seen in Rendlesham Forest. We can also argue with confidence that the main focus of events was a series of misperceptions of every days things encountered in less than everyday circumstances."*

Wikipedia – Reported UFO sightings in the UK. Quote: This is a list of notable alleged sightings of unidentified flying objects or UFOs in the United Kingdom. Many more sightings have become known since the gradual release of the MoD UFO sighting reports by the National Archives in 2008. In recent years there have been many sightings of groups of slowly moving lights in the night sky, which can be easily explained as Chinese lanterns. *Project Condign*, undertaken from 1997 to 2000, concluded that all the investigated sightings of unidentified aerial phenomena in the U.K. could be assigned to misidentified but explicable objects, or poorly understood natural phenomena.

> Chinese lanterns now 'old hat 'have been replaced with drones! This is a ridiculous statement, which covers up thousands of sightings, many of them inexplicable which have been reported the length and breadth of the British Isles and USA over a period of now 80 years plus…. The alluded to catalogue of sighting reports shows sparse details and effectively camouflages many incidents of which we have investigated before without one single reference to our work despite having contacted *Wikipedia* asking them to make a note of our commitment.
>
> Poking fun at UFOs – year after year we are subjected to the authority's view on UFOs and the stance taken by the media who love nothing better than to poke fun at us, denigrating time after time reports published by concerned citizens who like us only seek one thing – an answer!
>
> This now Worldwide UFO Incident still continues to attract enormous interest even now over 38 years ago. Irrespective of the evidence gathered here which documents many other incidents that have occurred around the East Anglia area involving UFO activity – which some may feel is very similar to what I and my companions witnessed. In addition to that, we wanted to show the reader some other incidents involving people who have suffered all manner of physical and psychological effects following a close encounter with something we still are unable to define to this present day. At the end of the day the reader will make up their own minds on what they believe these objects are and where they come from. Hopefully, the reader can draw their own conclusions on the comprehensive evidence that you are about to read, rather than base any opinions on what you read about what happened in *Wikipedia* by those that don't even bother to contact me!

Welcome from John Hanson & Vicky Hyde – 25 years research!

Vicky and Steve Hyde

THIS book catalogues a huge number of sightings of inexplicable objects seen in the sky by members of the public and those of the RAF/USAF during the middle part of the 20th Century. Unfortunately, due to the sheer weight of sightings involved, we have been forced to omit many reports of UFO activity in order to keep the size of this book down, which we apologise for.

The presence of Unidentified Flying Object should be treated with seriousness, rather than the opposite taking into consideration the trivial way in which legions of newspapers have over the years FAILED in the main to present this with concern, rather than a flippant attitude.

I would like to thank our colleague and now friend retired Colonel Charles Irwin Halt, who in private, is quiet in nature and unassuming, rather than the opposite as one may expect from a senior USAF officer that carried out many roles of high powered leadership while in the United States Air Force. It's clear from the many citations that were awarded to him from servicemen that served with him – which I had the privilege of seeing on display at his home in West Virginia during a visit there in May 2018-19; that he was very well respected and thought of by his colleagues at the many air bases he served during his time with the United States Air force.

Thanks also go to his Wife, Yong Ho and family for making us so welcome at his house in Washington. I would also like to thank Nick Pope for his unwavering support lasting many years for the *Haunted Skies* books. Having researched into thousands of similar sightings recorded worldwide over the last 70 years; including vast numbers of newspaper cuttings reporting on those incidents – one might wonder why the overall UFO evidence is never presented collectively by mainstream media but nearly always singularly. I think we know the answer to that one!

This book catalogues many reports and sightings which go back to the early 1940s' based on a number of personal interviews with the numerous witnesses concerned – some of whom are now sadly no longer alive. Bearing in mind the National reputation of my colleague and co-author, retired Colonel Charles Irwin Halt who is in constant demand by TV/Film company producers to talk about what he saw in December 1980, I felt that he should have the opportunity of being able to comment selectively on some of the British UFO sightings which took place before the 1980 period, if only to lend tremendous weight to what he and his colleagues witnessed in December 1980, and showing the reader that contrary to the way in which the media still continues to report with extreme sensationalism on those matters – the airmen were not the only witnesses to UFO activity!

In addition to the comments made by Charles Halt – there is an update with regard to the many comments directed at Colonel Halt and myself since the first book *The Halt Perspective* was published in 2016. Colonel Halt also asked for the opportunity to make some rebuttals with regard to attacks on his character, and 'set the record straight' with all manner of continuing theories put forward by those as to what they believed he and his colleagues had seen.

One man who has supported the publication of the *Haunted Skies* books is *Daily Mail* long – time journalist Michael Hellicar who was reporting on the UFO events of 1977 when many of the 'reporters' of today weren't even born.

"As a freelance journalist, I've investigated UFO sightings in France, the U.S. Roswell, Brazil, Suffolk, Devon, and Somerset. I've interviewed police and military officers – cool, trained observers, not given to hysteria – who have seen things in the sky and, in some cases, descending from nowhere to land on solid ground, and been impressed by their eye-witness accounts. Anyone who reads John Hanson's compelling research into UFO sightings, impartially, un-sensationally and straightforwardly reported, will be convinced (as I became, a long time ago) that 'we are not alone'. Their 'Haunted Skies' books will have you looking up into the skies for a long time to come. There have been too many authoritative sightings of UFOs for the whole subject to be dismissed as mere flights of fancy, so to speak, by cranks and obsessives about the subject. It is an unfortunate fact that ufology has been given a bad name by a few crackpots. But the evidence turned up by John, and now his daughter Vicky Hyde, over many years commitment confirms that out there are many, many sane, sensible people who have witnessed sightings that cannot reasonably be shrugged off as clouds or weather balloons or – a particular favourite by the naysayers – aircraft refuelling in flight."

BBC Presenter, Howard Hughes:

"At the end of the day – in the absence of revelation or 'disclosure' – there is only belief. Either you believe there is something out there or you don't, and the process of making a decision is assisted by evidence. Perhaps it's something you've seen or something you've been told. It's unlikely, but it might be something you read in a tabloid newspaper. Maybe you have read a book on the subject. Maybe you think you have been abducted by the 'Greys'. Evidence is the key to belief or dismissal. The 'Haunted Skies' series of books is the best-researched series of its kind. I have worked on news-desks all my life, *but I have never seen research so thorough – documents, photographs, statements, witness accounts, and many, many of them. I urge you to read and digest this new edition and let it help you come to an informed decision. Are the claimed craft 'theirs' or 'ours'? Do governments know more than they tell us, and is there a 'big truth' that has yet to be revealed? This book will help you come to a view. John Hanson and Vicky J. Hyde deserve great success for their hard work and the frequent wearing out of old-fashioned shoe leather in the quest for detail. The boy who loved 'The Invaders' and went on to be a broadcaster and journalist is impressed."*

John Hanson: Michael Hellicar is spot on! Having now published 10 books and written 17 cataloguing precisely the events that have dominated both TV and newspaper articles going back to the late 1940's, I have finally realised after talking to numerous reporters employed for the National Newspapers over in the UK that most editors have no inclination to publish articles involving serious research, but welcome publishing articles on light-hearted stories involving claims of alien abduction – laced with a liberal dose of humour. Why that is I have no idea! In my quest to obtain contact with people in the film and TV sector, hoping to attract support for the *Haunted Skies* books, I learned at an early stage that while many famous people on stage and screen have expressed their concerned opinions about UFOs in a newspaper or magazine article, actually making contact, was another thing! Like so many others, I was fascinated with the comments made by many political leaders – men of influence who had shaped the destiny of human beings on this planet, with regard to the UFO subject – about something that shouldn't even exist – it does!

Men in power fail to disclose true facts behind the UFO question WHY?

It appears puzzling and inconceivable that in a period of history which is fading away fast, with few grandparents and great grandparents left who served in two Great World Wars, that despite the curiosity expressed by people like Prime Minister Winston Churchill, (and so many others) who promised to reveal the true facts behind UFOs – nothing of the sort has happened. In addition, many modern-day Presidents of the USA have made statements about the existence of UFOs on occasions they have witnessed inexplicable phenomena.

President Ronald Regan, in 1974, reported *"My aircraft was followed by a bright white light, which to our amazement shot up into the sky and was gone".* President Jimmy Carter: *"If I become President, I will make every piece of information this Country has about UFO sightings available to the public and the scientists."* President Bill Clinton: *"I am resolved to investigate mysteries surrounding the murder of JFK and to get to the bottom of the understanding of the Government on UFO sightings."*

Changes of attitudes towards interest in UFO reports

We accept that World Governments have far more pressing matters to deal with, such as matters of survival, health care and other broad-based human concerns which take precedence over esoteric questions as to the credibility of UFO reports. But why has this deplorable state of affairs manifested to such a degree that any attempts to raise the subject to serious scientific investigation appears to be nigh impossible? MP Sajid Javid was Home Secretary – (heavily tipped to be a future Prime Minister) was given some *Haunted Skies* books and thanked us in a personal letter stamped with the House of Commons logo . . . making a reference to the UFO archive and the *Halt Perspective* book. Former Prime Minister David Cameron: We sent ex-Prime Minister David Cameron two of the books a couple of years back and we received a thank you from him. He had himself while in office promised publicly to be open and entirely frank about what the Government knows about Close Encounters.

Buckingham Palace enjoys reading *Haunted Skies* books! (Or at least they did!)

HRH Prince Philip has also been receiving the books for a number of years, which we have never disclosed publicly – sadly, due to circumstances beyond our comprehension, we appeared to have breached Royal Protocol! In September 2019 we sent a *Haunted Skies Revised Volume 4* book, which covers the Jubilee year of 1977, to his secretary, Brigadier Archie Miller-Bakewell, recorded delivery. After having not received any acknowledgement by way of letter, which was unusual, we wrote two letters to the Palace but heard nothing more. Could it have been the front cover which they might have felt was 'over the top' with its depiction of alien beings? We shall never know…

Toyah Wilcox

Liz Kershaw

Gloria Hunniford

Toyah Wilcox, British actress, singer and producer, was driving along the A36 heading from Bath towards Warminster at 11.30pm, on the 22nd May 1996. She was about six miles out of Bath when she saw *"triangular lights"* coming over the brow of the hill and heading upwards into the night sky. She wrote a report to Essex UFO researcher, Ron West, along with a signed photograph a short time afterwards.

Disc jockey 'Liz' Kershaw, presenter at *BBC's* Coventry & Warwickshire radio station, was driving along the M62 Motorway towards Liverpool one Sunday evening in December 1991.

"I was terrified to see this huge triangular-shaped object float across the motorway. It had three red lights – as it glided in front of me – and was the spookiest thing I had ever seen. I pulled up near the bridge and saw a number of police cars parked with police officers watching it. When I got home, I rang the Liverpool Police to find out what it was; they denied all knowledge of it."

Oddly we were unable to obtain a photo of Liz despite being promised one by her and other BBC representatives at the radio station, many of whom had invited me to speak at the radio station on the UFO subject previously – before any books had been published. We even asked the *BBC Radio* station for a photo in 2010 but were told this wasn't possible and they declined to give us a reason why. A different situation existed back in 1992 when Liz's photo was used in an edition of the *Sunday Mail,* Glasgow, dated the 5th January, 1992 . 'DJ Liz in UFO terror'. Another unknown newspaper showed an even larger photo of Liz on the 6th January, 1992.

'Liz claims I saw UFO'

Her version of events being identical to what she had told us apart from describing having seen *"Three red lights hovering in the sky over the US Army base at Burtonwood near Warrington."*

Gloria Hunniford – After coming across an article about some friends of hers that had seen UFOs, hoping that she might be inclined to discuss the matter further. She telephoned a mutual colleague in July 2019 and while not wanting to enter into any further conversation about the subject, wished us well and the book's success.

Betty Driver – TV actress, who played barmaid Betty Turpin of the long-running British ITV soap, *Coronation Street*. She and her sister Freda were very helpful in providing details of some UFO sightings, including being followed by one of them many years ago. RIP ladies.

Hillary Clinton has a long political history advocating for children and families, gender equality and health care reform, but in 2016, during her bid to secure the Democratic nomination for President, she had the courage during a radio interview and then later on *'Jimmy Kimmel Live,'* to tell the listeners that she wanted to review files about UFOs and the mysterious Area 51 site in Nevada and make them public. *"I would like us to go into those files and hopefully make as much of that public as possible,"* she told Kimmel. *"If there's nothing there, let's tell people there's nothing there."*

I also felt privileged to have also entered into written and verbal conversation with many people over the years who gave their support to the *Haunted Skies* books. They include Edgar Mitchell, Paul Hellyer, Erich Von Daniken, and Trevor James Constable, a man of immense knowledge on the UFO subject, world-renowned author and historian, who has produced ten non-fiction books, and served 31 years at sea, 26 of them as a radio officer in the U.S. Merchant Marines. His first book, *They Live in the Sky*, published in 1958, advances the shocking theory that UFOs were mainly invisible and that our atmosphere was the home of huge, invisible living creatures, confused with spacecraft when they became visible.

"UFOs are space ships, but their vibratory make-up is not fixed in the physical-material density. They are mutants. UFOs have their main existence in a density that is invisible to human beings of normal vision. The intelligences behind the spaceships are various orders of etheric beings, that is, beings differently constituted to man and normally invisible to him, yet capable of materializing at will when necessary or required. There are normally invisible, living things in space that are not spaceships. Space is filled with primary energy currents of which some exist on earth."

A native of Wellington, New Zealand, he authored several books on the aerial warfare of World War II, together with co-author Raymond Toliver. Trevor fully supported the research that I was doing and told me he was very impressed with some of the *Haunted Skies* books sent to him. Trevor James Constable 17 September 1925 – 31 March, 2016 RIP.

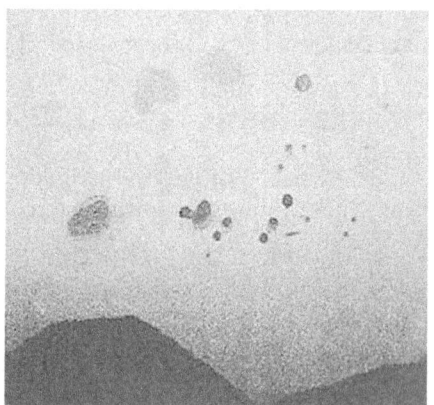

Despite the tremendous research and commitment carried out by so many, now defunct, groups going back 70 years, attempting to create awareness of the existence of a UFO presence that defies understanding to this present date. No scientific-based research, is currently being carried out and is unlikely to happen because I don't think anyone has the answers! This is an age where it appears convenient to those in authority and now the media to publish sightings of UFOs as an object of ridicule, rather than being treated seriously. We have asked ordinary citizens from all walks of life to simply tell what they saw, rather than depending on the garish sensational accounts published by newspapers that still in the main treat the subject with disdain. It's impossible to include all of the UFO sightings made from the early 1940's – because we don't have the space in this the second volume of the *The Halt Perspective* to outline some astonishing reports, many from pilots – in the main now forgotten. But we will endeavour to give the reader an idea of just how prolific UFO activity was – if only to show that Colonel Charles Irwin Halt and his colleagues were not the only ones to sight inexplicable phenomena – despite skepticism continuing to be aimed at the subject of UFOs, by the media who continue to focus on individual events, while deliberately ignoring the thousands of sightings reported by courageous citizens and the armed services, the reason why eludes us all!

It's clear that there has been a successful campaign by Governments going back to the 1940s to **deliberately mislead the public** by explaining away the majority of UFOs reported to them as misidentified mundane objects; such as weather balloons, planets, flocks of birds, etc . . . whether those 'incursions' were deliberate or the necessary criteria (unknown) which allow us to sight what we commonly refer to as UFOs is, of course, open to speculation . . . It's chilling, though to consider the possibility that these 'unidentified flying objects' are manifesting and going about their everyday business in all probability well outside the field of human electromagnetic optical vision.

Meeting Colonel Halt – ©Rob Swiatek

In July of 1991, I found myself in something of a 'pickle'. Big matters loomed on all sides – the Gulf War had ended, but the Middle East was scarcely an oasis of tranquility; the UFO field continued to be rocked by putative secret government documents and the crash of *something* in Roswell back in 1947; I was between girlfriends – when word came from the manager of my apartment building that the exercise facility on the ground floor would be closed a month for renovation. What!? The exercise room closed! I'd been in the building – at the northern end of Crystal City, Virginia, and a mere half-mile from the Pentagon – for six years, merrily walking to and from work each day at the U.S. Patent and Trademark Office and staying fit, thanks to the building's nicely-equipped exercise room. Going without workouts for a month, as per the manager's disconcerting announcement, was anathema to me; moreover, driving to a gym, miles away during the monstrous evening rush hours typical to the area never, I believe, entered my mind. However, an alternative that might provide a different outcome occurred to me after some thought: A *Doubletree Hotel* with a rotating lounge occupied the plot of ground immediately adjacent to my apartment building; might it have a gymnasium I could join on a temporary basis? Upon checking, the answer turned out to be yes, and on 8 July 1991 I handed a cheque to the staff of The Fitness Company – which ran the exercise facility – and immediately began my short-term membership amidst the weight machines and barbells collected there.

THE HALT PERSPECTIVE 2

Overheard conversation about UFO sighting

Some short time after I'd completed my workout one evening, I was walking out through the reception area, when I heard a male voice relating details of a UFO encounter. Amazing! Something about beams of light, objects, a military patrol: A quick sentence or two, not loudly spoken. Overhearing casual UFO conversations in the workaday world has never been an adjunct of my life – once or twice prior to 1991 it had happened, perhaps, and not thereafter. The words came from a man some feet away speaking evenly and in serious tones to a woman, who listened intently.

Not one to normally interrupt conversations that didn't involve me, I nonetheless *did* (how could I not?) and asked if he were describing the Rendlesham UFO case – well-known to ufologists of the time, but not the general public in the way, say, Roswell was. Although he didn't appear taken aback, he probably thought, *my God, can I not escape UFO people even at a fitness centre?* – Before he gamely answered in the affirmative. In response to a second query, he added that he was Colonel Charles Halt (*the* Col. Halt, I thought, amazedly). Standing there in workout attire and feeling somewhat the fool, but needing a bit more information before I disappeared, I quickly noted I was with the Fund for UFO Research, a Washington, D.C. based organization of veteran researchers, and inquired as to his availability for a follow-up contact. Although after 28 years my memory of his exact response is hazy, I recall he gave me a phone number or a place of employment and said to call at my convenience. I made the short walk back to my apartment.

Informed Don Berliner and Richard H Hall

Within a day or two, I had informed Don Berliner and Richard Hall, both fellow executive committee members of the Fund and long entangled with the UFO field, about my chance meeting with Col. Halt and the desirability of scheduling a meeting with him, if possible. They agreed this would be a valuable opportunity to question the principal first-hand witness to what, even then, was turning out to be a remarkably convoluted event – an event that had occurred almost 11 years before, had been widely written about in the UFO Press, yet whose puzzle pieces still presented a largely inchoate picture to investigators. I spoke to the Colonel several times that summer and fall, filling him in on the Fund for UFO Research, its members, and how we approached the UFO subject. But it wasn't until the second week of December 1991 that a dinner meeting was convened at the Hyatt Regency Crystal City in Arlington, Virginia. I recall that, in addition to the Colonel, Richard Hall, Don Berliner, Fred Whiting, and myself were present. All proceeded smoothly and cordially, the food was good: Halt related in measured words the details of what had transpired in the pinewoods of Suffolk back in 1980, questions were asked and answered, and the Fund members emerged with the conviction that, whatever the precise origin and nature of the phenomenon that had manifested before the Colonel and his party for an extended period of time, it wasn't the Orfordness lighthouse or radioactive rabbits. Fred Whiting summarized the Hyatt Regency get-together in the minutes of the Fund's December 1991 executive committee meeting: Fred and Rob discussed the dinner meeting earlier in the week with Col. Charles Halt, one of the primary witnesses in the Bentwaters AFB UFO case in December 1980. They were impressed with his account, which may be the focus of a forthcoming book. The Fund kept in regular contact with Colonel Halt after the initial December 1991 meeting; in August 1997, for example, he appeared at the Fund's annual *Mysteries of the Sky* seminar, where, of course, he spoke on the Rendlesham

Forest affair. (I recall the plaster cast he displayed of the imprint purportedly made by the object in the forest still had pine needles adhered to it.)

In due course, Charles Halt became a close friend of Richard Hall, long-time UFO researcher and author who, at various times throughout the decades, served in official capacities with the National Investigations Committee on Aerial Phenomena, the Mutual UFO Network, and the Fund for UFO Research (as its chairman, for a time). Hall once told me that he was one of the few people Halt trusted for accurate information about people and events in the oftentimes-murky UFO field, and that he would periodically receive phone calls from his friend in this regard. In due course, when Hall was writing his magnum opus, *The UFO Evidence, Volume II: A Thirty-Year Report*, around the turn of the century, he had "extensive personal interviews" with Col. Halt for the entry on Rendlesham in the volume. Richard wanted it to be precise and factual. That entry still stands as one of the most succinct, accurate accounts of what has become a veritable Hydra of a UFO encounter, one that is seemingly still growing.

Memorial to Richard H Hall – paying respects

In October 2009, some months after Richard Hall had passed away, Colonel Charles Halt and his wife, along with a number of other invited guests, attended a memorial to Richard Hall organized by *Susan Swiatek in the aftermath of that year's *Mysteries of Space and Sky* conference. In conjunction with the memorial, a large number of Hall's paintings were gathered together in an impromptu showing, which the late artist and UFO researcher Budd Hopkins took the opportunity to expound upon for several minutes.

Richard possessed a bachelor's degree in philosophy from Tulane University in New Orleans and lived most of his life in the Washington, D.C. area. He was a proponent of the extraterrestrial hypothesis to explain UFO sightings. Richard was also a member of the Authors Guild and wrote numerous books and magazine articles dealing with the role of women in the American Civil War. Between 1958 & 1969, Richard worked for the National Investigations Committee on Aerial Phenomena (NICAP). He began as executive secretary, and eventually became NICAP's assistant director. In this role Hall was both an eyewitness and participant to much of the early history of the UFO phenomenon in the United States. He never claimed he had been abducted by aliens or that he has seen a UFO. Yet his life became a quest to delve into the unending, mysterious universe and find life beyond Earth. "*I am, in the legitimate sense, in the philosophical sense, a skeptic,*" Mr. Hall said in a 1997 CNN interview. "*I think there is evidence of something. I am critical about it. I am open-minded, [and] I am trying to find out.*" Mr. Hall's interest was triggered when as a boy growing

---

*Susan Swiatek. When the book *"Interrupted Journey"* was published in 1966, Susan became hooked on the UFO and abduction mystery. Even as a child, she was fascinated by the nature of *"flying saucers."* A long time Mutual UFO (MUFON) member, Susan hosted the 1999 Symposium near Washington, DC. She has lectured and created artwork for several book projects such as Richard Hall's "The UFO Evidence—Part II" and the "Extraterrestrial Encyclopaedia" compiled by Ron Story. She was also a major consultant on *"Grassroots UFOs"* by Michael Swords. Susan is currently the MUFON Virginia state director and on the executive committee of the Fund for UFO Research. Susan holds a BFA degree from the Maryland Institute College of Art, Baltimore and works in the publishing field. Robert's degrees in physics and earth science paved the way for a career at the US Patent Office where he is a Physics Examiner in Aerospace Technology. Robert has lectured at conferences throughout the US and contributed writing to numerous UFO projects and titles, especially for the Fund for UFO Research (FUFOR). Robert is frequently seen turning up on the Discovery or History channels in various productions. He has served as Secretary-Treasurer of both FUFOR (since 1986) and the UFO Research Coalition (URC) since 1997. Robert has been on the Board of MUFON since 2004. MUFON (Mutual UFO Network) is a private organization that investigates and compiles data on reports of unidentified flying objects. Sue and her husband, Rob Swiatek, an oft-cited UFO expert, are the first couple of Virginia ufologists.

THE HALT PERSPECTIVE 2

up near Hartford, his mother told him that she had seen something strange in the night sky. *"Could there be something out there?"* he asked himself at the time, according to his friend Susan Swiatek, Virginia director for the Mutual UFO Network. [John: whom we had the pleasure of meeting during a lunchtime talk in company with Colonel Halt in May 2018/2019. Susan asked me to sign the *Haunted Skies* books which she had amassed over the years and I was pleased to do so.] The Colorado-based group, of which Mr. Hall was once a board member, is an organization of UFO enthusiasts and "ufologists" – those who study unidentified flying objects. Charles Halt was a very good friend of 'Dick' and attended the family funeral in 2009.

Working with NICAP director Donald Keyhoe

Richard helped lobby the United States Congress to hold public hearings and investigations into the UFO phenomenon. In 1964, Richard Hall researched, edited, and wrote much of *The UFO Evidence*, a compendium of UFO incidents from the 1940s, 1950s, and early 1960s that NICAP considered being the most persuasive for the belief that UFOs were a *"real"*, physical phenomenon. A copy of *The UFO Evidence* was sent to every member of Congress in 1964. Following Keyhoe's removal as NICAP director in 1969, Richard left NICAP to work as a technical writer and editor. He continued to work in the UFO field. He served as the director of the Fund for UFO Research, which provided grant money to researchers working in UFO studies. He was also the editor of the *MUFON Journal*, the official publication of the Mutual UFO Network (MUFON), the largest civilian UFO interest group in America today. In 2001 he wrote a sequel to *The UFO Evidence;* it covered prominent UFO incidents from the mid-1960s through the 1990s. He was also the founder and chief editor of the now-defunct *Journal of UFO History*, which featured articles on the history and growth of the UFO phenomenon in the United States. Hall was a vocal proponent of the theory that UFOs are extraterrestrial spacecraft from an advanced alien civilization, and he was an active member of the now-defunct *"UFO Updates"* message board and website. In 1964, he told of *"high level White House discussions on what to do if an alien intelligence was discovered in space"* took place. CIA director John McCone initiated a review of the possibility that UFOs might represent a threat to the United States and CIA agents interviewed Richard Hall, who provided them with data about UFO sightings from NICAP's records

CIA admits lying about causes of UFO report for decades!

In 1997, the CIA released a report called *CIA's role in the study of U.F.O.'s 1947-90* by Gerald K. Haines, which admitted that the agency had routinely lied about the causes of UFO reports for decades, blaming the incidents on weather conditions such as "temperature inversions" or "ice crystals". Instead these sightings were of secret aircraft, such as the SR-71 or U-2 spy planes. Pulitzer Prize winning science writer William J. Broad wrote about the release of the report in the New York Times, quoting Hall: *"It's very significant,"* said Richard Hall, chairman of the Fund for U.F.O. Research, a group in Washington. *"Certainly, they've lied about not having any interest in the subject. But I don't know of any other deception like this."*

John E. Pike, head of space policy at the Federation of American Scientists, also based in Washington, said the admission raised questions about other Federal cover-ups involving UFO.'s adding that *"The flying-saucer community is definitely onto something,"* in charging that the military is hiding something. While Mr Pike and other aerospace experts accepted much of the government's explanation of the earlier deceptions, Richard Hall continued to believe that the government was covering up evidence of the extraterrestrial origins of UFOs. To supplement his income as a UFO researcher, Hall worked for many years as an abstractor-indexer for the Congressional Information Service in Bethesda, Maryland, and he did similar work for the National Institute on Alcohol Abuse and Alcoholism, Columbia Telecommunications and the National Council on Ageing. Under the circumstances we felt it appropriate to include the article written by Richard about the UFO incident at Woodbridge following a number of interviews held with Charles – later published in the *International UFO Reporter* in the 'fall' of 2000 – Volume 25. Number 3. It seemed befitting and emphasises the thoroughness of someone who was so well respected in and out of the UFO community.

UFOs over RAF Bentwaters Air Force Base ©Richard H Hall 2002

Richard H Hall

"On two nights between Christmas and New Year's Day in December 1980, UFOs were observed by US Air Force and enlisted men outside the gates of Bentwaters AFB England. Numerous personnel positioned in various locations also reported lights in the sky that no doubt included some IFOs, as is common in complex multiple witness cases. My contribution focuses on the sightings made by officers and men who left the base and went into the forest to investigate odd lights. I have had extensive interviews with Colonel Charles I Halt and have studied the packet of documents from the Citizens against UFO Secrecy (Barry Greenwood files) which seem to have confused some of the British investigators. Also, I have read other relevant books and Internet postings.

My focus has been establishing the facts about the encounters in the woods guided by Halt. I do not claim to be an expert on this case or as thoroughly versed in its myriad details as Jenny Randles. What I am convinced of is that the facts of the encounters in the woods establish this as an extremely strong and convincing case, quite independently of what other witnesses may or may not have seen and whether or not the lighthouse momentarily fooled some people. Furthermore, the case fits a strong pattern of military base intrusion cases that can be traced back at least to 1966 at the ICBM missile bases in North Dakota and Montana.

In outline the details of the forest encounters – as confirmed by Colonel Charles Halt are these: At approximately 3am on the morning of either the 27th of December or 28th December.

THE HALT PERSPECTIVE 2

Colonel Halt's original memo to the MOD which he has since publicly described as deliberately oversimplified reported that two USAF security Police had left the back gate at RAF Woodbridge to investigate a strange glowing object in the woods.

These men were SSgt James Penniston and AIC John Burroughs who were accompanied by Ed Cabansag who according to Colonel Charles Halt was stationed at the gate to serve as radio relay since they were experiencing radio transmission problems. (They also reported wildlife "acting in a frenzied manner".)

When Penniston and Burroughs entered the woods they encountered a metallic, roughly triangular object on the ground approximately seven by ten feet in size, its brilliant glow illuminating the entire forest. It also has pulsating body lights. Penniston approached and touched the (apparent) craft, but they retreated when the luminosity increased, and it flew through the trees.

A couple of days later a party of officers and men led by Halt found three tripod-like depressions in the ground where the object had been seen. Scintillation counter readings registered unusual levels at the site. Some of the British Investigators are bothered by what they perceive to be 'contradictions' between the original statement made by Penniston and his public comments, many years later when he gave me more detail. These are easily explainable. Halt acknowledged understating his experiences since they feared for their reputations and possible damage to their careers. Penniston did the same. Halt gave me a very positive character and reliability reading on Penniston. We have highly credible witnesses reporting incredible things. What they witnessed fits exactly with decades of other reports by credible witnesses, down to details of brilliant luminosity, pulsating body lights, EM effects, animal reactions, radioactivity, landing gear-like imprints in the ground and an apparent radar confirmation. A very strong case indeed. About two nights later the encounter personnel involving Colonel Halt occurred. Halt was notified about 10.30pm that there was another 'glow' in the woods which some people interpreted as a return of the UFO. Determined to get to the bottom of this Halt personally led an investigation into the woods, along with Lt Bruce Englund, the security police shift commander. This time they took 'Light-Alls' portable lighting devices, radiation counters, a night scope and other equipment. They experienced power problems with the *Light-Alls*, and interference with radio transmissions.

This trek through the woods resulted in the now famous audio tape recorded by Colonel Charles Halt as the party progressed and began seeing unusual things. If the glow was from the UFO again, they did not immediately see it. After gathering evidence at the apparent landing site they were leaving the woods and entering a clearing when Colonel Charles Halt saw the red sun-like light that moved about and pulsed . . . appeared to throw off glowing particles and then broke into five separate white objects and disappeared . . . the lighthouse . . ? I think not!

Immediately after this, three star-like objects were seen moving rapidly and making sharp angular turns, displaying body lights and appearing elliptical then circular. All very typical UFO features. Two of the objects were to the north and one to the south. All about 10 degrees off the horizon.

In 1994 Colonel Charles Halt reported that during these sightings one of the objects suddenly flew directly overhead and beamed a thin pencil like light down to the ground about ten feet in front of them. He also heard chatter on the radio about the beams coming down into the weapons area of the base. As Colonel Halt described: *'We just stood there in awe, wondering whether it was a signal, a warning, or what it was.'* In a public talk made in Maryland a few years ago, Charles Halt obviously was still in awe, although he refused to speculate about possible extraterrestrial origins. It was clear to him that these objects were nothing in our inventory.

As had been reported on the Internet, Charles later became Base commander, promoted to full Colonel, and finished out his career in a highly responsible job in the Pentagon. My meetings and conversations with him and his vetting of my report on the case for the *UFO Evidence* Volume 11 (*Scarecrow* January 2001) convinced me that he is a very careful and responsible person highly credible. He is working on a book about the case which we all need to read in order to sort out some of the unanswered questions. He was not voluntarily forthcoming with me having been burned by UFOlogists in the past, but finally acknowledged that I had the facts straight to the best of his knowledge. I have the distinct impression that he knows and can document a lot more than he has told."

In an interview conducted with Sally Rayl on the 13th May 1997

Jim Penniston tells of being accompanied by John Burroughs and heading towards the tree line approximately 50 metres away, behind which was a clearing where 'the lights' were coming from. *"As we started getting closer, it was apparent that it wasn't an aircraft downing or a crash, we weren't sure what it was at that point, so we radioed it back to the CSC. We entered the tree line and moved in about 20 more metres. There was an object sitting in a clearing. It was emitting mostly white light at that point, very bright. Both Burroughs and I had to squint when we looked at it. I found it strange that there was no sound coming from the object, but the animals around us were in a frenzy. We had wildlife running by us and lots of birds. Outside that noise, however, there were no others. That was when I decided to have Burroughs stay there as a radio link. He did not seem calm. He didn't acknowledge what I was saying, but I thought he understood. I was more concerned at that moment with what was going on in front of me.*

As I continued into the woods, I started seeing the outline of the object itself. The lights that had just been a blue from 300metres away were now definite, distinct colours – light blue, yellow, and red and they were pulsating. Looking at the silhouette of the object I realized it was not a conventional aircraft; meaning that it was not one that was already published in 'Jane's All the World Aircraft'. It was no aircraft I had ever seen, and it wasn't one that I knew any prototype of. I had my notebook and camera while I was out there, so I began taking notes.

This is what I wrote – Triangular in shape. The top portion is producing mainly white light which encompasses most of the upper section of the craft. A small amount of white light peers out of the bottom. At the left side centre is a bluish light and on the other side red. The lights seemed to be moulded as part of the exterior of the structure, smooth, slowly fading into the rest of the outside of the structure, gradually moulding into the fabric of the craft. As I was taking notes, I also memorized what was in front of me for what seemed like hours but was in fact only minutes. Finally, I unleashed my camera case cover and brought the camera up to focus. The air was electric. It made my hair and skin feel as if I were surrounded by static electricity or some type of energy. I began snapping photo after photo. It was still eerily quiet. I got to within 10 feet of the craft and the clearing where it sat. I estimated it to be about three metres tall and about three metres wide at the base. No landing gear was apparent, but it seemed like she was on fixed legs. I moved a little closer. I had already taken all **36 pictures** on my roll of film. I walked right up to the craft. I noticed the fabric of the shell was more like a smooth, opaque black glass. The bluish lights went from black to gray to blue. I was pretty much confused at that point. I kept trying to put this in some kind of frame of reference, trying to find some logical explanation as to what this was, and what was going on. It was dead silent. No animals were even making noises anymore.

*On the smooth exterior shell there was some writing of some kind, but I couldn't distinguish it, so I moved up to it. It was three-inch lettering, rather symbols that stretched for the length of two feet, maybe a little more. I touched the symbols and I could feel the shapes as if they were inscribed or etched or engraved like a diamond cut on glass.

At that point I backed away from the craft, because the lights were starting to get brighter. Still there was no sound. There was no physical contact with any kind of life form, but there did seem to be a life form presence. It was mechanical this ship and it seemed to be under intelligent control. The next thing I knew, I was standing about 20 feet away from the craft with Burroughs, who I thought I had left back near the tree line. The craft moved off the ground about three feet, still with no sound. It started to move slowly, weaving back through the trees at a very slow pace, maybe half a foot a second. It took about a couple of minutes for it to manoeuvrer itself back to a distance of about 100 -150feet, then it rose up just over the trees about 200 feet high. There was a pause and then literally within the blink of an eye it had gone, all with no sound that still boggles my mind.

We thought it had left, but then both Airman Burroughs and I saw the same array of coloured lights maybe a half a mile away. So, we pursued it, trying to follow its course as best we could on foot. We only got about 300 yards into the woods before we turned around. We still had no radio contact which I thought was strange. We weren't even getting squelch. We went back to the clearing. There, Airman Burroughs noticed the impressions, the indentations in the ground, we found three of them, all triangular in shape about three metres apart. Then I decided we should head back."

Dedicated to the memory of Richard H Hall – Born 25.11.30 – died July 17th, 2009

---

*Colonel Charles Irwin Halt – This was the first time Penniston mentioned touching the craft and noting symbols.

THE HALT PERSPECTIVE 2

THE JOURNEY BEGINS: EARLY YEARS . . .

ON the **24th / 25th February 1893** – During a winter cruise sailing between Shanghai and Japan, the officer of the watch aboard *HMS Caroline* reported strange phenomena, involving the **sighting of a 'mass of unusual lights'** moving across the sky spread out in irregular lines heading northwards just before midnight. The fiery globes were seen to alter their formation now a massed group with an outlying light. When the isolated light disappeared, the others would form a **crescent or diamond**. **1896/1897** – During these years a number of **mystery 'airships'** were reported in the sky over California, often seen heading in an eastwards direction. Some reports claimed that occupants were visible on some of the airships. Others spoke of personal encounters with the pilots who often appeared to be human, though their behaviour, mannerisms and clothing appeared unusual. Not only were these mystery airships bigger, faster and more robust than anything then produced by the aviators of the world; but **they seemed to be able to fly enormous distances, and some were equipped with giant wings.** We were to come across reports from the end of the Victorian era **(1899)** of **luminous glowing *'balls of light'*** heading through the sky, changing direction while in flight. **On 30th October 1906,** several crew members of the steamer *St. Andrew*, including Chief Officer V.E. Spencer saw **three objects fall into the sea** about 8 kilometres away. This was followed by a huge 'meteor' disc-shaped, metal object, 16 feet in diameter, which fell into the sea about 2.5 kilometres away in a rocking motion, leaving a red streak. **(Source:** *New York Times*, **5.Nov.1906)**.

At 10.30pm on the **7th May 1909,** a long dark **cylindrical object** was sighted hovering above cliff tops at Clacton-on-Sea, by Mr. Egerton Fee. A few minutes later the object, which carried no lights, flew away, heading north-east. Mrs. Wigg from Lowestoft, Suffolk, was awoken at 1.30am, in the summer of **1909** by a noise similar to a motor car. She looked out of the widow and saw: "…*a dark bottle-shaped object, heading south-west at low altitude, and what looked like a **man steering at the front of the machine**"*. Several others also heard engine sounds and saw flashes of light. **(Source:** *Flying Saucer Review***)**

On the **31st of December 1909 at Huntingdon, West Virginia,** *'three huge luminous disks'* of equal size were seen in the early morning sky. **In 1910** – Mrs. F. Ryder, of 42 Ward Road, Cambridge (a young married woman) – accompanied by her father and husband – was walking over the railway bridge in Mill Road, heading towards the town, at 8pm. "*We saw a **cigar-shaped 'light'** – its edges well-defined, showing what looked like square windows in the side* – heading silently through the sky. Inside was a flickering light. One end was tapered with flames coming from the base." (It reminded her of a V1 'flying bomb', which missed their house during the Second World War many years later) "*It looked about 6-8 feet in length and was moving in a north-east to south-west direction.*" **(Source: Kath Smith, Isle of Wight UFO Society.)**

THE HALT PERSPECTIVE 2

Cigar-shaped objects 'like a flying bomb', **with square windows,** were seen crossing the sky in **October 1910**, as man struggled to master the aerodynamics of flight. In **1913** a number of luminous bodies were seen flying over Toronto Canada by thousands of people, moving in V formations of **three** – far too slow to be meteors. **(Source: The Royal Astronomical Society of Canada (November &December 1913)**

Similar sightings go back to the beginning of the 20th Century – the most spectacular involving a young man from Shuttlewood Derbyshire on the **22nd of January 1919** – a full account of which has already been given in previous books. This one is of interest as it took place at Sandhills a few miles from Shuttlewood involving a mysterious globe of light that meandered about the garden in front of the witness over a period of time. Could it have been the same phenomena which were to trouble our next witness? Are these objects in a different category from the glut of UFO sightings that have plagued our skies?

British runner plagued by mysterious light – now over 80 years ago!

Harry White (then aged seventeen), was a keep-fit fanatic who often went for a three-mile run at night. In **October 1932** he was running on a minor road that leads from Bolsover to Sandhills, Derbyshire, approaching the junction with the main road to Rotherham, on a clear evening, with the moon casting a subdued glow. *"Approximately 120 yards from the intersection I noticed a bright 'light' playing 'tag' with me at about 8pm. I stopped still. The 'light' also stopped still.* **It was hovering three yards away from me on the far side of the hedgerow which lined my route. The 'light' then also started up, maintaining a level pace with me, at a height of three feet above the ground. For the next fifty yards or so, this silent race between me and the 'light' continued until it suddenly moved towards me. Not so fast as to be a blur, but a calculated move which I could easily follow with my eye, the object left the hedgerow and suddenly moved towards and around my legs and in between my feet as I ran. I felt it had come to investigate and had become aggressive.** *But this could have been a nervous reaction on my part. It was, however, very real and not an illusion. I began to kick out at the thing, really scared and now in a panic."*

Seemingly undamaged by this vigorous retaliation, it remained close to Harry, evading his kicking, and easily moved around him without making physical contact. Upon reaching the road junction, the 'light' left him and returned to its position behind the hedgerow. For another hundred yards it kept pace with his now fast run. Then it just disappeared. He estimates the 'light' to have been a perfect sphere, twelve inches in diameter. **This is somewhat puzzling: how could a 'light', that size, have passed between a pair of running legs?** Harry was a schoolmaster by profession, a captain in the infantry during World War II and saw many horrors and felt intense fear on many occasions – now dim memories, but the 'light' still remains a vivid memory. When he arrived home his grandfather remarked, *"You look scared to death."* Upon recounting his story, his grandfather propounded a simple explanation: the area where Harry had seen the 'light' *"***was the traditional burying place of suicides, and one must expect to see the occasional tormented soul in such nether regions."** In June 1932, a **similar 'light'** was seen on a farm 18 miles south of Erie, Pennsylvania. Its reported manoeuvres and size – fourteen inches in diameter – make a noteworthy comparison. **(Sources: Ananda Sirisena/***Mysteries of the Skies: UFOs In Perspective,* **by Gordon Lore & Harold Deneault, published by Prentice-Hall, 1968.**

1940's – **A saucer-shaped object was sighted at RAF Woodbridge Suffolk, on the 6th June 1940** – In **May 1942** – a silver object sighted making a swishing noise was seen over London. During **1943** a '*Flying Saucer*'-shaped object was seen over Barking Railway Station London.

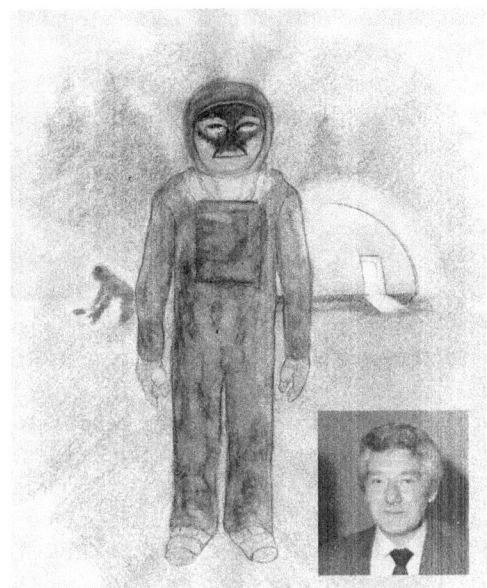

In the same year – RAF Serviceman John Warren reported a '*Close Encounter,*' with what he perceived to be an '*Alien Being*' near RAF Ludham Norfolk, *"wearing what appeared to be a greyish-white 'boiler suit'. Attached to the front of the 'suit' was a box that cast a greenish glow onto the face of the figure, visible beneath what looked like an old-fashioned diver's helmet. It had a round face, without any noticeable cheekbones, or chin. The figure stared at me as I approached, with a smile on its face that terrified me. As I passed the figure, standing behind the bushes that bordered the field, about thirty to a hundred yards away, I saw a large, domed object in the field behind this grinning entity."* **(Source: Philip Mantle** *Flying Disk Press*)

1944 – **Metallic 'Flying disc'** sighted over Streatham London during Air Raid on **20th February. 27th April** – Crew of Lancaster bomber sight UFOs over Germany – July. **'Flying Discs'** seen over London during Blitz. German 'doodlebugs' followed by UFOs.

Ronald Claridge, DFC, AEA – a radar operator aboard Lancaster Bomber 'F' for *Freddie* – was returning home on **11th August** from his 68th mission over enemy territory,, on their way back from Pellice, flying over France, when he noticed the 'Fishpond' radar screen had gone blank. *"I advised the pilot, Brian Frow what was happening. All of a sudden, he shouted out,* **'What the hell is that?'** *I peered out of the astrodome next to my seat and noticed an* **enormous 'ring of lights'***, stretching across the sky. As my eyes became more accustomed, I saw the lights formed part of a* **huge 'disc' flying parallel to the aircraft***, at an estimated height of 20,000 feet, at an approximate speed of 280mph. Then a strange sense of calm seemed to envelope the aircraft. Nobody opened fire. It seemed odd no turbulence could be felt from the presence of the object. A few minutes later it moved away at a colossal speed, ruling out any possibility that it was a conventional aircraft. When the bomber landed a full report was submitted to one of the officers, who debriefed the crew.*

THE HALT PERSPECTIVE 2

*He didn't seem surprised by what the airman had seen but **ordered them not to discuss what had happened.** To this day I don't know what it was we saw, but I am convinced it was not constructed by human hands. Don't forget we didn't even know what UFOs or 'flying saucers' were."*

Summer – Landed '**Flying Saucer**' sighted at Arnhem by a soldier **who was warned to keep quiet! September UFO paces V1 'doodlebug'** over London. **28th September** – German aircraft **harassed by orange globes** over Nova Scotia. **1944** – Mysterious 'Dark shadow' seen over Bass Strait Australia. **27th November**–American Aircrew Henry Giblin, of Santa Rosa, California, and Lt. Walter Cleary, of Worcester, Massachusetts, sight orange '**globes of light**' – US Pilot reports huge glowing **orange/red lights** in sky near German border.

On the **5th of August 1944, Prime Minister Winston Churchill banned the reporting for 50 years** of any alleged UFO incident, because of fears it could create mass panic. More importantly the effect it would have on the Church was considered! Reports given to Churchill included a Royal Air Force (RAF) reconnaissance plane returning from a mission over France or Germany toward the end of the Second World War, when over or near the English coastline it was intercepted by a **strange metallic object** that matched the aircraft's course and speed for a time before accelerating away and disappearing. The plane's crew were reported to **have photographed** the object, which they said had *"hovered noiselessly"* near the aircraft, before moving off. According to the documents, details of the cover-up emerged when a man wrote to the British government in 1999 seeking to find out more about the incident. He described how his grandfather, who served with the RAF in the Second World War, was present when Churchill and U.S. **General Dwight Eisenhower**

discussed how to deal with the UFO encounter. On the **28th of July 1952**, Winston Churchill ordered a top-secret inquiry into UFOs, asking: **"What does all this mean, what is the truth? Let me have a report at your convenience."** This note was unearthed from the Public Records office by Philip Mantle in 1989, who said, *"These documents clearly show that there was Government interest in UFOs from many years back."* (Source: *Daily Star* 19 Apr 1989 'Winnie's secret probe on saucer sightings. He led search') (Declassified records released 5th August 2010).

1945 – RAF Lancaster Bomber opens fire on UFO! – Was this one of the reports brought to the attention of Winston Churchill? Flt. Lt. Vernon Wilkes, DFC, formerly based at RAF Hemswell, Lincolnshire, with 150 Squadron was part of the crew aboard RAF Lancaster Bomber NG264 IQB, piloted by Flying Officer G. Markes. On the night **2nd of January,** he was flying over Nuremberg, Germany. *"Visibility was clear. There were bags of the usual queer lights and flares all over the deck. A light appeared on the starboard quarter and began to follow us. **I had seen plenty of these before at different times, but this one closed in***

Vernon Wilkes

steadily – *almost going out at times, and then blazing up again. It came close enough to light up my turret and the rest of the aircraft before diving into the ground, where it burned for a time.* **The skipper told us to open fire** *if we saw another one. A short time later, another one appeared and acted in the same manner as the other, so I told Danny (Sgt. Danny Driscoll, rear gunner) to 'have a squirt at it' with his guns.* **I saw the tracer appear to go pretty close to the object. I cannot say if it hit it or not, but it dove straight down and hit the ground."**

26th March – RAF Pilot sights **'glowing ball'** over Berlin. **Summer** -Pilot attempts to intercept UFO over Germany **UFO hovers over Nuclear Power Station during the summer .** US Pilot Ensign Roland D. Powell, based at the US Naval Station Pascoe, Washington, one of five F-6F Hellcat pilots scrambled to intercept a UFO, described as *"being the size of* **three aircraft carriers***, side by side, seen hovering at high altitude above this top secret plutonium production facility"* for the world's first nuclear bombs at **Hanford.**

1947 – During the period between **January and April, UFOs were plotted by radar on a number of occasions, crossing the East Anglia coast**, near Norwich, at estimated speeds of 400mph. **On the 5th May,** Mr. and Mrs. Olavick from Tucson Arizona reported sighting **ten flying discs,** nine of which were smaller than the tenth, seen *'playing around the cloud'* for over 5minutes before regrouping in a 'V' formation behind the larger object , then flying away at great speed. **O**n the **14th of June**, an experienced pilot and boy mowing a lawn at Bakersfield California sighted **ten round objects** moving across the sky in a loose 'V' shaped formation.

21st June – UFOs sighted over Maury Island, Washington State. **'V' shaped formation** seen over Birmingham, England on the **22nd June**. **23rd June,** a luminous object with what appeared to have a **polished aluminum surface** was sighted crossing the sky over Greenfield Massachusetts. **26th June** – UFO sighted over Montgomery. **June** – **Spinning silver 'ball'** sighted over Lancashire. **June** – Mysterious **ring-shaped UFO** seen over Dorset. **28th June** – **'Flying saucer'** reported over Wisconsin. **29th June** – UFOs sighted over Iowa. **30th June** – **Half Moon**-shaped object seen Boise Idaho. **30th of June,** Mr. Walter Nicholson from Hailey Idaho was one of a number of people that saw a **flight of 8-10 objects moving in a 'V' shaped formation.** At the time of this sighting he was with Forest Ranger Hunter Nelson who was marking trees three miles from Galena Summit. The men estimated the objects to be at a height of about 10,000 feet heading north-east. Walter: *"The left 'wing' of the V formation contained five discs in a perfect line, while the right seemed to weave about in flight."* Two UFOs sighted over Chester. **1947** – **Hundreds of UFOs** were sighted over Andover Hampshire. **1st July** – Large object seen over Phoenix Arizona. **2nd July** – Fireball sighted over Six Miles Mountain. **2nd July** – Claims that 'Roswell UFO' was struck by lightning. **3rd July** – **Aluminum objects** seen in the sky over San Diego. **3rd July** – **Alien craft with occupants found near Magdalena New Mexico. 4th July** -**'Flying Discs'** sighted over Oregon, Portland. At 2.30pm on the **4th of July,** Mr Kjell Oval a car salesman in Alameda and former Navy Pilot for four years was with a group of **50** witnesses at 2.30pm when they saw *"***A triangular formation of disc like objects** *over Auburn California, they looked to be made of metal and were bright silver, their outline perfectly discernible. They were in view for 3-4 minutes and were not aircraft. They disappeared one at a time high in the sky rather than over the horizon."* **5th July** – **Five 'Discs'** seen over New Mexico. A number of UFO sightings were reported for the **6th July**. They included a report of a UFO sighted, over Fairfield **– Suisun Air Base, California**. Then a **'V'** shaped formation of objects were reported over New Orleans by US Army Private Robert G Hellman who **told of seeing,** *"***Four discs** *flying over Canal street, like flashing whirling coloured saucers, pink and silver in appearance flying in a 'V' shaped formation."* During the same evening John Heathcote (14) reported seeing *"***Three plate-like objects** *over Valley Stream New York which were in a 'V' shaped formation heading westwards."*

THE HALT PERSPECTIVE 2

7th July – 'Flying Saucer' seen over East Troy, Wisconsin. **7th July – Flying Discs** sighted over Louisiana and Hawaii. **7th July – Flying Disc** seen over Phoenix Arizona. At 5.20pm **on the 7th of July,** Miss Louise Sheffield, a secretary at DuPont's Chester, Pennsylvania Division, sighted "*Five dull grey objects heading silently across the sky in a V formation."* At 6.30pm the same day at Tampa Florida, George Gortez and several others saw "*A formation* **of three golden** *coloured objects flying slowly overhead."*

Mollie Tilley from Tamworth, Staffordshire, England contacted us in the mid 90's– a sensible, down-to-earth, friendly woman then in her late 70s, who remains curious about her Uncle Frank Handford's close encounter, in **early July 1947**, following a *'flying saucer'* landing at the family farm in Fishpool Hill, just outside Hereford. Mollie: "*My uncle and mother Betty were not the sort of persons to make up wild stories. They were the exact opposite, not given to flights of imagination. My mother told me this: "We saw the incredible sight of a dome shaped craft, glowing with light, descending onto the ground, and watched as a pair of steps slowly came out of the craft, followed by the entrance of* **three silver suited 'beings', who stood next to the spaceship, picked up some apples and a piece of turf, before re-entering the 'ship' and leaving.*"*

The next morning, they ventured outside and discovered a large circular impression burnt into the ground and scorching to a nearby wicker gate. Frank telephoned the police, who later arrived with men from the Air Ministry, as well as military personnel, they conducted a search of the area with a Geiger counter, "*which revealed high levels of radiation*." The men then left, threatening Frank with dire consequences if he told anybody what had happened. Despite publicity in the *Hereford Times* about this incident and searches through local newspaper archives, we were unable to find any other witnesses. Enquiries made into the matter discovered the farmhouse located in **Lower Fishpool Hill** had been demolished in 1948. (WHY?) According to the 1946-1948 Herefordshire Electoral Roll the residents in July 1947 were Margaret E. Handford and Frank Handford, ordnance survey grid reference for the site being **603339. (Source: Personal Interviews – Marilyn & Robert Aldworth, Birmingham UFO Society)**.

On the 8th July -Two silver 'discs' seen over Muroc Army Airfield, California. **9th July – Black 'disc'** seen by Idaho Statesman. Police Officer sights '**Jelly-fish**' shaped object over Newfoundland. **10th/11th July**. Lincoln La Paz sights UFO over New Mexico. **12th July** – **Silent Disc** seen over Washington. **14th July** – UFOs sighted over Lake Mead Nevada. **16th July** – **Pilot paced by UFO over Kansas. Thanks to declassified operational records**, previously kept by the British Eastern RAF Fighter Sector, we learnt of the RAF response behind a number of operations implemented in a bid to identify an *'unidentified flying aircraft'*, officially designated as **X306** but nicknamed by the pilots as '**C' for Charlie**.' Army commitments were met by 595 Squadron and Meteors of 245 Squadron operated under Neatishead Control on intercept practice. Mr. William Kent, the pilot of the aircraft, now a retired Group Captain, had this to say: "*I remember the incident well. It took place on the* **17th July**. *I discussed what had happened with the Neatishead Flight Controller and a report was later sent to the Commanding Officer of the Group, who decided* **the unidentified aircraft was most probably a leaking meteorological balloon."** **UFOs sighted over Oregon USA** – Pilot Kenneth Arnold was flying over Baker Oregon on the **24th of July 1947**. (a month after his now famous UFO sighting) intending to land at La Grande, "*I noticed a cluster of about twenty to coming straight towards me at what seemed like a terrific speed. I grabbed my camera and started filming, even though I thought they were ducks. As they came within 400 yards approx. of me, they veered sharply away from me and to their right, gaining altitude as they did so, fluttering and flashing a dull amber colour. I was a bit shocked to see that they had the same flight characteristics as the ones I had seen previously. They disappeared eastwards at a speed far in excess of airplanes or ducks."* Mr Arnold, curious as to what was on the film, had it developed. But it showed: *"only one or two of these objects could be found on my film and you could only see them under a jeweller's glass".* Incredibly, what promised to be one of the most important pieces of film appears to have been lost from history. We wrote to Kenneth Arnold's daughter, Kim living in Boise, Idaho, but never received a reply.

July 1947 – Lt Colonel 'death bed 'confession meets Roswell 'Alien'

An amazing deathbed confession (our condolences) happened in 1997 from highly feted well respected Squadron Leader Lt Colonel Marion 'Black Mac' Magruder – a fighter pilot who had served with distinction during the 2nd World war in a number of theatres of war, which included his squadrons involvement at Okinawa, that witnessed some of the bloodiest battles of the entire Pacific war, crucial in ensuring Allied domination of the skies at night.

In July 1947 Lieutenant Colonel Magruder began his year's posting to the National Air War College at Maxwell Field in Alabama. (July was a fateful month in his life, according to his son Mark because it was in that month that his class took a special trip to Wright Field in Dayton, Ohio.) As Mark Magruder recounts, his father told him that he and the rest of his class were told that the military wanted his feedback on a strategic decision in the field of military and political planning. Basically, the higher-ups in the military were looking for guidance on a critical decision they had to make. The Air War College students were led into a room where they were told about the crash outside of Roswell, New Mexico **earlier that same month**, and shown debris from the crash – **then shown one of the Aliens who survived the impact!** Even more incredible was an invitation to meet a surviving occupant of one of these craft – surely something that appears

incomprehensible in its implications, never mind shattering earthly conceptions and our human belief system. In that fateful conversation made to his sons over 40 years later as he knew his time was near, Magruder described the being in specific detail to his sons, *"**the being seemed "squiggly" to me, the creature was not like the aliens you see depicted on television, except for the large head. Actually, instead of a grey colour, the being had a flesh tone. And it resembled a human being more than anything else. It had a large head, it had large eyes – larger than usual – and it had only a slit for a mouth and hardly any nose."*

Mark said his father told him that it didn't really have a nose the way human beings have noses. The creature was human-like. Yet, despite its humanoid appearance, it was clearly not from this planet. It was unlike any human being he had ever seen. My Father seemed also impressed with the way the 'alien' moved and the disproportionate length of its limbs. He said "**It was small, like a child, but not like a child, because of its large head and long arms. It was five feet tall or smaller, a little creature, but it did not look like a small adult. It was clearly something different. It was wearing a coverall that reminded me of a flight jumpsuit. It was alive. And we killed it. It was a shameful thing that the military destroyed this creature by conducting tests on it."** LT Colonel Magruder said that his group was shown photographs of the craft, and that it was more like **a disk than a crescent or a triangle. He said he also saw some of the crash debris and** remembered that certain beams had something inscribed on them, but he was

never told what the writing meant or whether it was ever translated into English. The debris that his father handled, Mark and Merritt Magruder said, convinced him that whatever the material was and whatever function the parts served, this stuff was not of this World! **(Source: /UFO Magazine)**

Recently in (March 2020) I had the pleasure of speaking personally with Mark's brother Merritt about what is, one of the most sensational accounts I have ever come across during many years research into the subject. Merritt: "*My father was always reluctant to discuss what he knew about the Roswell incident, although he hinted that he knew far more than he could ever tell us. When we asked him to elaborate he declined. Occasionally during the screening of some TV documentary or film relating to the UFO subject, there would be that inane comment about 'little green men' This would draw the comment from Dad that "They weren't green and weren't anything like the popular stereotyped image of the 'gray alien, I learned that there were in fact two different types of species of aliens, labelled as either a 'Green or a Gray. Apparently one breed was friendly the other the opposite and regarded by the military as hostile."* In addition Merritt told me that on one occasion his Dad received a visit from two men who warned him the consequences of keeping quiet – needless to say they were promptly ejected!

James V Forrestal

His father was also a friend of James V Forrestal, who became a Presidential Assistant, Under Secretary of the Navy, Secretary of the Navy, and then the nation's first Secretary of Defense. [At the height of Forrestal's career, it was widely thought that he would be elected President or at least the Vice President.] Merritt Magruder: "*My Dad told me that the Roswell debris and the dead aliens were never destroyed. The 'captives' were kept at Wright Field, later renamed Wright Patterson Air Force Base. The 'material', was moved to Eglin.*" (We would like to thank William J. Birnes, Mark, Merritt and Natalie Magruder, Stanton Friedman, and access to the article in *UFO Magazine*.

Frederick 'Busty' Taylor – considered one of the world's leading researchers into the crop circle phenomenon –was a primary school pupil in Andover, Hampshire, England in **1947**.

THE HALT PERSPECTIVE 2

*"I can clearly remember seeing, even as a child, **hundreds of tiny 'silver balls'** moving across the sky at high altitude. The oddest thing was they appeared to be playing 'tag' with each other and were accompanied by one or two larger objects heading towards the south-east. Not long after this my father, who worked for the MOD as a crane driver, was with some other men when they noticed an object, stationary in the sky, which vanished about ten minutes later."*

28th July – United Airlines sights '**Flying Disc'** over Idaho. **July** – **Close Encounter 'Aliens seen'** Edinburgh Scotland. **4th August** – **Elliptical object** over Boston Massachusetts. **4th August** – **Black 'Flying Saucer'** seen by Pilots over Alaska. **7th August** – Montana resident Peggy Mitchell living at 610, North Logan was stopping overnight with five other girls, on a 'sleepover' when at 2am they saw about **twelve light orange objects** moving at speed through the sky in a '**V**' formation. **10th/11th August** – 'Long flame' seen over Silver Springs, Ohio & **airborne objects reported over St Louis**. **13th August** – Unidentified Flying object seen over Twin Falls.

Death of Captain Mantell attempting to intercept UFO!

1948 – The Captain Thomas Mantell UFO incident was among the most publicized early UFO reports. It resulted in the **crash and death** of 25-year-old Kentucky Air National Guard pilot, Captain Thomas F. Mantell, on **7th January 1948,** while in pursuit of an alleged UFO. Thomas was an experienced pilot; his flight history consisted of 2,167 hours in the air, and he had been honoured for his part in the Battle of Normandy during World War II.

The official file of investigation shows that the incident was explained away as a '**BALLOON'** which appears to be universally accepted. **NOT SO**! Following an excellent investigation made by **NICAP – The Mantell Incident Anatomy of a Re-investigation by** Francis Ridge with Jean Waskiewicz and Dan Wills. **(Francis Ridge NICAP-*The Reality of what actually happened*?)** Proves to us that the official explanation of it being a skyhook balloon is wrong!

Francis L Ridge of NICAP – *The Reality of what did actually happen*?

"There were about 100 launchings of Skyhooks per year, about two a week. Skyhooks were written about (highly publicized) and discussed in unclassified documents. **But there is no launch date and location that even comes close to producing a Skyhook over Godman at that time.** *There WAS, but that has been changed twice and apparently turns out to be completely wrong. I'm open to new evidence and won't be upset if it indeed turns out to be a balloon explanation, but now is the time to place these events where they properly belong for the record.* **We now know that the Jan-6-48 Skyhook launch was from Milaca, Minn**., (NOT Camp Ripley 43 miles away, that was a fabrication. It reached its MAXIMUM HEIGHT of 80,000 ft in three hours of launch, or presumably at **about 11 am on the 6th. It could therefore not go any higher.** *Thus, the nonsense about 100,000 ft is sheer*

THE HALT PERSPECTIVE 2

falsehood. It had gone almost DUE SOUTH from Minnesota, slightly to the West, at about 190degs. It did not get tracked heading SE towards Kentucky, so it is anyone's guess where it actually went, unless there are lots of news reports charting its course along the way. There is no upper winds data in 1948 from 80,000 ft so no way to check using meteorological records. That means that when Lt Orner tracked the object by Godman's theodolite at 5:35 PM CST at 240° azimuth and 8° elevation, **if it was a Skyhook balloon at 80,000 ft it had to be about 100 miles away to the WSW, which would be the vicinity of HOPKINSVILLE, Kentucky. YES, THAT HOPKINSVILLE from the 1955 incident. It would NOT be anywhere near Nashville, Tennessee.**, where famed astronomer Carl Seyfert sighted from 4:30 to 4:45 PM CST what he called a balloon with cable to a suspended basket (the Skyhook pictures of Jan-6-48 do not show a "basket" or any other large object hanging beneath, only relatively tiny payloads). Even worse, when Lt Orner lost track of the UFO in the theodolite it was at the horizon (0 degrees elevation) still farther north at 250 degrees azimuth. **An 80,000 ft balloon would have to be at about 350 MILES away at that point over southern Missouri!!!** Even more discrepant with Seyfert's sighting in Nashville, which would also be about 350 miles away? IN PITCH DARKNESS!!!!! The Skyhook could not have been seen."

On **7th January, newspapers** across the U.S. carried headlines similar to the *Louisville Courier*: '**F-51 and Capt. Mantell destroyed Chasing Flying Saucer.' Quotes:** The **"Mantell Incident"** was the most thoroughly investigated sighting during that time. Captain Thomas Mantell died trying to reach a Skyhook balloon, launched from Clinton County AFB. He didn't know that he was chasing a balloon because he had never heard of the huge, 100-foot-diameter skyhook balloons, let alone seen one! Mantell's death was ultimately caused by the hype over UFOs, which no doubt caused him to chase after it at all costs "Skyhook" balloons measure **(73 feet in diameter and 129 feet long)** and ascend to altitudes as high as 100,000 feet, the translucent polyethylene plastic (of which the balloons were made) gleams brightly in the sun. At higher altitudes, Skyhook balloons tend to lose their spheroid shape and undulate slowly in air currents, often assuming the shape of eggs or discs. Skyhook balloons were released regularly from west coast launching sites by the Air. Force under Project '**Moby Dick.**' They have been known to drift across the entire United States on their mission of obtaining weather data in the upper reaches of the earth's atmosphere.

His oldest son, Thomas Mantell III of Louisville, said he had heard mention of the Skyhook theory in some of the many stories on the incident. A spokesman for the Office of Naval Research in Washington confirmed that Skyhook balloons, which were classified "**confidential,**" were being used for atmospheric testing by the Navy during 1948 in central Minnesota. Thomas was skeptical, however, that a balloon could have been flying half the speed of a P-51, as his father's radio message indicated. "**The cover-up is the big thing. They were very vague with my mom...she, like me, believed that he was too good a pilot to have gone up that high and blacked out from lack of oxygen. He'd flown too many missions without oxygen, and he knew his capabilities. I would really like to know the real cause of the crash. That's what befuddles me more than anything."**

Wife prevented from seeing the wreckage of the plane, why? Captain Mantell's wife, Margaret, who later remarried and continued to live in Louisville, was not allowed to see the wreckage of her husband's plane. She was told that pieces of it were sent to Dayton, Ohio, for investigation, and that her husband had passed out from oxygen starvation before the crash. It appears that the "**Oxygen system was not serviced: but the system was in working order."**

THE HALT PERSPECTIVE 2

A slur on the memory of an honourable man, whose name has been sullied, NOT forgetting a UFO sighting from Lockbourne Air Force Base at 7.25pm on the same date, involving an oval large yellow and orange object seen in the sky for over 15 minutes. Our condolences go to Thomas Mantell's wife Margaret. His parents Elsie (1897-1971) and father Thomas Francis (1888-1953) Captain Thomas Mantell, was among the first fliers to cross the Cherbourg Peninsula on D-Day and was awarded the **Distinguished Flying Cross** for heroism during World War II. He is buried at **Zachary Taylor National Cemetery in Louisville**. (**Sources:** *The Boston Daily Globe* 9.Jan.1948 'Army Air Hero killed chasing Flying Saucer'/*The Albuquerque Tribune* 9. Jan. 1948 'Flier Killed in 'Saucer chase'/*Providence Journal* 9.Jan.1948 'National Guard Pilot killed in hunt for Flying Saucer' over Kentucky/*Los Angeles Times* 9.Jan.1948 'Flyer killed in futile chase of Flying Saucer'/*Denver Post* 9.Jan.1948 'Kentucky Pilot killed chasing sky vagrants'/ *Rapid City SD Daily Journal* 'Killed Chasing Flying Saucer')

Thanks to the **Aerial Phenomena Research Organisation** we learned of an interview in (1977) conducted by Jack Pickering investigator an Attorney in law, with William Jones of Zollinger Road, Columbus Ohio, then aged 28 who was on duty in the direction finding Shack – situated some three quarters of the way down the North to South runway, about a mile away from the Control monitoring aircraft activity and weather conditions. Jack described the cloud cover which was overcast and around 12000 feet with a 10 mph wind. *"It was dark. I was lying on my back looking out of the window when I saw right over my head at a 30 degree angle from vertical, appearing through the overcast a* **great big red object**. *I thought it was an aircraft on fire. I jumped up and started to reach for the microphone or telephone when I realised it was no aircraft. At this time the Control Tower operative called me before I could reach them. He asked me "What the hell is that out there?"*

I told him I didn't know; it was just a **great big round ball**. *I told him to call Airways, which he did and, then the Op's man and Captain plus the meteorologist came to the shack to have a look at it.* **It stops just as it comes through the overcast and hovers in the air completely silent. It then makes a circle of the entire base, which is about six miles in total. It accelerated to a speed in excess of a thousand miles per hour but came back and stopped instantly; it didn't coast to a stop. It stopped like it ran into a wall. It's now still right over my head. Then it moved south-west against the wind. When it got down nearly to the edge of the base, just a little past the end of the runway, it descended to the ground vertically. It came clear to the ground and stayed there 10 – maybe 15 seconds and then rose vertically** *back up to the overcast. By this time we had been in touch with an airplane which was coming from Wright Field, he said he couldn't see anything [too far out] It's an assumption, but I think the object detected the airplane approaching because as the aircraft came closer the object went back up into the overcast.*

I estimated the size of it based on the fact that I knew how high it was away from me 1200 feet. If I hadn't had the weather reports in front of me and it had been a clear night, I couldn't have told you how big it was. Since it was at a 30 degree angle it wouldn't be much more than 1200. It was bigger than a one car garage but not as big as a two-car garage. I went out to have a look to see if the grass was burned, mashed or if there were prints where it had landed. There were none. I don't know if the Army of the Air Force examined the area for radioactivity, not while I was there". Jack was flown to Wright Field three times for an interview about what he had witnessed. He confirmed that four people were also witnesses to this incident. Jack says it was **7.10pm** when the object appeared –and was visible for about 20minutes. Jack was adamant that this **happened the same day as the Mantell crash**, after learning of the death of the pilot earlier that day. Following a lengthy but thorough interview conducted by William, Jack was again asked about what had been circulating around the base about Mantell. "**The report was that he ran out of oxygen. He exceeded the safe altitude and** didn't have any oxygen aboard and he was at 15000feet. Part of his transmission was – now I can't say for sure – he either said it's gigantic and it's metallic or it's monstrous and metallic. But I think he said it's gigantic and metallic. I didn't read this. I heard part of this as it was coming over the radio and telephone. There was an hour or so discussion after it was over and when they found the wreckage. They determined 2-3days later that he had become unconscious and the airplane disintegrated in the air because it dived."

Ex-RAF Spitfire Pilot – Desmond Arthur Peter Leslie (his Father was a first cousin of Winston Churchill) **In** '*Flying Saucers Have Landed*' **written by Desmond Leslie and George Adamski** in 1953, commented on this sighting: "*The wreckage of his plane had been found in tiny pieces, scored by peculiar deep lines, as if he had got into a shower of some terribly unexplainable something, as though he had flown into the tremendous exhaust stream – or worse – against which no terrestrial metal could survive.*"

In *Flying Saucer Review, Volume 1, No.5, November/December 1955*. Desmond tells of meeting an engineer from Godman Field, who witnessed the event, during a trip to the States. The man told Desmond that the object came across the county slowly, at a speed estimated to be 110 miles per hour, at a height of 5-7000ft, and was 250-350ft in size. It passed over Benning Field, who notified Godman Field that a UFO was approaching their position. It is then said that although three F51 Mustang Fighters were available, only *one was fuelled and ready to scramble. According to the witness, "*It was a huge dull silver, circular, disc and flew along at an angle with a heavy list, so that the upper structure was plainly visible. The structure was a huge, flattened dome and everyone on the field had a perfect view of it; it was breath-taking. This was no weather balloon or atmospheric effect. The wreckage of the plane was spread over an area of six square miles, it did not fall in pieces but came down like confetti.*" He watched the flight leader – Captain Mantell – try to intercept it. **In addition to what was reported, he also described it as** "*having a ring of portholes surrounding the rim, but this was deleted from the voice transmission.*"

Leonard Stringfield, who wrote *Situation Red – The UFO siege* – worked with the Air Defense Command from 1953-1957 in the investigation and reporting of UFO activity, as well as an early warning co-coordinator for the Colorado Project under Dr. Condon. He was a man of great integrity and possessed impeccable credentials. He served in several important posts with **NICAP, IUFOR, MUFON, and the Center for UFO Studies**. Stringfield wrote: "*My informant, preferring anonymity, related that he had talked with Mantell's wing man, who witnessed the UFO incident. The pilot stated that Mantell pursued the UFO because he was the only pilot with an adequate oxygen mask. The pilot also related that he saw a burst of what appeared to be tracer fired from the UFO, which hit the P-51 and caused it to disintegrate in the air! Since the Mantell case, all other military encounters ending in disaster have been hidden from the public.*"

Incoming message!

To Dept. of Army, Washington DC to Wright Patterson AFB, Dayton, Ohio. 'Flying Turtle' UFO reported by Pilot! Air Material Command – 'Pilot from 15 Air Force at 0955 – **1st April** heading 180 degrees altitude 1,500ft indicated at 124 degrees 3 minutes east, 12°52 minutes north, weather scattered cumulus 3/10 base three thousand top 6000 visibility unlimited sighted flying object approximately 3 miles east IA heading 360, altitude, estimated one thousand feet below him. Unidentified object estimated speed at time 200 miles per hour; pilot turned left attempting to intercept unidentified flying object for more positive identification. At this time flying object made a turn of 90 degrees left levelled out and accelerated disappearing in approximately 5

THE HALT PERSPECTIVE 2

seconds, heading off 270° 'Pilot had phenomenon under observations for about 60 seconds, **described as having a turtle back and an indistinct dorsal fin, the shape of the object was that of a half moon, closely resembling a flying wing-type aircraft, esti***mated wing span 30ft length 20ft, silver*, no exhaust trail was observed, five seconds elapsed, time for disappearing would indicate exceedingly high speed.' **3rd April -UFO sighted; occupant descends! 4th April** '*Huge bird'* seen flying over Alton by Army Colonel. **5th April** – Two objects seen over Holloman air base. **8th April** – **'Flying Disc'** found in New York Town. **9th April** – '*Giant Bird'* sighted over Illinois. **12th April** – '**Missile**' reported over Los Angeles. **June 2nd** – 'drumming' sound and **mystery object** over Ontario Forest. **7th June flaming red cone'** reported over Army air base.

Pilot Clarence Chiles and co-pilot John Whitted were flying an Eastern Airlines Douglas DC-3 from Mobile, Alabama to Montgomery, at a height of about 5000 feet on the **24th of July** at approximately 2:45 a.m., Chiles spotted a hazy red cloud, somewhat similar to aircraft exhaust. It was slightly above them, and to the front-right of the DC-3 by about half a mile. Following the sighting which lasted for about 10 to 15 seconds, both men described the object as "***cigar – or torpedo-shaped, about 100 feet in length, and about three times the diameter of a B-29 bomber. The "fuselage" was entirely smooth, with no wings, projections or fins***. A bright red-orange exhaust emanated from the object's rear and was more orange at the outer edges of the exhaust but grew redder when it rose in altitude. The exhaust extended approximately 30 to 50 feet behind the object. They heard no sound from the object as it sped past the DC-3." Intriguingly, the witnesses described the object had what appeared to be "**two rows of rectangular windows**."

They weren't on their own. Walter Massey, a ground-crew chief at Robins Air Force Base, Georgia, about 150 miles from Montgomery; claimed to have seen a very similar object about an hour before Chiles and Whitted's encounter which he described as a "***Cylindrical object*** *that seemed to be two or three times larger than a B-29 "with a long stream of fire coming out the tail end … I noticed a faint glow on the belly of the wingless object."* (**Sources: Clark, Jerome,** *The UFO Encyclopedia:* **2nd Edition; Volume 1, A-K; Omnigraphics, Inc, 1998,** *Encyclopaedia of UFOs*, **Ronald Story, editor; Garden City: Doubleday & Company, Inc, 1980, 3** *The Report on Unidentified Flying Objects***, by Edward J. Ruppelt, 1956)**

July 24th/25th – **Numerous sightings of UFOs** over the **United States, 25th July** – **UFO sighted over Yakima Airport Washington. 31st July**– **Domed 'disc'** seen over Indianapolis. **27th July** – Dr **Lincoln Paz offers explanation on 'flying saucers.' August** – **Fluorescent green objects** seen to descend over Essex. **Summer** – **UFO tracked by Radar by NORAD-Explanation:** *high flying seagulls*!

Two 'flying persons' sighted near Grassy Butte, Oregon, Fred Scott (then aged 63) was walking from Antelope to Rome Oregon and passing near Grassy Butte just before dawn on the **16th of September**, when he looked up and was amazed to see, "***Two flying persons in the sky, one behind the other some 8-10 feet to the south of my direction at a height of about 150-200 feet up in the air, heading slowly in a west to east direction. They had wings narrow and rounded at the tip, which didn't flap, and their legs were unusually short, almost as if cut off from the knees.***" (Source Kenneth Arnold interview 12.July.1950//letter from Jerome Clark to Ted Bloecher 26.Sept.77)

23rd September – '**Amoeba**' object seen over California. **October 1st,** – **US Pilot chases 'ligh**t 'through sky (written off as **Weather balloon** later!) **24th October** – Silvery object seen over Winnipeg. **November 18th,** – Pilot sights UFO over Andrews Air Force Base Maryland. **December 3rd** –Air Traffic Control reports sighting UFO.

THE HALT PERSPECTIVE 2

1949 – January 4th, USAF Captain sights UFO circling the sky. **March** -Strange phenomenon sighted over Staffordshire. **March –** Paratrooper sights **yellow 'disc'** in the sky. **17th March – Eight UFOs** sighted over Texas. **April 3rd,** –Object, shaped like **two plates** seen over Montana. **4th April – Curved UFO** sighted over California. **5th April –** Police Officer sights UFO – then **Triangular UFO** seen. **6th April – 'Flying Disc'** sighted over Stapleton Airfield, Denver. **8th April – UFO** seen over Indiana. **14th April – Four rectangular UFOs** sighted over New Jersey. **24th April – UFO sighted over Skyhook balloon. 24th April – 'Sausage'-shaped object** sighted over Arizona. **May 2nd,** – **Three 'flying discs**'seen by an air traffic controller. **5th May – Two 'flying discs'** seen by Army Officers. **18th May –** a New Orleans housewife was outside watering her lawn when she noticed a **silver disc-shaped object, resembling a dinner plate in appearance**, approximately the size of a small aircraft, apparently travelling east to North-North-west direction on the outskirts of the City, in the vicinity of Lake Pontchartrain, two miles away, at an angle of 45 degrees off the horizon. **19th May –** Two **flat objects** sighted over Arizona. On the **21st May** an F-82 Fighter aircraft was dispatched from Moses Lake AFB, near Hanford, Washington, to intercept a **'flying disc'** that was observed hovering in restricted airspace over **Hanford Atomic Power Plant** at an altitude of 17-20,000ft by personnel and confirmed on radar. Before the aircraft could take off the object shot off in a southerly direction at a speed greater than the jet fighter. A short time later another aircraft was observed on radar in the restricted area of the Hanford Atomic Power Plant. This one was positively identified as a commercial aircraft, dropping leaflets announcing a rodeo!

Three men and two women were out fishing in a boat near the mouth of Oregon's Rogue River, on a clear day, with the sun behind their backs, at 5pm on the 24th of May, when they noticed a strange circular object approaching from the north-east. After watching it hovering in the sky to the east of them for about two and a half minutes, it shot away silently at high speed in a southerly direction. The fishermen (and women) – then employees of the Ames Research Laboratory at Moffett Field, near San Francisco – were able to look at the object through binoculars for about a minute each when they saw an object they described as being, *"circular and thin, relative to its diameter, with a shape similar to that of a pancake, with some sort of vertical fin on the upper surface at the trailing edge. No wings, antenna lights, propellers, engines or exhaust ports could be seen or heard; its trailing edge looked wrinkled and dirty."*

About three weeks later the Ames employees reported their sighting to the security office at Moffett Field. The security office then requested AFOSI agents to investigate the sighting. Examination of Blue Book archive material reveals the Rogue River UFO report had been inexplicably split into two separate accounts; the one taken from Olive Elizabeth Macbeth, giving the address: PO Box 207 Gold Beach, Oregon was not matched up with the other statements obtained from her companions Dr. Gilbert Rivera, of California; and James Heaphy of 152, Sherman Avenue, North Bend, Oregon. **Dr. Allen Hynek** pointed out the *Blue Book* files carried this UFO sighting under the classification of aircraft, based on the assumption the UFO and aircraft were one and the same, despite the comment made by the investigating officer that 'two separate and distinct alert conditions existed on the afternoon of 24th May 1949'. **24th May** – UFO sighted over Rogue River Oregon. **July 24th,** –A Pilot sights seven UFOs in a 'V' shaped formation at midday over Mountain Home Idaho. He estimated the height to be eight thousand feet at a speed of about 600mph. **30th July** – Pilot and ATC sight object over Mount Hood, Oregon. **August** – **'Operation Bulldog'** launched. **November –** Strait of Hormuz: Three objects sighted under the sea by USN Commander J.F. Bodler.

1950 – February 5th, two Illuminated cylindrical objects sighted over Teaticket, Massachusetts. 24th February , elongated object seen over Albuquerque New Mexico, second UFO sighting later over Los Alamos, New Mexico. March – Three UFOs sighted over Minnis Bay

Kent, 13th March, cylindrical UFO seen over McClellan Air Force Base, California. 17th March, large number of strange objects in sky, some 'flying saucer' in shape over Farmington New Mexico. 20th March, 'Flying Disc', with 'portholes', seen by pilots over Stuttgart Arkansas. 29th March, six 'bomb' shaped objects seen over Marrowbone Lake Tennessee. April 27th, – *TWA* pilots sight UFO over Goshen Indiana. 29th May, American Airlines Pilot sights UFO over Maryland.

During the summer Dennis Maycroft from Nottinghamshire was carrying out electrical installation work to the *BBC* transmitter at Holme Moss, Yorkshire, near Holmfirth. He was working on a mast platform approximately 600ft off the ground with Mr. Frederick Binchell, a senior engineer from the BBC, and four steel erectors from the Birmingham area. At 2.30pm they noticed something in the sky, roughly two miles away over the Huddersfield area. *"It was shaped like an upturned saucer, silver in appearance, and approximately a hundred feet in length. We watched it move slowly up and down in the sky, noting when it was in the 'up' position, the underside appeared dark. When it was 'down', you could see a bluish 'energy' around the top of it. Details of the sighting were passed by telephone to Mr. Binchell, who was now on the ground."* After some two hours had elapsed the saucer-shaped object climbed upwards at tremendous speed before being lost from view. When Dennis returned to the ground, he discovered over twenty people had seen the unidentified flying object, including the senior engineer who had already left on his way to the *BBC* in London to report the incident. *"A few weeks later, when somebody enquired about the sighting, he was told 'it had been a weather balloon'. If this had been the case, how could it have hovered in the same position for two hours and move at such fantastic speed?"*

RAF Test pilot on ground sights UFO over airbase!

On August 14th, Stanley Hubbard, then a Flt. Test Pilot with the RAF had this to say: *"It was a warm day and unusually quiet for a base that normally resonated with the sound of general noise and aircraft engines. As I trudged across the runway, heading towards the Mess where I was billeted, I became aware of a strange sound coming from somewhere behind me. I stopped and turned around, curious as to the source of this noise, and was very much taken aback to see an object, looking like a* **'flying sports discus'***, rocking from side – to – side in a regular rhythm of movement, (approximately 20 – 25 degrees either side) heading across the sky at about a thousand feet off the ground. I watched as it moved over, noting that the exterior of the craft appeared to be light grey in colour – a bit like mother-of-pearl – blurred, rather than sharply defined. As it passed overhead, it allowed me to determine it was obviously reflecting light because, as it rocked, it reminded me of a* **pan lid, rotating segments of light. Around the edges were what looked like tiny crackling, sparkling lights, accompanied by a powerful smell of ozone.***"

The next thing I was aware of was the arrival of the female dispatcher from the radio shack nearby. She was hysterical. She screamed out my name and said, 'Did you see that horrible thing go over?' I walked over to the Wing Commander's office and explained what I had seen. He made a telephone call to the Air Ministry, who interviewed me a few hours later, following which I was advised not to make any enquiries about the incident, or discuss it with anybody else." **(Source: Personal Interview).**

Flt. Lt. Stanley Hubbard

THE HALT PERSPECTIVE 2

What would have been Stan's reaction, then, if he had learnt of a sighting **the following day** involving Colonel Robert Willingham, of the USAF, who was navigator aboard a F94 jet, when, *"A saucer flew right over [us], put down three landing gears, and landed out on the dry lake – bed. [The cameramen] went out there with their cameras toward the UFO. I had a chance to hold [the film] up to the window. Good close – up shots. We got to watching how it made 90° turns at this high speed and everything. We knew it wasn't a missile of any type. So then, we confirmed it with the radar control station, and they kept following it, and they claimed that it **crashed somewhere off between Texas and the Mexico border.**"* Both incidents were explained away officially as either hallucinations, or misidentifications!

During our communication with Mr. Hubbard in 2006 about what he had witnessed, he told us he had been inundated by requests from T.V. and film-makers in the United Kingdom, including the BBC, to take part in further documentaries. Stan: "**Such matters are now of no interest to me, especially after what I saw as a most embarrassing performance, broadcast by a group of total incompetents!**"

Three disc-shaped objects seen over Dover, Kent

Joyce Mary Tyson (born 25.Nov.1919) and her husband an ex-army officer who had served in the military Police – well versed in the use of small arms and military vehicles were enjoying a picnic not far from the Radar Station at St Margaret's Bay, Dover Kent in August. They noticed three disc – shaped objects over the town of Deal, coming in from the direction of the English Channel. As the objects approached closer her husband took a photograph of them. Joyce, *"The 'Discs' now looked more like a child's flattened spinning top with the top being slightly rounded, with a bulge around the outside and underneath, looking like an inverted saucer, with a sort of glittery effect which could have been caused by the sun in the stern part of the sky reflecting off the objects. The objects appeared to be sharply defined, with one of them being slightly higher than the other two on either side of it. As they flew over the cliff top, they appeared to be heading out to sea, but then changed direction and headed straight towards where we were standing. My husband shouted out, 'Good God! – what are those?' "* At this point, Mr Tyson took a second photograph – then a third, as one of them split and headed away eastwards . . . Mr & Mrs Tyson sent copies of the first two photographs to the *Daily Mirror*, asking them if they would be interested in publishing them. After some time had elapsed the couple contacted the paper asking them for an update. The Daily Mirror denied having received any photos from them. **(Source: Chris Rolfe)**

September 3rd, three, bronze 'flying discs' seen over Spokane Washington. 5th September, Stan Hubbard sights UFO for second time over RAF Farnborough. 20th September; – Two objects with three smaller ones inside seen hovering over Colorado. 21st September, – UFO tracked on radar over Massachusetts. – 1st October; object seen to land by Philadelphia Police Officers. 12th October, four blazing orbs of light were seen sweeping backwards and forwards in the sky over England. 15th October, UFO, shaped like a bullet sighted over Oak Ridge Tennessee Atomic Power Station. 19th October, workmen at Tallington near Stamford, Lincolnshire reported having sighted **three 'flying saucers'**, one of which was seen to break slowly away and head north – westwards. 25th October, – formation of UFOs seen heading towards Cardigan Bay. 30th October, two big glittering 'stars', showing long pointed 'tails', were seen moving slowly through the sky over Hirwaun, near Aberdare, Merthyr Tydfil, Wales, by a number of people in the town and surrounding areas, who contacted the authorities. Many of the reports told of seeing what looked like stars either travelling together or 'attached to each other', approaching from the west and heading eastwards. Some people even described seeing them divide in flight. (**Sources:** *South Wales News,* **31.Oct.50,** *'Flying Saucers in Wales?' Western Mail,* **2.Nov.50, 'More say they saw Flying Saucer',** *Western Mail,* **4.Nov.50 'More about Flying Saucers',** *Western Mail & South Wales News,* **4.Nov.50**)

A 'Cigar'-shaped object seen over Chiswick London. Police officer sights mysterious 'bars of light' in the sky over Gowerton Wales. 5th November, 'Cigarette-shaped' UFO seen over London. 5th November, Bean shaped UFO sighted over Oak Ridge, Tennessee. 6th November 'Comet-like object' sighted over Southampton. 22nd November, Former RAF Officer sights UFO over Yeovil.

1951 – January, Two objects described as resembling 'silver shillings', one behind the other, sighted travelling high in the sky over Ipswich, Suffolk. 8th January, three lights forming a Triangle seen over Fort Worth Texas. 12th January, object sighted stationary over Fort Benning Georgia leaving Fan – shaped trail. 16th January – Two members of General Mills Aeronautical Research Laboratory, Artesia, New Mexico sighted a dull white, round object in the sky. February 26th, Metallic object seen hovering over, Ladd Air Force Base, Fairbanks Alaska. 5th April, Triangular object showing **three lights** seen hovering over Portsmouth. May, Formation of five 'V' shaped objects seen over Isle of Wight. **Project Blue Book**

In a letter sent to Captain (later Major) Hector Quintanilla by John G. Young – then living at Klamath Falls, Oregon: *"Dear Captain Quintanilla, I saw in the paper recently how you take UFOs seriously. I have had a little secret for about 13 years, but always feared of being labelled as a crackpot, but at this stage I couldn't care less. Our home in England was about 500 yards from the River Thames, half – way between the towns Kingston and Richmond, Surrey. I was home on a 3 – day pass from the Army,* in **June 1951,** *when I happened to glance up and was startled to see a* **very big, bright, circular object. It stayed over our position above the river for what seemed a long time**, *although it may have been only a minute. I longed for a camera, or other witness, but there was none to be seen or heard. I had heard of 'flying saucers' with portholes around the side, but this was just a silvery bright object, the size of an average parachute.* **It was as a plate, or saucer.**" **1st June – glowing yellow saucer-shaped** object sighted over Niagara Falls. **24th July, Tubular fin-shaped object** sighted in the same year.

Leonard Burrell from Kessingland, Suffolk, was completing his National Service at RAF Church Lawford, just outside Rugby, Northamptonshire in July when he saw something that caught his eye – *"... a bright light, brighter than the sun behind it. It seemed to flash on and off at one second intervals, clearly visible against a blue sky with a few high feathery clouds far away on the horizon. I looked at my wristwatch (12.35pm) and continued to observe the object.*

Approximately ten minutes later, the object had descended low enough for me to make out precisely what it looked like. I estimated it to be between five and ten feet long and three to six feet wide in the middle. It was silver metallic in appearance, with a very high gloss to its outer surface, and seemed to have been constructed from glass – like material, with a mirror finish. It reminded me of a very large diamond, with finely cut edges. The object was now at its lowest point, about 500 feet off the ground and 2 – 300 yards away, appearing to rest for a while, for several seconds, over a group of trees near the school buildings.

A short time later the UFO began to move slowly upwards, still turning at the same speed and

THE HALT PERSPECTIVE 2

flashing regularly, with bright sunlight reflecting off each facet of its surface. Within 20 minutes it had gone." Len contacted the nearest RAF weather station and explained what he had seen. They confirmed that no weather balloons were in the area that day and were unable to offer any logical explanation for the sighting. **(Source: Personal Interview).**

11th August, Over Portland Oregon, **three objects** seen flying in a perfect 'V'-shaped formation. 31st August, 'Pear' – shaped object sighted over Matador Texas. Scotland: Orange UFO (like two soup bowls joined together – 70ft off ground) seen following a tractor. Schoolboy sights RAF jets followed by 2 or 3 white discs over Norwich. September 6th, Six orange 'lights' sighted over Claremont, California. 20th September– 'oblong airships' seen by family, over London. **Police officers confront landed UFO**!

On the 1st of October 1951 the *Sunday Express* published a report relating to a report of an object seen to land by two Philadelphia police officers; unfortunately, the actual date or location isn't known but appears to have taken place in this month. Quote: "Patrol – man John Collins and Joseph Kennan saw a large spherical shiny object float gently downwards onto a field. The officers called for assistance and were joined by James Caspar and Sergeant Joseph Cook. Warily they approached the object which sat there, silently gleaming in the light of their flash lamps. After observing it for some moments, John plucked up the courage and prodded it, '*I touched it and it just dissolved, leaving my fingers sticky, there was no smell, just stickiness. Over the next twenty minutes the thing slowly began to disappear. Thirty minutes later it had gone, leaving no trace in the ground.*' "

October 2nd, UFO with clipped tail seen over Columbus Ohio. 9th October – Civil Aviation Authority Chief, reports sighting silver shaped UFO. 11th October – Balloonists sight UFOs over Minneapolis. October 12th, 'flying saucers' seen over Lincolnshire. November 24th, P-51 Mustang pilots sight 'Flying wing' UFO over Mankato Minnesota. December 7th, Square UFO sighted over Oak Ridge Tennessee. **[More than a thousand sightings were reported to the authorities that year involving unidentified objects reported over airports military bases and atomic energy centres.]**

The Colonel comments

It's odd to be commenting on UFO sightings from a period of time when I was only a young boy around 10 years of age living in Pittsburgh, Pennsylvania to a middle class family.

My Dad worked at a steel mill, until he joined the Navy, training for the Merchant Marine Fleet. Then the War ended and he became an insurance salesman. People think that because I retired as a Colonel

that I had come from a well to do background. I wish! In fact both my parents were products of the depression – no doubt this was why my mother was always concerned about money and meeting household bills etc., but we always had food on the table. My Mother recently celebrated her 100th birthday! It was a happy childhood but tight finances meant most of my clothes were quality hand-me-downs as we were fortunate to have several well to do family friends with older boys. When I was nine or 10 years of age I inherited a large, slightly used

erector set for Christmas, from one of those families. It provided countless hours of entertainment and I learned a great deal about engineering principles. It was big step from the mostly homemade toys I had become accustomed to. When I was nine I inherited a morning paper route with the Pittsburgh Post Gazette. The paper bag was so heavy that I had to make several trips around the neighbourhood at 5:30 am – this was a bit of a drag but provided an income and I did it until I was 17, by which time I had saved up enough for my first year of college. The following year I received a hand me down chemistry set for Christmas. I quickly became a budding Chemist. I discovered *Fisher Scientific* with their major outlet based in Pittsburgh.

Well the years have flown by. I never expected in my wildest dreams that because of an amazing incident in which I was involved in during December 1980 – that I would find myself 40 years later, scrutinising reports of UFO activity from so many members of the public, including members of the armed forces not only in the UK, where I served, but in the States.

Looking at a period of history, now 70 years ago, it's important that we don't allow peoples' experiences which *do change your life* slip away to be lost in the mists of time. People will point out that one only has to research the Internet to find out who, what, where, and when, with regard to reported UFO activity. The drawback to this is that very few people have been able to interview those witnesses. In this book there are many primary sources which are what the book is about.

Look at what RAF Test Pilot Stanley Hubbard, witnessed – further evidence of inexplicable aerial phenomena this time over RAF Farnborough Airbase, England in 1950, over half a century ago during a period of intense Worldwide UFO activity! All he wanted like me and so many others are answers – none are forthcoming.

Then we have the saucer-shaped object seen over the BBC transmitting aerial explained away later

as a weather balloon! To complicate matters even further, the illustration drawn from interview with RAF serviceman Len Burrell shows what at first glance appears to be a kite, but unlikely to be the case, another mystery unsolved!

Are they seriously expecting us now to believe this was the case – not forgetting a few years ago when what appears to have been a similar object was reported over a US Atomic Power plant when after a fighter jet appeared the object shot away

There is no reason to dispute what is being seen visually, but what it is and where it originates from is a matter that still continues to baffle those few who treat the matter seriously, rather than the flippancy now attached to the subject which doesn't make sense?

Rationally if one concedes that serious research has been secretly conducted into the subject by scientists with unlimited budgets, then some answers must have been obtained. If this is the case, why aren't they then being made available to the public? For some inexplicable reasons, some UFOs have been seen hovering over Nuclear power stations and Military Air Bases. What would be the attraction there? Energy, curiosity, I wish I knew – or do I?

One man that has researched into this aspect of UFO activity is Robert Hastings who is a friend of mine. He has sought out and interviewed former and retired U.S. Air Force personnel regarding their direct or indirect involvement in nuclear weapons – related UFO incidents. These individuals – ranging from retired Colonels to former airmen – report extraordinary encounters which have obvious national security implications. In fact, taken to their logical conclusion, these cases have *planetary* implications, given the horrific consequences that would result from a full – scale, global nuclear war. Numerous cases include reports of mysterious *malfunctions* of large numbers of nuclear missiles just as one or more UFOs hovered nearby.

(Declassified Soviet Ministry of Defense documents confirm that such incidents also occurred in the former USSR.) To date, Robert Hastings has interviewed more than 150 military veterans who were involved in various UFO – related incidents at U.S. missile sites, weapons storage facilities, and nuclear bomb test ranges. The events described by these individuals leave little doubt that the U.S. nuclear weapons program is an ongoing source of interest

Robert Hastings

to someone possessing vastly superior technology. Significantly, UFO activity occasionally transcends from what many people believe to be just mere surveillance and involves direct and unambiguous interference with our strategic weapons systems. The reasons behind such actions are, of course, unknown generally, those that have studied UFOs for years wonder if 'they 'or 'it' are driven by some schedule or is the phenomena random in its movement. One thing is assured, the forces that lie behind these manifestations have time on their hands which we don't; bearing in mind the strong likelihood that the phenomena has been around for hundreds, if not thousands of years.

Robert has presented his research findings at more than 500 colleges and universities nationwide, and possesses hundreds of highly favorable letters of recommendation from sponsors. *"I am not condemning any government agency for its policy of secrecy regarding UFOs, but I believe that the public should be given the facts."* Hastings believes that UFOs are piloted by visitors from elsewhere in the universe who, for whatever reason, have taken an interest in our long – term survival. He contends that these beings are occasionally disrupting our nukes to send a message to the American and Soviet/Russian governments that their possession and potential large – scale use of nuclear weapons threatens the future of humanity and the environmental integrity of the planet. In short, Washington and Moscow are being warned that they are "playing with fire."

To suggest that this scenario is the only explanation for widespread UFO sightings during the modern era would be presumptuous, simplistic, and undoubtedly inaccurate. Nevertheless, Hastings believes that the now well-documented nuclear weapons-related incidents are integral to an understanding of the mystery that confronts us. Sometimes reality is indeed stranger than fiction.

I wish I could explain what it was that I saw in the sky over Rendlesham Forest, Suffolk and what the other airmen experienced and could offer an explanation for a myriad of inexplicable objects that appear to roam the skies at free will, despite our best efforts to curb their movements. But it's important to record the truth which always seems to be under attack by those who weren't even there and some who weren't even born!

'Flying saucer' sculpture marks the wrong spot!

The Suffolk Forestry Commission spent some £15000 on commissioning a sculpture of a 'flying saucer' which was then placed a short distance from the boundary fence, proclaiming this is where I or Jim Penniston saw the UFO – but it's in the wrong place! Something like this attracts many visitors who flock there to pose next to it but its location is inaccurate.

I refuse to go there and pose next to it. It's nowhere near where the event took place and just unfortunately, albeit unintentionally, adds even more confusion as to what took place. Looking at the UFO events that took place in 1951, the reader can see what forms a common thread to the background of this book; the appearance in the sky of three globes of lights of approximately equal distance from each other forming a visual triangle of light.

Not forgetting as I will point out many times, while the Media often see the funny side of UFO reports (an unintentional course of action based on superficial education on the chosen topic) the opposite prevails!

1952 – In January, W.R.A.F officer sights 'flaming oblong UFO' over Canterbury. 29th January, glowing 'Pear-shaped UFO' sighted over Hampshire. February 11th, Pilots sight a yellow-orange comet-shaped object, pulsing flame for a few seconds. 20th February, red, fiery object seen zig-zagging in the sky over Long Beach California. 20th February, Greenfield Massachusetts Church Minister sights three silver objects travelling in a 'V'-shaped formation. 21st February – Three green 'balls of fire' seen in the sky over Richmond. 28th February, Cambridge Students sights UFO heading north east. March 20th, saucer-shaped 'light' seen over Maryland. 23rd March, mysterious red fireballs sighted over Washington. 24th March, UFO Tracked on radar – at speed of 3000mph over California. April 4th, UFO Tracked on radar over Texas – speed 2,160 mph. 5th April, three dull grey circular objects sighted over Phoenix. 6th April, Huge formation of 'flying discs' witnessed over Texas.

14th April pilots sight 'inverted bowl' UFO over Tennessee. 17th April, deep orange coloured object seen over Arizona. 18th April, number of lights forming 'V'-shaped formation seen over Maryland. 19th April, Toronto, Canada, 10.30pm, 50 – 60 pale orange objects sighted in 'V'-shaped formation – seconds later out of sight. 24th April, Vancouver 7:30pm 'V' formation of objects with second 'V' formation inside appeared from the south direction and then shot upwards into the sky.

24th April, pilots sight **three UFOs** over Vermont. 27th April, Cigar-shaped objects observed over Michigan. 29th April, pilot encounters pulsating object. May 1st, – Five flying 'discs' sighted over *Moses Lake* Washington. May 7th, silver white object sighted over Nevada. 9th May, 'flying' blue bubble' sighted over Malvern Hills, Worcestershire, England by radar personnel. May, 'flying disc' sighted over Kensington, London. May 5th-6th-7th, objects sighted over New Jersey. 7th May, silver cylindrical object over Keesler AFB. 9th May, arrow-shaped object over George AFB California. 10th May, UFOs sighted over Savannah Nuclear Power Station. 19th May – Seven objects sighted by pilots over Texas. June 1st – *Sunday Dispatch* newspaper, Cigar-shaped UFO sighted over Dorset.

July 14th, – two Pan American pilots were flying on a heading of 60° near Norfolk Virginia when they saw eight objects in the sky over Chesapeake Bay near Old Point Comfort Virginia.

THE HALT PERSPECTIVE 2

Washington DC National Airport – Seven UFOs tracked on radar – then over White House!

At 11:40 p.m. Saturday, July 19, 1952, Edward Nugent, an air traffic controller at Washington National Airport (today Ronald Reagan Washington National Airport) plotted seven objects on his radar scope located 15 miles (24 km) south – south – west of the city; no known aircraft were in the area and the objects were not following any established flight paths. Nugent's superior, Harry Barnes, a senior air – traffic controller at the airport, watched the objects on Nugent's radar scope. He later wrote: *"We knew immediately that a very strange situation existed . . . their movements were completely radical compared to those of ordinary aircraft."* Barnes had two controllers check Nugent's radar; they found that it was working normally. Barnes then called National Airport's other radar centre; the controller there, Howard Cocklin, told Barnes that he also had the objects on his radar scope. Furthermore, Cocklin said that by looking out of the control tower window he could see one of the objects: *"a bright orange light. I can't tell what's behind it."*

At this point, other objects appeared in all sectors of the radar scope; when they moved over the White House and the United States Capitol, Barnes called Andrews Air Force Base, located 10 miles from National Airport. Although Andrews reported that they had no unusual objects on their radar, an airman soon called the base's control tower to report the sighting of a strange object. Airman William Brady, who was in the tower, then saw an *"object which appeared to be like an orange ball of fire, trailing a tail unlike anything I had ever seen before."* As Brady tried to alert the other personnel in the tower, the strange object *"took off at an unbelievable speed."* Meanwhile, another person in the National Airport control tower reported seeing *"an orange disk about 3,000 feet altitude."*

Capital Airlines pilot, S.C. Pierman was waiting in the cockpit of his DC – 4 on one of the airport's runways, for permission to take off. After spotting what he believed to be a meteor, he was told that the control tower's radar had picked up unknown objects closing in on his position. Pierman observed six objects – *"white, tailless, fast-moving lights"* – during a 14-minute period. Pierman was in radio contact with Barnes during his sighting, and Barnes later related that *"each sighting coincided with a pip we could see near his plane. When he reported that the light streaked off at a high speed, it disappeared on our scope."*

At Andrews AFB, meanwhile, the control tower personnel were tracking on radar what some thought to be unknown objects, but others suspected, and in one instance were able to prove, were simply stars and meteors. However, Staff Sgt. Charles Davenport observed an orange-red light to the south; the light *"would appear to stop and then make an abrupt change in direction and altitude . . . this happened several times."* At one point, both radar centres at National Airport and the radar at Andrews AFB were tracking an object hovering over a radio beacon. The object vanished in all three radar centres at the same time. At 3am, shortly before two jet fighters from Newcastle AFB in Delaware arrived over Washington, all the objects vanished from the radar at National Airport. However, when the jets ran low on fuel and left, the objects returned, which convinced Barnes that *"the UFOs were monitoring radio traffic and behaving accordingly."* The objects were last detected by radar at 5.30am around sunrise, E.W. Chambers, a civilian radio engineer in Washington's suburbs, observed **"five huge disks circling in a loose formation. They tilted upward and left on a steep ascent."**

A famous photograph widely available, that purports to show a formation of UFOs overflying the nation's capital, was examined by *Major (retired) Colman S Von Keviczky and determined

THE HALT PERSPECTIVE 2

from subsequent analysis to be **lamps on the building's balcony** overlooking the White House! Photographs like this and other faked images hinder rather than help any cause! **(Sources: Clark, Jerome,** *The UFO Book: Encyclopaedia of the Extraterrestrial.* **Visible Ink, 1998 – 1997. Peebles, Curtis,** *Watch the Skies! A Chronicle of the Flying Saucer Myth.* **Berkley Books,** **1994. Randle, Kevin D.,** *Invasion Washington: UFOs Over the Capitol. Harper Torch,* **2001. Ruppelt, Edward J.** *The Report on Unidentified Flying Objects*)

At 6.22pm while over Portland, Maine, the crew of a US Navy P2V Neptune patrol plane sighted a group of five **'lights',** while a long, thin blip was being tracked on radar. Although some consideration was given to this being USAF KC – 97 airplanes, involved in a refuelling operation, it appears unlikely to be the case. The sighting lasted 20 minutes. At 7.30pm the same day, three USAF officers and two civilians from Warner Robins Air Force Base, Georgia, sighted two white 'lights' heading across the sky, side by side, at an estimated speed of 100 miles per hour, over a period of 15 minutes observation. At 8:15 p.m. on Saturday, **July 26, 1952**, a pilot and stewardess on a National Airlines flight into Washington observed **some strange objects** above their plane. Within minutes, both radar centres at National Airport, and the radar at Andrews AFB, were tracking more unknown objects. A master sergeant at Andrews visually observed the objects; he later said that *"these lights did not have the characteristics of shooting stars. There were no trails... they travelled faster than any shooting star I have ever seen."*

NATO's first Exercise, 'Operation Mainbrace' begins!

In September 1952, NATO's first Exercise, 'Operation Mainbrace', was conceived by General Eisenhower to show NATO members Norway and Denmark that their land could be defended in the event of war with Russia. It involved the use of 200 ships from eight nations and over 80,000 men, and it was held in the North Atlantic, between Ireland and Iceland. During the night of September 13th 1952, Lieutenant Commander Schmidt Jensen and several members of his crew aboard the Danish Destroyer *Willemoes* were north of Bornholm Island when they saw an unidentified object, triangular in shape, emitting a bluish glow moving at high speed towards the south – east at an estimated speed of over 900mph. *"I was in charge of the bridge and the Captain had just turned in. The sky was clear when, suddenly, we heard a whistling sound and saw a 'flying triangle' passing at speed. It was luminous, with a greenish light, and flew with one corner pointing forward. From its rear jetted three rays of fire backwards. I have no idea how high it was, so I could not judge either its size or speed, but I believe it went at more than 1,500 km/hour. It disappeared in a north – westerly direction. I have studied some astronomy and have also learned to identify most of the modern planes, and I am sure it was neither."* (Although this may appear to be a 'one off' case, the reader should be aware of a particularly heavy period of UFO activity taking place in the USA at that time, involving over 580 reports of unidentified flying objects seen, beginning in July 1947. This information is taken from the files of *'Blue Book Unknowns'* kept at Maxwell AFB). (Source: Don Berliner Fund for UFO Research)

At 11.40am 17th September 1952 over Tucson, Arizona, Mr. and Mrs. Ted Hollingsworth sighted: *"...two groups of three large, flat, shining objects, flying in tight formations. The first group was slow, the second faster – both out of sight, two minutes later."* On 19th September 1952, two RAF officers and three members of the ground crew stood near Coastal Command, Shackleton Squadron, at RAF Topcliffe Yorkshire, were watching a Meteor Jet descending to land at the nearby

THE HALT PERSPECTIVE 2

Dishforth airbase, at 10.30am. In an interview later held with a reporter from the *Sunday Dispatch* (21.Sept.1952), Flight Lieutenant John W. Kilburn from Egremont, Cumberland, had this to say:

"It was something different from anything I have ever seen in 3,700 hours of flying in a variety of conditions. As the Meteor crossed from east to west, I noticed a white object in the sky. It was silver and circular in shape, about 10,000ft up, some five miles astern of the aircraft. It appeared to be travelling at a lower speed than the Meteor but was on the same course. I said, 'What the hell is that?', and the chaps looked to where I was pointing. Somebody shouted that it might be the engine cowling of a Meteor falling out of the sky – then we thought it might have been a parachute – but, as we watched the 'disc', it maintained a slow, forward speed for a few seconds, before starting to descend."

"While descending, it was swinging in a pendulum fashion from left to right. As the Meteor turned to start its landing run, the object appeared to be following but, after a few seconds, it stopped its descent and **hung in the air, rotating as if on its own axis**. It then accelerated at an incredible speed to the west, turned south-east and disappeared. It was difficult to estimate the speed of the object, as it was all over within 15-20 seconds. During that time, we could see it was flashing in the sunshine. It appeared to be about the size of a Vampire Jet aircraft, at similar height. We were all convinced it was some solid object.

We realised it could not be a broken cowling, or parachute. There was not the slightest possibility it was a smoke ring, or vapour trail from the Meteor or from a jet aircraft, nor a weather observation balloon. The speed of which it moved discounts this altogether."

The other air crew – Flight Lieutenant Marian Cybulski, Master Signaller Albert W. Thompson, Sergeant Flight Engineer Thomas B. Dewey and Flight Lieutenant R.M. Paris – confirmed the account given by F/Lt. Kilburn. In addition, LAC George Grime told of seeing:

"...a sort of halo shining on the centre of the object; it appeared to be going rotating and shining as it turned. It was a solid object, with no marks on it."

(Source: *North Evening Gazette*, 29.Sept.1952 – 'Flying Saucer Seen /*Sunday Dispatch*, 7.Dec.1952 – 'RAF's Saucer – Still A Mystery')

Kathleen V. Wilson-Sharp of High Lawns, Colchester, was enjoying a picnic with her husband near Crayke, in September 1952. *"I was watching some Fighters coming in to land at Dishforth Aerodrome, about 20 miles away to the North, when I noticed a circular object emerge out of two very dark clouds and hover above the Aerodrome. At first, I thought it must be a weather balloon, as it appeared stationary, when suddenly it turned and streaked off in a very un-balloon-like horizontal and speedy manner. When I first saw the object, it caught the light of the sun. As it turned, it had a brilliant light of its own. It seemed to me to be more like an inverted cup and saucer, not unlike a lemon squeezer."* Mrs. Wilson-Sharp was so puzzled about what she had seen that she wrote to the commanding officer at Dishforth Aerodrome, asking if anyone there had seen it. He wrote back by return, thanking her for the clear description of it and stating that *"six of my officers had seen it and their description tallied with yours."* He also told her that he was *"collecting all the evidence he could and had written and published a book on the subject"* – what a pity we do not have a copy of this letter, or the book! [It is believed that this officer may have been Wing Commander John Arthur Charles Stratton who was awarded an OBE in 1953 by Her Majesty the Queen.]

We learnt RAF personnel at Neatishead in the UK had also witnessed something on the radar scope during the same year, according to one airman plotter, who spoke of a particular night when, as the night jet fighters were due to be stood down, they began to receive new plots on the radar scope, originating in Cornwall and extending north-east to the North Sea, involving a track with six plots, with a time lapse between each plot of seven seconds. This indicated that whatever it was had travelled three hundred-and-fifty miles in thirty-five seconds – six thousand miles per hour! Another RAF Neatishead witness was Frank Redfern, father of Nick Redfern. *"In September 1952 during 'Operation Mainbrace', I was manning the radar screen when just after 4.00am the scope picked up an object, which at first I thought may have been an aircraft; travelling at 50,000ft over the North Sea, and parallel to the English Coast. Then I realised, due to its enormous speed, this could not be so. Aircraft from RAF Coltishall were scrambled to intercept. One of the jets attempted to intercept the object, but it shot off across the sky at tremendous speed, heading towards Norway. The next day, a group of people from Coltishall arrived. They included a photographic team and additional radar equipment. To our surprise the UFO showed up again, on the scope and they scrambled the aircraft. As far as I know, they did capture it on film. The following day, the radar tapes and records kept of the incident were seized by a group from Coltishall, and that was the last I heard of it."*

Questions raised in the House of Commons about this matter, seven years later!

According to *Hansard, on* February **2nd 1959,** (seven years after the Topcliffe sighting had taken place) Mr. Mason asked the Secretary of State for Air – Mr George Ward – for the results of the enquiry into 'the unidentified flying objects' sighted by airmen, during NATO's '**Operation Mainbrace'**, on 19th September 1952. Mr. Ward replied, "**No object was ever identified**". 20th **September 1952** – **white object** seen over Sutton, Surrey, three RAF jets then seen to pass overhead. **21st September 1952** – **UFO sighted by six RAF jets – tracked on radar over, North Sea**. **22nd September 1952** – Milton Keynes motorist sights **illuminated 'dinner plate'**. **24th September 1952 – Flashing particles stream past B-29 aircraft over Charleston, West Virginia. 29th September 1952 – five or six objects** seen in the sky over Colorado. **September 1952 – UFO tracked on radar over North Sea** – RAF Scrambled – attempted to intercept. **September**

THE HALT PERSPECTIVE 2

1952 – Saucer-shaped object seen over Bexley Heath, Kent. **Giant black object, seen hovering just above River *Debden*, Suffolk – 5 miles from RAF Woodridge. October 1st, 1952 – South Carolina pilot attempts to intercept UFO**. 10th October 1952 – **'Blinking' white light** seen over Otis Air Force Base, Massachusetts. **17th October 1952 – rectangle of ten 'lights'** seen over Killeen Texas by Church Ministers. **19th October 1952 – 'V'-shaped formation of three UFO seen over San Antonio.**

Air Commodore Michael Swiney, OBE, from Norfolk, spoke to us during an interview at his home address in 1998 of what he witnessed on the 21st of October 1952 then 68 years ago, whilst a RAF Flight Lieutenant stationed at the Central Flying School, Little Rissington, Gloucestershire. At the time of the incident he was instructing Flight Lt. David Crofts – a naval officer – on a high-level exercise.

"As we broke cloud cover, I saw what at first I took to be three parachutes in front of the path of the aircraft. Instinctively, I grabbed hold of the control stick and pushed it to one side in an evasive movement, at the same time looking over my left shoulder and directing David Crofts' attention to what I had just seen. At this point, I realised the three objects were not parachute flares but two perfect circular objects, with a third object being on edge showing a fuzzy white. I contacted Little Rissington Control Tower by radio and told the Controller, after some deliberation, he had three UFOs in front of the aircraft, asking him what action should be taken. He replied they would contact the Senior Officer at the airbase for guidance. A check made with Box Radar Station, Wiltshire, confirmed the objects had been plotted on Radar as three 'blips', which then merged into one echo."

Air Commodore Michael Swiney, OBE (right)

The pilots made their way back to Rissington, flying back through their own contrail in an effort to establish whether they were being followed by the UFOs, bearing in mind the 'blip' on the radar scale had disappeared when the contrails did. After landing at Little Rissington, they were interviewed separately about the incident but gave identical accounts of what had been seen.

Michael Swiney: "I can't give any explanation for what we saw. I can't say it was any 'alien' craft, or indeed, representative of any 'alien' technology. All I can tell you is what we saw. ***I was frightened***; I make no bones about it. It was something supernatural, perhaps, and when I landed someone told me I looked as if I had seen a ghost."

THE HALT PERSPECTIVE 2

Meeting H.R.H. Prince Philip

Air Marshal Sir Peter Horsley – former Deputy Chief of Strike Command, later Equerry to HM the Queen and HRH Prince Philip – was to take an interest in the following matter on behalf of the Prince, whom it is claimed has always been interested in UFO reports.

Air Marshal Sir Peter Horsley

Stephen Derbyshire (13) and his cousin Adrian Myers (8) set out to photograph bird life at The Old Man of Coniston, close to the Cumbrian village of Torver, (The locality of a sighting involving strange figures seen many years later). At 12.30pm on the **14th of February 1954** an object was seen descending through the sky, glistening in the sunlight, its outline well defined, showing **'portholes', a hatch and a 'bump' on top**. Stephen took two photographs of the object as it climbed rapidly upwards into the sky, accompanied by a swishing noise. He was later interviewed by the **Duke of Edinburgh's secretary** and invited to Buckingham Palace where he spoke to the Prince about what had taken place

In conversation with Mr. Swiney about the version of events as given by Sir Peter Horsley, obtained from their original report, Mr. Swiney still felt that while his memory of the event was reasonably accurate, he would have liked to have seen a copy of his original report, last seen by him in 1974. In the (**Operational Record Book**) kept at the Central Flying School, Little Rissington, it contains the following entry, dated 2lst October 1952: *"Flight Lieutenant M.I.E. Swiney, Instructor and Lieutenant D. Crofts, Royal Navy Student, sighted* **three mysterious 'saucer-shaped objects'** *travelling at high speed, at about 35,000 feet, whilst on a high-level navigation exercise in a Meteor 7. Later A.T.C.C Gloucester reported radar plots to confirm this, but the Air Ministry discounted any possibility of 'extraterrestrial' objects.*

MOD – UFO files routinely destroyed!

As the years went by, Mr. Swiney attempted to obtain sight of his original report but was informed that, in accordance with MOD procedure, all files had been **routinely destroyed** at five-year intervals, (this practice was halted in 1967, the earliest records being from 1962) which meant his was no longer available for scrutiny – or at least this was the impression the MOD wanted to give! In 1974, during a posting to the MOD itself, Mr. Swiney – now an Air Commodore – asked for sight of his original UFO report from 1952 and was handed the document, which contained his and David Crofts' account, without any fuss, after being told it had been previously filed in the Air Intelligence Branch's Blue Book! After examining them, he placed the files into the out-tray and thought no more of it – until retirement in 2002, when he expressed an interest in having sight of the reports again, and wrote to the RAF's Air Historical Branch, now based at Bentley Priory. He was advised that UFO reports submitted to Air Ministry Intelligence could have been preserved for transfer to the PRO or, alternatively, marked for destruction – which, it was suggested, to have been the likely fate in this instance.

Enquiries made with GCHQ – Blatant denial!

Dissatisfied, Mr. Swiney wrote to the Director General of GCHQ to enquire if their department had retained a copy of the incident and was later told that while a search of the archives had failed to find the document, his request had been passed to the MOD. They wrote to him explaining, quote: *"It was generally the case that before 1967, all UFO files were destroyed after five years but, since 1967, following an increase in public interest, UFO files are now routinely preserved. Any files from the 1950s and early 1960s are available for examination at the PRO."*

Michael Swiney: **"*If it was generally the case that before 1967 all UFO reports were destroyed after five years, how was it that I actually saw and read it in 1974, some seventeen years later, while serving at the MOD?*"**

We spoke to David Crofts, now living in Hampshire, who corroborated the account given to Mr Swiney, adding: *"After a debriefing with two officers from the Air Ministry, I was told by them that the objects were moving at a speed of some* **6,000 miles per hour**.*"* In 2015, we learnt that David had passed away. – Our condolences to the family. **Air Commodore Michael Swiney died of cancer on September 30, 2016, aged 90. RIP'.**

John: "What a pleasure it was to meet you, when I left your house after spending time talking to you about the incident you said to us: **'Would you like to use the hospitality of the house?' I replied: I'm driving, thinking he meant a wee tipple. He replied 'no – the toilet' and he laughed saying 'you could have had a gin and tonic!'** "

On the same date, but this time over Knoxville, Tennessee, employees at an airport weather station logged the sighting of *six white 'lights'*, which were seen to fly in a loose formation for one to two minutes and make a shallow dive at a weather balloon. 24th October 1952, UFO shaped like a plate, sighted by pilot over Elberton Alabama. 31st October 1952, orange object sighted by off duty pilot over Fayetteville, Georgia. November 3rd, 1952, Laredo AFB Control tower sights UFO. 4th November 1952, whirling 'discs' sighted over New Jersey. 11th November 1952, oval object seen over Bromley Kent.

12th November 1952, four lights seen over Los Alamos New Mexico. 13th November 1952, oval objects in 'V' formation sighted (and tracked on radar) over Montana. 18th November 1952, object showing several lights follows aircraft over Washington DC. 20th November 1952. 'Flying tadpole' sighted over English Counties.

Three blinding lights seen over Tangmere Aerodrome Surrey. Police sight 'flying tadpole' over Bognor, breaks up over Tangmere area. 24th November 1952, round glowing object sighted over Annandale Virginia making right angle turns in the sky. 30th November 1952, Washington DC, radar operators at Washington National Airport track on radar similar targets to those plotted on 26th July 1952.

The Colonel comments

Any scholar seeking to acquaint themselves of the history of UFO activity should read these books, if only to learn what our citizens witnessed – many of whom are now no longer alive. Over 60 years later people argue as to the identity of what is labelled the 'Triangular UFO' which was the scourge of the skies over Belgium in the mid 1980's. Some insist that the objects were top secret aircraft – others believe they represent examples of alien technology. The interesting thing is that not many people know, there was a glut of just as many reports of similar objects seen over the East Anglia area. John has showed me many witness reports, along with illustrations.

Based at Belgium – Triangular UFOs

In this year I was coming up to being a teenager, looking back I gained a Bachelors Degree in Chemistry and Economics and an MBA in Business Management. Then I served 29 years in the Air Force retiring as a Colonel. Assignments included Base Commander at RAF Bentwaters and Kunsan AB, Korea.

I never had any real interest in UFOs until what happened at RAF Bentwaters. I did everything I could to keep what was happening from going public. It was not career enhancing and I knew my life would never be the same; despite my efforts my memo and tape were released. Since then I've been stuck out in the public while my former superiors hid. I've tried to get the real story and truth out but every time the media has made it into a sensational story and misrepresented the facts. It really is frustrating. There are very few people that I really trust. One is Leslie Kean, who I assisted with her book. She and Budd Hopkins were trusted friends.

Now four years later on from the first book, here I am again seeking to put the record straight, after further attacks on my character, by all sorts of people including those that I thought I could trust, because otherwise the misleading version of events will be given credibility by those in power that want to hide away the exact nature of what actually took place.

Exercise Mainbrace – Largest peacetime military exercise – UFOs sighted!

'Triangular objects formed by three lights' have been reported over military installations that include Fort Benning, and Ladd Air Base. Why the attraction with Army and Air Force bases, but not seemingly with naval locations can only be open to speculation. The 1952 period is an important one, as it shows further sightings by RAF and USAF aircrew of what appears to be some sort of controlled interference by Unidentified Flying Objects whose origins and agendas can only be guessed at by the Navy and Air force during Exercise Mainbrace.

While I can't say what those objects were – what is patently obvious are the correlations of perceived visual imagery, ('Triangular shaped') with some of the UFOs seen in the 1950's ('V' shaped) suggests that they are one and the same! Not forgetting the numerous occasions when three lights are seen which form a triangle. Similar objects were seen long before this! This doesn't stop people continuing to draw erroneous assumptions as to what they believe the objects are! A similarity of behaviour exercised by those many of whom weren't at RAF Bentwaters, Woodbridge, but continue to come up with crazy notions as to what they believe we saw or didn't!

This was the first large-scale, naval exercise undertaken by the newly established Allied Command Atlantic (ACLANT), one of the two principal military commands of the North Atlantic Treaty Organization, (NATO) part of a series of NATO exercises jointly commanded by Supreme Allied Commander Atlantic Admiral Lynde D. McCormick, USN, and Supreme Allied Commander Europe General Matthew B. Ridgeway, U.S. Army, during the Fall of 1952. I seem to recall that the aircrew of the plane who witnessed UFO activity over RAF Topcliffe/Dishforth had been previously involved in Exercise Mainbrace. If so, this means the strongest likelihood that the aircraft were followed from the North Atlantic back to England. This is not rare in the annals of the UFO phenomena. There are many others who report being paced by these objects both in their vehicles on the ground and planes in the air. I'm not happy with the hypotheses that these actions are hostile because if they wanted to be antagonistic, we would certainly know about it!

UFO activity close to where I live now

I live close to the Washington area, so I found the report of seven UFOs tracked on radar over the Capitol in July 1952 interesting. (I was aged 12) One of the objects was described as a bright, orange light by the Air Traffic Controller, or ball of fire leaving a trail according to a spokesman from Andrews Air Force base who also saw the over flight. Here is a piece of history showing, the media's take on what happened which appears to be straightforward, in the first instance , as published by a newspaper in Washington in comparison to the *New York Times*, well I rest my case, nothing has changed there! Nice picture of Marylyn Monroe. What should really concern us because it concerns me, was the claim made by the well respected nuclear physicist Stanton Friedman, who allegedly stated that some of the U.S. fighter jets involved in the intercept disappeared in the predawn darkness that morning! If true then concern gives way to fear!

Ironically my final assignment at the Pentagon, Washington was Director of the Inspection Directorate for the Department of Defense Inspector General. In the latter capacity, I was charged with inspection

oversight of the entire Department of Defense. In addition to responsibility for the armed forces I directed inspections of many agencies to include NSA and the DIA. Many have attempted in the face of scepticism to bring the public's attention to something that should be the subject of serious scientific research rather than the butt of continuing humour, unfortunately it can bring one under the spotlight and attract the attention of those that seek to denigrate something they have no idea about – unless they fall into the same position that I did, then their attitude changes. So, I have great respect for

THE HALT PERSPECTIVE 2

Flying Saucers Seen Over Washington For 2nd Time In 4 Days

Washington, D. C., saw flying saucers again for six hours early today.

Eight to 12 objects showed on radar screens, flying a 10-mile arc around the capital. Radarmen estimated the objects, or flying saucers, were clipping along at about 120 miles per hour.

The last time the saucers were spotted over Washington, on Saturday, the air force sent jet fighters up to chase them, and when the word of the new appearance was flashed around, it was expected that the jets would be ordered up again, to try to shoot down the objects.

But the jets stayed on the ground. An air defense official explained, "We were too busy with other things, and besides objects aren't hurting anybody."

However, civil aeronautics officials did direct an Eastern air lines pilot to check the objects as he flew over the city. But the pilot didn't see a thing. The officials said the saucers disappeared from the radar screen when the plane reached the area where thy had been tracked.

So it remains a mystery.

The second appearance of the saucers in four days leaves th experts just as stumped as ever. Some think the saucers are space ships from another planet. Some think they're just natural phenomenon we haven't figured out yet.

The air force doesn't know what to think. But it's determined to find out. Top scientists have been called in to launch a major investigation.

people that have tried to flag up the reality of the existence of a very puzzling phenomena, many of whom I have met which should be of concern to us all.

I then Retired in 1991 and for 12 years managed a large gated community of 7,000.

James McDonald senior physicist

It's so important to remember the efforts made by those that in the face of adversity and often ridicule, stood up to be counted.

Look at the late James McDonald from Arizona. (May 7, 1920 - June 13, 1971) a senior physicist at the Institute for Atmospheric Physics and professor in the Department of Meteorology, University of Arizona, Tucson. He campaigned in support of expanding UFO studies during the mid and late 1960s, arguing that UFOs represented an important unsolved mystery which had not been adequately studied by science. He was one of the more prominent figures of his time who argued in favour of the extraterrestrial hypothesis as a plausible, but not completely proved phenomenon. James interviewed over 500 UFO witnesses, uncovered many important government UFO documents, and gave important presentations of UFO evidence. He testified before Congress during the UFO hearings of 1968. McDonald also gave a famous talk called "Science in Default" to the American Association for the Advancement of Science (AAAS). It was a summary of the current UFO evidence and a critique of the 1969 Condon Report UFO study.

James McDonald senior physicist

RAF Bentwaters personnel track UFO on Radar

In a meeting held at the Boston, Massachusetts, symposium on UFOs, on 29th December 1969, James told of three significant radar sightings made by RAF Bentwaters personnel, prior to their alerting RAF Lakenheath. He commented, *"One could easily be enmeshed in a semantic dispute over the meaning of the phrase, 'one genuine UFO', so I shall simply assert that my own position is that the Lakenheath case exemplifies a disturbingly large group of*

THE HALT PERSPECTIVE 2

UFO reports in which the apparent degree of scientific inexplicably is so great that instead of being ignored and laughed at, those cases should since 1947, have been drawing the attention of a large body of the World's best scientists. Had the latter occurred, we might now have some answers, some clues to the real nature of the UFO phenomena. But 22 years of inadequate UFO investigations have let this stunning scientific problem out of sight and under a very broad rug called Project Blue Book, whose final termination on December 18th 1969, ought to mark the end of an era and the start of a new one relative to the UFO problem." James is spot on; had we as a race of people bothered to do something about this, instead of burying our heads in the sand and hoping it will go away – which of course it won't. The 'Pandora's Box' of this unsolved enigma of what UFOs are and where they're from is a tempting challenge! So many of us seek answers, one wonders at what stage in the evolutionary history of man on this planet will he accept the reality and move on to a greater understanding of something that appears to live unseen alongside us.

Demise of UFO witnesses

John told me that Air Commodore Michael Swiney and Lt Croft had passed away, my condolences to their families. At least we have their account. The sighting of three objects in the sky is, of course, always of interest to me as it strikes a chord with what we saw in December 1980. What should be of concern is that despite the release of UFO files into the public domain by the authorities over the years – it's clear the policy of the MOD on this occasion (and no doubt many others) was to deliberately prevent UFO reports from being made available to the public. Ironically, the only way Mr Swiney was able to obtain sight of his original statements in 1974 was when he was employed by the MOD in a senior role of responsibility. But, of course, he was then later advised that all pre-1967 UFO records were destroyed, so what the heck is going on here, further evidence of concealment, but for what reasons and why, never mind who?

The Flying Saucers Are Real, by Donald Keyhoe

Why don't people see what's going on here, don't they care or are they too frightened? Reading these reports from the 1950's strikes an accord with me because as a teenager growing up into adulthood, I never had much interest in the UFO subject, but I can clearly remember reading a book I came across during a church rummage sale, while assisting my mother, who was organizing the event, entitled The Flying Saucers Are Real, by Donald Keyhoe. This book published in 1954 outlined numerous encounters between USAF fighters, personnel, and other aircraft and UFOs between 1947 and 1950. I found Keyhoe's book fascinating but, after reading and putting it aside, forgot all about it. Having refreshed my memory from what Donald wrote in his next book, 'Flying Saucers from Outer Space' which contains reports from Pilots involving objects that have nearly crashed into their aircraft and 'V' shaped formations of objects seen moving through the sky, it should be a source of concern that the majority of these incidents, some involving tragic loss of life, following claims of airplanes being struck by unidentified flying objects have been 'swept under the carpet.' These were

real people they are owed an answer. Just because these events took place now 66 years ago, why are truths still kept from us?

I have no idea why or what conditions are required which allows us to see them or 'it' – maybe some subtle shift in the electromagnetic fields – if so, then one may ponder that the atmosphere of our planet could be flooded with 'ethereal manifestations', but we lack the optical range to see them. Of course, their incursions could be random, but while we cannot identify the reason for their appearances, we have learnt much about their characteristics which remain unchanged over the years. Sightings of UFOs and their unexplained arrivals in the sky have and still do whip up all manner of crazy theories, to this present day. Unfortunately, they have long been the subject of interest by *Hollywood* and other science fiction film producers who continue to produce the depiction of confrontations between human beings and alien beings that want to dominate the Planet. Those fire fights are legendary, and we all have grown up and enjoyed the films. But there is a succinct difference between our own belief systems that interprets what we believe these things are and where they come from – and the REALITY – an indecipherable commodity which eludes us completely. Memories of it were resurrected in December 1980, when I found myself confronted with an experience I could not explain. The incidents that occurred over a three-night period in Rendlesham Forest, Suffolk, left a lasting impression on me, and tragically affected the lives of many concerned.

1953 – January 1st, at 8.45pm, Mr. Warner Anderson – a Craig, Montana resident – and two women reported sighting **a silver, saucer-shaped object with a red glowing base**, flying low over a river and then climbing horizontally into the sky, at speed seconds later. **8th January 1953** – At 7.15am, over **Larson Air Force Base**, a number of men from the 82nd Fighter – Interceptor Squadron, including the squadron commander, sighted a **green, 'disc'-shaped, or round object**, flying south-west for 15 minutes, in a vertically bobbing motion and sideways movements, below the clouds. **9th January 1953** – Captain George Madden was flying a B29 over California on that evening accompanied by Lt Frank Briggs when a '**V**' formation of blue lit objects were seen moving towards them. Five seconds later they were gone. **10th January 1953 –** Retired Colonel Robert McNab and Mr Hunter of the Federal Security Agency were in Sonoma, California, at about 3.45pm, when they saw a similar object to that above. Mr. Lloyd Mason was walking up a steep hill in the Don Valley, Brightside, Sheffield, England in the early 1950s, at 6.30pm, on a clear, but cold night. "*Suddenly I was surprised to see, about 500 – 1,000 feet in the sky above me, a* **bright orange large metallic looking 'flying saucer', showing lights around its sides, with a dome,** *hovering in the air. It then suddenly shot off across the sky at incredible speed and vanished.*" In late **January 1953,** Mrs. M.L. Martin – wife of a RAF serviceman, stationed at RAF Marham, Norfolk was looking out of the window at 3pm, when she saw what she took to be a jet aircraft, crossing the clear blue sky at high altitude. To her horror, "**both 'wings' left the fuselage. However, instead of crashing to Earth, they rushed across the sky, one behind the other, before coming to a halt, glinting as they caught the sun, before suddenly rising upwards and disappearing out of sight**. When I later discussed what I had seen with my husband, he told me all personnel at the airbase **had been warned not to breathe a word about a UFO which had, apparently, been seen by other airmen.**"

At 1pm on the 28th of January 1953, Mr. R.W. Love the owner of *Love Diving Company*, Point Mugu, California, saw a 18 – 20 feet white, flat 'disc', heading through the sky overhead on a straight trajectory – gone six minutes later. At 6.05pm the same day, California, USAF T/Sgt. George Beyer sighted: "…*five 25 foot green spheres, flying in 'V' formation through the sky. They then changed formation to one behind the other, the end objects turning red, kept under observation for 12 minutes*".

THE HALT PERSPECTIVE 2

February 4th, 1953 – at 1.50pm Arizona Weather Bureau observer – Stanley Brown sighted "...*a white oblong object, flying straight upwards, which then levelled off in flight and was joined by a second, similar, object. The second object was seen to move away but return to the first object on two separate occasions. After five minutes, both were lost to sight behind clouds."* During the afternoon of the 13th February 1953, a grey, cigar-shaped object was seen darting backwards and forwards through the sky over Inverness, Scotland by local resident George Macpherson. **(Source: *Glasgow Herald* and *Greenock Telegraph*)**

Virginia – At 5pm on the 7th of February 1953, Mrs. B Eagen of Ellers St, Norfolk, Virginia contacted the local newspaper after seeing a bright white light which she thought was a *'flying saucer'* moving over the area heading in a south east direction. A bright light was then seen over Virginia Beach which sparked off a deluge of telephone calls made to Preston Charles chief of the *Suffolk New Bureau* 20miles south – east of Norfolk. Enquiries made with the Norfolk Naval Air Station about recent balloon launches were able to rule out this possibility, taking into consideration that residents were used to seeing the eight feet in diameter balloons moving over the sky. But these sightings involved the appearance of objects that were seen to dart about in the sky! A familiar background to the noted activities of a phenomenon that still will not be accepted as a reality of everyday life!

US Pilot encounters UFO – goes on the attack!

At 10pm on the **11th of February, 1953,** Marine First Lt Edward Balocco who was the only pilot on 'Intercept ready status' was driving around the Air base at Edenton North Carolina, in his jeep when an alert disturbed the tranquility of that Saturday evening. Edward made his way to the F-9 Panther fighter jet parked on the tarmac ready for take – off. He climbed in and fired up the engine, asking the tower what was happening. "**Unknown bogey at two three zero".** Edward took off and in a few minutes was heading north towards Virginia Beach, while being vectored to the UFO by the Cherry Point Tower. After 20 miles of flight Cherry Point handed him over to the Norfolk Naval station. When he reached the allocated position, the object suddenly disappeared off the radar at Norfolk Tower. After searching for about 15 minutes, Edward radioed Norfolk and informed them he was running low on fuel and was returning to base As he headed south towards Edenton at a height of 20.000 feet, he noticed a bright light on his port side below him on or near the ocean. He flipped on his navigation lights so other pilots could identify him and glanced back astonished to see the 'light' had risen to his altitude. It was now hovering motionless in the sky about 2000 feet away. Edward made a head on plunge towards the object, which as he approached closer saw was disk shaped with red blinking lights on its hull.

As he continued to close in, he reached for the trigger on his stick and squeezed it with full force, to his shock he realised that the gun canister was empty. As he closed in to about 350feet away from the object the canopy was drenched in white light, everything seemed to hang motionless for a second or two then just as suddenly as it stopped, everything started again – the *'saucer'* broke away in a flash and headed south at incredible speed. On landing at Edenton, he was told that he would be taken by plane to Cherry Point for a debriefing. Following an interview that lasted some hours, **he was told that he should say absolutely nothing about what had taken place.** We shouldn't be surprised to hear that somehow the news leaked out, despite Edward keeping his mouth shut, when someone posted up a comic poster on the notice-board in base headquarters, depicting a squadron of F-9s flying in formation with one pilot in the centre (Balocco) stating that he had seen a flying saucer . This of course attracted sneers and jeers from other pilots. Was this deliberately contrived to draw attention to the incident so that it could be made the butt of ridicule? Quite likely in our opinion, knowing the lengths the authorities will go to in desperately covering up something or someone whose identity is still not known now nearly 70 years later. Things became more personal when a letter was sent to his Mother containing two band aids with a cryptic note saying: *"The next time your son goes up, have him put these over his eyes."*

On the 17th February 1953 at 10.4pm two officers and three airmen of USAF AC & W Squadron, Port Austin, Michigan, sighted both visually and on radar an object which appeared to be larger and brighter than any star, changing colour as it moved slowly across the sky for five minutes, until 10.09pm. At 10.08pm, the radar picked up a target moving in a similar direction for 17 minutes. 24th February 1953 – At 7.43pm over Sherman, Texas, Warrant Officer and Mrs Alden saw two bright, red round objects, with large halos, flying around in small circles; they were then seen to climb and fade away during the three to seven second sighting. 27th February 1953 – USAF pilot sighted: *"…five, fluttering yellow 'discs', making circular turns in the sky over Shreveport, Louisiana, at 11.58am. Three of them then vanished, leaving the other two – which performed a number of erratic square turns for a total of four minutes."* March 11th, 1953 – at 4am, Mrs Nina Cook – an experienced private pilot and wife of a Pan Am flight engineer – reported having seen a large 'light', flashing 10 – 15 times per minute, moving up and down along a mountain range at Hackettstown, New Jersey. 21st March 1953 – At 3.05pm over Elmira, New York, a member of a Ground Observer Corps observation post sighted: *"…six 'discs' in a group, flying high across the sky – gone in a few seconds."* 25th March 1953 – At 3.05pm, USAF Captain and a Mrs D.E. Cox from San Antonio, Texas, saw several 'lights' in the sky – some of which moved straight, others making 360 degree turns for one-and-a-half hours.

27th March 1953 – At 7.25pm, a USAF *F-86* Jet fighter was flying at 700 miles per hour over Mt. Taylor, New Mexico, when the pilot saw a bright orange 'circle', moving through the sky at an estimated speed of 900 miles per hour. The plane gave chase but lost it, minutes later. 29th March 1953 – At 3.45pm, Mr. L.C. Gillette – a Spooner, Wisconsin resident – was outside when he saw *"an aluminium, circular, object flying high and fast through the sky, during which it was seen to reverse its course on two occasions over the 15seconds sighting."* Mr. Gillette said he had seen a similar object in 1938.

In the Spring of 1953, RAF Serviceman Sidney Yeakes stationed at RAF Felixstowe, Norfolk, England sighted *"…a dark, wedge-shaped 'craft', trailing six separate yellow and blue flames from its rear, at a height of about 7,000 feet – totally unlike any aircraft I had ever seen. Frightened, I dismounted and watched it move over, feeling the hair on the back of my neck stand on end, as the object disappeared in the sky towards the direction of Harwich."* April 12th, 1953 – Major Fred G. Padelford was co-pilot aboard a *C-47* at 10,500 feet, when ten objects were seen in a loose changing formation, flying at 140 miles per hour. April 15th, 1953 – At 5.45pm, three orange 'lights' were seen in the sky for three and-a-half minutes over Tucson, Arizona, by S/Sgt. V.A. Locey.

An object resembling 'two plates, face-to-face trailing a red glow, performing a number of strange movements in the sky' was seen on the 20th of April 1953 by three youths – Terry Platts, Brian Davies and Allan Green – over Rawmarsh, Sheffield, England. According to the boys: *"For most of the time it appeared edge on, but towards the end of the observation it banked and went away, and we saw its circular shape. On moving, it left a long trail of flame ending in black smoke; this stopped when the craft stopped."* The boys were amazed how slow the object could fly, and the fact that it could dive and stop and start as it flew across the sky. Strangely, the sketch they submitted to the newspaper was not published; instead, another one was showing what appeared to be a rocket, rather than saucer shaped. Was this Intentional or accidental? **(Source: *Star & Sheffield Telegraph*, 24.Apr.1953)**

At 7.45pm 21st April 1953 – a brightly lit object was seen hovering in the sky over Norwich, by spectators at a football match before being lost from view at 8.15pm. It is likely this was the same UFO sighted by a member of the Royal Observer Corps, at 8.15pm, North of Lowestoft. Through the lens of a telescope, he saw *"what looked like a plastic lighter refuel capsule, with a sharp pointed end"*, move towards the south-west, before turning north-east and disappearing, 30 minutes later. 26th April 1953 – At 7.35pm, Mr. A.C. Carter, Mr. and Mrs. H. Hopkins and their daughter, from Athens, Georgia, sighted fifteen to twenty yellow objects, flying across the sky in a 'V' formation, heading in a south to north direction – lost from view ten seconds later. May 10th 1953– US Marine Corps Squadron Leader D.R. Higgin was flying an *F3D -2* Jet fighter over Elsinore, California, at 12.40pm, when he saw a *"dark gunmetal delta-shaped object, 22 feet long by 10 feet wide, showing a fin on the top."* This was then seen to descend at a 25-30 degree angle under the lead airplane of the formation, and over the airplane of the Squadron Leader – gone in seconds. 27th May 1953 – At 8.30pm, several people living in the San Antonio area of Texas reported the presence of nine separate lights, 'wandering' through the sky over a period of 15 minutes.

June 2nd 1953 – Mrs Dawn Gould, (92 in 2019) described to us what she saw at midday: *"I was living at Melplash Court, Bridport, Dorset, and pegging the washing on the line, I happened to look upwards and see five saucer – shaped objects, like white circles, high up in the blue sky, 'line abreast' – just hovering there. Before I could shout out or fetch someone, they changed to 'line astern' and moved forwards and upwards until out of sight. I've never forgotten what I saw."* August 3rd 1953 – Amarillo, Texas airport control tower Chief – Mr. C.S. Brown – was on duty, at 12.04pm, when he saw: *"…a round, reflective, or translucent object flying across the sky, which stopped in flight for seven seconds, and then sped away before halting again. It was then joined by a similar object and both flew off in different directions, after a total of 56 minutes."*

On the 16th of August 1953 Valerie Frostick (15) from Orchard Road, Market Hill, Maldon, Essex, was on her way to bed, one evening, when she happened to look out of the bedroom landing window and see: *"…what I took to be a shooting star, moving across the sky. It stopped and I continued looking, when I realized that this was no shooting star. It was a 'flying saucer', which was rotating, and had a smooth creamy metallic outer surface. As it passed opposite to me, I saw that it had a dome on top, with portholes all the way around. The 'saucer' then headed off, westwards. Instead of feeling frightened, I felt very peaceful and rather smug to think I had seen such a lovely object."* 20th August 1953 – crew on board a *TB-29* Bomber/trainer aircraft were near Castle Air Force Base, California, at 9.05pm, when they saw a greyish, oval, object in the sky, which made four passes at the airplane(three times at 10-20 miles distance), before diving vertically now two objects.

UFO over East Anglia

Mr. F. W. Potter from Norwich – then aged 34, owner of a local window cleaning business, with over twenty years' experience as an amateur astronomer, member of the British Astronomical Association and the Norwich Astronomical Society – was in the process of leaving his house with his wife to attend a meeting on 6th October 1953. As the couple stepped out of the house, Mr. Potter was the first to see a bright yellow 'star' moving slowly across the sky, unlike anything he had seen before. The couple rushed back into the house and brought out a three-inch reflecting telescope, which they set up in the back garden. During an observation period which lasted three and a half minutes, they were able to describe the following: *"It had a dark grey hull and a caged dome shape, with the cube of the dome hanging towards the ground, the flat side emitting a pulsating light that was much stronger when the object was stationary, but decreased in luminosity when the object moved. In the centre of the caged dome was what looked like a conning tower containing eight windows?"*

As a result of considerable publicity given to the sighting, with strong comparisons being drawn with what the Potters had seen and a similar photograph of a 'flying saucer', taken by Mr. George Adamski, (as shown in his book, *Flying Saucers Have Landed*), the couple received scores of insulting letters ridiculing them for having reported the incident, all of them having been written, according to Mr. Potter, *'by people without any scientific training'*. Our enquiries revealed several other witnesses had also seen this unidentified object over the Norwich area during the same evening. One is bound to wonder if there was any connection with the saucer-shaped 'craft' seen by Mr. Potter and other inhabitants of Norfolk when a UFO was plotted on radar, by RAF Neatishead just before dawn the following morning. **(Source: *Eastern Evening News* 11. Oct.1953, Letter sent to Newspaper/Source *Daily Mail* February 11th, 1954 "was it a 'Saucer 'they saw over Norwich?").**

RAF testing New Radar tracks UFO following aircraft!

In the winter of 1953 Flt. Lt. Cyril George Townsend-Withers, principal scientific officer at Boscombe Down, Wiltshire, responsible for testing experimental aircraft radar equipment, was conducting tests with new radar installed into a Canberra aircraft, accompanied by his science officer. *"We took off at 11.00am and flew over the Salisbury area, gaining height to 55,000 ft, when a 'blip' appeared on the Radar scopes, representing an object five miles behind us. After establishing the anomaly was not being caused by any malfunction in the equipment, I climbed up into the turret and, on looking back, saw a glistening object following us at the same speed. The pilot tried unsuccessfully to shake off the intruder, accelerating to speeds up to 225 knots, finally executing a 'U' turn to give us a better view of the UFO. Unfortunately, it also put us on a collision course.* **The object was very brilliant – almost fluorescent – with two stabilising fins at the rear and about the same size as a small jet fighter, with a thirty feet wingspan.** *As we approached within four miles of each other, it suddenly shot vertically upwards, at terrific speed, and vanished, 50, 60, and 70,000 feet – as quick as that! There wasn't even a vapour trail. Radar experts were very interested, but there was no reaction in the sense they thought it was an enemy aircraft, posing a threat. The attitude in those early days was, 'we'll look into it, but if it isn't Russian, then we are not really bothered".* **(Source: Peter Hough and Jenny Randles of the Manchester UFO Research Association)**

THE HALT PERSPECTIVE 2

The Colonel comments

1953 was a year of apparent increased UFO activity with all manner of strange things seen in the skies. They included a now all too familiar description over 50 years later of 'V'-shaped formations of unidentified objects travelling with impunity through our atmosphere, *'Saucer' shaped objects 'and 'green spheres'* moving majestically through the air, which were the subject of considerable concern by the military authority judging by the warnings handed down to military personnel to keep quiet.

SCHOOL DAYS 1953-54
MIFFLIN

Numerous reports from West Virginia

It seems that little has changed, despite the overwhelming UFO sightings provided by so many people who include numerous pilots – even some reports over West Virginia, not forgetting what was seen over the White House! Those guys on the RAF Canberra must have had a surprise while out testing experimental radar. I have no idea what this object could have been – two stabilizing fins on the back with a 30 foot wingspan. Could it have been some sort of covert top secret aircraft or missile? If my memory recollects, looking at the hundreds of sightings in this vast archive, most of the UFOs don't have obvious wings...problem is that I wasn't there, so aren't qualified to form any judgement! But that doesn't stop me bringing these matters to your attention – because I am unprepared, like John, to accept the official line on the subject. You only have to look at the rubbish printed by *Wikipedia* about me!

I don't believe these objects can be explained away as plasma fields or balls of light – even covert human technology on test – but who knows? What we do know is that the sheer weight of evidence most of it indisputable, identifies that we aren't alone, but what's the attraction is it energy? Or is the interaction deliberately orchestrated for another purpose?

What has changed with people's attitudes?

East Anglia was the venue again for a dome shaped object seen by Mr. Potter and his wife. After they reported it, they were besieged with letters attacking them – nothing changes! This was in October 1953, followed by the RAF Pilots sighting a month later over Salisbury Wiltshire.

I was unaware of the USAF standing order issued in 1953 forbidding personnel not to talk about 'genuine UFO reports,' and that if they did, they could be sent to prison for 10 years or a ten thousand dollars fine.

THE HALT PERSPECTIVE 2

WARNING!

26th August 1953 – USAF standing order, issued in the United States to military personnel, 'All genuine reports of UFOs must be kept from the public. Paragraph nine informs ranking Air Force officers that they are warned not to probe beyond the first reporting stage. Under section 111 of a joint army, naval and air publication (JANAP.146B) any pilot who reveals an official UFO report, can be imprisoned from one to ten years and can be fined $10,000.'

Even civilians were warned with dire consequences should they tell others – after having seen inexplicable things moving around the sky an example being the wife of an airman stationed at RAF Marham Norfolk. Then the guy who was shown secret Files!

First Lieutenant Felix Moncla

In Donald Keyhoe's book, the former Marine Corps naval aviator wrote about an incident in his 1955 book *The Flying Saucer Conspiracy* – as was "one of the strangest cases on record, involving an Air Force jet which mysteriously disappeared over Lake Superior on a stormy November 23rd, 1953. It began near the U.S – Canadian border, when U.S. Air Defense Command noticed a blip on the radar where it shouldn't have been: an unidentified object in restricted air space over Lake Superior, not far from *Soo Locks*, the Great Lakes' most vital commercial gateway. An F-89C Scorpion jet, from Truax Air Force Base in Madison, Wisconsin, took off from nearby Kinross AFB to investigate, with two crew members on board. First Lieutenant Felix Moncla – who had clocked 811 flying hours, including 121 in a similar aircraft – accompanied by Second Lieutenant Robert Wilson was observing radar. The U.S. Air Force reported that Moncla had crashed and that the object of the intercept was a Royal Canadian Air Force (RCAF) aircraft. According to the report, the pilot of the Canadian aircraft was later contacted and stated that he did not see the intercepting plane and did not know that he was the subject of an interception.

However, on several occasions, the RCAF denied that any of their aircraft was involved in any incident on that day, in correspondence with members of the public asking for further details of the intercept. Once again I wonder what the hell happened here. Was it an accident? If so – then the aircraft and the brave crew have never been recovered. If it was a UFO then why shouldn't I be surprised, but each and every incident has to be carefully scrutinized to ensure that the wrong conclusion can be made……In this instance I honestly don't know, I mean who does? ….Very sad and my thoughts are with the surviving relatives, whatever the cause.

The case file from Project Blue Book, the Air Force's own UFO investigatory team, reiterated the Air Force assertion that the jet *"successfully accomplished its mission,"* and that the crash was an accident, *"probably"* caused by an *"attack of vertigo."* It attributed the abnormal radar behaviour to unusual *"atmospheric conditions"* and deemed the inability to recover wreckage as understandable, given the deep water.

Meanwhile, investigators from the National Investigations Committee on Aerial Phenomena (NICAP) discovered that any mention of the mission had been expunged from official records. And the Aerospace Technical Intelligence Center's official line on the case was: *"There is no record in the Air Force files of sighting at Kinross AFB on 23 November 1953… There is no case in the files which even closely parallels these circumstances."* All the more reason for highlighting this incident these are men's' lives, and we owe them an explanation or at the very least to ensure that matters like this aren't expunged from official records!

THE HALT PERSPECTIVE 2

The amount of reports for just one year (a sample according to John) should be frightening, as well as illuminating in its presentation……. When you consider the massive response of so many people who have spent many years of their lives researching and investigating all manner of sightings and close encounters brought to their attention, now 67 years on from the 1953 period it's easy to wonder what has been achieved, because there seems little evidence of increased AWARENESS with regard to the Public's interest in the subject. Better to try than not bother at all! That's why I have never given up despite the lengthening of the years to ensure that at least the public will have the opportunity of seeing for themselves the TRUTH about what happened to me and my colleagues, backed up by other citizens who having little to gain but everything to lose in a culture where just telling what you saw, can bring ridicule down onto your shoulders!

1954 – March 1st, Mrs. Edith Capes from Lowestoft (UK) contacted her local newspaper, The *Eastern Evening News* (2.Mar.54), after sighting an object, *"looking like a child's spinning top with a light underneath it, travelling over the town."* At 7.30pm the same evening Mr. P. Goreham from Norwich reported seeing a spinning 'ball of light' in the sky, which changed into a 'triangle' as it headed across the sea. In 1954 amateur astronomer Michael Wilson from Farnham Surrey – later technical director of *Flight International* during the 1970s – had just completed a six-inch reflecting telescope and was carrying out some final adjustments in the evening when he became aware of a series of lights moving across the sky from west to east. *"They had the appearance of first or second magnitude stars and were heading across the sky in groups of three, there were probably fifteen or twenty of them taking 15-20 minutes to silently cross the sky. Coincidently, there was considerable night flying activity going on with the RAF from RAF Odiham some six miles away. I rang RAF Farnborough and they immediately sent a dispatch rider and radio operator to Farnham where I was living, since they were unable to pick up the objects themselves. It transpired in conversation they had alerted Odiham to the presence of Unidentified Aircraft and had notified a flight of Hunter Aircraft."* **(Source: Bob Tibbitts, Coventry UFO Research Group)**

May 14th – At 3.45pm, USAF fighters (from 91st Fighter Squadron, RAF Bentwaters, Suffolk, piloted by Captain Kenneth Scott, Jnr., Lt. Harry Joseph Eckes and Lt. David Clarby, were scrambled by GCI Radar type 7 at Bawdy, to intercept a UFO eight miles from their position, travelling at 240 knots. After it had been sighted visually as a 30ft. in diameter, silver/grey round object, showing a thin silhouette estimated at a height of 50-60,000ft. On the same day, Marine Corps pilots chased a formation of sixteen UFOs near Dallas, Texas. **(Source: NICAP *'The UFO Evidence'*, 1964 – Personal Interview with Jill Clarby)**

On the 15th of May, it was the turn of Berlin, Germany to experience the beginning of a wave of UFO sightings over the capital, often on cloudless nights that was to last six weeks. This sighting at 10.15pm involved two amateur astronomers, Wolfgang Kobski and Rudi Fibich, who reported seeing three round and luminous 'bodies' flying at great height on a zig zag course. Over the next few weeks, a total of 300 people saw these 'strange bodies.' All reports told of sightings that occurred at between 10-11pm, for a few minutes at a time involving **three objects** on each and every occasion, flying on a zig zag course. The American authorities interviewed many Berliners and took statements from them. A new Radar station was installed on an airfield, presumably to track the objects. 24th May – At daybreak, three (unnamed) pilots, flying over eastern Taranaki, at 135mph, sighted: *"…three strange orange objects, oval in shape, with reddish flames coming from them; they appeared to be hovering at about 7,000ft above us, but it was difficult to tell whether or not they were moving. We flew on and noticed a number of others, flying in a single line formation.*

Suddenly they all climbed rapidly upwards, at great speed, and disappeared from view." The pilots were later interviewed on the radio about their sighting and told of, *"observing 15 huge 'discs' in the sky*!

In June, Dr H.P. Wilkins, director of the British Astronomical Association, was on a flight from West Virginia to Georgia. His attention was caught by two *"Brilliant oval shaped objects apparently suspended above the tops of two masses of clouds. They were yellow like polished brass or gold reflecting the sunlight. A third appeared this one dull grey in colour. They moved slowly northwards in the opposite direction to the clouds and were all rectangular in shape. I estimated them to be 500 feet across. Four such objects have been seen over West Virginia within the last five years."*

On the 29th June (some accounts give the 30th) Captain James Howard was piloting a Stratocruiser Centauries airliner on a flight from Idlewild Airport New York to London, at 9.05pm, accompanied by co-pilot First Officer Lee Boyd. Other crew included George Allen navigating officer, Douglas Cox radio officer, Dan Godfrey engineering officer, Bill Stewart and Stewardess Daphne Webster. They were flying north over Seven Island, Quebec, heading north-east at about 230 knots, when he and five other passengers saw: *"…a large object, the size of an ocean liner, and six smaller ones flying north – west of us. Three of the smaller UFOs led the 'mother ship', the other three brought up the rear. They flew parallel to the BOAC for about 80 miles although the six 'escort ships' stayed the same; the 'mother ship' "appeared to change shape occasionally."* Interviewed by the *News Chronicle* reporter, later, at his home in Coombe Dingle, Bristol, Captain Howard said: *"There was a big central object which appeared to keep changing shape, sometimes wedge-shaped, sometimes like a dumb-bell, sometimes like a sphere with projections."* An interview was arranged by Graham Knewstub – Vice President and research Chief of the Bureau.

2nd July 1954 – USA: Did a jet crash after attempting to intercept a UFO?

The *Flying Saucer News*, in their edition of summer/autumn 1954, gave information on what they regarded as a parallel with the Mantell case, when they disclosed that a USAF jet had crashed after attempting to intercept a UFO over New York. According to official sources, the USAF had confirmed there had been a successful intercept, but declined to identify what had been intercepted because of the active nature of its mission. Ironically there had been an intercept all right, when the plane crashed into a car and buildings, killing four people, after the crew bailed out when the cockpit had become unbearably hot.

A ridiculous explanation for the surge of 'flying saucers' reported in the press was offered by *The Lancet*, who wondered if some 'flying saucers' might have been *"froth blown from sewage works on washdays, when suds go down the drain"* – no doubt an explanation based on an article in the *Ludlow Advertiser* (15.July.1954), relating to a report from a garage man working near a sewage farm, who claimed he had seen six 'flying saucers' take – off over the area. On 7th July, Mr. Lee Boyd and navigator – Mr. Allen – were guest speakers at the monthly general meeting at *Carwardine's Café*, Baldwin Street, Bristol. Mr Lee Boyd and Mr. Allen accepted the offer of honorary members of the Bureau, Captain Howard having already been granted this accolade. **(Source:** *Evening News,* **30.June.1954 – 'Jets Hunt Flying Saucers'/***News Chronicle,* **July 1954 – 'Flying Saucer – 30 people in airliner watch seven of them')**

George Hortrop, contacted us in 2003, and described what he and his companion saw at

THE HALT PERSPECTIVE 2

5.45pm, on the 6th of August while sitting on the beach at the 'Knap', when they saw a stationary object in the clear blue sky, south – west, towards Rhoose Point, Glamorgan, Wales. *"It was brilliant silver although there was a slight westerly wind, the object continued to remain stationary... It then altered its shape to a silvery dumb-bell before eventually disappearing from view, two hours later."* A few days later the National Press wrote that a number of observers from RAF St. Athan and Rhoose had sighted an object 'resembling a large double convex lens', stationary in the sky. George wrote an account of the incident and sent it to Lord Clancarty (formerly the Hon. William Francis Brinsley Le Poer Trench, – a major figure in British UFO research – who spoke on the subject in the House of Lords, and wrote many books on the UFO subject. He wrote back to George, informing him that *"the UFO sighting would be referred to during a debate on the subject in the House of Lords."* An hour and a half later, two silver circular objects were seen over Cheltenham, at 7.15pm, by a number of people. One was Eric Jones, who through binoculars noted that one of the objects was tilted and showed a conical tower, similar to the Adamski-type 'saucer' illustrations then in vogue at the time. Between 6.30pm and 8.15pm on 26th August at least five people saw a bright, shining, oblong object, *"As if cut out, with light shining through it, in the sky over Bath. Through binoculars, it looked like an upside-down saucer. Around the bottom rim was a white light. Occasionally, you could see flashes of blue and red lights. It then faded away, leaving a ring of white lights where the edge had been."* (**Source: Bath Chronicle**)

RAF Pilot 'Jimmy' Salandin encounters three objects over East Anglia

RAF Auxiliary Officer, Flight Lt. James Salandin, MBE, (89 in 2015), was stationed at RAF North Weald, Essex, near Epping (then attached to 604 County of Middlesex Squadron) James described the mysterious encounter he had while on an air test, climbing towards Southend, Essex, on 14th October 1954 – *". . . still vivid in my memory, despite it having happened over 50 years ago. I took off at about 4.15pm. Flying conditions were perfect. When at a height of some16,000 feet, I noticed a number of contrails in the sky, approximately 30-40,000 feet over North Foreland. Through the middle of these trails I could see three objects, which at first I took to be aircraft, although there was no sign of any vapour trail that one would associate with the movement of an aircraft in high atmosphere. When they got within a certain distance, two of them went off to my port side; one was gold in colour, the other silver. The third object headed towards me and closed to within a few hundred yards, almost filling the middle of the aircraft windscreen, before departing towards my port side. I tried to turn and follow but it had disappeared from view. The object I saw through the front cockpit of my Meteor 8 Jet aircraft was* **saucer-shaped, with a 'bun 'on top and underneath.** *I didn't see any portholes, windows, or other exterior extrusions that one would associate with the passage of an aircraft through the air. There weren't even any flames coming from the objects."*

In 2008, we met up with James Salandin at his home in rural North Yorkshire (one of a number of visits made) to discuss personally with him what he had seen: *"It is now 54 years since my sighting of three UFOs in October 1954. At the time I was bound by the Official Secrets Act and, if it hadn't been for*

THE HALT PERSPECTIVE 2

leaks, nothing more would have been heard of the incident. I have always said that I know what I saw, and my story has never varied over the years – the picture is still clear in my mind. However, I have not at any time given an opinion as to my thoughts on the subject, but I feel that now is the moment to do so. Since my wife, Margaret, passed away nearly two years ago, I've had plenty of time to reflect and would like to voice my true feelings, as most people appear to be skeptical or just not interested in UFOs. I was a volunteer in the Fleet Air Arm, from 1943 until demobilization in 1947, my flight training being with the United States Navy,

after which I served with 604 County of Middlesex Fighter Squadron 'R' Auxiliary Air Force from 1947, until we were disbanded in 1957. The last five years of my service I was 'B' Flight Commander. During this decade, 604 were equipped with Spitfires, Vampires, and Gloucester Meteors, the Squadron motto being, 'Si vis pacem para bellum', (If you want peace prepare for war!) **I mention all of this because I was an experienced pilot and I have never seen, in all the years of my service, anything like I saw on that day."** (Source *London Daily Sketch* **24.Feb.1955 'A flying saucer buzzed me, says meteor jet pilot. It flew straight at me at staggering speed')**. There is a problem here about the universal date of this incident – as, in the newspaper write-up Jimmy **(then aged 29)** said it was a **Sunday afternoon**; many other entries found on the Internet identify the **14th October 1955** as the date which appears to be incorrect. **The correct date is 17th October 1954**. Sadly, James passed away in 2018 and we wish him bon voyage – what a privilege it was to be friends with him – RIP James Salandin.

Patricia Hennesey from Chase Road, Southend, was walking home at 10.35pm Saturday 16th October, when she saw "*. . . a silver-coloured cylindrical object with a large corrugated tube or scaled pipe attached to one side, approximately six to twelve feet in height by ten feet in width, standing across Park Lane, its silver light blocking out the street light*" (other accounts mention the location as Caldwell Park). We discovered Mr. Alex S. Jennings had carried out an investigation into the incident, which had attracted the attention of the Press, whom it was said visited the location and found dark patches on the road – apparently neither oil, nor grease. Could there have been a connection with what RAF Pilot James Salandin reported on the following day, Sunday 17th, rather than the incorrect date of the 14th? Taking into consideration the locality given in both incidents? **Source:** *Sunday Express,* **17.Oct.54. Alex S. Jennings,** *'Flying Saucer News'* **winter 1954/1955/)**

Mrs. Jessie Roestenberg was living at a farmhouse in rural Ranton, Staffordshire with her husband Tony (a Dutchman by birth), and their children, Karin (2), Ronald (6), and Tony. On 21st October, she witnessed something that was to totally change her conceptions of life on this planet

Mrs. Jessie Roestenberg

– still very much evident when we met and interviewed her on a number of occasions over the years – the events she described still crystal clear in her mind. She was first interviewed in November/December 1954 by Shropshire UFO Researcher Gavin Gibbons and local UFO Researcher Wilfred Daniels (later published in an edition of *Flying Saucer News*, Winter 1954/55).

Needless to say, what was told to Gavin was identical to what she was to tell us half a century later. In the version of events given by Gavin, he outlines the arrival of what Jessie and her boys first took to be an aircraft. They watched it hovering over the chimney of the farmhouse, after hearing a noise like 'water being thrown on a fire'. They described the object as a dome, part divided vertically and horizontally, making four sections, the front two being transparent in material, the back two metallic, with an upper revolving part like aluminium/silver.

"The 'saucer' tipped at an angle, creating an impression it was going to land, causing the children to throw themselves to the ground, enabling them to now see two men with skin like ours, very high foreheads, their features being in the lower part of their face, with shoulder-length hair, dressed in what looked like ski suits, with a stern and forbidding expression on their face, wearing something resembling 'glass bowls' over their heads, with what looked like breathing apparatus. After about 15 seconds, the 'machine' ascended at an angle of 45 degrees, showing a flashing blue/purple light mounted on its front, and began to move away. When Tony arrived home, I told him what had transpired and he called the police." They sent a sergeant and five constables. Jessie was very perturbed to see the following local newspaper headlines, boldly declaring, **'Staffordshire housewife sees hairy men from outer space'**.

After the sighting she felt revitalized for a short time, until discovering a strange rash covering her face and front part of her body. She also lost a considerable amount of weight over a relatively short period, which was cause for concern. Jessie sought the advice of her doctor, who was aware of the UFO incident and intimated there was something wrong with her mental health. Offended by this suggestion, Jessie contacted psychiatrist Dr. Wilson, who confirmed, after a medical examination, there was nothing wrong with her mental state. *"He asked me if I had been given a chest X-ray and blood tests. When I told him this had not been done, he personally escorted me to hospital, where a chest X-ray was taken, but found to be clear. Unfortunately, blood tests showed the blood count was very low. The haematologist said to me, 'If it didn't sound so ludicrous, I would say you have been exposed to a massive dose of radiation'. I was given injections of iron, twice a week, which caused all sorts of problems before the correct dosage was established."* History was to record that Jessie and her two children were not the only witnesses that afternoon. RIP Jessie.

On 25th October, a railway-man and police officer from Aberdeen sighted five objects described as *"silver, luminous disc-like things, flying silently across the sky in neat formation followed by three more at 6.10pm."* **(Source: *Aberdeen Press and Journal,* 26.Oct.1954)**

RAF Bawdsey tracks saucers shaped UFO – fighter jets launched to intercept!

John Cotton SAC 2590718 was a National Service fighter plotter stationed at RAF Bawdsey, Woodbridge, Suffolk in 1954 (Ground Control Interception). One night in late 1954 he was in the middle of an exercise when they were told on the intercom that the radar had picked up an unidentified flying object. *"At the time I was working in the RT recording area. As soon as the Meteor NF11s were sent to investigate, I started recording the intercept, which was normal procedure".* As the interceptors approached the UFO, they obtained a visual and reported it as being stationary in the sky and saucer in shape. On being instructed to approach closer, *". . . the target shot off at high speed and began hovering again. On the second approach the object shot off and disappeared off the Type 13 height radar. Afterwards, the Chief Controller that night, either Flt Jack Smith or Flt Clifford, asked to hear the recording – but for the first time ever there was no recording. I should point out that it was a simple continuous loop of clear film on which the voices and time signal were 'scratched' and supposedly fool proof."*

The next morning the plotters who should have been allowed to sleep in were told to parade for the C.O. who reminded them of the Official Secrets Act which was being applied to the events of the previous night. Later that day the Chief Controller tried to contact the two pilots involved but was told they had gone on leave. *"There was an unconfirmed rumour that the aircraft were contaminated by radiation. But I was told they hadn't seen a weather balloon as none had been launched in that vicinity. That was the last I heard of it. My wife confirms the story as she was the assistant of the C.C at the time. It was such a vivid experience I can still picture it after 50 years!"*

Earl Mountbatten of Burma . . .

. . . wrote a personal letter to the editor of the *Sunday Despatch*. This letter followed an earlier article concerning a 'wave' of UFO sightings in America, in the town of Orangeburg. The letter read as follows: *"These extraordinary things have now been seen in almost every part of the world – Scandinavia, North America, South America, Central Europe, etc. Reports are always appearing, and the newspapers generally try to ridicule them. As a result, it is difficult for any seriously interested person to find out very much about them. I should therefore like to congratulate you on having had both the intelligence (and, incidentally, the courage) to print the first serious helpful article which I have read on the 'Flying Saucers'. I have read most other accounts up to date and can candidly say yours interested me the most".*

[John: I had the pleasure of meeting Lord Louis many years ago at a *HMS Kelly* Reunion dinner in London, after being invited by my late Father in Law Edward 'Ted' West who was a Chief Petty Officer on the ship and shot down a German Stuka which was dive bombing the ship as it sank off Crete in 1941.]

In the same month Flt Jack Hunter with 24 years in the service was taking a guided missile course at Henlow Bedfordshire, when he saw a UFO flying over *Toplers* hill which he claimed **"was**

THE HALT PERSPECTIVE 2

no aircraft or missile – not part of a stunt. I admit I had been a skeptic before, not now" The officer wasn't on his own – many people saw the saucer shaped object. However, the officer didn't make this information available till some months later

1955 – January 1st, at 6.44am, a 'metallic disc' was sighted at Cochise, New Mexico, described as resembling 'two pie tins, face-to-face'. On the same date were reports from Brazil, involving a family and an employee who were out fishing, just past midnight, when they saw a 30 metre in length disc-shaped object, at an estimated altitude of 200 metres. The light from the descending object lit up the surrounding area. When about a metre off the water, a figure was seen within the light on the cupola, believed to be about 5-6ft in height. **(Source: Project Blue Book)** 10th January, At 4.00pm, Staffordshire housewife – Jessie Roestenberg – sights an orange cigar-shaped object, followed by the appearance of an RAF Jet. 18th January – A disc-like object was reported over the sea at Southport, by Mr. Peter Walsh, who contacted the Police and coastguards. **(Source: *The Daily Express*, 19.Jan.1955)** 17th January – Luminous object described as being circular with a rounded base was seen moving over Norwich and Wrexham at 7.10pm. **(Source: *Eastern Daily Press*.19 Jan 1955 'reports of disc like object over Norwich')** 27th January – Richard Street (14), Charles Bender and Edward Wettstein (14) rushed into the Burton Ohio Sheriff's department at 9pm and told law officials that they had been tobogganing at the rear of Chardon Avenue school when they "... *saw a brilliant object stationary in the sky, which suddenly took off at a fantastic rate. It had a brilliant amber light on the smaller top with a light dividing the space underneath which wasn't lit.*" **(Source: *Burton Ohio Times* Leader, 27.Jan.1955 'Three boys report seeing 'Flying Saucer' while playing in Chardon')**

Air Marshal Lord Dowding head of RAF Fighter Command comments!

The previous head of the RAF Fighter Command whose brave pilots 'The few' won the Battle of Britain. Air Marshal Lord Dowding told the Flying Saucer Club, in London: on the 23rd of January 1955, "*It's rude to fire AA guns and send fighters to shoot them down; you never know what they could do to you. I believe these objects come from planets hundreds of years ahead of us in scientific knowledge; there is no material we know that could travel 9,000 miles per hour, which was the recorded speed of one saucer, without becoming white hot.*" On the 28th of January it was the turn of residents living in the Valley Centre – to see what we have labelled as an example of UFO display, the purpose of which remains elusive, although we don't believe their antics are for our amusement! Mrs. Rubalcaba, her son, and daughter first spotted them during the early part of the evening. "*They played some sort of tag with each other, darting about in the sky. Through a telescope, they were perfectly round. One of them had two distinct lights towards the front, they seemed to be signalling each other, and would grow dim and then bright. At 10.30pm they disappeared from view.*" **(Source: *California Times Advocate* 29.Jan.1955 'Flying saucers reported over Valley Centre').** At 9am on the 2nd of February, several people living in the Swindon area of Wiltshire England saw a strange object in the sky described as having "a curved end like a boat and something like a turret on the top" **(Source: *Swindon Evening Advertiser* 2.Feb.1955)**

It appears the same phenomenon was seen over South Florida, USA, causing pilots to swerve out of the way to avoid striking it. Pilot Captain Charles Elmore reported seeing three bright white 'lights' due south of the DC-6B, at 8.35pm, 7th February as they crossed Biscayne Bay at 1,200ft. *"The lights were 15° higher than the plane and had fuzzy edges and were round. They appeared to hover with the front two connected by a line of light between them. Suddenly they blinked out. The tower also saw them but couldn't identify them."* **(Source: Mr. H.B. Williams/*The Daily Telegraph*, 7.Feb.1955).** On the 8th a brand-new B-57 jet bomber exploded over Maryland under test. 9th February – two jet fighters crashed at Goose Bay. The air force reported they collided in the air, but authenticated Press reports said they crashed separately, five minutes and some miles apart! With no explanation as to what occurred! On the same day, two jets crashed in New Brunswick! **(Source: *The UFO Annual* MK Jessup).** 11th February, six 'flying saucers' were seen in the sky over Chichester. On the same day 11th February – Captain King was flying between Miami and New York. *"Suddenly, close to the plane and under the wings, two strange reddish-green objects passed by. They were also seen by some of the passengers. I hadn't believed in 'flying saucers' before, but after this incident my opinion had quickly changed."*

12th February, three girl secretaries working in East St Chichester, Miss P Coom, Miss P Vigar, and Miss E E.M. Rogers told of sighting six flying objects in the sky *". . . frisking like tadpoles in a pond, they looked like bubbles but were flat and disc-like, they disappeared at speed towards Portsmouth."* **(Source: *Portsmouth Evening News*: 12.Feb.1955 'cigars over Sussex').** On the same day, it's reported that a USW Stratojet bomber on an arctic flight at 35000 feet exploded mysteriously. There were two survivors who were unable to shed any light on the disaster. While we can't say that there is any connection between accidents like this, it seems very odd and quite frightening. On the 13th of February, a Belgian airliner carrying 29 persons vanished after radioing Rome's Ciampino Airport that it was preparing for a landing. The pilot radioed he had seen a fireball in the sky, before the disaster! On the 15th of February Tom Mallion (58) and Leslie Streeter (35) who were employed on the construction of a new telephone exchange, in Best Street, Chatham, Kent sighted an object in the sky described as *". . . smooth the underside like a plate or saucer with no wings or holes in it heading towards London at 11.30am."* **(Source: *Kent Messenger Maidstone* 16.Feb.1955 'Workmen see Flying Saucer it was certainly not an airplane we saw')**

USAF Secretary of State for Air discounts the existence of UFOs!

In 1955 – after eight years of study by the USAF into reported UFO activity the secretary of the Air Force, Mr Quarles made public a 316-page booklet based on the investigation of 5000 reported sightings. This showed that all but three per cent (150) proved to be balloons, aircraft, astronomical bodies, birds or mirages. *"In some cases other than the three per cent there has not been enough information to say what gave rise to the reports. Mr. Quarles disclosed that the USA in cooperation with Avro Ltd of Canada was building a disc-shaped aircraft with jet engines that will look rather like the public conception of a flying saucer. He added that there is no evidence that any objects mistaken for flying saucers are of foreign origin. I am sure that even the three per cent of the unexplained objects were in fact conventional phenomena or illusions."* March 2nd, – At 3.00pm a hovering, rectangular-shaped, object was seen rocking in the sky over Tucson, Arizona. One hour later, at about 5.00pm, a car driving ten miles north of Huntley, Illinois, was followed for ten minutes by three elongated 'balloons.' The objects were each about seven metres long and showed eight red lights. 19th March

THE HALT PERSPECTIVE 2

– At Manchester, New Hampshire, Joanne Crowley and her friend Gene Tobias both aged 13, eighth graders at Straw School reported having seen a "... *shiny disc in the sky with a yellow glare around it turning over and over, moving at high speed before disappearing out of view seconds later*" **(Source: Manchester *New Hampshire Sunday News* 20.Mar.1955)**

April 8th – At 9.30am over Rockford, Illinois, USAF Pilots open fire on a large object, which explodes after discharging a small round object. Balloon-like objects observed. Two balls of light observed by more than four military witnesses. April 9th, a member of the Civil Defense Ground observation corps stationed on the top of Physicians Hospital at Plattsburgh New York, reported having "... *sighted a rust-coloured mist, round in shape, surrounded by misty cloud moving away from the post, at 1.30am at a height of about 1600 feet. It then banked to the left and went down behind the ridge of mountains on the Vermont side of the lake*". He called the Vermont State Police, thinking it may have landed. At 3,34am an odd vapour trail was seen stretched across the sky. Further observations revealed that it was likened to a pencil or cigar-shaped object, giving off green light from the edges, glowing gold in colour. It was visible until sunrise. At 4.10am, a strange glow was seen towards the north east horizon over the Vermont area as if something was on fire. Enquiries made revealed nothing had been reported; such as plane crash or fire. "*A bright star appeared in the sky which began to change colour from white to greenish white to pink and then red, blue and white again. It then rose upwards as the sun came up. Through binoculars, it resembled an inverted dish, glowing deep red on top with flanged lines along the bottom, giving off a green vapour in a series of eight exhaust-like trailing underneath, with a brilliant yellow light beneath it. Three apertures could be seen near the top of the 'dish.'*

May 17th – At 8.20pm over Mojave, California, nine grapefruit-sized objects were seen for 10 minutes over the desert. Radio and television interference were reported. Explanation: aircraft. 25th May, the crew of a Portuguese Airlines 'Sky master' aircraft, landed at London Airport, and reported having "... *sighted a long silver cigar-shaped object, without wings, passing under the nose of the plane...*" while flying between Epsom and Dunsfold. Astronomer Royal, Sir Harold Spencer Jones told Canadians in May 1955 that: "*Stories of Flying Saucers were bunk – I am certain that no life exists in the solar system, except that on Earth and primitive planets.*" In the same month, jet fighters were launched from Norton Air Force Base after reports of three silvery disc-like objects over the Mount Wilson area between 7.15pm and 8.15pm. One witness was Lt John Elliot of the Pasadena Police who went to have a look after receiving numerous calls from the public reporting something very odd in the sky. "*I could see the silver disc-shaped objects changing formation, as if playing tag in the sky.*" 23rd June – Near Utica, New York, the pilots of a Mohawk Airlines sighted a "... *grey, round UFO with portholes emitting blue green light heading at great speed, heading across the sky. Its speed was calculated as being approximately 4.700 miles per hour.*" Apparently two other aircraft also saw and tracked it on radar. **(Source: *UFO Investigator*)**. July 7th, at midday Ruth Murray from Beccles, near Lowestoft, sighted, "... *a flat, glistening silver object, heading silently, at tremendous speed, towards the south-east. It was the most beautiful thing I had ever seen. It couldn't have been an aircraft, nor was there any smoke. I watched it for a few seconds, and then it turned black and disappeared.*" 8th July – James Carey of Leona Lane, Connecticut, sights orange 'disc' at 9pm. **(Source: *Hartford Connecticut, Courant* 9.July.1955 'Flying Saucer seen in New Britain sky').** 10th July – Mr Killian of Dewey Oklahoma, sighted, a "... *round silver object in sky heading north east at an estimated height of about 15,000feet. It stopped, circled twice and then headed away.*" **(Source: *Bartlesville Enterprise* 11.July.1955 'Dewey man thinks he saw saucer')**

THE HALT PERSPECTIVE 2

11th July – Long Beach, California. Coastguards were contacted by a motorboat owner, told of having sighted a *'flying saucer'* over the Santa Catalina Channel. Further investigation revealed that the owner of a 22 foot boat, San Bernardino resident, Mr. George Washington was cruising with his wife Elsie and daughter Marie towards Catalina Island during the afternoon about nine miles west of Newport heading for Avalon Harbor 13 miles away. *"We saw a round, grey rotating cylinder about 2500 feet above the boat, surrounded by a haze of fumes."* George contacted the coast guard – minutes later Air Force jets appeared and gave chase to the object which shot away in a zig zagging motion at colossal speed, outrunning the jets. Others also testified to having seen what appears to have been the same UFO during the morning over the same location. **(Source:** *San Bernardino Sun* **12.July.1955 'Man describes object seen over Channel' –** *Santa Anna Register* **11.July.1955 'Saucer skims channel, so say fishermen').** The following day, on the 12th of July, Palmdale family Mrs. Isaac Jones and her son Bob (14) saw a long, thin silver object which split into three shiny triangles which then darted about the sky before heading away at speed. Bob called his father who works on Air Traffic Control at Palmdale airport. He and a colleague William Kane confirmed they also had them under observation. **(Source:** *Southern Antelope Valley Press* **14.July.1955 'Silvery Flying saucers objects sighted in manoeuvrers over Palmdale').**

'Flying Saucer' descends over Kent suburb!

On the 17th of July 1955, Margaret Fry, then a young housewife, living in Hythe Avenue, Bexleyheath, Kent, was on her way to the doctor's surgery, in King Harold Way, accompanied by the emergency locum, Dr. Thukarta, to collect some medication for her son, Steven, taken ill with suspected sunstroke. Within minutes into the journey, the 'Austin 7' car was plunged into darkness, as a black shadow fell across it, cutting off the bright sunlight.

"We turned right into Chessington Avenue. The engine of the car began to splutter. The car then came to a halt, near the junction of Ashbourne Road and Whitfield Road. Wondering what on earth was going on, we got out of the car, to be confronted by the amazing sight of a light-grey, elliptical mass, with well-defined edges, about 25 ft in length, sprawled across the junction, roughly 20ft above our heads.

Out of the base of this unusual shade of **grey/silver, pewter-coloured object – divided into sections**, apparently riveted together – **descended three objects that resembled huge, ball-bearing wheels which retracted upwards, followed by a swishing noise** *as it began to spin. After a few minutes, it rose slightly off the ground, by which time a group of children had arrived. They shouted, 'flying saucer'. A few minutes later, it tilted at an angle and rose up to about a hundred feet, where it stopped still in the* air. A 'porthole 'opened. It then immediately moved quickly upwards, making a 'swishing' noise, and rose about another hundred feet, where it began to slowly rock backwards and forwards, before heading away and out-of-sight."

(Other witnesses were tracked down by us including a local police officer – full report with authors.)

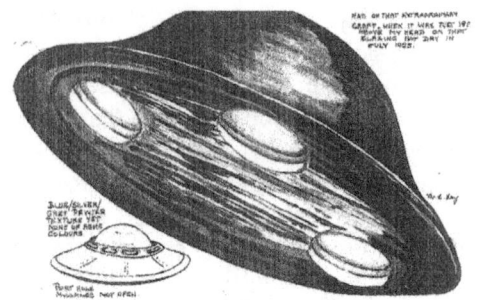

Did a UFO crash in England and was it captured by the authorities?

In 1955, US journalist and TV regular host of the 1950s and 1960s, Dorothy Mae Kilgallen and her husband, Richard Kollmar, were on holiday in England. On May 23rd, 1955, following conversation with an unnamed person of British Ministerial rank, Dorothy, in a wired communication to the States said, *"I can report today on a story which is positively spooky, not to mention chilling. British scientists and airmen, after examining the wreckage of one mysterious flying ship, are convinced these strange aerial objects are not optical illusions or Soviet inventions, but are flying saucers which originate on another planet. We believe, on the basis of our inquiry thus far, that the saucers were staffed by small men – probably – fewer than four feet tall. It's frightening, but there's no denying the flying saucers come from another planet. The source of my information is a British official of cabinet rank who prefers to remain unidentified."*

Apart from Churchill who resigned as Prime Minister on the 5th of April 1955, whose remarks about the UFO subject are well known, we were unable to identify any one in the British Cabinet who had expressed any interest in UFOs/aerial phenomena. We should also entertain the possibility that the information disclosed to Dorothy may have been deliberately passed to her as disinformation! Who knows? Whatever their visit and length of it, we couldn't find any mention in the English newspapers relating to their holiday/visit to England, which seems odd for suggesting the couple who thrived on publicity. – Was it a clandestine pre-arranged visit?

1955 – British Government's attitude towards reports of 'flying saucers'

Many people wrote to the Ministry of Air wanting to know their views on the question of whether 'flying saucers' existed, taking into consideration reports published in the Press. This was a matter brought to the attention of Parliament. The under-secretary of State for Air, Nigel Birch, stated that: "Flying saucers do not exist. Reports of flying saucers, as well as other abnormal objects in the sky, are investigated as they come in, but there has been no formal enquiry. About 90% of the reports have been found to relate to meteors, balloons, flares, and many other objects. The fact that the other objects are unexplained need be attributed to nothing more sinister than lack of data." [Some sources give a figure of 15,000 sightings between 1947 and 1954 – only a few of which have survived.]

THE HALT PERSPECTIVE 2

It is suspected that the 'informant' taking into consideration his well known interest in the UFO subject was Lord Louis Mountbatten, who the couple presumably may have been introduced to after being invited as guests to attend the Coronation of Queen Elizabeth in 1953. Especially as Lord Louis Mountbatten had an interest in reported UFO activity and even wrote an official report about an 'alien' in a silver spaceship seen to land on his estate, by one of his employees, on the 23rd of February 1955.

A total of 8,251 guests attended the Queen›s coronation ceremony at Westminster Abbey. There were more than 2,000 journalists and 500 photographers from 92 nations on the Coronation route.

Dorothy Kilgallen's articles about the coronation won her a Pulitzer Prize nomination. Even if the couple had been invited by the Royal Family to England two years later in 1955 – it is extremely unlikely, conversations of this sort would have taken place, bearing in mind it would surely have been a breach of Royal Protocol? Although it is claimed the couple were regular guests at Royal cocktail parties! This may put things in a different light! But is puzzling as to where there is a complete absence of references to such visits?

George Filer: *"I believe the most likely source was Lord Mountbatten. He was first Sea Lord (1955-1958) and Chief of Defence Staff (1959-1965). Mountbatten was murdered while sailing near his holiday home in Ireland in 1979. His experience in the region and in particular his widely known Labor sympathies led to Prime Minister Clement Attlee appointing him Viceroy of India after the second world war. In his position as Viceroy, Mountbatten oversaw the granting of independence to India as India and Pakistan were partitioned in 1947. I had dinner with Prince Phillip due to his interest in UFOs at Sculthorpe RAF Base. He told me his nephew Mountbatten had seen UFOs while in the Navy."*

John Hanson: The Editor of *Flying Saucer Review*, Gordon Creighton, told me about his interest in this matter, many years ago – after coming across an anonymous one-page written document referring to a crashed UFO, signed by 'Creighton' something Gordon denied saying 'he wished he had been involved!' Presumably the document was malicious! Gordon wrote to Dorothy hoping to identify the informant but never received any reply. Creighton suspected the source of the information to Kilgallen as being Lord Louis Mountbatten.

Derek Dempster – another man of courage

Another man to whom we spoke, also keen to set the record straight, was Derek Dempster, M.A, RAF test pilot with the North Weald Squadron from 1948 onwards, and personal friend to RAF FLt. James Salandin – who inspired his interest in UFOs.

Derek was educated, initially, at the French Lycee Regnault in Tangier, and completed his schooling in England, in 1942, when he then volunteered for the RAF and was sent to Southern Rhodesia for pilot training.

On his commission, after receiving his 'wings', he qualified as a flying instructor. In the mid-1950s he left the RAF and took up a

THE HALT PERSPECTIVE 2

position as air correspondent for the *Daily Express* newspaper. He was then able to sift through reports of UFOs and decide whether further investigations should be carried out. He was asked to review a copy of *Flying Saucers have Landed,* by George Adamski and Desmond Leslie, which increased his curiosity into the UFO subject. Unfortunately, owing to a disagreement with the editor of the newspaper over the grounding of the world's first passenger jet, the *Comet*, he left the *Daily Express* and started his new job as first editor of *Flying Saucer Review,* at Werner Laurie Publishers, in Doughty Street, London. He was assisted by the following people: Waveney Girvan (publisher), Lewis Barton (editor of *This Week*, illustrated magazine), The Honourable Brindsley Le Poer Trench (an accountant at the South African Embassy), Dennis Montgomery (librarian) and Gordon Creighton (diplomat).

Derek Dempster: *"We held meetings at Westminster, Caxton Hall, near Scotland Yard. We believed these things were coming in from outer space, and we were trying to prove this with science. We had some allies, such as Peter Horsley, who had been Station Commander at North Weald, and was then equerry to Prince Philip. We received collaboration from Henry Chinnery, who was Horsley's successor.* **Both men had a keen interest in keeping the Palace posted on 'flying saucers' and we used to exchange files with them**. *There was also a shorthand writer for Lord Mountbatten, named Dan Lloyd, who was an ex-Royal Navy man. He was also very interested in 'flying saucer' matters and shared this interest and new research material with Mountbatten. It was said, at the time, that Mountbatten kept lever files of UFO photographs to show visitors on the bridge of the warships when he was at sea. I met George Adamski at this time. I could see how terribly keen everybody was to embrace people like him, who claimed he had travelled to Venus. I was sceptical of him but wished to remained objective. What we were all living on, then, was hope and expectation. We kept being shot down due to the activities of the lunatic fringe, who began to attach themselves to Ufology. I had to leave FSR because of the effect it had on my business interests in the aviation industry; apart from that, I was being regarded as a 'nutcase', whose opinion in aviation matters was in question."*

Derek's literary output includes **The Inhabited Universe** and **Worlds in Creation, The Tale of The Comet** with Kenneth Gatland, and the award-winning **The Narrow Margin** with Derek Wood, which served as a source book for the film **Battle of Britain.** Derek passed away on the 25th January 2012. RIP

Lord Louis Mountbatten took 'Ted' my father-in-law on his final journey

John Hanson: *"I met Lord Louis Mountbatten myself, during the 1970s, at an* HMS Kelly *reunion dinner, as my father- in-law was retired Chief Petty Officer 'Ted West', who shot down a German Stuka dive bomber at Crete, in 1943, as the ship foundered. He was later awarded a medal by the King at Buckingham Palace for his bravery. I found Lord Louis a charismatic figure and was saddened of his assassination by the IRA in later years, but proud of the fact that he [Lord Louis] officiated at the funeral of*

Ted West

Ted, when his ashes were cast into the sea at Portsmouth. What an honour that truly was!

Obviously, then, I had no inkling of the existence of UFOs. If I had, no doubt I would have been regarded as a 'nutcase' as well, by my fellow police officers.

(Source: Personal Interviews held with Mr. Salandin/ Derek Dempster/*FSR***, Volume 1, No.1, 1955/***FSR***, Volume 3, No.2, 1984/** *Above Top Secret***, Timothy Good)**

Washington Post obituary 18.11.79 '**What did Dorothy know?'** Rita Mae Brown **the author of the novel** *Six of One***.** In one article which is too lengthy to include, there are no punches pulled. **Her death is treated as extremely suspicious, one of the motives being she was ready to publish details about the assassination of John F Kennedy. It would have been the 'scoop of the century'.** Quote: "Nothing larger than her own life or her own needs motivated her until she had a fateful, secret interview with Jack Ruby early in 1964. She could have chosen to forget it, what appeared to her to be horrific implications of conspiracy in the death of the president; she could have backslid into her life of glamour. The more she probed the more she felt her own life was in jeopardy. She thought the JFK assassination touched the soul of America and she wasn't going to stop. She put the truth first and paid the price." **(Source: Book by Biographer Lee Israel's** *'Kilgallen'***)**

Dorothy Kilgallen

On November 8, 1965, Dorothy Kilgallen, born in Chicago, the daughter of newspaper reporter, James Lawrence Kilgallen (1888–1982) and his wife, Mae Ahern (1888-1985), was found dead in her New York City home at the age of 52. She had, apparently, succumbed to a fatal combination of alcohol and seconal. It is not known whether it was a suicide, murder or an accidental death. Her death certificate cites the cause of death as "undetermined".

Because of her open criticism of the Warren Commission and other US government entities, and her association with Ruby and recent interview of him, some speculate that she was murdered by members of the alleged JFK conspiracy. Kilgallen had become a friend of Marilyn Monroe and the break up with the Kennedy's, the rumour was she had secrets such as the visit by the President at a secret air base for the purpose of inspecting things from outer space. In the mid-fifties Kilgallen learned of secret efforts by US and UK governments to identify the origins of crashed spacecraft and dead bodies, from a British government official. Having read the circumstances of her death I can only regard them as suspicious as I did with the suicide of MK Jessup! The facts, never mind a Detectives 'gut instinct', speak for themselves.

The only incident we have ever come across involving a captured 'flying saucer', is as follows!

Did the Allies capture a landed 'flying saucer in 1944?

Leslie Grant was a soldier with the British Army, on his way to deliver vital supplies to Arnhem, in summer 1944, with a colleague, when he found his route blocked by a bridge destroyed by Allied bombers. Seeking another way around, he managed to get his lorry bogged down a steep valley and went to look for help. After coming across a captured German tank, manned by a British crew (it had a yellow triangle on it), he asked them to tow his lorry to the top of the hill. The man agreed, but said a very odd thing: *"Don't be surprised when you see something strange at the top."*

Leslie: *"I hadn't got a clue what he was on about and continued on the journey. When we reached the top, I saw this huge grey circular 'thing', approximately 100 feet in diameter, just resting above the ground on three tripod legs, with a dome on top and what looked like slatted windows around its circumference."*

Leslie stood there, trying to work out what it was – bearing in mind he had never heard of UFOs or 'flying saucers' – and decided to walk towards it, but found when about 70ft away, his passage was blocked by what felt like an invisible force stopping him, *"...**like pushing against rubber**"*. Frightened, he returned to the lorry and drove away. When he finally reached his destination he went over to the commanding officer and told him what had been seen, but was shocked when the man warned him to keep quiet about it.

We contacted Mrs Phyllis Moonie – then a UFO investigator for the well respected Essex UFO Group, run by Dan Goring, editor of *Earth-link* – hoping to glean further information about the incident. Mrs Moonie told us she saw no reason not to accept as other than genuine the version of events given to her by Leslie, who was then employed as a bus driver at the same depot as her husband. Unfortunately we were unable to speak to Leslie himself, as he had passed away.

This was not to be the only occasion when we were to come across reports relating to what appears to be some type of invisible force-field surrounding the perimeter of the UFO. Could this sighting in some way corroborate the highly controversial alleged developments of 'flying saucers' produced by Nazi Germany, during the Second World War, which some people maintain were capable of flight to the moon and beyond, or are the German 'flying saucers' just a myth? Did German fighters attempt to chase UFOs then? They certainly reported the same phenomena as the Allies.

We know that Winston Churchill clamped down on UFO reports from Allied pilots fearing that it could cause panic and that it may threaten the teachings of the Church. No doubt other Cabinet members were made aware of what was happening not only in the UK but also in the States. But the 'whistleblower' that was alleged to have confided in Dorothy of course remains unidentified!

In August Bradford lorry driver Ernest Suddards (35) was on his way home, from work, accompanied by his son Raymond (l3). As they drove down Roundhill Street, at 4.00am a short distance from the family home, they saw something, approaching in the glare of the headlights.

Ernest: *"It looked about 4ft tall, dressed in skin tight black clothes, with arms close to its sides feet together, and hopped, or jumped forwards, in a series of jerky movements. On its chest was a circular silver disc, with holes cut into it, below the throat. It then turned down a nearby passage. We were literally paralysed by the* sight. After arriving home, we talked about it and then contacted the police, who had a look around, but found nothing." We spoke to Ray Suddards (aged 63 in 2006) – like his father, a lorry driver by occupation.

Ray: *"I remember it clearly – like yesterday. It had this silver plate, with holes on its chest, hopping up Roundhill Street. After my dad reported what we had seen, he was subjected to a lot of ridicule. A few days later, he picked up a newspaper and read about a similar 'figure' being seen in Horton Lane, close to where we had seen it."*

The sighting led to much speculation. Some people believed that what the Suddards had witnessed was the lone occupant of a downed 'flying saucer'; others thought it might have been a ghost. Following an appeal in the *Bradford Telegraph & Argus*, we were contacted by Detective Sergeant Paul Jackson (retired) who recalls the incident very well, because his partner at the time was Police Constable Victor Briggs – the officer who interviewed them and made a search of the area. *"He* (P.C. Briggs) *often brought up the subject in conversation, as he believed they had genuinely sighted something highly unusual."*

What happened at Hopkinsville Kentucky?

There have been numerous books, documentaries and debates, regarding this incident, which alleges a close encounter with extraterrestrial beings on the 21st August. The incident became famous and well-publicized. It occurred at Gaither McGette's rural farmhouse rented at the time by the Sutton family, located between the hamlet of Kellyand the small city of Hopkinsville, Christian County, Kentucky.

Many people believe that it had nothing to do with any alien incursion and more in keeping with a paranormal report, involving some sort of demonic presence. The seven

THE HALT PERSPECTIVE 2

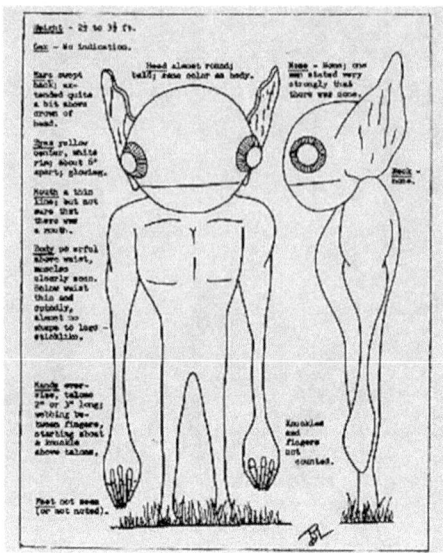

people present in the farmhouse claimed that they were terrorized by an unknown number of 'creatures' – often referred to as the '*Hopkinsville Goblins*'. The residents of the farmhouse described them as:

"*…around three feet tall, with upright pointed ears, thin limbs, long arms, and claw-like hands or talons. The creatures were either silvery in colour or wearing something metallic. Their movements on occasion seemed to defy gravity with them floating above the ground and appearing in high up places, and they 'walked' with a swaying motion, as though wading through water*".

23rd August – At 10.45am, Mr. G. M. Park from Arlington, Virginia, watched, for 30 minutes, "*several orange lights moving singly or in groups, circling and stopping through the sky.*" **(Source: Project Blue Book).**

Three UFOs sighted over control tower!

At 12.10pm on the same date, according to Leonard H. Stringfield, editor of *ORBIT*, USAF fighter aircraft from Lockbourne Air Force Base, Ohio, were scrambled to intercept three UFOs which had been hovering over the control tower. The aircraft climbed to 20,000ft, but the UFOs shot away at incredible speed. Officials at Forestville and Loveland also told of having sighted the erratic behaviour of UFOs on the same day – described as round, brilliant white spheres and discs.

25th August 1955, at 7.30pm, fifteen UFOs were sighted crossing the sky over Birmingham UK. Later during a dark and breezy night, Frank and Eileen Bordes, of The Bronx, were out fishing on Titicus Reservoir, near Bush Pine, New York State. Eileen was the first to see an iridescent pink mushroom-shaped object rise about 2ft above the water, before disappearing below the surface. She brought this matter to her husband's attention and then asked him to row ashore. When this was done, the couple looked out into the darkness, which was illuminated by twinkling stars. They then noticed a light, followed by two long lights below this, apparently emanating from an elongated object some 15ft long, which *was partially submerged,* around which appeared a good deal of turbulence. Frank and Eileen rowed along the shore, feeling they were being watched in some way. They also remarked on the curious fact that whenever they headed towards the object(s), it would speed towards them; when they moved back, so did it. **(Source: Dr. Paul Gray).**

The Reverend Pitt-Kethley, from West London, was travelling on an Uxbridge train to East Harrow, London, at 4.10pm., on the 18th of October, when the train was halted by a signal at West Hampstead Viaduct. As he casually looked through the window, he saw a strange craft approaching in the sky, at a height of about 120ft, described as being reddish brown and grey in colour, reminding him of: "*…a German troop carrier, about the size of a small bus, containing about 30 immobile helmeted figures, with human faces, all apparently dressed in khaki uniforms, some of whom were seated and staring fixedly forward. I was puzzled how such an object, with its low trajectory, could possibly clear London.*"

US Secretary of Air replies!

28th October – former Marine Corps Officer Donald Keyhoe who has written several books on flying saucers accused the United States Air Force of a deliberate attempt to conceal the facts from the public. This was in response to a report issued by the Secretary of the Air Force Donald A. Quarles, who stated, "*Flying saucers were imaginary and that only three per cent of the year's sightings were unexplained.*"

Gigantic object seen by astronomer Frank Edwards – author of *Flying Saucers, Serious Business* – tells of an interview conducted with Frank Halstead, curator at Darling Observatory, Duluth, Minnesota, who spoke of what he witnessed on the 1st November, when he and his wife Ann were travelling on a Union Pacific passenger train. "*We were about a hundred miles west of Las Vegas, when my wife called my attention to an object moving just above the Mountain range, in the same direction as the train. At first, I thought it was a blimp, but as I watched I realised it could not be, as this thing was 800ft long. It was then joined by another object, which was disc-shaped – very shiny, flat on the bottom, with a low dome on top. They then began to rise upwards, slowly at first, then much faster, and in about 15secs disappeared from sight.*"

Disturbing letter – if true, not the only one!

A disturbing letter was sent by David Bell to M.K Jessup author of the *UFO Annual*, on November 13th, – '*An Air Force jet fighter radioed McClellan Air Force base in Sacramento that it was preparing to land. It had not been heard of since. The whole area of our central valley is thickly populated, and it seems unlikely that a crashed plane would go unnoticed. A burned-out area, some 30 miles away, was investigated, but yielded nothing.* **The plane has simply vanished.** *This seems to follow along with other cases cited by both you and Harold T Wilkins. Like the ones you have given, it disappeared after asking for landing instructions and usually very close to its landing point.*'

17th November – At St. Louis, Missouri, twelve round, flat objects, silver on top and dark on the bottom, were seen to fly across the sky in a four-deep formation, tipping in pitch and roll, for 45 seconds, at 6.10am by local resident Mr. J. A. Mapes. 20th November at 5.20pm over Lake City, Tennessee, Capt. B. G. Denkler and five men of the USAF 663rd AC&W Squadron sighted two oblong, bright orange, semi-transparent objects flying at terrific speed and erratically, toward and away from each other. The sighting was explained away as being a mirage. November 1955 – at 10:30am over La Veta, Colorado, a dirigible-shaped object, with a fat front, tapered toward the tail was sighted by State Senator S. T. Taylor, described as luminous green-blue and jelly-like, appeared overhead diving at a 45° angle, reducing to 30°. (**Source:** *Blue Book*)

RIP Colonel Joseph Lee Merkel

1956 – At 2.50pm 31st January 1956, Lt. Colonel Joseph Lee Merkel – a member of the 123rd Kentucky Air National Guard – took off from Standiford Field, Louisville, Kentucky, in an F-51D aircraft, with the intention of carrying out a maintenance test flight for a carburettor and propeller change. He climbed to 20,000ft and made contact with Oak Hill Air Defence Command Radar Station. A course was then set for Terre Haute, Indiana, at 3.pm. As the flight continued,

THE HALT PERSPECTIVE 2

the pilot was contacted by Oak Hill, who told him that the aircraft was fading on their radar scope. Lt. Colonel Merkel replied he had Terre Haute in sight. 3.24pm: Oak Hill received a message from Lt. Colonel Merkel to say he was returning to Louisville on a heading of 1350, at 34,000ft, climbing to 35,000ft. At this point, the pilot was informed of an aircraft approaching from his right. The pilot replied he did not have this in sight and the 'blip' then faded from the radar scope. 3.35pm: Communication ended between the pilot and Oak Hill – presumably caused by the aircraft crashing onto the farm of Mr. Ormel Prince, near Bloomington, Indiana.

Lt. Colonel Merkel

Mr. Prince later told the Aircraft Investigating Officer – Grady Bishop – that he was sure **the aircraft had exploded in mid-air!** The Official Air Force accident report into the incident left an impression that this was due to oxygen starvation. In April 1980, Mr. B.F. Greene Jnr., of Brookline, Massachusetts, contacted the son – Lee Merkel – who told him the Air Force had given the cause of the accident as malfunction in the oxygen equipment. Lee also recalled having read in an Indiana newspaper report about a UFO detected on radar, and planes being scrambled to intercept. His father headed towards the object but, sadly, crashed and died. **(Source: *FSR*, Volume 32, No. 3, 1987 – AIRCRAFT ACCIDENTS AND UFOs: A REVIEW OF SOME UFO RELATED AIRCRAFT DISASTERS, T. Scott Crain Jr., State Director for MUFON)**

Lee was survived by his wife Catherine and four children; they lived at 1104, Manning St, Louisville. An examination of the 1956 *Congressional Senate Records* for that year: (ref- 9609) shows us that Lee was promoted to full Colonel posthumously . . . It was claimed that he crashed on a test flight and witnesses reported the plane was smoking and that he apparently attempted an emergency landing.

On the Kentucky Guard Memorial Page 2020, there is a glowing tribute to Lee accompanied by the statement there was no fire or explosion. In 1956 Frank Edwards gave a talk in New York for the Civilian Saucer Intelligence Group. A screen shot is shown *(left)* from his talk... Something seems amiss here? The reader may not agree...

THE HALT PERSPECTIVE 2

April 19th, 1956 – a black delta/triangular winged aircraft was sighted in the sky over Derbyshire at 1pm, circling a propeller driven Anson aircraft, before breaking away in flight and heading off at fantastic speed in a long curve across the sky – gone in seconds. 27th April 1956, a UFO described as having a chequered outer surface covered with small dots, like rivets, was seen over Limehouse Lane, Wolverhampton, before being lost from view as it headed into a cloud, making a humming noise. June 1956, UFOs were sighted over the town of Cheltenham Spa, Gloucestershire and the surrounding area. They included reports of an object showing blazing lights streaming out of its square windows, seen at 11.30pm over Bishops Cleeve, a high point overlooking the town of Cheltenham – (the scene of other UFO sightings). July 8th 1956, a white 'disc' with a small white dome on top was seen at 3.30pm passing across the sky over Surrey. Within a short time, it

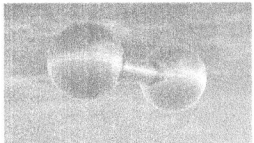

changed to half-white and brilliant red, before shooting straight up into the sky, and ejecting two spheres or globes as it did so. On 10th July 1956, an object resembling *'two spheres or globes, apparently joined by a bar-like structure'*, was seen over Stonewall, Oxfordshire, in broad daylight. (Similar to that seen by Elsie Oakensen in 1978.)

A strange object was seen crossing the sky during the late morning of 13th August 1956, by Eric Rush, then living near St. Mary Cray Railway Station, just off the A224, at Bexleyheath, in Kent. *"We lived close to Biggin Hill Aerodrome, so it was a common sight to see 'Spitfires' and other aircraft flying across the sky, with the occasional sound of jet aircraft, which were pretty rare in those days. I was shocked to see what looked like a light bulb crossing a gap in the blue sky, faster than anything I had ever seen before. When my father arrived home, I told him what I had seen. He suggested I contact the Daily Mirror newspaper, which I did, but despite scouring the papers over the following days, I never saw my letter, although I was sent a ten shilling Postal Order and a thank you note for reporting the sighting of a 'flying saucer'."* At 5.00pm on 13th August 1956 Paul Porcher from Flixton, Manchester, was leaving work when he noticed a red object in the sky, framed between the two roofs of the nearby Barton Power Station. *"It was about 50 yards across, a few hundred feet up in the air, and seemed to have bevelled edges, resembling an upside-down cup and saucer. After about 15 seconds, it moved away towards Eccles. I don't claim to have seen a 'flying saucer'. I can't say what it was that I saw."* **(Source: FSR, 1956, Volume 2, Number 5, Sept/Oct. 1956).**

UFOs tracked moving in from the East Coast-fighters scrambled!

At 9.30pm, 13th August 1956, radar operators at RAF Bentwaters and Lakenheath tracked a group of 'dots' moving in over the East Anglia coast, from the direction of Holland. The 'dots', which could also be seen visually, were then 50 miles distant and closing at nearly 5,000 mph – well over the speed of sound but failed to produce any sonic boom. At this point, the radar then picked up a number of other 'blips', showing as an irregular group of twelve to fifteen in number, heading north-east at a much slower rate, **"being led by three UFOs, forming a triangular formation"**. At 10pm, a United States Air Force jet was scrambled to intercept but returned to base a short time later, after failing to make contact. Fifty minutes later, a UFO – described as 'an oval-shaped white light' was seen crossing the sky over RAF Bentwaters, at speed, apparently connected with the report of a similarly described object seen hovering over RAF Lakenheath, for a short time. A RAF *Venom* night-fighter aircraft, already on patrol over the Bedford area, was instructed to intercept the UFO. After making airborne radar contact, the object began to zigzag behind the jet – both 'vehicles' being tracked by ground radar. Despite a number of high-speed manoeuvres, the plane was unable to shake off the UFO until another fighter appeared. According to the *Daily Express* (22. Feb.78), quote: *"The UFO was seen to shoot off at right angles and split into two separate objects, before locking onto the tail of the fighter in a deadly game of 'hide-and-seek', before eventually disappearing."*

Freddie Wimbledon – the flight controller on duty that evening, at RAF Neatishead told us: "*The incident was released into the media by a retired USAF Officer NCO, who wrote his version of what happened, twelve years after the event, which became known as the Lakenheath incident. The article in the* Daily Express *was full of errors and inaccurate conversations.* **The Venom was not a single seater and did not possess the onboard capabilities to apply to any gun lock onto the target.** *I can tell you that details of the matter were brought to the attention of the* Sunday Times *who contacted the MOD but denied any knowledge of the incident. Apparently, the American ambassador was advised the same.* **Because of the restrictions of the Official Secrets Act,** *I wasn't even allowed to discuss what had taken place – even with my wife. However, as the years passed and more servicemen came forward to tell what had happened, I became pestered by people who wanted to ask me questions about this incident. When I explained my position to them, some of them became quite nasty towards me.*

My memory of the event: I was chief controller on duty at RAF Neatishead, East Anglia, on the night of 13th/14th August, 1956. My duties were to monitor the radar picture and scramble the battle flight, which were on a 24-hour call-out to intercept any intruder over British airspace, not possibly identified in my sector of responsibility. I remember Lakenheath United States Air Force Base contacting me, by telephone, to inform me there was something buzzing their airfield. I scrambled a Venom night fighter from the battle flight, through sector and my controller. The interception cabin then took over. The interception control team would consist of one fighter controller (an officer, corporal, tracker and height reader) consisting of four highly trained personnel, in addition to myself, who could clearly see the object on our radar scopes. After being vectored onto the trail of the object by my interception controller, the pilot called out 'contact', and continued to close on the target, but after a few seconds and in the space of one or two 'sweeps' of our scopes, the object appeared behind our fighter. Our pilot called out, 'lost contact – more help'. He was advised the target was now behind him and given fresh instructions. I then scrambled a second Venom, which was vectored towards the area, but before it arrived on the scene the target had disappeared from our scopes. Although we continued to keep a careful watch, nothing further was seen again. The fact remains that at least nine RAF ground personnel and two RAF crew were conscious of an object, sufficiently solid to give returns on radar. Following a report made of the incident, a senior officer from the Air Ministry came down and interviewed us about what had taken place."

Ivan Logan

Mr. Ivan Logan – RAF Navigator from 23 Squadron – one of the pilots involved in the incident – was also anxious to bring to our attention the subsequent exaggerations in the public domain, which included the ridiculous suggestion that one of the Venoms was chased by the UFO. "*At the time, we didn't consider the incident to be of any great significance. According to my logbook, we took-off at 02.40 hours, on the 14th August 1956. My pilot was Ian Fraser-Kerr, and we were airborne for 45 minutes. On this particular night, we were the second

THE HALT PERSPECTIVE 2

Venom aircraft used to attempt an intercept and were scrambled at low level, 2-3,000 feet, looking for a target near RAF Lakenheath (USAF). Normally we were controlled by RAF Neatishead or Trimingham, but on this occasion, we were with RAF Lakenheath Control Approach Radar, who advised us where the 'target' was, rather than controlling us. The difficulty with low altitude operations was the amount of ground clutter produced on the radar when we turned or scanned low. We had no radar 'lock-on' facility. It was all done manually, moving the scanner by means of a tiny joystick – pointing up, if turning towards the target, and down if we were turning away, the amount depending on how much bank the pilot was using. You can imagine the difficulty involved with trying to manually strobe the 'target' and, at the same time, advising the pilot, verbally, about visual height and target positions. I remember picking up a contact, several times, usually at about three to four miles. It may have been the same  *one, as it appeared to be virtually stationary. We were unable to turn behind it, as it was closing at high speed. Eventually, we were forced to return to base, as fuel was running low. After landing, we met up with the other crew – pilot David Chambers and his navigator, John Brady – in order to debrief. I don't remember UFOs being mentioned as the cause of the scramble. There was certainly some conversation about the possibility of it having been a Meteorological balloon, or something similar."* We contacted Mr. Chambers about the incident, but there was little he could tell us, other than of a feint signal picked up on the corner of the radar screen and that no visual of the object was made.

John Brady ©David Clarke

John Brady – *"At the time I was a navigator on 23 Squadron, equipped with the De-Havilland Venom NF3 night fighter, based at Coltishall, but attached to Waterbeach, near Cambridge, where it provided quick reaction alert to protect the integrity of UK airspace in that area. About an hour or so before we took off, my pilot – David Chambers, and I, were on two minutes' readiness. At about 2am on 14th August, the controller at Neatishead asked for a Venom aircraft to investigate a contact for the Americans near their Base, at Lakenheath. After scrambling, we were instructed to climb to 7,000 feet, where we were handed over to Lakenheath, who gave us indications as to where the contact was positioned. On the first search, I saw nothing, but on the subsequent three or four runs I obtained a contact of around four miles. However, the contact was not as strong or bright as a contact from a large aircraft, but it was quite firm. The approach speed was high and gave the impression it was stationary, but at the same level as our aircraft. The Americans confirmed, at one stage, the contact was stationary. Unfortunately, you cannot intercept a target like that, and my pilot could see nothing in the dark. The Americans didn't offer close control, but what they did was sufficient, and our radar AI21 was good enough to obtain a contact. At the end of the fourth or fifth run, we heard a Venom aircraft had been scrambled, so we returned to Waterbeach, landing at 02.55 hours. At debrief, Ivan and I agreed that we had obtained good contact but could not come up with much idea as to what it was. My own belief is that it was probably a Meteorological balloon, but little was made of the incident at the time and it was soon forgotten. I heard, recently, this was the first time a RAF aircraft was scrambled to intercept a UFO. Whilst I do not believe in the existence of alien craft, I did have a firm contact that night."*

One cannot ignore the evidence looking at the number of UFOs reported from the East Anglia over the years that the direction of these objects was from the Holland/Belgium area. This is of interest bearing in mind the Belgium wave of the mid 1980 period. Presumably other factors or criteria need to be met in order for the 'UFOs manifest visually?

14th August 1956 – David Hester and Brenda Wagstaff were in London Road, Leicester. At 7pm they sighted three orange-coloured lights join up in the sky, before heading towards London. 16th August 1956, a red UFO was sighted over Reading Berkshire-followed by a saucer-shaped object, seen heading south west. Three 'flying discs' were observed for three hours over Southampton. – Summer of the same year. UFO sighted over sea at Gower – also seen by residents of Swansea & a cigar shaped object seen over canal at Paddington London. At 2am Bolton night workers sighted three brilliant blue globes in the sky.

At 10.00pm the same day, an unidentified object was plotted on radar over London. Thirty minutes later Flight Lieutenant Harry Goldstone, navigator on board a Meteor Mk.X1, was preparing to land at West Malling, Kent, at 2,000ft, after being asked to look out for an unidentified light in the sky that could be seen visually by Ground Control. *"The light was a few thousand feet above us, but it didn't have a star's intensity of light. I don't subscribe to 'flying saucers' but I don't know what this light was, nor does anyone else."* **(Source: *Flying Saucer Review World Round-up of UFO Sightings and Events*)**

1st September 1956, radar stations in the UK were on alert after an unidentified 'blip' appeared on the screen. Aircraft were scrambled but failed to sight anything, despite flying straight through the plotted location. This was explained away on the 3rd September by the Air Ministry, who blamed electrical storms. **(Source: *Evening Chronicle*, 3.9.56 – 'Radar image was due to storms').** At 8.44pm on 8th September 1956 Charles Longcroft from London was waiting to catch the train at Box Hill, Surrey, with some friends when they saw a round, scintillating object in the sky, flickering with light and constantly changing in colour from white to red, red to white, white to green and green to white. After seven minutes they lost it in cloud cover but saw it again at 9.20pm. Apparently the object was also seen by other rail passengers, as well as the porter. **(Source: *FSR*, Sept/Oct. 1956, *Volume 2*, No.5).** Knowing that sightings of unidentified objects can occur at locations like Box Hill, it's no surprise to learn of another sighting which took place at 11pm on the 29th of July 1997 – 41 years later! A couple reported having sighted a *"Weird white object in the sky resembling a circle with a rectangle on it."* In addition there have been reports of a mysterious *'brown fur covered creature'* seen on the hill. Another witness described seeing what looked like an *'ape',* or *'bigfoot'* in the forest. On 17th September 1956, pupils and staff were travelling to school at 8.30am through Glendean (seven miles from Dunoon) when five flat half circular objects, with aluminium-like surfaces, were seen stationary in the sky. In the same month, Janet Redman sighted a cigar- shaped UFO over Lincoln – from out of which smaller objects were seen to fall out and then go back into the main object. Was this connected with the sighting of six silver discs over the Lincoln railway yard?

On the 22nd September 1956, what looked like a glass globe some 80 feet in diameter with something or someone inside was seen over Cleethorpes. The RAF scrambled fighter aircraft seen for a short time before it vanished from sight. On 24th September 1956, a huge 'white bird' was seen in the sky over Beamsley Beacon near Bolton Abbey, Yorkshire, by a party of hikers, next to a strange orange sphere. 23rd October 1956 – Two UFOs sighted over Coventry by retired RAF Squadron Leader Ernest Booker.

THE HALT PERSPECTIVE 2

Over Jackson, central Alabama, on the 14th November 1956, Viscount Airliner, Captain W. J. Hull and co-pilot Peter Macintosh were cruising the aircraft when they saw an 'object' which halted in mid-air and hovered in front of them. It then began to dart all over the place, rising and falling in flight, making sharper turns than any aircraft, before shooting out over the Gulf of Mexico at a fantastic speed. **(Source: UFO Investigator/Condon Report).**

1957 – In early January (exact date not confirmed) a resident of Lanarkshire, Scotland, sighted a bright star moving northward across the sky. Then, a second 'star' appeared alongside the other object before heading towards him. Suddenly they halted in flight, enabling him to see a very large black oval-shaped object, and then there was a flash of orange red light followed by a silver oval object seen to descend from the larger one. The objects began to move away, accompanied by a faint whirring noise. After travelling for about a quarter of a mile, they stopped again, there was another flash of light. Once again, a small silver object dropped downwards. Finally, the larger object moved out of sight (Source: Glasgow UFO Research Society)

2nd January 1957 – UFO sighted moving across the sky over St. Helens, Lancashire, at 3.30pm before shooting upwards and vanishing from sight. At 4.30pm the same day a glowing orange 'cigar' was seen in the sky over Staffordshire by Mrs. Jessie Roestenberg who alerted her next-door neighbour Mrs. D. Osborn. The two women watched as it crossed the sky, heading westwards, leaving a trail twice its length. *"An RAF jet appeared in the sky and approached the object, which ascended vertically and vanished into the sky."* On the 3rd January 1957 Mrs. I. Hurcoop looked out of the window of the Cowan Ward at the Royal South Hampshire Hospital, Southampton, at 2.20am and sighted *". . . an unusual bright star, moving slowly across the night sky. I shouted for the night duty sister and attendant nurse, who stood watching with me as the 'star' slowly disappeared below the roofline of the Grimston Ward, followed by the appearance of several more stars, which began an aerial display lasting until 5.30am."* At 10.20am Halifax Yorkshire schoolboys David Weeks and David Tracey – reported sighting two 'solid' silver or grey oval objects spinning on their axes, about the size of a moderate plane, heading eastwards, over the town.

9th January 1957, two objects were seen hovering in the sky over Saville Park, Halifax, Yorkshire at 11.30pm one in a vertical plane, the other horizontal. By the time the witness shouted out to his friends, the objects had accelerated towards the south and were out of view. In the same month two strange objects were seen in the sky over Lesmahagow, Lanarkshire, out of which smaller objects were seen to merge. 21st January 1957, a fast-moving red glow, looking like . . . *'a large fire in the sky, with several rays running through it',* was seen flying across the Bristol area, ruining television reception for many viewers, who contacted the *BBC* after the screens dissolved into wavy patterns and jagged edges between 10pm and 10.30pm, followed by reports of an object seen over Downend, Portishead and Clevedon a few minutes later, lighting up the sky with red light, before moving over Whitchurch. January 23rd, 1957, another multi-UFO display, this time over the Royal Hospital in Southampton.

8th February 1957 – UFO seen over Eastney, Portsmouth, at 10.15pm by Mrs. F. King. *"The object seemed to enclose a dark form of some description, surmounted by a lighted spar – somewhat like a radio mast. The whole appearance vaguely resembled a humming top, in black and white. I'm convinced I saw a 'flying saucer'."* 11th February 1957 – "five 'tadpole'-shaped objects, dark in colour, with black 'tails'", were seen heading across the sky, over Mansfield, Nottinghamshire. 15th

THE HALT PERSPECTIVE 2

February 1957 – A partly-transparent, glittering, egg-shaped object was seen to descend into Sandstone Harbour, Portsmouth, at 11.40am by three boys – Geoffrey Bolt, Dudley Heywood, and John Whiting – who were on a school cross-country run at the time. (**Source: Nicholas Maloret, WATSUP, Southampton**) 20th February 1957 – residents of Paignton, Devon sighted a bright flashing light, **encircled by a grey ring,** hovering over the centre of the bay at 3.45pm. *(Source: The Paignton News* **(21.Feb.57).**

UK Secretary of State for Air answers question!

On the 26th February, 1957, Mr. J. A. Leavey – MP for Heywood and Royton – tabled a question to the Secretary of State for Air, following incidents brought to his attention, which included a report of a commercial aircraft seen flying over Wardle, allegedly taking the same route as the UFO, and the discovery of a minute radio transmitter belonging to the Air Ministry, suspended for a meteorological balloon. Then, two boys found another piece of meteorological equipment attached to a parachute, lying on Brown Wardle – also on the flight path of the UFO. (How coincidental!) During the afternoon of 28th February 1957, Mr. K. Maskery from Reddish, Greater Manchester, sighted a saucer-shaped object in the sky, showing many coloured lights, with flecks of red shooting out from its edge. At 6.07pm a 'flying saucer' was seen over Weymouth by Mr. C. Fooks and Mrs. E. R. Newman, who said: *"I have never seen anything like it before. It seemed to come from out of a cloud, larger than any star. Its sheer brightness impressed me the most".* March 10th, 1957 – At 7.00pm two separate lights; one red, the other white were sighted by astronomer Paul McCormick from Fishponds, Bristol, who was observing Jupiter. 13th March 1957 – an object resembling a shining, silver cigarette was seen hovering just over the sea at Scarborough by a group of men fishing.

UFOs tracked on US radar over Los Angeles

The first of four UFOs appeared on the radar scope at a civilian airport in the Los Angeles area, at 1.50pm. on the 23rd of March 1957, According to the C.A.A operator: *"…it was moving faster than anything I had ever seen; about 40 miles north-west, it came to an abrupt halt, and then reversed its course in just a few seconds."* Five minutes later, two more UFOs appeared, also heading in the same direction. These were tracked at a distance of 30 miles in 30secs, at 3,600mph, before they disappeared off the scope. A fourth 'target' appeared and also went off the scope at 3,600mph; by this time some of the objects were at 10,000ft, or lower. On the 26th of March, 1957 – RAF Church Lawford, Rugby, reported having tracked an object from a stationary position in the air to 1,400 mph a copy of the radar plot was requested by the Air Ministry. **(Source: Declassified MOD records).**

On the morning of 4th April, 1957, radar operators at the Ministry of Supply Bombs Trial Unit, West Freugh, near Stranraer, in Scotland, picked up on radar, five stationary 'objects' at 70,000 feet – the size of battleships – later explained away by an Air Ministry spokesman as an air balloon, sent up from Aldergrove Airport in Northern Ireland. This hardly seems in character with the attitude of the base commander – Wing Commander Whitworth – who was quoted as saying: *"I was not allowed to reveal 'its' position, course and speed",* adding: *"From the moment of picking 'it' up, it was well within our area. It was an 'object' of some substance – quite definitely not a freak. No mistake could have been made by the Ministry of Supply civilians, who operated the sets – they are fully qualified and experienced Officers."* – A different picture to that depicted, at the time, when investigators of the Deputy Directorate of Intelligence (Technical) confirmed a stationary 'object' had first been tracked on radar at Balmalloch, at heights varying from fifty thousand to seventy thousand feet, and another radar station, twenty miles away, had 'locked on' to the target. Later, four more targets, moving 'line astern', were plotted by both radar stations. The size of the radar echo was considerably larger than would be expected from normal aircraft – more like the size of a ship's radar echo. Even if balloons had been in the area, these would not have accounted for the sudden change of direction and the high-speed movement against the prevailing wind. The report concluded that the incident was due to the presence of *"five reflective 'objects' of unidentified type and origin".* **(Source: AIR 20/9321.DDI.Tech., 30.4.57/*Sunday Dispatch*, 7.Apr.57)**

Later, the same evening, tanker driver James Emmerson was driving thirty miles south of Penrith, at 11.30pm, when he noticed a reflection in the windscreen of his vehicle, which he took to be the headlights of an approaching vehicle. Seeing nothing arrive, he pulled into the side of the road and switched off the tanker's lights. He was shocked to see: *"…a yellow, glowing object, in the shape of a perfect half-moon, with a distinctive gold rim and a straight edge on top"*. Was this one of the UFOs tracked earlier on radar at West Freugh? It is worth bringing the reader's attention to a strange phenomenon which occurred at Ypsilanti, Michigan, United States, in early 1957, where, during some research work on a radar scope, 'points of light', resembling circular ripples, were seen to appear – some extending for 20 miles. Two years later, these 'ring formations' were observed on radar sets in Britain and the United States. 5th April, 1957 – two UFOs, looking like silver three-penny bits, were seen motionless in the sky over Glasgow, followed by a report on the 7th April 1957, when three 'silver globes' were seen over Rothesay Bay by golfers on the course. 10th April 1957 – At 4.50pm, three people living in the Kensington area of London sighted what appeared to be a 'flying saucer' in the sky above them. They were James Collins of Dancer Road, Fulham, Mr. B. Kell of York Street, and Mr. J. Colly of Bridge Buildings, Hammersmith. All three of them described seeing: *"…an elliptical object – like two saucers, rim to rim – suspended in mid-air, swaying slightly in a pendulum motion."* **(Source: *Flying Saucer Review*, Volume 3, Number 4, July/August 1957, Page 6).** At 11.30am on 27th April 1957 – a bright sunny day, with a slight wind – Mr. K. Solomons of Taunton, Somerset, was standing by his van, when he sighted: *"…an unusual, black silhouetted object – apparently stationary in the sky – glinting brightly, a quarter of a mile away. It then moved off, gathering speed and disappeared in the north-west direction, before dropping down behind some houses. I estimated its speed to be about one-and-a-half times that of a jet plane."* **(Source: *British Flying Saucer Bureau/Flying Saucer News Bulletin*, number 9).**

Two days later, at 8.50pm on the 29th April, 1957, a squadron of *Javelin* jet aircraft were scrambled from RAF Odiham, Hampshire, in response to anomalous radar returns tracking an object over Orr, St. Margaret's Bay, Kent. No contact was made, owing to the extreme speed of the UFO. Declassified MOD documents (AIR 20 9994) tell of two metallic objects sighted in the sky, at an estimated height of 30,000 feet, by Shanklin, Isle of Wight, resident – Mr. L. Humphreys – and that no visual was made of the objects. It is alleged the presence of the UFOs caused heavy interference to TV sets, during the screening of *'Come Dancing'.* At 9.30pm, Mrs. Olive Webb of Leckhampton, (just outside Cheltenham, Gloucestershire) noticed what she took to be the *Comet* airliner, moving low over the sky, and called her husband. The couple watched it for several minutes, noting: *"…superstructure on top, showing three lights, went faster in a reverse direction, without appearing to* turn around. When near to the crest of Leckhampton Hill, it rose at a slight angle and was joined by a second object, both blinking at each other – as if signalling one another. Both objects then closed on each other and were gone."

At 11.31pm, on the 30th April, 1957 a round, red/orange object was sighted over Fulham Palace Road, London, by a party of six people. They included Mr. T. Barton, his brother John, and his wife. The object was seen to perform two complete circles in the sky, apparently spinning as it did so, before heading away in a southerly direction. At 11.48pm, Mr. Brian Philips of Brookside South, East Barnet, sighted a strange object in the sky, heading northwards. At one stage, the object turned through 360 degrees. Brian telephoned the Police to report what he had witnessed, which lasted about a minute. **(Source: Gordon Creighton).** May 1st 1957, Jack Martin (51) from Stow Road, Wisbech, Cambridgeshire, was outside during the early morning, at around 7am when he happened to look upwards into the sky and see: *"…a golden object – the size of a dinner plate – flat in appearance. It disappeared over the village of Guyhirn, flying in a peculiar jerking movement."* It was also seen by several other men in the same locality. At 11.30am on the same day ex-Royal Navy Petty Officer Eric Pengilly was delivering mail in the Coverack area of Cornwall, when he noticed a 'dome-shaped object' in the sky, flying slowly from west to east, for ten minutes. When it reached the coast, just north of Manacle Point, it tipped at an angle of 45 degrees and shot upwards, climbing faster than any jet would have done. It then disappeared from sight. Eric later received a visit from RAF Intelligence Officers, who questioned him for a couple of hours on what he had seen. **(Source:** *Flying Saucer News***, no. 9).**

Questions asked in the House of Commons about UFOs!

On the 15th of May 1957, questions were asked in the House of Commons by Major Patrick Wall, MP, who enquired of the Secretary of State for AIR: *"How many unidentified objects had been detected over Great Britain this year, as compared with previous years, and whether the object picked-up on radar over the Dover Straits, on the 29th April, has been identified?"* A further question was put to the Minister, by Mr. Frank Beswick, as to what the nature of the aircraft was, or other aircraft, sighted on the Radar Defence screen, which occasioned the dispatch of Fighter Command, (Air 20/9321/1957). Mr. Ward replied, **(Source:** *Hansard* **1957/393/4):** *"**that five flying objects reported this year are, as yet, unidentified, compared with last year – none in 1955 and six in 1954**. The object sighted in the Channel, on the 29th April, turned out to be two of a large number of 'Hunters' of Fighter Command, engaged in a training exercise. Their movements, as observed on radar, were somewhat unusual and aroused the suspicion of the radar."* **(Air 20/9322/57 Crown Copyright).**

USAF pilot scrambled to intercept UFOs over Lincolnshire

During a visit to see veteran UFO Researcher – Frank Marshall, living in the Dorset area – a friendly man, who allowed us access to his UFO files and memorabilia collected over the last 30 years, despite failing eyesight, which didn't dim his enthusiasm and knowledge of the UFO subject, we came across a handwritten letter sent to Frank, many years ago, by an unidentified airman, whose account is of great interest, as it took place on the same evening when two USAF F-86D jets from the Fighter Intercept Wing were scrambled to intercept a UFO. Contents of letter: 'This *'saucer'* came into view at 10.48pm on Monday, 20th May 1957, over Digby, Lincolnshire, about eight miles

THE HALT PERSPECTIVE 2

away to the west. Its speed was estimated at about 900mph, while completing turns, but increased when climbing to about 1,500mph. The UFO was visible for 15 to 20 minutes. It first appeared to be diving and then it completed four circles in the sky. The circles had a slightly flattened top and bottom. When the circles were completed, the 'disc' must have then turned onto its side, as it was only seen during the dive. It was of oval-shape and slightly larger than the nearest star, shining bright, rather than twinkling.' At 2.15am. 20th May, 1957, Mr. L. Wetland, from Blackfield Road, Fawley, near Henley-on-Thames, was working on the top of a fuel tank at the Esso Refinery, Fawley, when: *"I happened to look up at the sky and see this object, shaped like a 'disc', flying in an arc, south-east to south-west, at 45 degrees elevation, high up. It went through the 'arc' in about four seconds and was elliptical – like a black ring, with a reddish/orange glow in the centre and around its edge. It appeared to be spinning, like a 'Catherine wheel'. In a few seconds, it had gone out of sight. I've served in the RAF & Merchant Navy but never seen anything like that before"*. **(Source: '*Echo*' Newspaper, 20th May 1957).**

Pilot ordered to intercept and attack UFO!

Can we say this was the same UFO tracked on radar in the late evening over East Anglia, initiating an order sent to pilots from the 4069-111 Fighter Wing, based at RAF Manston, to intercept? Extremely likely, in our opinion, notwithstanding that over 50 years later, in interviews held between Milton and UK UFO Investigator – David Cayton, (following information supplied to him by Manchester-based UFO Researcher Harry Harris (2008) – it was established the likely date given for the incident, from review of the personal flight log, may have been 27th April, 1957, rather than 20th May, 1957, although the contents of a letter written by the unidentified airman to Frank Marshall, during the early 1960's, is endorsed with the date of 20th May 1957, as opposed to the earlier date.

We contacted Milton Torres – now a Professor of Engineering, with over 260 hours spent flying combat missions over Vietnam, to find out what had taken place on that night.

Milton Torres

"The 406th FIW (Fighter Interceptor Wing) were committed to Metropolitan Sector RAF to have F-86Ds standing by as an operational requirement. I can clearly remember the call to scramble, although I don't remember such specifics as the actual vector to turn after take-off. We were airborne, well within the five minutes allocated to us, and basically scrambled to about flight level 310, our vector taking us out over the North Sea. Normally, the other pilot would take the lead. However, for some reason, I was the leading Pilot. I was advised by GCI (Ground Control Intercept site) that they had been observing, for some considerable time, a 'blip' on radar, orbiting over East Anglia. From my conversation with GCI, I was told that all normal procedures of checking with the other controlling agencies had revealed the UFO, with a very unusual flight pattern, was motionless in the sky for long intervals. The instruction

came to select the afterburner, to expedite the intercept, and to proceed to a height of 32,000ft. By this time, the aircraft radar was on and I was looking for any sign of the UFO. I was asked to report any visual observation, which would have been highly unlikely – as the weather had closed in, with very poor visibility. I complied with the instructions given to me by Ground Control, predicted to reach some theoretical point for a lead collision course type rocket release. At this time, the aircraft was travelling at Mach .92, which is about as fast as the aircraft could travel in a straight and level position.

Ordered to attack!

The order then came to fire a full salvo of rockets at the UFO. At that time, I was only a Lieutenant and very much aware of the gravity of the situation. I asked for authentication of the order to fire and received it! This further complicated my difficulty, as the matrix of letters and numbers to find the correct authentication was on a piece of printed paper, about 5x8 inches, with the print not much bigger than normal type, not forgetting that it was totally dark, with the lights down for night flying. I used my flashlight while trying to watch the radar which, as you will appreciate, was no easy task. The authentication was valid, and I selected 24 'Mighty Mouse' rockets on salvo. The final turn was given, with instructions to look 30 degrees to port, the UFO exactly where I had been told it would be, at an angle of 30 degrees, 5 miles distance. The 'blip' was 'burning a hole' in the radar with its incredible intensity. It was similar to 'blips' received from B-52 bombers and seemed to be a magnet of light. What followed next, I remember with much clarity. I ran the range gate over the 'blip' and the 'jizzle band' faded, as the marker superimposed over the 'blip'. I had a 'lock on' that had the proportions of a flying aircraft carrier – by that I mean the radar return was so strong, it could not be overlooked by the fire control system on the F-86D. The larger the aircraft, the easier the 'lock on' – this almost 'locked on' by itself. **It was one of the best targets I could ever remember having locked onto**.

I called to the GCI, 'Judy', which signified that I would take all further steering information from my onboard radar computer, rather than depending **on instructions from GCI**. At this point, I was travelling at about 800 knots, with 'dot' centred on my radar screen, requiring only the slightest correction of course. At 20 seconds before launch of the missiles, the circle on the radar screen began to shrink, requiring increased precision to keep the 'dot' centred, while keeping the trigger depressed. At 10 seconds from the 'target', I noticed that the overtake position was changing its position. It moved rapidly to 6 o'clock – 3 o'clock, then 12 o'clock, before coming to rest at 11 o'clock position. This indicated a negative overtake of 200 knots. There was no way of knowing what the actual speed of the UFO was. It could have been travelling at very high Mach numbers and I would only see the 200-knot negative overtake. The circle, now down to about one-and-a-half inches in diameter, started to open up rapidly. Within seconds, it was back to three inches in diameter and the 'blip' was visible in the blackened 'jizzle band', moving up the scope. This meant it was going away from me. I reported this to GCI. They asked me, 'Do you have a tally-ho?' I told them I was still 'in the soup' and could see nothing. By this time, the UFO had broken lock and I saw it leaving my 30-mile range, (soon off the radar screen at GCI). **Following my return to RAF Manston, I was advised that the mission was considered classified and I would be contacted by an investigator. The following day, I was approached by a civilian in the Squadron operation area. He asked me a number of questions about the mission and told me it was highly classified and not to discuss it with anybody – not even my Commander, threatening me with a National Security breach if I ever breathed a word about it to anyone."**

This is an incident which still captivates Milton's attention, who is now actively involved in organizing annual RAF Manston reunions. Like us, he wonders on whose authority that order was given and what precedent was in force for allowing the discharge of weapons over civilian airspace.

UFO researcher, David Cayton

*"In response to my FOI request to the MoD's Air Historical Branch (RAE) confirmed this to be the RAF's Sector Operational Command Centre cold war bunker, at Kelvedon Hatch, Essex, responsible for controlling the Military London Metropolitan Sector area, at the time (now open as a privately run museum). This Unit had advised Milton the target 'blip' had entirely gone off the scope in just two sweeps of the GCI, and then instructed him that the mission was considered classified. The next day, he was debriefed by an Officer from the National Security Agency. The Commanding Officer, at Kelvedon Hatch, would report up to the ADOC (Air Defence Operations Centre), at Fighter Command HQ, Bentley Priory, Stanmore. I suggest that almost certainly the order to fire would have been authorized by the ADOC, at Bentley Priory. The order would have been issued by the Met. Sector, Kelvedon Hatch, and then related to the pilots via the **GCI Signal Unit, at Bawdsey. I firmly believe this would have been the chain of command. Milton knew for certain that his USAF 406th Fighter Wing was operating under the control of the RAF's control and the USAF would most definitely have not been allowed to independently fire missiles over the UK airspace.**"*

Milton was never really sure who the other pilot was. He seemed to think that it might have been Major Dave Robertson, but then rejected that idea. Whether this was because the Officer had chosen not to get involved would be pure speculation. However, we did come across an account of the incident published by the *Daily Star* **20.Mar.1991:** '**How fighter pilot took on a giant alien spaceship – MY DOGFIGHT WITH A UFO!**' in which there is a reference by the journalist Dick Durham, quote: 'Major Dave Robertson was also alerted that night in his own Sabre jet. He recalls leaving RAF Manston and then landing at RAF Bentwaters at Bawdsey, Suffolk, to have his jet armed with live rockets. "***I was advised that more than one ground control site and multiple UFOs were involved and that the area extended into Scotland, I gave chase to several of the UFO's but was unable to maintain radar contact long enough to go to lock on***" he revealed, which appears to have been direct quotes from him rather than Milton.'

20th May, 1957 – A 'short, fat cigar-shaped object' was seen hanging vertically in the sky over Bletchley, Hertfordshire at 3.30pm, attracting the attention of shoppers and local children, who stood watching the object, which remained completely motionless, despite a strong breeze blowing. At 5.10pm, it altered its position to that of horizontal and, within seconds, was heading towards Leighton Buzzard and soon out of sight.

'Operation Vigilante'

Three days later, on 25th May, 1957, the RAF held an Exercise, named '*Operation Vigilante*', over the Nottingham area – hardly likely to be connected, one would have thought, with the appearance of a rectangular object, seen over Woodthorpe, at 11.00am, occasionally catching the rays of the sun, before disintegrating into what looked like white vapour. This was followed by the spectacular sight of two silver 'discs', seen to emerge out of the vapour and then head off across the sky, leaving the now purple vapour to drift downwards onto nearby rooftops. A yellow cigar-shaped object was seen in the sky, east of Ben Lomond, diving and climbing in the air, between 4.00am and 5.00am, on 26th May 1957, by two Police Officers on patrol near the Torpedo factory, at Alexandria. **(Source:** *Flying Saucer Review,* **July/August 1957, Volume 3, No. 4).**

June 8th, 1957 was designated as a worldwide International *'Flying Saucer'* sighting day

It attracted the attention of the London *Daily Herald,* The *Yorkshire Evening Post,* and numerous others. At 5.35pm, Margaret Millington of Alexandra Road, London NW8, accompanied by her father, sighted: "*...a circular, apparent solid object, showing a flat base with the upper part mushroom-shaped, clearly visible against white cloud in the sky".* **(Source:** *Flying Saucer Review,* **Volume 3, No. 4).**

At 9.15am on 14th June, 1957, plumber Albert Brown was returning home to Long Eaton, Nottingham, when he saw an unidentified flying object "*. . . resembling an artist's impression of a 'flying saucer' – aluminium, or silver, in colour – about a thousand feet up in the air, over the road bridge at Chilwell".* Later that day, at 10.30pm, an object was seen zigzagging across the sky over Ilkley, Yorkshire, followed by a green flare-like object – roughly square in shape, with a piece missing at the rear – by Mr. E. Gregg, while visiting Middleton Hospital. At l1pm, Mr. R.F. Andrews from Malabar Road, Truro, was sitting in his garden when it lit up – as if a powerful searchlight was shining on it. *"I heard a swishing sound and looked upwards to see a cigar-shaped object pass overhead, throwing out sparks, with a very bright glow from the one end. It left a thin wisp of smoke in the air after it had gone."* Other witnesses to this event were local brothers – D. and E. Drew – who were walking from Tregolls Farm, at 11pm. *"We were walking down the lane; there was no moon. Suddenly, the place was lit up by a brilliant light and I stepped into the side of the hedge, thinking a car was coming. My brother turned around and pointed at the sky. I looked up and saw a cigar-shaped object, glowing red at the head and throwing out a very brilliant light from its 'tail'. The object was travelling at terrific speed, approximately 300 feet in the air."* At 6.15pm on 15th June 1957, Mr. G. Marsden from Chorley, Wigan, was standing at the side of the road, taking a break from cycling with his son, near Mawdesley, when he noticed a silver point of light, with a bluish tinge to it, moving in the skynorth-west, at a height of 6-7,000 feet. *"It appeared to be 25 feet in diameter and moving at 600 mph. We watched it for about twelve seconds in horizontal flight, until it whisked vertically upwards. In seconds, it had gone."* **(Source:** *Uranus,* **Volume 14, number l, August 1957).**

On the same evening, Mr. and Mrs. L.H. West were driving along the road, between Norbury and Hungerford, when they saw what looked like a large white plank, vertical in the sky. They stopped the car to take a closer look. It then altered its position to horizontal and shot upwards into the sky and vanished out of sight. A few minutes later, an RAF jet aircraft appeared over where the UFO had been. **(Source:** *SCAN* **Magazine,** *Jan/July 1978* **– Leslie Harris).** At 9.15pm on 18th June 1957, Mrs. G Pennells and her daughter, June, sighted a cylindrical, silver-gold object with a 'blunt end', about half a mile away, moving across the sky over Stafford. Twenty or thirty minutes later, the object, now more orange in colour, reappeared in the sky – this time moving at the speed of a piston-engine aircraft, before slowing down. At 9.30pm, a silver, cylindrical, object was seen over Gailey, Staffordshire, by Mr. L. Broomhall, following a curved path across the sky, before remaining stationary for a short time, and then proceeding on its journey at a height of between 5-10,000ft and speed of 30-50mph. At 9.45pm, the same evening, Ann Poulton and her boyfriend were walking near Bee Lane, close to Bushbury Hill, Wolverhampton, when they saw what looked like: "...*a glowing saucer-shaped object, heading in a straight line towards Stafford. We don't think it was a plane. It was oval and orange/red in colour. After a few seconds, it gained height and disappeared towards the North".* **(Source: Wilfred Daniels, British Flying Saucer Bureau).** Is it possible this was the same UFO seen by ex-RAF serviceman Ian Charters, from Glasgow, at the other end of the Country – then a member of the Royal Observer Corps, who, with others, sighted an object *'showing a fiery red 'tail',* moving over the City, which made a sharp turn near the horizon, before moving out of sight?

At 8.30pm 19th June, 1957, a grey 'rectangle' was seen for over ten minutes, projecting from the underside of a cloud above the setting sun, over Stafford, by Mrs. M. Wilkes – a civil servant. **(Source: Wilfred Daniels, British Flying Saucer Bureau).** A short, stubby, cigar-shaped object was seen over St. John's Wood, London, on 20th June, 1957 heading northward, at great speed, by a number of people – later explained away by the Air Ministry as being *"probably one of the newest meteorological balloons, which, having shed its instruments, got into an air current at great height.* ***These are cigar shaped****".* Was this same object seen at 3pm over Haddington, East Lothian, by Mr. J.M. Spark, his wife, and the Reverend J.S. Ritchie? *"It had a red top and was motionless in the sky, despite a north-east wind – Seven minutes later it vanished from view."* At 10.15pm, Lorna Horgan of St. Joseph's Convent, Stafford, was looking out into the night sky, after having just watched a TV program on Saturn. *"I saw a large bright object in the north-west direction of the sky, which I took to be a planet, until – to my amazement – it moved away, travelling parallel to the horizon towards the direction of Shrewsbury, before disappearing into low cloud."*

At 5.30pm 21st June, 1957 – Mr. A. N. Haskett of Chiddingfold, Surrey, was resting by the side of the Brighton Road about four miles from Capel, Surrey when he spotted a shining pinpoint of light high above him, underneath which a DC-6 Airliner passed was seen descending towards London Airport (at an estimated height of between 5-7,000 feet). As soon as the aircraft had passed over, *'. . . a saucer-shaped object'* (believed to be a few thousand feet higher than the aircraft) made an extremely rapid ascent and vanished within seconds. **(Source: *Flying Saucer Review*, Sept/Oct. 1957, Volume 3, No. 5).** At 10.15pm, 28th June, 1957 – Dr. Bernard E. Finch of 851 Finchley Road, London NW11 was in his garden, watching a BOAC *Viscount* airliner pass overhead. *"My attention was drawn to a whitish-green circular object, which passed east over the plane. It then veered southwards. The UFO was extremely high and moving at phenomenal speed."* Other witnesses to this incident included Mr. R. Richardson from Wimbledon. He described it as being *"a slightly pear-shaped object, brilliantly lit."* **(Source: UFOLOG, Isle of Wight).**

July, 1957 – Retired Sales Managing Director, Victor Godding, contacted us in August 2006, after reading an appeal from us in the *Cheltenham Echo* Newspaper. *"In July 1957, I was playing cricket at Wycliffe College, Stonehill, near Stroud, one afternoon, when a saucer-shaped object appeared in the sky, towards the south. It resembled two saucers, one on top of each other, light grey in colour. There were four of us that saw it. It's something I've never forgotten, although I don't, as a rule, mention it outside the family."* At 8.20pm during July 1957, a woman living a few miles north of Sheffield was at her home address, when she saw *"a strange 'light' dropping down from the sky, followed by the appearance of a thin golden cone".* Ten minutes later, people at Firth Park, Sheffield, sighted a similar phenomenon. This was to be just the start of a 'flurry' of UFO reports brought to the attention of the authorities, over the next few days. A bright silver cigar-shaped object was seen over Stokeley, eight miles from Middlesbrough, just after 9.00pm on 22nd July 1957, by Mr. D. Rowland, his brother, and a friend – T. Gundry.

During the early morning of the 27th July 1957 Longmont, Colorado resident – Mr. J. L. Siverly, sighted: *"...a thick 'disc' – ice blue, with a toplike **honeycomb (interconnected hexagons)** – hovering and rocking below the hilltops, for 10 minutes.The middle band was scalloped, and the bottom showed four kidney-shaped forms"*. Two days later at t 10.31pm on the 29th of July 1957 – this time over Cleveland, Ohio, *Capital Airlines* Captain R.L. Stimley, and First Officer F. J. Downing, sighted: *"...a large, round, yellow-white object in the sky, which dimmed once, and then crossed the bow of the airliner. We gave chase but were unable to catch it and lost sight of it, eight minutes later."* Captain W. J. Hull found himself involved in another UFO sighting, this time on the 30th August 1957 while piloting a Viscount over Chesapeake Bay, near Norfolk, Virginia. He saw a brilliant object in the sky which flew fast across the sky before coming to a dead halt in front of the plane some 20 miles away from them. The object was picked up on radar by both the Viscount and a DC-6, before *"... dissolving in front of our eyes"*

September 25th, 1957, a film, entitled *Out Of Step,*was shown on *ITV*. It included contributions from Sir Brinsley Le Poer Trench, editor of *Flying Saucer Review,* Gavin Gibbons, and Dr. Percy H. Wilkins. Sir Harold Spencer Jones – former Astronomer Royal – provided the 'opposition'.

19th/20th September 1957 – An Air Force Major was piloting a bomber over Fort Worth Texas when he saw a UFO which was being tracked on radar. The object seen as a glowing white light shot away at speed but was continued to be tracked before disappearing and then reappearing for a short time, before vanishing for good. October 8th, 1957 – At 9.17am, two US Army sergeants, stationed in Washington, sighted two flat, round, white objects, flying irregularly, one behind the other in the sky, frequently banking as they did so, before being lost from sight 25-30 seconds later.

The Air Ministry disclosed the following details: *"The Air Ministry is investigating the sighting, last week, of an unidentified' flying object' over the airfield at Gaydon, Warwickshire, one of the top RAF's 'V' Bomber stations. It was seen by a night fighter pilot and picked up by ground radar. At 9.18pm, last Monday, 21st October, 1957. Flying Officer Sweeney – a pilot of considerable experience – was flying a Meteor on a training exercise from RAF Station, North Luffenham, at 28,000 feet, flying west, when he almost collided with a cigar-shaped object, displaying six lights, moving slowly over Gaydon – then in use as a training base for atomic bomber crews. After taking violent evading action, Flying Officer Sweeney approached the object from the starboard side. Suddenly, its lights extinguished, and it vanished from view".* Enquiries made later revealed the UFO had been plotted on radar, at 28,000 feet over RAF Gaydon, a few minutes before the sighting.

Mrs. D. C. Lash of West Worthing, Sussex, was helping her elderly uncle in the garden, at 4.40pm on the 22nd October 1957, when she noticed a curious 'cloud' in the clear sky, as the sun was setting. *"It was cigar-shaped, apparently made up of thick pink cloud, hanging there motionless, with the southern end tilted upwards, many miles over the Channel, in the direction of the south-west, at great height. I watched it casually for about 15 minutes, noting that it never changed its position, and was unable to decide whether it was a natural phenomenon or not. After eating tea, uncle asked me to put the lights on while he drew the curtains. As he did this, I heard him say, 'what in Heaven's name* is that thing hanging out there?' I joined him at the window and saw, in exactly the same place in the sky where the 'cloud' had been, a great sparkling object hanging amongst the stars, looking like an enormous chandelier, high in the sky. My uncle fetched a pair of binoculars. Through them, it looked like a cloud, with a double row of lighted portholes, rising to a triple row in the centre, sparkling with red, blue, and golden light. When I arrived home, at 6.10pm, I looked out for the object, but it had gone." Was this the same UFO seen by the RAF pilot over Gaydon, the previous evening?

At 4pm on 2nd November 1957, Mr. I. Andrews of Highlands Road, Andover, was watching a football match at the London Road ground, when he saw a dozen *"circular, disc-shaped objects apparently composed of vapour, resembling dark grey clouds, twisting and turning in the air – like an aircraft performing aerobatics".* **(Source: *Echo* newspaper, 4.Nov.1957).**

At 11.00pm, 2nd November, 1957, Levelland, Texas – Police patrolman Fowler was one of four officers who received the first of fifteen phone calls from people reporting having encountered a landed object in the road. Two men, four miles west of the town, noticed a brilliant object approaching the vehicle. As it passed overhead, the headlights went out and the engine died. After the object moved away, the lights and power were restored. At midnight, the officer received another phone call from a driver on the opposite side of the town. He told of coming across an egg-shaped object, about 200ft long, in the middle of the road, followed by the lights and engine of his vehicle failing. The phenomenon was explained away by *Project Blue Book* as ball lightning, but later dismissed by Dr. Allen Hynek. Further enquiries into the matter revealed that the other police officers involved were Sheriff Weir Clem, and his deputy – Pat McCulloch. One of the sightings involved Pedro Saucedo, who was driving along Highway 116 towards Levelland, with his passenger – Joe Salav, when an immense object, showing blue-green lights swept over the truck. Straight away, the engine and lights died. Frightened, the men jumped out of the truck and watched, in disbelief, as the object settled onto the highway. Both of them later said they heard what sounded like a faint clanking or hammering, and other noises which they interpreted as voices. The red glare given off by the object was so bright that the men were unable to look directly at it. A few minutes later, the dirigible-shaped object, estimated to be 200ft in length, rose up into the night sky and was soon gone. **(Source: *Flying Saucers – Serious Business,* Frank Edwards).**

Kirtland Air Force Base – reports UFO hovering over weapons storage area!

A UFO was seen to fly right-to-left along the East-West runway at Kirtland Air Force Base on the 4th November, 1957 and then turn south-west toward the tower, where it then halted near the nuclear weapons storage area for about a minute. The object was reported by CAA tower personnel, Mr. R.M. Kaser and Mr. E.G. Brink, who were reliable observers, with 23 years of airport control tower experience between them. According to them, the lighted object came down steeply at the east end of a runway, left the flight line, crossed runways, taxiways and unpaved areas, at about a 30° angle, and proceeded south-west towards the control tower, at an altitude of less than 100ft. Through 7x binoculars, the object appeared to be egg-shaped, having no wings, tail, or fuselage, and was elongated vertically. It appeared to be 15-20ft tall, about the size of an automobile, standing on its nose, and had a single white light at its base. After the UFO left the area it was tracked on surveillance radar, where it exhibited some amazing flight characteristics. The object also came back towards Kirtland, until it took up a position behind an Air Force C-46 that had just taken off. It stayed in position behind the C-46, until they both moved out of radar range. There have been several UFO incidents in and around Kirtland Air Force Base through the years. **(Source: Dr. J. Allen Hynek, James McDonald, Francis Ridge, NICAP).**

At about 1.10pm on the same date, James W. Stokes – a high altitude research engineer of the USAF Missile Development Centre, near Alamogordo, reported that he saw an *"elliptical UFO sweep twice across the highway."* The car radio and the engine failed. Stokes claimed that ten other drivers were also on the road, and their engines had also failed. Stokes reported a wave of heat and, later, his face appeared sunburned. This case was explained by the Air Force as a hoax**. (Source: *Daily News,* Alamogordo, 8th November, 1957).**

At 5.10am on 7th November 1957, Commander Waring of the United States cutter *Sebago* was informed that the ships radar had picked up an object, which was racing around the ship. On one occasion it halted in mid-air, before darting ahead at speed. At 5.21am, four men on deck – Donald Schafer – Quartermaster, Kenneth Smith – Radioman, Thomas Kirk and Ensign – Wayne Schottley, were able to obtain a visual image of the circular object, which was described as **shiny and moving at speeds beyond the capabilities of known aircraft.** The UFO was later explained away as being a piston-engine aircraft!

Truck driver Melvin Stevens (48) was driving home, at 7.25am the same date when a large egg-shaped object dropped out of the sky and landed on the highway in front of him. Melvin thought it was a weather balloon, at first. *"It had a propeller on either end and on top of the object. I got out and was confronted by three people – two men and a woman – all about four and a half feet tall, with pasty white faces. They were dressed in grey suits. They tried to talk to me, but I couldn't understand them; one of them tried to shake my hand. They then got back into the object and flew off."* The location isn't given but on the same date, according to *Project Blue Book,* UFOs were sighted at Boerne, Texas, and Radium Springs, New Mexico **(Sources: Aerial Phenomena Research Organization).**

8th November, 1957 – At Merrick, Long Island: a New York housewife sighted a bar-shaped object, three and a half feet long, giving off blue flashes, making a swishing sound as it headed through the sky, at 10.10am.

At 9.15pm on 14th November, 1957, a mysterious orange-red 'light' was seen over Mitcham, Surrey, by Mr. A.B. Martin (who was out driving with his father, between Rose Hill and Mitcham) – which vanished but reappeared, a few minutes later, over Mitcham Common, before disappearing for good. **(Source: *Evening Standard*, 14.11.1957).**

In the same month, Gloucestershire Police Constable Donald Hibbard, from Dursley, was in his back garden in Woodsfield Road, at 8.00pm, when he saw a round object, sharply defined, brilliant white in colour, moving across the sky under the cloud (which was very low) – only a hundred feet in height. It then circled the locality, about half a mile away, moving at an estimated speed of 500mph – whatever it was it caused some interference to the television set, which was on at the time**. (Source: Mrs. Hibbard).**

At 10.07am, the 26th of November, 1957, three control tower operators, stationed at Robins Air Force Base, Georgia, were on duty, along with a weather observer and four others, when they saw a silver, cigar-shaped, object in the sky, which suddenly vanished after eight minutes of observation.

THE HALT PERSPECTIVE 2

A most peculiar object was seen at 4pm on the 27th November, 1957, high over Southampton Water, drifting towards the direction of Hythe, before disappearing from view. A number of people who saw the object described it as a 'stubby, rigid cross', with solid looking appendages hanging from it. Enquiries with the Police, Coastguard, and Southampton Airport met with no success. The sighting was even brought to the attention of the Top-Secret Aircraft Establishment, at Boscombe Down, who stated: *'they had no experimental object up and that, if they had, they wouldn't disclose the information to the public!'* **(Source: *Echo* Newspaper, 30.Nov.1957).**

At 9.30pm, John Heard – a full-time worker in the Boy Scouts – was out walking his boxer dog in the Bedfordshire area, when his attention was caught by an object hovering beyond the houses, directly in front of him. *"It was a dazzling white 'light', shaped like the tin hats the ARP wardens used during the last war, with a shimmering haze around it. It appeared to be over the River Ivel in the direction of Holme Mill. Suddenly, within seconds, the 'tin hat' moved away leaving only a vapour trail and was gone from sight."* According to Miss Thelma Roberts (who we met some years ago) – the area UFO investigator for Hertfordshire – other witnesses were later found. **(Source: *Flying Saucer Review*, May-June 1958, Vol. 4, No. 3).**

At 2.30am on 29th November, 1957, a lorry driver was travelling along the desolate Brecon Beacons, in mid Wales, when he saw an object with a blue 'nose' and red 'tail' silently crossing the sky. Minutes later, a greenish-blue 'delta'-shaped object was seen by two police officers on duty in the Rhonda Valley. It was then seen by people living in the Isle of Man, crossing over the sea, four miles off the coast of Douglas. One man described it as being: *"...bluish/white, leaving a sheet of orange flame. There was a boom of an explosion as it vanished from view".* James Harvey – a Coastguard from Scarlet Point – saw the blue/white object, with a red glow, moving from west to east, *'... tapered like a carrot, miles high, going at a terrific speed'.* Any idea that this was some natural phenomenon could be dismissed, perhaps by the nature of the previous reports Three US Coast Guardsmen from New Orleans, Louisiana, were on duty at 2.11pm, on the 30th of November 1957 when they saw a white, round, object in the sky, which turned gold – then separated into three parts and turned red, over a period of 20 minutes.

Housewife sights UFO and then its occupants!

Mary M. Starr – a resident of Old Saybrook, Connecticut, and a former teacher with a master's degree, from Yale – retired to bed, at 10.00pm on the 15th of December, 1957. Between 2.00am and 3.00am, she was awoken by a 'bright light' and first thought it was an aircraft in trouble. Looking out she saw: *"...a cigar-shaped object, brightly lit, with square portholes, hovering just above my clothes line; I could see men inside".* The object, no more than ten feet from the north side of Mrs. Starr's home was approximately 20 to 30 ft long and dark grey or black in colour. It hovered motionless, about 5ft above the ground, between the house and the tool shed. No wings, fins, or other appendages were seen. Through the object's lighted windows, Mrs. Starr saw two figures that passed each other, walking in opposite directions. *"I could see that the object was so shallow that the men could not have been more than three and a half or four feet tall. The occupants' right arms were **raised but no hands were visible**. They wore a kind of jacket that 'flared out' at the base and their heads were unusual – **square or rectangular, red orange, with a brighter red 'bulb' in the centre. I thought they might possibly be wearing some kind of helmets**.*" **A third 'being'** came

THE HALT PERSPECTIVE 2

into view from the left. Mrs. Starr leaned forward to see more clearly, then the portholes faded, and the entire shell of the object began glowing brightly. From the top end, closest to her, there arose a kind of six-inch *'antenna'* that oscillated and sparkled. After five minutes of glowing steadily, the *'antenna'* was retracted, and the craft began to move. It retraced its original path, gliding smoothly in the direction from which it had apparently arrived. It then made a very sharp right-angle turn, now appearing oval in shape. The hull had changed to a dull grey-blue, and small circular lights now outlined the entire rim. The UFO dipped and undulated, following the contours of a small depression to the north of the witness' house, then tilted sharply and shot up into the sky, at terrific speed, in total silence. **(Sources: NICAP, Richard Hall & Isabel Davis, Charles Bowen,** *Flying Saucer Review,* **Jan/Feb.1968, Vol. 14, Page 15-16. 'The Spectre at Winterfold'/***Woking Review/* **SIGAP).**

1958 –10th February, an RAF jet was seen passing over Ipsley, Worcestershire, during broad daylight, being followed by a silver 'disc', to the surprise of the witness. Later, the same afternoon, three similar objects were seen flying over Studley, Warwickshire a few miles away. **(Source: UFOsIS, Birmingham)**. 17th February 1958 – Regents Park, London, a silver aluminium coloured oval object, with a greenish rim of light around it, trailing a spurt of red flame, was seen moving over the Capital at tremendous height. Seconds later, it was out of view. The Air Ministry *'Flying saucers were either hallucinations or, alternatively, reflections from something on Earth'.* **(Source: Gordon Creighton,** *Flying Saucer Review,* **1958, Volume 4, No. 5).** 13th of March, 1958 – Newcastle-on-Tyne *". . . a silver-grey coloured disc, with its outer edge revolving, tilting towards the east at 3.30pm heading southwards tilting towards the west, allowing me to see what looked like a conning tower".* **(Source: UFOLOG).**

Retired RAF employee Ernie Sears – a long-standing veteran of the UFO subject and previously a member of the Southampton Group, (SUFOG), run by Steven Gerrard, was out walking, in March, 1958, when he noticed a cigar-shaped UFO hovering over the experimental Radar Base, on Portsdown Hill, Portsmouth. *"It was a blustery morning. I watched the object for a full minute, assuming it was an aircraft fuselage caught in the sun. Approximately thirty minutes later, two RAF Fighter jets raced over the town at low altitude. As an ex-RAF man, I knew their actions were very unusual. I watched as they climbed in a gradual curve, towards the gleaming 'cigar'. As they closed in, it slowly turned on end and vanished, leaving the aircraft circling the area. I rushed to a telephone box and rang the Control Tower, at Thorney Island Airbase, (where the 'Meteor' jets were based) and asked the official what the object was which the 'Meteor' jets were chasing? He replied, you didn't see any jets!"* **(Source: Personal Interview).**

UK Under Secretary of State for Air answers questions

On 19th April, 1958, aircraft from RAF Lakenheath were scrambled to intercept UFOs plotted on the station's radar, ten miles away from the airbase – later explained away as being due to freak weather conditions. On 10th June 1958, the Under-secretary of State for Air – Mr. Charles Orr-Ewing, was asked, *"How many instances of unidentified flying objects had been reported during the last 12 months, and what steps were taken to co-ordinate such observations?"* He replied: *"Reports of 54 unidentified flying objects have been received in the last 12 months. Such co-ordination as is necessary is undertaken by the Air Ministry. Most of the objects turn out to be meteors, balloons, or*

THE HALT PERSPECTIVE 2

aircraft. Satellites have also accounted for a number of reports." Due to lack of space we would like to comment that according to our sighting reports, there were a number of occasions when the RAF were scrambled to intercept after UFOs were not only tracked on radar but seen visually by members of the public during this year. On 16th July, 1958, Peter Smith, then aged 13 – a pupil of Rickmansworth Grammar School, Hertfordshire, situated on a hill close to electric power generators and main railway line – was looking out of the window at an overcast sky, as dark storm-clouds gathered, a few minutes before 4.00pm. *"Suddenly, a bright white glowing hat-shaped object appeared in the sky and performed a number of movements, slowing slightly on the downward 'runs', travelling faster than a jet and disappeared out of sight behind trees."* **(Source: Thelma Roberts International Unidentified Flying Objects Observer Corps)**. On the 31st August, 1958 William McGregor, who had seen service in the Royal Navy, as a Meteorologist, was returning home after walking his dog, at Bilton, Coventry, when he noticed a silver-coloured object moving in circles across the sky and alerted his wife, daughter and neighbours who came outside to watch the object. *"I looked at the object through a pair of powerful binoculars when I saw an object rotating on its axis, at a height of some 30,000ft surrounded by half-a-dozen smaller spinning 'discs'. I watched the object as it moved northwards, but then lost sight of it."*

US sailor sights UFO and then its occupants!

Chester Grusinski – a member of crew aboard the Aircraft Carrier USS Franklin D. Roosevelt – found himself, once again, witnessing UFO activity, while en-route from New York to Cuba, in the Caribbean, during September/October, 1958. *"I was below decks at the time, one evening, when a group of excited men came running up from the engine room, followed by another group, a few minutes later. Curious, I made my way onto the flight deck and noticed they were watching a small 'light', apparently following the ship. As it approached closer, I saw it had a row of windows along its side, with what appeared to be alien figures, rather than humans, looking out. While all of this was going on, the bridge watch was screaming on the ship's intercom for the Officer of the Deck to 'get up, on the double'. It took off so quickly, I could feel the heat of it passing on my skin."* **(Source: Personal Interview).**

1959 – In January, Leonard Hewins, sighted an object surrounded by blue haze land at Stratford-upon-Avon, Warwickshire, inside which were seen four seated occupants. When it took off, he heard what sounded like rushing water. **(Source John D Llewellyn. Full report in Volume 1/RV1** *Haunted Skies***).**

23rd February, 1959 – Mr. George Wild from Honeysuckle Road, Sheffield, was one of a number of people who sighted a 'flying saucer' hovering 200ft off the ground over the city, at 6.40pm, after experiencing unusual interference on the television sets. The sighting was later explained away by the Commanding Officer, at RAF Brize Norton, who suggested they had seen the *Fairey Rotodyne* – the world's first vertical take-off Airliner – although this appears unlikely, as the object seen was totally silent. **(Source:** *Sheffield Star/ Sheffield Telegraph***, 25.Feb.59).** 13th September 1959 – A white, pear-shaped object, metallic in appearance showing a trail under it, was sighted at 4pm over Gills Rock, Wisconsin, Bunker Hill Air Force Base, Indiana. It involved at least two control tower operators and the pilot of a Mooney private airplane. The object showed little movement during the three hours observation. An attempted intercept by a USAF T-33 jet trainer failed. **(Source:** *Blue Book***) Police Officer sights UFO Air Force jets scrambled and attempt intercept!**

THE HALT PERSPECTIVE 2

Police Officer Robert Dickerson was on police patrol at the edge of Redmond, a city in King County, Washington, United States, located 16 miles (26 km) east of Seattle on the 24th September, 1959, when he saw a glowing disc-like object drop down out of the sky and hover some 200ft off the ground. A few minutes later the object climbed upwards and headed past Redmond Airport, where it once again stopped in mid-air – now hovering in a north-east direction. Robert contacted Flight Specialist Laverne Wertz at the airport. He and other Federal aviation men went outside to see the object, which had 'tongues of flame' around the rim. Wertz telexed the Air Force Traffic Control, at Seattle, who told him Air Force jets from Portland were being scrambled and that Air Force Radar at Klamath Falls, Oregon, was tracking the UFO. At Redmond, the ground observers were still watching the UFO when they heard the roar of jets. As the planes dived towards the UFO, the flames emanating from it vanished. A fiery exhaust blasted from the bottom of the 'disc' and it accelerated upwards, at terrific speed – close enough to cause one pilot to frantically move out of its path. Another struggled to control the plane, after being struck by the object's exhaust. Three planes headed-off in pursuit but were quickly left behind. When the pilots landed, they were ordered not to discuss the incident. The Air Force explained it away as being a routine check-up, following a false radar return. It is claimed that Laverne Wertz checked one of the aircraft with a Geiger counter but that the results of the examination were never released, although it is believed it was no normal reading. The explanation then put forward was that it had been a weather balloon. Unknown to them, copies of the F.A.A logs had been handed to NICAP. When they pressed for further information, they were told it had been Venus! **(Source: *Aliens from Space... The Real Story Of Unidentified Flying Objects,* Major Donald E. Keyhoe).** 1st October, 1959, UFOs reported on this date over Telephone Ridge, Oregon. **(Blue Book).** 6th October 1959, Military sight UFO over Lincoln, Nebraska **(Blue Book).**

Virginian youths fire shotgun at UFO!

19th October, 1959, at 6.15pm, Mark Muza (15), and Harold Moore (14), sighted a circular object – about 4ft in diameter, making a whirring noise – hovering above the ground in a desolate area known as the Big Marsh, at Poquoson, Virginia. The object, apparently metallic, was seen to have a dark centre, surrounded by a 6ins wide silvery rim. On seeing the object descend, Muza, who was in possession of a 12gauge shotgun, fired three times – the last shot ringing on the 'metal' when about 50ft above him. The object then went straight upwards, like a spinning top, making a noise like a tornado**. (Source: *Newport Daily Press,* 21st October 1959/23rd October 1959 – 'Boys fire at Creature!').** November 18th, 1959, UFO sighted South of Crystal Springs, Mississippi.

SELF-IMPOSED RESTRICTIONS

Due to self-imposed restrictions, because of the sheer volume of reports, which we don't have the room to incorporate into this book, we have decided to select one or two incidents that we believe the readers will find of importance from the 1960's onwards.

1962 – Ronald Wildman, from 42, St Margaret's Avenue Luton, Bedfordshire, a car delivery driver for the Car Collection Company was driving along the A.41, Ivinghoe Road, through Aston Clinton, Buckinghamshire, at 3.30am, **9th February 1962**, to deliver a new vehicle when he noticed: *"a large, metallic-looking object, hovering approximately 30ft off the ground, over some* *nearby trees."* From a tape-recorded interview conducted by Stratford-upon-Avon UFO Researcher, John 'Dennis' Llewellyn, a more comprehensive account was obtained. *"I left home at approximately 3.00am, as I had a delivery to make in Swansea. I proceeded to Dunstable, and was on the Ivinghoe, Aston Clinton Road, going towards Aylesbury. I had just passed some cement works. Approximately two miles past this, I rounded a slight bend at 40mph. As I did so, I came across a terrific glare from an object in front of me.* **It was approximately 30-40ft across, and 20ft high. I didn't have time to brake, as I was within yards of it. My engine started to slow up. When I was within 20ft of it, the car just lost power. I changed down to second gear, but the car didn't pick up any 'revs'. I proceeded at 20mph.(approximately), with the object in front of me. It was oval in shape and was – quite honestly – fantastic.** *It was a clear night. There had been a frost. You could count the stars. There was no cloud, or mist, of any description. I followed the object 200 or a few more yards. It did appear to come lower at one spot. At this spot, a halo appeared around the base; I should say a couple of feet away from the object. On the object itself, I could see what looked like* **black marks –** *at regular intervals – which* **could have been portholes, or air vents.** *The haze (or halo) could have come from that, but I wouldn't like to say. But when the halo appeared near to trees on the left, at this point, (there is a slight bend), the object veered off to the right at fantastic speed. At the time it veered off, I don't know whether it touched the trees, or whether the power of it moving away thrust the particles of frost on the trees onto the car. My car automatically picked-up its 'revs'. I changed back into top gear, and proceeded as fast as I could to Aylesbury. I didn't pass anybody. On the way, I met a* **Police Constable** *at Aylesbury lights and explained what had happened. He called over a colleague, and – after explaining to his colleague – he said I had better come down to the Police Station. When the Police Sergeant saw me, he said I looked shaken, which I was – rather scared. He said, 'give him a cuppa'. After they gave me a cup of coffee, half an hour later, I left the Police Station, and proceeded on my way to Swansea."*

Mr. Wildman was asked if he could explain why the appearance of this object should have caused any engine faults. *"I should have said that the headlights of my car, when coming onto the object, threw back a solid reflection, approximately 40 ft across the clear sky. Knowing it was there 'really put the wind up' me."* (End of tape recording). Close by is Upper Icknield Wayand, Icknield Way. A map drawn by Mr. Wildman shows the presence of overhead power cables, and a cemetery to his left. At 11.45pm on the same date, Mrs. James Manley from Carryduff, five miles south of Belfast saw *"A thing appear in the Eastern part of the sky, heading in a North West direction shaped like a* **'Whale' with the head glowing red and the rest yellow.** *It was so bright it lit up the room, a few seconds later, it had gone out of sight."* (**Sources:** John 'Dennis' Llewellyn/*Daily Herald,* **Feb 10th 1962,** 'Flying Saucer slows driver'/*Daily Express,* **10.2.1962,** *Daily Mail,* 'I saw IT says scared driver'/*Daily Telegraph* **10.2.1962**).

USAF Jet Tanker attempts to intercept UFO!

United States Air Force Major George A. Filer, *"I was stationed at the 420th RAF Air refuelling Squadron Base, at RAF Scunthorpe, Lincolnshire, in* **February 1962.** *I was in orbit over the North Sea in a six engine K5-50 Tanker Aircraft, when we received a call over the radio from London Control, who excitedly asked us to have a look at an* **unidentified flying object, which had been picked-up on radar, hovering between Oxford and Stonehenge.** *After being given the intercept heading, the aircraft headed in towards the target, with further transmissions from London Control, informing us that all commercial aircraft had been cleared from our path, in order that we could intercept safely. We*

THE HALT PERSPECTIVE 2

realized we were exceeding our maximum speed and had great trouble slowing the aircraft down. At about 30 miles, my APS-23 radar seemed to pick up on the hovering object, directly ahead of us. **It was exceptionally large radar return, reminding me of a huge bridge, or a ship, such as a destroyer, bigger than anything I had seen on radar in the air before.** The return was sharp and solid, as compared to the fuzziness of a rain cloud. My impression was that this UFO must have been made of something substantive, like metal or steel. As we approached to now ten miles from the target, at a speed of around 425 miles per hour, it apparently sensed us, **because we could now see a series of dim lights, directly ahead of us, on what was a dark night. At five miles from intercept, the UFO seemed to come alive.** The lights brightened and the object accelerated in a launch similar to the Space Shuttle, at night. Within a few seconds, it moved vertically

George Filer

We asked London Air Traffic Control if they had any rocket launches in the area. They replied in the negative and told us we were now clear to return to our mission. The incident was recorded in my navigator's log and mentioned the next day, on Operations, but no intelligence briefings ever took place."

Late April, 1962 – NASA pilot Joseph Walker was making a record-breaking attempt at piloting the X-15 Aircraft when he saw "**five disc-shaped or perhaps even cylindrical objects.** It was impossible to estimate their size or distance from the camera. I don't feel like speculating about them. All I know is what appeared on the film which was developed after the flight." (**Source: Daily Telegraph, 12th May 1962/The Calgary Herald, Friday, May 11, 1962).**

George Filer, 2020: "Prince William is the newest member of the Royal Family to become obsessed with researching space aliens, keeping alive a family precedent started in the 1950's by his grandfather, Prince Philip, a serious UFO believer, who has chased a UFO in the Royal family aircraft. When I chased a huge mothership over England, Prince Philip was the speaker at Sculthorpe Officers Club Dining Inn and asked to talk with our crew. We spoke for at least an hour about our sighting and his interests in UFOs. I asked the Prince why he was interested in UFOs, he said 'Earl Mountbatten, his uncle had raised him and he had seen UFOs on several occasions. Admiral Mountbatten was the Commander of a fleet of British ships in the Mediterranean Sea when a UFO buzzed the fleet and thousand of sailors saw the craft.' According to private visitors, Prince Philip kept a map on his office wall in Buckingham Palace indicating UFO' hot 'spots.

Prince William, the young heir second in line to the British throne and Princess Diana's oldest son, is said to be star struck by Michael C. Luckman's controversial book, 'Alien Rock: The Rock 'n' Roll Extraterrestrial Connection' featuring many rock stars who have spotted UFOs. In January 2009, William transferred his commission to the RAF and was promoted to Flight Lieutenant. He trained to become a helicopter pilot with the RAF's Search and Rescue Force. In January 2010, he graduated from the Defence Helicopter Flying School at RAF Shawbury, on 26 January 2010, he transferred to the Search and Rescue to receive training on the Sea King search and rescue helicopter; he graduated from this course on 17 September 2010. This made him the first member of the British royal family since Henry VII to live in Wales. He allegedly spotted a UFO while flying but no details are known and some were seen during his marriage."

At 11.45pm, 5th February, 1963 – following a report of a yellow-white glowing UFO, about 3ft in diameter, seen over a missile site at Charlottesville, Washington (located in west Central Virginia, approximately 100 miles south-west of Washington DC), aircraft were scrambled to respond. It appears that a pulsating yellow '*light*' was also seen to manoeuvre around their plane, by a private pilot and a newsman passenger. In February 1963 at 3.15am, a contingent of the Royal Navy's North Atlantic Fleet was participating in exercises off Norway between Spitsbergen Island and Norway – 30-50 miles off the Norway coast– when an object was tracked on the ship's radar, at 35,000ft, and then by sonar after it entered the water 50ft below the surface before continuing into deep water at a range of 20,000yds. The radar signature indicated it was 100ft-120ft in diameter. The object was also tracked by other ships and the order was issued for the fleet to execute an evasive 'Z' pattern manoeuvre. Air Force jets were scrambled. **(Source: *MUFON Journal*, 1984).**

Mr. Dennis Wright, from Kent, and his two brothers were installing new hoppers at the Dover Gasworks, in March 1963, when three objects appeared in the sky, moving from the direction of France, transparent in colour and cigar-shaped, closely followed by two others. "*We watched as they moved over. The first one flipped on end and went straight up at a 90 degree angle, followed by the other two, perfectly round and metallic silver in appearance. To our amazement, they began some sort of 'aerial display' above us. A twin-engine plane appeared, one of the 'saucers' flew directly at it. The pilot must have been terrified. The object was so big in comparison to the aircraft.*" Dennis made a telephone call to the nearby RAF Manston Airbase to report the incident, when – all of a sudden – the three 'saucers' shot off in the direction from which they had come, gone in seconds. "*About a minute later, two RAF jet fighters appeared, and began a search across the sky, presumably looking for the UFOs.*" **(Source: *Probe*/ Peter Tate, UFO Bristol).** 18th March, 1963 – A strange object was sighted over the Atlantic coast of Florida a few moments before a Minuteman missile launched from Cape Canaveral, which then veered off course and had to be destroyed. **(Source: *UFO Investigator*, March-April 1963, page 4 – 'UFO SEEN AS ROCKET VEERS OFF COURSE').**

Peter Finlay – an engineer from Stakeford, Newcastle-upon-Tyne, was driving between Rothbury and Whittingham on the 8th of April, 1963. He noticed, through his windscreen, an object reminding him of: "*... a black wagon wheel moving across the sky, at a height of approximately 800 feet high, and two to three miles away. Minutes later, an RAF jet shot across the sky.*" Mr. Finlay rang the Duty Officer at RAF Boulmer, to report the incident, but was told by the man that "*he was not prepared to comment on the matter*". **(Source: *Newcastle-upon-Tyne Journal*, 9.Apr.63).**

Triangular object, Hertfordshire – RAF Bentwaters scramble jet fighter!

At about 8pm on August the 1st 1963, Mr. David Ogilvy an ex-High altitude RAF Pilot and qualified instructor for 14 years, was in his garden at Garston Hertfordshire when he saw an object the shape of a barrage balloon in a pronounced tail down attitude. "*I thought this was the case but when I checked ten minutes later, it was still there – so reasoned that if it had been a balloon, why would it have been in the same place? I examined it through binocular and saw 'fins' but soon assumed a more Delta form which resembled a Vulcan. This change of shape could, of course, have been due to a declining sun which might have altered the parts visible from the ground. Under the nose was, what looked like, a pod and in front of the trailing edge a long protrusion resembling full span flaps. The*

THE HALT PERSPECTIVE 2

'machine' or whatever it was faced about 300 degrees 'T' for most of the time but then slowly tuned to about 240 'T' It altered course three times in a period of about one hour. I rang the Air Ministry and a very disinterested official told me that the object was a met balloon from France. I cross examined him about this, he said little and appeared to have been briefed to keep quiet. With an airstream that was prevalently north east it could not have come from France, nor would a balloon remain stationary for so long a time." David rang Elstree Aerodrome and spoke to the duty Air Traffic Controller. He confirmed he could see the object and told him that someone from No 5 Group Royal Observer Corps, Watford had phoned him and told him that they had logged it as a UFO and that a USAF F-100 from RAF Bentwaters had endeavored to reach the UFO but failed to climb high enough. He continued to keep observations on it until it went dark by which time, he lost sight of it. David later discovered that two ATC cadets at Elstree Aerodrome had reported seeing an object that might have been a met balloon at 2pm on the same day. "Although I am reluctant to estimate its height it could have been at 80,000 feet and 400 feet wide. I know of at least eight witnesses including two cadets, two flying instructors, the duty controller at Elstree, my wife and two neighbours. This was no met balloon!"

An object, described as 'V' shaped *"like a shiny plastic triangle with red glow at the bottom which changed into a circular shape,"* was seen moving slowly across the sky, heading north to south over Gillingham, Kent, at 8.30pm before going upwards and out of sight. (**Source: *Chatham Rochester and Gillingham News 2nd August 1963,* 'Was it a 'flying saucer' over Medway towns').** The Air Ministry explained away the sightings *"as probably being one of many varieties of meteorological, radiosonde balloons, made of plastic, which, when inflated, look like an inverted pear. At certain altitudes, they burst and parachute down equipment used for examining the atmosphere".* We interviewed a number of witnesses, including RAF servicemen who had attempted to unsuccessfully climb up to the object in their aircraft. One of these was Mr. John Nightingale, who had photographed the object, which we later confirmed to be a French weather balloon, adrift from its moorings – but was this what was seen, bearing in mind the other sightings?

John Kimber was watching a number of Westland Whirlwind helicopters and Seahawks flying over the Isle of Wight, at 10.30am on the 18th of November, 1963. Weather conditions were described dark and misty sky to the east, but blue sky, with small clouds to the west. *"I was just in time to see a small silver disc disappear into a tiny cloud, hardly much bigger than the UFO. I waited for it to come out, but nothing appeared. The puzzling thing was that the 'cloud' had been moving in the opposite direction to the UFO."* During another period of intense aerial activity over the Island, he saw a small white, dome-shaped object appear in the sky during that afternoon. *"No sooner had it gone out-of-sight when the RAF Sea Hawks flew over once again."* **(Source: Isle of Wight UFO Society).**

Rider encounters landed UFO, Epping!

Following reports of UFOs being seen in the Essex area, Pauline Abbott, then aged 17, a trainee riding instructor at the Ivy Chimneys Riding School, Epping, was exercising her horse, *'Leberstram'*, in the yard of the Riding School, at 4.00pm, on a misty afternoon on the 27th December, 1963.

She heard a squelching noise coming from the nearby field, which she took to be a duck quacking – then wondered if there was somebody in the field itself, and shouted out, *"Who's there?"*, but received no answer. Looking over towards the field: *"I saw this thing on the ground. It was about three feet high and eight feet wide, greyish in colour, with a glow coming from the one end. I sat on the horse, too frightened to move. Whatever it was took-off slowly and disappeared into the distance. When I later went to have a look in the field,* **I found a number of deep indented marks in the ground, approximately 8ft across, by one and a half feet deep, with four lines radiating outwards from the circular marks, with 'cup' marks at the end of each line."*

Pauline borrowed my pencil and did a rough sketch of what she saw. (Fig. 1.)

Dr. John Cleary-Baker, Editor of BUFORA, suggested the incident, involving Pauline, *"Was a reflection of light. The marks in the ground were lightning, striking the ground. The evidence of a single witness, described by a responsible person well acquainted with her as 'imaginative', is a somewhat precarious foundation on which to erect a narrative of a UFO landing. I will not go so far as to accuse this young lady of hoaxing, but I feel that a pennyworth of fact has been augmented by a pound's worth of invention. The evening was misty and a light reflection from a vehicle on the road nearby, distorted by a swirl of vapour, could afford a fanciful mind all the prerequisites for a UFO landing story. Miss Abbot's story impresses me as representing much ado about little."*

I was almost mesmerized and just sat on Leberstram and looked at it. It was a bit like a dream. And as I watched, it took off very slowly and disappeared into the distance.

"I realized what it was because U.F.O.s had been sighted around the area, and I notified the local paper. But I didn't mention it to any of my friends, because I was afraid they would laugh at me and think I was nuts. Then, the next day, we found

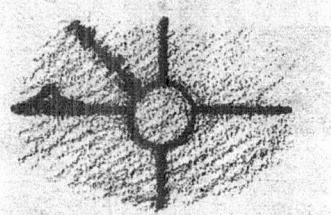

some strange marks on the ground which looked like this . . ." She did another quick drawing (Fig. 2). ". . . and I knew they had been left by the saucer."

Is it any wonder that Pauline Abbot became the subject of much ridicule; to the extent that she regretted intensely having ever reported the matter in the first place? We doubt very much that the object she saw and drew was a swirl of vapour caused by a passing motor vehicle! This was one of those cases where the reader was left with a number of unanswered questions, such as: What happened to material recovered from the scene? Was it ever analysed? What were the views of the original BUFORA Investigator – Mr. Paul Webb? He attended the scene, and discovered a thick, silvery, slimy, deposit on top of a fence post, in 'line of flight' identical to what was found on the ground where the object had landed. No disrespect intended to John Cleary-Baker who passed away many years ago, but your comments attract the same sentiments! Would you have felt the same if confronted with what we feel is overwhelming evidence of so many that *also* had the courage to come forward? Pauline would be 64 now – we have been unsuccessful in tracing her **(Source: *BUFORA Journal*, Vol. 1, No. 1, Summer, 1964).**

Everyone is familiar with the sighting made by US Police officer Lonnie Zamora on the 24th of April 1964, but Lonnie Zamora wasn't the only person to sight something clearly out of the range of everyday events. On the 28th of April, 1964 Albuquerque, New Mexico children – Sharon Stull (10) and Robin Stull (8) – sighted an egg-shaped object, hovering near the Lowell Elementary School for about 10 minutes. Robin refused to look at the object and ran off. The object bounced up and down about three times in the sky and then left. Later, [Sharon was treated for *'infra-red'* burns on her face. According to Police Lt. C. K. Jolly, the physician said he believed Sharon saw something and it had burned her.] **(Source: Dan Wilson).** At 8.15pm, Mr. E. J. Haug – of the San Francisco Orchestra and

Conservatory of Music – and C. R. Bubb – High school teacher – were camped out at Benson Lake, Yosemite. California. *"At 8.15am, we were by the side of the lake when we heard the sound of rushing air, and were surprised the branches on the trees didn't move – then we heard it again and looked up to see three objects, heading east to west across the sky at incredible speed – gone in seconds. In the brief moments that I observed them, I was able to clearly see the three bright silvery objects moving on a parallel course but at variable forward speeds. As one of them moved ahead of the other two, there was an adjustment and they would line-up for a moment, before another would get ahead – then the adjustment would be repeated."* **(Source: NICAP).**

12th July, 1964 – An orange-white oval shaped object was sighted over Park Avenue, Washington, County Durham, at 8.20pm flying in a north-east to south-west direction. According to the witness Mr. W D Muir, a member of the Tyneside UFO group *"The object flew back along its original course at a height of between 1000-1500 feet. A few minutes later a RAF jet aircraft appeared and circled the sky."*

13th July, 1964 – *"A dull coloured black round machine making a swishing noise, showing a thin rod on top with a flashing small white light",* was seen heading north to south over Worthing, Essex, at 5.30pm by Miss Louise Franklin gone in a few seconds. 16th July, 1964 – Mr. R.M. Glazier, from Edgware, Middlesex, saw *"what appeared to be a star crossing the sky, followed by a similar object seen at 12.30am which came to a sudden stop in the sky before, proceeding forwards in a sweeping 'S' movement, of flight, through my 60 mm. telescope. I managed to get a glimpse of what looked like a bicycle wheel."* **(Source: UFOLOG Information Sheet No. 3, 9.Sept.64, handwritten).** Later on that day a *"brilliant cone-shaped object was seen hovering over the sea,"* about three miles west of Point of Ayr, by observers from Wallasey Coastguard Station, Cheshire, including Mr. R. W. Lambert at 3.45pm. After five minutes, **the 'cone' inverted and moved out to sea**, where it was soon lost from view. **(Source: Isle of Wight UFO Society).**

Cone-shaped light sighted over Washington – Did the US Air Force respond?

At 10.30pm, 28th July 1964, a former Navy pilot and another man, working in a field at Lake Chelan, Washington, saw an intense cone-shaped light project up from the ground to a similar light in the sky, alternating on and off. A round, aluminum-looking object, about 30 feet in diameter, with a red and white light, then appeared and descended to the ground. This was accompanied by a strong whistling sound, like a small jet, followed by high-pitched voices heard – similar to children playing. Before this object took off, a low-flying Jet circled its position. The densely wooded area was explored by helicopter and on foot, a few days later, by Sheriff Nickell and a USAF officer – but nothing was found. **(Source: Jacques Vallée, *Magonia*, 619).**

Virginian businessman sights UFO landing – Alpha radiation recorded at scene!

Mr. Horace Burns – a gunsmith, who ran a small business on North Main Street, Harrisonburg, Virginia, was driving his station wagon on Route 250, towards Waynesboro in the Shenandoah Valley, at about 5pm on the 21st December 1964, when a huge metallic object came down out of

THE HALT PERSPECTIVE 2

the sky from the North, and passed over the road 200 feet ahead of him. His car engine stopped with an abrupt jerk, while the UFO landed lightly 'like a bubble' in a small meadow, some 100 yards away. Mr. Burns pushed his car to the side of the road and stood watching in amazement. *"The UFO resembled an inverted spinning top, some 125 feet in diameter and at least 80-90 feet high. In addition, I noticed that its circular sloping sides rose in six concentric convolutions, which decreased in diameter to the dome on top. Darkness was falling, but I was able to clearly see that the object was metallic. All around the perimeter of the object, at the base, was a glowing bluish coloured band, about 12-18 inches wide. I didn't see any doors, windows, or portholes, and neither any seams or joints; I couldn't see any landing gear either. The 'machine' had gently settled its base on the ground; its underside seemed to be slightly curved. Suddenly, with a whoosh, it rose straight up to about several hundred feet, and then headed away towards the north-east."* Mr. Burns got back into the car, which started straight away, and drove home. He told his wife what he had witnessed but was reluctant to tell anyone else, until he heard an announcement on a local radio station about a UFO investigation club based at the Eastern Mennonite College, in Harrisburg. Relieved, he contacted them and later received a visit by one of the group. On the 30th December; Professor Ernest Gehman of the Eastern Mennonite College went to the location with a Geiger counter and quickly identified the spot where the incident had taken place. The Geiger counter recorded over 60,000 counts per minute. At this time he was joined by a Mr. Harry Cook – a research engineer from Duponts – and a Mr. Funk, also an engineer. They ascertained that the radioactivity was the alpha type and not the more dangerous gamma waves...

Multiple UFOs seen over Washington – US jets scrambled

After being alerted of something unusual in the sky six army signal corps engineers including Paul M Dickey, and Edward Shad based in the Munitions Building, Downtown, Washington looked out of the window at 4.20pm on the 11th of January,1965 and saw a number of 'spots' in the sky which they estimated to be at a height of 12-15.000ft. The objects now disc-shaped began to zig zag across the sky towards the Capitol building. At this point two Air Force jets entered the sky and headed towards the objects which easily out ran them. It is said that this was one of many such incidents that occurred around the Capitol in the same month. The Defense department denied it had ever happened! One newspaper published an article entitled 'The Pentagon can't see spots in the sky'. **(Source:** *Strangers From The Skies,* **Brad Steiger)**

Virginia police officers report encounter with UFO

Two motorists travelling in opposite directions along Highway 60 near Williamsburg sighted an aluminum inverted 'ice cream' cone-shaped object hovering over a cornfield. According to one of the men whose car stalled he said, *". . . it was about 75ft in height and making a swishing sound. It then shot upwards at great speed."* The Virginia State Police confirmed they had been contacted by a motorist who reported while driving along highway 60 near Williamsburg, on the evening a huge aluminium coloured machine dropped down onto the road and caused his car to come to a stop. After hovering for about 25 seconds the object took off with an audible whooshing noise. Another motorist reported a similar encounter with what appeared to be the same UFO during the same evening in the Virginia area. One of the witnesses was Police Officer 'Woody' Darnell and several other officers who watched a glowing object hovering over them for several minutes before it took off in an explosion and shower of sparks on the 23rd January, 1965. Examination of the locality revealed that some of the trees were bent over another was still on fire. A short time later at Fredericksburg 275 miles from Marion people there saw a UFO described as a 'Christmas sparkler' spinning at great velocity and spewing sparks from its base as it headed over the Rappahannock Valley. Explained away.

West Virginia woman sights UFO with alien occupants!

At Rivesville, West Virginia a woman was up at 8am on the 23rd of April 1965, when she saw a 25ft object land near her house while in the kitchen. *"It was shaped like a disk, with portholes, from a cylinder about 3 ft high, a sliding door opened out of which a small being, about three foot tall, wearing white clothing, emerged and jumped to the ground. Its face was not clearly visible but it had pointed ears, a sort of tail, and was linked to the main object by a cable. It picked up something from the ground, then re-entered the cylinder, which slid up into the larger white disk. The outside rim of the object started spinning in a counter-clockwise motion then with a soft whistling sound, it rose straight up out of sight.* **(Source: Jacques Vallée** *Magonia* **644).**

Virginian TV personality reports UFO encounter near Philadelphia

Arthur Morton Godfrey (born 31.Aug.1903 – died 16.Mar.1983) was a television personality, broadcaster, and entertainer, who worked for the *Columbia Broadcasting System,* in New York, during the mid 1960s to 1979. Arthur commuted from his home in Virginia to New York by means of piloting his own private aircraft. During a conversation on the show with comedian Orson Bean, on the 26th of June, 1965 Arthur told of an incident which befell him and his co-pilot, Frank Munciello, while on a night flight from New York to Washington, in a twin-engine Convair. [The date was not mentioned but it appears it was fairly recent, as opposed to some time ago.] *"We were near Philadelphia, when a brightly-lit object suddenly appeared off the right wing of the aircraft; I immediately rolled the plane sharply to the left, to avoid a collision, and contacted the FAA Control tower at Philadelphia. I asked them if there was any traffic near us; they replied in the negative. At that moment the object reversed its course and circled us, before coming up sharply behind our left wing. I again banked and tried to increase the distance between us, but it banked right with me – every move I made, it copied. Suddenly it veered upwards and away into the night."*

Two UFOs tracked on radar – Jet fighter launched. According to the *Steubenville Herald-Star* July 13, 1965, an unidentified flying object was spotted on Monday, July 12, 1965 by thousands of persons over much of Ohio, Pennsylvania, West Virginia, and Maryland around 7:5 p.m. They included a report of an object seen hovering over Findlay, Ohio, which was tracked on radar for a period of 24 minutes. It is claimed that the Bellefontaine, Ohio, Air Station picked up two objects on radar screen. Another or the same object was picked up on radar at Oakdale, Pennsylvania, and observed visually near Eastmont, Pennsylvania and was tracked on radar for about one hour. Lockbourne AFB, Ohio, ordered a jet fighter to get a closer look at the object but it was unable to reach the object reportedly hovering at 60,000 to 80,000 feet. During the 2nd and 3rd of September 1965, it is claimed tens of thousands of people in a swathe stretching from South Dakota to the Mexican border watched a display of UFO activity involving formations of bright lights moving backwards and forwards across the sky. Some people said they had seen diamond-shaped formations, others single lights, which dropped down from the sky before heading upwards again.

At 4.30pm, 8th November, 1965, the pilot and passenger in a light aircraft reported they had been 'paced' by two UFOs and that military jets turned up and attempted to chase the UFOs. At 5.16pm on November 9th, 1965, New York State as well as portions of six neighboring states and eastern Canada was plunged into darkness for several hours. Besides the loss of power, the blackout triggered sensors that placed the Mt. Weather facility (to house the President in time of nuclear attack) on red alert. There were also a number of reports of anomalous lights, and speculation that the blackout may have been related to the UFO activity. At 5:20pm, while en-route between Syracuse and Rochester, Renato Pacibi, conductor of the Indianapolis Symphony Orchestra sighted a bright light in the west which was seen to rapidly descend and then head towards Syracuse. Moments later, word came on the radio of the power failure. At Camillus (near Syracuse) a housewife and three of her children reported seeing a 'huge dome-shaped' fireball for five minutes just prior to the blackout. It then rose over the moon and moved forward, as it did so the lights began to dim. It then moved back, and disappeared in a flash, and then the electricity went off.

Testimony given by Dr. James E. MacDonald in the House Committee on Science

On July 29th, 1968 Dr. James E. McDonald testified in part before the House Committee on Science:

Mr. Ryan: Let me ask a further question: In the course of your investigation and your study of UFO sightings, have you found any cases where contemporaneously with the sighting of UFO's allegedly, there were any other events which took place, which might or might not be related to the UFO's? Dr. McDonald – "Yes. Certainly there are many physical effects. For instance, in Mr. Pettis' district, several people found the fillings in their mouth hurting while this object was nearby, but there is car ignition failure. One famous case was at Levelland, Texas in 1957. Ten vehicles were stopped within a short area, all independently in a 2-hour period, near Levelland, Texas. There was no lightning or thunder storm, and only a trace of rain. There is another which I don't know whether to bring to the committee's attention or not. The evidence is not as conclusive as the car stopping phenomenon, but there are too many instances for me to ignore. UFO's have often been seen hovering near power facilities. There are a small number but still a little too many to seem purely fortuitous chance of system outages, coincident with the UFO sighting. One of the cases was Tamaroa, Ill. Another was a case in Shelbyville, Kentucky, early last year. Even the famous one, the New York blackout, involved UFO sightings. Dr. Hynek probably would be the most appropriate man to describe the Manhattan sighting, since he interviewed several witnesses involved. I interviewed a woman in Seacliff, N.Y. She saw a disk hovering and going up and down and then shooting away from New York just after the power failure. I went to the FPC for data; they didn't take them seriously although they had many dozens of sighting reports for that famous evening. There were reports all over New England in the midst of that blackout, and five witnesses near Syracuse, N.Y., saw a glowing object ascending within about a minute of the blackout. First they thought it was a dump burning right at the moment the lights went out. It is rather puzzling that the pulse of current *that tripped the relay at the Ontario Hydro Commission plant has never been identified, but initially the tentative suspicion was centred on the Clay Substation of the Niagara Mohawk network right there in the Syracuse area, where unidentified aerial phenomenon has been seen by some of the witnesses. This extends down to the limit of single houses losing their power when a UFO is near. The hypothesis in the case of car stopping is that there might be high magnetic fields, d.c. fields, which saturate the core and thus prevent the pulses going through the system to the other side. Just how a UFO could trigger an outage on a large power network is however not yet clear. But this is a disturbing series of coincidences that I think warrant much more attention than they have so far received."*

Mr. Ryan: As far as you know, has any agency investigated the New York blackout in relation to UFO? Dr. McDonald: *"None at all when I spoke to the FPC people, I was dissatisfied with the amount of information I could gain. I am saying there is a puzzling and slightly disturbing coincidence here. I'm not going on record as saying, yes, these are clear-cut cause and effect relations. I'm saying it ought to be looked at. There is no one looking at this relation between UFO's and outages."*

Mr. Ryan: One final question, do you think it is imperative that the Federal Power Commission, or Federal Communications Commission, investigate the relation if any between the sightings and the blackout? Official explanation The Great North-East Blackout began when the north-eastern region of Canada and the United States was plunged into blackness at 5:16 p.m. on November 9th 1965. It was the largest single power failure in history that plunged thirty million people (one-sixth of the population of the North American) in eight American states and the eastern portion of Ontario into total darkness. Power was subsequently restored within three hours in most parts of the province. New York City was without power for as long as 13 hours. Electrical power failure began when a single transmission line from the Sir Adam Beck # 2 Generating Station tripped into the open (shutdown) position. The malfunction of this backup relay was on one of the six lines linking the Sir Adam Beck # 2 Generating Station with the rest of the eastern power grid. Within 2.5 seconds, the remaining five transmission lines became overloaded and tripped (shutdown) open, isolating the 1,800 megawatts of power being generated at the power station. The generators at Sir Adam Beck became unstable and began automatic shut down. A sudden surge of power tripped the circuit breaker and the backup relay failed. This power surge was the catalyst for what occurred. The overflow of power leaped to the other five lines, the relays of which overloaded and tripped their circuit breakers. The process continued along lines in New York State until the entire grid of thirty-one interconnected power utilities had broken down. The north-east power system became unstable and separated into isolated power systems within 4 seconds. Outages occurred throughout New York, Ontario, most of New England, and parts of New Jersey and Pennsylvania. Dr McDonald: *"My position would call for a somewhat weaker adjective. I'd say extremely desirable."*

Sources: *Time Magazine* **(November 19, 1965) Canadian Edition, p.24. (2) Ibid. p.23B. (3) John G. Fuller, 'Aliens in the Skies: The New UFO Battle of theScientists' (New York: G.P. Putnam and Sons, 1969), p.85. (4) Toronto Globe and Mail, November 16, 1965. (5) Ibid. (6)** *Ontario Hydro, Hydroscope,* **Vol. 2. No. 40 (November 19, 1965)p.2. (7) James M. McCampbell, 'Ufology: New Insights from Science and Common Sense' (Belmont, Ca.: Jaymac Company, 1973), p. 57. (8) James E. McDonald,** *Statement prepared for the Hearings before aCommittee of the U.S. Federal Power Commission.* **(9) Frank Edwards, 'Flying Saucers: Serious Business' (New York: Bantam Books, 1966), p. 147. (10) Ibid. (11) Donald E, Keyhoe, 'Aliens From Space' (Toronto: The New AmericanLibrary of Canada Limited, 1973), p. 172. (12) Frank Edwards, op.**

THE HALT PERSPECTIVE 2

cit., p. 148. (13) Donald E. Keyhoe, op., cit. p. 176. (14) Ibid. p. 172. 15) *Time Magazine, op. cit.,* p. 28A. (16) Frank Edwards, op. cit., p. 149. (17) Ibid. (18) Donald E. Keyhoe, op. cit., p. 177. 19) Ibid., p. 182. (20) *Toronto Globe and Mail,* op. cit. (21) Ibid. (22) Donald E. Keyhoe, op. cit., p. 180. /Errol Bruce-Knapp).

The Colonel comments

This period straightaway triggers off early memories of my days spent scouting, from an early age right up to very many years later. From a personal point of view I've always held great affection for England. My Grandmother was of Scottish descent; no doubt research into our family background would provide interesting reading! I was very active in scouting having early on become an Eagle Scout and was representing my unit at numerous events. I was selected to attend at 17 years of age the 1957 National Jamboree at Valley Forge and represent the US at the International Jamboree at Sutton Park England.

This was the 50th anniversary of scouting and a real privilege. All the events took place on adjacent sites within Sutton Park located in Sutton Coldfield. As well as the 33,000 participants from 85 countries, an additional 17,000 British Scouts were camping on other organised sites spread over a fifteen-mile radius from Sutton Park and attending the daily organised events at the main campsite, giving a total attendance of 50,000 Scouts in residence, with a further

JUBILEE JAMBOREE. SUTTON COLDFIELD. 1957

7,000 being bussed in from locations all over England for day-long visits that were spread over the 12 days of the Jamboree. The Jamboree was formally declared opened on 1st August by Prince Philip, Duke of Edinburgh, accompanied by the British Prime Minister, Harold Macmillan.

The Jamboree was closed on 12th August 1957, by the World Chief Guide, Olave, Lady Baden-Powell, who gave her speech alternately in both English and French. Lady Baden-Powell was accompanied by the Lord Mayor of Birmingham.

This was the first occasion when postage stamps were produced by the British post office to celebrate

THE HALT PERSPECTIVE 2

the event. Looking back to those days utilising the resources of the WWW . . . I discovered the following: One day Queen Elizabeth visited the camp hospital where many were being treated for the flu. The weather during the 12 days ranged from an oppressive summer heat wave to two days of torrential rain that turned many pathways into quagmires. Many of the American Boy Scouts were fortunate in that the US Air Force brought in cots to avoid sleeping in water that flooded many campsites. The event is commemorated by a short stone pillar in the centre of Sutton Park that still stands near the site of Lady Baden-Powell's closing address.

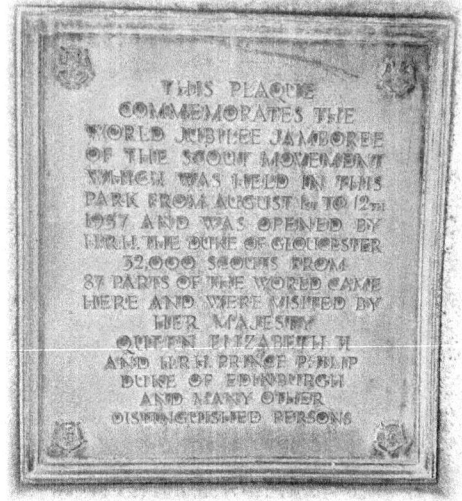

I spent the remainder of the summer travelling in Europe – what an education. When I returned I stayed active in scouting and through scouting made friends with Bob Graham, who was Executive Vice President of US Steel. In those days US Steel was a major corporation. When asked about my future plans, and I told him I wanted to be a chemist or chemical engineer, he told me their big laboratory was in Duquesne, not far from my grandparents' home and asked if I would be interested in being an intern. I immediately accepted the offer. I learned the routine of all the chemists and filled in for them as they took their summer vacations. Additionally, I worked with the Chief Chemist on a research project trying to find a practical way to extract Germanium from iron ore. I quickly realized that being cooped up in a lab for a career and, with luck eventually becoming the Chief Chemist, was not what I wanted. If I had then I wouldn't in all probability be writing this up in a book about UFOs!

It's an irony that in 2016, when the *Halt Perspective* was published, a copy was sent to Prince Philip – then 93 years of, age. His Secretary, Brigadier Archie Miller-Bakewell, thanked me and John in a personal letter. Incredible to think Prince Philip was at the same venue as I was back in 1957.

Years later while at RAF Bentwaters I was to actually enjoy lunch with Princess Anne, who came to the airbase. It's a small world! She was visiting a Woodbridge Orphanage that the base had assisted and wanted to thank me for the support. Many good times were spent with the Territorial Army (the equivalent of our National Guard) celebrating their Remembrance Day and numerous other social events. I especially remember all the great friendships, good times and fond memories of the times spent with the Anglo-American Friendship Council. All in all, Bentwaters was a fantastic tour.

Since retirement

Over the years, since retiring, I've lectured at a lot of UFO conferences – a few in England – many in the States, and served on discussion panels telling people what happened to me and my colleagues on that momentous last weekend of December 1980 when, as Deputy Base Commander at RAF Bentwaters, my life was turned upside down by something I regarded as initially with curiosity many years ago and in all probability worthy of investigation had I been inclined to do so. But UFOs were the last thing on my mind! Being responsible for the every-day events, involved in ensuring things went smoothly in running a large community of people that lived on and off the airbase kept me busy, as I am sure you can imagine. The fact that I ended up writing an unprecedented memo to the MOD about what took place in the leafy forest just outside the base, in rural Suffolk, England as I have said before changed my life!

THE HALT PERSPECTIVE 2

It's been a roller coaster of a ride – I've met so many others like me who just want to spread the word about the reality of a subject which isn't treated with a great deal of seriousness, generally speaking, by the media. For me it's about ensuring that they hear the FACTS about what happened – not the fiction which has sadly dominated what took place, now 40 years ago – more about this in due course. What I witnessed is still as clear as a bell in my memory. It's also about realising that so many others have also had to come to terms with what they saw, often in the face of adversity, the frustration they feel about what happened to them and the way they were treated; it is an emotion I have also had to deal with, especially as I have been the target for a number of years of attacks against my character for simply telling the truth!

So while my life doesn't revolve around what happened while Deputy Base Commander at RAF Woodbridge, now 40 years ago, I've been 'ensnared' by what took place and can't escape it to this present day – mainly because I know what I saw and will continue, to the best of my ability, to keep it in the public eye – rather than sitting back and having to hear from those that weren't there and the never- ending explanations offered by those who think they can explain it away!

Family life

People very rarely ask me about my family life, which is fair enough as I value my privacy, but for those that might like to know, I'm a family man with some great children, now adults, of whom I'm very proud. I reside in a quiet suburb of Woodbridge, Virginia with my South Korean wife, who loves the garden complete with its family of tortoises! On some weekends we head off to the family 'retreat' in West Virginia, accompanied by the family dog 'Caesar' situated close to the grounds of the adjacent forest teeming with wildlife overlooking the Blue Ridge Mountains. I was pleased that John and his two friends David and Julie Boardman have visited us now twice in the last few years. There is nothing like sitting outside on the balcony and taking in the beauty of the natural surroundings, captivated even more so when an occasional deer wanders in to the space that we took 10 years to clear (never mind construct a house)! As John and his friends David and Julie can testify to. Apart from that there is quite a lot of maintenance to do to keep the place and the grounds up to scratch. It keeps me busy I can tell you that! It's also thirsty work!

THE HALT PERSPECTIVE 2

Here is a document that I came across on the internet, which I found of interest.

Department of the Air Force Washington Office of the Secretary SEP 28 1965 – MEMORANDUM FOR MILITARY DIRECTOR, SCIENTIFIC ADVISORY BOARD: SUBJECT: unidentified flying objects (UFOs)

In keeping with its air defense role, the Air Force has the responsibility for the investigation of unidentified flying objects reported over the United States. The name of this project is Blue Book (attachment 1). Procedures for conducting this program are established by Air Force Regulation 200-2 (attachment 2) The Air Force has conducted Project Blue Book since 1948. As of 30 June 1965, a total of 9267 reports had been investigated by the Air Force. Of these 9267 reports, 663 cannot be explained. It has been determined by the Assistant Deputy Chief of Staff/Plans and Operations that Project Blue Book is a worthwhile program which deserves the support of all staff agencies and major commands and that the Air Force should continue to investigate and analyze all UFO reports in order to assure that such objects did not present a threat to our national security. The Assistant Deputy Chief of Staff/Plans and Operations has determined also that the Foreign Technology Division (FTD) at Wright Patterson Air Force Base should continue to exercise its presently assigned responsibilities concerning UFOs. To date, the Air Force has found no evidence that any of the UFO reports reflect a threat to our national security. However, many of the reports that cannot be explained have come from intelligent and technically well qualified individuals whose integrity cannot be doubted. In addition, the reports received officially by the Air Force include only a fraction of the spectacular reports which are publicized by many private UFO organizations. Accordingly, it is requested that a working scientific panel composed of both physical and social scientists be organized to review Project Blue Book – its resources, methods, and findings – and to advise the Air Force as to any improvements that should be made in the program in order to carry out the Air Force's assigned responsibility. Dr. J. Alan Hynek who is the Chairman of the Dearborn Observatory at North western University is the scientific consultant to Project Blue Book. He has indicated a willingness to work with such a panel in order to place this problem in its proper perspective. Dr. Hynek has discussed this problem with Dr. Winston R. Markey, the former Air Force Chief Scientist. Signed: E. B. LeBailley Major General, USAF Director of Information.

In this section of historical sighting reports we have accounts of strange lights halting in the sky over Arlington Virginia and an alert at Lockbourne Air Force base Ohio when Jet fighters were scrambled to intercept UFOs.

Further evidence from so many people of a variety of inexplicable flying objects seen by them in the sky, going back now well over 50 years ago, covering a 11-year period from 1954-1965 – eleven years, a tremendous amount of ground covered with all manner of reports of UFOs and the response by the Air Force in both Great Britain and the United States to try and intercept 'targets' in the sky after being tracked on radar. Not forgetting we have had to ignore (space does not permit) a huge number of reports. So, why now 60 years later does the subject still attract little 'serious' interest within the wider community?

It's because we don't know how to deal with something that is so far out of human comprehension – so rather than frighten folk we adopt a humorous response as can be seen from the way the media treat the subject. Don't forget the fear induced by the Orson Wells radio broadcast *'The War Of The Worlds'* warning people that the Martians were invading, on 30th October 1938.

A wave of mass hysteria seized thousands of radio listeners between 8:15pm and 9:30pm when a broadcast of a dramatization of H. G. Wells's fantasy, *"The War Of The Worlds,"* led thousands to believe that an interplanetary conflict had started with invading Martians spreading wide death and destruction in New Jersey and New York. The broadcast, disrupted households, interrupted religious services, created traffic jams and clogged communications systems and a score of adults required medical treatment for shock and hysteria. In Newark, in a single block at Heddon Terrace and Hawthorne Avenue, more than twenty families rushed out of their houses with wet handkerchiefs and towels over their faces to flee from what they believed was to be a gas raid. Some began moving household furniture. Throughout New York families left their homes, some to flee to near-by parks. Thousands of persons called the police, newspapers and radio stations here and in other cities of the United States and Canada seeking advice on protective measures against the raids. Maybe that's one of the reasons why Governments have played down the phenomena, I don't know – just surmising. Are we ready for the whole truths? Of what they know – if they know, they aren't saying!

Another example from a newspaper cutting dated 1947 is shown. It tells its own story.

THE HALT PERSPECTIVE 2

RAF Bentwaters scrambles aircraft in 1954!

Obviously this was something I found of interest personally, as it involved pilots who were scrambled from RAF Bentwaters, Suffolk after radar at RAF Bawdy plotted something worth investigating in May 1954 – over 26 years before my encounter with a UFO in the nearby Rendlesham Forest.

On this occasion, they described seeing a 30 foot diameter object – whether there was a connection with what the US Marine Corps chased over in Texas, nobody can say because we know so little about these objects, despite the passing of many years. In the same year, airmen at RAF Church Lawford were threatened with the Official Secrets Act should they speak about any UFOs they saw, following the sighting of one over the base.

Then we have what is now within the annals of UFO history, a 'classic incident' which once again involved aircraft being scrambled from RAF Bentwaters two years later in 1956. The outcome was of course doomed to failure as whatever these things are they can easily outrun our jet fighters!

It began when radar operators at RAF Bentwaters and Lakenheath tracked a group of 'dots' moving in over the East Anglia coast, from the direction of Holland. These 'dots', which could also be seen visually, were targeted at 50 miles distant and closing at nearly 5,000 mph – well over the speed of sound but failed to produce any sonic boom. At this point, the radar then picked up a number of other 'blips', showing as an irregular group of twelve to fifteen in number, heading north-east at a much slower rate, "being led by three UFOs, forming a triangular formation" – strikes a chord with me; knowing what I saw. Problem is, trying to make sense of this, but of course none of it does or is supposed to! I certainly wasn't aware of the full facts behind this incident, although I had heard about it. Of course, it wasn't until I had my own personal experience that I became aware that there was a reality to reported UFO activity, rather than the opposite!

John tracked down and interviewed the RAF Air Traffic Controller Freddie Wimbledon, whose account has already been included, but the letter is evidentially paramount. Here it is....

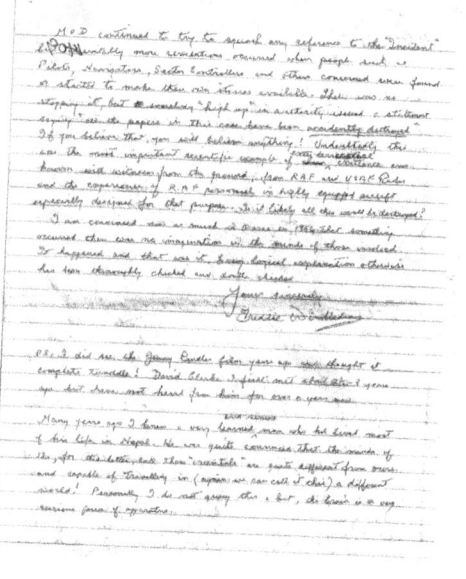

Through tracking down original witnesses we can see that an embellished inaccurate report was published in the newspapers about this incident – nothing surprising there when it comes to this subject. John was also able to track down other witnesses who reported seeing UFOs on the same date which can only corroborate the validity of something or someone – whose reason for being there in the atmosphere cannot be determined.

I had a look at *Wikipedia* with regard to their assessment of this incident; taking into consideration the inaccurate information published about my role in the events that took place at Suffolk in December 1980 – a matter they have never contacted me about!

Their quote: 'Most significantly, the aircrews originally involved in the incident, Flying Officers David Chambers and John Brady from the first aircraft and Flying Officers Ian Fraser-Ker and Ivan Logan from the second, were located and interviewed. The aircrews involved all flew with 23 Squadron from RAF Waterbeach and were scrambled at 02:00 and 02:40 on 14 August – around two hours later than Wimbledon and Perkins claimed the interceptions occurred.

In contrast to the reports given in the original classified Tele-printer message and in the accounts of both Wimbledon and Perkins, the aircrews both stated that the radar contacts obtained were unimpressive and that no 'tail-chase', or action on the part of the target, occurred. They also asserted no visual contacts were made. The first pilot, Chambers, commented that "my feeling is that there was nothing there, it was some sort of mistake", while Ivan Logan, the second Venom's navigator, stated that "all we saw was a blip which rather indicated a stationary target." At the time 23 Squadron decided that the radar contact had, if anything, been with a weather balloon.' End of quote.

The Condon Committee also included this case in its analysis. Aside from the Blue Book file, it was able to obtain a previous classified Tele-printer message, transmitted three days after the incident, from 3910th Air Base Group to Air Defence Commandat ENT AFB; the Tele-printer message›s description of the events, including the 'chase' episode. Based on the information available, the Committee's researcher (Thayer) felt that while anomalous propagation was possible, the lack of other targets on radar scopes at the time made it unlikely. Focusing on the later phase of the incident at Lakenheath, he came to the remarkable conclusion that "this is the most puzzling and unusual case in the radar-visual files. The apparently rational, intelligent behavior of the UFO suggests a mechanical device of unknown origin as the most probable explanation of this sighting." Aviation journalist and noted UFO sceptic Philip J. Klass concluded, however, that the incident could be explained as a combination of false radar returns and misperceptions of meteors from the Perseid stream. Why I am not surprised!

In this year (don't forget I was around 16 years of age) this film was advertised:-

Lord Louis Mountbatten – John met him through his late Father-in-Law who served under him as a Captain on HMS Kelly and learnt some years later from a confidential source that Lord Louis had files of UFO reports kept aboard his ship – Sadly, Lord Louis was assassinated by the IRA, many years later.

Interesting to read about Dorothy Kilgallen – sounds like some very dangerous assignments she set herself. I have no opinions on the manner of her death. Guess we will never know who the British source was but like John I have my own suspicions. It's one thing to make such fantastic revelations based on hearsay, which may be true for all I know, but as you will hear in due course, strikes a familiar chord with me personally as many such allegations or claims involving alien beings and communication with base commanders, have come to my attention over the years with regard to what happened in December 1980. These FAIL miserably to stand up to any proper investigation, and are the perambulations of a vivid imagination.

I'm sorry to hear that RAF Flt James Salandin has died. He sighted 'three bun-shaped' objects while on patrol over Southend Essex, in 1954, part of East Anglia; an area which has attracted a huge amount of sightings over the years and many in the mid to late 1980's of which John has on file and seen by me when I visited him at his home address in England in 2018 while talking at a Hull Conference, never mind the material he physically carried over to the States. John and 'Jimmy' were good friends and met up a few times over the years and regularly spoke to each other every few weeks. John recorded by way of film, much of what Jimmy spoke about and like him I agree that it's important to preserve the imagery, as so much has slipped away and continues to do so from official files, because these are ordinary citizens from all walks of life whose accounts should be saved for posterity.

John told me that 'Jimmy' had become disenchanted with the Press and the *BBC* because of their attitude towards the subject and the scepticism expressed by people following publicity towards his sighting, which he believed was some sort of 'control' exercised to balance reports of UFOs, rather than tell the viewers that this was not a singular sighting over a long period of time and that so many others had seen similar objects, which of course is dammed harder to explain away – nothing new there then! But, why does this situation continue to occur?

Privately, of course, one thing – publicly, that's another matter!

In private many people, especially those in positions of social and political influence, have obviously discussed the long-term problem of a very puzzling phenomena, but publicly – that's another matter – why do they keep quiet? Getting a book like this out into the public domain ensures that future generations will be able to read the truth about what went on, rather than other, very dubious, accounts which can, like 'Chinese Whispers', change drastically over the years; sadly of course, this is what the media seem to enjoy. I know all about this too well, because of the incredible amount of rubbish and lies that have swamped the internet about what we did or didn't see in Rendlesham Forest way back in December 1980. John has also told me about Staffordshire woman Jesse Roestenberg and his friendship with her . . . my only comment about that particular incident is that she's clearly not the only one to witness something so extraordinary, beyond the conceptions of everyday events – no wonder it literally takes over people's lives, and I should know due to the never-ending inaccurate accounts published!

Official response towards the subject laughable – but no laughing matter!

How many times have the RAF scrambled jets to intercept UFOs which have been tracked on radar? Ample evidence is given of the way in which politicians in powerful positions such as Secretary of State of Air, find it convenient to explain them away as being an aircraft, meteor, balloon, satellite, anything rather than admit they DON'T HAVE A CLUE! Hence the line of defence taken by them to denigrate and minimize reported UFO activity.

Why the interest in Nuclear installations?

The incident at Kirtland Air Force Base involving an unidentified object seen to fly along the runway and turn towards the tower before halting near the nuclear weapons storage area for about a minute, brings back memories for me. In 2017 I was invited back to the UK by the *Travel Company* from Las Vegas, and after meeting up with John and the guys from the States, I found myself walking down the 'Hot Row' (Weapons storage area) once again, which, as always, brings back powerful memories. Looking at the encounters described by the pilots at RAF Bentwaters some 24 years before ours in 1956/57 – why should I not be surprised to learn of this incident involving claims of something 'buzzing the airfield' and reports of a saucer-shaped object seen – never mind a target being tracked by radar which elicited a response. I also found the report of a ball of light seen over the 'bomb dump' of much interest, but without being able to identify the authors of the report, I can't comment, other than 'they' appear to be attracted to nuclear fission locations.

According to NICAP, UFOs were tracked by NATO radar for over three weeks, during the period from August to September 1956 – moving between 2,000-3,500 mph over Denmark. The response by the Air Force action following UFOs (ambiguous as that term dictates) tracked by radar will of course quite rightfully elicit the scramble of jet fighters to investigate further, bearing in mind possible threats of hostile action. I'm stunned by the amount of mostly now forgotten sightings of 'high strangeness' from those early years of something so odd that once seen, it *does* change a witness' outlook on life. The amount of occasions when they have been scrambled but haven't been able to identify the objects following reports from the public and after being tracked on radar speaks volumes.

Navy reports seeing them as well – ships buzzed by them!

UFOs are also seen over the sea. Look at what the commander and crew of a US navy ship reported in November 1957 'buzzing the vessel'. Clearly, this was no weather balloon, but we can rest easy, knowing that this was explained away as an airplane! Then there's a spectacular sighting from aboard the USS Franklin D Roosevelt in October 1958, when what looked like alien figures rather than humans were seen. Of course cases like this demand explanation . . . in some cases rational explanations are found! In a perfect world we could advise the reader that 99% of sightings brought to their attention in this book have explanations. If only! Thereby lays a problem! You can't find an explanation because there isn't one. What happens is that mundane or silly reasons are put forward to try and 'write off' what has been

seen. This is evident as shown by the number of crazy sensational stories still being brought to our attention now nearly 40 years later by those who seem to want to capitalize financially about what they think happened at the Air Base. There is a glut of sceptics, most of whom have never witnessed anything and feel well qualified to pontificate on something they know nothing about, rather than confront reality! That's something I know only too well. I was there! I know that logically some of unidentified objects plotted on radar will turn out to have natural explanations, but not all! It is clear from the staggering number of sightings shown involving apparent incursions of mysterious flying objects into our atmosphere – that we are dealing with something inexplicable which we should be taking very seriously, rather than taking a flippant attitude towards the subject. I grow tired of the never-ending crackpot explanations put forward to explain what I and my colleagues saw nearly 40 years ago.

After eight years of study the USAF published over 300 pages of their study into 5000 sightings and concluded that three percent proved to be balloons! One might ask how long can this deception

THE HALT PERSPECTIVE 2

go on? The answer is painfully obvious! One of those reports was over Kirtland AFB, involving an object which was seen to hover over the nuclear weapons storage area . . . As the reader can see, irrespective of whether you live in the States or England, when the Governments are questioned by their politically voted representatives, acting on behalf of their constituents, the answers are swept away in a plethora of inane answers which don't stand up to scrutiny. Remember Donald Keyhoe? He accused the Government of concealing the facts from the public *'flying saucers were imaginary'* he was told! So is this what this book is about!! Imagine that!

US pilot ordered to attack UFO over East Anglia!

I find it amazing that USAF Pilot Milton Torres was ordered to fire on a 'target' while over British civilian populated areas (East Anglia). The ramifications of that could have been horrendous to the population if the 'thing' had come to earth. Milton is shown here with my colleague Nick Pope who has given us some great support over the years.

What do we make of this? The report makes disturbing reading, because of the secrecy surrounding the now long forgotten investigation with no idea of the cause. I accept for all I know that there may be a natural explanation, but the content of the witness statements raises suspicion never mind the huge amount of other evidence of other witness sightings, that there is more to this than meets the eye!

In October 1957, an RAF officer nearly collided with a cigar shaped object, displaying lights moving over RAF Gaydon where bomber crews were trained. Coincidently or not In spite of the high level of security surrounding such a sensitive military installation, people living in that part of south Warwickshire soon found out that literally on their doorstep, were several huge bunkers filled with nuclear bombs!

The following month, it was the turn of airmen at Robins Air Force Base, Georgia, to report sighting a silver, cigar-shaped, object in the sky, which suddenly vanished a short time later. There was a time I would have firmly rejected any consideration that UFOs existed. After what I saw, the situation for me changed. As I have said before, each case must be judged on its own merits, but incidents like the one published here involving Mary Starr, the lady from Connecticut, and having a former teacher with a master's degree – baffles human conception. Did she really see the small alien occupants of an object hovering just above the ground? Or was it some form of subtle manipulation? Unlike others, there is no reason to doubt the genuineness of incidents like this which are not uncommon to the background of this phenomenon, as the reader will discover for themselves? So, many times we ask the same question about, what on earth lies behind this puzzling phenomenon? No answers are forthcoming, because we STILL cannot comprehend the nature of something that defies human conception and understanding, despite the technology of the 21st Century!

A British Air Force spokesman tells us in June 1958 that "*54 UFOs were reported in the last 12 months.*" This is just over one a week! Well, if you look at the number of statistical sightings recorded in this book for that period, you may arrive at another conclusion! There is no getting away from the serious concern felt 'behind the scenes of public view' about the way incursions of UFOs were treated by the RAF, and the USAF! Contrary to speculation, of course the Armed services take the whole subject of UFOs with seriousness, because even if they are harmless – it's clear that interaction with them can have catastrophic implications for human beings, never mind machines. On one occasion, six RAF jets were seen converging on a UFO over Cheshire which made a quick exit. We have seen on countless

THE HALT PERSPECTIVE 2

occasions involving attempted intercepts by the military to no avail; almost as if the UFOs don't wish a confrontation – rather than fear one. I wish I had the answers to this, but with all due respect, if the objects possess some modicum of intelligence, (whatever or whoever they or it are) then they must know we would have no compunction about firing on them – no wonder they leave the area.

I am once again amazed at the amount of recorded sightings of strange objects seen in the sky over this period, many in my own country even in my own state of West Virginia. One thing is assured, it's clear there is no distinction between what was seen, – has been seen, and in all probability maybe still seen moving around in the sky throughout the World. For all we know! Sightings of these objects hovering over power stations and air bases appear to be a common background to this phenomena rather than isolated cases. The amount of times people have reported seeing three globes of light forming a triangle can no longer be ignored, and surely indicates we may be dealing with something that depends on three fissures or openings in its body to orchestrate its flight through the air.

Not forgetting the fact that these objects 'possess' the propensity to split up into separate globes and move about in the sky. Time after time, the RAF or the USAF responds to what they no doubt perceive as a threat in the sky – possibly foreign aircraft after being tracked on radar – but due to the speed and manoeuvrability of the objects – find themselves completely out of their depth. In my home state of Virginia, one of them was even seen over a missile site, attracting the response of the military. Another example of the old, wearing thin, explanation proffered by the authorities was when a formation of 'silver saucers' were seen over Lancashire heading towards the direction of a local RAF Base could have been weather balloons! Rubbish! I imagine that these were tracked on radar, but you try and find any of this information in public records.

Are they monitoring us?

They have even been seen to enter the ocean on many occasions and tracked on sonar; one such example took place while Navy ships were exercising off Norway. Are they monitoring us, if so for what reason? Are they utilizing the energy fields around our equipment? The simple and frustrating truth is we just don't know! I can't praise enough the courage of the ordinary men and women in the street for coming forward to report what they have seen – often in the face of ridicule – as a witness myself I know exactly what happens after one does this . . . It appears to me that, while very few can fault my testimonial of what took place at Suffolk in December 1980, and continue to support the reality of what took place, others adopt a different tact by seeking to denigrate what did happen by offering all sorts of silly explanations . . . they never give up. Much more about this in due course.

Triangular marks found after UFO sighted! Radiation detectors used

Schoolgirl Pauline Abbott witnessed something out of the ordinary, but her testimonial was rejected because she was just a single witness! If we applied that sentiment to every incident involving single witnesses – then what would be the point of this book? No wonder she regretted intensely reporting the matter. John tried to find her current whereabouts, as I'm sure she may have further information, but he wasn't successful. Not only that, but three marks found afterwards in the soil were explained away by BUFORA as a lightning strike? Difficult to believe, one mark but surely not three and if so, then why isn't this phenomena accepted scientifically as a by-product of lightning strikes?

If you want further evidence look at what we found after the UFO sighting in the forest – three marks in the soil. Some people in the UFO community have suggested that the radiation levels might not be as significant as MoD suspected, suggesting that the Geiger counter used wasn't appropriate for the task and even speculating that the dial might have been misread. I'm wary when ufologists start

THE HALT PERSPECTIVE 2

trying to second guess the measurements taken by the military personnel who were actually there, or questioning the contemporaneous scientific assessment. Monroe Nevels used the equipment available to him and the DIS assessment used the readings reported to MoD. We can only use the data we have, not the data we'd like to have, or the data we think we should have had. That's the way science works. In any case, such speculation misses the key point: the radiation readings peaked in the three indentations found where the craft was seen to have landed. It's like using a metal detector and hearing a bleep; in a sense, it doesn't matter what make or model of metal detector you're using, or whether its dial reads 7 out of 10, or 8 out of 10; the key point is that it bleeped – that tells you there's something there. It's about cause and effect. Something caused the spike in radiation levels where the craft landed; the key question is: what?

Another very serious incident took place in my home county of West Virginia involving the sighting of a UFO which actually landed in a small field a short distance away from a Mr. Burns who used to run a gunsmiths shop in Harrisonburg. A Geiger counter recorded a massive number of 'alpha' counts per minute rather than gamma. The matter was reported to the authorities; they dismissed the sighting, and claimed no such landing took place and no radioactivity! Why did they believe that was the case, was Mr. Burns lying – I doubt it – if he was telling the truth then clearly the authorities had something to really worry about, hence their attitude.

Radiation

I know all about radiation because we picked up above average readings at the location in Rendlesham Forest, on this occasion in West Virginia the radiation was alpha which isn't harmful, but illustrates once again that these things can be dangerous to health.

Then I read the report about the triangular object (three beams of light) which appears to have landed in the Wiltshire area; a couple passing stopped to have a look. A burnt patch was found; tests revealed the area had been heated up to 12,000 degrees. This is well above the melting point (or sublimation point) for all chemical elements. It is above the boiling point for all but two elements: tungsten and rhenium. The effects of such temperatures on the human body will depend upon the length of the exposure. Extremely short exposures might only cause the sweat on the skin to evaporate and the outermost layers of clothing and hair to ignite. Any kind of prolonged exposure would completely vaporize the human body. As in – nothing left. No charred remains, no bones, no ashes. With the exception of any traces of tungsten or rhenium on your body, which would be reduced to near-boiling molten metal, everything is gone. The carbon in your body will sublimate. There won't be anything left. Folks should start treating this subject seriously. UFOs are dangerous. The guy himself appears to have sustained some physical ailment on the skin which aggravated him up to when he passed away according to his wife who John spoke to.

Seeing a UFO does change your life – I should know, otherwise I wouldn't be commenting. What should be of concern to us all are the uncommon (not rare) occasions some of which are documented in this book when the witness sustains physical injury, that manifests in a variety of ways – they include rashes, burns, and damage to the eyes, tanning of the skin to those that happen to be in the wrong place at the wrong time although others see it the other way round! Not forgetting the physiological trauma that can develop afterwards.

Further reports of three objects seen and tracked on radar – in this case over East Anglia which was where I was stationed when I had my sighting of UFOs. This one sparked off an alert – which was explained away as a weather balloon – although radar had picked up three objects which of course wouldn't have been considered of any relevance. Despite the passing of time, sightings continue to take place.

THE HALT PERSPECTIVE 2

Guy opened fire on a UFO can you believe that?

An encounter over my home county, this time at Poquoson, Virginia on the coast – when it was alleged the guy opened fire on the UFO which may sound an impossible state of affairs – but I'm sure he's not the only one!

I mean how you do know what your reaction will be when faced with something inexplicable and for many people very frightening. Invariably when people do report these things like the British bus driver who saw a cylindrical object crash into the river – he's told by the police it was four ducks! It's an insult to intelligence but that's how it works.

Tim Mayhew contacted us in 2019 wishing to bring to my attention through John what he saw while living on the RAF Bentwaters flight path during the early 1960's. He spoke of a conversation held with his late father, World War 2 Lancaster Bomber Sgt pilot Edward Mayhew (Teddy) assigned to 227 Squadron flying Lancaster B Mk1 and B Mk111, out of RAF Strubby and RAF Bardney Lincolnshire. Edward told him: *"No such things as ghosts, and UFOs were a load of rubbish. On bombing raids over the Ruhr, my plane was followed many times by these orange balls of light, which I believe was some type of top secret German weapon. It was apparently a common occurrence and we were told by higher authorities to disregard them as they seemed benign."*

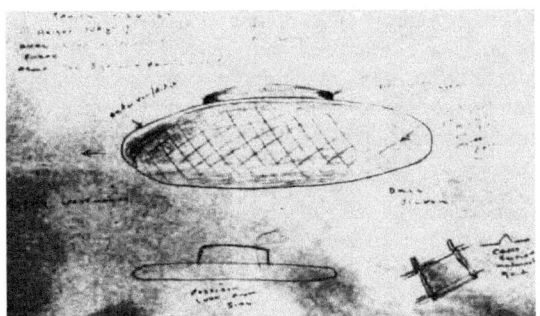

Tim: *"I was running from the Thorpeness road back to school, we had a large play area, and the bell had gone when I saw this flying object hovering above me quite low. Now I was used to all sorts of aircraft as I lived on the Bentwaters flight path, this was new to me and strange. It was a dull silvery steel colour; the underneath had the shape of a filled-in tennis racket, slightly oval with lots of crossed metal; what I could make out of the top was like a flat cowboy hat shape, again dull silver but darker. It was a lovely day; I can still smell the gorse bushes, little cloud, so I can only guess at spring or early summer. Since then I have had an interest, and your books may fill in some of the pieces for me. Please pass this on to Colonel Charles Halt as I'm sure he would be interested."*

USAF Major George Filer & The Socorro Incident

In 1962 USAF Major George Filer, who is a champion of the UFO cause to this present day, found himself in a highly unusual situation after being directed to seek a 'visual' on an object tracked by radar over the Oxfordshire area. Following his sighting of the gigantic 'thing' it took off at high speed. I spoke at a conference in the United States during which one of the other speakers outlined what took place at Socorro on the 24th April 1964 when an egg shaped craft with three legs along with small men in white coveralls were reported by New Mexico Police Officer Lonnie Zamora. Sounds crazy stuff and at first glance, unbelievable, especially as we are being asked constantly when it comes to discussions on the subject *"where is the hard evidence to to support the presence of these unidentified flying objects in our skies."* As you can see he was not the only one to find himself witness to something very out of the ordinary, emphasizing that these things can be harmful to health of human beings, look at what happened to the girl whose face was burned by the intrusion of something into our atmosphere a couple of days after

THE HALT PERSPECTIVE 2

Lonnie saw his UFO, then there's the guy from Santa Fe who appears to have witnessed what may have been the same UFO?

If these incidents were few and far between well then maybe one might be inclined to look for rational explanations, but therein lays the problem – the statistics speak for themselves! Like John, I am puzzled at the number of instances of where 'humanoids' or 'beings' are seen near a landed UFO. I'm not sure that the entities originate from far off planets, I may be wrong because nobody really knows, but could the images be projected in some way into our consciousness – making us perceive something which is clearly beyond our comprehension? Why don't people bother to do any background research into not only the witnesses but other incidents around the same locality before jumping to conclusions?

If the whole subject was on trial before a Court of Law, the massive evidence of first hand witness testimonials would return a verdict of case proved for the UFO subject. Why UFOs have been mostly treated by the media and newspapers for over the last 70 years as the butt of humour rather than something of serious scientific research defeats me!

Nick Pope comments

"The levels of radioactivity in Rendlesham Forest are an important piece of physical evidence, and a better understanding of this aspect of the story may prove critical when it comes to resolving the question of what took place back in 1980. In the original Ministry of Defence investigation, the Defence Intelligence Staff assessed the levels of radioactivity documented in Lieutenant Colonel Halt's official report as being 'significantly higher than the average background'. This new radiation survey gives us considerably more data and is the sort of serious research and investigation that I wish more people in the UFO community, be they sceptics or believers would undertake. An MOD spokesperson said: "*All our historic files which refer to UFOs, including Rendlesham Forest, have either been released, or are in the process of being released to The National Archives. The MOD continues to have no opinion on the existence, or otherwise, of extraterrestrials.*"

UK SPOTLIGHT ON 1966

150 UFO SIGHTINGS FOR THIS YEAR!

Selected sighting – British Police Officer's Close Encounter with UFO!

POLICE Constable Colin Perks was checking the back door of a shop behind '*Hoopers* 'in Alderley Road, Wilmslow, Cheshire, near the A34 road at 4.10am 7th January, 1966, when he heard a high-pitched whining noise. Turning around, he was amazed to see a greenish/grey flying object hovering, about 35 feet off the ground about a hundred yards away. The officer estimated the object was about twenty feet in width, and thirty-five feet in length, elliptical in shape, and emanating an eerie glow. After a few seconds the object moved away at a fast rate, heading in an east to south direction, where he soon lost sight of it. His official report into the matter was later sent to the Ministry of Aviation, by the Deputy Chief Constable, and filed as secret until declassified, over 30 years later, although some details were released to newspapers, a few months later. This is what he had to say some years later:

"On Thursday evening, 6th January 1966, I was posted to night shift working the town centre beat, my only means of communication being ten minute check ins from a telephone box every 30 minutes situated along my beat. At 4.5am I was checking the rear of a property on the east side of Alderley road from north to south behind the *Rex Cinema, the car park being empty as was the Finnegans car park." (Situated a short distance from the A34 Manchester to Alderley road).

"I then walked over the narrow service road and made my way to the rear of the first shop's backyards. I had taken just a couple of steps into the back yards when I heard this high pitched whine, (at about 4.10am); my first instinct was to suspect intruders at the jewellers or other close shops along

---

*The Rex Cinema sits on the main junction in the centre of Wilmslow in the south of Greater Manchester. Built by, and operated by the Stansby family throughout its entire lifespan as a cinema. It is an Art Deco styled red brick building with cream rendered panels and tall windows; it still retains the 'REX' signage above the front doors. It opened on 15th October 1936 with Errol Flynn in *"Captain Blood"*. The auditorium had a 35 feet wide proscenium and there was a 40 feet deep stage which was well used until 1985, when plans were proposed to seal off the stalls area and create a cinema in the circle. There was a cafe provided for the convenience of patrons. The auditorium runs parallel to the street and it is now a mix of retail and leisure units. The lobby, cafe and part of the auditorium are a furniture store; the rear of the auditorium is split into bars and cafés. Next to the front doors is the archway entry to the car park (still in use). The cinema closed on 8th June 1995 with *"An Awfully Big Adventure"*, by that point the cinema was just operating in the 338-seat circle area and the stalls were a large book shop.

THE HALT PERSPECTIVE 2

the route; I stood still and analysed the situation then decided to make my way to the jewellers. I turned round and was literally stopped in my tracks, when I saw an apparent **metallic object about the size of a single-decker bus approximately 30 feet by 18 feet, symmetrical in shape appearing elliptical (though this appearance may have been due to the object being so low.) It had a flat bottom and was quite dark underneath;** *I could see two tiers* **plus what looked like a handle on top like a dustbin lid.** *It was emitting this greenish grey 'ghoulish glow' about fifteen feet all around except for the bottom. I did not notice any windows doors aerials or portholes neither did I see anything resembling an undercarriage. The object was about 100 yards away appeared stationary, and approximately 35 feet above the ground. It remained in this position for about five seconds although it seemed like a lifetime then without any change in the sound it moved at an incredibly fast speed in a east south east direction and was lost from view before it reached the treetops and houses some 500 yards away.*

Mrs. A Walker, then living on the A538 Altrincham Road, Morley, Wilmslow, was retiring to bed on a clear starry night twenty minutes later at 4.30am, 7th of January 1966 when she saw a *"pearly green coloured object hovering over the Linden garage area opposite her house as big as a shilling at arm's length, just at the side of the garage roof it seemed then it shot away moving at a speed I estimated to be 70mph"*. Bearing in mind the close proximity of the nearby town centre, **and the similarities in description** it is likely this is what PC Perks may well have seen. When PC Perks arrived back at the Police Station he told a fellow Constable and Sergeant what he had seen, as a result of which the three of them returned to the scene of the incident at first light. They discovered the car park of Finnegan's (Now *Hoopers Store* 2009) was covered in 2-3 inches what looked like broken windscreen glass which disappeared one and half hours later. (**Source: *Evening News*, 2.Mar.66. 'Cops and Saucers'/*Daily Mirror* 3.Mar.66 'Beg to report sir one flying saucer'/*Daily Sketch* 3.Mar.1968 'PC claims he saw a flying saucer'/*Flying Saucer Review*, 12(2), March-April 1966, p.3.)

MAPIT UFO Researcher Derrick Woods from Sale, Manchester, to whom we spoke, in 2006, told of being contacted by a local farmer, from Adderley Edge, (two miles from the town centre), who said he knew a nurse, who was near the Rex Cinema, Wilmslow, on the 7th of January 1966 when she saw what she believes to have been the same saucer-shaped object moving through the sky but chose to keep quiet, fearing ridicule.

According to Nick Redfern there is a considerable file held at the Public Records Office available for public scrutiny relating to this matter which reveals a visit was made to the location by two MOD officials who recovered some of the 'glass debris' which was analysed but found not to be of any significance (whatever that means). We emailed the PRO in November 2009 asking them for a copy of the papers, and were advised this would cost us £112.95pence, which seemed extortionate. **(National Archive file: AIR 2/17983.)**

Mr. Terrence Kelly wrote a letter to the *Manchester Evening news* who published it on the 5th of March 1966. "*I was driving along Waterside Lane in the direction of Strines Road, Disley about six weeks ago. My wife and I saw an object approaching us at slow speed about 300 feet in the sky. It had a bright green light or lights beneath and white lights above. I stopped the car to try and make out what it was. As it was quite dark we couldn't make out any general shape. There were no flashing navigation lights as one would find on an aircraft just these white 'cabin 'lights .It then moved away doing about 35 mph towards Whaley Bridge fifteen minutes later it was out of sight*"

Visits have been made to the scene by us after a similar sighting in the same locality took place a few years ago.

On the 18th of January 1966 -John Wright – a schoolboy from Dean Low Road, Wilmslow – Cheshire was standing near the Bluebell Garage, at 7.45pm, when he saw a pinpoint of light approaching in the sky. As it moved closer, he saw: "*…a silvery-grey object with a lighted porthole, flying through the air towards the direction of the* Bluebell Hotel, *on the opposite side of the road, close to Manchester Road, about 60 feet in the air and 20 yards away from where I was standing.*" **(Sources: *UFOLOG*/Joan Nelstrop, DIGAP)**

Selected sighting – UFO over field, Wiltshire – Flint fused, and mark left on the chest of witness!

At 11.30 pm 30th April 1966, Dennis Tilt – a local Building Contractor and his wife, from Warminster, Wiltshire, were driving past Chitterne, on the B390 – a clear night, no wind, with a nearly full moon, when they noticed three luminous 'beams of light', forming a triangle, a few feet off the ground in a nearby field. In a letter written to UFO researcher, Ken Rogers, Dennis had this to say "*We stopped the car and got out to have a closer look. To our amazement, the three 'lights 'merged into one 'ball of light', changing into what looked like a frying pan, without a handle, now hovering 50 feet, or so, off the ground. We felt very nervous and decided to leave. Upon our arrival, at Battlesbury, we were surprised to see what appeared to be the same object passing overhead, going towards Chitterne*". We were unable to speak to Mr. Tilt, due to him having passed away but his wife confirmed the sighting and told us, the next day, that Dennis "*. . . reported the incident and took Ken Rogers to the scene to have a closer look. He later told me they had found a burnt patch on the ground, some 50 feet in diameter, near to where we had seen the UFO – completely out of character for the geology of the*

THE HALT PERSPECTIVE 2

area. To the best of my memory, we weren't physically or mentally scarred by what happened, although, very oddly, Dennis brought my attention to a peculiar red mark (about the size of a ten pence piece), on his chest, a few hours after the sighting. This mark was the source of occasional irritation and was still there right up to his death." Scientific analysis of soil control samples, taken from outside the burnt area, revealed the presence of tin, flint, and an absence of mineral or organic matter. Samples of soil taken from inside the burnt area revealed Lime, Wolfram 2%, Carbon 3%, Tin 1%, Cassiterite 1%, organic matter, flint and traces of silver, suggesting the surface area of the ground had been subjected to an estimated heat of 12,000 degrees centigrade or more, and that the elements of Tin, Wolfram and Carbon had been created by flint being fused together by a tremendous heat source. This application of heat caused through interaction between a UFO and the ground was hot enough to vaporise anything in its way – sobering in its implications; God help anyone who gets that close to these objects! When are we going to comprehend the real danger, albeit maybe not intentional but still fatal to human life, and take the subject seriously! **(Source Ken Rogers/Arthur Shuttlewood)**

Prime Ministers Question Time – Question on UFOs – On the **22nd of June 1966,** during Prime Minister's Question Time, Sir John Langford-Holt asked the Secretary of State – Mr. Merlyn Rees: *"What arrangements are made for the reporting and receipt of reports of sightings of unidentified flying objects? And how many of these reports have been received in the last ten years from civilian and service sources?"* Mr. Rees replied: *"Reports of unidentified flying objects are received by my department from both service and civilian sources and are investigated. Between* **1959 and 1965, 351 reports were received**. *I regret that earlier figures are not available."* Sir John also asked Mr Rees: *"What estimate he has made as to the value, courses and origins of reports of sightings of unidentified flying objects as well as the objects themselves?"* Mr. Rees: *"Reports are examined at their face value in the light of their possible air defence implications and we do not carry our study beyond this point. No Defence implications have been found."* **(Source: AIR21/19126)**

Selected sighting – Washington physicist and electronics expert encounters UFO

During the late evening of the 1st of August 1966, high-speed objects performing manoeuvres in the sky were reported by police officers, state troopers and civilians, over Prince George County, Maryland. In the adjoining State physicist and electronics expert – Dr. Basil Uzunoglu was driving on the Capitol Beltway, at 11pm, near Washington, when he noticed an unusual object in the sky, about 18,000 feet above the highway. It then descended to 200 feet above a house, approximately 200 feet away from the Beltway. Shaken by the sighting, he drove away and later reported the matter to Andrews Air Force Base. On the same evening a group of young people who had been picnicking on Erie Peninsula, Pennsylvania told the Police they had sighted a UFO which landed not far away from where they had been sitting. As some of the group watched to see what was going to happen next, one of the girls (who had returned to her car) saw what she described as: *"…a strange 'hairy creature' that tried to break into the car and then climbed onto the roof. I sounded the horn and the 'creature' jumped down and then disappeared."* **(Source: NICAP)**

Former Army Security Investigator Mr. J. J. O'Connor – now a lawyer – then in Florida, was piloting his plane near Sebring, Florida, at 9,500 feet, on the 20th of September 1966 when a UFO

THE HALT PERSPECTIVE 2

hovered above him. As its shadow covered the aircraft, O'Connor reduced power and dived. He pulled out at 3,500 feet, and saw to his consternation that it was still with him. He reached for a .38 revolver he kept in the cockpit, but the size of the enormous object stopped him from firing it at the object. A few moments later the UFO circled upwards and went out of sight. **(Source: NICAP)**

Selected sighting – Spectacular photos of UFO, later seized by Home Office Security!

Anthony Rider Russell (then aged 36) – a hairdresser by occupation – was standing by the window of his flat in Lewin Road, Streatham, which lies at the southern end of Streatham High Road, South West London at 2.30pm 15th December 1966 carrying out resolution tests on two new 2x converter lens (focal length increased from 135mm to 270mm by one converter) he had just purchased for his Zenith 35mm SLR camera, loaded with Gratispool colour film. While aiming his camera at the gable of a house opposite, some 60 feet away, his attention was caught by a peculiar object dropping through the sky, which suddenly stopped dead in mid-air before slowly drifting downwards in a pendulum motion. Tony managed to take

Anthony Rider Russell

the whole roll of film, after first setting the camera to infinity, before losing sight of it. Although excited by what he had seen, he decided (as it was near the Christmas period) not to bother having the film developed, but to write down a report and send it to *Flying Saucer Review* (after finding

THE HALT PERSPECTIVE 2

their address in the telephone directory), relying on his memory of the events rather than what he had hopefully captured on film. After sending the letter off, he decided to have the film processed and was disappointed to find that only four of the photographic transparencies (out of 12 exposures) matched the image of the UFO, as seen through the lens of the camera, being convinced he had taken the whole roll of 12 exposures. In due course, he sent three of the exposures to Gordon Creighton, Editor of *Flying Saucer Review*, who asked his photographic expert – Mr. Percy Hennell – to examine them, after taking prints from the negatives, and concluded that they were genuine. The first of the photos was depicted on the front cover of *Flying Saucer Review*, January/February 1967, Volume I3, No. 1, 'UFO Photographed over London', accompanied with an article on

page 29, as a late item –'The Russell Photograph', which showed all three photos. The first was taken at 1/125 sec. f.5.6.focal length 270mm. The second photo was taken at 1/125 sec. f5.6.focal length 270mm; the third at 1/25 sec. f11 focal length 540mm. The incident and the three photos were shown again in the next edition of *Flying Saucer Review*, in March/April 1967 – 'The Tony Russell Photographs' in an article 'written-up' by the Editor of *Flying Saucer Review* – Mr. Charles Bowen – following a visit made to Tony, accompanied by Mr. R. H. B. Winder and Gordon Creighton.

Comparisons were drawn between them and the illustration provided by PC Perks. We traced Tony Russell, who told us that his father – an artist by profession – had designed the cover for the first Adamski book, although it was later rejected for publication (but another one was approved and published). *"I was sceptical of the existence of UFOs until December 15th, 1966, and decided to hang on to the fourth photo because of what it showed, feeling it to have been a very valuable photograph, as it showed a 'disc' or saucer-shaped object, dark maroon in colour, with what appeared to be some lettering or marking on the underside. I would like to say I was upset to find the photos published in black and white, rather than colour, and although many magazines and books over the years have used the photos, I never gave anyone permission to publish them at all; worse, I never got my photos back from Flying Saucer Review."*

Sometime after the event Tony received a visit from two men, who showed him ID cards, identifying them as being from the Home Office Security. **They searched his house and found the fourth and best slide, after threatening him with the police**. He did write to the MOD, some years later, asking for it back. They denied ever having been to his house or any knowledge of the UFO photos. Another interested party that came to see Tony was Finnish film producer – Veikko Itkonen, (whom we were unable to find little about, other than that he was born on the 16th April 1919 and passed away in San Diego, California, on the 23rd March, 1990). Our attempts to track down any of his material relating to that interview, or the recovery of any of the colour photographs, was unsuccessful – despite Tony having seen them in a foreign magazine, many years ago. Unfortunately, he cannot remember the name of that magazine. Sadly, Tony passed away in late May 2010, so we were never able to finally meet him face-to-face, but treasured the many conversations held with him, not only about the UFO he photographed but many other subjects in which he showed lively interest and felt privileged to be invited to his funeral by his daughter, Janet. **(Source: Personal Interviews, Tony Rider Russell)**

THE HALT PERSPECTIVE 2

UK SPOTLIGHT ON 1967

400 SIGHTINGS FOR THIS YEAR!

Selected sighting – Civilian pilot encounters four red UFOs!

AT 10pm on the 13th January, 1967 pilot Carl M, and a passenger Jimmie Moran, were aboard a Lear Jet 23 en route from Houston to Las Vegas, at 41,000 feet and 300 knots airspeed on a 300° heading when they saw a red oval luminous object in the ten o'clock position which split into four similar red oval objects vertically a number of times, each separated by about 2,000 feet and emitting a "*red ray*," before retracting the lowest objects up into the top object. Albuquerque radar tracked the object 39 miles ahead of the Lear jet moving on the same heading, with no transponder signal and at that moment the object blinked off visually for 30 seconds then blinked on. Albuquerque control contacted a National Airlines DC-8 over Casa Grande, whose pilot confirmed the Lear pilot's reports. Albuquerque control warned the Lear that the object suddenly darted towards the jet at high speed within seconds until the radar blips merged (possibly 39 miles in ten seconds or roughly 14,000 mph). The object flooded the Lear with intense red light so bright the pilot had difficulty seeing his instrument panel; the object maintaining its position in front of the Lear jet for a few minutes. Then the object blinked off – came on again – and started falling back behind the left wing, before pulling forward. When the object blinked off, radar controllers at Albuquerque would lose the object, but then regain it when it blinked on again. Both the UFO and Lear jet made left turns over Winslow, and then Los Angeles Center radar picked up both targets. Past Flagstaff the object climbed at a 30° angle, disappearing to the west in under 10 seconds.

Selected sighting – UFO hovers over nuclear missile silos – NORAD jets on standby

During the evening of 5th March, a UFO was tracked by radar from a tracking station at Minot, North Dakota, heading for one of the Minuteman grids where the missiles are kept in deep pits, pointed upwards for launching. The alarm was raised and flashed to Minot Air Force Base and to the '*strike defenders'* – the men that defended the missiles. A minute later the UFO appeared – *a metallic craft, over 100 feet in diameter*. The guards watched as it descended; lights flashing around the rim shone onto a dome in the centre. The object turned towards the nearest missile site with three 'strike teams' in pursuit. Suddenly the UFO stopped and hovered about 500 feet off the ground, under the watchful eye of the guards below it, with their guns trained on it. The seconds ticked away; fighter pilots at NORAD had been scrambled and were awaiting take-off. A radio call was received from the base to say the UFO was circling the launch control. As the pilots readied to take off, the object swerved upwards and out of sight. **(Source: *Aliens From Space*, Donald E. Keyhoe)**

Sir John Langford-Holt questions the Prime Minister about UFOs! – 19th July 1967

"Whether in view of the fact that that the Secretary of State for Defence is responsible only for the air defence implications of the reports of unidentified flying objects, he will allocate to a department the duty of assessing the wider implications of these reports." Prime Minister Harold Wilson replied: *"No Sir."* Sir John continued: *"Is the Prime Minister aware that enormous numbers of reports are coming into the Government from people not all of whom are cranks? Would it not be appropriate without me knowing very much about the origins or significance of these items that somebody in the Government should at least take a serious interest in them?"* The Prime Minister replied: *"These matters are taken seriously when the reports which are received are sufficiently detailed to enable a check to be made. In very many cases there are natural phenomena such as balloons, aircraft, and so on. Where it has not been possible to get a satisfactory explanation, it is usually because the information has been too inadequate or imprecise for investigation."*

Questions asked in Parliament. Another question was put to the Secretary of State for Defence – Merlyn Rees, by Edward M. Taylor, on the 24th July 1967, asking him, *"What information has he regarding reports of unidentified flying objects, in recent months, and if he will make a statement"*. Mr Rees: *"Such reports are investigated, but nothing of defence interest has been found."* What would Mr. Rees have made of an object seen to drop down from the sky over Walton, near Peterborough, on the same date? It was described as a thirty foot silver sphere. Even if he had known about this, and the other hundreds of UFO sightings from that year, we cannot be that naïve to believe he would have admitted it to the public. **(Source: *Peterborough Evening Telegraph*, 28.July.1967)**

Letter from the Prime Minister Rt Honourable Harold Wilson. In July 1967, Julian Hennessey received a communication from The Rt. Hon. Harold Wilson, OBE, PC, MP – then Prime Minister of the United Kingdom, stating: *"As reports of these objects (UFOs) continue to appear from many parts of the world, it is quite understandable that there should be a growing interest in seeing some responsible effort made to seek explanations of these phenomena."*

Selected sighting – Devon and Cornwall police officers chase UFO!

Police Constables Roger Willey and Clifford Waycott, of the Devon & Cornwall Constabulary, were on mobile patrol at 4am when they saw a **star-shaped light at Anvil Corner**, two miles east of Holsworthy. The officers attempted to give chase but were unable to catch up with the UFO, which they estimated as being approximately four hundred yards away from the police car. Roger told us many years later: *"My regular observer was off that night, so I picked up Clifford Waycott – a County 'bobby'. I'd never thought about UFOs before because it didn't concern, or* interest, me up to then. I'd been in the Force for 12 years but I do know that I saw something I couldn't explain. I drove at high speed, to try and catch up with it, but it didn't make any difference. I stopped the car at Bassetts Corner and woke up a man, sleeping in a car, to show him the object. (Chris Garner, on holiday, from Luton, Bedfordshire). I then told traffic control that I was seeing something I couldn't explain in the sky, not unnaturally, this attracted all manner of derogatory comments, such as "had I been drinking, etc". I admit I felt a proper 'Charlie' afterwards. When I returned to base, the Press were waiting for me. When I woke up off nights, the Press were outside the house. This went on for a few days. I never described what we saw as a 'flying cross'. **It didn't look like a cross, to begin with, but then neither was it globe or saucer-shaped. It was like looking through diffused glass."*

Roger Willey

At a later Press conference, held by the Chief Constable of the Devon and Cornwall Constabulary PC Waycott said, "*The light wasn't piercing but it was very bright. **It was star-spangled, just like looking through wet glass, and although we reached 90 mph, it accelerated away from us."** The Times* newspaper disclosed Mr. Peter Mills, Member of Parliament for Torrington, in Devon, intended to ask questions in Parliament about the recent spate of UFO activity – a statement which appears to have galvanised the MOD into some action, judging from a report submitted on the 26th October, by the Head of S4 Air, Mr. I.E Carruthers, who confirmed arrangements had been made with the Deputy Chief Constable of Devon & Cornwall, for an MOD Officer, (a member of the Defence Intelligence Service staff), to interview the police officers who had seen the UFO, at Exeter Police Station.

On the **27th October 1967**, the police constables were interviewed by Mr. J. Dickinson, from the MOD, at Okehampton Police Station, who later 'wrote-up' the following report, (now declassified): 'The police constables first saw a bright light on the horizon shortly after 4.00 am. 24th October. At this time they were sitting in a police patrol car. They decided to try and discover the source of the light and started to drive in what they believed to be the general direction of its source. The road, along which they were driving, from Holsworthy to Hatherleigh, near Okehampton, is a winding country road and, as they drove along, the light appeared to move. After driving some

THE HALT PERSPECTIVE 2

ten or twelve miles, the constables realised that they were no nearer the source of light and they stopped and got out of their car. The light no longer appeared to be moving. Shortly afterwards, it disappeared. From a scientific point of view, the observation of the light through the windscreen of a moving vehicle does not provide a sound basis for concluding whether the source of the light moved or not. It is possible that it was the movement of the car which gave an illusion that the light itself was moving. Although the planet Venus would have appeared over the eastern horizon between 3 and 4 o'clock, the police constables state that they observed their light to the north-east, **therefore it is not possible to state they observed Venus**. When questioned about the disappearance of the light, one of the police constables indicated that by the time he had decided that the light came from a spaceship. They did not see a spaceship but only saw a light and his conclusion appears to have no factual basis."

Police Constables Clifford Waycott and Roger Willey (right).

THE HALT PERSPECTIVE 2

UK SPOTLIGHT ON 1968

96 SIGHTINGS FOR THIS YEAR!

Selected sighting – 'Hank the Deuce' paced by a UFO!

HENRY Ford II, sometimes known as "HF2" or "Hank the Deuce", was the eldest son of Edsel Ford and eldest grandson of Henry Ford. He was president of the Ford Motor Company from 1945 to 1960, chief executive officer from 1945 to 1979, and chairman of the board of directors from 1960 to 1980. He was aboard a Jet Star plane, accompanied by his executives, flying at 35,000 feet en route from San Antonio to Detroit on the 16th of April 1968. While near Austin, Texas the pilots (and passengers) sighted a huge, round, object overhead. They thought, initially, that it might have been an unusually large research balloon – until it began to move with them. A few minutes later it was still there, pacing the aircraft at 616 miles per hour. The senior pilot said *"It looked twice the size of the DC-8 and was 5-600 feet in diameter.*

Henry Ford II

No protrusions or windows could be seen." During the hour-long sighting Mr Ford asked the pilot to radio the Air Force and send up a jet fighter to intercept. The pilot, fearing ridicule, declined to do so. **(Source: NICAP/Photo- ©copyright By Hugo van Gelderen/Anefo [originally uploaded to Wikimedia Commons by Mr. Nostalgic before being cropped and reuploaded by Emiya1980] – File: Henry Ford II in Nederland om zijn jacht te bekijken. Hier op Schiphol, Bestanddeelnr 914-9054.jpg, Nationaal Archief [Dutch National Archives])**

Selected sighting – Tremendous light displays over New York State

On the 26th of September 1968, around 9,15am, Mr Earl Fickelsher from Gowans Road, Angola, a village in the town of Evans, Erie County, New York State, left the house to collect his son from a scout meeting. As he did so a bright light like a searchlight swept the porch of the house and surrounding area. The beam then swung its light up onto the clouds between the house and fields nearby. Earl called his wife outside who joined him with a flashlight. They stood in the drive and watched the light which appeared to be scanning the clouds as if looking for something. Earl flashed the torch two signals short and one long one, three times at the light. It shot up through a hole in the cloud and immediately vanished. Earl advised his wife Doris, (who was the director of 'ALLIED SAUCERS' Association, Eden, New York) to keep flashing a signal as he had to get their son. He was halfway up the road when to the left of the roadway a beam of light responded in the same pattern. Two red light signals short and one long.

Doris: *"I couldn't see the object, only the light signal. This went on for about eight minutes, me flashing the 'same flash being sent back' making a half circle around the house until it reached the back of the property and stopped. I went into the house and called our next door neighbour to come over. She joined me and I explained what had been happening. We walked around with me flashing the torch again.*

Suddenly a dull yet strong circular light appeared above our heads, and then joined by a second, both circling above us very fast. It made us very dizzy to watch and at each completed circle, they seemed to merge as one big light. They circled in opposite directions once then separated, one settling above the front of the house, the other towards the telephone pole on the front lawn near the road. Then they merged into the clouds and we lost sight of them."

The objects were estimated to have been moving at a height of between 800 feet and 1000 feet. It appeared to be 60 feet in diameter and was so bright no discernible shape of any possible craft was seen. **(Source: OUTERMOST Magazine 1970 Gene Duplantier)**

Eugene Arthur Christopher Duplantier RIP

Gene Duplantier, whose illustrations grace the pages of several classic saucer publications, was the editor of the UFO magazine 'Saucers, Space & Science.' In 'The Night Mutilators', he presented a round-up of cases up to 1980. This book contains plenty of unsettling details about various abduction and mutilation incidents, culminating with the incidents in New Mexico, around the Dulce area, as investigated by researcher Gabe Valdez. Some years ago I corresponded with him with regard to an incident that took place in Rainsford Cheshire. He passed away in December 2019.

THE HALT PERSPECTIVE 2

UK SPOTLIGHT ON 1969

80 SIGHTINGS FOR THIS YEAR!

Selected sighting – Schoolteacher encounters landed object with occupants!

A retired schoolmistress, living a few miles from Bridgnorth, in Shropshire, was exercising her dog 'Stanley', a short distance from the house on the 12th April 1969. She picked up a stick and threw it over a nearby hedge. The dog ran after it but came straight back, yelping, and clearly distressed. Thinking someone had thrown something at the dog, the woman barged through a narrow gap in the fence.

Her annoyance changed to excitement, then fear, when she saw the amazing sight of an object, resembling a spinning top in appearance, with three legs, around which stood three 'figures', bending down, picking something up from the ground and placing whatever it was, into an object that looked like a large mirror, situated beneath or close to the front of the 'craft', which she estimated to be approximately the length of two cars. Fearing for her safety, the woman ran back to the house with the dog and, after a sleepless night, packed her suitcase and went to stay with friends, in London, for a few days.

Following her arrival back home, she contacted Derek Samson – an investigator for NICAP, living in Shirley, Solihull, in the West Midlands – and told him what had happened. Derek decided to pay her a visit and arrived at the house, two weeks after the incident.

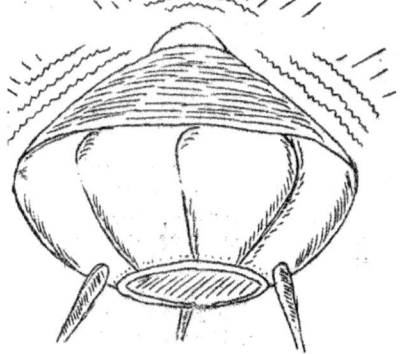

"I found her to be a charming, capable lady, who took me to where it had happened, 25 yards away from a group of trees. I searched the area and found no definitive landing marks, although I did discover three small holes, each having a circumference of seven inches, to a depth of five inches. The distance between each hole was three, four, and five yards, in a triangular shape. If these were made by the landing legs of a craft, then the vehicle was very light. I took some soil samples

THE HALT PERSPECTIVE 2

– (nothing untoward was found). After more thorough investigation, I was convinced an area of some several feet in diameter had been used, or trodden down. This area seemed devoid of the longer blades of grass and plant life. When viewed from a short distance away, it could be seen as a little clearing."

We spoke to Derek about this incident, hoping to discover where this had happened and obtain details of the witness. Unfortunately, owing to his deteriorating health, Derek was unable to assist further, although he saw no reason to treat this woman's extraordinary account as being anything other than genuine. We also contacted NICAP, GB, with regard to seeking further information as to the location of the incident, but they, too, were unable to assist any further as they had no record of this incident. As a matter of interest I'm sure that Derek would have got on with Colonel Halt as they both shared an interest in firearms!

During the evening of the **23rd of July 1969** a number of people – including Bedfordshire Police Sergeant Martin Burgess – chased a UFO for some distance, before losing sight of it at Brickhill, Bedford. Martin: *"When we first saw the object, it seemed quite high up and then dropped rapidly –* **until it was floating a few hundred feet in the air.** *The 'light 'was very bright, so it was impossible to gauge its size accurately, but I would say it was between 6-8 feet across. It looked like it was coming down over the centre of Brickhill, but then veered off towards Manton Heights. We chased after it, but lost it amongst the houses. I don't know what we would have done if we had seen 'little green men' coming out of the thing – either breathalysed them, or run away, I suppose."* A police spokesman said no official report was made of the incident. (**Source:** *The Bedford Record*, 29.July.1969 – '**UFO chased by police patrol'/DIGAP**)

The Colonel comments

A cursory look at UFO reports for the period between 1966-1969 shows that in addition to the UK Police officer's sighting of January 1966, for the whole ONE month, there was a total of 20 other sightings. They included reports of, red spheres, spinning discs, triangular objects, luminous globes and saucer-shaped objects seen. Over 100 public sightings, reported to various UFO groups in England as opposed to figures later released by the MOD – far too numerous to list here. Never mind the United States which gives you an idea of the problem facing the authorities. They included a report of a UFO that crashed into a tree in a London suburb during August 1966, followed by the authorities moving in straight away to 'contain' the incident. Gauging the seriousness of the occasion the witness who later complained of a *rash on his neck* after the event was then taken to MOD HQ where, along with according to him, 15 other people were interviewed there about what they had seen. One wonders if any of the others were afflicted physically but the chances of obtaining access to official reports like this are nigh impossible I would have thought. This was a matter that he felt sufficiently aggrieved about to write to the MOD and the British Prime Minister Harold

Wilson, emphasising his concern. I couldn't even begin to guess what happened here, there may have been a natural explanation as opposed to a fanciful one involving all manner of crazy ideas including, of course, alien beings colliding with a tree! Doubt that very much. So why the blanket of secrecy covering what happened? Still in force to this day one supposes. This is just one of hundreds investigated by John over the years; if you want further information about this, please contact him. He has tried to chase up official documents from over 45 years ago relating to other personal UFO accounts obtained through interviews with the witnesses who told him they had reported the sighting to the MOD at the time. But he has been unsuccessful. On other occasions the MOD stated that the classified files relating to their investigation would be released after a thirty years period of retention had elapsed. These were earmarked for release in 2001 – guess what? He's still waiting!

The spectacular photographs shown taken by Tony Russell in December 1966 over London, who John spent time talking to on the phone a few years ago, is believed to be absolutely genuine according to John who has no reason to think that this is fabrication. Apart from that, rigorous testing was conducted by photographic specialists, who worked for the *Flying Saucer Review*.

Tony knew he was seriously ill but was adamant about what he saw, and photographed all those years ago. Whatever the source of the photo was, it was important enough for Home Office security authorities to come along and seize some of the photographic slides one of which was in colour, and has never been seen since. The family invited John to the funeral after Tony passed away which he attended.

Here is another photo taken a year before the UFO sightings in the Forest. This one was taken over Leiston, Suffolk where Brenda Butler lives; it's been checked out and is again believed genuine. Are we looking at the same or an identical object? I am told that this object wasn't too far away from Sizewell B Nuclear Power Station, whose presence may well be connected with its appearance.

THE HALT PERSPECTIVE 2

I can understand that on those periodic occasions throughout history when faced with the unknown, humans respond with a variety of emotions which includes fear and hostility. One might think that in our advanced technological age that we might consider a different approach. One of the reasons for this is the fact, first of all, there should be a different attitude towards the subject, rather than flippancy and whipped up hysteria by the Press, whose presentations often include scenarios something more akin with Star Trek or Star Wars. It is time for a change in the subject; it should be part of the school curriculum – unless it is, we are never going to be able to come to terms with something way out of our present level of understanding.

Look what was reported over Maryland close to the borders of my 'weekend retreat in West Virginia' during August 1966, witnessed by a Physicist, Police and State Troopers, followed by a report on the same day by youngsters picnicking on Erie Peninsula, when they claimed to have seen something land and what appeared to be some sort of entity. It doesn't make sense – but of course it's not meant to.

Scientists sight object over Harwell Nuclear Power Station, Berkshire!

In England, highly intelligent scientist, Peter Wroath (and UFO Investigator) employed at Harwell Atomic Power Station, Berkshire, who helped to build and run a series of particle physics experiments on the Proton Synchrotron at Rutherford, at the DESY laboratory in Hamburg and at CERN in Geneva, told John Hanson about an amazing sighting of a triangular object, seen high in the sky over Harwell, ˙Didcot, Berkshire Atomic power station (˙where John was born) accompanied by a colleague, that defied explanation. If guys like this with very impressive credentials couldn't come up with a rational scientific answer then surely it's pretty clear that something serious is going on that we have not the faintest idea of even comprehending.

Why are so many UFOs being reported near nuclear facilities and why wasn't there more urgency on the part of the government to assess their potential national security threat?

Peter Wroath

In the last 75 years, high-ranking U.S. military and intelligence personnel have also reported 'UAPs' near sites associated with nuclear power, weaponry and technology – from the early atomic bomb development and test sites to active nuclear naval fleets. All of the nuclear facilities – Los Alamos, Livermore, Sandia, Savannah River – witnessed dramatic incidents where these unknown craft appeared over the facilities and nobody knew where they were from or what they were doing there.

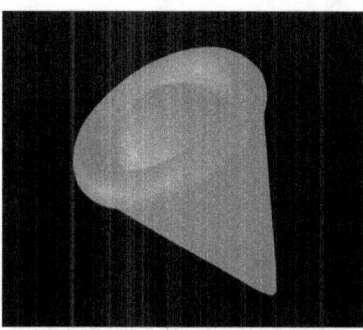

Look at the evidence obtained by my friend, Robert Hastings, a UFO researcher and author of the book *UFOs and Nukes: Extraordinary Encounters at Nuclear Weapons Sites*. He states that nuclear-adjacent sightings go back decades, and has interviewed more than 160 veterans who have witnessed strange things in the skies around nuclear sites. *"You have objects being tracked on radar performing at speeds that no object on earth can perform; you have eyewitness [military] personnel. You have jet pilots. Witnesses to these incidents are often highly trained personnel with top security clearances. In recent years, their reports are being corroborated by sophisticated technology".*

THE HALT PERSPECTIVE 2

Authorities unable to determine source of objects invading our airspace!

What was the purpose behind the 100 foot wide object that was tracked on radar and then seen visually as it descended over Minot US air force base, North Dakota, in March 1967? Here we have the ingredients of a particularly disturbing incident with guards training their weapons on the object hovering over the silos that housed atomic weapons. As the planes were readied to intercept the object flew away, pretty frightening stuff don't you think? For all they knew this could have been the forerunner of an attack launched by a foreign power. A scenario that has been re-enacted so many times now...

I can understand perfectly how they must have felt, as it was my job while based at RAF Woodbridge/Bentwaters, to know what was going on in the fire departments in the Police Squadron on the A10 flight line, because our mission was to send those aircraft into Germany and Poland should the Russians mobilise!

December 1980 was one of the most unstable periods of the Cold War. Soviet troops were gathering across the borders of Poland. On a serious note it's a wonder that World War Three never started following so many incursions over military bases by unidentified flying objects, many of which were tracked on radar and certainly not the product of over active imaginations or hovering celestial objects!

Another incident now long forgotten – but which once again brought back the memories of what I saw and discovered in Rendlesham Forest, Suffolk – took place in North Dakota when, after a dome-shaped object was seen hovering over a field, they found TWO groups of three depressions at the site. This was 14 years before the events at RAF Bentwaters!

With regard to reported encounters between motorists and UFOs many of which can be found in this book, it's strange that diesel engines seem to remain unaffected by the presence of nearby UFO fields of energy, presumably because the engine doesn't need a current of electricity to maintain its motion. On a more serious note one wonders how many times petrol driven aircraft engines have been rendered inoperable (albeit for a short period) during an encounter with a UFO. Oddly, and rather fortunately, such incidents seem very rare, although there have been claims, from other parts of the world, that some aircraft attempting to intercept UFOs have crashed.

Three lights forming a triangle in shape were reported hovering in the sky, over a Cheshire RAF Radar installation. Was it monitoring our transmissions or was there another reason for its presence over this type of installation? Time and time again reports of these objects have been noted over power stations and atomic sites. Some people speculate that they are an alien intelligence – who really knows the answer? Therein lays the problem!

During this year (1967) all manner of strange unidentified objects were seen in the sky over England. We are not talking about indistinct light sources which could for all we know have a rational answer but what appeared to be structured objects resembling a variety of shapes which includes: – *'three pronged, orange disc-shaped UFOs'*, *'spinning tops'*, *'green cylinders'*, *'egg'*-shaped objects*', and something that caught my interest a *'flying saucer'* sighted over a school in Nottingham involving dozens of people – **official explanation optical illusion**! – It's crazy and an insult to the witnesses. I know that these objects can leave marks or depressions in the ground; I even have A PLASTER CAST OF THE MARKS LEFT IN THE FOREST – more on that later!

Towards the end of 1967 sightings of objects resembling *'Flying Crosses'* began to be seen moving through the sky over the UK (and also coincidentally over the USA during the October period). A short-lived phenomena visually, although other sightings of UFOs continued to be reported. Incidentally, Ian

THE HALT PERSPECTIVE 2

Ridpath, who I was to meet following the disclosure of my memo and subsequent publicity, dismissed the sightings of the 'flying cross' during this period of time, (including the police officers chase) as "... .spurious side-to-side and up-and-down movements of hovering celestial objects are common due to the auto kinetic effect in the eye. In addition, passing clouds can give the illusion that stationary celestial objects are moving. Or: The facts are consistent with Venus being viewed through semi-transparent clouds." Ian – with regard to the incident that took place at Rendlesham Forest explains it away as – "At its most basic, the case comes down to the misinterpretation of a series of nocturnal lights – a fireball, a lighthouse, and some stars. Such misidentifications are standard fare for UFOlogy. It is only the concatenation of three different stimuli that makes it exceptional. Those unfamiliar with the ways in which nocturnal lights can be misidentified should read my article on astronomical causes of UFOs."

Ian Ridpath

In April, 1967 British Coastguard, Brian Jenkins reported seeing a rotating object with a *triangular* opening seen hovering over the Devon Station followed by a jet fighter dispatched to investigate. Officialdom trotted out the unbelievable explanation that it was a car headlight, an insult to those that were involved! It happened in the day not the night! This was a year of intense UFO activity reports which included a black boomerang-shaped object motionless in the sky hovering over a power station, and multiple accounts of saucer shaped objects seen in the sky cavorting about.

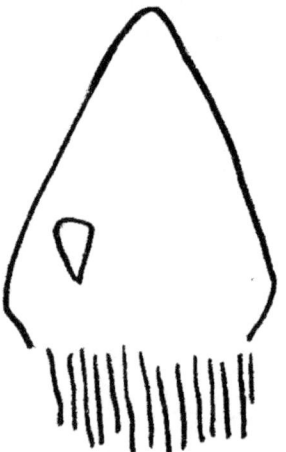

Like John, I am aware that quite often people's accounts can be altered or manipulated over the years – even embellished – so it's important to present wherever possible first-hand interviews for obvious reasons. I know all about that having spent time interviewing the men in my team and other US security servicemen after what they experienced at the end of December 1980.

John spoke to me about the Devon and Cornwall police officer, Roger Willey, who was with PC Clifford Waycott, when they chased what was later referred to by the British media as an object resembling a 'flying cross' in October 1967 – many such examples are given around that time. John also met his son Mark, who has been most helpful in providing many photographs and information about his dad, who used to live on a canal boat in Leicestershire, when he first met John. Later, John visited Roger and his girlfriend Michelle in the Isle of Wight, as shown in the photo. Roger is reading a copy of the *Flying Saucer Review* of which John was a consultant! Roger passed away some years ago. Condolences to Mark, Michelle and family.

I may have mentioned before, and no doubt will again – at the end of the day we are dealing with people whose lives are changed forever, not only by their sightings of inexplicable objects in our atmosphere, but by the attitude of authority and worse, the media – examples of which will be seen as we delve deeper into the book.

More worrying are the accounts of these domed objects seen hovering over roofs and buildings, the purpose of which eludes me completely. Quite often single sources of light, sometimes in clumps of three are seen moving in from different directions and meeting up, before splitting away in different directions. There are even reports of the two or three UFOs merging into one separate object, giving an impression of a pre arranged schedule mystifying to say the least!

THE HALT PERSPECTIVE 2

John has sent me many UFO report files to look at, which he has investigated over a span of 25 years! He also brought me a ton of paper work containing files for me to read personally to the States that we discussed over a beer. I was taken aback to see over 300 UFO sightings for 1967, with a huge surge in late October of that year. Far too much information to fully ingest never mind include in this book! However he has asked me to comment on some of the interesting ones.

They included a sighting in Wales, a place that I am familiar with having spent many vacations climbing some of its lofty peaks.

This related to a Close Encounter by a local man, Ernie, who was out walking at night time when he was confronted by a "... *large, black, silent mass, pulsating with lights, hovering above the ground accompanied by a horrible smell – like a mixture of burning rubber and something rotting, trees were swaying at the side of the road. A lorry, pulled up its lights extinguishing so I jumped into it and saw the driver, who seemed mesmerized by the sight of this 'mass'.*

He kept shouting, 'What's that?' It then banked over to the left and took up a position over a nearby house. I asked the driver (who was very frightened) to drop me back home – which he did. When I arrived home, my mother took one look at me and asked if I had seen a ghost! A short time later, after feeling sick, I noticed this rash all over my body, and had swollen eyes. I was taken to Ruthin Hospital by my mother, where the doctor examined me and suggested the allergy may have been caused by diesel, although I now believe my symptoms were caused by exposure to the fields of energy surrounding the UFO. Furthermore, I still suffer occasionally with a rash on my chest". Another casualty of phenomena which we are told doesn't exist!

John interviewed him at the home of Margaret Fry – author –

in Abergele, North Wales, now in her 90s (2020), some years ago. Margaret is one of those forgotten heroes of the UFO cause. Her experience goes back to 1955 when as a young housewife she and a number of other witnesses witnessed the near landing of a saucer-shaped object in Kent. I applaud her dedication and commitment, still ongoing at 93!

Lessons that were learned!

On one of my early trips to Wales, we (my daughter and I) stayed at a bed and breakfast. On the first night after climbing I went to the shared bath for a shower. You can imagine my surprise when I came out of the shower to find no towels. I finally dried on the bath mat. I went downstairs to inquire with Mrs Sutherland and was told I was supposed to bring my own towels. A lesson well learned. I will say she was a good host and her cooking was great.

On another occasion we rented a stone cottage in Capel Curig. It turned cold so I foraged and found a bag of coal in the shed. We got the stove going and all was well until my daughter turned on her hair dryer. Suddenly all the lights went out. I accused her of blowing a fuse only to discover the electricity was metered and required coins. Quick trip to the local pub solved that problem. Upon returning home I got a bill for the coal we used. Another lesson learned.

Letter intercepted or lost?

It's no surprise to read about that a letter sent to Washington DC, by a Reading man, who tells of seeing something without wings or propellers moving over the Royal Ordnance factory – a serious matter which should have been treated with concern – went missing! If that is what happened well the authorities obviously felt it was easier not to comment.

Waves of sightings

Why do such 'surges' of UFO activity take place? The dominant factors that create this situation are of course like the UFOs themselves – frustratingly unknown. The background to the sightings reported over England and some from the States is familiar in description and behaviour from the previous and following years. Over the years there have been reports involving UFOs and vehicle interference, ranging from dimming lights and spluttering engines at one end of the scale, to a complete breakdown at the other. As far as the reported displays of lights moving around the sky, which appear to form a backcloth to the phenomena itself – are we looking at one central light moving at incredible speeds creating an optical illusion of multiple objects? Which, by the way, sometimes appears to precede the appearance of what many refer to as a 'craft' or something structured, whose presence inhibits understanding. Could those movements in the sky be a way of energizing themselves, in order to achieve the metamorphosis from swirling lights to something apparently far more structured? Why the apparent interest in nuclear/military installations?

From my own personal point of view I'm naturally curious about a similar incident that occurred over another USAF base, this time in Berkshire, at RAF Welford. This one involved disc-shaped objects overflying the base and took place in early December 1967. Then seen again on the 25th and 26th of December 1967. Incredibly there was also a sighting of a cigar-shaped UFO which ejected a 'disc' on the 27th of December over Yarmouth on the Isle of Wight. Reading eye witness accounts like this brings it all home again to me.

I was a little perturbed to read in the files, many with signed statements, what lorry driver Mr. Carl Farlow encountered in November 1967 – 13 years before our UFO sighting in Suffolk. This involved other witnesses and the presence of this object inflicted severe damage to the electrics of the lorry which Carl was driving through Hampshire, UK. John told me that he was lucky to interview Carl, who was very reluctant, after pointing out the amount of ridicule he had faced after reporting it and the inaccuracies published by the media about the incident. Here is a short passage which the reader will find of interest. No doubt should any of the readers wish to find out more – contact John.

Carl was astounded to discover the four 6 volt batteries were dry. *"Every fuse had blown. It needed a new starter dynamo and wiring harness. When I drove past the scene, the next day, I noticed they were putting chippings onto a newly covered strip of tarmac by using a black tar barrel, mounted on a trolley, traffic being restricted to one lane, with a 'stop and go' board in operation. There was a bulldozer doing something to the ground at the side of the road, with workmen washing down the telephone box."*

During a visit to the States to see his son, Carl met Michael Wallace, from NASA – Engineer of Apollo Space Missions – by now feeling dissatisfied with the number of inaccurate accounts published of his sighting, over the years. *"I just wanted to set the record straight. I know what I saw to this day. It wasn't ball lighting or anything I could explain. I can't say it was any alien spaceship. All I know is what I saw. The 'Mickey taking' that went with it was unbelievable. I thought long and hard before I even spoke to anybody. There have been many things published about it. Why it's stirred up so much interest I don't know."* Carl received a visit from two men, who showed him their ID, announcing themselves as MOD Officials – one of them, Mr. Perks, (The MOD deny they had anyone of that name serving with them) – asked him a number of questions about what had taken place. Carl: *"The one never said a word; the other did all the talking. He was the youngest and had a grey briefcase. After 15-20 minutes, I'd had enough. I was tired, with lack of sleep. I told them to leave, suggesting if they wanted more to check with the police, who had taken my statement."* End of quote. Fortunately we now have the truthful version of events and I'm sorry to hear that Carl has since passed away. My condolences to Sue his wife, – who has been in contact with John over the years.

At Heathrow airport, London, employee Mr. Percy Grieg sighted a Saturn shaped object over the site. When he contacted the Control Tower they denied all knowledge. John also interviewed Brigitte Kelly and spoke to her on a number of occasions when she was living in the Shropshire area about what she endured while driving home. He found her account very genuine – without embellishment and similar in event to so many others that he has come across over the years. I can only praise the courage of people like Brigitte Kelly who, like so many others, just want to tell about something highly extraordinary and devastating which can change your life and attitude towards a subject which they had no interest in before because, of course, such things don't exist. Problem is they do! These people are 'Victims' of something so out of their everyday comfort zone are looking for support and empathy, and don't realise that they're not the only ones. The problem is that when they write/report it to the MOD they receive a standard letter – which is non committal. Often they then contact a UFO organisation and are then at the mercy of individual belief systems. What puzzles us is why people like Brigitte and others, whose stories are outlined here, report medical anomalies after the event and complain about unusual marks found on the skin – matters that I have discussed with John but neither of us know why this happens and for what purpose – if there is one – it's disturbing to say the least.

Once a sceptic – now a believer!

Once I would have questioned reports like this wondering if they were figments of a vivid imagination or seeking self attention; a trait of behaviour which appears more in common with many of the so-called UFO researchers who treat this business as a commercial enterprise rather than wishing to document some amazing experiences which have been brought to my attention over the years during the many lectures I have given both in the States and in the UK.

THE HALT PERSPECTIVE 2

Correlations of UFO activity on Earth when Mars is at its closest?

The fact that there was such a heavy rise in UFO activity, especially during October 1967, makes interesting reading, especially taking into consideration forecasts of such by Dr. Olavo T. Fontes, of Rio de Janeiro – a researcher of the UFO phenomena – who predicted correctly the autumn of 1967 would record more UFO sightings than any previous period in the 20-year history. This was due to UFO 'waves' occurring in *"cycles of every 26 months, with a peak period every five years"*, and that these 'two' would merge in late 1967 – Britain and Canada being selected as most likely to experience rises in UFO activity. Why that situation arises I have no idea – others claim that UFO activity increases when Mars is at it's nearest, but nobody can actually prove conclusively the association between rises in activity and other criteria.

Not surprisingly given the huge increase of UFO activity during 1967, the MOD tried to downplay sightings, as we can see from official documents. What concerns me as a United States Air Force Officer, who served his country for many years and witnessed for himself UFO activity close to the Rendlesham Forest, Suffolk, next to RAF Woodbridge airbase in December 1980 – is why all of this has been more or less forgotten and why the media publishers pour scorn on those that continue to come forward to this present day? We can see the many number of occasions when RAF aircraft are seen following reports of UFOs by the public – but rarely confirmation by the MOD or the military that these actions were sanctioned as a result of incursions into British and American airspace by unidentified flying objects.

In fact there have been a number of denials, which is of course official policy about something which doesn't exist – when, of course, it undoubtedly does! The attached document dated November 1967, which has been declassified summarises the attitude of the authorities towards the UFO subject!

Confidential Police reports 'Not in the interests of the Public to report'!

The Rt. Hon. Harold Wilson, OBE, PC, MP – Prime Minister of England

In July 1967, the Prime Minister of Great Britain was taxed about the wider implications relating to the mass of reported sightings of things which didn't fit into the parameters of what our ordinary citizens expect to see flying in our air space. The PM fobbed off the question by falling back on the old excuse that these are representative of natural phenomena – such as balloons, aircraft etc, or that the information was inadequate for investigation! None of this should be happening but it has – and it still continues to do so!

However The Rt. Hon. Harold Wilson, OBE, PC,

THE HALT PERSPECTIVE 2

MP – then Prime Minister of the United Kingdom, did write to one researcher (stating what is fairly obvious) quote: "*As reports of these objects (UFOs) continue to appear from many parts of the world, it is quite understandable that there should be a growing interest in seeing some responsible effort made to seek explanations of these phenomena.*" So on the one hand the PM declines to enter into any 'official investigation' but oddly, writes to one researcher acknowledging that there should be a "*responsible effort made*" If one takes into consideration the mass of sightings for this year and contrast the figures stated by the MOD who officially stated that they had received only THREE reports of UFOs seen during April 1967, two of which were satellites and one celestial object, – it's obvious there is something wrong with the statistics! The reality as the reader can see is completely different! This is the same Prime Minister who received a letter from a London man in August 1966, who was so affected by what he saw from the family home one evening, from which he suffered slight burns as a result of the experience, which on that occasion, he failed to acknowledge?

Over the years I've spoken to so many people from all walks of life that have witnessed extraordinary incidents some similar to what I saw, some of them have been police officers, pilots and members of the public who I judge as genuine. Many of them ask me what I think they are and where they come from. Answer: I don't know – who does?

The MOD stated that during the period of May 1967, they received a total of 15 reports, of which they judged four to be satellites, one a celestial object, one a balloon, three aircraft, one miscellaneous and four unidentified (insufficient information), but nothing earmarked for investigation. If we examine as an example reports from the public for that particular month, they include a black '*boomerang*'-shaped object, a black flying '*disc*', a *large globe showing three lights,* a '*disc*' over the London area, a '*dome-shaped object*, a '*flying saucer*'-shaped object, objects showing bars of lights and more – if someone knows the answer, please let us know!

When you witness the inexplicable it changes one's outlook on life – it certainly changed mine. I mentioned seeing an object like an '*eye*' looking down on me while I was out in Rendlesham Forest in December 1980, and couldn't help but contrast the account given by witness Ronald Martino whose account I've read. He tells of seeing an amber ball of light drop down and hover over a nearby field. I presume that there might have been an alert at the nearby RAF base because according to Ronald an RAF jet fighter was seen to circle overhead. Indicating the seriousness with which such reports are received by the Air Force – could it have been tracked on radar?

John asked me about my knowledge of a Colonel Robin Olds who left Ubon, Thailand (8th Tactical Fighter Wing) several days before I got there. He set the wrong example and the officers were out of

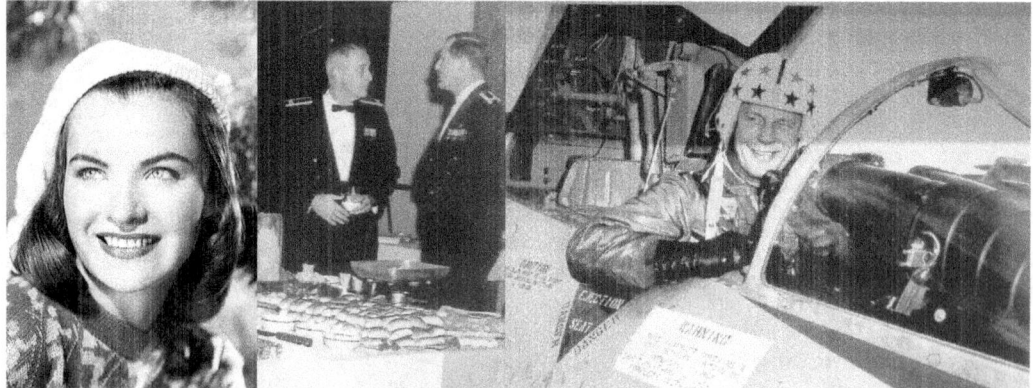

Ella Raines • Robin Olds (right), Bentwaters Officer Club • Robin Olds sitting in the cockpit of a 81st TFW F-101 Voodoo

THE HALT PERSPECTIVE 2

control. He was a larger-than-life character and I was told one of his games was riding his motorcycle through the Officers Club with several Thai girls of, shall we say 'ill repute', hanging on the back. His deputy was just as bad. He (Olds) returned to the States and caused a lot of problems for his movie star wife Ella Raines, who later divorced him. He became the Commandant of the AF Academy and continually crossed those above. I don't know anything about his alleged UFO experiences but what he described sounds like a jettisoned external fuel tank to me.

Sightings of strange aerials objects continued to make their presence known in the following year of 1968 a multitude of reports of *'cigar 'shaped objects,* and *'triangular ones'* reported in a variety of colours which the media continued to treat generally with humour. How on earth can they still adopt this policy NOW, given the depth of the enormous number of reports covered in this book (and so many hundreds of others) from ordinary citizens who just want answers.

UFO sightings reported to me personally from the UK

In December 2010, Penney Poyzer living in Nottingham, UK emailed me about what she had seen in July 1969 while, as a child growing up in Britannia Road, Ipswich Suffolk . . . *"I remember seeing three UFOs flying in formation as dusk fell in the summer of July 1969. There were ten of us kids that saw it move over in an arc heading in an east to west direction. It stopped overhead for what seemed like ages but was probably only 20 seconds. Then as swift as they came they left on the same trajectory, completely silent showing no signs on any propulsion. We all ran home and told our parents who rang the Police. The next day we had a visit from two men in plain clothes who asked us what we had seen. I don't think they were police officers but from the Air Ministry. Although our stories were the same, our parents were told that it was probably the result of over developed imagination. I have never forgotten the sense of shame in not being believed and anger at feeling so disempowered – I can't explain it to this day."*

In 2018 John Hanson spoke to Penney after reading about the event that I had been involved in – which had triggered off her own memory of the incident. She asked him to pass on the following message to me. *"Dear Colonel Halt, I do hope that you remain in good health, I am sure you have extraordinary and ordinary memories of Suffolk but hope that they are very happy. I went out with a couple of chaps from Bentwaters, they were great company and I am still in touch with one of them. Everybody seems to hold nothing but the fondest memories of the bases and as a Suffolk Gal that makes me proud... I never had the pleasure of meeting you but the respect and affection in which you were held by your personnel I am sure remains."* (Penny has presented *'No Waste Like Home'* a *BBC 2* eight-part series, first screened on the 18th of August 2006.)

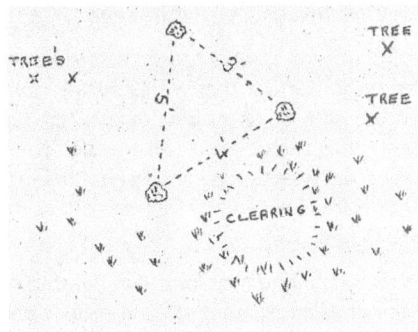

An incident from Bridgnorth, Shropshire involving a teacher who was out walking the dog when she came across an object in a nearby field supported on three legs, with what

appeared to be figures moving around on the ground caught my attention, not that I'm giving any credibility to the incident, which seems genuine enough, but the marks left behind may well correspond roughly with what I myself and others saw following the UFO sighting in December 1980. These were 9.8 feet across x 3 inches – compared to the ones found at Bridgnorth that were around 9 feet x12 x15 feet, forming a triangle.

Another report from Barry Preece, who contacted John in 2017, asking him to forward his sighting of what he saw to me while living at Lowestoft approximately two years before the incident I was involved in. Barry: *"I've never talked about it as I've never seen anything like it since. I would have been around 12/13 years old at the time, but strangely enough I can remember the encounter as if it happened yesterday. One evening, I was with my friend – Andrew, walking over to his house, so he could get some money for some chips, when we noticed a group of three lads around eight to ten years old looking up at the rooftops, transfixed. I thought they might have lost their ball or something, until one of lads pointed between the rooftops into the sky. I saw a tiny metallic 'disc' that seemed to be slightly shaking; it was still light at this time but getting darker by the minute. The object stood in one place for around a minute, until it flew off like a blip, incredibly fast – it was a blink … then gone – but the story doesn't end there! I lived in a little terraced house in Sudbury Cottages, off Bevan Street – you have to walk down an open alleyway to get to it.*

On our way back it was dark. When this 'ball of light' came over a wall and headed straight towards us. It was totally controlled – definitely not a balloon or anything man-made; it was glowing red and orange in colour and had no noise to it whatsoever. It stopped a foot above our heads and pulsated; it was spellbinding. We were just speechless, as we were face-to-face with something that we both knew wasn't from this planet. I'm sure it was reading my thoughts, as the moment I contemplated touching this, it shot off like a bullet, heading towards the back of these other terraced houses. I thought it was going to crash straight into the side of this house, when it shot up vertically – higher and higher into the night sky. As it went up, another object came across towards the 'ball of light'; they joined together – then shot off again, and that was that! It was just an incredible experience that I feel privileged to have experienced, but still wonder what the hell I had seen. I always look up into the night sky now and hope that I get another chance to see something."

Inexplicable events like this are very intriguing but the source of frustration to witnesses, who initially look for a rational explanation, then find out to their dismay there isn't one.

While lights in the sky could be anything – objects resembling what appears to be craft not constructed by human hands is another matter entirely. Reminds me of the incident which happened to the runner guy way back in 1938. John has many others like this. Is there a connection with the UFO phenomena, are they just a deviation of the same source, are they a form of intelligence? I wish I knew.

I would never have guessed that there was so much UFO activity during these years – a matter of just over a decade before we had our own experiences. It's important that we allow the public the opportunity to see just how much of it went on during the early to latter part of the 20th Century, because people have the right to know the extent of what was seen by our citizens, not only in the United States but by the British Public, whom I regard with great affection having spent time in Suffolk as Deputy Base Commander of RAF Bentwaters/Woodbridge and made many friends both at the time and afterwards during further visits to England and also to Wales.

What Dr Joseph Allen Hynek said in 1971 shows that little has changed (not for trying I hasten to add). Quote: Of practical research Dr Hynek said: *"I've gone to damn many meetings, which turn out to be nothing but 'coffee clutches'; we just sit and talk about it and nobody does anything."*

PART 2

COLONEL CHARLES IRWIN HALT
A MAN OF IMPECCABLE CHARACTER!

JOHN: It's an appropriate moment to pay our respects to a man who I now look on as a friend that is well respected within the community of UFO research and investigation, both here and in the United States. He is in constant demand as a speaker because he *tells it how it was*, not how others perceive it to have been, many of whom weren't even there!

CHARLES: It's time to take a break from the never-ending rush of all manner of strange craft seen in the skies of our planet – 99.9% of which can be explained or so we are led to believe by those sceptics in the scientific domain, who try to convince us that they are top secret covert aircraft, mind control programs, and more recently experiments using holograms, who knows? What we do know is that there are undeniable similarities in behaviour, not so much with what I saw, but with so many other reports, that have been brought to the attention of the public by responsible people whose accounts have never been explained by the authorities. **Why is that one may wonder?**

Declassified document of interest!

In a declassified CID document released in 2001 December 1980 – CIA – RDp96-607890010014200013 May 1988, Maxwell AFB, **Colonel John B Alexander** US Army authorised an article in *Military Review* entitled, *The New Mental Background 'Beam Me Up Spock'*. Air War College/Air University Dolan M McKelvy LT Colonel USAF 'Psychic warfare exploring the mind frontier'. A research report submitted to the faculty in fulfilment of the research requirement Maxwell unlocking mental capabilities to create an entirely new battlefield dimension which if ignored pose a threat to self and country, more serious than nuclear weapons . . . This top secret project encompassed the arts of faith healing, dowsing and remote control/viewing, with a view to using psychic capabilities in a variety of subjects including military use. In this article he challenged the imagination of his readers when he stated, to be more specific there are weapons systems that operate on the power of the mind and whose lethal capacity has already been demonstrated. He discussed psychotropic weaponry and provided eye opening unclassified information on both Soviet and American research into para-psychological phenomena. There is much more including experiments with rats and frogs in laboratory conditions, whose demise were caused by psychic powers to harm sicken or kill.

THE HALT PERSPECTIVE 2

Frightening stuff

But to my knowledge projected holograms cannot leave marks in the soil or create all manner of medical ailments to those unfortunate enough to encounter these object at close range, which goes way back before man could even fly!

We now leave the 1960's, a tremendous decade that saw activity peak in 1967, which appears to have eased off as we entered the 1970s before slowly building up – to a crescendo in 1977, then appearing to ease off over the next few years. The answer to all of this continues to elude us all to the present day! Often I wonder if the activity, generally measured by its incursions into our atmosphere or time continuum, and recorded by so many people over the years is constant but due to certain criteria being met – what those conditions are, well that's another 64 million dollar question – the answer is of course speculative. We are not dealing with ambiguous reports of lights in the sky, from a fair distance away no matter how strange they perform, but what appears to be structured craft. Not that there may necessarily be any difference between the two, judging from the number of occasions when following a display of '**luminous phenomena**' seen darting all over the sky, often described as carrying out what appears to be manoeuvres – then on occasion – witnesses have reported the arrival of what appears to be a structured object.

I'm just a guy that merely wishes to ensure the FACTS are given rather than allowing the fictional conglomerate of continual explanations put forward to explain what it was that happened over those fateful nights in December 1980 by mostly, people that weren't even there!

Those that were – well that is, of course, another part of the story which needs to be dealt with accordingly, as recently I still continue to come under further criticism as to my role in what occurred now 40 years ago by people such as Jim Penniston and Gary Osbourne in their latest book, which will be discussed further on.

Of course they're not the only ones – they join an ever-increasing number of others who also seek to cloud the judgement of what actually happened! Is it because the incident attracts so much attention, now in its 40th year? The irony here is that it's a 'Catch 22' situation: on the one hand, as you can see for yourselves in this book leading up to and including the 1980 period, we weren't the only ones to see inexplicable objects in the sky and (as has been alleged) objects on the ground. On the other the continuing media's attention has created a myth. *(Encyclopaedia: Traditional story especially one covering the early history of a people or explaining a natural or social phenomenon, and typically involving supernatural beings or events).*

I've even climbed mountains!

I'm not just about Rendlesham that only fills a tiny part of my life. As some of you know I'm an accomplished mountaineer and a man that has enjoyed a career-filled life. It's ironic that I nearly didn't join the USAF – then when I did I wasn't actually posted to England! But fate decreed otherwise and I ended up holding senior posts in Washington. Now things are a little more quiet since retirement . . . while I like to get up early and exercise the family dog Caesar! Catch up with family and get on with life, the interest in this incident, now 40 years ago, never stops . . . judging from the constant emails I get from folk who want to discuss what took place and my part in it!

People ask me: 'What you do think it was like for the men to serve under you Colonel?' Answers I can't give, but I'd like to think that I was fair and very much a 'hands on' with the men that I worked with. I was the sort of man that liked to get things done quietly and with a minimum of fuss, rather than the opposite.

THE HALT PERSPECTIVE 2

I will continue to fight my 'corner' to the bitter end to ensure that history records my determination to ensure that the FACTS – not FICTION about what happened outside the air base while as Deputy Base Commander – should be preserved. This book and my many talks, both in England and the United States, are, of course, one way of doing it. At the risk of repeating myself, I am passionate about ensuring folks should see the true picture! How can you ignore the important evidence of what is being published in this book, showing that so many people (including myself) can't be mistaken and want answers? When John came over here he took some photos of the numerous citations and awards which adorn my wall showing, if nothing else, that I was respected for being a Colonel that cares for his men!

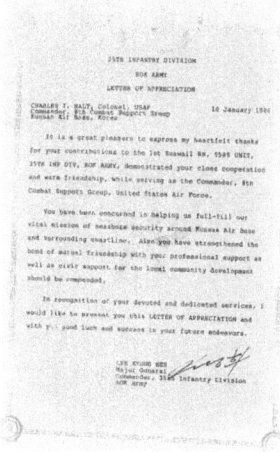

THE HALT PERSPECTIVE 2

LT COL C. HALT
HONORARY ADVISOR
TO THE ENLISTED WIVES CLUB
RAF BENTWATERS 1983

THE HALT PERSPECTIVE 2

THE HALT PERSPECTIVE 2

THE HALT PERSPECTIVE 2

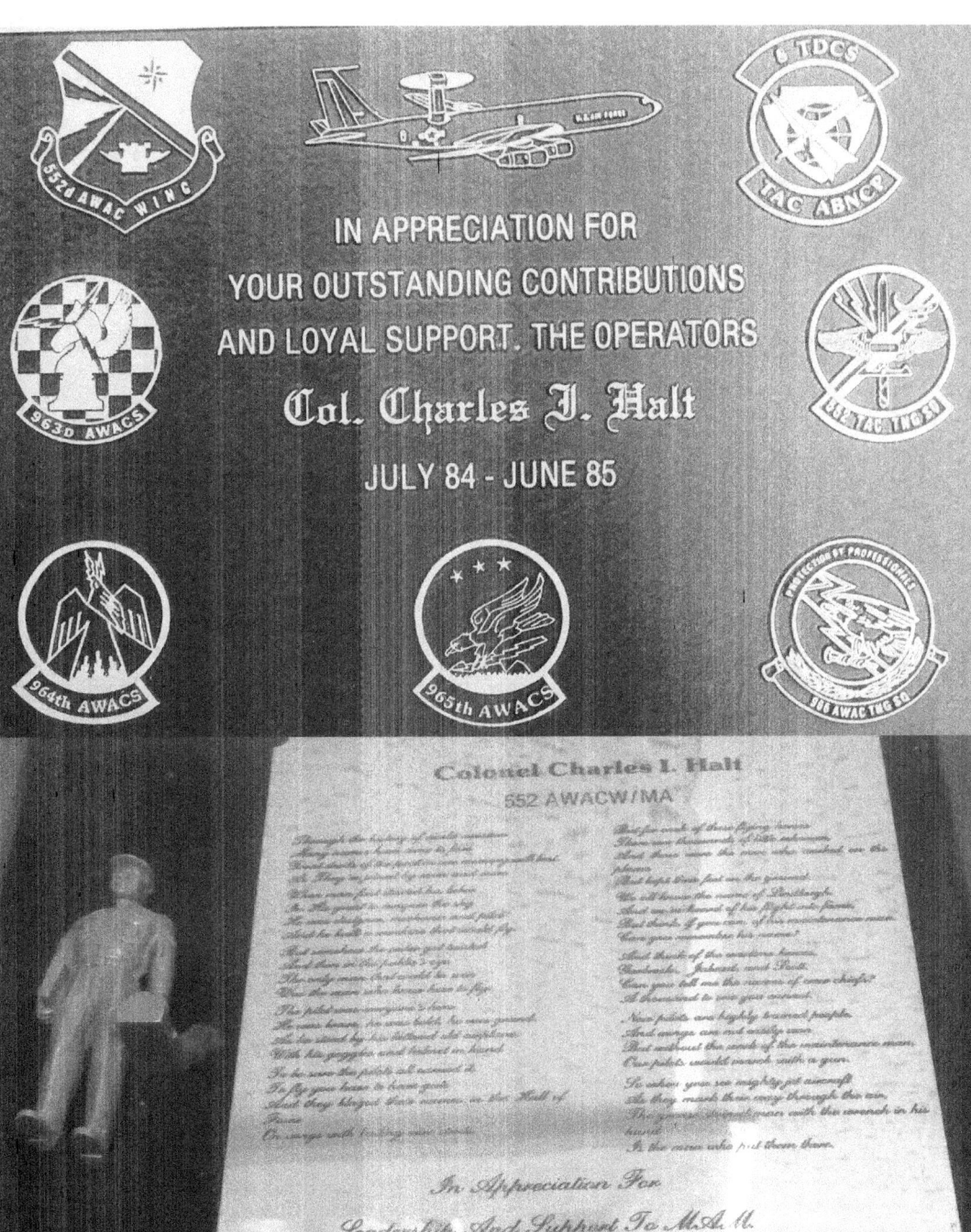

THE HALT PERSPECTIVE 2

THE HALT PERSPECTIVE 2

JOHN HANSON ON PATROL

– EARLY DAYS AS A BEAT COP!

WE will now continue our voyage of discovery through in the main the now unforgotten period of history, half a century ago. But before we do that I'm going to take a pause and reflect those now halcyon days of 1966 when I was a young British Police Constable initially walking the beat in south Birmingham from Sparkhill Police Station with four years experience, '*shaking hands with door knobs*' to ensure premises were safe under a starlight sky, with the odd hooting and foxes running across the now deserted streets. The joys and pain of trudging a few miles before stopping at the West Midlands boundary marked by the arrival of Robin Hood Police station for a cup of tea and natter with the office man, was part and parcel of working nights – before the issue of personal radios!

A year later I was riding a Police Velocette (motorcycle) through the leafy suburbs of Hall Green, wearing a long cape. A short time later I undertook a driving course and ended up driving a panda car, an Austin A40, equipped with two tone horns and blue light. These were exciting days as you can imagine – especially during the quiet period of a set of nights, when parked up in the car trying to ward off sleep, the radio would then crackle into life reporting a 'break in' or stolen car. The adrenalin kicked in and excitement mounted.

Looking back I wouldn't have changed a thing! One incident out of so many comes to notice. At around 4.30am a report came in about a bakery shop being entered and the contents of the safe stolen. I decided to respond slowly, rather than quickly and instead of racing to the scene, I waited at a junction. The suspect car went rushing past and I gave chase. During a 'blue lighting' journey which lasted a couple of hours, I managed to stop the car and arrested the driver – a very large, strong man – and handcuffed him. "*One in custody control.*" I then joined the CID which in those days was measured on ones drink capacity and being interested in catching criminals! I was not a big drinker and have always been amazed at some officers' capacity to imbibe such copious amounts! I spent the middle to the end of my career in the CID, which if nothing else makes one scrutinise most things, instead of accepting them carte blanch.

I had no interest in UFOs – such things couldn't possibly exist – until an incident in January 1995 sparked off my interest, involving Birmingham police officers who were directed to a report of a UFO seen. The rest is history.

THE HALT PERSPECTIVE 2

John Hanson ... From the days 'on the beat'

UK Spotlight on 1970 – Over 100 sightings recorded for this year!

Reported sightings included objects in a variety of shapes – cigar, triangular, boomerang, pulsing orange objects, rotating spheres, yellow discs, diamond, 'Mexican hat', three objects, 'chandelier', square objects, red orange flashing lights, shining discs, objects sighted over airports, UFO activity around transmission masts. Of interest: Dr. Joseph Allen Hynek visited the UK for a covert meeting.

Selected sighting – Spring 1970 – Were RAF jets scrambled?

David Bryant – a retired Royal Navy helicopter pilot – was stood at a bus stop in Hanging Hill Lane, Hutton, Middlesex, just before dawn, in spring 1970, waiting for a bus to arrive. *"It was still dark but with a hint of sunrise. Suddenly, three huge globes, scintillating with light, passed overhead at a height of about a thousand feet. I shouted out to a group of women waiting alongside me, pointing upwards into the sky. Much to my surprise, some of them became hysterical. A few minutes later, two RAF English Electric Lightning jets thundered across the sky, following the same path taken by the UFOs."* It is a matter that still causes him puzzlement, despite the passing of years. Were the aircraft scrambled to intercept the UFOs, or was it a coincidence

David Bryant with astronaut Al Bean

that they were in the locality? David – who is also a retired teacher, wildlife photographer and rock guitarist – and his charming wife, Linda, who have met many of the US and Russian Astronauts through their 'Space Rocks' business, helped us organise a visit by retired Colonel Charles Halt (former Deputy Base Commander at RAF Bentwaters/Woodbridge) to Woodbridge, Suffolk, in July 2015. David has published four books under *Heathland Books*, which range from ghosts, religious apparitions to evolution, planetary astronomy and the Apollo missions. Did the Americans go to the Moon? Ask David Bryant!

Selected sighting – Nurse reports UFO over Hospital Wisconsin

During the early hours of the morning, a nurse's assistant at the Memorial Hospital, received a call at 4am, 5th October 1970, from a patient. She made her way to one of the three bed wards and asked the man who was sat on the edge of the bed what he wanted. He told her that he had seen some monkeys swinging from trees and also sitting on the window ledge. *"I didn't bother looking out of the window and told him to go back to sleep; he had rung the bell off and on for a long time and each time I answered it. The curtains were closed but he could have been looking outside before I came in. I settled the patient back down in bed. As I was doing so, I saw a bright light coming through the sides of the curtains. I went to the window and opened the drapes and immediately saw a pulsating balloon-like object, about a hundred feet long by over 30 feet in diameter, a diffused yellow-green, showing a stream of intense white light protruding from the object. I was shocked and startled, and stood there paralysed for about five minutes."* It then started to move upwards and, as it did so, the colour changed to an orange glow around the outer edge of the object. By this time she had come to her senses and went to fetch another nurse, all that remained was a streak of fading light. She never gave it another thought, until speaking to a UFO investigator – Mr A.J. Andropolis, of Sturgeon Bay, who told her about the incident at Sutton Farm, near Kelly, Kentucky, and wondered if there was any connection. **(Source:** *APRO Bulletin*/**Kathleen Smith,** *UFOLOG***)**

UK Spotlight on 1971 – Over 160 sightings recorded for this year!

They included objects in a variety of shapes, such as Bowl, Cigar, Three objects/lights, Flying Cross, Diamond, five sided, saucer, 'L' shaped, and square. On the ground people reported seeing 'Monsters' strange figures and not unsurprisingly three scorch marks were found in a field after a landed object, took off.

Selected sighting – Close encounter with UFO over Maryland

Between 7.30pm and 8pm, 21st January 1971, Mr Elvis Arnold (20), and his wife Sharon and her sister Lynn Holding (16), were driving north on Oldfield Point Road, about three miles south of Elkton, Maryland. Mr Arnold sighted a 'light' in the sky and joked *"There's a flying saucer".* They were stunned when the object moved to the left of them and appeared to halt over trees. Mr Arnold instructed his wife to stop the car; as she did so the object veered away in the direction of Elkton, heading westwards over Route 40. The family decided to give chase and then saw another object in the northern sky, which met up with the first one over a farmer's field. After a minute or two the second one flew away towards Elkton and was out of sight. The first UFO came back towards the car, crossed over the road just ahead of them, and halted over a farmer's field 60 yards away.

THE HALT PERSPECTIVE 2

The couple switched off the lights and engine, and Mr Arnold got out, by which time it was at 70 degrees to the horizontal, allowing him to see: *"…something the size of a Piper Cub – dull in colour, grey not shiny, shaped like an aircraft. It had a fuselage and slight swept-back wings placed in normal airplane position, except it had no tail assembly. At the front end was a very large and very bright white searchlight where the nose of an airplane would be. On the underneath was a circle or cluster of lights, the outer one being plain white, with flashing red lights in the middle. The latter blinked constantly and increased the pulsing as the object moved or picked up speed. I heard a sound like the hum of a muffled generator. When it changed direction it merely pivoted rather than banking as an aircraft would do."*

The entire sighting lasted between 15-20 minutes. Shortly afterwards it flew off towards the direction of Elkton, circled the area before heading south-east, and disappeared from sight. **(Source: *APRO Bulletin*)**

Selected sighting – RAF tracked 35 UFOs on radar – warned to keep quiet!

RAF Wing Commander Turner, who was awarded an MBE in 1983, was guest speaker in October 2007, at the *Close Encounters* conference in Pontefract, West Yorkshire, organised by Philip Mantle, of *UFO Data* magazine, who said: *"His testimony is remarkable."* In summer of 1971, RAF Air Traffic Control officer Alan Turner was the duty military supervisor at RAF Sopley, a joint military/civil air traffic control radar unit. He said: *"I saw a series of radar blips, one at a time, travelling south-east, at regular six or seven-mile intervals, climbing fast for about 40 miles, before disappearing. I calculated their height at 3,000 feet, climbing to 'in excess of 60,000 feet' – the instrument wouldn't read any higher. I knew I was not watching military aircraft. The only craft with that rate of climb were supersonic 'Lightnings', but they wouldn't have held such perfect formation. They're also noisy."*  The phenomenon was also witnessed by four civil and six military controllers. Afterwards, everyone had to write a report. Wing Commander Turner says six military radars in southern England picked up the craft, as did operators at Heathrow. He also instructed a 'Canberra' aircraft, returning from Germany, to turn around and investigate. *"There was something about a quarter-mile away from him which, to quote him, was 'climbing like the clappers', but he didn't see anything really, nor did his crew."* Wing Commander Turner plotted the course of the UFOs. They travelled from near Marlborough, in Wiltshire, to near Alton, Hampshire, before disappearing. He said, a few days later, that they were interviewed by **two anonymous men and told not to talk about the incident.** He kept quiet until 11 years ago. *"They were unidentified, they were flying, and they were objects. I've got to keep an open mind. It's arrogant to believe that we're the only ones in this universe."*

UK Spotlight on 1972 – Over 110 sightings recorded for this year!

They included objects in a variety of shapes, such as bowl, cigar, three objects/lights, flying cross, diamond, five-sided, saucer, 'L'-shaped, and square. On the ground people reported seeing 'monsters', strange figures and not unsurprisingly three scorch marks were found in a field after a landed object took off. In addition two cases we investigated, apparently judged very genuine in our opinion related to objects sighted from the residents houses, which were seen to contain what appeared to be humanoid or alien figures!

THE HALT PERSPECTIVE 2

Selected sighting – USAF scrambles Fighter Jets-ordered to destroy UFO!

At 6.00am on the 14th September 1972, a UFO was detected by USAF radar in Southern Florida. This led to two military jets being scrambled into the pre-dawn skies by the North American Air Defense Command, after a glowing circular object appeared on the radar scopes? The fighters were dispatched from Homestead Air Force base, south of Miami, and ordered to use their onboard radar systems to search for the UFO. According to an Air Force spokesman, who was later interviewed, he said: *"If it had proved hostile, we would have destroyed it."* Although no trace was found, one of the Pilots – Major Gerald Smith – confirmed there was definitely something in the sky over the City: *"We were getting height cuts from two different military installations."* Enquiries revealed the object had first shown up at 4.20am and was attributed as being a *'hard target'* by FAA Air Traffic Controller – Mr. A.W. Brown, while his associate – Mr. C.J Fox said: *"It was a good clear target."* Visual reports came in from witnesses on the ground, who described the object as: *"…being a silver/white in colour, and cigar-shaped."* Other reports told of strange lights – some blinking, others unusually bright over the County. Amazingly, the Air Force explained the incidents away as being weather phenomena, or Venus, which was exceptionally bright at that time of the year. **(Source: *UFO Investigator*, October 1972 – 'Jets scrambled to intercept UFO)**

UK Spotlight on 1973 – Over 70 sightings recorded for this year!

They included objects in a variety of shapes, similar to what has already been laid out in the previous years. In addition was a number of reports from RAF Alconbury involving claims of paranormal activity, strange figures seen on the runway, and a wolf-like humanoid who breached the perimeter fence, near to the where the nuclear weapons were stored – and was shot at by sentries, before making 'its' escape! Adjacent to the base was 'Monks' wood where up to the present date, strange figures resembling monks and ghostly apparitions have been reported from inside the Centre for Ecology and Hydrology.

Selected sighting – RAF pilots encounter UFO!

We spoke to ex-RAF Pilot, Jeremy Lane, who had served with 85 Squadron, flying Canberras, from West Raynham, having logged a total of 1,400 hours flying time, with two tours in Germany. He was on a night-time sortie from RAF Leuchars, together with other aircraft, on 2nd May 1973, flying north, to test the northern Radar Defences. After reaching an altitude of about 38,000ft, they noticed a strange sight ahead and above, completely stationary in the sky, resembling a Concorde aircraft in shape, with lights flashing around its perimeter, orientated in a North-South direction.

"I reported the sighting to the Radar Controller, who confirmed nothing was showing on Radar, but he had received other reports from earlier aircraft of a similar object. All of the crew on my flight deck could clearly see the vehicle. As we continued North, I climbed the aircraft with a view to being some 10,000ft higher on the southbound leg, which would give us an idea of whether the vehicle was close, or far away, and its apparent size, depending on how close it was to us. As we came south, the vehicle was still there. I again contacted the Radar operator, who confirmed fighters had been

scrambled to intercept, although the Radar had still not picked it up. The lights were still flashing and the orientation of the vehicle was still North-South, but the apparent size of the vehicle remained as it had been, suggesting it was at very high altitude. It was an incredibly clear night and from 46,000+ feet, we could see well into Northern Europe. At some point, as we approached the 'vehicle' from underneath, it became brilliant light and accelerated to the South at an incredible speed; within one to two seconds it had disappeared from view, travelling 500 to 800 miles."

When they landed back at Base, all the crews independently drew what they had seen. A report was submitted to Group Operations, as they understood there was no official channel for submitting reports of such nature, and that was the last they heard. On a subsequent visit to RAF Kinloss, on 25th June in the same year, Jeremy was discussing the incident with a friend of his – then flying Nimrods – when he was told: *"This was a frequent visitor, often seen by the pilots."*

Selected sighting – 'Orange mass' sweeps the sky with 'searchlights' over West Virginia

Another UFO incident that captured our attention took place, at 10.30pm, during the summer of 1973, and involved Mr James V. Coste (a banker from Hinton, West Virginia, and President of Hinton Television Cable Company) his wife, and a Mrs Oliver Porterfield and her husband – the principal at a local school. They were returning from dinner at a mountain resort along Greenbrier River Road, about 13 miles from Hinton, when a blinding light lit up the sky. Puzzled, they stopped the car. James – a former radio/radar engineer for the US Marine Air Corps in World War Two – said: *"We saw an object showing **four giant searchlights**, pointing upwards and moving in a circle."* His wife said: *"It looked to me as if the thing was searching the earth for a place to land, as it lit up the ground for several hundred feet in every direction."* Mrs Porterfield: *"I was just a little frightened. I couldn't believe my eyes, but there it was."* The group moved about hoping to get a better look at the object, which was described as a round '**orange mass', with shafts of light sweeping downwards from the bottom.** After observing it for approximately 15 minutes, the object then flew quickly away.

Selected sighting – US helicopter encounters dome-shaped UFO over Ohio

On this date, a four-man crew of an Army Reserve helicopter was flying ten miles east of Mansfield Air Force Base, Ohio, around 11pm, 18th October 1973 ,when they *"encountered a near mid-air collision with an unidentified flying object"*, according to the official report, signed and submitted by the crew after the incident. A full explanation for this terrifying UFO close encounter has never been offered and, to this day, the helicopter-UFO incident remains one of the most credible – and terrifying – in the history of the subject.

The commander of the helicopter Major Larry Coyne (35) and his crew – Staff Sergeant John Healy, First Lieutenant Arrigo Jezzi (at the controls) and Specialist Robert Yanasek – thought, at first, that the light on the horizon was a radio tower beacon."*We were flying along at about 2,500 feet, when the crew chief on the helicopter observed a red light on the east horizon. He then informed me that the light was closing on the helicopter, and that it was coming at us on a collision course. I looked to the right and observed that the object became bigger and the light became brighter, and I began to descend the helicopter toward the ground, to get out of the collision course path. We were descending and this object was like a missile locked onto the helicopter – only it came at us on a perpendicular angle, to hit us almost broadside. It looked like we were going to collide with it and we braced for impact,*

THE HALT PERSPECTIVE 2

and then I heard the crewmen in the back say, 'Look up!' and I observed this craft stopped directly in front of us – stopped – it was hovering, right over the helicopter!"

Further research by Jennie Zeidman, reveals further eyewitness testimony from a family on the ground. In addition, the exact location of the incident was about a mile and a half away to the west and the helicopter at lowest altitude and closest approach of the object was about 700 feet high, not 400 feet above the terrain as initially believed. The witnesses – a mother and four children – were returning from their rural home, following a visit to the grandmother in Mansfield. As they drove south, they observed a single steady 'red light' – brighter than a normal aircraft port wing light – which was flying south, *"like a jet, at medium altitude"*.

UK Spotlight on 1974 – Over 73 sightings recorded for this year!

They included objects in a variety of shapes, similar to what has already been laid out in the previous years. Now notable for the Berwyn Mountain incident, something that has been the subject of hundreds of newspaper articles over the years, involving claims of an alien spaceship and occupants recovered by the army! Wishful thinking! John Winston Lennon UFO sighting-UFO material found Harborne Birmingham.

Selected sighting – Animal mutilation in the United States

Following a spate of reports of animal mutilations, centred on Meeker County, Minnesota, NICAP researcher – Jack Bostract (who lived 100 miles away) went out to investigate. He discovered that Sheriff Mike Rogers had received a complaint from cattle owner Frank Schiefelbein, at North

THE HALT PERSPECTIVE 2

Kingston Township, on 1st December 1974, after discovering that one of his female Black Angus calves had been mutilated. Rogers drove out to the scene and examined for himself the deceased animal which was being examined by vet Dr. Nelson, who performed an autopsy and took samples which were later sent to the University of Minnesota, Veterinary School for further analysis. *"The lips of the animal had been cut off one inch above the nose to behind the rear of the left jaw bone. The tongue was cut out deep in the throat, and the jugular vein was slit. One cup of blood was found at the scene which indicated that the majority of the blood have been collected and moved from the scene. The edge of the left ear and the reproductive organs had been removed."* The location where this had happened showed a perfect circle, with no traces of footprints in the snow.

Selected sighting – Police Officer encounters strange 'globe' on Ben Nevis

Police Constable David Dawson, of the Strathclyde Police and his companion both veteran climbers were descending Ben Nevis after a gruelling climb lasting 16hours in the winter of 1974. The two men decided to stop and take a break at the Red Burn halfway down the Mountain. David, *"I was lying down exhausted, Kerr shouted out in an alarming tone,' look at that Dave' I forced myself up and looked outwards seeing an object the size of a full moon approaching, increasing in size as it grew closer. It was about the size of a double Decker bus, and silver all over making a noise like an electricity transformer moving at about 30mph, barely a hundred yards, just above the ground. I studied it trying to determine a regular shape or windows to it there were none, we watched as it headed towards Polldubh, where we lost sight of it"* **(Source: Personal Interview)**

Spotlight on 1975 – **Over 125 sightings recorded for this year!**

They included Crescent, saucer, red glowing orbs, rectangle, cylindrical, strange figures seen, a landing in Cornwall, and much more...

Selected sighting – Close Encounter with UFO, then threatened!

Just before 9pm in September 1975 Steven Smith a part time soldier from Queens Park Billericay Essex, was motorcycling along Wickford Road, near Burton on-Crouch, with two other friends, when he noticed two lights in his rear view mirror. After a few minutes had elapsed, without any sign of being overtaken, Steve shouted to Jackie his pillion passenger to take a look behind – one look at her horrified face, told him something was wrong, instinctively he took immediate action by slewing the machine into a ditch. *"Looking up I was astonished to see a bullet shaped object showing a single flashing light underneath pass silently over our heads moving southwards, I later reported this Incident to the Police and my regiment, and tried to forget about it until I received a visit from two plain clothes men, who identified themselves as military, they asked me to accompany them to my army base where I was interviewed, and warned in no uncertain terms the Incident hadn't happened"* A week after the event, he noticed the paint had began to peel off the tanks of the motorcycles, and told the Regiment what had happened, who replaced the tanks with new ones **(Source: Brenda Butler & Ron West)**

Selected sighting – Loring AFB, Maine ... UFO circles airbase

At 8.45pm, 27th October 1975, Sgt. Grover K. Eggleston, of the 2192nd Communications Squadron, was on duty at the tower when he received a call from the Command Post of an unknown aircraft reported. Six minutes later, while watching his radar screen, Eggleston noted the 'unknown' appeared to be circling approximately ten miles east-north-east of the base. Object disappears off radar screen – emergency situation declared

Forty minutes later the object suddenly disappeared from the screen, indicating either the object had landed, or dropped below the radar coverage. The Wing Commander arrived at the weapons storage area, seven minutes after the initial sighting was made. Immediately, other units of the 42nd Police began pouring into the area, security vehicles with blue flashing lights converging from all over the base.

Air Support requested

Through the Loring Command Post, the Wing Commander requested fighter coverage from the 21st NORAD Region at Hancock Field, New York, and the 22nd NORAD Region at North Bay, Ontario, Canada. However, fighter support was denied by both regions. The Wing Commander then increased local security posture and requested assistance from the Maine State Police in trying to identify the unknown craft, which they presumed was a helicopter. A call was made to local flight services for possible identification, without results. The 42nd Security Police conducted a sweep of the weapons storage perimeter inside and out. An additional sweep was made of the areas that the craft had flown over. All actions produced no results. The craft broke the circling pattern and began flying toward Grand Falls, New Brunswick, Canada. Radar contact was lost in the vicinity of Grand Falls, bearing 065 degrees, twelve miles from Loring. Canadian authorities were not notified. No further unusual events occurred throughout that night. Priority messages were sent to the National Military Command Center in Washington, D.C., the Chief of Staff of the US Air Force, the USAF Forward Operations Division at Fort Ritchie, Maryland, and Strategic Air Command headquarters at the 8th Air Force and the 45th Division, informing them of what had taken place. The base remained on a high state of alert for the rest of the night and into the early morning hours of 28th October.

UK Spotlight on 1976 – **Over 150 sightings recorded for this year!**

An increase in UFO activity from all over the United Kingdom, stretching in a great swathe across the Country that included Manchester, Aldridge, Banbury, Mildenhall, Sheerness, Southampton, and St Austell, in Cornwall, which was the scene of a number of 'Flying Saucer' sightings. They included an assortment of various shapes and sizes, and a number of reports of humanoid and alien figures seen.

Notable case – 6th January 1976 – Close Encounter at Stanford, Kentucky. Louise Smith, Mona Stafford and Elaine Thomas, were driving home to Liberty from a late dinner at the *Redwoods* restaurant, located five miles north of Stanford, when they encountered a saucer-shaped object. As a result of which they sustained, burning sensation to their hands and face a red mark on the backs of their necks, measuring about three inches long and one inch wide, with clearly defined edges, giving the appearance of a new burn before it blisters – burning and tearing of their eyes, case of conjunctivitis.

THE HALT PERSPECTIVE 2

Selected sighting – Close encounter with UFO – serious injuries caused!

A terrifying incident that happened involving 'Shelley' from Bolton, Lancashire, on the 23rd of January 1976, without doubt one of the strangest and disturbing UFO encounters ever brought to our attention, involving the appearance of a 'spinning metallic 'disc', ablaze with lights, flat on the top, with sloping sides, three lights and three legs, which swooped over her, while walking home past Rumworth Lodge Reservoir – causing a catalogue of various physical ailments. They included crumbled dental fillings, burn marks on her arm and side, nausea and vomiting, and the discovery of a strange purple rash on her neck and shoulders.

Selected sighting – UFO landing, figures seen Wisconsin!

At Egg Harbor, Door County, Wisconsin, Dean Anderson was cutting grass on a golf course under the bright full moon, at 3.30am, 11th July 1976 when he noticed two round 'discs' *"coming off the moon"* side by side. One flew off; the other dropped down and landed 200 yards away. A ladder appeared at the side and three 'figures' ran quickly down it, after which Anderson, heard *"pounding coming from under the 'ship', toward the back"*. A few minutes later, the 'figures' ran back up the ladder – which was hauled back in. The 'men' were five feet, eight inches, to six feet tall and very agile. Three landing 'balls' or spheres on the UFO left depressions two feet deep and 15 inches wide, 20 feet apart. The witness took photographs of these indentations. **(Source: Keta Steebs, *Sturgeon Bay Advocate*)**

Selected sighting – *Close Encounters of the Fourth Kind*

This Hollywood blockbuster film began in May 1976, and was released in November 1977. The film received numerous awards and nominations at the 50th Academy Awards, 32nd British Academy Film Awards, the 35th Golden Globe Awards, the Saturn Awards and has been widely acclaimed by the American Film Institute. In December 2007, it was deemed "culturally, historically, or aesthetically significant" by the United States Library of Congress and selected for preservation in the National Film Registry. Bizarrely it was alleged that while making the film a series of terrifying events occurred which was to change the lives of many of the cast and crew members. According to *The Enquirer*, who launched an investigation, a ghostly presence frightened Steven Spielberg and his two associates, forcing them to flee from the hotel where they were staying. The set was lashed by at least a dozen storms. Eerie cloud formations, resembling precisely the one used in the film to hide a UFO, repeatedly floated over the set. A *'real UFO, complete with four flashing and glowing lights',* soared above the set while a scene depicting the landing of the UFO was being filmed. Was this publicity just a ploy to advertise the forthcoming film or not? Not so according to Melinda Dillon, who reported having sighted a UFO herself at her California home two weeks before she was offered one of the star roles! She wasn't the only one – Elke Sommer herself reported having sighted a UFO.

UK Spotlight on 1977 – **Over 215 sightings recorded for this year!**

Many people will be aware of the extraordinary UFO events that took place in and around South Wales during a 'wave' of activity, including the now immortalised sighting at Broadhaven

Primary School, Broadhaven, Dyfed, on the 4th of February 1977 when a silver shaped 'craft', and its occupants, were seen by the children on the slope of the nearby hill. There were many reports of UFOs seen by schoolchildren, multiple reports of strange figures, landed craft and what looked like aliens.

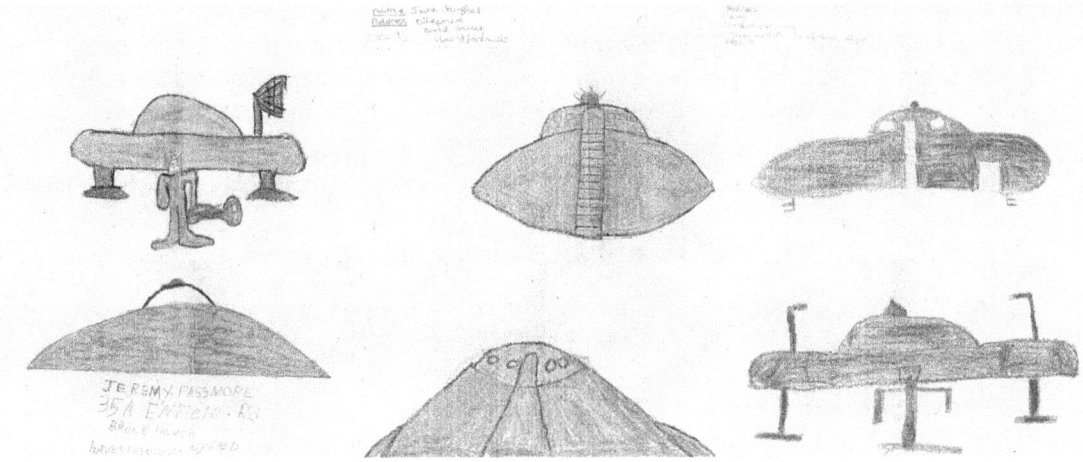

Selected sighting – *'Coronation Street'* TV Star and sister sights UFO!

Actress Freda Driver, the sister of Betty Driver – more familiar for her role as evergreen Barmaid, Betty Turpin of *Coronation Street* fame – spoke to us about a strange incident she and her sister witnessed, during August 1977.

Freda: *"I was sitting in the lounge at the farmhouse where we lived at the time, one stormy evening, and happened to glance through the window, when I saw this large circular yellow 'ball of light' hovering above some trees, apparently unaffected by the gale force wind blowing outside. I watched it, noting it had a slightly misty halo around it, and thought to myself it's watching me as well! After about 15mins, I decided to summon up the courage and venture outside, asking my sister, Betty, to come with me. When we opened the door, accompanied by the three boxer dogs, the wind was so strong we had trouble standing. As soon as the dogs saw the UFO they ran back inside and hid under the table, at which stage we began to feel frightened and went back inside the house. After 5mins or so, it shot up into the sky and disappeared, followed by the wind dropping dramatically. We found out that others had also seen this UFO, which was explained away as a weather balloon!"*

Freda described another incident which took place, while home with her sister, Betty, one evening, approximately ten miles from Ellesmere Port, when they noticed a curious 'ball of light' travelling in tandem with their vehicle, about a hundred yards away. *"I stopped the car to have a closer look at this object, and was surprised to see it had also stopped, motionless in the air, as if somehow watching us. Unsure of what to do, we got back into the car and continued on our journey, noting, with fright, it was still following us – always at the same distance away from us, irrespective of whatever*

THE HALT PERSPECTIVE 2

speed we were doing. It stayed with us for about 20 miles and was clearly seen by other motorists, some of whom stopped their cars. To our relief, when we entered a built-up area, it shot off upwards into the sky and disappeared." A few days after the incident, Freda was not surprised to learn, from reading a local newspaper, that the UFO had been seen by other drivers on the road, one of whom launched an appeal, asking for any other witnesses to contact him. Needless to say, Freda and Betty decided to keep quiet, fearing ridicule. In 2011, we wrote to Betty and she sent us a signed photo of herself and Freda. Sadly, although we sent her a copy of *Haunted Skies*, she passed away a week later. Did she read our inscription on the inside cover to her? We shall never know.

UK Spotlight on 1978 – Over 170 sightings recorded for this year!

Selected sighting – RAF scrambles over Suffolk

In **April 1978**, Staff Sergeant Thomas W. Wharton of the 91st FS (stationed at RAF Bentwaters, Suffolk, United Kingdom, between January 1977 and 1980) was to sight something inexplicable during April 1978. Whether there was any connection with the extraordinary event that took place a few years later, in December 1980, at RAF Woodbridge, is something we will never know. Sometime between midnight and 1.00am, during April 1978, Thomas was a front passenger in Staff Sgt. Mike Bugno's VW van, heading towards RAF Wethersfield, where he was living at the time with his wife, Helen. He had just passed through the small town of Finchingfield, off the main A12 road. As they approached the crest of a small hill, with the base lights of RAF Mildenhall clearly seen (although approximately thirty miles away), they noticed a bright 'light' in the sky near Mildenhall, which illuminated the night sky. After a few seconds, it appeared to get bigger and brighter.

Thomas said: *"I remember saying to Mike, 'Mike look at that light!' It was the brightest landing light (least I thought it was) I had ever seen. It lit up the entire sky near the base. I thought it was a C-5 or maybe a C-141 with new, bright landing lights (I had never seen anything so bright from so far away) before. We both looked at it for a few moments longer. Since Mike was still driving and it was dark, he needed to watch the road, too, but I noticed it appeared to be headed our way. I said, 'Mike, look, it is headed this way!' He pulled over. He wanted to see what kind of aircraft this was. The lights got brighter and it was headed in our direction. We got out of the van. Just as we did that, within seconds (I mean this) it was right over our heads and there was no noise, none at all. The entire sky above us was so bright, we could not look up at the object . . . it was so weird, no noise, no shape could be seen of whatever this thing was. We both looked at each other and said, 'What the hell is this?' We could not believe this. We kept trying to look up at it, but could not because it was so bright. We felt nothing – no humming, no noise, no movement of the grass around, nothing was happening. It was like we were in a void of some kind".*

British fighter jets appear!

"It hovered over us for a few more seconds, then I heard a noise from behind me – it was a jet engine sound. I looked up, put my hands over my eyes to see better, and I saw two British F4s headed right towards our location. They got so close; we could see the 'Union Jack' flag panel on their aircraft fuselage. They were deploying photo flash cartridges; we could hear and see what they were doing with them but nothing else above us. They were taking pictures of this thing (not that they needed more light, this thing was extremely bright) as it was. Mike yelled out to me, 'What the hell is happening here'? I did not know either but a moment later, whatever this thing was, took off to the west, towards London. It was like looking at a 'light sabre', or something like it, because it left a single line of bright light in the sky, as it headed away from us. It was like someone drew a white line in the sky. It was instantaneous. I could not believe it".

Fighters give chase!

"One second it was above us, the next it was over London (you could see the lights of the city from our location). The British F4s took off after it. They kicked their aircraft into 'burner', trying to catch or chase this thing. It was amazing to witness. They never caught it, but were headed towards London, too, when all of a sudden, this thing appeared over our heads again (no kidding, it was like in the wink of an eye) . . . that fast. We tried to look up at it again, but it was useless to do so. I turned my head and saw the F4s headed back towards us again (I guess they were still taking pictures of this thing). We were right under it when it shot straight up; I mean it, straight up. All we saw was a white line in the sky until we could follow it no longer – still going straight up, without a sound, into space."

Mike and Thomas waited, but after nothing further was seen, drove home to the base which was just a few minutes away. As they approached the base main gate, it was clear from the excitement and behaviour of the American and British Security Guards stationed there, that they, too, had seen whatever this thing was. They told the security men what they had seen and were advised to report the matter to the MOD Police, which they subsequently did. When Thomas arrived home, he awoke his wife and told her what he had seen. She thought he had been drinking. Thomas had this to say:

"I decided to turn on the BBC radio. It was now two o'clock in the morning. The BBC radio stations were flooded with calls about a UFO sighting over London and fighters that were reported chasing it. It was an amazing night, to say the least. Of course I (we) also filed a report with the RAF Bentwaters OSI. They (OSI) took the report and that was that. We never heard another thing about it. During the rest of the tour, Mike and I talked about it often, but never really understood what happened that night. I (we) know it must have been a UFO, least that is what we think it was (so did all those folks in London) You know, I am sure many of you have had something strange or something happen that was so exciting or important happen to you, that you said to yourself, I will never forget this day or date in my life. The very day after the event, the very next morning, I and Staff Sgt Mike Bugno (Maintenance Operations, Weapons Controller) reported this event to the USAF, OSI at RAF Bentwaters, Suffolk, United Kingdom, and that was the last we ever heard about it."

Thomas is a credit to the USAF. He is man with an illustrious career, and we had the pleasure of talking to him recently, with regard to seeking permission to write-up this incident. Thomas started

THE HALT PERSPECTIVE 2

his military career as an aircraft mechanic (basically) stationed at: Clark Air Base, Philippines (June 1970, F-4s) then DaNang Air Base, Republic of Vietnam (February 1971, flying F-4s) between 1972 and 1975 he was posted to RAF Lakenheath, Suffolk, England. This was followed by a posting to Edwards AFB, California (1975 & 1976, F-4 Tow Target Operator – In-flight) then he was sent back to RAF Bentwaters, Suffolk, England (1977 to 1980, flying F-4s, then converted to A-10s). From 1980 to 1982 he served at Nellis AFB, Las Vegas, flying F-4s, then converted to F-16s. His other secondments included Hahn Air Base, Germany, 1982 to 1985, flying F-16s, Luke AFB, Phoenix, Arizona, 1985 to 1988, flying F-16s and 12th AF F16 Demo Team). Nellis AFB, Las Vegas, Nevada (1988 to 1991, F-16s – USAF Thunderbirds and two months with the Navy Blue Angels, F-18 Maintenance Exchange Program). RAF Lakenheath, Suffolk, England (1991 to 1996 F-15C/D/E). Thomas retired in Feb 1996 – 26 years later and sixty (60) countries, either TDY/Deployed (countless deployments globally) or just vacationing with the family. As he says, *"What a ride the USAF was for me!"*

Selected sighting – UFO flies over M4 Motorway!

4th October 1978, Mr Lloyd Meeking: *"I was 12 years old; it all started on a trip from Torquay Devon to Heathrow airport for a two week winter holiday to Malaga Spain, with my parents and brother. While on the M4, we stopped at the Granada services for our evening meal at about 7.30pm, and then continued up the M4 motorway. When some 20 miles further we noticed in the distance red and white lights, moving along very slowly followed by an object with lights that flew over the top of us about came over about 500 feet, high. It was so big it blotted out the sky above us. We wound down our windows to get a better view, and could see it very clearly. It was absolutely silent, and stayed above us, it seemed for a long time, we could see the under body of this object which consisted of cubes and squares with brilliant lights displayed. My mother and my brother and I were screaming at my father to pull into the hard shoulder, so we could get out and stand under it, he was so petrified; he would not stop the car. This object was the size of the Wembley arena, it eventually drifted away towards the Swindon town area at which point two gold lights shot off it, then came back up the M4 again, and crossed in front of us, before disappearing into the Wiltshire countryside."*

Spotlight on 1979 – Over 150 sightings recorded for this year!

Ansted, West Virginia restaurant owner Norma White (43), sighted what she took to be a bright star motionless in the sky about five degrees, some 2000 feet above the mountain to the north of the town at 5.55pm on the 5th of December 1979. It then moved towards the witness, rising to another 2000 feet (approx) over her head, its bright light extinguishing allowing her to see, a 'Y'-shaped form which emitted dim green light. At the three points of the 'Y' were clusters of red lights, the bottom cluster accompanied by a white light. The object silently moved away eastwards descending as it did so over the course of the next few minutes. It sat there in the sky for 15 minutes. Then six lights flew off it followed by another six lights ten minutes later.

Over in the south west part of the sky another six lights appeared, making a total of 18 small coloured lights flying around the sky. By this time two police officers arrived at the scene and watched the lights, along with the daughters of Mrs. White, her husband and a student. Police officer Cohenour told the family that they had received between 10-20 calls from the public about this incident. Mrs. White posted a notice on the wall of her restaurant inviting UFO witnesses to contact her. She collected 200 names. One of these sightings came from Gary Poling who was driving east of Ansted after dark on the same road as Mrs White's restaurant when he saw light as bright car headlights coming out of trees off the road some 3-400 yards away. At this point his Plymouth Fury car began to misfire and he could only achieve 45mph with the pedal to the floorboard. The digital clock gained three hours. These effects only lasted just under a minute before things returned to normal and Gary sped away up to 85mph. (**Source:** *International Reporter 1 UFO* **January 1980)**

Spotlight on 1980 – **Over 125 sightings!**

7th January 1980. Cameron Wyatt (12), from Willow Crescent, Market Harborough, Leicestershire and Adrian Goldthorpe, were out playing, when they saw: *"A saucer-shaped object, with a round dome underneath, showing five flashing lights, following a tractor across a nearby field. Seconds later it disappeared."* **(Source: Crystal Hogben, *'Magic Saucer' Marlborough Mail,* 10.Jan.1980)**

January 1980. Schoolboys – Darren Sinar and Dean Basford – were out playing, near Highfield Road, Birmingham, West Midlands, when they saw, *"An object – which looked like a saucer, with another saucer turned upside-down and placed on the top – moving up and down above us in the sky, with flashing lights on its top, bottom, and along its sides."*

11th January 1980. Mrs. 'Pixie' Revell, from Whitstable, Kent, was driving home along Thanet Way, near the Long Reach roundabout, at 8.55pm. When she saw: *"Two shafts of piercing light to my left, above which could be seen a number of small red lights in a square, about 50 yards away and a hundred feet off the ground. In between the beams of light were what appeared to be criss-cross metal strips, like angle-iron? The next thing that happened was that I actually drove underneath whatever it was, as it landed on the ground over nearby ancient woodland."* **(Source: Personal Interview)**

14th January 1980. A truck driver was crossing over a railway bridge at Heald Moor, Lancashire, at 3.00am when he became aware of a loud humming sound. Seconds later, the headlights of his vehicle picked-up a strange shape on the road ahead, described as a large, dark, metallic object, showing three red 'beams of light' projecting from the top onto the ground. *"I recalled seeing several men moving around it, as if doing some type of task. As I came closer to the object, I realised it was a tortoise-shaped 'craft', with a curved pipe on top, with two 'figures' that appeared to be inspecting the red beams. Reducing my speed, I noticed one of the 'figures' wore a peaked cap and a dark two-piece uniform. His arms were at his side. The second 'figure' was wearing a one-piece suit, grey or silver in colour, and he was stooping down looking at the object, as if inspecting it for damage."* As the motorist drove slowly away from the scene, his headlights suddenly cut off and he was forced to slam on the brakes – apparently then losing consciousness. A sudden jolt woke him up and he realised the headlights were working again and that the truck had moved about a quarter-of-a-mile further along the road. When he arrived at his destination, he was stunned to find out he had lost more than three hours of time. **(Source: Carl Nagaitis, Phillip Mantle, book *'Without Consent'*)**

20th January 1980. Milkman Fred Smith, of Cove, near Farnborough, Hants saw a light in the sky approaching his position from the North at 4.07am. *"The 'light' had now increased in size and was beginning to take on a crescent shape, with a bluish haze around it. It didn't look man-made. I began to feel uneasy. By now there was no doubt it was crescent shaped, with a bluish glow all around it, flying quite fast, at a high altitude, when I realised it was slowing down. Suddenly it came to a stop; hovering in*

THE HALT PERSPECTIVE 2

the sky above Farnborough. I could feel the hairs on the back of my neck standing on end. After a short time, the 'craft' slowly turned around and accelerated away northwards, and was soon gone from sight."
(Source: Personal Interview)

2nd February 1980. At 9am a silver-white metallic object was seen in the sky over Epsom Downs. Later the same day, at 1pm, an object resembling a 'cap' was seen in the sky over Stone Cross, West Bromwich, by a number of people. A yellow light was seen moving through the sky over Dartford, Kent, at 10.45pm on 2nd February 1980.

6th February 1980. Mrs. Stella Edge from Hoylake, Wirral, Merseyside, was at home on when she heard a high-pitched sound resonating through the house. Despite a check of the electrical appliances within the house, and examination of the nearby street, the source of this noise could not be traced. After a couple of hours, the sound began to recede, but returned to its original high-pitch during the evening meal – a matter brought to the attention of Stella, by her husband and daughter, who burst out laughing when somebody suggested, in conversation, that the noise sounded like a spaceship taking off. How ironic those words would turn out to be!

7th February 1980. An orange-yellow coloured 'ball of light' was seen moving through the sky over Chertsey, in Surrey at 6.15am. The following evening, Stella noticed an intense 'glare of light 'emanating from behind the drawn curtains. Wondering what was causing this 'glare', she pulled back the curtains and was confronted by the sight of "... *a brilliant white 'disc' of sharply defined light, surrounded by haze, motionless in the air, just above the gable end of a nearby house. After a few minutes it began to rise slowly upwards, out of the range of my vision. I rushed out into the street and, at first, couldn't see it – then, as my eyes adjusted to the darkness, I saw it almost resting on the rooftop of a house, a short distance down the street, accompanied by a tiny object that looked like a' star'. I stood watching – now very frightened. All of a sudden, the 'star' shot away from the disc shaped object and went out of sight. The 'disc' then tilted slightly and rushed away through the sky, in a blur of speed, towards the direction of the churchyard. The next morning, I telephoned the Police to report the matter."*

February 1980. Earlier that month Mr George Smith, landlord of the *Pilot Inn* at Berwick, was taking a walk on the local golf course accompanied by his wife, child and dog. As he was walking past a nearby holiday camp on his way home, he became aware of a bright yellow object which had swept in from the sea. The object proceeded to make its way soundlessly up the Tweed Valley whereupon it stopped and started to 'float'. The family stood still staring at this object for around two to three minutes. They described the object as being as big as a big 'light bulb' but a different shape – slightly oval. Mr Smith was reported to have said: *"It was just a light, you couldn't see doors or anything like that. It was around several thousand feet up and travelling fairly fast, it would be around 50 miles away when I lost sight of it".* **(Source: Malcolm Robinson)**

11th of February 1980. Margaret Fry, her daughter Jacqueline Fowler and niece Julia Lewis, were at the front of the house in Bexleyheath, Kent, when they noticed bright star-like object in the sky. It then began to expand and as it did so descended until it was approximately 200ft above their head. They were then surprised to see nine small lights moving in and out of the larger object as it moved overhead. The larger object described as being the size of an aircraft carrier, and apparently silver metallic in appearance, maintained its position in the sky for about an hour before moving away. (**Source: Personal Interview**)

THE HALT PERSPECTIVE 2

13th February 1980, at 06:45am. Dave Rawlinson was on his way to work when he happened to glance up in to the early morning sky and saw a 'flashing light'. The 'light' came down from the sky and started to follow the railway embankment at Tweedmouth, travelling towards Berwick. As the light approached *'One Tunnel'* leading to the trading estate, it completely vanished as if switched off. Dave stated that there was no way that this light was a helicopter or aircraft and was in his sight for around ten minutes. **(Source: Malcolm Robinson)**

13th February 1980, at 4.15pm. Three lights were seen in the sky over Beare Green, Surrey. According to the witnesses, they were constantly changing patterns they flew overhead.

18th February 1980. The Police, in March, Cambridgeshire, confirmed that they had received a number of calls regarding UFOs sighted over the town, described as looking like *'a massive ball of orange flame'* in the sky – apparently also seen by some of their own officers.

25th February 1980, at 8pm. Halifax resident – James Carter – and three friends, saw: *". . . a rectangular object, showing a scarlet light",* moving across the sky towards the direction of Mytholmroyd, for five minutes, before it moved behind a cloud and disappeared. A spokesman at Leeds/Bradford Airport suggested it was probably an airplane or helicopter. **(Source: *Daily Express*, 26.2.80 – 'Five see UFO')**

2nd March 1980. Bradford resident – Lorna Mandell – was driving along Micklethwaite Lane, near Crossflatts, between 4-5pm, with her two children, when they saw a flashing red circular object with a glowing red twinkling centre and shimmering edges, descending vertically through the sky, despite a strong wind blowing at the time. As it touched the ground, the light in the middle disappeared and the object was lost from view. **(Source: Graham Birdsall, Yorkshire UFO Society)**

6th March 1980. Richard Courtney – the civilian Flight Controller at Plymouth Airport – was looking towards the Caradon TV mast, at 8.23pm, *". . . when a' bright light' shone through the clouds between the TV mast and Kit Hill. I radioed an incoming 8.45pm flight and advised him I was going off the air for a few minutes to confirm a UFO. I made my way out of the flight tower. When I looked over into the sky where I had seen the UFO, there was nothing to be seen. By this time, the Manager had joined me. Suddenly the 'light' came on again. The Manager couldn't believe his eyes."* He said: *'The hairs on the back of my neck are standing on end'.* The 'light' – now flashing on and off a brilliant diamond blue in colour, with a large area of diffused light around it – was above and shining through the clouds, at a height of two thousand feet. The glow from the object spread over a large area of the sky. You could make out clearly the disc in the centre.

The 'light' then went out again; at this point I had to go back to the Control Tower and the 'light' was still there in the sky. I radioed the incoming aircraft and asked him to confirm a visual on the UFO. He told me he could see the 'light' but was unable to assist further, as he was preparing for landing. At 8.31pm, the light disappeared for the last time." **(Source: Bob Boyd, Plymouth UFO Group)**

9th March 1980. A mysterious cluster of red flashing lights was seen in the sky over Baildon and Ilkley Moor, West Yorkshire at 5.15pm by a number of people, who contacted the Police at Shipley, who in turn telephoned the Air Traffic Control, at Leeds/Bradford Airport, thinking it might have been a distress flare, but were, told they had no knowledge. The Police themselves admitted their own officers had sighted UFOs, at an altitude of 6-700ft, north of Ilkley. **(Source: *Bradford Telegraph and Argus*, 12.3.80)**

THE HALT PERSPECTIVE 2

11th March 1980. Nicholas George – a subcontractor, from Stratford-upon-Avon – was driving home along the A422, just after 7.00pm approaching the Temple Grafton turn-off, when he noticed a 'blob of light' in the sky towards the south-east through the windscreen of his car. Feeling uneasy, he began to slow down, in order to obtain a closer look. To his horror, a large brilliant cigar-shaped object appeared, with dark red patches on its curved end. He said: *"I took my left hand off the steering wheel and applied the brakes. This caused the vehicle to veer off the road and hit the kerb, coming to a stop. Very shaken, I got out of the car and lit up a cigarette, looking out over the open countryside for any sign of the object, at which point I noticed my left-hand felt tender and oddly dark in places. There was a circle of damaged skin, with a blue/purple narrow ring around its edge. The centre was made up of dead skin. Next to this was another large blister, filled with fluid."*

Mr. George contacted the Worcestershire-based UFO Group – *Sky Scan* – who tape-recorded an interview with him, in which he had the following to say: *"Only one hand was affected because I was smoking, at the time, with my right hand – the left thumb hooked under the wheel. The funny thing is that it didn't hurt like a normal burn. At the time it felt tender, but it was dark outside and I didn't pay much attention. When I arrived home after work, several hours later, my hand was sore. The blisters came later."* The Investigators – Tony Green, Derek Lawrence and Margaret Webb – confirmed the base of the thumb was swollen and red. There was a circle of damaged skin, approximately 1.5-2.0cm across, with a blue/purple coloured narrow ring around its edge. The centre was made up of dead skin.

Next to this was another large blister – 1.5cm filled with fluid. Under the metal expanding watch strap was a small blister and mark – still visible a week after the incident. Emphasising the professionalism of this select UFO group, was the decision to have the vehicle examined by a fully-qualified mechanic then to contact the manufacturers of the windscreen, to ascertain whether a burst of microwave energy, striking the windscreen from a nearby microwave tower, could have explained away the incident. (This stretch of road was to be the subject of other sightings of UFOs over the years.)

13th March 1980, at 8.30pm. A woman from Tyersal, Bradford, reported having seen a brightly-lit glowing, revolving object, travelling swiftly across the sky, heading towards the direction of Leeds.

17th March 1980, at 7.30pm. Two unusual 'red lights', one brighter than the other were seen motionless in the sky over a densely populated area of Swindon. According to the woman concerned: *"The larger 'light' had a dome on top. It disappeared from sight first, followed by the other. Both were seen above rooftop level".*

17th March 1980. Steven Dayman-Johns and his wife, Julie, were travelling back home to Frome, Somerset, in a 1973 Datsun Cherry car, along Ridgeway Lane (a narrow road approximately one and-a-half miles long) at 10.35pm when Julie brought her husband's attention to a white object she saw move through one quarter of the car's windscreen, before coming to a halt in the sky. John stopped the car and, after switching off the headlights, stood on the sill of the car and sighted the object in the sky – which had no definite outline but appeared to have a darker ring running around it. After a few minutes, he got back into the car and continued on his journey, keeping the object under observation until it suddenly moved away at a phenomenal speed towards Wanstrow, emitting a faint light from its front and rear. Steve decided to make his way to higher ground and drove to the end of Ridgeway Lane to the T Junction, being overtaken by a motorcyclist who sounded his horn several times at them. They turned left at the junction and pulled into a lay-by, about 150yds from the junction. After getting out they looked across the sky but couldn't see the object, although they did notice a whitish glow on the horizon in the shape of an upturned letter 'U'. Their curiosity now aroused even further, they got back into the car and drove to where they had originally seen the object, along Ridgeway Lane. Just before reaching the lay-by, they saw a bright vertical beam of light behind the trees, catching them in its brilliant glare.

Once again, they made their way towards it, driving along Marston Lane and up and over Cheese Hill, where they caught sight of it, two to three fields away – a bright 'beam' projecting downwards from its centre, solid in appearance, rather than a beam of light. At this point, Julie began to feel frightened and refused to get out of the car. Steven observed that the top of the 'beam' had a 'V'-shaped darker area inside it. A few minutes later, he decided to walk over and have a closer look, but Julie pleaded with him not to go.

Getting back into the car, the couple drove along the road – still keeping an eye on the object, which was glowing brighter and apparently closer to where they were positioned. Stopping once again, he switched off the car headlights. Within seconds, the object dropped in height and approached them silently; at highspeed, passing over their car (now the size of an outstretched hand at arm's length) some 50ft off the ground, before disappearing, finally, from view. **(Source: Martin Shipp/***Probe Report***, Vol. 4, No. 2, October 1983)**

17th March 1980. Margery Sherrard, her daughter, Deborah, and friend, Teresa Malvaney, were on their way to Knowsley, to drop off Teresa, after a keep fit class. As they drove along Holt Lane at 11pm Margery noticed a bright light descending through the sky, which they first took to be an aircraft on its way to Liverpool Airport, several miles to the south-west, described as being 'orange, with white lights; the other, a red diamond'. As they continued on their journey, they passed a *'strange figure'* walking along the road, with long grey hair and thin face – about 50yrs of age. After arriving at their destination, they made the return journey back along the same route, when they were forced to swerve to avoid striking the same man (a coincidence you may say) but as they reached Knowsley Lane, they encountered a third similar 'figure' walking along the middle of the road. At no time did either of these 'men' acknowledge the presence of the vehicle.

Brenda Butler: *"1980 was a year of considerable UFO activity for me and my colleague, Dot Street, from BUFORA. It started in March 1980, when a lady from Gorleston, near Yarmouth, Norfolk, telephoned me, reporting having seen a huge orange 'light' in the sky, heading towards the coast, which she believed came down somewhere near the sea. The woman told me that she and her neighbours had gone outside at 10.30pm, after the house lights had began to flash on and off. This was when they saw the UFO. I also remember interviewing another woman in Gorleston, living on the Yarmouth Road. She saw this orange 'light' going across the sky. After having watched it, they went back inside the house.*

About an hour later, they were watching TV. A shadow went across the front room curtains. They opened the curtains and looked out and saw the figure of a man, wearing what looked like a helmet. Frightened, she sent her terrier dog outside but it ran back inside. Looking upwards, she was amazed to see the orange 'light' in the sky again. One of the young boys in the family told her he saw a man, dressed in a funny hat and black clothes, running out of the garden."

THE HALT PERSPECTIVE 2

30th March 1980. Off duty Police Constable David Cathro, living on the Gowrie Park Housing Estate, was awoken by a metallic humming noise, at 4.45am, which increased in sound.

"From my bedroom window that overlooks the Carse of Gowrie, I saw four 'dull glows' moving across the sky, about three quarters of a mile away, in a diamond formation, accompanied by the noise, which grew louder but changed its pitch. They then stopped and appeared to be over Star Inn Road. Suddenly, one of the 'lights' came away and slowly descended to the ground in the vicinity of Benvie, where I lost sight of the formation, although I could still hear the noise for a short time afterwards. I alerted the neighbours and we all stood outside watching. One of them produced a pair of binoculars. I looked through and saw an object, shaped like a rugby-ball, with a white top and glowing orange base. I telephoned the Police, at Forfar, and explained to them what I had seen. They checked with the Airport and told me there was nothing plotted on Radar for that area. Enquiries made the following day revealed the object had been hovering over a Compressor Plant at Forfar."

31st March 1980, at 4.50am. Off duty Police Constable Graham Irving and his wife, also living on the same estate, were awoken by a strange metallic humming noise and low frequency vibrations. Graham and his wife dashed to the window, which faces north-west over the Carse of Gowrie, and saw four dull orange lights travelling from right to left, north to north-west. The couple then went back to bed, as the lights and noise were beginning to fade. Graham said: *"Suddenly the noise became loud again; once again, we went to the window and looked out. We saw four objects hovering approximately 1Km away, to the north-west, in the Benvie area. After about five minutes one of the objects slowly descended towards the ground until it was out of sight. After hovering for a longtime, the other three lights departed northwards."*

A subsequent search of the area by local police, who were contacted, revealed nothing untoward. A 132kV power line runs across the area to Benvie. It is said that similar noises were heard by two milk delivery boys in the Menziehill area of the City. **(Source: Personal Interview)**

1st April 1980. The pilot of a civilian aircraft, en route from Nottingham to Bristol, sighted an object, likened to *'a car headlight, shining through the mist',* moving through the sky at about 40mph. Enquiries made later revealed the UFO had been tracked on radar by Birmingham Airport. **(Source: UFOsIS, Birmingham)**

5th April 1980, at 1.30am. A flashing mass of what looked like 'white spikes' was seen in the sky over Upper Dicker, Sussex. Later that evening, at 8.30pm, two objects, described as 'golden basket in shape', were seen in the sky over Looe, Cornwall. **(Source: Mr. D. Cutler)**

7th April 1980. A white star-shaped object was seen over the M11 Motorway at 9pm.

8th April 1980. Two UFOs – described as one being red in colour, the other white and spinning – were seen heading north-eastwards, across the Firth of Forth, and Dalgetty Bay, Fife, at 8.30pm. Was this the same UFO reported over Edinburgh, at 9.30pm on the same day, described as red and white 'lights' moving slowly through the sky?

9th April 1980. Dorothy Smith (mother-in-law of Shirley Smith) from Offmore Farm Estate, Kidderminster, was walking along the road at 10pm, when she noticed a bank of coloured lights forming the lower edge of a transparent circle in the sky, under a single bright light. **(Source: Crystal Hogben, *Magic Saucer*)**

THE HALT PERSPECTIVE 2

10th April 1980. An unusual light was seen in the sky, said to be almost as bright as the Sun, throughout the North of England, early today. In Manchester, 40 people telephoned the police, saying they had seen flare flashes in the night sky. In Stockport, police, fire and ambulance men, were called to a field where it was said an object had landed, but nothing was found. Air traffic controllers at Manchester Airport said that the whole sky was brilliantly lit up for afew seconds. People from North Wales to the Scottish border contacted the police. An airport spokesman said the most likely explanation was that an unusually large piece of space debris had re-entered the atmosphere, causing the sky to flare up. **(Source: *Burton Daily Mail,* 10.4.1980 – 'Spacerubbish light sky')**

11th April 1980. During the morning an unusual object was detected close to Fuerza Aerea Peruana (FAP) base in La Joya, Arequipa, and a thousand kilometres south of the city of Lima (Peruvian Capital). The object, like a balloon glowing in the sun's reflection, was sighted hovering in the sky, by many people, approximately 3 miles away, and at an altitude of approximately 1,800ft altitude. FAP directed Lieutenant Oscar Santa Maria Huerta, a pilot of the Peruvian Air Force to take-off in his Sukhoi 22 aircraft and take down the spherical glowing object, as it was without clearance in a restricted airspace. (One presumes that they may have thought this was a balloon). Oscar complied and approached the object, which was hanging motionlessly about 600 meters above the ground, at 7.15am. After landing, the object reappeared and hovered in the sky above the base for two more hours. Lt. Santa Maríadescribed the object as follows: *"It was about 30ft in diameter. It was an enamelled, cream-coloured dome with a wide, circular, metallic base. It had no engines, no exhausts, no windows, no wings or antennae. It lacked all the typical aircraft components, with no visible propulsion system."*

When within firing range, Oscar pulled the trigger, launching sixty-four 30mm shells, some of which missed the target and went towards the ground, but the majority hit the object directly, without exploding or causing any harm. (Approximately 1,800 men at the base witnessed the event).The UFO then started to climb in height, and proceeded farther from the FAP. It made a sudden stop at 36,000 ft, forcing Lt. Santa Maria to move aside, now approximately 1500 feet away. The Lieutenant then decided to fly up higher, to approach it from above, having slightly below 100 rounds left. Just ashe locked on to the target, ready to attack, the UFO performed a straight vertical ascend, evading the approach. He had the object locked for an attack for two more times subsequently, but just when he was about to hit the trigger, it moved away, always eluding his attempt. At this point, being nearly out of fuel, Santa María was forced to abandon his mission and withdraw. He was 84 kilometres from his base, and 22 minutes had passed since his initial contact with the object. Following the declassification of documents by the U.S. Department of State, Oscar Santa Maria was subsequently interviewed by many researchers and reporters, over the years and became known worldwide through cable TV.

14th April 1980. A circular UFO showing a number of 'portholes' along its length, spilling out yellow light, was seen travelling 30-40ft off the ground, over fields on the outskirts of Grantham, Lincolnshire. **(Source: Richard Thompson)**

29th of April 1980. Mrs Everett of Penhill, Swindon, Wiltshire was leaving the house at 9.05pm when she saw two red lights circling around the sky. Five minutes later one of them disappeared leaving the other one, which circled again, before dropping down vertically growing in size showing a dark vertical band in the centre, then split into two. Another UFO report for the Swindon area during April 1980 came from Miss Ann Williams of Pinehurst, Swindon, who saw: *"A rotating beam of yellow glowing light motionless in the sky showing several smaller red lights shimmering and bobbing up and down, before disappearing from view 15 minutes later."*

15th May 1980. Gareth Hughes – then a teacher from The Wirral, Merseyside – was driving home along the northbound carriageway of the M53 Motorway at about 4.00am, approaching junction 2 opposite Bidston Hill, when he noticed a bright light close to the ground, estimated to be 300ft away and massive in size. *"It resembled two curved, black artillery shells, angled at 45° towards me, showing two beams of light projecting from the rear, which didn't go all the way to the ground but stopped in mid-air. I could see two pink-reddish jets of flame behind each 'shell' as I now continued on my journey."*

At 6.30pm the same day, Brian Murphy and his friend – Andrew Keen – were fishing off Orford Quay, Suffolk, when they saw a silver, cigar-shaped object, motionless in the sky. *"It moved away and then came back. It was as bright as the sun ,and kept flickering and making a buzzing noise. It was a clear night. I would say it was about the size of a football in the sky. We watched it for about an hour, and then it just vanished in front of our eyes."* (**Source: Brenda Butler/Ron West, EAPRA**)

29th May 1980. Marion Kennedy from Framlingham, Suffolk, was driving to Baldock, Hertfordshire, in the early evening, accompanied by her eldest daughter Sarah (driving) and youngest daughter Pamela, aged 11 (in the back), when they noticed a *'dark red, flickering, light that looked like lightning in the sky unlike anything they had ever seen before.'*

As they approached Framlingham, still daylight, they noticed a peculiar 'bright white light' motionless in the sky, just above the horizon. When near Bury St. Edmunds, a curious thing happened: the light, still prominent in the sky, seemed to 'hop over' to a bank of built-up black cloud, and disappear – much to their relief.

"After leaving Bury St. Edmunds, we continued along the A14, when my eldest daughter, Sarah, drew my attention to the fact that the journey seemed to be taking forever to complete, and that the local countryside – a familiar route of ours – did not look right. Suddenly, without any prior warning of unusual weather conditions we entered what we took to be a patch of thick fog. Actually, it was more like dense smoke, alternating between thick patches, and swirling up from holes in the ground – the most remarkable thing I had ever seen in my life. By now, tensions inside the car were considerably heightened. Pamela, who had previously been asleep, was now wide awake. As we reduced speed, in order to cope with the hazardous driving conditions along this straight stretch of dual-carriageway, in complete contrast to what had been a clear, dry, evening, illuminated by a full moon, we noticed what, at first, we took to be the outlines of a number of heavy lorries travelling towards the East, passing through this bank of 'fog'.

In a way I find difficult to explain – there seemed to be something horribly wrong about this part of the journey, although I cannot put my finger on what it was that created so much fear with the appearance of these strange lorries. Pamela remarked that it was almost as if the lorries were driving themselves and that they had evil faces. Naturally, I dismissed this as an overactive imagination. After arriving at the house in Baldock, we settled down for the night – the three of us sharing the same bedroom, trying to forget about all the problems we had encountered – when my eldest daughter suddenly jumped out of bed, at 12. 45am, shouting to me that she had just seen a 'red light' flash across the sky. We all rushed to the window, but there was nothing to be seen. It was a brilliant moonlit night – just like daylight. We stood at the window for a little while, and then I told the two girls we were going into the garden. Later, thinking about my actions, I was curious why I decided to go into the garden on my own, as I am a nervous person, but felt impelled to go into the garden, when I was amazed to see the appearance of an object travelling from the left, behind some barns in the near distance. It was enormous – the size of a house, totally silent, showing a number of curious red brick-shaped lights along its base and at the top. I couldn't distinguish the outline of the object because of the dazzling white lights on its 'body'... then it dipped downwards, the white lights appearing to squash down – as if they had been withdrawn, somehow, allowing me to see the outline of a 'flying saucer' shaped object, with a dome on its top. It moved very slowly and went behind the bottom half of a tree, a few hundred yards away, and then dipped, once again, went straight down to earth and disappeared, followed by the frenzied barking of dogs in the locality. Incredibly, a 'white light' – identical to the one we had seen earlier that evening – appeared in the right-hand part of the sky, at great speed, before also disappearing."

According to Pamela: *"It had a flat bottom. Inside I could see, running horizontally across, a number of red 'blocks of light'. In the top of the object I could see what looked like two 'pylons', forming a triangle – a bit like a heart in shape. When it tilted, this 'pylon thing' went shorter and it looked more like a saucer. I reported the matter to the Police and then telephoned the local United States Air Force Base (it may have been Mildenhall) and spoke to an officer there, when it became obvious the questions being asked of me were being read from a previously prepared pro forma. The next morning we went to have a look around and realised whatever we had seen had not occurred at the bottom of the garden, as we had first thought, but over a cornfield, about two fields away, bordered by a group of electricity pylons."* Marion told us that following the UFO event, the family were to experience unusual things occurring at the family home. They included household objects going missing but reappearing a few days later, and problems with the electrical system on their Austin Mini. **(Source: Brenda Butler/Personal Interviews)**

3rd June 1980. Peter Francombe was travelling along the Clevedon Road, through Tickenham Village, Cleveland, Avon, at 10.45pm, with Barbara Shakespeare and her two young children, when they saw a peculiar light in the sky and pulled in to take a closer look. *"It flashed brightly, approximately three times every couple of seconds, and then moved erratically across the sky, made a 90° turn to the north-west, and began to hover again. We continued on our journey and saw it, once again, before it disappeared from view into the clouds."* **(Source: BrendaButler/Ron West)**

5th June 1980. Peter Jones from Billericay, Essex, was driving along the A127 arterial road towards Southend-on-Sea and had just passed the turning for Orsett and Brentwood at 10.55pm when he saw, *"... a vivid green, glowing light – the size of a bus, with brighter parts that looked like lights – heading at terrific speed across the sky, about a mile away, as it came over the top of my car. I thought it was going to crash. It then disappeared behind trees in the distance."* Five minutes later, Bill and Mavis Jones from Billericay, Essex, were travelling along the A127, towards Southend-on-Sea, at 11.00pm: *"As we passed the Brentwood turnoff, a vivid green cigar-shaped object, illuminated inside with a number of bright lights, shoot across the top of our car – so close, we thought there was going to be a collision."* **(Source: BUFORA/Mavis Jones/Brenda Butler/RonWest)**

18th June 1980. Mr. Andrews, from Rainbow Close, Ipswich, was walking past Ipswich Hospital, at 10.30pm. When: *"I saw a long, narrow object flying through the sky. It had five square* *windows on the side. One end was thicker than the other. I watched it for several minutes until it was lost in the distance."* **(Source: Brenda Butler /Ron West)**

20th June 1980. Graham Lee and his wife, Elizabeth, were driving between Clare and Cavendish, West Suffolk, when they sighted a bright orange *'light '*hovering just above the road and stopped the car to have a closer look. Ten minutes later the *'light shot* away, leaving a small trail behind it'.

21st June 1980. Switchboard operator Alma Millard, from Horfield, Bristol, was out walking with friends, at Bossington, near Porlock, Somerset, when she noticed, *". . .what I first thought was a small cloud, breaking away from a much larger cloud – then I suddenly realised the small cloud was moving much faster than the large one, making a pulsating movement, which made me keep my eyes fixed on it. Inside the cloud was a rounded to oval outline, which was forcing the cloud forward slightly in a pointed movement. There was no sound. It came out of a large cloud from Porlock Hill, travelling into a large cloud over Selworthy Beacon. Unfortunately, I tried to get my friends to see it but the sighting was over. The object, although travelling fast, didn't appear out of the cloud it travelled into."*

June 1980. Mary Sinton, the owner of a successful bed and breakfast farm accommodation in the Cotswolds, spoke about an extraordinary sighting that happened in June 1980, while on a camping holiday in Torver, Cumbria. *"I was with my boyfriend, Paul, at the time, and returning back to the campsite in our 'Hillman Imp' car, along the A593, Ambleside to Coniston Road, (Grid reference Longitude 323, Latitude 999/8, No. 7 English Lakes, South-East area). As we turned a bend in the road, close to the campsite, I was astonished to see nine tall 'figures', stood in a group of trees near the side of the road, caught in the glare of the spotlights fitted to the 'Hillman Imp' I was travelling in. I estimated they were at least seven feet tall and identically dressed, wearing silver-white coloured helmets and body armour, carrying what looked like a rod, carried vertically in front of each of them, reminding me of a regiment of soldiers stood to attention on the parade ground. As we drove past, I left it for a few seconds and then shouted out, in great excitement, 'Did you see them, Paul?'. One look at his face confirmed he had, although, oddly, he had only seen one 'figure'. When we arrived at the campsite, we felt very nervous and had trouble sleeping, wondering if anything else was going to happen. The next morning, we discussed what had happened and wondered whether we should let the Police know but, on reflection, thought they would never believe us."* We spoke to Paul, who confirmed the events given by his ex-girlfriend. He told us, *"It was the most unusual thing I have ever seen in my life. It defies explanation."* **(Source: Personal: Interviews)**

24th June 1980. Plymouth resident Tony Lloyd – aged 17, was at home at 10.30pm when a large 'flash of light' lit up the room. *"I shouted for my mother to come and have a look, and rushed outside just in time to see a bright orange 'globe' hovering low down in the sky, over the sea, a few miles away – too large to be an aircraft, or flare. I telephoned the Coastguard. A few minutes later, a white 'light', or 'beam', shot out of the larger object and headed northwards …then the orange 'globe' disappeared."* Other witnesses to these phenomena were PC John Daniel, and friend – retired Metropolitan Police Commander, Ivor Thorning, who viewed the object through binoculars." *We watched it for five minutes before it began to fade away. It looked like a bright light, with a white circle underneath, hovering over the sea off the coast of Totnes, Devon. I have flown thousands of miles in helicopters and it was no helicopter we were watching."* Another witness was Mrs. Todd, of Southway, Plymouth, who saw flashing lights in the sky at about the same time and called her daughter. *"We went outside and saw this cigar-shaped object, with flashing lights all around it, before extinguishing a minute later, allowing us to see a dark grey cigar shape – quite visible in the night sky, directly over Porsham Wood, about 500 yards away from the house, before it slowly faded from view." Other reports described it as looking like a black sphere, with wings, hovering in the sky. Mrs. J. Hamar, of Venton, just outside Plymouth, tells of seeing a 'bright golden light' in the sky at 10.30pm. Rushing outside, she saw, "What looked like a bird, or glider, motionless in the sky. I rushed to my neighbours and borrowed some binoculars, and on looking through them saw what looked like a 'flying saucer'. I alerted other neighbours and we continued to watch it, although I didn't see it go." The Authorities and Police were inundated with reports of UFOs from all over South Devon, including Ashburton, Brixham, Teignmouth and Newton Abbot – later explained by the Police as being unusual cloud formations and lightning flashes, whilst the Brixham coastguard suggested it was a helicopter using a powerful searchlight, which was reflecting off the clouds! **(Source: Bob Boyd, *Plymouth UFO Group* / Personal Interviews)**

2nd July 1980. Christine Harris of Baildon, Bradford, was amazed to see a *"silver and black metallic 'flying saucer'"* hovering in the sky, above Lister Mill, Manningham, Bradford, before heading off towards the direction of the City Centre.

7th July 1980. Mrs. Joyce Westerman from Normanton just outside Wakefield Yorkshire, close to the M62 and M61 Motorways, was to sight something extraordinary on the afternoon that defied explanation. There were seven witnesses, six of whom were the children of Mrs. Westerman. Joyce: "*I was at home. My six children were outside the house behind some fields containing electricity pylons, playing a ball game. When my eight-year-old daughter suddenly ran into the house shouting and crying and telling me to "come quick, an aeroplane has just landed in the field. I ran outside and saw, a few hundred yards away, in the fields, an object on the ground – dull grey in colour which had the appearance of a Mexican hat. Around the object stood three very tall 'men', all of whom appeared to be dressed in silver suits, pointing a dark instrument at the ground.* The children and Mrs. Westerman made their way over the field towards this object and stopped at a fence. The 'men' walked to the rear of the object and it rose vertically, stopped in mid-air, and then shot off at an angle at a high rate of speed. **(Source: Philip Mantle and Mark Birdsall)**

Mid-July 1980. David Cheesman, from Lewisham, London, was at home one evening with his brother, Michael, when they heard a cracking noise – like *an aircraft, breaking the sound barrier, followed by a bright 'light', which struck the blinds on the window, scattering light into the bedroom.* My brother went out to have a look and upon his return told me he had seen a *pitch black triangular object, displaying a light in each of its corners, moving slowly across the sky."*

18th July 1980. Six off duty nurses, living at *Cox's &Bramley Cottages*, in the bottom grounds of High Hurlands Nursing Home, Gentiles Lane, Bramshott Road (near to the village of Passfield, Hampshire) were disturbed by the sound of a strange humming noise at 8.30pm.

Two of the nurses – Georgina and Elona – decided to take a look outside and then shouted for the others to join them. The group then watched with disbelief as 'a saucer-shaped' object, flashing with red and green lights, began to slowly descend over the nearby apple trees, some 30 feet off the ground. One of the girls, Hazel, fetched a camera and took a photograph before it eventually disappeared about 15-20 minutes later. At the top of the hill, Nurse Diane Edworthy and Helen Monger were on duty when they heard the sound of someone moving about at the back of the

THE HALT PERSPECTIVE 2

building, followed by the dogs barking furiously, at 12.15am. Diane: *"A short time later, Helen told me she had seen a 'figure' by the back door, so I decided to ring the Police from the first floor office at the left-hand side of the building and ask them to attend, fearing we had prowlers. After making the 999 call, at 12.35am, I happened to glance up at the French windows that give access to an outside balcony 15-20 feet off the ground and was astonished, but not frightened, to see a 'figure' in black, at least six feet tall, peering through the window at me. He was covered in black and wearing a huge helmet over his head, preventing me from seeing if he had any neck or face, and covered all over in what looked like a leather outfit, with fabric that glistened. By the time I had regained my senses he was gone, making a thudding noise as he left."* A few weeks after the event a police officer brought an American around to the house who told Diane he was from Cape Canaveral and questioned her about what had occurred. Unfortunately she began to receive a number of telephone calls from all sorts of people who wanted to see her including cranks, so put a stop to it, but was intrigued to hear from a man, living in Headley Down, who told her about an identical 'figure' he saw 25 years ago in the area. **(Source: Personal Interview/ Omar Fowler, 'PRA')**

19th July 1980. George Morton, from Stratford Road, HallGreen, Birmingham – an ex-Signalman with the RAF, during the Berlin Airlift of 1949 – presented toPrince Charles, in a ceremony held at Bushy Park, London, over 50 years later: *"At that time, my mother, Ada, was alive and used to sleep downstairs in the front sitting room, due to ill health. At about midnight, I went over to the curtains and drew them back. I was stunned to see a grey domeshaped object, just like a 'flying saucer' with a blue/white field, of presumably 'energy' surrounding it, covering the width of Pembroke Croft, which backs onto Robin Hood Cemetery. It looked to be only a few feet above the houses. Excitedly, I shouted for my mother, who came over to have a look. Within a minute or so, it moved a fraction to the right and then headed off across the sky, towards Shirley, Solihull, very quickly. A few days later, I was looking through some Newspapers, when I came across a report of a UFO seen over Shirley."* So many people had seen it that the switchboard at the Police Station was jammed with callers. **(Source: Personal Interview)**

22nd July 1980. Mrs. Yvonne Howard and her husband were driving hometo York after holding a 'Disco' at Sutton-on-Derwent, at 2.00am, when they sighted a red flashing light in the sky. Within seconds there were two, three, and then six, of the objects moving in a cluster across the night sky.

14th August 1980. Andrew Nightingale was walking towards Helmshore Bay, Lancashire, at 8.50pm., accompanied by his friend, looking for somewhere to fish, when they saw nine pulsating lights forming a circle under the water. Within ten minutes the light had faded away. **(Source: Mr A Bramhill)**

17th August 1980. At 3.30am Mrs. Ethel Gatward ofTilbury, Essex, was finding it difficult to get to sleep when she noticed a white light in the clear sky. She got out of bed and went to the window, and was astonished to see a cigar-shaped object moving slowly through the sky, towards the north-east direction, about 200ft off the ground, approximately100yds away. In the middle of the object was a red flashing light. She then opened the window andheld it steady with her arms outside, over the ledge and continued to watch the object – now at roof top height a mere 50ft away. She then switched on the bedroom light and awoke her husband. He wasn't interested, and went back to sleep. Ethel: *"I first saw it to the right of my bedroom window. The object seemed to hover*

THE HALT PERSPECTIVE 2

for a few seconds and then came in a straight line past my window. The red light on top, in the middle, kept appearing like a flapping light that seemed to go on and off – like a signal. There was no sound, or wings, of any sort. The lights were brilliant; the middle was in complete darkness. There was grey metal visible at the end – this seemed like a ring. It was the shape of an elongated bullet, and about the size of a car. I could see light beams emitting from its nose and tail. There were no wings seen, or appendages, and it was totally silent." After watching it move away and out of sight and she then went back to bed. When she awoke on the Sunday morning she felt very sick, her arms were 'tingly' and she was unable to keep food down until later in the day (it is speculated that the medical condition may well have been caused by her having had her arms out of the open window during the time of observation). She also told of having experienced a roaring noise in her left ear, which lasted for about 30 mins. **(Source: Personal Interviews)**

18th August 1980. Reporter, Jeremy Finney, from the *'Hereford Times'* newspaper was travelling home from work at 5.50pm, *"I was driving along the A49 past Dinmore Hill – a regular route home – when I saw this 'blazing ball of red light' fall from a spherical cloud, silently in an arc, over fields, about half-a-mile away and disappear. I don't believe what I saw can be explained naturally as I experienced a period of missing time which I am unable to account for, but I prefer to leave things as they are."*

Nurse, Margaret Freeman, from Powys, was with her friend Carole, travelling towards Leominster at 10.00pm. on the 18th August, *"as I turned onto the main Hereford to Leominster Road, after commenting on the reddish colour sky, we saw what looked like a railway carriage, with different coloured windows in front of us. My recollection of what took place next is somewhat vague, but it felt like I was floating. I remember a journey along an ancient lane, with a hedge on both sides. I saw a sign – a triangular one, with a circle in it, hanging out of the* hedge. I then became aware of approaching a bend. Desperately, I tried to force the car around - acutely aware I was in no position to drive at all. Oddly, I saw no other vehicles. I heard Carole *remarking we were in* Leominster. Although I was coming around from whatever had ailed me, I still didn't feel right. My next memory was having a cup of tea with the Nursing Sister at the Hospital, and Carole pointing to her watch, telling me it was 10.00pm! This seemed impossible. It was 10.00pm. when we set out. I continued on my journey, dropping Carole off at her home. As she got out of the car, she asked, "Are you going to tell John (my husband) what happened?" I replied, "What on Earth are you on about?" Immediately I felt this terrible pain in my head and it all came rushing back to me."* **(Source: Personal Interviews)**

20th August 1980. Ruth Sutherland – then aged 14, was stood outside her house, at Poundsgate, Dartmoor, some four miles away from Newton Abbot, South Devon, talking to a friend at 9pm, when they noticed a *"small spinning egg-shaped object, gold in colour, heading across the sky towards them, which slowed down and changed direction, two huge objects appeared in the sky, side by side, filling up the sky – so big we could barely see the sky at the side of them making it three dimensional. We could see the nuts and bolts on the structure. One was saucer-shaped. The other resembled a gigantic 'T'-shaped object. As they came nearer we could see lights underneath, flashing in sequences. The object looked solid in appearance, as if constructed, so in the space of a few minutes we had seen three different types of UFOs."* **(Source: Personal Interviews)**

Just 45 minutes later, Mr. Leslie Gary Frost – an Engineer by occupation, from Sidegate Road, Hopton, on the Norfolk coast, was helping his wife, Margaret, bring in the washing, as dusk fell, on a

THE HALT PERSPECTIVE 2

cloudless, moonlit, night, when he was staggered to see two jet black massive structures, showing a pattern of red and white lights moving towards him, approximately 150 feet above the ground. *"The top one was about two hundred feet off the ground. They appeared solid, rather than translucent. I stood there with my son, who had come out of the house, mesmerized by what we were seeing. The one reminded me of a huge manta ray, with three large red lights at its front, with two brilliant lights at the rear. It halted in mid-air, throwing a shadow over us, and then there was a terrific flash of light and a small triangular object appeared, which began to circle the sky, for ten minutes, over a nearby water tower."* Margaret: *"I went to fetch in the washing. Lots of lights came over very slowly, from the back field. They looked like a formation of planes coming in, displaying red and white lights. One of the red ones shone brighter than the others. They couldn't have been planes – they were moving too slowly and making a droning noise. My husband wanted to see more, so he and my son went to have a closer look. I went inside."*

Anthony Mark Frost (10): *"We went up the garden to get the washing in and Dad said, 'Look at that!' Me and mum looked and saw three red lights and two white lights. My dad and I went to get a better view. There were two, because one broke off and it gave a flash and the big one went away, but the little one went around me and dad. We then went inside the house, then we went down to Hopton to phone the Police, and a Police lady came and she asked me some questions - then I went to bed."*

Mr. Frost confirmed he was interviewed by a Policewoman, who told him she would be sending a report to the MOD. After nothing else was heard, Mr. Frost contacted Brenda Butler and Dot Street, who went to interview him; otherwise, we would have been none the wiser. After details had been given to the Press, Mr. Frost was dismayed to find the published article failed to accurately reflect what had really happened and contacted the Police at Lowestoft, when he was then advised his report had been passed to the MOD.

Mr Frost: *"I've often wondered if there was any connection with heavy interference to my television set, about a week before the UFO sighting took place. I knew it wasn't the TV, as a replacement set showed the same problem. Sometime after the incident, I did receive a visit from two men, who told me they were from the University of Swindon, and very interested in looking at some scale models I had built of the UFOs I had seen, after taking a number of photographs of those models. They told me, in a very threatening manner, 'Leave it alone', which is exactly what I did until you contacted me."*

It appears that no such place existed, which should not come of any surprise. What gives these nameless, unidentified, persons the right to threaten people like Mr. Frost? We presume that they are fearful of reports such as this being brought to the attention of the Public. **(Source: Brenda Butler / Dot Street / Personal Interview)**

Late August, 1980. Kim Sergeant was driving his girlfriend home towards Blofield on the A47 – not many miles away from the scene of the previous UFO incident, at Hopton, when they noticed a glowing red 'ball of light' hovering just above the skyline which suddenly appeared to 'latch on' to their car. Much to the couple's consternation, the UFO continued to follow them, *"It reached the end of the road, just in front of us, and began to slowly descend. I stopped the car. To our further fright, it stopped motionless in the air and started to float towards us. I started up the car and raced away. To my relief, as we neared my girlfriend's house, it vanished behind some trees."* **(Source: Borderline Science Investigation Group)**

THE HALT PERSPECTIVE 2

28th August 1980. Anthony Richard Constable – a cafe proprietor by employment – his wife, Josephine, sister Carol Frisk, and the couple's two children – Dean (10), and Scott (8) was driving his Ford Escort along the Aveley Road, Essex heading towards Aveley, at about8.30pm on a warm and pleasant evening, along Romford Road: *"We noticed two bright red 'lights', motionless in the sky, 30 degrees above the eastern horizon, and decided to take a closer look, our curiosity aroused, and drove along Mill Road into Aveley High Street. At a point near Aveley roundabout, we noticed the 'lights' were approximately 200 yards away over the Stifford Road, and drove cautiously along Stifford Road (now almost directly underneath the two red 'lights'). We discussed getting out but decided against it, feeling frightened."* They sat watching: *"three red lights, spaced equidistantly apart from each, together brighter than street lights, showing from the underside a large light grey oval to circular-shaped mass, estimated to be at a height of 4-500 feet, its diameter equivalent to approximately three inches at arm's length."* Anthony decided to approach the object from the opposite direction and, after turning the car, looked up and was astonished to see it had vanished from sight. **(Source: Maureen Hall / Robert Easton, 'BUFORA' / Dan Goring,** *Earthlink***)**

29th August 1980. A resident of Todmorden, Lancashire, was driving home with some friends at 12.30am when they saw a red 'light' heading eastwards across the sky, towards another similar object: *"They met up and began to make these up and down movements – as if communicating with each other in some way. After a few minutes, the second 'light' disappeared. The other then headed off along the way it had come. We heard a noise like the wind and decided to continue our journey, thinking that was the end of it, when, all of a sudden, some 'lights' appeared on the road in front of the car and disappeared from sight, leaving us all shaken."* **(Source: Mr. A. Bramhill, BUFORA)**

30th August 1980. Crystal Hogben, Editor of the *'Magic Saucer'*-a magazine devoted to children's UFO sightings, was at her home address when she received a knock-on the door at 9.30pm by Keith Barker (13), who asked her to come outside, as it was National Sky watch night: *"I set off with Keith and a friend, Daren (8), on the way to a nearby farm, offering clear views of the sky, when Darren shouted, 'Look at that!' I looked out and saw a white 'light' in the sky, moving out from Cassiopeia. It seemed to divide into three lights moving across the sky in a great zigzag arc of movement, forming a triangle, before moving away.*

August 30th 1980. At about 1am several policemen and medical staff at a hospital (hospital not named), were amongst many people who reported seeing a UFO hovering over Dumfries. They described it as being oblong in shape and having multi-coloured lights. It hovered in the air for roughly 20 minutes before it vanished over some hills.

31st August 1980. A number of residents from various parts of Derbyshire contacted the authorities and newspapers after reporting an Unidentified Flying Object moving across the sky. It began at 12.20am when two separate groups of people (some in a car, were travelling back to their campsite, at Beresford Dale, Derbyshire) when the others (already on the campsite) noticed a number of 'lights' moving towards their position from the south-east. As they moved closer they saw a large oval shape, carrying two broad 'beams of light' at the front with six smaller red lights below the base. It then moved away towards northwards making a faint buzzing or humming noise. At about the same time the other group, who were already on the campsite, sighted a square-shaped object in the sky with rounded corners, showing two bright white lights – like those carried by a medium sized aircraft. The object, flying straight and level across the sky at an

THE HALT PERSPECTIVE 2

estimated altitude of 1,500-2,000 feet was in view for 6-7 minutes as it headed away in a northwest direction, making a humming noise. At 12.30am a woman resident of Ashbourne was saying goodnight to a friend, when they saw a mass of flashing and pulsating red, blue and green, lights approaching from the Ormston direction, (Southeast). *"It was larger than a four bedroom house and made a humming noise. As it passed overhead, calves in a nearby field scattered. Our dog rushed into the house, clearly distressed."* At about the *same time*, over Chaddesden, some 12 miles away from Ashbourne, a householder noticed a large bright star in the sky. Curious, she looked out and saw, with amazement, *". . . a large dome-shaped object, covered with yellow/white lights hovering above the rooftops of houses opposite, level with my position. It reminded me of a bright chandelier and was about four times the size of a full moon. I watched as it headed away westwards."*

At 12.35am a cluster of red, white, green and blue, lights (higher than the rest) were seen moving across the sky over the *Nestles* factory, in Ashbourne. As it approached closer, the witness received an impression of two fuselages and five or six portholes. It then banked a few degrees to the left enabling the witnesses to see, *"a distinct impression of a high tail fin and something apparently ducting from the bottom of the 'craft' – like steam, or vapour."* At 12.37am a local disc jockey and his wife were driving home through the outskirts of Mapleton, towards Mayfield, when they noticed a group of lights, surrounded by what appeared to be mist, heading in their direction. *"It looked like two car headlights, shining upwards, with a row of blue lights and a green light, with a yellow flashing light underneath. It was so low it narrowly missed colliding with the corner of a house before flying away, towards Dovedale, accompanied by a buzzing noise."* Another report for the same day – from Shelton Lock, Derbyshire – told of a silver *'upside-down saucer-shaped object, with a 'cup' on top, rotating around a centre flashing light',* which was sighted hovering over power lines.

At 1.40am Edna Proctor and her daughter, Edith, sighted what they took to be a helicopter hovering above a reservoir, at Golborne, near Wigan, described as, *"an oval or rectangular object, surrounded by a sort of orange 'mist' at the rear, out of which came out red sparks. Through the 'mist' a slowly pulsing red light was seen. On the side of the object was an orange 'patch', or window; at the end were two yellowish lights"*. Another witness was Mrs. Brenda Hollins – also from Goldborne – who appears to have sighted the same object over the reservoir, although she did not see the windows or the lights on the object, probably due to the angle of observation. According to her, *"the object lowered something into the reservoir and then raised it up, before shooting across the sky and disappearing from sight".* **(Source: Jenny Randles, 'The Pennine UFO Mystery'/ Peter Hough)**

2nd September 1980. Shirley Skinner, a housewife from South Town Road, Great Yarmouth, watched with amazement as at 7.30pm an oblong-shaped object, with a glowing light in its centre, crossed the sky. *"I tried to settle down for the evening and started to watch the TV. At about 8.00pm, I glanced through the kitchen window and saw, with some fright, what looked like two shiny black pointed crash helmets, with red 'bands' sticking up, a few feet above the hedge. I wondered what on earth they were, but lacked the courage to go out and have a look. I shut the curtains. When I next looked out, they had gone."* **(Source: Ron West)**

6th September 1980. Christina Campbell and her daughter, Barbara, had just finished clearing up at the family-run Public House, *The Commercial Inn*, at Colinsburgh, Fife, at12.35am when they saw, *"a dull red coloured cigar-shaped object in the sky, towards the direction of Anstruther, in the centre of which was a brilliant flashing light – like a flashgun going off",* before being lost from sight behind buildings in the NNW direction, five minutes later. The matter was reported to RAF Leuchars, who could offer no explanation.

6th September 1980. Tony Caldicott, from Kings Norton, Birmingham, was out fishing at the side of the canal, at Parsons Lane, Kings Norton, at 4.00pm. "*A man came up to me. He said, 'Have you ever seen a cloud like that?' I looked and saw an object inthe sky, bell-shaped – then it changed to a 'cigar', or 'tube', in the sky – a process of behaviour itrepeated, seven times over in the 45 minutes period we watched it.*"

7th September 1980. At 8.45pm four boys, fishing at Trimpley Reservoir, *close to Habberley Valley (just outside Kidderminster, Worcestershire)* sighted "three 'lights' in the sky – '*the first, moving in a straight line; the second, zigzagging – then two of them entered a cloud, leaving the third to carry on, which descended over nearby trees, about 200 yards away, surrounded by haze, before moving away out of sight*". (**Source: Crystal Hogben,** *Magic Saucer*)

8th September 1980. A triangular formation of 'three lights, with a red light inset' was seen over Tyneside by a number of residents who contacted the Police. Enquiries made with RAF Acklington confirmed they had received other UFO reports, adding, "*We have no further information about this and, if we did, we would not be allowed to release the information.*"

11th September 1980. Gipton, Leeds, West Yorkshire Police officers, PC Warner and WPC Firth, were directed to have a look along the A64 York Road, after an anonymous call was made at 3.41am reporting a UFO over that location. A short time later the Police officers sight a bright light in the sky moving eastwards towards the village of Scholes. It then halted and began to flicker in brightness, but suddenly shot upwards to an estimated height of about a thousand feet in seconds. Due to sparsely scattered clouds they lost sight of it initially, but saw it again moving southwards. The Officers gave chase but lost it down York Road, Leeds area. At about the same time Police officers near Garforth Golf Club sighted a bright object in the sky, giving off red white and blue bursts of colour. It hovered in the sky and then as before shot upwards in a second and was gone out of view.

13th September 1980. Two days later a similar if not the same light was seen over Wetherby by several officers. They chased the object to Fulford York some 13miles away before being lost from observation. Discreet enquires made revealed this had been tracked by radar (Police confirmation later revealed this to be Staxton Wold Early Warning Station). Other officers interviewed were, Sgt Craig, PC Bowe, PC Quinn, PC Roy Allen, PC Richard Gordon. Inspector Blanchard, and WPC Cranidge, who described it as, "*cone-shaped through binoculars. At5am, a smaller light detached itself and hovered silently with the larger object which was seen topoint in movements upwards then down to the left.*" The illustrations made by the officers resemble the object seen by Coastguard Brian Jenkins on the 26th of April 1967, at Devon – later explained away as a balloon. Radar tapes were destroyed (sounds an all too familiar response!).

13th of September 1980. Humberside Police was contacted by a member of the public at 10pm reporting having seen a UFO. PC's 1077 and 3056 were sent to the Long Hill and Brandshome estates in Hull. They interviewed the witnesses who described seeing what looked like an oval pink coloured bright flare in the sky at 9.55pm which was lost from view over Sutton Golf Club area. The conclusions reached by Graham Bridsall, who wrote to many people in authority including the

THE HALT PERSPECTIVE 2

MOD and Professor Jakeways, were that this could have been Venus. Could this incident have been the reason why a senior officer from Humberside Constabulary went to see Colonel Dick Spring at Bentwaters. They couldn't have known about the incident in the forest – or did they? Is it possible that details of an alleged incident which had taken place near an Air Base had been telexed to all forces? Unlikely. During an interview with the secretary of Colonel Richard Spring – Chief of Base Operations & Training, at Woodbridge/Bentwaters – Georgina Bruni was told of that visit made by Hull police officers, with regard to a UFO incident under investigation by them, and that Colonel Richard Spring had himself gone to the railway station to pick up the officers. Initially, we were puzzled why the Hull Police should have contacted Colonel Richard Spring about any UFO incident which occurred hundreds of miles away from them. We originally believed the visit by the Hull police officers was as a result of a UFO incident which took place at Ganstead, near Hull, during early January 1981. It involved members of the local CB Radio – the *'Hull Citizens Band'* – who, after hearing of the incident through eavesdropping on police transmissions, involving a landed UFO, made their way to the location concerned. Information from 'Peter' then a serving officer divulged that two police officers known to him had been directed to the UFO incident. As a result of what they had witnessed, it was alleged that the woman officer suffered some trauma. Both of them were warned never to discuss the matter again. Details of the incident were subsequently published in the *Hull Star*, on 16th January 1981. Could it have been the Police UFO sightings which took place in Leeds and Hull that had precipitated the enquiry and visit to an Airbase hundreds of miles away? Or was it a combination of the two incidents?

15th September 1980. Dovercourt, Essex, housewife Jean Cook was hanging out her washing just before 1pm when her husband, Derek, directed her attention to something he could see in the sky. *"I saw a bright, round, silvery object – the shape of a children's swimming ring, gliding through the sky, about 200 feet above us. It had a small dome on top and, as it flew, it wobbled slightly, allowing view of a black underside, before it disappeared behind some trees."* **(Source: BUFORA Journal 10, No. 2, April, 1981)**

16th September 1980. Pam Blakey, from Perton, near Wolverhampton, formerly employed as a Secretary at RAF Cosford, Shropshire, was driving home with her husband. *"We had been out visiting some friends and were returning home to Perton, just after 3.00am, when we saw what, at first, we took to be the headlight of a farm tractor, stationary, over a farmer's field. As we continued on our journey through unlit countryside, with Peter driving, we noticed the 'light' was now following us. All of a sudden the darkness was flooded with brilliant silver light, turning night into day. My first thoughts were that it was a Police helicopter, hovering over our car. Panicking, I shouted out to Peter to get us home as quickly as possible, realising that it was only a few feet above us. As we entered Perton, driving along The Parkway, with this luminous object still behind us, I admit to being terrified. When we pulled up at the front of the house and dashed in the 'ball of light' shot upwards into the sky. Thinking this was the end of it, I rushed upstairs to the bedroom window and looked out, where I saw the object, now triangular in shape, hovering over a small coppice in Sedgewick Drive, before it once again shot upwards into the sky, where I never saw it again."*

Pam told us that although she went to work a few hours after this incident, she was disinclined to bring the matter to anybody's attention, fearing nobody would believe her and that her position of employment may have been in jeopardy. She believes there was a link between the sighting of this unidentified object and a marked deterioration in her health, involving nosebleeds, persistent headaches, depression and the lack of co-ordination. In addition to this, the couple reported a number of electrical malfunctions around the house, necessitating the replacement of some of the domestic appliances installed in the property. Peter: *"We noticed something very unusual about the red Allegro company car that was only twelve months old. When I examined the vehicle, the day after the incident, I found the red paint on the roof had turned to orange. The car had to be scrapped later!*

17th September 1980. Civil Servant, Gary Moore, accompanied by his friend, Andrew Johnstone – an electrical fitter by trade – was driving home to Portsmouth, southwards, along the A3, after having just gone through the village of Cobham at 12.30am. While descending ahill, with a good clear view of the open countryside, their attention was drawn to a 'bright light' in the distance, which, as they travelled closer, was seen as two lights, similar in appearance to two car headlights, approximately 200 feet off the ground, stationary in the sky. Gary decided to pull into a lay-by and get out of the car, curious as to what the lights could be. *"Suddenly, we were able to make out other lights on the 'craft', which consisted of a red light on the front left-hand side, and a green light on the right-hand side. In the centre section of the object appeared a flickering square of lights -something like three rows of five lights – glittering in amber, white, blue, sequence, as the lights rippled backwards and forwards. At the rear could be seen two amber lights, about the same width apart as the 'headlamps'. Whatever it was, it was massive."* After passing overhead the object, estimated to be at least 200 feet long, with its huge rectangular body reminiscent of some majestic airborne oceanic liner, was soon lost from sight as it passed over a nearby hill. **(Source: Omar Fowler, 'PRA')**

18th September 1980. The West Mercia Police were called to the Church Hill area of Redditch, Worcestershire, after four schoolboys – Tim Belmont, Peter Bevington, Stuart Heath and Colin Humphries – contacted them, reporting having sighted a clover-shaped UFO hovering about ten feet above a house in Sandhurst Close at 9.00pm.Tim was the first to see the object, which he took to be a bird – then realised it was stationary, with a red flashing light on each wing. We traced one of the youths, Colin Humphries. *"I was out walking, with three other schoolboys, in the Church Hill area, on what was a stormy evening, with lightning flickering overhead. All of a sudden, we were shocked to see a cigar-shaped 'thing', metallic in appearance, with red flashing lights along its 'wings', hovering about ten feet above a house in Sandhurst Close. Our excitement soon turned to fear, so one of us telephoned the Police. By the time they arrived, the 'flying cigar', or whatever it was, had moved away. The Police told us it was probably lightning, following a heavy storm in the area."* **(Source: Derek Waugh, Redditch UFO Study and Investigation Group /** *Redditch Indicator***, 26.Sept.80, 'Close Encounter with a 4 feet UFO')**

19th September 1980. Mrs. Rina Oakes was returning home, at 9.00pm, driving past Coughton Court – a Stately Home, situated just off the Alcester Road, a few miles from Studley. Warwickshire, *"It was pouring with rain, at the time, but I noticed what looked like a 'cigar of light' stationary in the sky, over Coughton Court. Then the windscreen wipers failed, but after I had driven a few hundred feet along the road, they came back on again. This was the first and last time they would ever let me down. Was there a connection with what I saw?"* **(Source: Personal Interview)**

21st September 1980. A motorist and his family were returning home along the A530, near Wimboldsley, Cheshire when they saw what appeared to be two 'stars' in the sky, followed by a heavy burst of static on the VHF Radio, installed in the vehicle. Curious as to the source of these two 'stars' in the sky, the driver stopped and got out of his vehicle. As he did so, *"the top 'star' dropped* downwards and headed straight for me but stopped in mid-air, about 500 yards away, approximately 200 feet, high. Then it took off and met up with the second object. Both of them then sped across the sky, where they were soon lost from view."

23rd September 1980. Mr David Munday contacted Warminster based friend, UFO enthusiast Steve Wills in 2015 wishing to tell him about an incident that took place at 6pm. *"I was looking forward to going to the Bristol Rovers league cup evening game at 7.45pm kick off being played at Ashton Gate, Bristol City ground I and my brother Michael met Mark Haslam and got onto the Diesel pulled train bound for Bristol. We departed Portsmouth and Southsea Station around 4.45 and travelled past Cosham , Salisbury, and when south of Warminster noticed from the train window on the right hand side looking in an easterly direction, a round shiny bright, sun like light object moving in the sky above the tree line on hills between Stockton and Warminster for at least two minutes as the train slowed down. Many other 'fans' in the carriage also saw the object which was the subject of great curiosity and astonishment as the train went past Warminster we lost sight of it."* Michael: *"I noticed a bright round orange red object moving up and down silently over the tree line, on the east* side of the train was a telephone mast visible up the hill". **(Personal Interview)**

23rd September 1980. At 6.30am Julie Box, of Pans Lane, Devizes, Wiltshire, got up to see her soldier husband, Michael, off to work at the Queen's Lancashire Regiment, Warminster, when he told her, *"I've just seen six UFOs, one behind the other, pass over the brow of a nearby hill (some 2-3 miles away) while looking through the kitchen window".* Julie looked through the window and saw two objects, moving from left to right, flying across the *clear blue sky*, which inexplicably vanished from view, accompanied by heavy interference on the radio.

October 1980. Schoolboys – David Prytherch & Gerald Kellahan, from Sir Thomas Jones School, Amlwch, Anglesey North Wales sighted, *". . . a brightly lit saucer-shaped object, full of coloured lights, which made a swishing noise as it passed overhead. It looked like a crab underneath, as it passed directly above our heads, at around 8.00pm, before heading on towards Parys Mountain, joined, shortly afterwards, by a bigger version of the first."* **(Source: *The North Wales Chronicle*, 16.Oct.80 – 'UFO lands on Parys Mountain')**

9th October 1980. Nurse Diane Edworthy, stationed at High Hurlands Hospital, Liphook, Hampshire, found herself once again witnessing another example of UFO behaviour – this time over the orchard, close to the main building. *"I was working with a girl, called Cathy, at about midnight. She drew my attention to an awful humming noise she could hear. I listened but couldn't hear anything at all. A short time later, I happened to glance through the window overlooking the rear of the building, when I saw some bright lights moving slowly across the sky, towards the front of the building. I thought that was very odd and, although I couldn't give any distance, they seemed close enough to be over the grounds of the hospital, rather than high up in the sky. If they had been high up, I wouldn't have seen them. I alerted Cathy and we stood there, watching what looked like a huge star in the sky, as it changed colour from white to intense blue in an explosion of light.*

After twenty minutes, or so, it changed colour again from blue to red, green and orange, before going back to white again. At this point we had to get on with our duties, so it wasn't until 12.45am. We had another look and saw flashing lights coming from the 'Star'. We opened the window and saw it was now only a few hundred yards away from us, and about 20 feet off the ground, with lots of flashing red and green lights over the edge of the orchard. It stayed there for some time, spinning and throwing off lights, until at 3.30am it and the 'Star' just disappeared." **(Source: Omar Fowler /SIGAP Journal *'Pegasus',* November/December 1980.** *FSR* **Volume 30, No. 6, 1985 /Personal Interview)**

22nd October 1980. Julie Noutch, aged 18, was a front seat passenger in a car being driven by her Aunt, along Tabor Road, Criccieth, Gwynedd, Wales at 7pm. *"As we turned a right-hand bend, we noticed seven orange lights forming a circle in the sky, just above the horizon – presumably connected with the appearance of a moving green light, about a mile away. I asked my Aunt to stop, so we could have a closer look. She refused, as she was frightened. I later contacted RAF Valley. They told me no aircraft had been flying in the area at the time. Although over 20 years has passed since I saw the UFO, my memory of it is still clear."* **(Source: Police Constable Kevin Babb/Personal Interview)**

28th October 1980. At 4.40pm Eric Rush, from London, was standing on the platform of Peckham Rye Station. *"I glanced up into a clear sky and noticed a 'bright light' almost directly above me, motionless in the sky. I knew it wasn't Venus, or Mercury. It was far too high to be a planet. I noticed there was a black smudge underneath it, which began to form a longer line as it corkscrewed downwards. I watched it for about five minutes, wondering what on earth it could have been – then I suddenly had this awful feeling ... 'Was it an ICBM Missile, with a nuclear warhead?' If it was, there wasn't much point in running anywhere. When the black line reached about 30,000 feet, it broke, or split, into three separate objects, that slowed in descent to about a 1,000 feet, before soaring like a Red Arrows bomb burst display, towards the East, South, and South-west – out of sight in seconds. I tried to telephone 'BUFORA' and Heathrow Airport but in the end, I gave up."* **(Source: Personal Interview)**

29th October, 1980. Police Constable David Philip Jones, from County Police Station, Llanerchymedd, Amlwch, Wales, was awoken by the sound of the family cat, crying to go out, at 5.00am. While returning upstairs, his attention was attracted by a source of bright light filtering through the closed curtains. Curious as to the cause, he opened the curtains and recoiled from a glare so bright it pained his eyes to look at. Opening the window he looked out and, as his eyes adjusted slowly, he noticed a large *'ball of silver light, with hazy rings around it, underneath which could be seen a smaller silver sphere'.* Excitedly, he called his wife, Helen Mary Jones. The couple then stood watching the dazzling object until the cold of the night proved too much, when they decided to go back to bed. **(Source: Personal Interview)**

1st November 1980. Accrington resident – Mrs. Maureen Turner – was stood outside her house, with her children, at 5.45pm when she sighted, *". . . an object hovering in the sky. It looked like a Frisbee and then the shape of a lemon. It was orange to start with but then there was a blue flash which completely lit up the object, now metallic and blue-grey in colour. It made this loud humming noise and was in view for some time before moving slowly away."*

13th November 1980. At 4.30pm six schoolboys – Richard Gilson, Lee Perkins, Anthony Rayment, Matthew Anderson, Vincent Jones and Abdul Shahid, were playing football on a stretch of land, bordering Poole Harbour, known as *Baiter Point*, when they saw an object, resembling *"a hamburger, with 'bumps', bisected by a black line, showing red yellow and blue lights, apparently mounted on some sort of propeller projecting from the underneath, with a red poppy shaped underside, out of which protruded a single central yellow light, twice the size of a helicopter, stationary in the sky, at a height of about 300 feet.' After a few minutes, the object – making a low humming noise – rose upwards and flew away on a diagonal course."*

THE HALT PERSPECTIVE 2

19th November 1980. We were to come across a remarkable report involving a 'close encounter' with an alleged Alien 'craft' and its two occupants, during the late evening according to Mario Luisi – a resident of Burneside, Cumbria, whom we met up with in 2000, wishing to find out more about what lay behind his extraordinary claim. Mario – an affable friendly man – advised us, straightaway; he did not really care whether we believed him or not. After all, he said, "I *didn't have to answer your letter*" and, after some conversation, produced an elderly, poorly typewritten but thorough, original, 5,000 word document, entitled, '*My Close Encounter*', compiled a few weeks after the incident, showing the 'craft' and its 'occupants'.

28th November 1980. Police Constable Alan Godfrey, was on mobile patrol, at Todmorden, West Yorkshire during the early hours of when he received a number of calls on his personal radio, reporting a herd of between 20-30 cattle roaming the street on the outskirts of Todmorden. After having made various searches of the area, without finding any sign of the missing cattle, Alan called in at the local Police Station and left, a short time later. Having travelled acouple of hundred yards, west –north-west, along Burnley Road, when he noticed a glow, low down, on the road in front of him, which he took to be an early morning bus, approximately 200 yards away."*I quickly changed my mind when I saw this very strange object hovering about five feet above the road, resembling a spinning top, with windows. I estimated it had a width of 20 feet, and was 14 feet high. I drove up to a hundred feet away from it and stopped. It was dome-shaped; with the top more flatter than the base, and projected fluorescent light from the top. I saw it had a row of dark 'square' windows beneath it. The object was white in colour and rotating anticlockwise. The top of it came to within two feet of the tops of nearby lamp-posts. The leaves on nearby trees were shaking, although there was no breeze. The headlights of the Police car were reflected away from the object, showing me it was something physical. I tried to radio the Police Control – there was nothing, just static, although the area does have its 'black spots'.*" Alan remained calm and sketched the object onto his Police notepad, before driving away from the object, now feeling disorientated. When he returned to the scene, a short time later, there was nothing to be seen.

December 30th 1980. The Northumbrian Police received a number of calls from the Public reporting UFOs being seen crossing the sky over Tyneside and South Northumberland between 4.35pm-4.45pm. Mr Leslie Balsdon, a draughtsman by trade from Ashington – who was previously a non-believer in the existence of UFOs – was with his two sons, Gary and Darren, when they saw, '*five or six quite distinctive, saucer-shaped craft heading out towards the sea, each showing a bright white light at the front, with a red glow at the rear, flying just under cloud cover. They seemed to be in formation with one leading the others fanned out behind*' Invariably the sighting led to all sort of speculation by the press and media; one suggestion being the witnesses may have seen the 'RAF Woodbridge UFO' returning to outer space after its landing in Suffolk. Other witnesses were Mr & Mrs Ward from Crosby Road, Scunthorpe, Lincolnshire, they were sat in the living room of their top floor flat at 4.30pm when they saw, '*three objects resembling stars moving from the South in a horizontal line heading northwards, within a minute they had passed overhead and we lost sight of them*'. Enquiries made by Dick Thompson (the Lincoln-based UFO researcher whom we met to discuss the matter) revealed that between five and ten tadpole-shaped objects were seen a short time later passing across the sky over Messingham near Scunthorpe, during the evening of the 30th of December 1980. **(Source Richard Thompson)**

Events important enough to be brought to the attention of The Lord Hill Norton (whom we wrote to; wondering why such a prominent figure had taken an interest in a matter, which still attracts ridicule to this present day). In one of a number of letters sent to us he gave this reply, *"My position is and always has been that there are physical objects, almost certainly not man-made, regularly detected in Earth's atmosphere. I want to know what they are, who, or what is directing them and what is their purpose."*

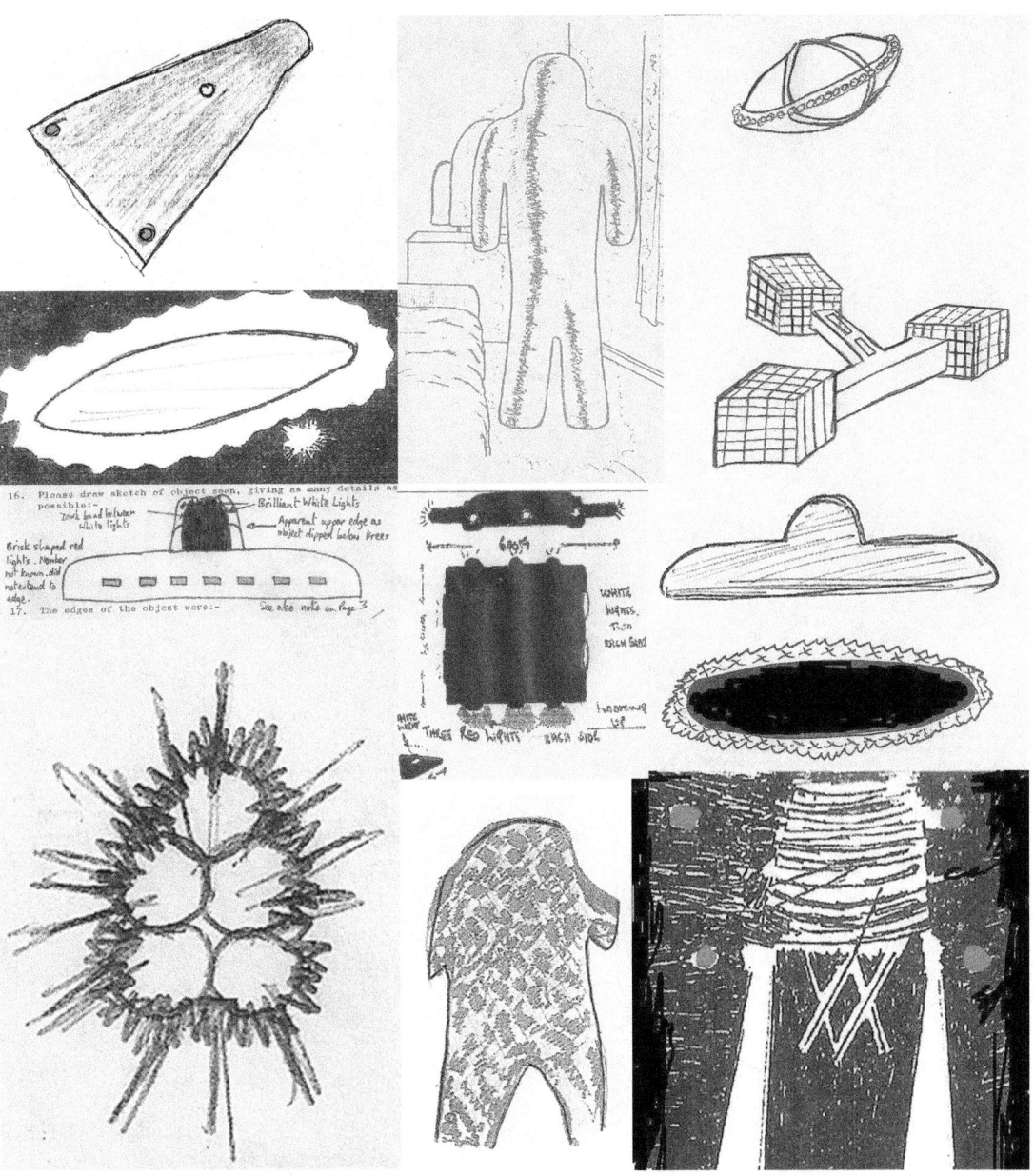

THE HALT PERSPECTIVE 2

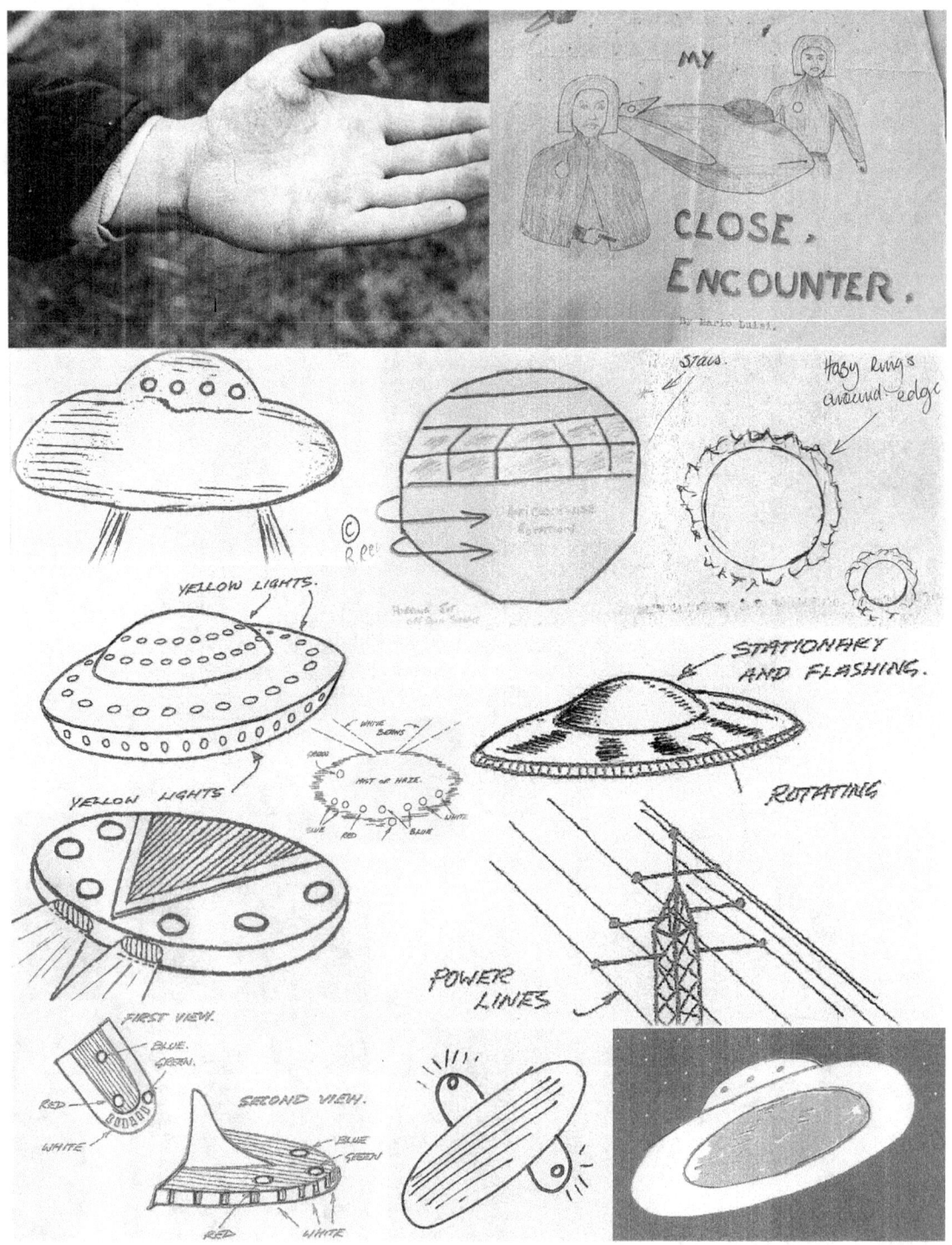

THE HALT PERSPECTIVE 2

1980 – A time of tension on the World stage

In September 1980, the Iraqi army carefully advanced along a broad front into Khūzestān, taking Iran by surprise. Iraq's troops captured the city of Khorramshahr but failed to take the important oil-refining centre of Ābādān, but by December 1980 the Iraqi offensive had bogged down about 50–75 miles (80–120 km) inside Iran after meeting unexpectedly strong Iranian resistance.

On 29th November 1980, the commanding general of the Group of Soviet Forces in East Germany announced that from the 9th of December almost all of East Germany along the Polish border would be closed to travel by members of the Western Military Liaison Missions in East Germany. East German air defence personnel reportedly had their leaves restricted pending a 'big action' that might be called in the coming week.

In his daily notebook the next day, Zbigniew Kazimierz Brzezinski, a polish American diplomat who had served as a counsellor to President Lyndon B. Johnson and National security advisor to President Jimmy Carter, characterized the situation as *"gathering clouds over Poland are getting darker."*

He records that he had openly stressed to the press the *"calamitous consequences of a Soviet military intervention,"* even though there was still disagreement within US policy agencies whether anything should be said publicly. It is clear that fears were raised by these developments which could have wrought many changes both political and military – dragging us into more conflicts over, in all probability, the most valuable commodity – oil!

Whilst 'normal' life went on in the UK, these international developments must have been the source of great concern, especially if a confrontation between either the Soviets or Iraq sparked off a military response. Obviously the US military and Government were worried, about the developing international crisis despite it being the Christmas period. Whilst the political issue has no bearing on what took place in rural Suffolk, there could have been ramifications for the US bases that operated in the UK for obvious reasons, should the situation have escalated. This was the backcloth to what happened not only in Rendlesham Forest but elsewhere in the Country involving the appearance of inexplicable objects that continued to make their presence known, apparently indifferent to the affairs of life on this planet!

Alan Godfrey

THE HALT PERSPECTIVE 2

Charles Halt with David Boardman during a meeting in West Virginia

PART 3

DECEMBER IN SUFFOLK!

Colonel Charles Irwin Halt comments . . .

O**NE** may consider from the apparent biased attitude in which the media have over the last 60 years presented reports of UFO activity, that it is deservedly being labelled The Greatest Show on Earth. If so, then I'm not on my own, talk of the lighthouse, cow's muck on fire, cops playing with patrol cars on the runway, moth traps, psychonitric holograms and a myriad of other silly explanations, should be totally discarded in favour of the FACTS, which follows.

First I'm going to comment on some other UFO incidents, which form the backcloth of this book, to show we weren't on our own, and that as far as I am concerned, what I saw cannot be explained. It's pretty obvious now that the wealth of reports already outlined for 1980 of which, of course, I had not the slightest idea existed, puts things in the right perspective!

What Jim and John saw . . . well there's going to be some discussion about that later, particularly following Jim's unprecedented out-of-character verbal attacks on me and surprisingly, his companion and fellow UFO witness, John Burroughs in his latest book '*The Rendlesham Enigma*' co-authored with Gary Osborne, published in July 2019 priced at £24.

Constant attacks on my character

Over the years there have been constant attacks on my character, because I merely told the truth, about what I witnessed, rather than pandering to those that seem to think I am covering up for something! Wishful thinking on their behalf! Then there are those who weren't there – they continue to scrutinise every facet of what happened, seeking tiny inconsistencies between the witnesses that were there and then casting aspersions on those involved.

Others cultivate the media and offer sensational explanations of what they believe *actually happened* – sometimes misquoting me. Not forgetting the silly explanations put forward by those who have not bothered to research into the UFO subject. Worse of all, are manufactured or fabricated versions of events by people like Larry Warren and others which only muddy the waters of what took place, in an attempt to whip up vivid imaginations based on individual belief systems influenced by the tabloids.

THE HALT PERSPECTIVE 2

Beams from the UFO had struck the WSA – so they say I claim!

Charles: In one program I was heard, (it begins to get very repetitive) describing the beams from the UFO had struck the WSA. It was later ascertained that my speech had been manipulated editorially to give that impression. Makers of these films/documentaries are so desperate to spice things up; they have been literally putting words into my mouth, by editing cut and splicing to make it sound like I was actually admitting a serious breach had taken place. On another occasion it was claimed in an interview that while out in the forest I had admitted being confused with the Orford Ness lighthouse- another fraudulent claim.

Here are some photos taken from a recent visit to the airbase, the tower itself is too dangerous to climb. Another one – somewhat period, shows 'Whisky' tower.

THE HALT PERSPECTIVE 2

How can you ignore the importance of what is being published in this book, showing that so many people can't be mistaken and want answers! It's odd that this incident has attracted the attention of the public for now 40 years. People wonder why that is? Taking into consideration the enormous amount of evidence unrolled before the readers eyes, over the last 70 years proving the existence of a phenomena which still defies understanding!

Emphasising the importance of what this occurrence meant to the British Government (albeit behind the scenes) ignoring the plethitude of ridiculous explanations offered – lies with the fact that this incident was later the subject of Questions in the British Parliament, on more than one occasion by Lord Hill Norton, Admiral of the Fleet who John was in touch with. He publicly stated he found this incident the most convincing.

Working with John Hanson of *Haunted Skies*

I've been working with John Hanson over the last five years sharing opinions, views, and looking at countless original UFO reports supplied to me from John, many that took place over the East Anglia area which, while not necessarily supplying the answers, shows that a concerted effort has been and will continue to be made to suppress the reality of what is going on. Why and for what reason?

1940 – Saucer-shaped object seen at the Base!

John Hanson even told me about a sighting he had come across in 1940 when a saucer-shaped object was seen by an airman guarding the RAF Woodbridge Airbase! Strange lights aren't rare! I'm told that

THE HALT PERSPECTIVE 2

records even go further back than this, which now doesn't surprise me. The East Anglia region has been prominent with UFO activity, on many occasions RAF RADAR has picked up multiple targets moving in from the east coast going back to this period of time. Here is the sketch drawn by the RAF airman, this shows that we weren't the only ones!

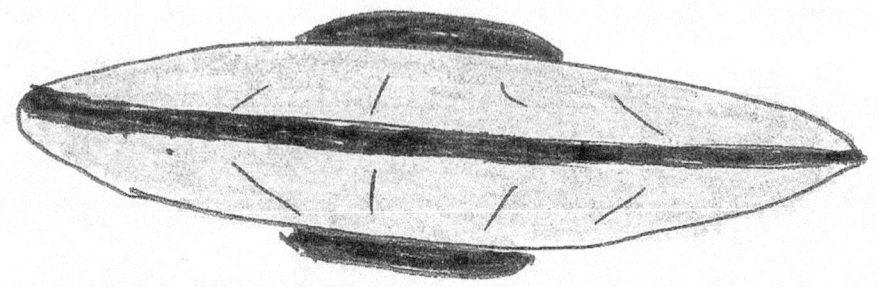

SUMMARY OF EVENTS

PLEASE DESCRIBE IN YOUR OWN WORDS THE EVENTS OF THE SIGHTING:

On approximately June 6th 1940, I was on night spotting duty on an ack ack site at Woodbridge, Suffolk guarding dummy aircrafts on a dummy airfield. Early morning I observed an object in the sky approximately 10-15 thousand feet distance away. Shape of a saucer and measured about 30-40ft across. I observed this with binoculars, and then took got a better look I used the identification telescope. On doing this I could not see through the object and it seemed to be hovering over the dummy airfield. I woke the Sergeant Major and told him and he said it was a weather balloon or meteor. I phoned Head Quaters and explained the situation and was told no search lights was up, no aircrafts or weather-balloons were about. I was probably looking at a gas cloud. The object started to move from left to right slowly and after a couple of minutes gathered speed then disappeared. It was logged and made a joke of.

1977 – Rendlesham Forest illuminated by bright lights!

Charles: Another example of strange lights which lit up the forest, this time a few years before the one that I was involved in, was given by Greg Ralston, a US security officer who was working swing shift 4-midnight in the 'B' area which backs onto Rendlesham Forest, near midnight, around 1977: "*We saw these lights which were so bright they lit up the woods, but couldn't see where they were coming from. This was an area well patrolled by our security force. Others that saw it included guys working on the aircraft. It was just like someone switching a light on and then off that quick. It was reported. Some years later I was watching* Unexplained Mysteries *on TV which covered a sighting at RAF Woodbridge, Suffolk and featured the Deputy base Commander Colonel Halt. So I thought he should know.*"

THE HALT PERSPECTIVE 2

1978 – UFO shines down light beams – sound familiar?

Another sighting of a strange airborne object took place a year later on 22nd November 1978 just off the *A5 road, Daventry, Northamptonshire, England, involving beams of light that moved around the vehicle in which head teacher Mrs Elsie Oakensen was driving at the time, which I would like to comment on.

She was another credible witness, married to a Police Inspector. John went to see her and spoke to her on a number of occasions about the incident. She wondered if there as any connection with what I saw two years later. I don't know but common sense dictates that there may well be.

Here is what Elsie had to say; what a pity we never met up: *"I was on my way home when is saw an object consisting of two globes linked by a tube hovering in the sky, during the late afternoon* (then her car came to a halt.) *To my relief, the car re-started and I made my way along a stretch of tree-lined road – a familiar route home. As I came to the end of this 'tunnel' of trees, total darkness engulfed everything around me. I couldn't even hear the engine of the car, or see any lights.*

Out of this blackness came a brilliant white 'circle of light', about a yard in diameter, shining onto the road to the left of the car, illuminating the landscape. To my astonishment, I recognised I was now near to a farm gate, some fifty yards further on, around a right-angled bend – something I had no memory of driving along. It then went dark and bright again, as a number of these illuminated 'circles of light' (there must have been 15 or 16 of them) switched on and off in a regular pattern, moving around the car in a semi-circle. Once again, darkness descended. I sat in complete silence, trying to analyse the behaviour of these 'circles of light' – apparently operating independently, rather than all together. When I reached my home, at 5.40pm, I realised the normal fifteen minutes journey had taken thirty minutes."

What Elsie and so many others reported just one year before our incident(s) serves to illustrate multiple times over that <u>what happened at Woodbridge, was not a single occurrence</u> which the sceptics try

*The A5 an old Roman Road, appears thick with UFO reports and encounters over the years, as John Hanson can testify to.

THE HALT PERSPECTIVE 2

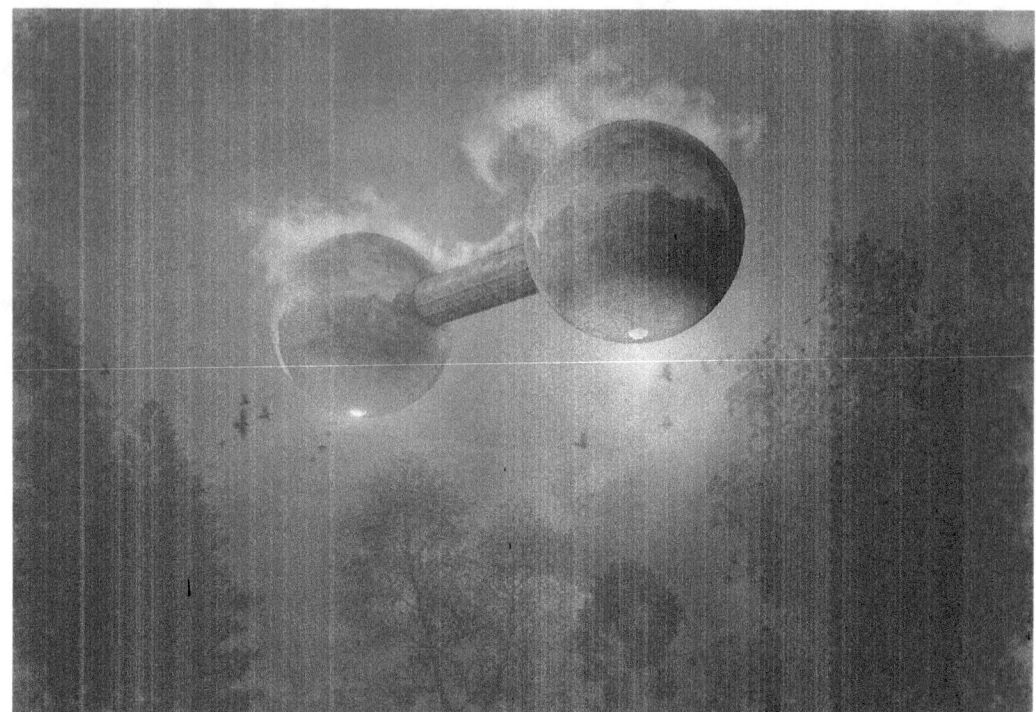

to explain away rationally, but completely ignoring the massive amount of other evidence made available over the years, so much of which has been forgotten . . . It's an insult to intelligence. Sadly Elsie and her husband, a Police Inspector, have passed away. I see from one of the photos shown to me that he was presented with a Jubilee Police medal from the Queen at Buckingham Palace. These are respectable citizens who seek an answer, not people given to flights of fancy or attention seeking.

1979 – Diamond-shaped UFO over RAF Coltishall

Retired UK Leicestershire Constabulary Police Constable 495 Brett Lyne's brought my attention to what he witnessed while serving with the Police at RAF Coltishall in 1979, wondering if there could be any connection with what happened in Rendlesham Forest, the following year. Common sense dictates that there is but I'm not qualified to reach that conclusion as I don't know, who really does?

Brett: "*In July 1979 (aged 18) I joined the RAF Police and, was posted to RAF Coltishall, in Norfolk. This base is about 12 miles north of Norwich and at that time had three squadrons of Jaguars and the 202 Search and Rescue helicopter squadron. My shift consisted of a substantive Corporal and two acting Corporals (one being me). Our office was situated on the side of one of the aircraft hangers – away from the runway and near to a fuel storage depot. The incident occurred during a night shift in either late August or early September 1980. We started work at 10.00pm and took over from the afternoon shift.*"

THE HALT PERSPECTIVE 2

Just before midnight there was a very loud boom from somewhere close outside. The men's initial thoughts were that the fuel depot had exploded, but on investigation found this not to be the case. *"At 7.00am. I said that I would drive over and unlock the gate, as it was light but a little overcast, with patchy clouds. This I did and I had just unlocked the padlock, when there was a terrifically loud 'boom' directly over my head. I instinctively flinched down and then looked up at the sky, where the noise had come from. There were now intermittent clouds, but moving between two of them was a very **large diamond-shaped craft**... It was certainly several times bigger than any aircraft I had ever seen and its shape was like nothing I'd seen before. The whole underside of this craft was covered in equally spaced sets of diamond patterned lights. Several of the lights were of different colours, such as reds, oranges, purples, greens, yellows, but kept in groups of the same colour. There was no noise at all and the craft moved silently across the sky between two clouds. Apart from being totally shocked, I managed to use my radio to call up the other two RAF policemen in our office. After about 20 seconds, or so, the craft disappeared fully into, or was hidden by, the clouds from my view and I didn't hear or see anything else of it, although I waited a few minutes just in case it should reappear. I drove back to the office and explained to the others what had happened and even drew a plan of the craft with the position of its lights and their various colours. Unfortunately I did not retain it, even though Cpl. Dinning suggested I submit an official UFO report. I had only been in service for 14 months and did not think it would do my career any good if people started to think I was a fantasist, or worse, so I declined."*

Charles: All I can say is that there have been many other sightings which have taken place all over the States as well as the UK, involving what people now refer to as **Triangular UFOs,** not forgetting the Belgium wave of similarly described objects during the 1980's. One sighting at 5.24pm on the 29th November 1989 involved two members of the Eupen gendarmerie who were driving the police car from Eupen to Kettenis when they saw a bright light over a field. The object then flew over the top of them, and was described as a *"... dark solid mass in the shape of an isosceles triangle; underneath were three blinding lights, in each corner, with a red pulsating light in the centre. It then flew away towards Eupen. We rang an airfield and were told no air traffic was in the locality. At 6.30pm the officers made their way to high ground close to the nearby lake of Gileppe, where they saw the object hovering over the watch tower of the lake."*

It's of interest to note that according to the witnesses, every now and then beams of lights were seen to shoot away from the side, and that a stationary white ball was seen to emit two clearly visible thin beams of light in opposite directions. A series of lights were then seen emerged from a row of trees. Behind the lights they observed the dark green silhouette of a triangle that rose upwards and executed a sharp turn. During the manoeuvre an upper structure was seen with what appeared to be illuminated windows, like a railway coach, before it took off towards the direction of the German border, disappearing from view at 8.39pm. **Official explanation: They had seen Venus!** The SOBEPS UFO group collected initially over 2000 eye witness accounts during an 18 month period of activity, which culminated as time went on in a total of 450 cases reported.

THE HALT PERSPECTIVE 2

John tells me that the Essex/East Anglia/Derbyshire area was swamped with reports of such craft, moving slowly over the landscape, often described as majestic in appearance and apparently completely oblivious to the affairs of man. While there appeared to be a multitude of UFO sightings around the English Counties, the States also witnessed similar phenomena.

I haven't the faintest idea what lay behind the 1979 'light display' reported by Ansted West Virginia restaurant owner, Norma White – an area I know well! She should be praised for her determination to conduct her own investigation into the matter, as a result of which she collected 200 names of others that had seen it. I wonder how many people know of this incident which like the thousands of others is already forgotten. Sadly for people like her and the majority of 'UFO' witnesses, they don't realise just how prolific the phenomena has been and instead of getting support by authority, are left 'high and dry' to try and come to terms with something that is so way-out of everyday life. Of course that's how it works, better to keep it under wraps, than create situations where people could be very worried feeling that the presence of UFOs, could be construed as threatening. Hence the Press's denigrating slant on the subject as we have all seen. **People deserve answers. But of course they don't get them.** The reason being is that most people who actually sight such objects don't realise that they aren't the only ones, although with the onset of the Internet it's now much easier to obtain information, which helps people come to terms with what they've seen.

February 1980 – strange light seen over RAF Bentwaters by USAF captain!

Another incident brought to my attention, during recent years, although I had no knowledge of it at the time, involved one of my officer's now retired, Captain Lori Rehfeldt, then a Law Enforcement Officer at RAF Bentwaters. *"I was on patrol with Airman Duffield, outside the Base, near RAF Woodbridge, at 3.00am in February 1980 – a place that literally scared the hell out of me – when we saw a strange 'light' in the sky moving up and down, left and right, a bit like an 'Etch-o-Sketch' board. I contacted the Police Control room at Bentwaters. They advised me to contact Woodbridge, which I did. They suggested we must have seen an aeroplane – an explanation I was not inclined to accept but decided to drop the matter, as some of the personnel had already begun to refer to Rehfeldt's UFO."*

Captain Lori Rehfeldt

I knew Lori, she was on the staff. What she saw doesn't surprise me. To be honest if I hadn't experienced what happened to me, I wouldn't have taken too much notice of people reporting strange objects in the sky, as I wouldn't really have been bothered. Yes I had read one of Donald Keyhoe's books as a teenager, but wasn't interested in books on the UFO subject. I was too busy helping to run an airbase. By the way it was only one book, taking into consideration a caustic comment made by a former Air Force colleague, a matter which will be addressed further into this book.

June 1980 – Orange globes seen hovering over parked US planes

Lori wasn't the only one from our airbase to witness strange phenomenon. Ken Kern – then a member of the Security Police posted to 'B' Flight, RAF Woodbridge Suffolk: *"I was cleaning my firearm, one afternoon, with other members of the Security Patrol, on the 15th June 1980, when I overheard a conversation taking place between one of the Airmen – A.I.C. Wagner, talking to Flight Chief Master Sgt. Faile, agitatedly. Wagner* and his partner, Campbell, were on A-2 Mobile Vehicle Control covering security of the aircraft parking area, where the A10's were kept, when they sighted an orange 'globe of light', about 20 feet in diameter, hovering over one of the aircraft. Curiosity gave way to fear when, in a flash of light, the 'orange globe' disappeared, leaving seemingly in its place the incredible sight of a pair of startled deer, who were not there a split second previously."

As you can see from this photo taken in more recent years by people walking around the forest using 35mm and digital cameras, could there be any connection with what Ken might have seen? I have no idea, interesting as these photos are, what on earth they can be. Such images seem common place to the forest, are they more prevalent to Rendlesham, rather than other Forests? Apparently not, according to John who has showed me photographic images from the collection of late East Anglia UFO researcher Ron West that shows Thetford Forest, Norfolk has been the venue for other sightings of **black saucer shaped objects** seen hovering over the trees.

June 1980 – Gamekeeper on Air Base reports strange figures!

Brenda Butler told John Hanson a strange story after being contacted by Mr Brian Jolly, and then employed by us on the Airbase, to keep the rabbit population down. She interviewed him with a Steve Meadows a colleague of hers from Saxmundham. I can confirm that Brian Jolly worked for us in that capacity but I never had cause to speak to him – just a passing nod if I saw him.

Brenda: "Mr. Jolly was walking near the Weapons Storage Area, at Woodbridge Airbase (known locally as the 'Bomb Dump') when he saw what he thought were three young children moving about behind some trees in the forest. Thinking they were from the Airbase he picked up his telescopic gun-sight and peered through it, recoiling in fright when he, 'realised they were all dressed in brown cloaks, flowing to the forest floor'.

Shaken, he quietly made his way out of the forest and contacted the Base Police, at Woodbridge, who assembled an armed party of Security Officers to escort him back to the scene. When they arrived at the location, one of the Airmen noticed a 'figure' disappearing into the forest and shouted out, to no avail."

Mr. Jolly: 'There was this strange luminous green sticky material covering the ground, but when picked-up, it just dissolved. I was advised not to go anywhere near the 'Bomb Dump' again on my own unless escorted by an armed guard.' In addition Brenda told of having spoken to a civilian worker, employed on the construction of a road to the new helicopter landing pad, who saw what he took to be 'a number of small children gathered in the forest, wearing fancy dress with brown coats and hats on their heads, near to where I was working, before realising these were not children.'

Charles: I've never seen any report pertaining to what Brian claimed, which might be odd bearing in mind that according to him armed security officers went traipsing into the wood to investigate, which must have been authorised, but not by me, as I have no knowledge of this incident other than what is posted here. So I can't form any judgement, the reader will have to make their own assessment. Once I would have laughed at stories like this not now. Could it have been a prank? If not well as a seasoned USAF Officer, how can I or anyone offer an explanation?

THE HALT PERSPECTIVE 2

An example of strange photographs accumulated by Brenda Butler taken over a long period many of which John tells me were obtained initially with a 35mm camera and then a digital one is shown above. I have no idea what causes these aberrations to appear – or what they represent. John tells me that some of them have been seen with the naked eye which may have been the cause of concern to some of the young airmen, who manned security points around the base. Your guess is as good as mine as to what they are and where they come from!

John: Stories, such as these, came as no surprise to us as, over the years, during a number of visits to Rendlesham Forest, we were to hear of all manner of strange things seen in and around the area, including strange objects in the sky , dazzling 'orbs', (some of them seen with the naked eye), reports of *tall spindly 'figures', with concealed faces,* wandering about on the Airbase. I tried to trace Mr Jolly, but was unsuccessful, although there are a number of people with that surname in the Norfolk area. Brenda told me that Steve tape-recorded the interview but later found that the machine had malfunctioned. In mid August 2020, I spoke to Brenda who told me that she was still picking up mysterious images captured on the digital camera. Admittedly we are unable to identify the nature of what causes these 'manifestations' to appear, and while aware of the scepticism attached to the subject of 'orbs' many of the photos taken can hardly be said to fit into this category, not forgetting the apports of stones, which can be a common feature of this forest, a phenomenon that is totally ignored! Why?

Charles: Whether these anomalies have anything to do with the events of December 1980 is of course open to conjecture! Strange things that have been seen in the forest, and elsewhere – Suffolk seems to have more than its fair share, as I can attest to!

I wondered what to make, of what Mrs Marion Kennedy from Framlingham, Suffolk and her family encountered after driving through a patch of thick fog? Followed by the sighting of a UFO after arriving at the house she was staying at in Baldock, Hertfordshire! Another example of the many times that motorists are followed by these objects – just *one* of a huge number of sightings that have taken place around the Suffolk area.

THE HALT PERSPECTIVE 2

She and her family were originally interviewed by Brenda Butler and Dot Street. John then contacted her some years later and interviewed her. He regards her as a very genuine witness who has not the slightest idea what on earth it was she and her family witnessed.

Maybe, for all I know, one day a rational scientific explanation will be found that suits all parties! Problem is that while this could be the case now for all I now, **then why the secrecy and need to cover up something which does affect lives**? Is it a case that the Real TRUTHS cannot be disseminated to the Public?

July 1980 – What the nurses saw? And the guy from Cape Canaveral!

With regard to the 'saucer' shaped object seen by nurses in Hampshire during July 1980, I remained very curious why the local British Police Officer brought an American around to the house, who told Diane one of the witnesses he was from Cape Canaveral, and then questioned her about what had occurred? No idea what the connection is there? Not heard of their role in UFO sightings maybe the US but the UK? Disinformation is an 'agency' speciality. It's obvious this was treated very seriously by the authorities.

Photographic evidence will never see the light of day and, one of the nurses who knew someone high up, left the day after! It doesn't make sense but it's not meant too! I thought that what I witnessed and what the others saw during the end of December 1980 was straightforward. That's why I sent the Memo in for the attention of Moreland as a talking paper; it was never intended to go anywhere else. Was I mistaken about that, because it never goes away and it never stops with all of the crazy stories still coming forward to this present day?

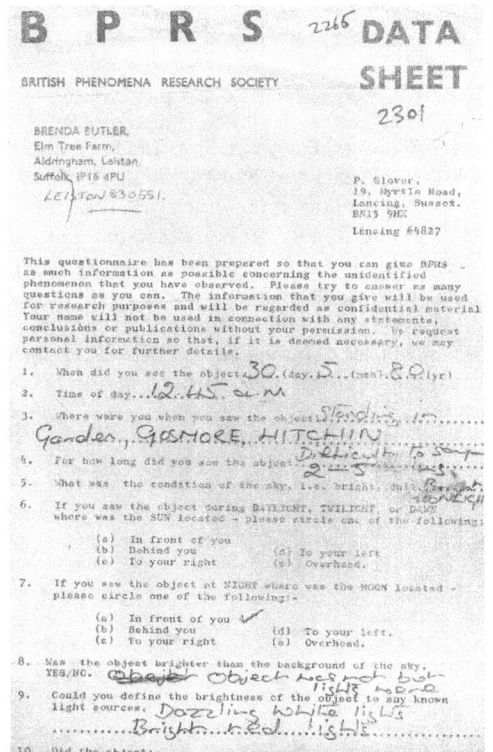
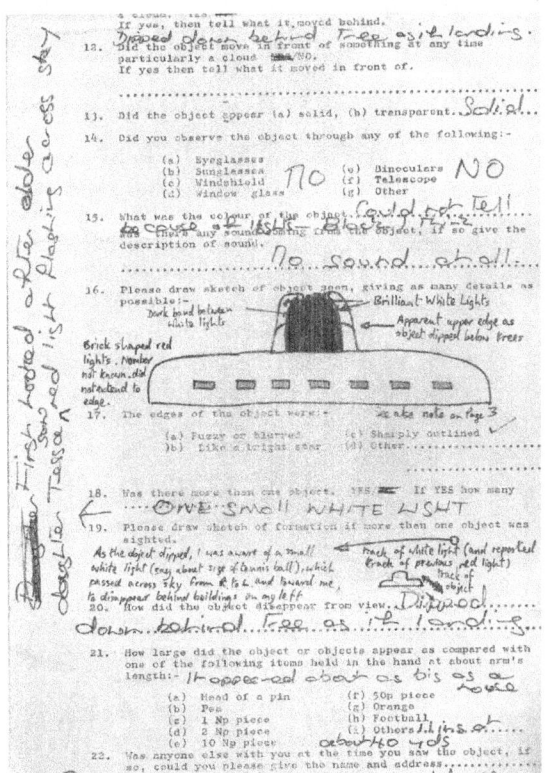

THE HALT PERSPECTIVE 2

Hotelier Barry Rey (70) passes away 25th November 2013 – R.I.P.

John: In the previous book, *The Halt Perspective*, we mentioned Barry Eric Rey's UFO sighting and his assistance to the authors following a visit to see him some years ago. Barry knew Brian Creswell, one of the police officers that had attended the scene of the 'landing' in December 1980; apparently his daughter was a friend of the family. We were shocked to find that Barry had passed away in 2013. It is worth while bringing to the reader's attention some fascinating facts about Barry we were not aware of. Here is a reminder first of what Barry Rey saw: *"It was in November, 1980. Definitely not connected with the incidents that occurred at the end of December 1980, when something was alleged to have been seen in the forest. I remember the sun was beginning to set, when I noticed a strange 'light' hovering over the village. I knew, from its shape and appearance that it wasn't like any aircraft, or helicopter, I had seen before – so I*

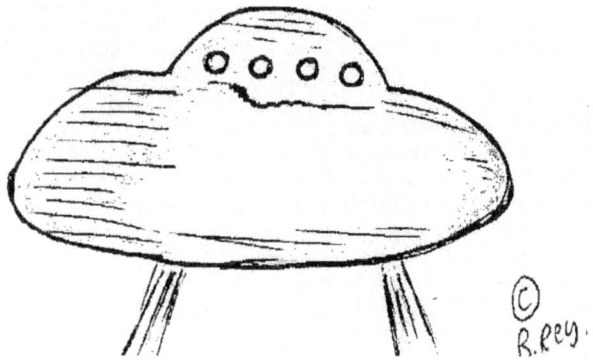

jumped into my car and followed it, as it headed over fields towards the coast. It was disc-shaped, showing portholes of light projecting a powerful beam from its underneath. At one stage, it was only 50 feet away from me before it passed overhead, rose up slowly, and dropped down over some trees at the other side of the field and landed. I drove along the road for a short distance and then saw it hovering over a house belonging to Robin Pendle, before it finally moved away for good." Barry wonders, as a result of what he saw, whether the date given for the now world-famous incident, involving Colonel Halt and others, is flawed – a supposition drawn rationally from his own experience. Unfortunately, Barry would not have realized, without the hindsight of many years research, that he was not the only one to sight UFOs over East Anglia – not forgetting other parts of the country, during this period.

Barry Eric Rey bought *Woodhall Manor* in the 1980s. He transformed the Grade II listed estate – parts of which date back to medieval times, into the *Wood Hall Hotel & Country Club*, adding a nightclub, squash courts and functions rooms. The manor is now a popular wedding and function venue. Born in south London in 1943, Mr. Rey's first career was as an officer cadet in the Merchant Navy. After which, he spent time in the Australian outback in the oil surveying industry. He went on to pursue several ventures, including a printing company, before buying *Woodhall Manor* and eventually settling in nearby Hollesley with his family.

Woodhall Catering Ltd – supplying the 'soaps'

During his time at the hotel, Mr. Rey began what became one of the largest film and television location catering companies in Europe, Woodhall Catering Ltd, supplying many renowned television shows including *The Bill*, *Eastenders* and *Lovejoy*, and films such as *Pride and Prejudice*, *The Englishman Who Walked Up a Hill – But Came Down a Mountain* and *Harry Potter*.

THE HALT PERSPECTIVE 2

Object seen over Woodbridge Suffolk

John: In Early December 1980 – Reginald Brown of Mill Lane, Waldringfield, Woodbridge, Suffolk was awoken at 2.30am by an extremely bright light, shining into the bedroom. On going to the window to see the source of the illumination, he saw, *"...an object – the size of a football – hovering in the sky. I watched it for about ten minutes until it shot silently away over the sea, before being lost from view."*

Three red lights seen over RAF Manston area

Charles: Arthur Munday was another person who wanted me to know about what he saw, wondering if it could be connected with the events that took place in the Forest. *"Between 11pm and midnight, in December 1980, I was (15 at the time, living in Margate, Kent) in the bedroom, playing records, when my mother came rushing into the house, telling me and my dad that she had seen 'three red lights, with a touch of gold', darting about in the sky towards the general direction of RAF Manston. We went outside, but nothing was seen. My mother telephoned RAF Manston and asked them if anyone had reported seeing strange lights, or whether an exercise was taking place. My recollection is that they weren't rude but less than forthcoming, although they admitted having received other calls. She felt a little stupid after reporting the occurrence, after being met with a cool response. My mum, who later passed away at 47, two and a half years later, was an incredibly realistic, rational, smart woman – not easily swayed or excited by most things. She was so emphatic and convinced of what she had seen, late Christmas night, that there was never any doubt in her, or mine or my father's mind, that she had experienced something quite uncommon and extraterrestrial. I'd like Colonel Charles Halt of the USAF, and all the other servicemen involved, to know that they were not alone in what they witnessed. I'm convinced both sightings are related, due to their similar and graphic descriptions."*

7.30am: 23rd December 1980

In December 1980, US Serviceman Donald Montgomery described seeing a **silver grey cigar-shaped craft** as day broke, hovering between two power lines, while driving to work at Bentwaters from Saxmundham, a regular route for him – around 7.30am. He said, *"Weirdly I have no idea what happened next, which is strange as I normally have excellent memory recall. I know about incidents that have happened at Amarillo Air Force Base in Texas during 1965 that as far as I know failed to make headlines and when talk of such things was forbidden. During a controlled deer hunt on the White Sands Test Range, which was closed down, I was with two people when we sighted what we took to be a missile fired down range and took cover as it overflew us in total silence. As it headed away into a south-north direction it just 'evaporated' in mid-air."*

This would be a few days before what happened to me in the forest. He also talks about finding three impressions in the ground at the rear of the farm close to Rendlesham where he lived following UFO activity a few days <u>before</u> the events that took place outside RAF Woodbridge. I can't say there is any connection but logic suggests there may be, unless Donald is fabricating, which I doubt very much, then we should treat this with seriousness rather than suspicion. I don't specifically remember Don personally although I knew the name; he was there when I was there.

I've come across so many people who have found the courage to stand up and confront the authorities who often dismiss such reports without even investigating them! In the main the majority of the worldwide public still look upon the subject as a niche one rather than something which may or may not be affecting our lives. I know it affected mine. If I had opted to go to Italy then I wouldn't have become involved in the subject. As I have said many times it certainly changed my life!

THE HALT PERSPECTIVE 2

24th December 1980 – UFOs sighted over Wyoming. Could there be any connection?

Another report brought to my attention by John was in the local *Wyoming Tribune* newspaper which told of a sighting involving eight flying objects, seen moving overhead, making a humming noise, projecting beams of light downwards on the 24th December 1980. This can't be a coincidence because as most of you know that's the sort of phenomena I witnessed while out in the forest – the purpose of which I have no idea. At the end of the day, I would like to know what 'they' are and where 'they' come from? Is that too much to ask? John tried to find out more but appears to have been blocked, despite entering into an email conversation with one of the staff personally at the local library where the archives are kept, who promised to send further details. Rather discourteous.

8pm: 24th of December 1980 – Half moon-shaped cluster of lights seen!

Julie Brown of Ravenscourt Road, Deal, Kent was a pillion passenger aboard her boyfriend's (now husband) Neil Brown's motorcycle heading home to Ripple, along Pommeus Lane, at 8pm, opposite *Sutton Vale* Country Club. They noticed some large red and green bright lights in the sky low down over open fields in front of them approximately 300 yards away on what was a cold and clear night. Neil then describes seeing approximately '*12 large lights forming a circle with four smaller ones set in the middle*.' Julie who was frightened after the sighting describes seeing a *'half-moon-shaped cluster of intense lights'* hovering over the fields close to Pommeus Lane, which was to be the subject of some trauma, still evident some years later when she discussed the incident with Kent UFO researcher Chris Rolfe of UFOMEK.

9.07pm: 25th December 1980 – Russian Cosmos 749 rocket re-enters North-West Europe

Charles: At 9.07pm (six hours before the first incident took place in Rendlesham Forest) the *Russian Cosmos 749 rocket re-entered over north-west Europe and was widely reported as a UFO. Some people claimed that the airmen mistook a natural phenomenon for something extraterrestrial!

From evidence obtained from radar personnel who were on duty that evening, this theory can be negated. I discussed this incident with David Bryant who felt it was "*extremely unlikely that Cosmos 749 could have been seen in Northamptonshire (or Woodbridge) It broke up during-entry and the last fragment is thought to have burnt out somewhere east of Clacton. Any surviving fragments would have fallen into the North Sea, and hence have been unrecoverable.* "

George Henry White contacted us about what he saw on the 25th December 1980. George aged 41 of Springfield Road, Kettering, in Northamptonshire – a welder by trade – was returning home at 9.10pm with his wife's parents in the car. "*We were approaching Findon on the A6, [a semi-rural clustered village, four miles north of Worthing, Sussex], on what was a clear night with just one cloud in the sky. We saw what I took to be an aircraft on fire to my right, and I stopped the car. My father-in-law got out with me and we watched these three lights, which were egg-shaped, silver – like mercury, speeding across the sky.*" Mr. White switched-on his aircraft band radio and heard a pilot in the process of either landing or taking off from Luton Airport, calling Air Traffic Control, telling them he had just seen *five UFOs in formation pass beneath his plane*. "*We could only see three lights still in the sky. We stayed there for some minutes, but after not seeing anything else, made our way to Rushden Police Station, where we reported the matter. In the paper, the next

---

*A report on the re-entry of the Cosmos 749 rocket can be found in the Journal of the British Astronomical Association (1981, vol. 91, page 561).

THE HALT PERSPECTIVE 2

day, it was reported as a meteorite or space debris entering the earth's atmosphere, which wasn't what we saw."

Logically taking into consideration the times given, one might feel that on this occasion what Mr White saw was the Satellite which was seen seven minutes later.

Charles: I still didn't say much publicly about what happened and my part in it, until people started putting out all kinds of garbage and nonsense... So much disinformation out there and people bugging me about what happened – I finally decided, it's time to tell the truth. I was *originally* a non-believer in the existence of UFOs, ambiguous term that that is! I never really gave it a second thought before the incident. For far too long the media and the national newspapers have become besotted with the UFO events that took place outside the USAF Base of RAF Woodbridge, completely ignoring the facts that surround this incident and the evidence of so many other sightings that can only in the end of course corroborate what some of the airmen saw rather than denigrate – one has to ask why this situation is continuing to occur?

Back in time – how it all began!

Ironically if I hadn't been involved in sighting something so strange which literally changed my life forever, I would have chilled out in retirement at my West Virginia retreat, drank a beer on the veranda and took Caesar out for a walk – a normal life . . . instead I have been inundated with requests from TV and film companies wishing to interview me – so many places, locations and people that I've met. Here is me with Nick Pope, too many years ago!

THE HALT PERSPECTIVE 2

In the spring of 1980, I was finishing my tour and had been hand-picked to go to Oslo, Norway, to be Commander of US Forces there. However, it seemed the CINC in Europe; the Commander-in-Chief's Exec, wanted the job and had a little more pull than I did. So I was given the option to go to Italy, or Bentwaters, England, maybe two or three other places. Fortunately, or unfortunately, I picked Bentwaters, England, arriving in the summer of 1980. At the peak of the Cold War. There was an awful lot of activity. Bentwaters-Woodbridge twin Base complex was home of the 81st Tactical Fighter Wing, which possessed six squadrons of fighters – being the largest fighter wing in the free world, charged primarily with stopping the enemy armour as they came across Germany, should that ever happen.

Huge number of sightings brought to my attention

Looking at the huge number of sightings brought to my attention by John Hanson, many of which I have read, some documented above, are of course particular interest to me especially those that were reported around the 1980 period for obvious reasons. I know what I witnessed and am naturally curious about other sightings of strange things seen in the sky, showing some similarities with what I saw. If only to show that I wasn't on my own. It's a strange thing and I know John will agree . . . The only time that you realise that there are things 'out there in the sky' that you can't explain, many of which defy explanation, is when, of course, you have your own experience! If I hadn't, well then I wouldn't have ever been involved in a subject that is treated in the main with considerable contempt, and humour by the media!

I don't know what the objects I saw were, whilst I doubt it could have been a foreign power, surely this should have been reported as we were in the middle of the 'Cold War.'

It's of interest to realize now that we weren't the only ones to be involved in UFO activity during December 1980, judging from the many UFO accounts given by people during this month. They include sightings of triangular objects in the sky, and other strange things over the English counties.

Those guys using mind control programs, deception, disinformation and holograms must have been busy!

The more I learn the more I'm convinced there's a concerted behind-the-scene effort to hide the real truths from us. Even some of our Presidents have witnessed something highly unusual and unexplainable. The problem is that so many of these incidents strike an accord with me understanding what happened in December 1980. I was very sceptical and found what allegedly had taken place in the Forest and what the airmen reported having seen place hard to believe, because such things couldn't exist could they? I was really going to debunk it quite frankly; and as events unfolded I became more and more concerned that there may be something to this . . . I kept telling myself that there had to be some type of logical explanation for it, but I certainly couldn't find one and even to this day I can't give an answer.

Nick Pope

In 1997, Nick Pope wrote to Brenda Butler about the radiation level. He said, *"I was able to confirm with the Defence Radiological Protection service that the radiation readings taken by LT Colonel Halt were **TEN times normal, not 25** as stated on '**Strange But True'**. I did check out the theory about nuclear material from a soviet satellite but found no evidence to support the hypotheses. I tried to get the investigation formally re-opened but was not successful."* Here is a 'period piece' photo of me and Nick, followed by a photo showing Brenda, Nick, myself and Chris Pennington outside Brenda's house in Leiston Suffolk, approximately 15 years ago when I was invited over to take part in a filmed documentary which, by the way, never came to fruition!

THE HALT PERSPECTIVE 2

Charles: What I find odd is the number of people that have **now** come forward to tell what they saw over that 1980 Christmas weekend. I'm sorry but I have to view some of these accounts with suspicion especially when the newspapers pick up on it. It's a shame that apparently genuine reports involving *what appears* to be 'alien figures' seen close to or near unidentified flying objects are ignored. Instead the nonsense involving fictitious underground bunkers on the airbase and close encounters with Base Commanders still proliferates as a backcloth to this incident by those desperate to sensationalize something which was in itself sensational! Others tell even more fairy stories, setting the stage for something I was totally unprepared for. John brought my attention to yet another 'late report', while work on this book was 'in progress' provided to him by UFO witness David Munday which saw its appearance on Facebook on the 24th of August 2020, from an Elaine Bines who stated: "*I was housed at an American air base and saw 'it' in the early hours of the morning. I witnessed what turned out to be the Rendlesham UFO back in the early 80s just after Christmas. Apparently visited over three nights and disabled nuclear weapons we were unaware were housed at the American air base, and supposedly neither was our Government. I witnessed it from my upstairs bedroom in Epping, Sussex in the early hours of the morning; sadly no mobile phones for filming in those days.*"

This incident was according to Facebook discussed by Nick Pope at a conference a few years ago. It may well be that this lady is genuine, but what is she claiming exactly, taking into consideration where did she get her information from, that nuclear weapons were disabled? I have no such knowledge and can neither confirm nor deny such a situation arose – unless she is getting confused with the Weapons Storage Area. Which USA base was she housed at? John left his number for her to contact him, because without obtaining a necessary interview with the witness, to ascertain the facts surrounding the claim, how on earth can we expect to take claims like this seriously? Is this going to be another example of someone jumping on the 'Rendlesham bandwagon'? Now 40 years later I think so . . . maybe I might be proved wrong! As Mike Sacks replied on Facebook to this post: "Bit late for this". Indeed, why did it take her 40 years to come forward? Silence is deafening!

THE HALT PERSPECTIVE 2

2.30am: 26th December 1980 – Suffolk, 'Rocket' seen by motorist

John: Dennis Porley from Harwich Essex – a mate on a tugboat – was travelling along the A137 and had just passed the turn off for Alton Water on his left: *". . . when I saw what I took to be a marine distress flare or rocket, going up over Mistley Quay, but then realised this could not be the case as it didn't explode in flight. I continued on my journey, now descending a steep hill at which point I lost sight of whatever it was. As I ascended the hill on the other side close to a nearby railway line I saw the object again in the sky, it **looked like a rocket, resembling how you would imagine a plane on fire**, about the size of a full moon but more red in colour. I lost sight of it once again, due to the contours of the countryside, but then saw it again this time behind me. I decided to pull up halfway between Brantham and Stutton to obtain a closer look, as it slowly moved over Stutton Point, before descending over Hollesley Bay, where I lost sight of it. When I returned to work after the Christmas period I happened to mention what I had seen to a colleague, he suggested it might have been a large meteorite, which I don't believe was the case. Neither could it have been the Cosmos 749 Russian Satellite as this had splashed down two days previously"* **(Source: Personal Interview with John Hanson).**

Early hours: 25th/26th December 1980 – UFO sighted

Charles: Senior USAF airman Carl Thompson Jr contacted John Hanson on the 3rd of July 2006, wishing to bring to my attention what he saw while on base. *"At the time, I was a Senior Airman with the 2164 Communications Squadron. I was a radio relay repairman. On the first night – Christmas night, if I'm not mistaken – I was at the Weapons Storage Area, working on a piece of equipment in the security tower, trouble-shooting it. I think it was a motion-detection component, used for the security of the weapons. At midnight, on the 25th/26th December 1980 the guy who was going to relieve me, AIC Don Snyder, called and said that he would come out to the area. So, I went back to the wide-band radio shop and finished up some paperwork. Now, I don't remember how much later it was, but he called me at the shop and said, 'We just saw a UFO!' He meant himself and the security guards. He was in the security tower cab at the time he called. You could plainly tell he was excited and maybe kind of anxious. He sounded matter-of-fact but also kind of half-scared. I asked, 'What did it look like?' He said, 'It was so bright that you couldn't look directly at it.' So I didn't get any details about its shape, or how large it was, any of that. It was just a really bright light. I asked him if the security police were going to report it and he said no. I told him that he could, but he would be on his own and how would it look if when questioned he was the only person there to have seen it."*

While not wishing to cast any doubt on the authenticity of what the airmen saw, what do we have exactly here . . . a report of a blinding light? We have no details of size, shape or height, which means while one wouldn't expect to witness something like this over the weapons storage area, adjacent to the forest, the fact that it was, is worrying. Any suspicious activity in and around the airbase is of great concern. As for answers I can't even speculate.

An unexpected briefing!

Approximately 5.30am to 5.45am: 26th December 1980

Just before Christmas, 1980, I was in the habit of going out and spending evenings riding around with the Police, visiting the Fire Department, going to the dining hall, into the medics, the clinic, 'doing my rounds' – the eyes and ears of the Base – finding out what was going on, when an unusual report was brought to my attention – the rest is well documented, but despite the passing of the years it still attracts so much attention – a lot of it very dubious to say the least. Others continue to parade what they think happened, often getting it all wrong. It's been like this for 40 years so no doubt it will continue!

THE HALT PERSPECTIVE 2

I've told the following account so many times, people probably know it by heart, but each and every time I tell it, I feel that I'm back there and facing something so extraordinary, which shatters the conceptions of what I thought was everyday life, boy was I in for a shock!

We normally kept two patrols, Police 4 and Police 5, Law Enforcement type, on Woodbridge Base, and three on Bentwaters Base, due to it being a little larger base – more aircraft –which were carried out hourly, or semi-hourly, whatever it was, checks at the back gate and East Gate, to check it for security, bearing in mind while it was fitted with a combination lock, sometimes the combination would be 'leaked', and people would take a short cut.

On 26th December 1980, I happened to be visiting the Security Police Operations Centre, known as 'the Desk', to pick up the 'blotters' for the previous 24-hour period – something I did if I happened to be out early and near the Police Station. The desk sergeant on that morning was Staff Sergeant 'Crash' McCabe. We called him 'Crash' for a very good reason – that's why he was on the 'Desk', instead of a patrol car. He said: *'Colonel, you're not going to believe this. Burroughs, Penniston and Bustinza were out in the woods last night, chasing a UFO'.* I said: 'What?' We both had a chuckle. I said: 'Now, be more specific'. He replied: *'Well, the Lieutenant said (the Lieutenant being the Flight Commander for the evening, or that early morning shift) he didn't put it in the blotter'.* I said: 'What happened? You got to put something in the blotter'. He said: *'I know they saw some lights, and something happened out there, and they think they saw something.'* I knew Jim Penniston was very credible ... John Burroughs probably so. I didn't know Bustinza, so I said: 'Well, why don't you just put in the blotter that they saw some lights in the forest', and, uh, I got a chuckle out of it and didn't think too much about it. I picked up the blotters and went up to the office and read through them. Didn't see anything else too exciting in there, shared them with my boss, and we kind of had a chuckle – UFOs in the woods, oh great – and didn't think too much more about it.

3am: 26th December 1980 – Lights seen over Forest – response initiated

Later I ascertained that following the initial report of unusual lights outside the back gate of RAF Woodbridge, that it was thought an aircraft might have come down. I managed to piece together what had taken place, over the course of time rather than any full-scale investigation taking into consideration, what befell me the following night!

At about 3am while carrying out security checks at RAF Bentwaters, Master Sergeant J.D Chandler overheard a radio transmission from Airman John Burroughs on law enforcement patrol, who told of seeing strange lights in the wooded area just beyond the access road leading from the back gate (East Gate, Woodbridge) about 300 yards out, so he called back to Law Enforcement and told Staff Sergeant Bud Steffens: *'It looks like there's been a crash – looks like an airplane, probably a helicopter's gone down'.*

Penniston and Burroughs investigate

Staff Sgt Jim Penniston security supervisor was contacted and asked to go to East Gate exit where he met up with Burroughs and confirmed he could also see the lights as well. Several minutes later Master Sergeant Chandler also arrived at this location, by which time John Burroughs, Jim Penniston and Airman first class Edward Cabansag had entered the wooded area beyond the clearing at the access road.

Staff Sgt Jim Penniston

Security Police Operations number 4 and 5 along with Sgt Bud Steffens, were also asked to assist the three officers who were now already deep in the woods. Sgt Coffee who was in Central Security Control (CSC), contacted Heathrow Airport in London, RAF Watton and Eastern radar, who'd all apparently tracked the 'manifestation' on radar 15 miles out over the east coast. A code 2 alert was ordered and other military jeeps were sent out. By this time the three patrolmen had lost radio communication with the base. This seemed very odd and between them they had two sets of radios, two law enforcement radios and two security NET radios.

At 04.11: From A.I.C Chris Arnold, law enforcement desk Bentwaters – A telephone message was sent to the Police: "We have a sighting of some unusual lights in the sky. We have sent unarmed troops to investigate. We are terming it as a UFO at present."

I understood that the officers had reported coming across a strange craft which was triangular in shape, two to three metres along its base and roughly two metres high. It had a pulsing red light on top and a bank of blue lights underneath, elevated off the ground by a tripod arrangement of three legs. Apparently Jim was overheard (according to MSgt J.D Chandler) to say that he thought it was a mechanical object and some 50 meters away. *"Each time he gave me an indication that he was about to reach the area where the lights were, he would give an extended estimated location. He eventually arrived at the beacon light but stated that this was not the light or lights he had originally observed, and was told to return, at no time did I see anything (lights)."*

Hieroglyphic-like symbols seen

As a result of a radio call to Sergeant McCabe –who then contacted Woodbridge and Bentwaters control tower – but found they were both down. (Although there was manning there, they just weren't up and operational.) They both said the same thing: *'There's nothing flying in the vicinity'.*

THE HALT PERSPECTIVE 2

The Master Sergeant is pretty smart. He says: *'Well, I'm not going out there. How about three, or four, of you guys go out there and see what happened? Check your weapons with me.'* So J.D. Chandler takes the weapons; bearing in mind you don't carry a gun in England. Penniston, Burroughs and Bustinza make their way out into the woods. They go down the forest service road, turn on a kind of a trail, and go up in the pines and actually approach something, describing it as **'approximately nine feet in length on the side, triangular in appearance, with a tripod-like set of legs**, showing various coloured lights, and according to Jim displayed Hieroglyphic-like symbols. Burroughs was to become so interested in what had taken place, we joked about sending food and blankets out as he spent so much time in the forest.

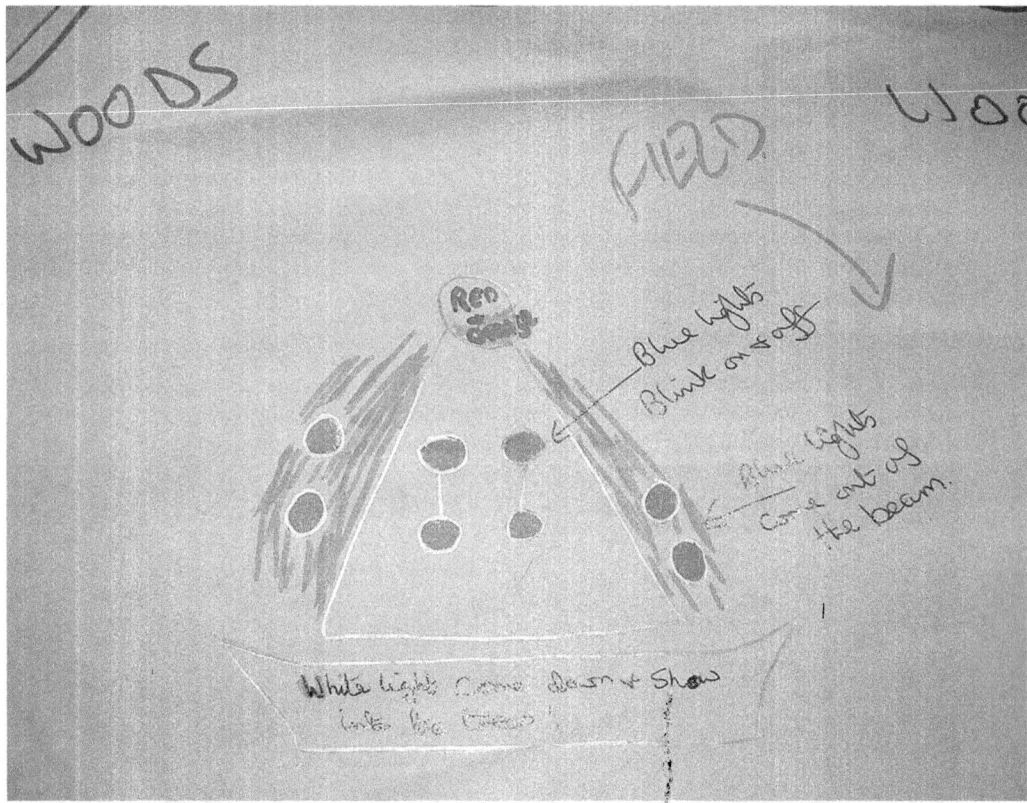

At 10.30am the police received a call from Bentwaters Law Enforcement – In reference to the UFO reported last night, we have found a place where a craft of some sort seems to have landed – two miles east of the East Gate at Bentwaters. PC Creswell attended and wrote up the police log as being... *"There were three marks in the area which did not follow a set pattern. The impressions made by the marks were of no depth and could have been made by an animal."*

Interviewed the three young airmen individually

I interviewed the three young airmen individually, who were involved in the incident, at the Base Commander's office, and obtained statements from them. Basically, what they said was that Airman John Burroughs was patrolling Woodbridge Base, as was one other patrol.

At some point, their stories become somewhat muddled. They are not really sure whether they were onboard a craft, whether they touched it or exactly what happened. We do know they were out there for probably **three to four hours** – in fact, to the point where people were very, very, concerned on the Base as to what happened to them. **Burroughs thinks he may have been onboard, or so he has told me.** They didn't tell me this initially, by the way, they were very secretive. They were concerned it was going to affect their military career, as we all were. They managed to find their way back onto the Base, after claiming the 'craft' levitated and went off at a high speed just prior to shift change, which would have been around four or five o'clock in the morning. Nobody knew quite what to do, so the Lieutenant, the Flight Lieutenant, decided nothing would happen – there would be no entries, although there was an entry made in the Law Enforcement Blotter at my insistence. The criticism by those who just wish to *'muddy the waters of what went on'* continues to this present day.

I also discovered something very worrying – the security blotters had been removed, and were missing! They were categorised in the paper chain as AF Forms 53. Not only that but the AF forms 1569s Incident and Complaints Report completed by the security controllers at Central security Control were AWOL! In contravention of Standard operating procedures!

Jim Penniston comments – Security blotters seized!

Jim Penniston claimed more recently: *"The removal and classifying of security blotters were part of the containment process initiated by others, outside the base command. Colonel Halt unknowingly asked the desk sergeant to include the first night's information that they had already omitted on the morning after. I think it disturbed him when he became aware the security blotters and 1569s had already been classified and pulled (without Colonel Halt's knowledge). It was much easier to put out a cover/containment story about the nights in question."*

Charles: **I have no idea about this, and was very surprised to learn that the logs were pulled ... by whom? Why was my order overruled and by who? If instructions from somebody higher, well, who knows? As for any containment process, not sure what that is about, clearly I wasn't consulted – maybe it was AFOSI gathering evidence? The radar at Bentwaters was on. We don't turn it off. The Controllers were on standby in case of an emergency.**

Claims that I, Ted Conrad and Gordon Williams were threatened to keep quiet!

(1) People claim that John was told by AFOSI to keep his statement brief and to only include the events of the first night. Penniston and Cabansag had their statements written for them by the AFOSI. Penniston and Burroughs being told by AFOSI: *"This is the version of events you will tell when questioned by anyone who asks what happened"*. It is also claimed that Wing Commander Gordon Williams, Ted Conrad and I were threatened to keep quiet.

(2) My memo to the M.O.D was a watered down version of events.

(3) The statements made by the witnesses were not signed – which means what exactly? **I didn't take the statements**. If Jim says the statement taken from him by the Air Force Office of Special Investigations almost resembled his original testimonial, and that he had to lie to his immediate chain of command well you have lost me! (4) Somebody asked me whether the AFOSI were brought in from an external force that leads this operation?

As most people are now aware the **drawing of the 'craft' sketched by John Burroughs**, during my debrief with the two men a few days later shows a cluster of lights, a red and orange on top with blue lights blinking on and off inside the 'beam' which would look red and orange on occasion. Presumably connected with what Jim saw, although John has no **conscious memories** of what he experienced while in the clearing? [Although I understand that this has changed in 2020, with claims that he has remembered what exactly?]

THE HALT PERSPECTIVE 2

Ian Ridpath, claims – No harsh interrogations by THE AFOSI!

Colonel Halt with Ian Ridpath (left)

On Ian Ridpath's website – bearing in mind he's been researching into this since 1983, not forgetting that he and I have also met many times, as this 'early period' photo shows – has this to say: *"In the days following the events of December 26 and 28, Halt and Penniston were debriefed separately by Col Ted Conrad, Halt's boss. These were the only two witnesses Conrad talked to. It is sometimes claimed in UFO circles that the witnesses were subjected to interrogation by the Air Force Office of Special Investigations (AFOSI), including injections by the so-called 'truth drug', sodium pentothal. However, in 2010 January Colonel Conrad told researcher David Clarke that . . .* **'No investigations beyond his own had been conducted. There were no conspiracies, no secret operation, no missile accident, and no harsh interrogations by OSI. I was in a position to know about the OSI. They had their own chain of command, but in practice the OSI commander kept me informed of any ongoing investigations they had.'** "

Charles: Well, as Deputy Base Lt Colonel, I can say I had no knowledge of any secret operation, missile incident, or conspiracy to do what . . . ? I'm not sure what Ted Conrad is on about. I have repeatedly, over the years, attempted to help Larry Warren personally, in setting the record straight. I really feel sorry for Larry, I think he's been used. At the time I thought that he and his colleagues were interviewed under normal protocol, I was shocked to learn, years later, of the involvement of the AFOSI and their harsh interrogations, which included the use of, I believe, Sodium Amatol, or something similar.

If the airmen were given drugs during the debriefing by OSI officers, which I believe happened following an extraordinary, highly unusual event, then logically this indicates the possibility this may have affected them psychologically – could be one of the reasons why there are so many inconsistencies, surrounding the claims made by them. Maybe this confusion was deliberately seeded in their memories, by drugs which were used to separating fact from fiction in this constantly ever-changing version of events.

THE HALT PERSPECTIVE 2

Air Force Office of Special Investigations

Each branch of the United States military has its own special investigative unit outside of their military police forces. According to the U.S. Air Force, the job of an Air Force Office of Special Investigations (AFOSI) special agent is the second-most sought-after career path within the USAF. While the U.S. Army Criminal Investigations Command enjoys a longer history that dates back to the American Civil War, the Air Force Office of Special Investigations (AFOSI) boasts a rich investigative tradition with ties to famed FBI director J. Edgar Hoover himself. Previously a command within the U.S. Army, the United States Air Force was created as a separate autonomous military branch in 1947.

Notebook produced – no codes seen then!

The RAF Bentwaters security guard that sat next to Jim on the pick-up crew bus the morning of their encounter, while riding back from guard Mount at CSC after they had come off duty, was Richard Bertolino. He remembers sitting next to Penniston. In an interview with the *Earth Files* podcast broadcast in 2009 September, Bertolino claims that Penniston *"pulls out the notebook and the diagrams what he saw out there. It was kind of diamond-shaped with tripod legs."*

It sounds as though Penniston sketched the object for Bertolino as they sat together. Bertolino does not mention seeing any existing notes or sketches of the craft in the notebook. And where is this diagram made for Bertolino in the notebook that Penniston now displays for the cameras?

In fact we did numerous programs together and the notebook was never mentioned until at the National Press Club 10 years ago (2010). John emailed Richard in June 2020, who put the record straight. *"Jim was meticulous to his job. This was the reason for the note pad. It was a small type. But to say he drew it for me I cannot say. If that was how it sounded I misspoke. I saw what he drew. My peice came from telling my story to Linda. It hurts me that these guys just can't all get together before it is too late and write the definitive book on Rendlesham."*

Wrong site!

Jim took us to a new site. Refer to the TV movie **UFO INVASION AT RENDLESHAM** (available on YouTube). When I asked Jim he stated ". . . there must be two sites". Now there are three or more sites? Jim further stated the existing trees were there in 1980. The Forester (Vince Thurkettle) added ". . . the trees are only 20 years old and would have been small saplings 13 years ago." – This is a serious issue. We know the plaster casts were made and photos taken at the original site.

Important claims like this should be scrutinised. Not automatically accepted as genuine just because someone said so! Unfortunately this is an attribute of behaviour, sadly lacking in a business dominated by people who are easily influenced. Remember Larry Warren and the vitriolic hate preached by him and his supporters against people like me and John Hanson without batting an eyelid. Unless you are at the receiving end then you haven't a clue how much distress it causes!

People continue to ask me what I think Penniston, Burroughs and Cabansag saw?

How can I say, I wasn't there with them? Jim Penniston said John Burroughs tried to get on the object. Burroughs said one side of the object was invisible, see through…the object had what appeared to be a license plate-sized object on the 'craft', was nine feet tall, pyramid-shaped and showed blue lights on the underside and a red light on top. The witnesses claimed the object levitated and hovered as it journeyed through the forest and was followed by the US patrolmen for some 90 minutes. A physical tri-pod arrangement, which could have been responsible for trace marks, was found at the scene during a later investigation – these were ten feet apart, and at a height of 25 feet, surrounding pine trees were damaged – the desk sergeant didn't even put that into the log.

Jim was regressed in 1994 by people from the future!

Jim was regressed in 1994, and talks about 'the visitors'. He describes them as being from our future – a dark and polluted world, with many difficulties. He explains that they are visiting in teams and each team is assigned a different task. **Apparently, the teams know exactly which people they are to target when they arrive in our time.** He claims that some of them are coming here to take sperm and eggs, which are necessary in order to help their species survive. It seems they have a serious problem with reproduction. In 2010, bearing in mind his close proximity to the object, Jim said: "*I believe the 'craft' is from the far-off future and that it contained our distant descendants, returning as time travellers, to obtain genetic material to keep their ailing species alive.*"

Budd Hopkins who I knew to talk to, claimed that his evidence showed the aliens were engaged in a sinister cross-breeding project with the intention of producing human-alien hybrids.

In 1994, Professor John Mack, a psychiatrist at Harvard University and a Pulitzer Prize winner, published a book on alien abduction claiming that these accounts are real. Initially there was great excitement as people thought this was a means of obtaining evidence which would identify the nature of what it was that we were dealing with.

The irrefutable facts behind a phenomenon – *Exposure*

John Hanson is in the process of putting together a number of new books, '**EXPOSURE**', which catalogue the medical after-effects of very close encounters with UFOs, through many personal investigations. The majority of these reports comes from memory recall shortly after the event, rather than regression. In Jim's case, who knows, but the use of hypnotic regression and administered drugs was used, as I suspect in this case, to seed false memory which would be later recalled under regression as being genuine.

The CIA cleaned up!

I was told by those "*interviewed*" that the OSI Doctor was there and involved but I don't remember seeing him. Contrary to what you have been told, the AFOSI and CIA have authorization to use hypnosis and have a published list of drugs to use. They include Sodium Pentothal, Sodium Amatol and even LSD. The AFOSI officers would not have had beards. But they would never, ever have turned something like this over to the Security Police. Discount anything John Burroughs says unless it fits. I think the spooks are trying to play with John. I should have never believed him. I was disappointed when, years later, I found out about the "*debriefings.*" None of the other senior officers wanted anything to do with the incident. Gordon Williams told me to get with Don Moreland and work with him. Rumours over the years suggest a CIA (clean up) doctor was involved in the "*debriefings*". According to information from several well respected UFO researchers it was a Dr. Christopher (Kit) Canfield Green. I am satisfied while he knew about the incident, he was not involved in any debriefings at the Base, although it is believed he has visited the UK during the later years.

Green is also a friend of John Alexander. I have again offended John Burroughs, so he's cut me off from some of his craziness for the third or more time. **John Burroughs is convinced activity on Orford Ness Island played a part in the incident.**

THE HALT PERSPECTIVE 2

Dr Green has, in recent years, worked with Rendlesham Forest UFO witness John Burroughs. The results of which were successful treatment for heart damage and, after years of dispute, the Veterans' Association (VA) finally agreed to pay for the treatment. Interestingly, John Burroughs claims he has a document proving that a weapon was developed off the back of what he encountered in Redlesham Forest. Although to date he has not released that publicly. While the reasons for treating these people are perfectly altruistic, the data gleaned could also be vitally important to certain interested parties. People still maintain that I was subjected to an interview/s by the AFOSI after the incident in the Forest. No way... But, it was a very interesting experience. I'm not sure if I had the opportunity to go out again, whether I'd do it again or not.

Dr. Kit Green

According to Dr. Christopher Green, Neuroscience Professor and Clinical Fellow at Wayne State School of Medicine, and a former CIA scientific analyst, there is already existing research showing the successful "extraction" of real data from a person's brain using brainwave analysis.

Sergeant Wayne Persinger – Head of AFOSI at Bentwaters

People have over the years asked me about *Sergeant Wayne Persinger who was the senior NCO of AFOSI at Bentwaters and worked alongside the Security Police Investigation Department. AFOSI had contacts with the FBI, MI5 and Special Branch, for fairly obvious reasons due to the nature of their work.

He had free reign to walk around and was not accountable to anybody including Gordon Williams. His terms of reference would have encompassed serious matters such as espionage, counter intelligence and checking new recruits in order to ensure their loyalty to the Air Force cause. I knew Wayne and his wife Diana but didn't have much to do with him after all it was a big base like a small town thousands of people on base. Although I kept my ears and eyes open, prior to the UFO events, usually the base Police or Woodbridge Police who had an office on base dealt with internal criminal activity quite efficiently, obviously I was updated as deputy base commander, generally speaking with what went on but not with the activity of the AFOSI.

During 'Christmas week' (Monday 22nd-25th December, 1980) Diana Persinger, the wife of the deputy commander of the RAF Bentwaters AFOSI *Wayne Persinger, and her young daughter was driving towards the Woodbridge base where they lived after having been out shopping. *"I saw this UFO; it was*

---

*Wayne arrived at Sculthorpe in 1961 and was assigned to the Air Police Squadron under the command of Major Winfred W. Charlot. He initially worked security, guarding the RB 66s and a KB50 Refueler in the Victor Alert section. They were armed and ready for battle dispatch. He later transferred to the Law Enforcement Section working as gate guard, controlling the entry and exit of cars, etc. to and from the base and patrol car duty. He then started duty as a Desk Sergeant on one of the Law Enforcement Flights. During that time he worked with TSgt Ferguson, TSgt James B. Holbrook, Horace Neal, Harold Deal, and others. Later he worked in the back office as a Provost Marshall Clerk. He frequently drove to Hunstanton, enjoying the facilities of the casino bar and club. There he his met his wife Diana Howell from West Newton and the couple are still married after 55 years. His best man was SSgt Leland D. Gee and he lived in base housing. Wayne also worked at the club, along with SSgt VA Keith and MSgt Herschel Ellis as "doormen". He left Sculthorpe in 1964 as the base was closing then went to Sembach Air Base, Germany. It would be fair to say that my information indicates he became well practised in the use of polygraphs to evaluate the truthfulness of suspects under interview, which formed part of his job.

suddenly on the top of me over the car. It was very low, with lights all around I couldn't define the shape but it seemed round. I pulled off the road to have a look but it just disappeared. I told some of the wives the next day. An officer's wife, I don't recall her name, but she went out there with some people camping in the forest looking for them. After that I never heard anything until I saw a TV programme and read about it in the papers. I was pleased as it confirmed my sighting. Wayne refused to accept that's what it was, he said it was a helicopter." I didn't know about this incident until I read about it in Georgina Bruni's book, although I knew Wayne and Dianna. John Hanson emailed him but he chose to consider about a response. Make of this what you will, according some he was a man that incited fear, but this is just gossip or idle rumour. He lives in the UK and we must respect his privacy.

Aliens were not seen by me or Gordon Williams in the Forest!

Despite claims from many people over the years, that weren't even there, including a quote from Manchester Solicitor Harry Harris – who was a member of the '*Sky Crash* team' I've met – **alleging that we surrounded a craft** – this is just not true! I never saw a structured craft. People keep getting it wrong. Only recently in a 2020 podcast someone stated that John Burroughs may have left the parked vehicles and gone across the field. I can tell you he and the others at the vehicles were ordered to quietly stay there and they did. When I came back to the vehicles, John asked to go to the site (he and Jim later told of having confronted a craft.) I said OK but make it quick. He and Bustinza did so. It was less than 100 yards and they quickly came back. They didn't mention anything unusual and were never out of our sight. I reported everything I experienced to the Command Post. They were in contact with those above me. Since no one seemed to care at the time we returned to the base tired and wet – after having stumbled into a small stream across from the farmhouse. Like most sensible people, I can only tell you what I witnessed, and have never changed or altered my version of what took place. This hasn't stopped so many embellished reports from the media claiming confrontations with alien beings, and of high-level talks with the Base Commander by those entities who asked for resources to repair their craft! Absolute rubbish – what next? Anything to sell papers!

Having said that, I would be the first to accept that over the years people have reported seeing strange things in the sky and moving along the forest tracks while walking through Rendlesham Forest. They include mysterious falls of stones, and what appear to be humanoid images captured on film. Even if I could offer an explanation, which I can't –there is no possibility in my opinion of any connection with these and any substance to malicious claims as above.

Orford Lighthouse demolished in 2020

Many still believe that we were confused with the light given off by the Orford Ness Lighthouse, but how many of those people were there, and how many of them have bothered to conduct any hard-line research into the subject? If they did, well, they would learn we are not the only ones to sight something inexplicable which can and does change peoples' lives. People should read the facts rather than blindly accepting official lines which can, on occasion, be deliberately misleading. But of course, that's how it works...I should know! Another claim alleges that discolouration of the surface of the soil on the field at Capel Green, is the residue of a UFO landing – according to Larry Warren and Peter Robbins in *Left at East Gate*. Surely unlikely, as this discoloration was photographed in the late 1940's by the RAF which negates the information, a matter that I agree on, having some considerable knowledge as a chemist and would like to point out "*that annual burning of the crop could have caused this effect*. Time moves on sadly, in this year the Orford Ness Lighthouse was demolished, not that it will change some people's opinions that this was the cause of lights in the sky over the forest 40 year ago!

THE HALT PERSPECTIVE 2

Looking back now and knowing what we now know about exactly what did happen, – it's clear that any facts were thrown out of the window and mixed up with fictionalised accounts, presented as evidence when even then Warren's account was treated with great suspicion (now proved to be lies and fabrication). Incredibly some people, granted a tiny majority, still believe him! What you have to understand is that on the one hand this man has caused colossal damage to the UFO subject and made us look like idiots to the public. On the other hand he has perpetuated the myth of what went on there who did what and who saw what?

Sgt John T Dressler wrote to me in April 1986 – asking about whether there was any official investigation conducted into the matter. Now Commander of 8.CSG, having left England, I wrote back to him from Hickam AFB Hawaii and explained his letter had caught me by surprise as I thought the 'dust' has finally settled on the Bentwaters affair. I told him I would be interested in how he had found a copy of *SKY CRASH* in Hawaii. I said in answer to his question, yes there was some unexplained phenomenon which occurred near RAF Woodbridge in late December 1980. By chance I was a party to most of it and had the opportunity to talk with just about all concerned. To this day I can't explain all the happenings. To my knowledge, the Air Force did not conduct any official investigation nor was there any official effort to cover up the activities. Most parties involved soon tired of curiosity seekers and rude 'investigators'– if there was any cover up, it was an individual effort to regain some privacy. I can speak from first-hand experience as my phone rang constantly, I was followed, my house watched, even my mailbox was full. Film crews from as far away as Japan showed up unannounced.

Sky Crash folks should have been on the payroll!

This is what I wrote to John Dressler: "*The authors of* Sky Crash *spent so much time in my outer office I should have put them on the payroll. By the way, the book does have some facts, but taken as a whole it should be listed under fiction. As far as potential in the Air Force as a UFO investigator, its nil and in fact as a hobby might put you in a difficult position as the Air Force does not investigate UFOs, and as best as I can determine, pretty much ignores such reports. There may be a specialized governmental agency that handles such cases – I have no knowledge in that area. I would suggest you complete your education and work on getting accepted into OTS. Assuming you are physically qualified and have the interest and aptitude I would recommend pilot training: with this background, you could then take career broadening assignments at various points in your career. I wished them the best of luck and success in what appears to be a well mapped out career."

The right Track... which is?

John Hanson: For me it gets more confusing as John Burroughs nominated another site at the edge of the forest adjacent to Capel Green where he says it happened, when he was over here with a film crew. This area is very familiar to me having spent a large amount of time in this area over the years both by day and night. His '**landing site'** was just a little further on from the 'seat', adjacent to the forest track furthest on the left that runs around Capel Green field. I was told that the film crew had cleared this small area. The next time I was there with Brenda Butler it was overgrown. To be fair it's easy to get mixed up unless you have spent considerable time down there, which I have and still get confused with so many landing sites apart from Colonel Halt's. I have to say that '*Area 1'* which Brenda showed me some years ago, lies a few minutes walk off the right hand side of the road as you enter the forest road and head towards the car park and entrance to East Gate/Folly House on your right; this is the site identified by Georgina Bruni in the photograph showing Captain Mike Verrano and PC Creswell.

Unfortunately some years ago the Forestry commission culled all the trees at this location leaving a flat barren landscape.

Brenda tells me that she showed the '**Area 1**' photo (as shown in Georgina's book) to Jim and John during a visit to the forest – they became excited and wanted to know where she had obtained the photo from. Clearly this location which is of some importance is not shown on the map, drawn by Georgina, probably because she believed 'the UFO landing site', is where the current Forestry Commissioned spaceship is now located, which is correct, but omits any reference to the earlier 'Area 1' landing' site on the other side of the forest.

Brenda Butler: "When I went up to see Georgina in London I pointed out the discrepancies to her but was told it was too late to make any changes as the book had been sent to her publishers. Looking back now I often wonder what happened to the huge amount of material that she had accumulated in her private possession, which included boxes of documents, some of which I had contributed to her. Fortunately I had copied everything or these would have been lost. I recall that Dot Street gave her some tapes and other information, but never had them back. I was like others, so sad to hear of her demise. Just to confirm where Area 1 is: You turn into the road towards car park past Folly House. Before you get to the runway lights there are 2 tracks almost side by side, both lead to Area 1. On the right hand side if you go up the one by the fencing, the sandy one, go up about 150 yards then turn right onto a track for about 50 yards then turn left into loads of bushes and trees. Then try and find the place now ... because it's all been cut down many years ago."

Who was Major Everett?

John: I am curious as to the identity of Major Everett (a pseudonym given by science Professor Ben Jamison, who Brenda met in 1991). He gave her a copy of the police log in 1990 which covers the period October 1980 - March 1981. The log covers various items that the Police on Base dealt with, such as drugs offences and three attempted suicides – but of course no reference to any UFO sightings.

One might consider that everyday occurrences which took place on the airbases that involved US

THE HALT PERSPECTIVE 2

Police response would have been copied to the Suffolk Police office on Base, for their information. But somehow I doubt it. Matters pertaining to 'in house' would be kept 'in house' – I might be wrong.

Everett, who was a pilot at the base flying A10's, supplied hand-written maps, **showing that the object had initially landed in Area 1 and then taken off before coming down near the perimeter** (fence was not there then) separating the forest from the field owned by Captain Boast.

He claims of having been present in a meeting that took place with Wing Commander Gordon Williams when he and others were told of a UFO landing which had taken place on the 25/26th and 29th/30th of December 1980. *"The first sighting of the craft over England was recorded on a radar screen at RAF Watten [sic], 50 miles away from where it landed. They reported: 'Tracing [sic] unidentified object.' Radar operators followed the progress as it flew over the East Coast until it disappeared."* But why is he not identified and why the anonymity? Puzzling …

Early hours: 26th December 1980 – UFO was tracked on radar!

Charles: Well I can only relate to the site of our encounter in the forest, which I have showed to the Press and Media over the years, near to the perimeter fence separating the field owned by Mr Boast of Green Farm, Capel St Andrew. I'm pleased that we can now offer additional evidence showing that a new witness has been found who corroborates that RADAR did track, albeit briefly, something during the early hours, when Jim and John were out there in the forest – thanks to David Bryant who brought the following to our attention.

> Green Farm
> Capel St Andrew
> WOODBRIDGE
> SUFFOLK
> IP12 3NG.
>
> Dear Mr Hanson,
>
> Thank you for your letter. Sorry not to have replied before. At the time the incident was supposed to have happened there was a lot of different stories and rumours in the newspapers. In fact that night we did not see or hear anything. Our four daughters were still living at home then and I can assure you that not one of them heard or saw anything. I am sorry not to be able to help you in any way. If you care to ring me up on 01394- . I shall be pleased to talk to you.
>
> David Boast

THE HALT PERSPECTIVE 2

The view over Capel Green field   *Charles Halt with David Bryant*

David Bryant: *"In the early nineteen eighties I spent my evenings running a hotel bar in the Norfolk Broads region. The location of the Hotel (near two major RAF bases) meant that service men and women from both the RAF and USAF regularly dropped in. One of these was David Moyes a serving Radar Operator/Fighter Controller at RAF Neatishead. His role was to monitor uncorrelated incursions into UK airspace: usually these could quickly be identified as Soviet 'Bear' bombers, probing the UK's state of readiness. Sometimes they would be American aircraft making emergency approaches to the nearby fighter station – I myself witnessed SR71 'Blackbird' and U2 spy planes doing just that. The RAF Sergeant and I shared an interest in space exploration and aviation which, on one memorable occasion, prompted him to discuss the strange events he had been witness to over the Christmas period in 1980. As his then wife was based overseas on Ascension Island, my friend had readily agreed to take the unpopular Christmas watch-keeping duty. Christmas Day was quiet, as was most of the evening.* **However, things became more interesting in the early hours of Friday, Boxing Day, 26th December 1980, when an uncorrelated return appeared on his radar screen. The station's Type 84 radar (with its range of over 400km) had detected a solid object apparently entering UK airspace over the North Sea before ultimately crossing the Suffolk Coast near Woodbridge.** *David Moyes discovered that this incursion had been detected by other radar bases in the Improved United Kingdom Air Defence Ground Environment and had been recorded by the Master Control Centre at West Drayton. I found my friend's account intriguing to say the least and have spent the intervening 38 years investigating what was to evolve into the 'Rendlesham Forest UFO Incident'."*

David was a good friend of David Bryant and lived in Langley, near Heathrow. He was a pilot and employed as an Air Traffic Controller at Heathrow for a period of time. Sadly Mr Moyes contracted MS and it is believed he may have passed away. If this is the case we offer our condolences. This means that we have some further proof unknown, to me for many years, that an object was plotted heading our way; was this the object claimed to have been seen by Jim and John that landed in the forest? Unfortunately we don't have an exact time, but its food for thought!

4pm: 26th December 1980 – Prison officer sights UFO

Former Prison officer at HMP Hollesley Bay Prison, Suffolk – Jeff Ralph – contacted John Hanson about what he saw, while out with friends, during the 26th December 1980. *"I had been working Christmas Day, 1980. When I arrived home after what had been a stressful day, I decided to 'let off some steam' and go out* with my wife, Christine, and our next door neighbour (who was a prison officer) and his wife, over farmland at Hollesley Bay, to shoot ducks. We had permission from the landowners. After picking up shotguns we made our way to Shingle Street, waiting for the ducks to come up. We lay down in the dyke, looking out to sea. It was twilight at the time, with darkness beginning to descend. At about 4pm, suddenly this 'thing' appeared in the sky, as if from outer space travelling in a shallow arc, of about 15 degrees the size of a small car, moving at fantastic speed heading towards the direction of Bentwaters. We all made a pact never to tell anybody about this, fearing ridicule – until now. I think that it's important Colonel Halt knows about this; whether it has any bearing on what he saw, I can't say."

Could it have been a fireball? There are none reported for that time by the British Astronomical Association. We spoke to Jeff again about the matter. He could only describe it as a light of some size, moving at terrific speed across the sky. He was unable to discern any shape to it, but felt it was very low, **about 60 feet above them,** and had originated from outer space. He was asked about any problems at the prisons and was surprised to hear that there had been claims of an alert at the Prison over the Christmas period.

Friday, 11pm: 26th December 1980 – Unusual lights seen over Forest

Gerry Harris, then living in a house situated in the centre of Rendlesham Forest, overlooking the twin bases of RAF Bentwaters and RAF Woodbridge, happened to look out of the window and noticed some unusual lights in the sky. *"The lights were going at a nice, steady speed and were moving about in the sky. I walked out into the front yard and stood watching them. I couldn't hear any sounds at all. They were bobbing up and down, and moving from side to side; they continued to move about in this manner for three-quarters of an hour when, all of a sudden, they disappeared. What I can't understand is that there were* **three objects in the sky.** *I must have looked away, because then there was only one. Whether they combined, I can't say – I got a bit fed up watching them. The bigger one in the middle descended down behind the trees. I thought to myself . . . it's crashed. All of a sudden it came back up and rose into the sky until I lost sight of it. However, just before they disappeared, there was a lot of activity on the base. I could hear vehicles driving about, and see flashing lights of vehicles moving about, and people shouting. I could hear voices calling to each other, which at that time of night was unusual. After hearing all the noise from the Base, I went down to have a look and found a military policeman there, standing next to a uniformed civilian Police Constable. They wouldn't let me on to Base. I had customers come to my garage the next day to pick up their cars; some of them were Base personnel. I asked them what the hell had gone on at the Base that night. One of them told me 'It's more than my life to talk about it'."* A few days afterwards, Gerry noticed that a large area of trees in the nearby woods had disappeared almost overnight. When he asked a forester who called into the garage what had happened, he was shocked by the answer – *"**The trees were radioactive; they had to go.**"*

Charles: This is interesting. John interviewed Gerry some years after Brenda Butler did. Could there be any connection with what took place during the morning of my encounter, two days later on the **28th December 1980**? Gerry is believed to be a genuine witness rather than others whose version of events are clearly fabricated. Not forgetting the important ingredient . . . this was a civilian witness and not bound under our constraints! He talks of **three objects**, trees felled after radiation was found; unfortunately we don't know exactly where the location is? His account appears to be corroborated by the landlord of the *Ramshott Arms* public house. Make of it what you will.

Friday, 11pm: 26th December 1980 – Bright lights seen over forest

The Landlord of the *'Ramshott Arms'* public house, Ramshott, near Woodbridge, was driving on the outskirts of Woodbridge, **at 11pm**. On his way home, after collecting his wife and children from

THE HALT PERSPECTIVE 2

Butley. *"As I came up the road, past the 'Butley Oyster' public house, I could see lights across the trees, over Rendlesham Way. Curious as to the cause I turned up the forestry road and saw trucks and jeeps, with men getting out of them. I thought it was an exercise and carried on up the road. A security guard then stopped me and ordered me to turn around and leave. I asked him what was going on. He refused to answer, and again ordered me to leave. I noticed more jeeps and lorries arriving up the road, and drove away, but decided to park up at the side of the road, when I heard lots of shouting and saw bright lights over the forest. About ten minutes, I decided to go home."* **(Source: Brenda Butler)**

Friday, 26th December 1980 – Orange sphere seen over Rendlesham Forest

Charles: Another interesting snippet of information was brought to my attention by John P Timmerman of CUFOs. J Allen Hynek (Centre for UFO Studies) Vice President/Public Relations Manager, was at a UFO Photo Project at the Park Central Mall on 18th October 1991, when a young man paused at the publications table, and told him that he had been on duty as a radar technician in the radar tower at Bentwaters on the night of the widely publicized event, 26th December 1980. The man said: "*I saw an object in the shape of a **large orange sphere with distinct edges** moving directly over the tower and pass silently right over the top of us . . . it had not been detected on radar at the time.*" He then told John that he was unable to give him his name for fear of penalties, for revealing what he had been told not to reveal. John had no reason to doubt the authenticity of what had been told him.

Another brilliant light is seen – this time the RAF attempt to intercept!

I must say that I pondered on the nature of what it was that was seen in April 1978, by Staff Sergeant Thomas W. Wharton of the 91st FS who was stationed at RAF Bentwaters, Suffolk, United Kingdom, between January 1977 and 1980. A man who had a very distinguished career, and whose account is considered to be absolutely genuine. This is yet another example of a mysterious unidentified object seen moving over East Anglia airspace, which despite the best efforts of interception, remains just that!

You know we've discussed strange things that have happened outside the twin Bases in the forest. Take the brilliant light that lit up the WSA area. I asked pertinent questions such as the size, height, direction – presumably eastwards; the answers, of course, remain unknown.

No doubt the sceptics will suggest that the illumination could have come from a spotlight, natural phenomena or even maybe light given off from bolides crossing the sky. John tells me that he has received a few reports from people who have been frightened by their passage across the sky, particularly during the night, over the years. But that isn't the answer. Can any association be drawn between what they saw over the WSA area and the incident involving Staff Sergeant Wharton, who sighted an enormous light above them in the sky, which shot away pursued by British fighter jets? What the heck was that about – two years before I took up command? He and his colleague were interviewed by the AFOSI and filed a report at RAF Bentwaters, which I have no knowledge about. Nothing was ever heard again. If a well respected and knowledgeable decorated Staff Sergeant who has served all over the world, met the President and flown all sorts of aircraft doesn't know, well that says it all!

Human beings from the future!

Jim now claims that what he witnessed was not any military covert aircraft, satellite re-entries or downed Russian aircraft, but rather, visits by human beings from the future!

THE HALT PERSPECTIVE 2

In 2010 while over here with John Burroughs and Linda Moulton Howe, during a conference at Woodbridge Community Hall, clips of films were shown to the audience, showing John and Jim recalling what happened under regression. The most amazing part of the regression conducted on the 10th September 1994 reveals an alien encounter at the scene of the incident!

Penniston talks about '*the visitors*' as being from our future – "*a dark and polluted world, with many difficulties. They are visiting in teams and each team is assigned a different task. Apparently, the teams know exactly which people they are to target when they arrive in our time.*" Penniston reveals that "*. . . some of them are coming here to take sperm and eggs, which are necessary in order to help their species survive. It seems they have a serious problem with reproduction. Could they be time travellers from the future?*" Jim was asked about this in December 2010, bearing in mind his close proximity to the object and that he had undergone regression, and Jim reiterated: "*I believe the 'craft' is from the far off future and that it contained our distant descendants, returning as time travellers, to obtain genetic material to keep their ailing species alive.*" I have enough information to back up my thoughts that Jim and John were either messed with in the forest or at the debriefing or some combination of both and that they have reality and fantasy confused. It's too bad as all they are doing is spreading unintentional disinformation.

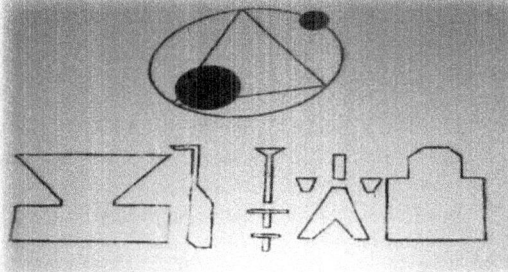

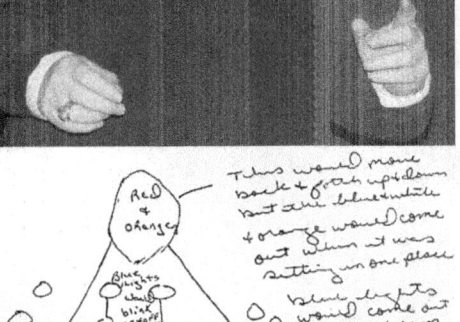

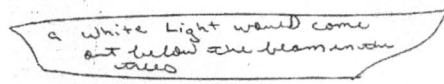

THE HALT PERSPECTIVE 2

In 2009, I was asked about the date of the first UFO incident (involving Penniston and Burroughs) by Robert Hastings, and confirmed the morning of **26th December** as now being correct. As I said before, there is no evidence to support the outlandish, unsubstantiated claims made that an alien craft landed and Gordon Williams entered into some sort of a dialogue with the entities by Warren. This is completely untrue. Major Zickler was not present in any of the proceedings that took place in the forest as he stayed at the party with Conrad, because didn't want to get involved.

Talk of photos taken – English Bobbies present! What next?

Captain Mike Verano, Palmer, Combs and Thompson were not there and John Burroughs was held back and ordered to stay on the service road. Now he talks about all kinds of things that I know didn't happen. The account from Bustinza is one of fabrication. I never ordered anyone to surround an object! There were no 'Bobbies' there. No-one, to my knowledge, was taking pictures (other than Nevels) and no film was confiscated.

It appears from this version of events that Larry may not have been present. Even if he was, well the evidence speaks volumes for itself. Warren has been proved to be a liar. If his agenda was to muddy the waters of what happened out there during the Christmas period he's certainly, along with a few others, done that. You have no idea how skilled these people are in fabricating disinformation. My advice is to be very cautious with regard to claims of this nature made, as they are untruthful.

Carl Thompson was one of the Air Traffic Controllers on duty that night (he and his partner saw the object both on the screen and visually, you have heard what he had to say. There's no way Bustinza could have known his name, as he didn't come forward until recently and their duty roster is not known but to a few – just further evidence that someone messed with Adrian. The plot thickens! I can only recommend that you proceed with caution.

Bentwaters Staff Judge Advocate, Lieutenant Colonel Arnold L Persky

Arnold L Persky pictured in 2018

John: According to the Bentwaters Staff Judge Advocate, Lieutenant Colonel *Arnold L Persky, he points out that the British authorities, including the local police, **would have been contacted** and expected to accompany the USAF patrols to the scene of the incident.

Although Lt Colonel Persky was aware that there had been an incident he assured Georgina Bruni **that if it had concerned an American air crash on British territory** someone from his office would have been summoned to investigate, in case the USAF were charged with damages to any property. Arnold Persky was sure that the British authorities were alerted and that they went to the forest sometime during the incident.

*Arnie Persky, last assignment before retiring, was Military Judge. During his career, he served as a military attorney, prosecutor/defense counsel, legal advisor to command staff, administration, etc. A licensed attorney since 1959. As of 1986, a Retired USAF attorney (JAG) who has been, since 1990, associated with the physician recruitment industry as a recruiter (nine years experience) as well as providing legal advice for 24 years to physicians concerning employment contracts.

THE HALT PERSPECTIVE 2

In mid May 2020, I received this email from Arnie: "*About two years ago you used Messenger to ask if I was at Bentwaters and knew Col Halt. I was the head lawyer, SJA, there and my immediate superior was Col. Gordon William's. Thanks for the reply. I will email you about my knowledge/experiences ASAP.*" This is what he had to say: "*Sorry for the delay. This pandemic has us all a little off schedule. As for Colonel Halt, I always liked him as a person as well as superior. Never had a doubt as to his honesty or loyalty to his oath as an officer. As zip mentioned earlier, my position during this period was as the "head" lawyer aka Staff Judge Advocate, and as such my boss was Colonel Williams whose Deputy was Colonel Halt. I had frequent contact with both over the years stationed there as most commanders looked to pass issues that might have a legal/practical/political effect on their decision. As to this UFO matter, as I don't recall when I first heard of it. It was not the night it happened nor during the remainder of my tour if memory serves. I like to tell others who ask what happened that,* **I have no memory of the incident because perhaps I was taken by the aliens who erased that part of my memory and then let me go**. *I find it strange that I was not informed on the date of the "incident"as the damage to land might have given rise to a claim against the USAF if caused by it. None of my staff was so far as I know. Airman Warren was not an ideal enlisted man. He was frequently involved in minor matters before this and as I recall was being considered for administrative action for discharge hearing. His comments in his book attributed to me are inaccurate. I do not find him to be an honest person, but in this matter my opinion is of no relevance. As to the book* You Can't Tell The People, *when contacted by the author from the UK while at our summer home in Connecticut, I told her pretty much what I have written here. I have no opinion as to the accuracy of the stories told as I find no reason how it would benefit the 'story tellers' to tell them. Sorry I can't provide any solid evidence one way or the other. Would like to be kept appraised, if not a burden. What about Zickler? He was the head of the Security Police as I recall. Be safe and well.*"

Setting the record straight about the space capsule being the answer!

Charles: At the Hull *Outer Limits Magazine* conference organised by Chris Evers in September 2017, where I was to give a talk in September 2018, UFO researcher Russell Callaghan produced images of a mock up space capsule that he claimed "*was actually used at RAF Woodbridge on the night in question.*" He said "*Documentary film makers in the Rendlesham case had always left out details about the ARRS crew and the capsule. This squadron was involved in the recovery of the command module capsules used during the Apollo moon missions and, during the 1980s, the recovery of film sent back to Earth in capsules from spy satellites. The ARRS practised on a mock up. This is the one that was at Bentwaters, it is in Florida now. What is interesting is it was on three legs.*" This was in addition to malicious admissions allegedly made by me to journalists and played to the audience admitting the lighthouse as an explanation! Although John pointed out the discrepancy and asked Russell to read a relevant passage from the *Halt Perspective* to clarify the situation this wasn't done. Read into that whatever you want. Russell could have contacted me and asked me what I thought but he didn't.

David Bryant sets the record straight!

Suggestions that the Apollo boilerplate capsule was responsible as the explanation for landing in the forest were ridiculous, according to Norfolk-based ex-pilot and author of several books David Bryant, who learned the following from Lowestoft-based man, 'Butch' Wilkes, who said: "*Sorry, this was not possible. I visited and worked on the Bases for a number of years from 1970 to now and back in late 1977 BP-1206 was sent back to NASA on a C-141. I was on the Base at the time and it had a big send-off. As a side note, the 67th ARRS got in the first of the shuttle mock-ups in the first two months of 1978. Moving on to the 1980's sighting: one more time, I was on the Base at the time and it is not possible that a helicopter from the 67th ARRS was flying that night, <u>as we had a bad ground fog for the days of the sighting</u> and ALL flights were grounded at the time. Plus the A-10 aircraft base at RAF Woodbridge and Bentwaters at the time did not have*

THE HALT PERSPECTIVE 2

night vision aids as they do now, so they did not fly at night." Mr Wilkes also disclosed an interesting snippet of information which *may* throw some light on the 1956 Bentwaters incident previously covered in this book, although no definite conclusions can be reached.

He says: *"This is not the first UFO sighting at RAF Woodbridge/Bentwaters they had a big sighting back in the 1960's. A ball of light was seen over the top of the nuclear bomb dumps at RAF Lakenheath, which then moved off at a high speed. A bit later a ball of light was seen over the nuclear bomb dumps at Woodbridge/Bentwaters. Some say it was the same ball of light that was seen at RAF Lakenheath that same day. The base had F-100s at the time and two of them were sent up to intercept the light but they were not able to keep up with it. I hope this puts an end to this mystery."*

Re-entry of Russian satellite

Charles: Chris Pennington, the ex-partner of Brenda Butler, who I met personally a number of times over the years, outlined a number of possible explanations as to what it was, that had landed in Tangham Woods, They included: *a 'craft' from another planet – a crashed aircraft? Defecting Russian Tupolev TU 142 'Bear'? – The re-entry of a Russian satellite – or even a drugs party?*

Chris: *"The 67th came to Woodbridge Airbase in about December 1969, with a complement of 250 personnel and their equipment, HC130 Hercules and HH53 Jolly Green Giants (helicopters) with in-flight refuelling capabilities, and was responsible for aerospace rescue operations over almost a million square miles. It was the biggest Search & Rescue Squadron in the World. These units were set up primarily to pick up astronauts, wherever they may come down around the world, as back-up to US Space Operations, NASA. Maybe it was just an excuse for the 67th to practice their arts. They never seemed to advertise their connection with the Space Race. They must have had equipment to practice with – if not the real thing, simulated models – which brings me to a conclusion that a Re-entry Module looks remarkably like some of the UFOs that were reported. If it were only a practice, why did John Warburton tell us that Colonel Halt's boss, Colonel Ted Conrad, said, 'not allowed to say what happened, as it would embarrass Governments'."*

Mind programming drugs! What next?

Charles: Let me think (re drugs). Would that have been sprayed into the forest or somehow gotten into their systems unknowingly? You see, there is a vast difference between possibilities, plausibility, feasibility and the reality of what actually happened. I still don't know and merely seek to tell folks what I witnessed along with others. I wasn't out with the other guys that night and don't feel there is any substance to such a claim. Maybe if the forest had been invaded by mind programming drugs then Jim and John could have been hallucinating about what they saw. In that case so must I!

Open letter from John Burroughs

In 2010, I received an open letter from John Burroughs to Gen. Gordon Williams, Wing Commander; Col. Theodore Conrad, Vice Wing Commander; Col. Sam P Morgan, Base Commander; Col. Charles I Halt Dept. Base Commander; Lt Col. Malcolm Zickler, Security Police Commander – in which he brought to my attention a number of personal matters relating to his health, having suffered following the UFO incident, and of an inconsistency with regard to his involvement in the first and third night. My mistake, the tape proved that he had been there and he did meet up with me on the night I was out. He then asserts that I have gone on record and claimed I had been exposed to something extraterrestrial in nature. That's my general view rather than believe whatever we encountered in the sky (and in the forest according to Jim) was of earthly origin, i.e. a mechanical device. I suppose you could argue till the

THE HALT PERSPECTIVE 2

cows come home as to the identity of what it was that we saw, but no one can offer irrefutable evidence proving what it was EXACTLY that descended over the Base, sending out beams of light.

3am, 27th December 1980, Oxfordshire – red, square lights seen!

John: David John Storer of Warwick Road, Banbury, Oxfordshire, was out with his wife driving near RAF Greatworth Airbase, Oxon., at 3am when they saw an unusual object for twenty minutes in the eastern part of the sky described as: *"various shapes, showing red square lights – a solid object with a glowing trail, on a cold but dry, windy night."*

Saturday 27th December 1980 – My account that led to the first MEMO!

Charles: Incredibly, if you look up Rendlesham Forest Incident on *Wikipedia* 2020, you will see that, quote: 'It was during this investigation that a flashing light was seen across the field to the east, almost in line with a farmhouse, as the witnesses had seen on the first night. The Orford Ness lighthouse is visible further to the east in the same line of sight. Later according to the Memo, **three star-like lights** were seen in the sky ... **Astronomers explain these lights as bright stars!**' End of quote. What a load of rubbish this is! I'm sorry but it's painfully obvious what is going on here, another slice of disinformation.

Now the facts! – We were having the Christmas dinner – a family dinner, a cover dish dinner for all the officers and combat support group – about 40 families – at the small Club at Woodbridge Base, known as the *'Twelve o'clock High'* Club, on the 27th of December 1980. While getting ready to start dessert and enjoy the evening's festivities – involving things like annual awards and the recognition for people who had done special things – the on-duty Flight Lieutenant Bruce Englund for the Security Police Squadron came bursting in, with his MI6, all red-faced and upset, and said to me, *'I've got to talk to you privately, right now'*, so I got hold of Ted Conrad, who was my boss – the Base Commander – and we went into the cloakroom. **(Ted Conrad told me that he had seen a UFO about a year ago but didn't report it knowing the hassle anyone got for reporting it to the command structure.)** It was the only private place to talk in the club, at that time. He said, *'It's back'.* I said, 'What's back? He said, *'The UFO's back'*. I said, 'How do you know that?' He said, *'I've seen something'*. I said, 'Where?' He said, *'Outside the East Gate, in the woods'*. I said, '...So what are you doing out in the woods in the East Gate?' ... (Bearing in mind England was a foreign country, as far as we're concerned).

Equipment fails

We were guests there, and our mission was not to patrol the woods but to maintain the perimeter of the base. He said, *'Some of the guys saw something, so we sent a patrol out there. We took some light-alls with us.* (The NF2 light-alls were motor generators. They were nothing but a small, I think, a five horsepower 'Briggs and Stratton' engine with a couple of big mercury vapour lights on top, and a gas tank, and a lot of sheet metal.) *The lights wouldn't work. The radios were acting up. When we looked in the woods with a starlight scope, we saw some strange things'.* I said, 'What did you see?' He said, '**We saw a glow and some red lights'.**

Ted Conrad instructs me to go out there to investigate

Ted Conrad and I looked at each other, as he had to make all the presentations – or maybe that was his excuse. He said, *'Why don't you go out and see what this is all about?'* 'Ok, I wasn't too excited, but I realised the cops had become preoccupied with this – both the Security Forces and the Law Enforcement – and they were more attuned to what was going on in the woods probably than what they should be doing;

in other words, guarding the perimeter of the base and providing law enforcement. So I went to see the Disaster Preparedness Officer, Sue….and said, 'Would you have one of your key NCOs – whoever is on standby – go over to your office, pick up an ANP-27 Geiger counter and calibrate it? She told me who was on duty. It was Sergeant Monroe Ruby Nevels.

I knew he was a professional photographer and had a degree in photography, so I said, 'Have him bring his camera along too', so she got on the phone and called him. I drove home. The police came by in a jeep and picked me up (Master Sergeant Bobby Ball) and I don't remember who else.

We then went over and picked up Sergeant Monroe Ruby Nevels. I watched him calibrate two ANP, ANP-27's, and we picked what I thought was the better. Actually, they were both probably very good … then we bundled into the jeep, and drove across the flight line. The two bases are about a mile-and-a-half apart – a little closer if you drive right across the flight line and in the back gate. We unlocked the back gate and drove across, and to what, what's known as East Gate, at Woodbridge. Lo and behold, there's a crowd out there. Well, I was quite concerned, so I said to them, 'Let's keep all these people back. We don't need the publicity. We are kind of trespassing. This was the Queen's forest – sort of like a National Forest. There's a lot of private property around here. We don't want to cause a lot of concern, or get people upset. They're going to wonder what we're doing stomping around out here in the woods', so he said, 'Ok'. At this time – there were probably 30 or 40 people in total, with three or four light-alls which were acting up. They wouldn't run right; kept flickering off and on. I could hear comments: *'He didn't refuel them'* and somebody else said, *'Yes, I did refuel them; I took them down to the motor pool before we brought them out'.*

Sergeant Monroe Ruby Nevels

Dull glow sighted in the Forest

Bruce Englund said, *'Let's look into the woods there'*, he had a first generation starlight scope. We looked into the woods and, sure enough, in one area there was a dull glow. When you look through a starlight scope you don't see things as you normally would. It's a greenish-yellow tinge to them. It's a different spectrum, or different, uh, frequency and there was something I could see in there, but I wasn't really sure what it was. It didn't make a lot of sense to me … and I'm not sure it's of great significance, but there was something. Sadly as the reader will see for themselves, in recent years following the publication of Jim's book, **I was savagely criticised by Jim and Ruby**, but plenty on that in due course….

Believed – Early morning Saturday 27th December 1980

Unknown to me at the time Communications Specialist Carl Thompson was working on the tower sensors in the WSA the nights of both incidents along with a co-worker who told Carl of having seen a UFO both nights and was threatened to keep quiet.

Carl: *"During the believed morning of 27th December 1980 we received some parts to repair the equipment. We were in the same situation as before. My colleague took the part out to the area. He called again. He said it was here again and the security police were going to report it because it seemed to go down in the woods as they watched it .They were looking from the tower cab in the Weapons Storage area towards Woodbridge.*

I told him to go ahead and report it. I heard a lot of radio traffic in the background as we were talking. Normally the radio was really quiet at that time. So that confirmed that there was something important going on. I was across the runway from them at the wideband site and could not go out to confirm anything. I do believe him. I don't remember how much time had elapsed when he was called for an interview with AFOSI. I think...When he returned to the shop he was highly agitated, **they told him that it did not happen and he was wrong, and not to talk about the interview.** *He never discussed the interview outside of what I told you. I have tried to search for him but with no results I just wanted you to know that there are a couple of more people who know it happened."* The next time Carl saw his colleague, he told him he had to file a report with the Security Police at their headquarters, approximately 30 yards away from the Weapons Storage Area. I know for a fact that Carl Thompson and his partner saw the 'object' both on the screen and visually). There's no way Adrian Bustinza could have known his name, as he didn't come forward until recently and their duty roster is not known but to a few – just further evidence that someone messed with Adrian. The plot thickens! I can only recommend that you proceed with caution.

Pocket Memo tape recorder

I had taken my small cassette recorder along with me, not specifically for this instance. It's just that any time I went around the Base, I would take this little recorder along, record things that need to be done, a fence that needed to be mended, or a road needing to be paved, or whatever I noticed, or something out of the ordinary ... and I'd bring it back and flip it to the secretary, and she'd type it up, then, at the next staff meeting, would mark who had the action on the items, and pass it them out for tasking ... so I'd taken it along that night, just because I thought I might need to take some notes and it was probably 35, 40 degrees, with a stiff wind blowing off the coast, and quite cold ...and I made a tape, which was later inadvertently released by a co-worker. I can't exactly repeat what's on there.

It's 1980, but I'll just go through what happened. I was afraid that wouldn't be too good, but the little pocket recorder I had has long since worn out. It gave up the ghost, and they've changed the format on tapes now so I put it on big tapes, while I could. Basically what happened, I took the pocket recorder along and just dropped it in my pocket, and I'd pick it up, and every few minutes I would say what was going on.

0148: Sunday 28th December 1980

Refreshing the readers memory from my pocket tape recorder

[3.05am-] – Two objects half moon shaped seen COLONEL HALT: 3.05: We see strange err, strobe like flashes to the, err ... almost sporadic, but there's definitely something there, some kind of phenomena. 3.05: At about err... 10 degrees horizon err directly north, we got two strange objects, err ...half moon shape, dancing about with coloured lights on them. But err. It has to be about 5-10 miles out, maybe less. The half moons have now turned into full circles as though there was an eclipse or something there for a minute or two. (Break in tape) 3.15am LT COLONEL HALT: 3.15: Now we've got an object about ten degrees directly south...SGT NEVELS: There's one to the left. LT COLONEL HALT: 10 degrees off the horizon and the ones to the north are moving; one's moving away from us. SGT NEVELS: It's moving out fast. LT COLONEL HALT: They're moving out fast. MASTER SGT BALL: There's one on the right heading away too. LT COLONEL HALT: Yeah, they're both heading north. Hey, here he comes from the south; he's coming in toward us now. MASTER SGT BALL: Shit. LT COLONEL HALT: Now were observing what appears to be a beam coming down to the ground. [Excited shouting in the background] MASTER SGT BALL: Look at the colours... shit. LT COLONEL HALT: This is unreal. (Break in tape) 3.30am LT COLONEL HALT:

THE HALT PERSPECTIVE 2

3.30: And the objects are still in the sky, although the one to the south looks like it's losing a little bit of altitude. We're turning around and heading back toward the base. The object to the south is still beaming down lights to the ground.

Eastern Radar RAF Watton contacted

During the sighting, I asked my command post to contact Eastern Radar at RAF Watton, responsible for air defence of that region. Twice they (RAF Watton) reported they didn't see anything, but we now know that one of those calls was logged at 3.25am on December 28th 1980.

Three indentations found on the landing site forming a triangle!

When we approached the site, we found the three indentations. We measured them, and you can hear the distance on there. I think there were eight or nine, seven feet apart, very triangular, and the dosimeter was picking up definite readings which were above background radiation, seven to twenty times, dependent upon whom you talk to, and it was, the site was hottest, so to speak, in the centre formed by the triangle. Also the trees, the pine trees that were there, were approximately, I would say, anywhere from 8 to 15 inches diameter. There were some marks on them. There were two, two sets of marks, or types of marks. There were blade marks that were done with an axe, that were very clear. Someone had come through the forest not too long before, and marked trees – probably for cutting, but there were some big rub marks and, if you looked overhead, branches were broken as though something could have come up or come down, although I can't say that for a fact. It appeared that way. You could see the sky there and you couldn't see it anywhere else. We were walking around.

Sgt Adrian Bustinza was present during the UFO events on the early morning of **December 28th 1980**. He later claimed there were a minimum 30 – 50 airmen out in the woods, which I would doubt and that he accompanied John Burroughs out into a field where 'lights' were seen, one of which shone down onto Burroughs causing him to be pushed to the ground.

Adrian also claims of having received a clear death threat from investigators who took him to a room, turned off the lights, shined a bright light in his face and proceeded to intimidate, and ultimately threaten his life. I have no knowledge of this. If true then no wonder his story has changed over the years. But of course he wasn't the only one to suffer.

A UFO appears in the sky!

An object appeared in the sky probably for, I'm guessing, 30, 40 seconds – maybe a minute, and all of a sudden, it just silently exploded into five white objects and they disappeared – just gone like that! While we were watching it, it appeared to be dripping the equivalent of a molten metal. Something was, like, dripping off it, so when the object disappeared, I said, 'Let's go out in the field and see if we can find some burned evidence, or some spots on the ground where something has fallen – there has to be something'... and we went out, of course.

In the meantime, we're having great problems with the radios. There were five of us present. We all had radios, and each (three of us) were on different nets. I was on the net with the command post. There was a cop on the security net with the Security Police, and one of the cops was on the Law Enforcement net, so we were talking to three different control centres, so to speak, all the time. Generally, we would have to relay, through one of the people that were back by the light-alls, because the radios would not carry that far and they were in the line of sight, yes, pretty much, but we were out in the open, in the clear, which was kind of puzzling because normally we should have gotten a good transmission right through.

THE HALT PERSPECTIVE 2

Indentations found in the ground

We identified one of the indentations as point one and I'm measuring them and taking readings, so we have a record of all this, when suddenly, Bruce Englund, the Lieutenant who was with me, looks out and says a few words I won't repeat, and says, '*There's something out there – look at that*', and it was a red thing. It's the only way I can describe it. It looked like an eye. It was oval and had a black centre, and it was winking. It just looked like an eye is what it looked like. It moved back and forth through the trees, horizontally, and not necessarily in a level plane. It was moving through the trees. It was in the forest at that time. We watched it blink. It moved through the forest, moved through the trees. We stood there in awe for quite awhile, watching this thing … and, finally, I said let's try and get closer, so we worked our way through the forest and, as we did, it receded. It moved out into the field. There was a large field on the other side of the forest. We came up to a barbed, an old barbed wire fence, and watched there for a few minutes. And it seemed to be centred almost in front of a farmer's house, and the farmer's house had a glow in all the windows, as though it were on fire inside. It's the only way I can describe it. It may have been a reflection off the glass in the windows. It probably was, but I didn't know for sure. I was quite concerned for whoever was in the farmhouse, if anybody was there, and it was an active farm. The animals were just going crazy on the farm. The horses, the cows, the pigs – everything was just making all kinds of noise. There was no activity that we could discern in the farmhouse at all. It was quiet.

UFO display begins!

It was a clear night, standing in the field, and somebody said, '*Look up there!*', and there were these objects in the sky. The best way I can describe them – they look like a **half, or a Cherokee moon**, well-illuminated, with multiple coloured lights, were moving about in sharp, angular, patterns – very fast, and as we watched them, they turned, from the equivalent of a Cherokee moon into a full circle. It was very amazing … and the way they were going, it appeared that they were doing some type of 'grid search, or doing some type of a pattern, or seemed to be some type of logic to their movement – really wasn't sure. We went around the farmer's house, (Boasts) went on out into a ploughed field, to get a better view, and all this time we could see the lighthouse. In fact, there was another lighthouse further down the coast we could see at that time, too. We're standing out in the ploughed field. We crossed it, and we all fell into a stream we didn't see and got good and wet. We came out of that, into another ploughed field, and, I don't remember who, but somebody said, '*Look!*', and we looked up to the North, and there were objects in the sky, to the North.

We probably watched them for twenty, thirty minutes, and suddenly, we noticed an object to the South. Contrary to what has been alleged I never told anybody any structure was penetrated by beams. I was several miles away. From my view, a beam or more came down near the Weapons Storage Area. I don't know for a fact that the beams landed there. I know they were in the area. I was too far away but relied on the radio chatter, which indicated the beams landed there.

This was a round object and it was approaching us at very high speed. It came in – and it's real clear on the tape. That's an interesting part of the tape, if you could hear it – it came in very, very close, I'm guessing within a quarter to a half mile, and stopped two, three, four thousand feet up, and sent down a beam. The best way I can describe the beam is a laser beam, because a light beam normally radiates out. This came down instead and it was six to eight, or maybe nine, inches in diameter and fell right at

---

*For those that are interested, John tells me that he can (space not permitting) include numerous reports like this which have been seen going back many years, involving the appearance of 'star-like objects, followed by half moon shaped or discoid in appearance that dominate the sky and appearing to conduct a grid like search as referred to by the witnesses. So I tend to ignore the bullshit thrown at me now over 40 years in an attempt to prove these things are a by product of natural celestial phenomena, or crackpot explanations by those that think they know better!

our feet. Well, that really had us upset because we weren't sure whether it was a warning, whether it was, you know, a shot at us, whether it was somebody trying to communicate, or what it was. We had no idea, and we just stood there and looked and nobody said anything and, all of a sudden, as fast as it came on, it was gone. The object receded.

New witness found 38 years later – also saw the strange lights over forest

I was having a beer with John Hanson and his two friends David and Julie Boardman, at my home address in Washington in May 2018 and discussing what we were going to put in the next book – as there were a number of up-to-date comments we wanted to include – plus new witnesses who had come forward, one of which involved my daughter who told me she had been out shopping and during conversation with local shopkeeper Jeff Weinhertz was astonished when he told her that he knew her father and had served on the Base with him. In addition to this he told of having seen strange lights moving around the trees on the same night I was out there. I telephoned him and also invited John to speak to him, he told us that he had indeed seen "*a strange light moving around the trees which wasn't the lighthouse or the flashlights used by the guys on the ground.*" Jeff remembered seeing me in the forest after weapons in the possession of the servicemen were placed into a vehicle parked at East Gate entrance. He was asked about Larry Warren and was adamant that the serviceman wasn't there at all.

Report made to senior officer – impressions found at location and plaster casts taken

Some five hours after the sighting, I informed my Commanding Officer about having seen '*red and white lights flying up into the trees, over the forest*'. He then said, '*let's go and see if we can find any physical proof of what is happening*' and, following a visit into the forest, we found damage to the trees and three depressions in the ground, forming a triangle, measuring 3.4 metres between each depression. Jim Penniston made three plaster casts of the impressions found in the ground without telling anyone he had them, until someone stole one of them from his luggage while going through customs. I gave him another one, which he buried at the bottom of his garden in the States. They didn't get mine, though. I did have some tests carried out on them by Melissa Tittl, a producer and actress known for '*Hanger 1: The UFO Files*' in 2010, but nothing untoward was found. The program turned out to be, despite promises, more entertainment that factual.

Penniston can describe to this day the hieroglyphic-like symbols he saw on the side of the object that appeared to be raised –"*sort of like they were burned on with a welding rod, or something.*" Soon after the incident, Jim Penniston asked me if he could be transferred to another base, as he was shaken after the event. So many people have had their lives changed because of what took place in this Suffolk forest close to the small town of Woodbridge.

Eastern Radar contacted – nothing tracked!

Squadron Leader Derek Coumbe was on duty as RAF Commander of Eastern Radar on the same night when I asked someone to telephone him, requesting confirmation of our sightings. He had this to say, later: *"They were very jumpy and panicky on the phone, but I personally checked the radar picture and there was absolutely nothing to be seen. They kept coming back and implying there should be something, but we kept a watch on it through the whole period and nothing was seen."* Coumbe told the *BBC*, in January 1981:

THE HALT PERSPECTIVE 2

"The radar tapes were removed by a joint RAF/USAF team from the Military Air Traffic Operations centre (MATO) at Uxbridge. This was not unusual but quite a common procedure that followed incidents such as a near-miss involving aircraft.'"

This is another example of a blatant cover up, regarding the events that took place over the skies of Suffolk. We had a situation where trained military personnel had seen something highly unusual and wanted confirmation, instead it was denied to us.

Derek Coumbe recalled for *BBC Radio 4* in 2003 that several calls had come through from Bentwaters asking them if they were seeing anything unusual in the Bentwaters and Woodbridge area. *"We scrutinized the radar time and time again completely, and kept a watch on it through the whole period when these phone calls were going on **and nothing was seen. Nothing at all,"*** A copy of the RAF Watton log obtained later reads, *Bentwaters Command Post contacted Eastern Radar and requested information of aircraft in the area – UA37 traffic southbound FL370 – **UFO sightings at Bentwaters.** They are taking reporting action.* UA37 was the code for an air corridor used by civilian aircraft which ran north/south approximately 40 miles east of Bentwaters. FL370 signified "traffic" at 37,000 feet in altitude."

Former RAF radar operator Nigel Kerr who was stationed at RAF Watton during Christmas 1980, told of having received a call from somebody at RAF Bentwaters, wanting to know if there was anything unusual on his radar screen. **He looked, and for three or four sweeps, something did show up, directly over the Base.** But it faded away and no official report was ever made.

If Monroe had been to the landing site prior to our visit, he never mentioned it when we went out. In fact, he wasn't sure where the site was. His reaction when we found it was surprise. It certainly didn't happen the night we went out. Conrad did not have time during Lt Bruce Englund's shift to go and Monroe was babysitting, as his wife spent the evening at a chapel program. Englund had to go and fetch him so he could participate. A day or two later I took Conrad and his family out and Conrad had no idea where the site was and never mentioned being there prior. Something doesn't sound right!

Several years ago, I challenged Monroe about his comment of having been there prior and he did not give me an acceptable answer. That all being said, Conrad may have been read in on the 'cover-up', but they would have never have trusted Monroe. Monroe claims he was out there before I ever recruited him to go out there too – very unlikely! It's certainly possible Conrad was out there earlier, but that puts him in the middle of the cover-up. Conrad isn't being honest. His wife and son have told John Burroughs there's more to the story. Maybe one of them will talk more?

People ask me 'what about photographs taken of the landing site?'

My only knowledge of that is Master Sergeant Ray Gulyas went to the scene and took a number of photographs and handed the roll of film to Captain Verrano. Subsequently, Mike was later told that the photographs were fogged. Mike returned to the location, two days later, and took his own photos and plaster casts of the impressions (these were later written-off by the police officer as being rabbit scratchings!). According to Ray Gulyas, the width from each ground indentation was 12 feet centre to centre. The marks on the trees, as described by Monroe Nevels, were found to be five feet off the ground. Ray handed the film over to Richard Nunn, in early January 1981, who processed six photographs and gave them back to him. In the spring of 1981, while returning to the US, the film negatives and plaster casts mysteriously disappeared from Ray's personal possession. Georgina Bruni managed to obtain a contact strip of **six photographs** from Richard Nunn's photographic files, in 1999; otherwise, there would be no photographs of the location. One of those photographs shows a tall policeman (PC Brian Creswell) and Mike Veranno.

THE HALT PERSPECTIVE 2

Michael Stacy Smith – fully loaded! Claims he was out there the same night?

In 2018, the following guy came forward to tell his version of events which took place in the Forest a month before what I and others sighted of which I hadn't any knowledge of whatsoever! Michael Stacy Smith a former Police Detective at Savannah Police Department living in Vidalia Georgia joined the US Air Force in July 1979 and after training was assigned to RAF Bentwaters, Woodbridge, Suffolk, England. He arrived in November 1979 and was posted to Delta flight.

Michael Stacy Smith

This is what he had to say . . .

In **November 1980** the base went on alert. All Security patrolmen were called out from the barracks. Michael was sent to a perimeter post located behind the East Gate on Woodbridge air base. "*About two or three in the morning I stood up on the bunker to urinate when I noticed about 150 to 200 yards down the fence line off Base, a glow in the forest moving in my direction. At first I thought it was someone with a lantern. When it got in front of me it stopped. I could see it clearly. It was a reddish orange glowing ball a little bigger than a beach ball. I then called for backup and a set team came to me. The object was still there. A black SSgt and a white A1C came. I didn't know them. I think they were. It happened. I will swear before God when I die – if you believe or not, I don't care – I have too many illnesses, mostly from radiation my doctors say. I know – Congress wants a private hearing. I assure you I will be more than happy to speak to them. From my experience, take it or leave it. I don't care. We are not alone . . . The A1C jumped the fence saying he was going to flank it to see what it was.* **I had an M-60 machine gun with over 500 rounds of live ammo. We were not supposed to but I locked and loaded my weapon** *all I had to do was release the safety – I was prepared to fire. As the Airman approached the object it left very quickly.*

*<u>**I was also there the night Lt. Col. Halt came out.**</u> I stayed on the base at the East Gate and had everyone's weapons in my truck. They posted a new guy on the gate that night. All of a sudden he started yelling what the F.... is that? An object flew over us coming from the Bentwaters direction. It made no noise and went into the Rendlesham forest.* **It was a glowing blue and triangle shaped.** *That's what I saw. I don't care who believes me. It truly happened. I will carry it to my grave. More of my brothers who were there need to speak out. I've had a few people on here say I wasn't at Bentwaters, Woodbridge from 1979-1981 because they*

never heard my name. They said they heard John Burroughs, Jim Penniston, Larry Lawrence Warren. So they think I'm lying. Just making it up – well I don't give a shit what you think. I was there and I saw what I saw. No one can take that from me. All my brothers' 81st. S.P.S. saw the UFOs. Some did, some didn't. I did."

Appearing in a film under production

Mike has posted his version of the events that took place up many times in the social media and is involved in a film documentary produced by film maker Dion Johnson aided by Gary Heseltine and Larry Warren. I'm sorry but I have no recollection of this incident in November 1980, involving Michael Stacy Smith. Why has it taken this man all these years to come forward? The very idea that one of the security cops would be armed with a fully loaded machine gun doesn't make sense. Who was it that gave authority for the use of such a weapon and authorized a visit into a British forest by a fully armed USAF security officer? If the British authorities had known about this it could have caused embarrassment and repercussions? He was left at the East Gate to guard the weapons for those in the forest. He could not have left the gate nor had an M-60 machine gun. The gun is a crew served weapon and requires a second person to carry the ammo. They were only issued at Bentwaters to guard the WSA and then only during an alert. He could not have radiation issues as he was <u>nowhere near the landing site</u>. None of us that were at the actual site had any issues.

Adrian Bustinza

Adrian Bustinza is another mystery. He gave me an initial statement and was then debriefed by AFOSI (Air Force Office of Special Investigation). His version of events gets better after each session and is the basis of much of what Larry continues to say. You obviously do not understand how the AFOSI and their counterparts operate. They don't report to anyone on the base and only notify the senior leadership when they feel it necessary. I personally confronted the AFOSI Commander, Chuck Matthews, and told him of the encounter. His reply was that they were not interested – **an obvious lie**, as I later learned of the 'debriefings' and that they took place in his building. I am convinced I was left out, as they had already done a good job of using Warren and others with a planted story that would make the incident, if it ever got out, as unbelievable.

In 1984 Sgt 'Busty' (Adrian) Bustinza was interviewed on the telephone by the now late Police Lieutenant Larry Fawcett. I sent John Hanson a copy of the typed notes taken. In it, Larry Fawcett tells Bustinza that he has a book coming out – based on the testimony with Larry Warren. Instead of asking Adrian Bustinza to <u>comment on direct questions,</u> put to him – Larry Fawcett leads him by quoting answers given by Larry Warren to him in a previous interview and then asking Adrian Bustinza for a response which in the main is quite short.

Example: "*Larry says at this point a light came down from the top of the thing and sort of jumped from head to head on the shadows, at which point Larry says he couldn't remember anything – then he woke up on his own in bed covered in mud in the barracks. Larry Warren was told by a roommate that he was brought in at 4am. Then he was asked to go down into the security shack.*"

Reply: "Right". The conversation continues with Larry Fawcett covering further comments from Warren who said, "*I was told not to say anything about the incident after a debriefing – then got picked up the next day by a couple of Chinese men driving an automobile and taken underground.*" Ok, I don't know if you know any of this is you there?" Reply: Sgt Adrian Bustinza – "*yeah I'm with you. I don't want to say anything else, it's with you.*" Larry Fawcett, talks about Larry being taken underground to a man-made cave – he looked down and saw "*one of the machines*" down there that they saw in the field. Does that sound anything?" Sgt Andrew Bustinza "*The underground part, I really don't know about the underground*

THE HALT PERSPECTIVE 2

part." Larry Fawcett then tells him about Larry Warren being hypnotized, and that his recall was being **petrified and seeing small beings, talking to an officer**, he (Warren) gave me (LF) the name escapes me – a big guy. Sgt Adrian Bustinza *"Lt Colonel Halt."*

Larry Fawcett, *"He (Warren) said the beings were conversing with Halt, something had happened to their machine when it came down and it got damaged, and at this point one of the beings – something happened on the other side of the craft because all the beings like got defensive, they all lined up real quick in a defensive move, their eyes got really big. One of them floated over and came over to him (LW) and that's the last thing he remembers – does this sound like anything like you remember?"*

Sgt Adrian Bustinza, *"Ok Boy let me see. I remember the conversation. I don't remember word for word the conversation, okay."* Sgt Adrian Bustinza is then asked if he had seen the beings. He replies, *"I just couldn't believe what was going on, I thought I was in a dream world or something."*

He is asked again if he remembers any of the conversation between Colonel Halt and the beings.

"No, I don't. To be honest with you I was just in the feeling of insecurity with it when you feel helpless – totally helpless, even though there were plenty of personnel there and they want you to feel secure but you feel like your whole body, your whole privacy has been invaded."

Further conversation takes place in which 'Busty' agrees with the statement made by Larry Warren that *"something happened to their machine'* it is also put to him that Larry Warren claimed *"Our Government helped them repair that machine – they flew a piece in from Germany."*

Sgt Adrian Bustinza: *"Hold on, let me see, Colonel Halt when we approached the machine, I remember Colonel Halt said, I remember Larry was going up there and I was so scared I didn't know what to think. I was in a foreign country you know."*

Further conversation takes place during which Adrian Bustinza describes *"some 'instant' communication between Halt and personnel (the men)"* he is asked about the 'beings' and says *"I remember seeing the craft and Colonel Halt talking but couldn't see who he was talking to – but I remember him saying that he would contact the electronics division which would be C.R.F – the call letters for the group, and they would have to get the parts from another world! The next thing I knew was waking up in bed."*

The gist of further questions put to Adrian elicits the answers that he didn't see who Colonel Halt was talking to, but that he did remember being driven back in the jeep with the Lt (Englund?) To the base and that he was advised not to tell anyone what had taken place.

Barry Greenwood told me that Larry Warren decided, as Bustinza was reluctant to go public, he would adopt Bustinza's story as his own.

A decision he made to flush out another's involvement. But it blew up on Larry anyway. I told Barry in later years that I remained puzzled, then as I still do, many years later how much of what are downright lies, and how much my later friend Budd Hopkins said was induced memories. I know Larry was regressed at Bentwaters in a debriefing and then again by him and Budd Hopkins. There was also a guy called **Ernie Frost** who alleged he was a witness to the events that took place and contacted the Massachusetts MUFON. As Barry recalled, Frost didn't want to be interviewed too closely about his involvement – then dropped out of sight. There seems to be a never ending number of people who claim to be core eyewitnesses, offering sensational eye witness accounts –then fade away. But they still keep coming, as we shall see further on into the book.

On the **25th of April 1985**, MUFON director Walter H Andrus wrote to Philip Julian Klass (Born: November 8, 1919 – August 9, 2005) an American journalist, and UFO researcher, known for his skepticism regarding UFOs and claimed *"that roughly 97-98 percent of the people who report seeing UFOs are fundamentally* *intelligent, honest people who have seen something – usually at night, in darkness – that is unfamiliar, that they cannot explain. The rest were frauds."*

The letter was a response to criticism made in the MUFON Newsletter of February 1985 in which it was alleged by Phil that it was riddled with malicious errors and falsehoods. A reference is then made to a conversation which took place between Phil and Chuck De Caro, when Phil suggested a polygraph test for Larry Warren. Following which it was intended that negotiations would take place to address this suggested action with Larry Fawcett.

Unfortunately due to some squabble between the parties about the polygraph proposal being made in confidence, this led to allegations of intimidation and a claim of no validity made against Philip, matters which, to be honest, appear confusing although sight of the previous allegations and claims may clarify the situation. MUFON then declined the 'generous' offer to underwrite half of the cost of a polygraph test for Larry Warren. This is where it gets interesting: *"Based upon our investigation into this case, Larry would <u>probably fail</u> any questions directly related to his having personally observed three occupants and their physical description as depicted in the CNN FILM. We have other witnesses that confirm that Larry was indeed present at the first sighting; however one witness, who now resides in Texas, said he personally **<u>did not</u>** see the small humanoids that Larry described in the CNN film. Mr. Warren apparently enjoys basking in this publicity, because he tends to embellish his story each time that it is told. We arranged to have a voice stress analysis test his device, using the CNN Video tape audio as the medium for the test. Larry Warren failed the questions where he was describing the occupants; therefore MUFON has no further need to conduct a polygraph test. We are relying on the testimony of other witnesses present, including USAF officers and enlisted security police, since Larry Warren is not the principal witness – just one of many to the two incidents"* Sincerely *Walter H Andrus Junior.*

Claims that British experimental airplane landed at Airbase

Ex Staff Sergeant Peter Tomaszewksi was stationed at the twin Air bases between July 1967 and April 1987 working in the missile maintenance shop. He contacted John wanting to let me know what he came across as he thought it might be of use. *"At the end of December, 1980, 1 heard a rumour about a supposed UFO landing but thought it was naturally a joke. Out of curiosity I telephoned the Police Security Squadron asking them if they knew anything about it, which they hadn't but a few days later I received a visit from a civilian who told me he was an investigator, and asked who my source had been, I told him it was just rumours, he said, 'I can tell you a landing took place in the forest at the East end of Woodbridge, the fern was pushed down and slightly scorched. Three imprints in the soil were found each one measuring 114 inches apart in a triangular pattern, there was a slightly higher than normal radiation count'. When I contacted the Security Office after he had left and asked them if they knew of this man, they told me they had no knowledge of any civilian investigator, but that I should keep quiet about it, as it had been a British experimental plane which had landed at the air base."*

Again I can only comment that I have no idea about this one…but would regard it as being disinformation. Why would the British land in a forest, next to a US (RAF) Airbase? Strange never heard of any aircraft which behave in this manner…Of course if you contrast the many other reports covered in this book, some of which have left similar marks in the ground, involving witness testimonial of 'landed craft' both in the States and the UK over the years, then you would apply commons sense and reject this out of hand. If you're a sceptic and believe all UFOs are covert man-made technology, then you might believe this explanation. You can't ignore the correlations of behaviour and physical appearances of so many 'craft' that have flooded our skies, the sightings of which go back in all probability to a period of human history when man couldn't even get his arse off the ground!

THE HALT PERSPECTIVE 2

Mysterious visit to RAF Woodbridge by unscheduled aircraft!

One aircraft which did make an unsolicited appearance during the height of the activity off Base was an unmarked C5 Galaxy transport aircraft that made an unscheduled landing on the main runway, at RAF Woodbridge. I was puzzled when the aircraft came to a stop at the end of the runway, rather than making its way to the parking slot. I set off in a jeep and drove towards the aircraft. As I approached, I saw numerous figures in white overalls emerging from the aircraft and making their way towards the adjoining forest. Armed guards were positioned close to the Galaxy. These wore no insignia to identity unit or rank. I spoke with one of the guards, who told me that as I did not have proper clearance I would have to leave the scene – which I did. You have to keep in mind that this was a foreign country to us. We had no authority here whatsoever, but I can assure you if it were within the US, we'd have had the place cordoned off with Military Police. Following that plane's arrival, unmarked helicopters were also seen over the landing site during the following days. I definitely do believe that there is a conspiracy covering this up and agents with a more than passing interest also attend various conferences too. I believe that there are agencies within my Government and at least one in your government that are actively working towards that. It's simple, if you do talk you could disappear – it's that serious.

Claim they were from CIA Langley Research Laboratory!

Jim Penniston says they were from CIA Langley Research Laboratory. I don't know but whoever they were, what they were doing was on British territory? How does Jim know when I didn't? So to summarise while we had a visit from what appears to be Government scientists, I still don't accept there is any connection with the alleged account that took place outside RAF Watton. I wish to make it perfectly clear that the UFOs I saw were structured machines moving under intelligent control and operating beyond the realm of anything I have ever seen before or since. I believe the objects I saw at close quarter were extraterrestrial in origin and that the security services of the United States and England were and have been complicit in trying to subvert the significance of what occurred at Rendlesham by use of well practised methods of disinformation. These events were and still are of tremendous defence significance to the United Kingdom and indeed the rest of the world. I have no knowledge of any such foreign aircraft or spaceship having been stored on this base, and would strongly deny any such allegation. If the 'space capsule' had gone missing then I'm sure I would have known about it. Did they contact me about it and even bother asking me for my view… of course not! It wasn't even there at the time. What a load of rubbish? Where is the evidence? I knew Conde well. I wouldn't have put it past him to claim what he did. He was nowhere to be seen the night I was out. One possible explanation is that several nights later he may have opened the back gate, while on patrol at Woodbridge, and driven down the paved road and displayed his lights to mock the earlier incidents. John Burroughs told me that Conde was not on duty so could not have been involved.

Colonel Alan Brown RIP

I asked John to visit Alan Brown, a retired Colonel from the Base, who lives in Woodbridge, Suffolk, to ask him (1) **How he got a control radio?** (2) **Who sent him to the ATC Tower when I was out there in the forest**? Bearing in mind at least three individuals confirmed he was in the Tower. Two of them to my recollection were either 'Gordy' Williams, or/and the director of Operations – Colonel Bowden.

On the 30th October 2015, John met up with Sally Brown a friend of the late Georgina Bruni. She and her husband Alan Brown (78), made him very welcome at their impressive family home, situated at Bromeswell, Suffolk, accompanied their two delightful Labrador dogs – '*Boycie*' and '*Misha*'. Alan expressed his concern about having lost touch with Gordon Williams, as they had been friends for many years and played golf regularly. Apparently 'Gordy' kept in touch at least once a week on the phone. But inexplicably this stopped some months ago. Alan described to John how he had become interested in flying, *"I literally fell into it. I didn't know whether I would like flying, but took to it like a duck to water. I joined the National Guard in 1956. I then moved to New Mexico. They were desperate for fighter pilots and that's how I got involved, until I retired in 1984. I still fly light aircraft as a co-pilot when I go over to the United States."* **He was asked whether he had been on duty at the airbase when the UFO incident took place, and strongly denied having been there telling John that he was off duty and at the local golf club, and that he did not learn of the incident until a few days later.**

Alan: *"I was actually playing golf with Gordy on the 28th December 1980, a Sunday. I told him that I had heard of some guys – a bunch of young people – were in the woods when they became frightened, after something scared the hell out of them. That's all I know, but I can tell you that something happened. The guys higher than me asked, as they didn't know. I heard that an air traffic controller saw some weird lights and one of the officers was out there, close to RAF Woodbridge. I asked Don Moreland, but he didn't know anything either."* He said: **"You have to be kidding. I know nothing. No one told me anything".**

Sally described the occasion when Georgina Bruni and her bodyguard – Jacqueline Davis – visited them while researching the background to her (Georgina's) book. At midnight the three of them went for a walk around Rendlesham Forest, curious to see for themselves the effect of the lighthouse on the landscape. As a result of this, Georgina rejected any suspicion that the beam from the lighthouse had played a part in what had taken place. I offer my sincere condolences to Sally for the loss of her husband Alan a few months ago. Thanks both for allowing John to take personal photographs which we show here, as the guy was well respected at the Base. **It's odd but later developments with regard to 'Gordy' Williams, who has also sadly passed away, was to be the subject of what I can only refer to as also odd…more on that in due course.** He's shown with Georgina.

THE HALT PERSPECTIVE 2

Georgina Bruni

Colonel Alan Brown

THE HALT PERSPECTIVE 2

John: Suffolk, spinning top UFO, 28th December 1980 – Bury St Edmunds, Suffolk resident, Charles Prentice, was outside at 1.45am when he sighted ". . . *an object about the length of a large car and the shape of a child's spinning top. It had a brilliant white light on the top of it, with a bright pulsating light just below it. At one point it was only three feet away from our bedroom window. The object continued to hover for about three-quarters of an hour before it left. There appeared to be two* **square-shaped panels on the outer body of the object***, it then shot upwards into the sky at phenomenal speed – soon only a tiny point of light before disappearing from view."* (**Source: Personal Interview**)

9pm: 28th December 1980

Robert Hulse was travelling home to Congleton Cheshire along the main Macclesfield to Leek Road at 9pm with his young son, following behind was his wife and other son. As Robert rounded the bend by the *Fools Nook* public house, he noticed a large red light hovering low down in the sky, further along the route he was taking. His curiosity aroused Robert pulled up into a lay-bye, and got out to have a closer look when he was astonished to see directly above him, at an estimated height of 200 feet, the underside of a disc-shaped craft approximately 85 feet in diameter: *"It appeared like a strange black sooty hole in the sky while around It the stars shone brightly, I could hear this deep rumbling noise emanating from the object, I knew straightaway that this was no earthly machine. It then slowly moved off towards Macclesfield at about 30mph, enabling me from its potion in the sky to see eleven and a half rectangular windows, out of which came a soft white light possibly six feet wide by three feet deep with a small gap between them along the side, I counted them to be sure. By this time my wife had pulled up behind me and we watched as whatever it was flew towards the direction of Lyme Green."* The next morning while on his way to work, still pondering on what he had seen, Robert was stunned when a silver cylindrical object flew out of a field to his left approximately a hundred yards in front of him, and shot off towards the nearby hills.

Radar operator tells of UFO plotted on radar – warned to keep quiet!

Charles: Someone I met on more than one occasion was Gary Baker, radar operator at RAF Neatishead from 1978-1980 from Ipswich, who had returned from leave at the end of 1980.

Gary Baker an intelligent, likeable man with a professional background with a career in nursing and the Territorial Army, now currently living in the Ipswich area of Suffolk.

He said: *"I was told* **this never happened***, by RAF officers, and that radar tapes and bridge logs from the evening of the incident disappeared. Whatever the radar picked up, it wasn't a subject of interest for interceptor aircraft because it didn't come from the east – this was the height of the Cold War. It would have been sensible to quash any evidence. If something had happened, and it wasn't picked up, it would have showed we weren't capable of dealing with something from 'above'. Later, I read the MoD said the radar had been switched off*

at the time, which is a load of rubbish; something extraordinary happened here outside the parameters of manned aircraft."

RAF Neatishead: UFO tracked in late 1980 – warned to keep quiet!

"Another UFO was tracked on radar in late December 1980. I was in the briefing room when high-ranking officers and personnel in suits instructed the Squadron Ops staff that it didn't happen and not to talk about it. This is rubbish; there were two radars and both had cameras. If the cameras were switched off, what was the point of 'them' removing the operating room bridge logs and radar tapes? This was followed by the warning to both Squadrons not to discuss the matter.

I can tell you that the US Air Force personnel at Bentwaters, in the first instance, dealt with RAF Watton, their radar picture – having been transmitted to them from RAF Neatishead. **I reject the MOD's stance, on radar evidence relating to this incident. Intelligence and high-ranking officers' squadrons were told it didn't happen – we were warned not to talk about it.** This refutes consistent claims that there were no radar tapes available, because the radar camera was switched off at Neatishead at 1627Z on that date. This was over three days and two radars, which both had cameras. The radar picture at Neatishead was also transmitted to West Drayton to Strike Command, to Eastern Radar and other radar stations, which came under the same umbrella of protection. I know for a fact that RAF Boulmer, in Newcastle, would have the coverage on their screens as well. Whether they would have picked up as much detail would depend on the curvature of the Earth that may have restricted the signal return, due to its geographical position. Neatishead, of course, was in excellent position being close to the source of the reported radar pictures and recordings, so they are lying about something. What exactly it is can only be is anybody's guess."

1983 – UFO sighted over Attleborough, Norfolk

Although Gary has little interest in either the UFO/Paranormal subject matters which he is the first to contend he knows little about, he remains curious about an incident which occurred in summer 1983, while out with his girlfriend in Attleborough. *"I never reported it at the time, because I feared, like others who had reported similar events, that I, too, would be the butt of ridicule. My girlfriend and I had been visiting a friend's house to play on one of the early computers. We left at about 3am on the way back to my parent's house, a short distance away. It was daybreak, just getting light, when we became aware of something large moving slowly in our peripheral vision. I looked up and saw a huge 'thing' – the size of* **several football pitches – about 200 feet above us, moving silently and slowly through the sky, accompanied by a sensation of electricity around us** *– as if the air was charged. We watched it move away – still very slow across Attleborough, where we lived – and head off over the Stanford Battle Area. The interesting thing is that neither of us talked about what we had seen for some years – never thought anything of it at the time – although something very odd took place. When we arrived home, minutes later, the sun was really quite high. It was much later than it should have been. Years later, I contacted my ex-girlfriend and discussed what we had seen.

She confirmed what we had seen, without me telling her anything from my recollection – which matched it."* Gary also told me about a series of **paranormal incidents** which had plagued him and his (now) ex-wife, many years ago: *"To be fair, prior to what we experienced, I treated such reports with great scepticism – until it happened to us. I've had framed graduation photographs inexplicably moved from the wall and thrown across the room, light bulbs ejecting themselves from the sockets, and decorative plates moving seemingly of their own accord and keys going missing. It got to a disconcerting point where we had no choice but to move house. This brought home the realisation that such things happen but I can't say what it is evidence of, as I have never seen a ghost and hope I never will."*

Conspiracy to pervert the Truth

1- Claim of UFO landing at RAF Bentwaters in November 1979!

Charles: There is something not right here; you've heard Gary Baker's account, his version of events is genuine, why would he make this up? He was there and we've chatted a few times about this in Rendlesham Forest during filming. Under normal circumstances if radar tapes are seized it's because there is an issue with a flight or maybe a near miss or even, perish the thought, an accident. That's common sense. But we know on this occasion there was a different reason. Surely we aren't expected to treat with any seriousness 'leaked out information' about **UFOs and aliens** by American USAF Intelligence officers, during a visit to the British run facility of RAF Watton to radar operatives?

Yet another likely example of disseminated disinformation, which may well have its roots in the same process of indoctrination that was to come to the fore, following the events of late December 1980 involving Brenda Butler and her then partner – Chris Pennington, an accomplished musician, both of whom I know – who were then socialising at the *Rod and Gun Club*, RAF Woodbridge, in November, 1979 talking to their friend – USAF security guard **Steve Roberts** – when the general alarm went off all over the Base.

Brenda: *"Suddenly there were blue lights flashing all over the place; outriders and security guards came to the Club. Steve had to go; but he came back about half an hour later, dressed in his security guard outfit, plus weapon. He stood at the door and told everyone to sit down, as no one was allowed to leave for a while. I went over and asked him what was wrong. He said that he was not allowed to say, but it involved an aircraft and a lot of high ranking officers up on the flight line.*

We were kept there for about three hours, and then we were escorted off the Base. There were still blue flashing lights all around and the alert conditions still held. Two days later, **word had got around that a UFO had landed on the runway at Bentwaters, and high ranking officers had gone out to it.** *This was the night we were at the Rod and Gun Club."*

NOW the facts not fiction or wishful thinking!

I can confirm that this was an 'Alert' a routine exercise, held at regular intervals on the airbase – not a UFO landing. One is bound to speculate who or what the source was behind this rumour which had the hallmarks of what was going to be disseminated a month later? This isn't coincidence but something deliberately orchestrated behind our backs but for what reason? What credence can we put on an admission made later by 'Steve Roberts' that he also had 'a finger in this pie'!

Steve told her and Chris Pennington that he had been tasked to bodyguard President Jimmy Carter when he flew into Mildenhall Air Base, to attend the 3rd G7 summit. He also met with the Prime Ministers of Greece, Belgium, Turkey, Norway, the Netherlands, and Luxembourg, and with the President of Portugal, addressed the NATO Ministers meeting. London, Newcastle & Sunderland between May 5th and 11th 1977.

Already we can see a pattern developing, almost as if there was a concerted effort to pervert the course of truth and dilute it with outlandish claims of aliens and downed spacecraft, to muddy the waters of what really happened! Look at the number of separate 'sources' of information who appear to have come together individually but collectively united in one objective, which in my opinion was to camouflage what took place, rather than accept the reality of what I and others service personnel saw.

2 – Suspicious claim of 'alien' figures seen outside RAF Watton airbase in 1980

Whistleblower Harry Thompson (pseudonym)

I read a report from Georgina Bruni who told of being contacted by a witness, who was given the pseudonym Harry Thompson. (Covered on page 310 in her book *'You Can't Tell The People'*). He claims that following radar tracking a large object moving just before midnight the **27th of December 1980,** two RAF police dog handlers were instructed to investigate a report of strange lights heading in from the north near the airfield fence to the west of RAF Watton. This incursion caused the station officer to get into a terrible flap. Two airmen arrived at the fence to find **several figures shining what appeared to be green and blue lights into the sky.** This is what he had to say: *"They were about 100-150 yards away from us and when we turned on our searchlights on them, they ran off very quickly, we only saw the figures for a little while in the searchlight, and these didn't always work. We got the impression that their clothes were silvery and bulky and appeared to suck in –or not reflect the light after a few seconds. They wore visors which looked like they were split into two halves like big eyes. We had to use infrared light because we couldn't see them in the normal searchlight. The dogs started going crazy and wouldn't obey the code words which was 'trifle' to bite and 'custard' to stop. We made our report and were told to continue our patrol."* The next morning a high ranking British officer questioned Thompson and his colleague. The men were advised to forget what they had seen because it was only poachers, and it was now a matter for the local police. Why was no background research conducted into this outlandish claim?

Note books, duty log and occurrence book went missing – heard that one before!

Thompson says that their note books, duty log and occurrence book went missing! Well I have to say that I regard this as nonsense or even disinformation. The reason is that if an incursion had take place, one would think that the base would have been placed on high alert, why didn't they send out more officers, why didn't they contact the police? Understanding that for all they knew this could have been the spearhead of a Russian advance force; this was at the height of a cold war!

If, as the informant says, they only saw the figures for a little while in the searchlight which didn't work properly, how much reliance can we place on their 'impressions' rather than clear cut visual observations of what they describe as silvery and bulky figures? Not forgetting distance, weather conditions, etc.

They disclosed they had to use infrared lights because the 'figures' couldn't be seen in normal searchlight. I'm sure that code names weren't given to the dogs, what's the point of that? Trifle and custard! I think that there is plenty of trifling going on here. 'They' then ran away!

28th December 1980 – Porton Down guys make an appearance!

To make matters worse (why shouldn't I not be surprised?) when commenting on what is after all another wild tale, we are told by the same source that the following day 28.12.80, a team of four scientists, 'supposedly' from MOD Research Centre Porton Down, were driven to the 'forest' by another RAF policeman, known to the informant, and that the Porton Down men changed into *'strange looking space suits'* before proceeding to wander off into the forest. On their return they changed back into their clothes and were driven back to the air base by the RAF policeman, who I presume wasn't wearing any personal protection equipment. If that was the case then how do we know they didn't infect nearby surfaces with whatever they were doing? To add further injury, it is then suggested *'that one cannot dismiss the possibility that there may be a connection between the Rendlesham Forest Incident and RAF Watton, because they occurred on the same date!*

Then even further unbelievable claims made by 'Harry', who says he was dispatched to the United States six months later. Hang on, if he was an RAF security policeman, why would he be sent there? It doesn't make sense. He then says he was assigned to **RED FLAG** a NATO air force bomber base at Miramar, New Mexico and saw a UFO in a heavily guarded hanger! Then explains his theory that the whole incident was hoaxed to put the Russians off the track, and that what was picked up on radar was not meant to be picked up at all! If anyone reading this believes it well I rest my case!

Georgina then ponders on the question that if the Porton Down guys had found evidence of any 'landing' with the presence of infectious agents, then Highpoint Prison and other like it would have been used to isolate those suffering with whatever virus or contamination the visitors might have brought with them! I can't agree, this lady was a champion of the UFO cause and had written a fantastic book, based on FACTS especially with having put the record straight with Warren. But this isn't fact, just speculation on something which will excite others with its depicted scenario of UFO landings and key personnel from Porton Down attending! So let me ask a question, if the scientists from Porton Down had attended, and made a search of the area following a report of a UFO seen, along with strange lights, reported previously near the perimeter fence at Watton, never mind their alleged attendance at RAF Woodbridge – then why is no mention made of any attendances by them during over 100 incidents that took place in 1980, up and down the country, some of which involved objects seen at close proximity by the witnesses?

Julian Horn, RAF Watton historian – the facts!

John contacted Julian Horn, responsible for the RAF Watton history website, in May 2020; also writer, and publisher of *The Wayland News* and resident of Watton, England, and asked him what he thought of this allegation. Julian: "*I worked at Eastern Radar at the time you mention and I have to say I am not aware of this incident. RAF Watton itself was almost dormant at that time. I do know at least one person who will know better than me and I can pass on your email and ask him if you wish? I will make your entry public in case other information is out there.*

At Eastern we were subject to incursion probing by the RAF Special Investigation Branch who tested our security by trying to gain entry – *this was at the time of the Irish problems of course when vehicles were regularly searched for bombs. I worked as a civilian on the technical side.* **On one of our regular remote building checks myself and a colleague caught two officers from SIB breaking in**. *I wonder if someone saw such an attempt to gain entry. But it sounds exaggerated to me. One other thought about the radar tracking John, Eastern had a 10 mile overhead – i.e. the nearest we could see an object was 10 miles away. RAF Neatishead was the only other radar that covered our overhead (that I know of) and that would not see low enough to trace an object to the point operators could say where something might have landed.*

I remember the Woodbridge incident – though not in any knowledgeable way – just what was in the media at the time. If I recall correctly, there were several UFO reports in those times but I think it is far more likely that, given the cold war and Watton's reputation for being involved in anti-Communist operations with CSE and RWRE and the U2s, that if they ever penetrated our airspace, they would be the ones everyone saw. Incidentally, I have connections with criminal justice – one brother, retired Inspector at Kings Lynn, another retired ACC BTP and my son is a Custody Manager at HMP Wayland. I also ran my brother's environmental scanning service for the police – Horn Ltd. – for some years in the late '90's and early '00's while he worked for HMG in Sierra Leone and later DRC – Interesting work but electronics has always been my thing."

I knew Nigel Kerr quite well, though not seen or spoken to him for some years. One of my duties when I worked at Eastern ('77-'82), was to change the tapes and film every midnight. The comms were recorded 24 hours a day and the local radar was imaged every 30 seconds on film. **Tapes and film were often impounded if there had been an air traffic control issue or more serious incident such as an 'air miss' (frequently misspoken as 'near miss' which is a hit of course!).**

On one occasion an A10 (I think) went down near Hockham. In cases such as that, tapes and films were taken by whichever agency was investigating so not surprising, indeed routine, to see tapes and films go. Sometimes tapes would be transcribed locally if it was an ATC issue, sometimes they would be taken away, especially if there was American involvement or an incident such as a crash.

Watton was on care and maintenance at this time and as far as I am aware there **were no dogs based here or even domestic patrols.** Certainly the kennels were dilapidated by this time. There would be the occasional sweep by personnel from RAF Honington – Watton's parent – sometimes with a dog, but that's all. Another job we did was regular (every 6 hours from memory) EFS (electrical fire and security) checks on the transmitters over on the south side of the airfield at Griston. I sometimes went with whoever was doing that and I don't think we were ever stopped or checked. There was no **'forest' adjacent to the perimeter either, just the odd copse and Wayland Wood.**

There were a lot of rabbits and hunting them with vehicles was a nightly occurrence. There were times when officers used to chase around the airfield in a Mini (I believe) standing out of the sunroof shooting anything caught in the headlights. I repaired the lights of a local pest control company from time to time and they used some pretty powerful beams then."

Footnote: Brenda Butler told John Hanson that she and Dot also paid a visit to RAF Watton and entered the base by telling the security staff they had permission. At some point while trying to set up conversation about any incursions at the base, they were followed into the room by the Japanese camera crew, which ended all talk abruptly with the Japanese crew making good their escape one way while Brenda and Dot ran the other way to safety! No surprise to hear about the sky crash crowd infiltrating another Airbase!

John: In a letters sent to Brenda dated the 29th of October 1984, Jim Yaoi Chief Director of the Nippon TV Network, thanked her for the interesting letters and photographs. *"As usual I am busy with the production of our TV programme and only have a few hours sleep each day. As promised, I am sending under separate cover two copies of my book, and a VHS Video tape of the programme broadcast in February. Since the tape was recorded under Japan's NTSC system, you will not be able to play it without converting it to the UK's PAL system. How about asking Dot to help you with this? In any case I must ask you to promise faithfully that you will not use the tape for commercial purposes of any kind. The scene in Group Captain Colonel Holt's office has been cut, since it might have got us into hot water, if it had been seen by anyone connected with the military."*

Lord Hill Norton asks questions in Parliament!

On the 25th of January 2001 Lord Peter Hill-Norton asked Her Majesty's Government: Whether they were aware of any involvement by Special Branch personnel in the investigation of the 1980 Rendlesham Forest incident.

Reply: Baroness Symons of Vernham Dean: **Special Branch may have been aware of the incident but would not have shown any interest, unless there was evidence of a potential threat to national security. No such interest appears to have been shown.**

Lord Hill-Norton asked Her Majesty's Government: Whether personnel from Porton Down visited Rendlesham Forest or the area surrounding RAF Walton (**presume this should be RAF Watton**) in December 1980 or January 1981; and whether they are aware of any tests carried out in either of those two areas aimed at assessing any nuclear, biological or chemical hazard.

Reply: Baroness Symons of Vernham Dean: **The staff at the Defence Evaluation and Research Agency (DERA) Chemical and Biological Defence (CBD) laboratories at Porton Down have made a thorough search of their archives and have found no record of any such visits.**

Lord Hill-Norton asked Her Majesty's Government: Whether they are aware of any uncorrelated targets tracked on radar in November or December 1980; and whether they will give details of any such incidents.

Reply: Baroness Symons of Vernham Dean: **Records dating from 1980 no longer exists. Paper records are retained for a period of three years before being destroyed. Recordings of radar data are retained for a period of thirty days prior to re-use of the recording medium.**

Lord Hill-Norton, asked Her Majesty's Government: What is the highest classification that has been applied to any Ministry of Defence document concerning Unidentified Flying Objects?

Reply: Baroness Symons of Vernham Dean: **A limited search through available files has identified a number of documents graded Secret. The overall classification of the documents was not dictated by details of specific sightings of UFOs.**

Lord Hill-Norton asked Her Majesty's Government: Whether they will detail the underground facilities at the former RAF Bentwaters installation; and what is the purpose of these facilities.

Reply: The Minister of State, Baroness Symons of Vernham Dean: **There are no underground facilities at the former RAF Bentwaters.**

Lord Hill-Norton asked Her Majesty's Government: Whether they are aware of any involvement in the 1980 Rendlesham Forest incident by either Ministry of Defence Policy or personnel from the Suffolk Constabulary.

Reply: Baroness Symons of Vernham Dean: **The Minister of Defence is not aware of any involvement by the Ministry of Defence Police in the alleged incident. The Ministry of Defence's knowledge of involvement by the Suffolk Police is limited to a letter dated 28 July 1999 from the Suffolk Constabulary to Georgina Bruni that is contained in the recent book.**

Lord Hill-Norton asked Her Majesty's Government: Whether they are aware of any investigation of the 1980 Rendlesham Forest incident carried out by the United States Air force, the Air Force Office of Special Investigations or any other United States agency.

Reply: Baroness Symons of Vernham Dean: **The Ministry of Defence's knowledge of an investigation by the US authorities into the alleged incident in Rendlesham Forest in 1980 is limited to the information contained in the memorandum sent by Lt Col Halt USAF, Deputy Base Commander at RAF Woodbridge, to the RAF Liaison Officer at RAF Bentwaters on 13th January 1981**

THE HALT PERSPECTIVE 2

Lord Hill-Norton asked Her Majesty's Government: – Whether, in the light of the new information contained in Georgina Bruni's book *You Can't Tell The People,* they will now launch an investigation into the Rendlesham Forest incident and the response to this incident by the United States Air Force and the Ministry of Defence.

Reply: Baroness Symons of Vernham Dean: **No additional information has come to light over the last 20 years to call into question the original judgment by the Ministry of Defence that nothing of defence significance occurred in the location of Rendlesham Forest in 1980. Accordingly there is no reason to hold an investigation now.**

Lord Hill-Norton asked Her Majesty's Government: Whether they have made any approach to, or received any approach from, any United States government or military agency concerning Georgina Bruni's book *You Can't Tell The People*; and, if so, whether they will give details of any such approach.

Reply: Baroness Symons of Vernham Dean: **As a matter of courtesy, the Ministry of Defence informed Headquarters 3rd Air Force at RAF Mildenhall about the book. The US authorities have not subsequently approached the Ministry of Defence on the issue.**

Lord Hill-Norton now asked Her Majesty's Government: Whether they now agree with the analysis of the basic facts of the Rendlesham Forest/RAF Bentwaters incident in the fourth paragraph of Lord Hill-Norton's letter to Lord Gilbert of 22nd October 1997, reported on page 429 of Georgina Bruni's book *You Can't Tell The People*; or, if not, in what respect they disagree.

Reply: Baroness Symons of Vernham Dean: **The Ministry of Defence's position regarding this alleged sighting remains as it did at the time of Lord Gilbert's reply to the noble Lord's letter of 22nd October 1997. From surviving departmental records, we remain satisfied that nothing of defence significance occurred on the nights in question.**

3 – Claim of aliens seen outside RAF Woodbridge airbase repairing craft!

Charles: US resident John Traylor, a former resident at Greyfriars Road, Woodbridge Suffolk contacted MUFON assistant Linda Zimmer in 2010. He alleged his Mother Yvonne had witnessed the landing of a UFO in Porters Wood, Woodbridge Suffolk – **and that two aliens were seen by local children**. In conversation with Yvonne and her husband John who worked at RAF Woodbridge,

Yvonne claimed: *"The airbase was closed down at the back of Rendlesham Forest and there were rumours of a spaceship actually in one of the hangers. All of the airmen that saw it were shipped back to the states."* John also claimed his father then worked for the Ipswich based factory *Ransome and Rapier* (steel constructors) and had been asked to *manufacture* a piece of machinery for the spaceship stored at RAF Woodbridge in December 1980! Secondly the 'spaceship' had initially landed at Kingston Middle School, Woodbridge before taking off again and then a short time later crashing into Rendlesham Forest!

His claim that a 'spaceship' was stored at RAF Woodbridge after having landed at the school before crash landing in the forest – followed by the 'aliens' asking us to manufacture a part to get them back in the air, did not happen! One can only despair! Having discussed this with John Hanson who has spoken to some of the parties concerned we both believe this to be the product of a vivid imagination based on matrimonial problems, matters that John was unable to get to the bottom of, because they declined to allow him to meet up with them personally. Stories like this excite the imagination of many people but both John and I are firmly grounded and don't feel there is any truth in this story – maybe this is another case of deliberate disinformation, we don't know. Whatever the reason what was the point in making this story available and then refusing John the opportunity to discuss it personally with the couple concerned, who he spoke to?

It's also been rumoured and claimed by some people that 'it' could have been a Russian aircraft which ditched or a satellite… I have had no knowledge of any such foreign aircraft or spaceship having been stored on the base, and strongly deny any such allegation.

Major General Gordon E. Williams USAF retired praised Georgina Bruni, by stating on the back of her book, *'You Can't Tell The People,'* **"Georgina has written the definitive work on this adventure near Rendlesham Forest. While 20 years has passed, she brings new light to this story that won't go away"**.

Adventure seems an odd word, ironically another reason why this matter has been in the fore front of UFO discussion, is the way in which harsh treatment was meted out to those servicemen under me who dared to waiver from the official stance, despite attempts to cover up what they had reported seeing.

4 – Suspicious claim of aliens seen outside RAF Woodbridge airbase repairing craft!

Whistleblower David Potts! (pseudonym)

Jenny Randles tells of being contacted by a David Potts (a pseudonym) around 1981 who told her that a couple of days after the radar tracking at RAF Watton the base had received a visit from a group of American air force officers supposedly from intelligence who had requested to see the radar reports. The Americans told the radar operators that a metallic **UFO had crash landed in the forest** near Ipswich and the patrols that had gone out to investigate had experienced difficulty with their vehicle lights and engines cutting out, thus having to continue on foot. It seems the object had been on the ground for several hours during which time **entities were witnessed**. A few years later Jenny found her original notes from Potts – which mentioned the Base **commander, and several officers had been called out to the forest from a party on the Base, and that the Base commander was communicating with alien entities.**

5 – Suspicious claim of aliens seen outside RAF Woodbridge airbase 1980 repairing craft!

Whistleblower Steve Roberts! (pseudonym)

Ironically despite outlandish claims made by Larry Warren and John 'Davey' Engalls aka Steve Roberts who served on the base – I never believed them right from day one, most sensible people didn't! Here we have a man who in early January 1981 gives Brenda Butler a drawing of a saucer-shaped object with landing legs that he says he witnessed. He then admits to Brenda during a visit to see her on his motorcycle in 1987 that he and several others had been ordered to go out and spread disinformation about it having been a UFO landing! Thank goodness we didn't rely on his information, no guessing about the identities of some of the others that were involved with him!

He told Georgina Bruni the same i.e. he didn't see any alien craft or any entities, but then admits having see a **saucer-shaped UFO** at close range in the sky – a UFO which he says was the same as the one I saw involving me, although he wasn't part of the same group. Georgina told him that I saw a triangular-shaped object, which is somewhat unintentionally misleading, if you read my account which includes seeing an object that exploded into five objects, dripping what looked molten metal, objects seen towards the north, half moon-shaped which turned into a full circle, followed by a separate object that sent down beams of light. One thing I can tell you is that contrary to the opposite this was no hologram being projected into the night sky by persons unknown to test our responses, which I will comment on further on! While others (they know who they are) have changed their stories or even made up tales out of thin air which have now been convincingly discredited – what I saw is crystal clear despite the passing of so many years because it became indelibly burnt into my memory.

6 – Suspicious claim of aliens seen outside RAF Woodbridge airbase repairing craft!

Whistleblower Larry Warren – a modern fairytale!

One of the contributory factors to why people now continue to suggest the most implausible explanations for what happened in the forest, is because of the publicity surrounding the disgraceful behaviour of USAF Airmen Larry Warren **who for over 39 years** claimed all manner of strange inconsistencies, built on a foundation of an immense number of lies which was later published in a book about the incident entitled '*Left At East Gate*' – now dishonoured. But of course he's not the only one to spread fabricated accounts as we have already seen.

In an article published by *UFO Magazine* in **January/February 1995** – Larry Warren tells of seeing British Policeman taking photographs, and that those photos were confiscated and flown to Germany. No evidence of this can be found. He then claims one of the men grabbed hold of the object and was carried ten metres before he let go! No evidence of this. Larry claims that '**my audio record was over four hours long.**' This is rubbish!

Larry says that one of the truck drivers claimed that a '**being**' was seen to pass through the windshield, and that the man kicked the windshield out with his boots. Others told of seeing small probes pass through the sides of the vehicle only to appear on the other sides. **No evidence of this.**

26th December 1980 – Another UFO sighting separate from what I witnessed

The information I have is that following John Burroughs visit to the Base, during the same evening, he was told about a sighting which occurred on the same night as mine the 26th December involving Lori Buoen and desk sergeant John Trementozzi. **They reported seeing red green and white lights in the forest, which appeared at one location and then reappeared at another place**. This incident was brought to the notice of Lt Bonnie Tamplin who went out to investigate, accompanied by Master Sergeant Bobby Ball. I gathered that the jeep had been struck by light beams and a blue light shot through the vehicle. Lori recalled that Bonnie was very frightened by the encounter. LT Bonnie Tamplin's whereabouts was traced but she chose not to answer about what she experienced!

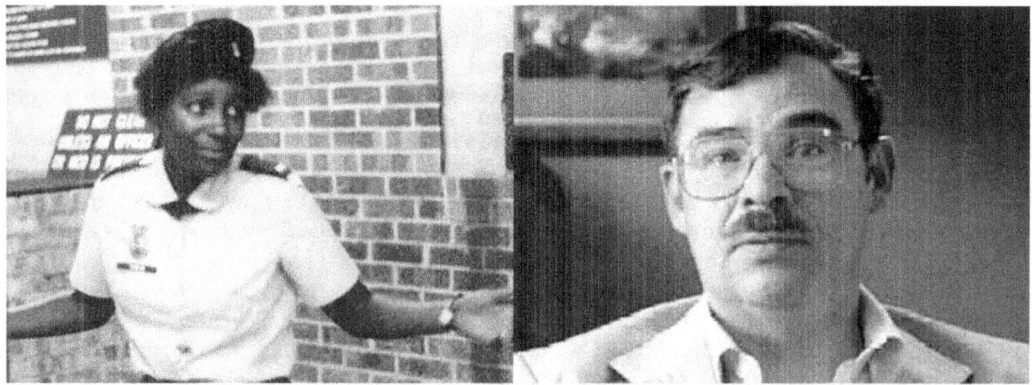

Lt. Bonnie Tamplin   *Master Sergeant Bobby Ball.*

Larry also tells us when faced with a fine or loss of stripes for making a telephone call to his mother from the Base. He settled for a fine! **What stripes are they? Surely there couldn't be a connection with references made to him being a Corporal in other articles?** Crazy stuff not forgetting the classic sketch of the UFO showed entitled *"A drawing made by one USAF airman following the encounter in Rendlesham Forest"* showing a number of small tile plates on its outer surface . . . Warren admitted to John Hanson that the "***The sketch only showed the spirit of what happened***."

John Burroughs says that he and Adrian Bustinza were given permission from someone on Base to approach one of the lights, in order to ascertain if there were any similarities with what he and Jim had seen the first night. This is what John had to say: *"All of a sudden in front of us we had a blue transparent light come streaking towards us and then a white object appeared up above and then floated down and was 'sitting' out there in the distance. I asked for permission to go towards it to see if I could get a closer look. As we started going towards it, it appeared to start coming towards us. Sergeant Bustinza was on my right. He went down to the ground. He saw me go into the light. He saw me disappear, he saw the light explode and I was gone for several minutes before I reappeared. I have no recall of it. I have no memory of what happened. The next thing I know was I was standing in the field and whatever it was, gone. It was like what just happened?"* John Burroughs in later years believes that this was a repeat performance of what took place on the first night.

28th December – Three 'lights' seen over Airbase

Brenda: Between 1am and 3am, twelve-year-old Sarah Richardson, from Woodbridge, was up late in the evening and happened to look out of the window, when she saw:" *…three bands of red, blue and yellow, 'lights' appear over the woods at the side of the runway. They were star-like; one in the north direction, the other two in the south. I thought someone was having a party and they were fireworks. It was a cold and clear night; the lights were low in the sky. I opened the window and leaned out. The lights appeared solid and looked metallic. No moon was shining. The light kept changing colour. They were there till well after 3am or 4am, when they suddenly shot straight away and disappeared from sight."*

At 11.45pm (approximately) on 28th December 1980

USAF Security Officer Airmen Lawrence 'Larry' Warren – then 19 years of age – was standing guard at Bentwaters perimeter post 18, when he overheard some radio transmissions being broadcast between the Bentwaters Weapons Storage Area and Woodbridge control tower. *"…about some funny lights having been seen, bobbing up and down over the forest, near Woodbridge Airbase, some five miles away. (I had no knowledge of the incidents that had occurred over the previous nights). Suddenly, out of the darkness came five deer, clearly panicked by something. Two of them actually jumped the fence and were out of sight in seconds."*

A few minutes later a Security Police truck arrived, driven by Sergeant Adrian Bustinza, accompanied by Second Lieutenant Bruce Englund, and two other Security Police Officers. Larry was then told to radio in. He was being relieved from his post, which he did so. Bustinza told him they were going to collect light-alls (generator mounted spotlights) from the motor pool. After collecting these, they arrived at the main gate at Bentwaters, which was attended by at least five or six other vehicles containing other security police personnel.

29th December 1980 – Three triangular objects seen in the sky!

Charles: Another guy who had an interesting story to tell about what he saw was Randy D. Smith, an Honour Graduate from Air Training Command. A Security Specialist, Randy's Certificate of Appointment assigned to RAF Bentwaters with the non-commissioned rank of Sergeant .At Christmas time, 1980. 'D'

THE HALT PERSPECTIVE 2

flight had been working the 3-11pm shift, while 'C' flight had been working the 11pm-7am shift. It was a quiet, clear night. Randy was working 'whiskey 5', the alarm response team in the weapons storage area on Bentwaters. He was unsure of his partner that night and had free range of one half of the WSA driving a pick-up truck. Clarence George was his area supervisor.

Sergeant Rick Bobo was the SPCDS Small Permanent Communications Display Segment [a 'computerized alarm system'] tower operator in the WSA. The next thing he recalls, not long after the shift began, perhaps midnight or so, on the morning of the 29th of December 1980 was when Master Sergeant Robert F. 'Bobby' Ball come over the radio and request that the aircraft control tower give him permission to cross the active runway; it saves 15 minutes driving time, as opposed to driving the perimeter road. At that point he knew something was happening because no-one ever crossed the active runway unless there was an extreme emergency.

Bob, accompanied by Lt. Bruce Englund, crossed the runway on Bentwaters and picked me up and some equipment, then returned by the same route. Rick: "*I would say that between 30 minutes to an hour had passed since Bob made his first request to cross. They then proceeded to re-cross the runway and went out the back gate, headed toward RAF Woodbridge. After that, the radio was quiet for a long time. It was a very quiet night – no planes, no helicopters flying. Clarence George came by to talk to me and he said that everyone in the WSA was in the SPcDS tower watching 'lights' and did I want to come check it out? So I did. Clarence thought they were all crazy. It's a small tower and people were jammed in there, body to body, overloading the tower I'm sure. More people than I've ever seen in the tower at one time. I asked what everyone was looking at, and they pointed out three objects that appeared like stars to the naked eye – **three objects which were triangular in shape**.*

Binoculars were being passed around. I looked through and saw very clear images of three triangular-shaped craft hovering a few miles away, and above treetop level. They were triangular in shape, larger than a fighter jet, but smaller than a C5 – Definitely triangular, with lights that were arranged around the bottom that were perhaps different colours, but unable to distinguish at that distance. I only stayed in the tower for an hour or so, and heard one of the guys with a turn on the binoculars, say: 'wow, it just took off'. Two of the craft left at a high rate of speed." The one remaining craft was still in position when Randy left the tower. The following night, he went on duty. At Guard Mount, Bob Ball was very serious; he's almost never serious, a very jovial person. He said, to Randy: '**I saw something last night, but I'm not at liberty to discuss it**'. *I later heard the morning after the first midnight shift; an A-10 was scrambled and sent to Ramstein, Germany, by Lt. Col. Halt*"

Randy described the object as effectively an upright pyramid, but was uncertain whether it may have been flat-surfaced or conical. However, he believed the objects were cone-shaped, as they "*didn't look to be as flat as an actual pyramid. The lights underneath, which created somewhat of a backlit effect, enabling the shape of the crafts to be seen clearly was observed as 8-10 rectangular blocks, arranged in a circle*".

Randy Smith was there and reliable. I'm not convinced he and a crowd were allowed in the WSA tower. He was part of the Immediate Response Team and should have remained on post. However, he could have gone up into the tower. I don't know of anyone else claiming to have gotten in the tower with Bobo. The remainder of his account sounds reasonably correct. A few years ago I heard from a former Security Cop that was on 'D' Flight. He was off the night of the event but told me Bobby Ball was so shaken by the event that the next day he went to the hospital for medication to calm down. Carl Thompson, a Communications Specialist told of him and a co-worker working on the tower sensors in the WSA the nights of both incidents. His co-worker told of seeing the UFO both nights and was frightened into silence.

The Security Police in the WSA looking through 12x power glasses claim the objects to the South had

a triangular shape. One of the patrolmen in the WSA claims to have seen a large object that could have been a 'mother' ship. The "eye" was oval less than a meter in diameter. It was glowing orange/red with a dark black oval like centre. The dark centre would disappear as though pulsing, like an eye winking I can account for all our time, and you know, I, I've had every possible explanation, from an air inversion to ball lightning, to a meteor shower, to just about the lighthouse. Everything you can think of. My original intent when I went out, was to put the whole thing to rest, so the 'cops' could get on with business, and here I was, kind of in a dilemma, and wishing 'Gee', I wish I hadn't got involved in this – this is the end of my Military career.

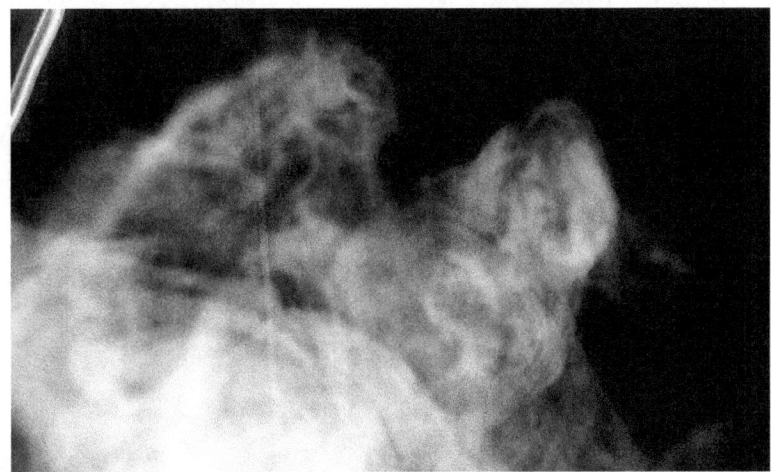

Reflections on what I witnessed on the second night

People ask me my opinion of what I witnessed? – I believe the objects that I saw at close quarter were extraterrestrial in origin and that the security services of both the United States and the United Kingdom have attempted both then and now – to subvert the significance of what occurred at Rendlesham Forest and RAF Bentwaters by the use of well-practised methods of disinformation. How much longer can we afford to ignore the presence of these mysterious objects that continue to be seen in our airspace...? Maybe at our peril who knows...? The Media still judge us overall on the events which took place on that weekend but completely ignore the wealth of evidence by so many others as shown in this book and others published by John that must surely to a great degree tend to corroborate the existence of a phenomena which we know very little about or seem to care – rather than the opposite. It's always important as well not to lose focus of the fact that the East Anglia area has been the venue for many other UFO sightings over the years, some going back to the 1940s.

People ask me about lasting health problems? – I did not experience any sustained ill effects. I cannot speak for the other individuals involved, as I'm told that several feel they have sustained lasting health problems.

People ask me are Governments hiding the truths about the UFO Phenomena? – The more I learn the more I'm convinced there's a concerted, behind-the-scenes, effort to hide the real truths from us. Even some of our Presidents' have witnessed something highly unusual and unexplainable. So many of these incidents strike a chord with me, understanding what happened in December 1980. Without the personal sighting I would have been sceptical and found what allegedly had taken in the Forest and what the airmen reported having seen quite frankly very hard to believe, because such things couldn't exist could they? I was really going to debunk it quite frankly; and as events unfolded I became more

THE HALT PERSPECTIVE 2

and more concerned that there may be something to this... I kept telling myself that there had to be some type of explanation for it, but I certainly couldn't find one and even to this day I can't give an answer.

People ask me if I believe Aliens exist – It's a shame that apparently genuine reports involving *what appears to* be 'alien figures' seen close to or near Unidentified Flying objects are ignored. Instead the nonsense involving fictitious underground bunkers on the airbase and close encounters with Base Commanders still proliferates as a backcloth to this incident by those desperate to sensationalize something which was in itself sensational! Others tell even more lurid fairy stories. Some people even suggest this could have been an invasion depicting a War of the Worlds scenario!

Now nearly 40 years later, once again I am having to continually put the record straight with my own

perspective of what exactly took place, and also rebutting ridiculous never ending claims made by people of what they thought happened or worse having to constantly read about what other people thought I had seen, often putting words into my mouth – which paints a misleading version of events that <u>history should not record</u>. Memories of it were resurrected in December 1980, when I found myself confronted with an experience I could not explain. The incidents that occurred over a three night period in Rendlesham Forest, Suffolk, left a lasting impression on me and tragically affected the lives of many concerned.

People ask me was I debriefed? – I can say without reservation I was never debriefed and have full memory of the events. The distance from the vehicles and light-alls to the identified site was less than 100 yards and was illuminated by both the light-alls and individual flashlights. The pines at that time were Corsican with a tall canopy and little if any low growth. That's the reason for being able to see that far from the East Gate the first night. I did not know Bustinzas name until years later I just knew there was security staffs Sgt. in the jeep when they picked me up and he stayed with us the whole time until we returned to the vehicles. Note his voice is on the tape.

It was their job to report above, sound an alarm and notify those above me. When I realized it was not an enemy threat but something way beyond our comprehension I backed off. That was in keeping with the then unspoken policy. Ask anyone in the military what happens when you report a UFO? That's why the B/W Air Traffic Controllers kept quiet until they retired. If I had seen a craft I would have reported it and things would probably have been different. Who knows? All I can say to people that now pick things apart, you weren't there. I still didn't say much publicly until people started putting out all kinds of garbage and nonsense … So much disinformation out there and people bugging me about what happened – I finally decided, it's time to tell the truth. I was a non-believer; I never really gave it a second thought before the incident. But I've got so much material from so many people, and talked to very credible people – people that do not want their names used – that are in very influential positions, including some that are as high in the government as you can get. I can tell you, we are not alone. I can guarantee you that. People should be careful and I'm not talking about something beyond us. My concern is that an agency with secretive powers might do something. You are the judge of that – several of the airmen were hypnotized, drugged and then threatened. John Burroughs was never the same after the event. I felt badly but couldn't do anything about it. I tell him that I've moved on with my life he should do the same. I've been accused of getting between him and Jim Penniston but that's not true. **What I described to Harry Harris and Michael Sacks,** was what occurred the first night. I never saw a structured craft. I reported everything I saw to the command post. Mike Sacks drew a sketch based on his assessment of what was seen **using his imagination rather than any sketch shown to him.**

People ask me was I harassed? – I have never been harassed by the senior command over the reports I made about the RAF Bentwaters UFO incidents – probably for a couple of good reasons; number one, my rank and some of the jobs that I have held, but also very early on, I sat down and made a very detailed tape and made several copies of everything I knew about it. Maybe I'm paranoid, but I think it was time well spent when I made the tapes.

Length of my tape recording in issue

It is claimed by Georgina Bruni during an interview made with her on page 237 of her book, *'You Can't Tell The People'* that I actually admitted to her I had 5 hours of tape recording, but would never allow folks to listen to the whole length (unlike the 18 minutes in the public domain). This is not the case – I wish! For a start while I was out there for some hours – the tape wasn't running without interruption. Sorry if could go back and change things I would have had a camera, and maybe a stack of cassettes, each 20 minutes in duration…

John Burroughs sent a number of emails to me in 2018 – accusing me of trying to discredit those involved, including him and Adrian Bustinza, which is absolute rubbish, and lies! It seems pointless nit-picking on an incident that took place over 40 years ago. It seems to me that people continually try to muddy the waters of what happened there when I was Deputy Base Commander. I'm not perfect, but my interpretation of what happened is standard now. Most people appear to have accepted my version of events which is straightforward, unlike other participants who have woven monstrous claims of absurdity now known to most people interested in the subject. Sometimes you can't do right for doing wrong! **But it gets worse as you will see soon….**

What people should be doing is not nit-picking on specific comments, but concentrating on the wider picture, taking into consideration that while people singularize the incident and argue till the 'cows

THE HALT PERSPECTIVE 2

come home' (excuse the pun) they conveniently fail to take into consideration the forgotten hundreds of similar UFO sightings that have occurred around the East Anglia area during that decade, some of them around the Base. Not forgetting the many UFO incidents which have been brought to my attention that occurred in 1980.

Threats of publishing private letters – As far as threats of possible publication by one British researcher of interesting correspondence between the *News of the World* and Harry Harris – 'hang on' – surely those private letters – of which I and John have a copy, are not in the public domain, *and cannot be published* accordingly at the whim of some individual who wishes to do so, as they are private, unless permission is granted. What constantly baffles me is why so many people wishing to set the record straight about what they think happened – or didn't – are so eager to catch the media's attention with their weird and wonderful hypotheses, don't bother to ask me? That's because they know my answer! I met him in 1994 as shown in the following pictures published in UFO Magazine!

Another guy who I met was retired Police officer Alan Godfrey who had his own UFO encounter in Todmorden, Yorkshire, in 1980. Mind you I wasn't aware that he later complained to the Press that he wasn't given enough time to tell his story. Next time we meet I will buy him a beer!

THE HALT PERSPECTIVE 2

FOCUS ON CHARLES HALT

Charles I. Halt, retired from the United States Air Force in June 1992, with more than 28 years commissioned service. He has a bachelor of science degree in economics and chemistry and a master's degree in business administration.

He is a graduate of Squadron Officer School, Air Command Staff College and the Industrial College of the Armed Forces. His assignments include several combat tours in South East Asia as well as being handpicked to serve as an escort/debriefer for returning American Vietnam POW'S.

In 1980 he was reassigned from Headquarters U.S. Air Force to RAF Bentwaters as Deputy Base Commander. He became Base Commander in 1984 and later served as Base Commander, Kunsan AB, Korea. From Kunsan he moved to Florennes AB, Belgium, where he was instrumental in bringing the Cruise Missile Wing on line and then phasing it out.

His final Air Force assignment was as Director of the Inspection Directorate for the American Department of Defense. In this capacity he had total inspection oversight for the entire American military establishment.

His security clearance was beyond what can be mentioned here.

Following his visit to Leeds, Halt travelled to London to record an interview for Michael Aspel's *'Strange But True'*, television series.

The documentary, broadcast on Friday 9 November 1994, created enormous interest, as Halt and several other important witnesses recounted the extraordinary events.

PART 4

UK SPOTLIGHT ON 1981

UFO reported over Rendlesham Forest again!

CHARLES: In January 1981, I found myself going out into the forest again with Colonel Williams to speak to USAF Serviceman – Steve La Plume, who was on duty at the East Gate [now in 2020 in the process of publishing his own book on this and other events!]

Steve La Plume

THE HALT PERSPECTIVE 2

He told us: "*We saw an object darting across the sky, continually changing course and altitude, in a series of up and down movements – almost too fast for the eye to catch, and contacted Security Control by radio, explaining what we were seeing. After about 30 minutes, the UFO returned – now much closer, allowing us to see it was cigar shaped, showing green, red and blue, lights on its underside. As it passed overhead, it illuminated the forest floor underneath it. What really annoyed me was that I couldn't remember what happened next. I have no memory of the object moving out of sight, or disappearing. We decided not to report the second sighting, fearing ridicule.*"

Unfortunately by the time we got there was nothing to be seen. I have no reason to doubt the version of events given. However I see that on Facebook in 2020 (unsure of when the post was put up) – presume recently – Steve makes a statement, t quote: "*My Name is Steven R. LaPlume. I was a security specialist at RAF Bentwaters during the UFO incident that some say never happened. If you read '**You Can't Tell The People**' then you may recognize my name from there. Larry Warren was a good friend of mine for quite a few years after we left the twin bases. I went on to be a Mercenary after I left the Service of my country. You may have seen my name in your guest book. I just wanted to say that the page by Chuck Dalldorf is actually a bit odd to me. Chuck admits he never saw anything. OK, I can buy that but then he states he would have heard about it. Well that's just it. It was hushed up the next day. When I had my sighting a few weeks after the one everyone focuses on, **I was told to go back to the dorm and forget about it**. I then talked to Larry about it a few weeks later and the next thing you know we are both civilians again. I know I was a good soldier as I make a living at it. I really don't know what it was that I saw but no aircraft I have seen since can do what this thing did.*"

Charles: As I've said before I went out there and have no memory of telling Steve to keep quiet, about what he saw, maybe General Williams advised him, but it's only a moot point, taking into consideration other sightings that were reported around the UK for this year which John has accumulated over a quarter of a century!

I read through many of these reports while Pat, his partner entertained a group of us, which included Steve Wills, during a barbecue at his house in Bromsgrove, Worcestershire following my talk at the Hull conference arranged by Chris Evers . . . If nothing else it reiterates the fact that on occasion the skies may, for all I know, be crowded with phenomena that is out of human visual range.

Time to hand back over to John, who wants to tell you about what happened in 1981 – which should be of interest as it contains a number of other reports relating to UFOs sighted in the sky over the UK – following on from the events that I was to become embroiled in; still the subject of discussion and controversy now 40 years later! If John included all of them the book would never get published! But it surely shows in stark contrast to the never ending media scepticism, with their uneducated attitude towards a subject which defies understanding, of the reality involving apparent incursions into our atmosphere by 'something' or 'someone' for an unsubstantiated purpose, into peoples' lives, leaving them with a variety of emotions which includes bewilderment, fear, excitement, and a need to know 'what the hell was that'? Instead many of them were to wish they

Charles, seated, with Steve Wills

THE HALT PERSPECTIVE 2

had never bothered to report it. So why, if as we are led to believe there are simple explanations for much of this, then why the cover up – which has gone on for over half a century?

John: Two people were driving from Stourbridge, West Midlands along the A491, during the evening of the **5th January 1981**, when they saw a stationary yellow 'light' in the sky, which began to approach them. As it passed overhead, they were astonished to see: an oval-shaped metallic object, showing a light at each end. Within minutes, the object was out of view – just a tiny yellow light in the sky. **(Source: Mark Pritchard, UFOsIS).**

On **7th January 1981**, David William Taylor of Hillcrest Road, Hornchurch – a telephone engineer by occupation – was with three friends, standing around a bonfire in Devonshire Road, Seven Kings, Ilford, Essex, at 8.pm, when a **long cylindrical-shaped object** was seen in the sky, moving in a straight line through the sky. On the **11th January 1981,** Tilbury crane driver – Mr. Simon Fitzgerald, was travelling to work from Grays, in Essex, along Dock Road, at 6.30am, when he saw, *"... an object, far too bright to be an aircraft, showing two bright lights, and a green one surrounded by a glare. I stopped at the side of the road and watched it before it went out of sight."* **(Source: Dan Goring, *Earth-link*).**

Just after midnight on **16th January 1981**, Eric Kempson and his brother-in-law, Tony Nicholls, were driving along Shooters Hill, London, when they saw: *"... a black Delta-shaped object, showing a number of coloured lights underneath. From out of the UFO's base projected a powerful beam of light that illuminated the road. I cannot say what it was that we saw, but I am convinced it was no aircraft, helicopter or weather balloon."*

At 7.00am on **21st January 1981**, a farmer's wife, living at Birdfield Farm – smallholding on the South Yorkshire/Derbyshire border, close to the B6054 road – happened to look through the window, when she saw: *"...something looking like a tent resting on the ground, about 8ft in height but more conical in structure, with a single apex, metallic-grey in colour. In front were three white blotches, like sacks or eggs apparently attached to it."* At 8.30am she left to do some shopping. On her return there was nothing to be seen. She then contacted the farmer on whose land the object had been observed, and was told he had no knowledge of anything like she described on his land. Unfortunately, details of the incident were not made available for investigation until 13 months later, following a visit to the location by Richard Adams and Paul Fuller. Rather surprisingly, they discovered an area, roughly 11ft by 11ft of disturbed furrowed soil, containing **three depressions, approximately 4ins deep. (Source: Paul Fuller/Jenny Randles).**

Three days later, at 6.00pm on **24th January 1981,** a cluster of five *'golf ball'*-sized lights, forming an oblong shape, were seen moving slowly across the sky over Bathampton, near Bath, in front of a much larger object, by local antiques dealer Maureen Woodgate, who was on her way home. According to the report, submitted on the same day to the British UFO Society, Maureen says she observed the objects for between 10 and 20 minutes. *"The lights/objects stopped for a few minutes before carrying on with their journey, at which point I left the scene as I needed to get petrol"* **(Source: British UFO Society).**

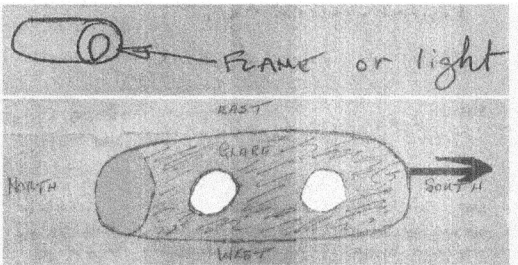 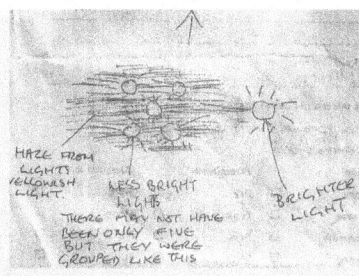

As seen in January 1981

THE HALT PERSPECTIVE 2

One of the original attending police officers sights UFO over Woodbridge!

Charles: Could there have been a connection with what Steve and Martyn Brophy, a local Suffolk Constabulary police officer, witnessed in the same year? He was one of the three officers that had attended in Rendlesham Forest in December 1980 following calls made from the base to them. He was driving a police car through Woodbridge, accompanied by another officer, during **March/April.** *"I happened to look upwards and see the amazing sight of a massive bank of lights, forming a rectangular shape, moving slowly across the sky. I felt the hairs on the back of my neck rising. I knew this was no aircraft and watched, in silence, unable to comprehend the sheer size of the 'craft'. From the look on my colleague's face, I knew he had also seen it."* The officers made their way back to the police station and sat down, trying to retain their composure. All of a sudden there was a frenzied knock at the front door, followed by the entrance of a man, wearing a crash helmet, who was shaking with fright. He said, to the officers: *"You'll never believe what I've just seen. I was riding towards Woodbridge, when this huge UFO swooped down over the top of me. I thought it was going to strike me – then it disappeared".* I remember when I did my talk at Woodbridge in July 2015, a Mr. Kim Tester stood up very nervously in front of the audience and told them about seeing two huge 'lights in the sky' while driving along the Woodbridge Road, not far from the airbase. He was traced by John Hanson, 35 years after the event, even though he didn't know his name! Not bad Detective work.

Kim Tester

My sons went for a swim around the Orford Island in 1981!

Just as matter of general interest, my then teenage son and friends 'on a dare', swam out to the island in the spring of 1981. It was foolish and very dangerous due to the rapid currents. I didn't find out until much later and was not happy. Additionally, my son and friends walked around the island and said there was no sign of life or activity. **No surprise as the entire highly-classified project had been wound down and removed.** During that time frame I occasionally had dinner at my favourite pub at Orford. I never saw any activity or lights. When I asked the pub owner he stated the lighthouse was now automated (which Keith Simmonds, the keeper, confirmed) and there was no activity on the island. I have no knowledge of such aerial devices capable of projecting hologram images kept at the airbase or elsewhere. I don't believe there was any connection with these claimed devices with what was witnessed by me and others involving lights in the sky and light beams seen to fall around us. But I don't know, speculation is fine – we need proof!

Orford Ness Lighthouse –highly sensitive area even in the 1960s'!

John spoke to Paul Sinclair, who I have met; he is well respected as a good researcher of the UFO subject, and has written a number of books entitled **UFO Truth Proof**.

Sometime during 2014 Paul was contacted by a former Flamborough lighthouse keeper who wanted to tell him about

unexplained sightings and other things that he had seen during his service as a lighthouse keeper before *lighthouses were automated. Paul arranged to meet him at his home on the outskirts of Bridlington a few days after he contacted him. Once inside he produced an A4-sized envelope containing notes and sketches of the things he had observed in his long career as a keeper. Some of the things that he told Paul were very enlightening and tied in with many of the unexplained events that he has looked into around East and North Yorkshire.

One of the things he spoke about surprised Paul when, while on duty at as a relief lighthouse keeper at Orford Ness, Suffolk, which would have been before 1965 . . . *"Everyday whilst at Orford Ness I was escorted to and from the lighthouse by military personnel. One day I decided to have a look around the outer perimeter of the lighthouse.* **In various places strange structures protruded from the ground, intrigued I walked up to one of them and began looking at it. I thought nothing about it at the time other than being curious as to what they were. However, after a short time I found myself in hot water as military personnel surrounded me and removed me from the lighthouse. They asked me what I was doing and gave me the hard word; I was then returned to the lighthouse and ordered never to walk in the unauthorised area again."

Summer 1981 – Girls' night out followed by frightening encounter with a UFO!

John: Valerie Walters (22) who I have met many times over the years and regard her and her colleagues version of what took place as absolutely genuine, was travelling on the A5 road after a sober night out with two friends in the summer of 1981, from the now defunct Shrewsbury nightclub, *Tiffanys*. The friends were laughing and joking with the windows down in the early morning when they saw a strange light in the field opposite the *Three Horse Shoes* pub. Val can remember the car stopping. But it was only under medical grade hypnosis that she could remember the finer details. She's not been in the best of health (2020) so we wish her well and send her our warm regards.

*The paraffin powered light was converted to electricity in 1959, and fully automated in 1965. The lighthouse (built in 1792) is not generally open to the public except on special days. Military defences have been part of the Orford Ness landscape since the 17th Century.

THE HALT PERSPECTIVE 2

Plymouth woman sights UFO – sustains burn on hand!

Just under a year later from the events that took place in Rendlesham Forest an interaction between an unidentified, apparently structured, object was to leave the witness burnt on her hand.

At 3.00 a.m., **11th September 1981**, Plymouth-based UFO Researcher, Bob Boyd, received a phone call from a man, who told him about an incident involving his girlfriend's sister, which had taken place a few hours previously, and that he had contacted the Police, who advised him this was not a matter they were able to deal with and had given him Bob's telephone number. *"I felt that I should see the girl immediately, amid dire warnings from my wife, and went out to see the girl, Denise Bishop – then 23 years old, and an accounts clerk – whom I found to be a very calm, self-possessed, girl. She had never thought about UFOs, and had not read any books on the subject. I interviewed her from 3.15 until 5.00 am, and took a couple of black and white photographs (the last on the film) of the burn to her hand."*

Denise: *"I was coming into my house at approximately 11.15 pm. As I approached the corner of the bungalow, in Weston Hill, Plymouth, I thought I saw some lights behind the house. As I got to the back door, allowing me to see up the hill behind our house, I saw an enormous unlit and dark metallic grey UFO hovering above the houses on top of the hill. Coming from underneath the object, and shining down on the rooftops beneath it, were six or seven broad shafts of light. These were lovely pastel shades of pink and purple and also white. I saw all this in an instant and I was terrified. I hurriedly reached for the door, but as I put my hand on the handle, from the unlit side of the ship, a lime green pencil beam of light came down and hit the back of my hand. As soon as it hit my hand, I couldn't move. I was stopped dead in my tracks. The beam stayed on my hand for at least 30 seconds, in which time I could only stand and watch the UFO. I was very frightened, although the UFO was a fantastic sight to see. It was huge and silent. In fact, the whole area seemed very quiet. The green beam, which didn't give off any illumination – like a 'rod of light' – then switched off and I*

continued to open the door. It was as if a film had been stopped, then started again. I had been stopped in mid-stride and when the beam went off, it continued the same movement. I opened the door and rushed into the house. As I did so, the UFO lifted into the sky slightly, and moved away and out of my sight. Rubbing my hand, I ran in and told my sister. We went back outside but there was nothing to be seen. Coming in again, my sister examined my hand but there was nothing there. I went and sat down and, a few minutes later, my sister's dog sniffed my hand, making it sting. On looking at it I noticed spots of blood and, after washing it, saw it was a burn. At 2.30 a.m. my sister's boyfriend came in and said we must report it to the police. He phoned the police but they couldn't help, except to give us Bob Boyd's number."

Bob: *"It appeared as a patch of shiny skin, with spots of blood and bruising about it. It looked as if a patch of skin had been removed, exposing the shiny, new skin beneath. I tried to get Denise to go to the casualty ward at a local hospital but she refused. When she complained that the wound was hurting, I told her to put her hand in cold water but this made it worse. Antiseptic cream was put on and this gave some relief. Denise had calmed down somewhat, but said she was terrified when the incident happened. Her first words to me were,* **"Will they come back to get me?" "What if it had been on my face or eyes?"** *and* **"Why me?"** *She was very frightened. After talking and allaying her fears somewhat, we called it a night."* (**Source: Bob Boyd, Plymouth UFO Group).**

Charles: The lady, who sustained a burn mark to her hand after sighting a UFO – how would the *BBC*, Andrew Pike and others, who have come forward in recent times, explain that one with their claims bandied about by the Pentagon scientists, spasmodically the subject of Press, relating to massive hologram weapons, beaming images over a battlefield to incite fear in soldiers on a battlefield, according to one researcher?

We aren't talking about individual or singular incidents, from which some logical explanation could be found, we are talking about a glut of similar reports brought to our attention over the years that are very worrying. If these objects (UFOs) are safe then why is it that so many people report all manner of medical problems? This should be the scrutiny of scientific research instead of being 'brushed under the carpet'; problem is – what exactly are 'the authorities' hiding?

Greensburg, Pennsylvania – UFO seen with occupants?

So many sightings during this one short year, 1981, which I was totally unaware of, not only in the UK but the States – citing just one example of the appearance in the sky of **'three white lights forming the point of a triangle'** seen over Greensburg Pennsylvania, believed to be some sort of a 'craft' according to the witness, who alleged she could see what appeared to be occupants. None of it makes sense but of course it didn't to me till I found myself witnessing something also out of the ordinary. Even now, long forgotten reports from astronauts both American and Russian are included. In the 59th anniversary of the Moon landings which were celebrated worldwide – *National Geographic* even has a copy of their original magazine printed in 1969 celebrating the landing published available to the public. It was claimed by Cosmonaut Major General Vladimir Kovalyonok, way back in 1981, quote: *"Many cosmonauts have seen phenomena which are far beyond the experiences of earthmen. For ten years I never spoke on such things".* Now, I can't say unequivocally that I have spoken to him personally, but see no reason to disbelieve him.

Another sighting report handed to me by John tells us about an incident that took place at 2.00am on **29th October 1981**, when Kevin Grimsby (16) from Hollesley, on the Suffolk coast, was out night fishing with a friend, when they saw: *"…a silvery object flickering and pulsating with light – the size of a car – hanging a few hundred feet above the sea, giving off a faint hum."* After hovering for 15mins, it moved away towards the direction of Woodbridge, and was soon just a speck in the sky.

THE HALT PERSPECTIVE 2

Charles: In addition to so many reports of mysterious things seen in and around the area, are examples of strange photographs accumulated by Brenda Butler taken over a long period, right up to the present date, many of which John tells me were obtained initially with a 35mm camera and then a digital one are shown. I have no idea what causes these aberrations to appear –or what they represent. John tells me that some of them have been seen with the naked eye which may have been the cause of concern to some of the young airmen, who manned security points around the base. Your guess is as good as mine as to what they are and where they come from!

Another visit by an unidentified flying object on home territory!

One such event involving a UFO sighted over the Rendlesham Forest area occurred on 'Guy Fawkes' Night, November 5th 1981, when a **large cigar-shaped craft** floated silently over the airfield and circled RAF Bentwaters Air Traffic Control Tower before drifting off. It was later estimated to be **huge and approximately 100yds long and 50ft in diameter**, moving over from the coast, floating silently over the Base, and completing a 'figure of eight' movement over the Control Tower, before heading back out to sea.

John: Stories, such as these, came as no surprise to us as, over the years, during a number of visits to Rendlesham Forest, we were to hear of all manner of strange things seen in and around the area, including strange objects in the sky, dazzling 'orbs', (some of them seen with the naked eye), reports of *tall spindly 'figures', with concealed faces,* wandering about on the airbase. I tried to trace a Mr Jolly, but was unsuccessful, although there are a number of people with that surname in the Norfolk area. Brenda told me that Steve tape recorded the interview but later found that the machine had malfunctioned. In mid august 2020, I spoke to Brenda who told me that she was still picking up mysterious images captured on the digital camera. Admittedly we are unable to identify the nature of what cause these 'manifestations' to appear, and while aware of the scepticism attached to the subject of 'orbs' many of the photos taken can hardly be said to fit into this category, not forgetting the apports of stones, which can be a common feature of this forest, a phenomenon that is totally ignored! Why?

Charles: Whether these anomalies have anything to do with the events of December 1980 is of course open to conjecture! Strange things that have been seen in the forest, and elsewhere – Suffolk seems to have more than its fair share, as I can attest to!

I wondered what to make, of what Mrs Marion Kennedy from Framlingham, Suffolk and her family encountered after driving through a patch of thick fog? Followed by the sighting of a UFO after arriving at the house she was staying at in Baldock, Hertfordshire! Another example of the many times, that motorists are followed by these objects just *one* of a huge number of sightings that have taken place around the Suffolk area. She and her family were originally interviewed by Brenda Butler and Dot Street. John then contacted her some years later and interviewed her. He regards her as a very genuine witness who has not the slightest idea what on earth it was she and her family witnessed.

Maybe for all I know one day a rational scientific explanation will be found that suits all parties! Problem is that while this could be the case now for all I know, **then why the secrecy and need to cover up something which does affect lives?** Is it a case that the Real TRUTH cannot be disseminated to the Public?

Mysterious occurrence on the flight line at Woodbridge Tower
USAF Master Sergeant tells of a strange experience at RAF Woodbridge!

Charles: Retired Chief Master Sergeant Randy Corey, currently living in Henderson, Nevada, was assigned to the Presidential security detail at Andrew Air Force Base MD from March 1977 to June 1981. He had a

THE HALT PERSPECTIVE 2

Top Secret, *Yankee White* **(White House Security Clearance)** and worked as a security guard for aircraft that transported US and foreign dignitaries throughout the US and all around the world. During this assignment, he was responsible for ensuring the security of these Special Mission aircraft 24 hours a day wherever they were in the World as part of a four man security team. At the time, Staff Sergeant Corey provided security for aircraft transporting the Vice President, Secretaries of State, Defense, and Treasury, Speaker of the House, as well as various Senators and Congressmen, who travelled around the world at the behest of the President, conducting Administration business. He also provided aircraft security to foreign dignitaries being transported within the US, to include Egypt's President Anwar Sadat and Israel's Prime Minister Menachem Begin.

After four years at Andrews AFB, he was promoted to Master Sergeant on his first attempt and posted to RAF Bentwaters, England, arriving there in July 1981. After arrangements were made to secure housing for his family at Kesgrave, near Ipswich in East Anglia, his family joined him there in October 1981 and remained with him through the four years in England.

After departing RAF Bentwaters, he spent another five years at Ramstein AFB, Germany, having been posted to the Headquarters, United States Air Forces Europe Security Police Staff as an Action Officer working War and Contingency Plans, now with a Top Secret, Cosmic Atomal clearance. While at RAF Bentwaters, Randy was initially assigned to C flight Security, a rotating shift working three Swing shifts, three Grave shifts, and then having three days off. He was the Flight Chief, leading a team of approximately 65 men and women, responsible for the security of four squadrons of A10 Aircraft at Bentwaters, a Weapons Storage Area, and two squadrons of aircraft at RAF Woodbridge for about two-and-a-half years. This was a joint base operation which was headquartered at RAF Bentwaters and sent people to RAF Woodbridge each shift. Security personnel were assigned on an alternating basis between the two bases, ensuring security to their assigned resources, Priorities A and C. After leaving C Flight, he was assigned as the NCOIC (Non Commissioned Officer in Charge) of the Quality Control Section, and Superintendent of Administration. He completed 28 years of active service in January 1998 at Travis AFB CA as the Chief, Security Forces Enlisted Manager.

Randy reported what he had encountered a few years ago on Facebook, so John contacted him and obtained the following details.

Randy: "**Around late November/early December 1981,** *I got a call from my Woodbridge Base Security Supervisor* **that they had heard a noise and believed something had come down on the flight line.** *The runway was closed and nothing should have been able to land. I drove over to Woodbridge, about seven miles away, and organised a search party with my troops that were assigned there that night. We commenced a 'line search' toward the flight line but it was so dark nobody could see anything, so I suggested we wait until daybreak, about 30 minutes away, and knelt down to wait. I laid down in an attempt to see the difference between the ground and sky, but was unable to see anything, While lying there,* **I felt the hair on the back of my neck standing up, although I still couldn't see anything, and felt as if a 'presence' was out there in front of me.** *As daylight began, we started our line moving forward, and about 20-30 feet from where we had been waiting, discovered a line in the dew on the grass across our front, as if something or someone had moved through across our front. The dew was shaken off the grass in a line, which we followed to the edge of the tarmac,* **where there was a 6' chain link fence with three strands of barbed wire above it. You could see where two of the three strands of barbed wire had been broken in a V section as if something heavy had gone over the fence at that spot. I also observed some broken branches on a tree just outside the fence line.** *None of us ever saw anything, we found nothing on the flight line, and therefore, never filed any type of formal report on the situation. I seldom ever even mentioned this "non event" to anyone. My daughter Jennifer knew of it and asked me to tell her about it, and when I did, she apparently videotaped my story and put it on YouTube.*"

THE HALT PERSPECTIVE 2

We learned from the Video uploaded to *YouTube* by Randy's daughter that this incident was kept confidential for many years presumably because of the implications of what may have been an incursion at such a sensitive location would have caused in the Press. Randy was told to keep the incident secret which he did for many years.

Charles: I remember the Chief Master Sergeant being on the base. I can't recall this incident but strange things were reported around that area, it sure was a spooky place, as I was to find out myself! But let me make this clear again – what I was involved in, now 40 years ago, became indelibly burnt into my memory as it was something out of the normal operational everyday events. I can't conclude as to what it was that we saw. All this continuing newspaper speculation claiming aliens were seen or some sort of invasion took place is absolute rubbish. But of course it wasn't just about the events of December 1980, other incidents involving sighted UFOs were brought to my attention. Many of the Security Police witnessed unexplained things at RAF Woodbridge. Several personally told of seeing **'East End Charlie'** (as they called him). He appeared to be a World War Two aviator that wandered near the back gate.

Reviewing historical cases – many over East Anglia

Over a period of some years, I've chatted to John and looked through his UFO files accumulated over a period of 25 years, many of which were reported in and around the skies of East Anglia, by ordinary citizens. The three objects I saw, John Hanson tells me, dominate in description – forming part of the backcloth to the UFO phenomena – whatever the period. The significance of this should be of major importance, bearing in mind that the UFO sightings reported in the 1980s – now referred to often as triangular UFOs showing a lighting pattern of **three lights; one in each corner and sometimes one in the middle,** may well have far more in common with earlier reports than we realize. I can't say whether we had aircraft which might have been mistaken for Triangular UFOs, whatever that means, but I can say that it appears from the many files I've seen in possession of John Hanson, that similar shaped objects were seen a long time before we could cross the channel, a huge number over the Essex and East Anglia area.

John: Over the many years, even back to the 1940's, I have researched into hundreds, if not thousands, of sightings involving the movement of an object(s) in the sky, described as **elliptical or half moon shaped**, never mind the huge number of times when witnesses have seen three objects sometimes in two groups of three – which performs manoeuvres well out of the capabilities of any human constructed aerial device. On occasion they have been observed to **rain down what look like particles of light** and have on occasion appeared to be carrying out a **grid search**. We have not included any of these reports in this book as we don't have the room. It's important for the reader to take these into consideration when forming any conclusion as to what they believe was seen in Rendlesham Forest, Suffolk by Colonel Charles Halt, and the other airmen rather than blandly accepting what now appears to be in favour as an explanation – testing of new weaponry!

More fanciful stories and outlandish claims!

Charles: A Mr Gilmore, whoever he is, claimed to John that I was transferred after the UFO event. I was not "transferred" after the event. I stayed at Bentwaters until late June 1984. I was never 'read in on any black project' during my tour. There was no Colonel named Bill Guin at Bentwaters. More nonsense! Ask Mr. Gilmore what he claims he was doing at Bentwaters. I certainly did not know him.

Claims that General Gordon Williams receives film of UFO?

Others claim that Gordon Williams received something while in the cockpit of an A-10 bound for Germany. Mike Verrano claimed it **was film of the UFO**. I think it was Mel Zickler's efficiency report that was late and they wanted it to get into his file before the promotion board. I remember talk of that happening. This was well after the event in the forest. I could be wrong but I don't think so. The only related film it possibly could have been is Monroe Nevels' 35mm film. To have gotten it someone would have to have broken into his home and done a substitute. Not likely! More on Mr Nevels in due course, following an unexpected and very disappointing situation, involving scurrilous **attacks on my integrity** made by him many years later.

Likewise, in a telephone call made to me by Ray Boeche in **April 1985**, during our discussion on the matter, I have no memory of ever having told Ray about an officer who drove Wing Commander Gordon Williams from the landing site to a waiting aircraft with a **motion picture of the UFO,** and that this was verified by me for the Senator James Exon.

If a film had been taken I would have been the first to know . . . yes there were claims of airmen being in the forest – and the more I learn the more I'm convinced there's a concerted behind-the-scenes effort to spread confusion and deception.

'Project Pounce', Colonel Steve Wilson – Special Report

It never stops – I have learned of the circulation of a 'Special Report' published by former head of *'Project Pounce',* **Air Force National Reconnaissance Organization Special Forces Unit** formed on the **28th of December 1980,** presumably as a result of what happened at Bentwaters. This alleged branch of the US government retrieves downed UFOs! USAF officer Colonel Steve Wilson is shown as head of the investigation which speaks of a meeting a special Delta Force Team on arrival at RAF Woodbridge, and to meet the Base Commander Colonel Dale C Tabor, and question me about the landing and film taken. His quote: *"This film was taken to OSIP, a special dept at the Pentagon, and then erase all arrival of the craft"!* Whoever he is – I have no idea. Claims that a '**Landing pattern' was produced in grass – wrong** there was no grass. He also alleges that the **physical marks were destroyed. Wrong.** They were still there after the 28th of December. It's even alleged that a crop circle appeared on the same date at Warminster – 'Crop' circle! Some people even suggest that he doesn't exist. There's more rubbish – common sense dictates that if the Government want something to be classified, whatever the reason, then I'm sure it stays that way…leaked documents pandering to those that believe the aliens are here and running the human race, are matters that I can't comment on further because it's a pointless exercise to do so.

Coincidently, I wonder if there is a connection between this 'communication' and a letter sent to Larry Fawcett by Robert Greer Todd who was a UFO documents procurer, analyst and source of the Roswell incident, (John has a copy). In October 1984 'Bob' wrote to the CIA asking them further questions about what happened at Bentwaters Air Base, because he wasn't satisfied with their previous response. By that time he had a copy of my memo sent to him by Colonel Bent. Bob mentions that the *Philadelphia Bulletin* covered the 'landing story'. Bob appears to have wondered if 'between the lines' of reply various letters sent to him if *Project Aquarius* existed, if so, was it set up to dealing with UFOs? Further comments about an NSA operation in England in 1980, that wasn't anything to do with Bentwaters!

Fanciful claims continue to be brought to RAF Bentwaters press office!

People continue to this present day to ask me why the media has an ongoing fascination for the events that took place in rural Suffolk at the end of December 1980. I suppose one of the reasons why this event continues to capture the public's attention, is because many people won't have a clue how frantic UFO activity has been in the past and will not be aware of the huge number of other worldwide incidents involving UFO activity that has in the main been forgotten! But these cases should not be consigned into forgotten history, as behind each and every sighting, men and women simply wanted an answer to what often was one of the strangest things they had ever seen or encountered. The fact that no answers

THE HALT PERSPECTIVE 2

were given by officialdom gives you an idea just how sensitive the subject is. People also appear to confuse the stereotyped salacious stories that abound mostly in pulp cover art depicting sparsely clad attractive women stalked by alien predators' intent on abduction! These scenarios appear to be confused with malicious stories spread by people such as Warren in his now infamous book *Left At East Gate*. An example of the way in which the 'grass roots of nonsense and wild allegations' take root and continue to flourish over the years, which provide people with escapism rather than confront the impossible.

Look at the way in which the Press Department at RAF Bentwaters was engulfed with letters asking for my whereabouts, suggesting that I and the other witnesses had been moved away, as part of some cover up! This was nothing of the sort, my posting ended – and I was re-posted in the summer of 1984, as were some of the other participants. One has only to look at some of the well meaning letters sent to Captain Victor L Warzinski of the Press department at RAF Bentwaters, by people like Jenny Randles and Mark Birdsall who wrote back to them: *"I'm not in any position to verify or disprove anything about our supposed UFO sightings. No official investigation of any kind was ever done. Current USAF policy is that we no longer investigate UFO sightings as we haven't done so for many years."* In another letter Victor said, *"I still regard various alarming scenarios which span across witchcraft, drugs, peace warfare and a near nuclear holocaust! To quote the advanced publicist flyer for SKY CRASH as fanciful! I still regard Art Wallace's (Larry Warren's) story as fanciful as reported in the News of the World. I still regard quite a bit more that has been written and said about this incident by a number of people beside you as fanciful."*

One time we had two senior Senators visiting the base. They decided they wanted to visit the WSA. We couldn't get them clearance!

US Senator James Exon: Born 9.8.1921 – 10.6.2005

I also spoke extensively with well respected US Senator James Exon who served as the 33rd Governor of Nebraska, from 1971-1979, and a US Senator from 1979-1997. He never lost an election and was the only democrat to hold Nebraska's class 2 US Senate seat. I told him the whole story. He was quite concerned about what I told him. After we talked he totally dropped the subject. Who got to him? I have the tape of Boeche's conversation with Bustinza and it doesn't make sense, as to an extent, he supports Larry. Remember Adrian was with me the whole time. Ray together with Scott Colborn made a joint effort to investigate the incident, and contacted Bustinza and Burroughs. Following their findings Ray contacted Senator James Exon. Ray asked me to contact James which I did as I have explained.

Senator James Exon

Those putting us on the wrong track!

If that's not bad enough then you have all the horrendous attacks and threats made against myself and John Hanson by Larry Warren, and his camp followers. His garish and unbelievable account of what happened proved to be the source of extreme interest by the British Press over the years. No surprise there! Although he **had** quite a lot of supporters including his co author Peter Robbins, it's indicative of the mentality of those that flocked to his side over the years, when careful scrutiny of what he alleged would have shown him to be a charlatan and fabricator. But the damage is done! My recently-passed friend Budd Hopkins wondered if these crazy stories could be induced memories, by other persons to deliberately confuse the real picture. I know Larry was regressed by Patricia Gagliardo and then by Budd Hopkins. Let's put this in the right context. This was no seasoned campaigner or seasoned serviceman of the 81st.

THE HALT PERSPECTIVE 2

On the 2nd of December 1980, Warren was assigned to the 81st Security Squadron. His shift commander was Major Malcolm Zickler. Flight Chief being SMSgt Farias. Warren was advised by letter that he would begin introduction training on the 5th of December 1980. His sponsor being Airman James C Gouge. Because of shift work it was suggested that Sgt Dennis K Hudson who was in charge of the sponsorship program would meet him a day or so before training began. If any problems arose he should contact Sgt. Hudson (Squadron Intro Monitor) SMSgt Swain (Squadron First Sergeant) – other points of contact SMSgt Farias/SMSgt Thornton (Law Enforcement)/MSgt Harrell (Law Enforcement).

Thank goodness those allegations made by Airman Larry Warren, who was at the Airbase in December 1980, have been proven to be lies. Over many years now he has made money out of promoting a foundation of fabrication and confabulation besmirching the reputation of honourable men that I served with. Incredibly he even sent me a Lawyer's letter asking me to cease and desist.

What really happened at Bentwaters?

I honestly don't know. Something very strange happened. I've been back many times. I've gone back to the site. I've sat down with any and everybody I can think that, you know, could shed some light on it. I've batted this around with Jacques Vallee. I've met the foremost Astrophysicist, from Great Britain, and gone through things with him, and I have a lot of unanswered questions and probably we'll never have them answered. I'd like to have them answered. But, it was a very interesting experience. So that, in essence, is what happened at Bentwaters.

1983

Publication of *Sky Crash* – misleading to say the least!

Obviously I have special interest in the events that took place around East Anglia following the arrival of the book *Sky Crash*, in 1983 – which whipped up by the media and I found myself the centre of interest and curiosity. I received various letters sporadically from people which I always answered as long as the sanity of the writer isn't apparently an issue!

You know I never fail to be surprised by so many books, magazines, and Internet articles now nearly 40 years on, postulating theory after theory about what people believe to be the 64 million dollar answer, to what happened out there in the forest on that fateful night. Often such 'offerings' are presented to whip up emotions and sell the product. Often I have been misquoted or my character has been maligned. So that's why I maintain my stance on what took place, if only to put the record straight. The annoying thing is that they use my Memo without bothering to contact me, yes I know it's in the public domain, but that doesn't mean you can use it without permission. Not only that but hardly any people contact me to ask a question. Here is Brenda Butler (right) who I have kept in touch with, showing the book!

Brenda Butler

THE HALT PERSPECTIVE 2

The 'Flyer' for the book – entertaining rather than educating!

The 'Flyer' advertising this book tell us about the 'World's first officially confirmed Close Encounter. The authors have been given dramatic information and documentation by the British Defence Ministry, who for the first time have come clean about their involvement in the UFO subject. This could be the book which finally ends the cover up. In view of the sensational, but absolutely verifiable and documented evidence presented, there can be no way *Sky Crash* can fail to attract excitement, controversy and huge sales. The British edition will be published in the summer of 1984, and the ripple following publication will spread across the world. Then this is followed by claims, of two protracted close encounters with an incredible and undeniably physical craft which had come down into the woods. Quote: 'A landing that lasted three hours, during which the entities held a long conversation with a high ranking officer. The craft had been damaged and was placed under military guard, while the aliens made hasty repairs. Enabling them to take off again. IT'S PILOTS, however were out of this world! They left strong pieces of evidence, including symmetrical trace marks, radiation, damage to surrounding trees and visual and auditory documentation which was immediately placed under strict secrecy. The traces were destroyed by the authorities in a calculated manner.'

Brenda: As far as the incident being an experiment as claimed, I do not believe it for a second. Even today it would be difficult to pull off. I am convinced Larry now really thinks all he says is true. I have more suspicions that he has personal problems or someone has done something to him. I have told him my thoughts and he indicated it might be true. The answer as to which, may never be known.

Charles: If you and Dot had not gotten involved this would probably all have only been known by a few. I was never excited about it being smeared all over the papers as I appreciate my privacy. Again the only reason why I went public is that too many people were running around telling wild tales. Every instance where I have spoken I have tried to keep it factual. When I interject opinion I state it as opinion. At one point, many years ago, I tried to steer you and Dot in the right direction but you kept insisting on some kind of accident or some kind of cover up. Any cover up was a desire for privacy. By the way I really did snatch my photo from public affairs and never gave them another. Keep in touch, let me know if you come across any new facts. I have as many unanswered questions as you

Dot and Brenda. Right, Brenda with Chris Pennington

THE HALT PERSPECTIVE 2

RAF Woodbridge (Alleged Incident). Question asked in House of Lords!

On the **4th of March 1983,** Lord Clancarty asked questions in the House – "About how many UFOs had been reported to them for the period 1978-1981?" The figures supplied to him were: 1978(750) 1979(550) **1980(350)** 1981(600). Lord Clancarty: "*May I ask whether or not it is a fact that over **2000** authenticated UFO reports were published in the Press?*"

John Hanson: Vicky McLennan has no problem in remembering her UFO sighting as it took place on her 18th birthday at 5pm, **29th September 1983.** "*I was on my way to meet my brother in Covent Garden travelling in the back of her boyfriend's MG sports car with my best friend sat in the passenger front seat, the road was quite busy at the time, as we drove over the bridge with about 60 people crossing over it. Suddenly we saw directly in front of us a **massive silver disk** it, almost dropped out of the sky in front of us, taking up a large area of the sky hovering on its side. I could see portholes all around the centre and what looked like lights on inside. Some of the windows looked dull as though people were looking through them. The craft was shining a lilac light from its underside. As it hovered I noticed **there was writing under it which looked like hieroglyphics, resembling what looked like a swastika in red, but I believe if my memory serves me right, the arms may have been going in the opposite direction from a swastika**.*" A similar object was seen in December 1966 around the London area, with similar 'imagery' on the surface of the object, they aren't the only ones...

1983 – 'Mystery of alleged UFO landing in Forest'.

This was the headline from the *Woodbridge Reporter* newspaper, on the 6th May, with once again a reference to an '*anonymous airmen*', who told of seeing three entities *'three feet tall, dressed in silver suits, levitating in shafts of light near their landed spacecraft'* in a remote part of Rendlesham Forest. A copy of the eye-witness' drawing of the UFO was included, followed by a denial of any contact with alien beings, according to the MOD. Other contemporary newspaper sources included *Sunday Mirror* – **'Flying Saucer lands in Britain – I saw UFO land American Officer'** and *News of the World* – **'We must be told'**. Although the incident(s) which occurred in Rendlesham Forest were now three years old, "*It continued to excite attention*", according to Squadron Leader Donald Moreland, who wrote to Peter Lord Hill-Norton at the MOD to this effect on the 9th May 1983.

On the 24th October 1983, **Sir Patrick Wall** asked Mr Stanley, the Secretary of State for Defence "*(1) If he had seen the United States Air Force memo dated 13th January 1981, concerning unexplained lights near RAF Woodbridge; (2) Whether, in view of the fact that the United States Air Force memo of 13th January 1981 on the incident at RAF Woodbridge has been released under the Freedom of Information Act, will he now release reports and documents concerning similar unexplained incidents in the United Kingdom; (3) How many unexplained sightings or radar intercepts have taken place since 1980?*"

Mr. Stanley replied, "I have seen the memorandum of 13 January 1981 to which my Honourable Friend refers. Since **1980 the Department has received 1,400 reports of sightings of flying objects which the observers have been unable to identify.** There were no corresponding unexplained radar contacts. Subject to normal security constraints, I am ready to give information about any such reported sightings that are found to be a matter of concern from a defence standpoint, **but there have been none to date.**"

In November 1983, *Michael Ray Dibdin Heseltine, Baron Heseltine, Secretary of State for Defence from 1983 to 1986, who was instrumental in the political battle against the Campaign for Nuclear Disarmament, wrote a letter from the MOD in reply to an enquiry made by the **Rt Honourable Merlyn Rees MP, who was contacted by Philip Mantle, in which it was suggested there had been a cover up with regard to the allegation made by the *News of the World* that alien beings had been seen in Rendlesham Forest. Baron Heseltine denied that such an event had taken place and also claimed that "**Nor was any unidentified object seen on radar**" [Events have proved him wrong with regard to any radar evidence although to be fair he would not have known of this at the time.]

1984

Letter of apology received from the '*Sky Crash*' crowd – invitation to dinner!

Charles: On the **28th February 1984,** I received a letter from Brenda and David Taylor: "*Would you please accept this letter from me, Mrs. D Taylor and Ms B Butler as an apology for the incident on the evening of the 23rd of February 1984. We are very concerned about the whole matter and feel that if we are to carry on with our interests in the investigation of UFOs we can both ill afford incidents of this nature. On this subject we went to see Mrs. Dot Street on the 26th of February 1984, she has promised us that she will not infringe on your privacy again. Mrs. Butler and I would like you to accept this invitation out to dinner one evening as a gesture of goodwill. We would like you to know that at no time do we intend to discuss the matter, appertaining to the incident that has been persistently discussed.*" Signed Brenda Butler and David Taylor

In late **October 1984,** I wrote to Brenda Butler at her home address, thanking her for the card she sent to me, telling her it was a bit early for Halloween! I told her my photos had come out alright and hadn't been mysteriously fogged, or any gone missing. I said I wasn't surprised "*Sarah's version of events with regard to sighting a UFO over Rendlesham Forest from her bedroom window at the edge of the forest had been cut out of the TV program I was involved in as her story changed with prompting.*" (Brenda Butler had herself checked out the location and established that it was unlikely a view of the chosen area could have been seen from inside the room concerned). I hope you finally believe me when I tell you that I am not an agent for anyone. I suspect that if you still believe me to be – then time will bear me out.

I also have in my possession copies of de-classified typed-up letter sent out from RAF Bentwaters in 1984 to Ramstein, Germany by Captain Victor L Warzinski who was one of the guys that responded to member s of the public when they wrote to the base enquiring about the incident. **In his letter to Ramstein he pointed out that the commander of OSI during period of incident did not carry out any investigation.** In another letter from the MOD he confirmed they didn't investigate as it wasn't considered as of being of any defence interest. A reference was made to the base commander Colonel Cochran who stated: "*That no audio visual documentation was done, nor was any report of investigation imitated by the USAF…base newspapers files and independent confirmation indicate first visit to Bentwaters was by SCEF following 'accident' was 24th September 1981. Advise Colonel Halt.*"

US Serviceman sights UFO over RAF Mildenhall – threatened by OSI?

Ex US serviceman Mark Miraglia spoke to John Hanson about what he saw over RAF Mildenhall, home of the SR71 Blackbird while based there between **1984** and **1986** – strange enough but what happened

---

*Michael Heseltine: British politician and businessman. (21.3.1933) having begun his career as a property developer, he became one of the founders of the publishing house Haymarket. Heseltine served as a Conservative Member of Parliament from 1966 to 2001, and was a prominent figure in the governments of Margaret Thatcher and John Major, including serving as Deputy Prime Minister and First Secretary of State under the latter. He resigned from the Cabinet in 1986 over the Westland Affair and returned to the back benches.

**Merlyn Merlyn-Rees, Baron Merlyn-Rees: (Born 18 December 1920 – 5 January 2006) was a British Labour politician and Member of Parliament from 1963 until 1992. He served as Secretary of State for Northern Ireland (1974–1976) and Home Secretary (1976–1979).

afterwards to him was not only even stranger but very traumatic. The aftermath of that trauma still forms part of his life to this very day. Mark: "*My role at the Airbase was to supply parts to the top secret SR71 Blackbirds which were kept under cover in guarded hangers on the base. There were two of them and a third which was under the control of the CIA. In the summer of 1986 I was outside talking to two men, just general chit chat, when I happened to look up into the sky and see a silver triangular shadow in the sky above the hanger. It wasn't sharply defined but appeared cloaked that the only way I can describe it. There was no mistake it was unlike anything I had ever seen before – not a SR71 that's for sure. As it was so unusual I reported it to the chain of command and was asked to see the sergeant; he told me to withdraw the report. I refused and was then ordered to see the Captain who again demanded I withdraw the report. I apologized but felt unable to comply. He said that if I didn't he would have to refer the matter to the OSI. I declined. A guy in a suit came over to me and escorted me over to a dark blue or black coloured car. I was reluctant to get in and he grabbed my arms and pushed me towards the car. The driver said to me, **"Not another RFI incident on my watch'** I hadn't a clue what on earth he was on about. I was more or less then forced into the vehicle. I was driven a short distance and taken to a basement room where I was surprised to see a group of men, about 15 of them, already gathered there. I wondered if they had seen the same thing that I had and didn't understand what was going on. We were then shown some film covering the USAF history and it contained various references to aircraft. I was then interviewed by two men in green fatigues and hats. They asked me to sign a consent form and the next thing was one of them stuck a needle in my arm. I tried to object but I was terrified. I was advised that '**I could be harmed if I said anything about what I had seen.' The next thing that happened was waking up in my bed in the dormitory** three days later! I couldn't understand why nobody had reported me AWOL. This is the first time I have summoned up the courage to tell what happened to me; I genuinely believed that if I told anybody about this I would be harmed. I have never come to terms with what they did to me and don't understand why. Who were the other men that were in the same room? In a way I feel betrayed – just for making a report of something strange in the sky which was over an RAF Airbase, I have no regrets for doing just my duty.*" John rang Mark and suggested we all meet up when he came over to see me, perhaps half way in Maryland. Surprisingly; he failed to answer any further communication. John felt there is little doubt in his mind that he may have been genuine but like many other witnesses I met over the years, he obviously had second thoughts, was he warned off, or was this another piece of disinformation?

1985

Claims that General Gordon Williams received film of UFO?

In a telephone call made to me by Ray Boeche in April **1985**, during our discussion on the matter, I have no memory of ever having told Ray about an officer who drove Wing Commander Gordon Williams from the landing site to a waiting aircraft with a **motion picture of the UFO,** and that this was verified by me for the Senator James Exon. If a film had been taken I would have been the first to know…yes there were claims of airmen being in the forest and the more I learn the more I'm convinced there's a concerted behind-the-scenes effort to spread confusion and deception.

Others claim that Gordon Williams received something while in the cockpit of an A-10 bound for Germany. Mike Verrano claimed it **was film of the UFO**. I think it was Mel Zickler's efficiency report that was late and they wanted it to get into his file before the promotion board. I remember talk of that happening. This was well after the event in the forest. I could be wrong but I don't think so. The only related film it possibly could have been is Monroe Nevels' 35mm film. To have gotten it someone would

THE HALT PERSPECTIVE 2

Monroe Nevels with Charles Halt recently in Rendlesham Forest

have to have broken into his home and done a substitute. Not likely! More on Mr Nevels in due course, following an unexpected and very disappointing situation, involving scurrilous attacks on my integrity by him many years later. Oddly he never said any of this when we met in Rendlesham Forest many years ago!

John: I would like to include further citations awarded to Colonel Halt during this year showing the respect felt by his colleagues, towards him during his service.

THE HALT PERSPECTIVE 2

1986

Another guy that wrote to me asking specific questions about my role in what had taken place at Bentwaters AFB was Dr Richard C Niemtzow MD of 1111, Boston Road, Andrews AFB. I replied to him on the 16th of June 1986, telling him I was surprised by his letter, as I had thought the *'dust had finally settled on the Bentwaters incident'*. In fact to some degree, my life then had more or less returned to normal. I told him I wasn't aware of any further investigation conducted by any US Governmental agency. To my knowledge at that time, none of the participants experienced any medical effects afterwards (although one was released from the Air Force for a drug related problem). As far as any information that would directly relate to an injury or a medical field, I wasn't able to assist further. One point that puzzles me to this day was the apparent lack of interest by the US Air Force as well as the British Ministry of Defence in the incident. All I can say is something unexplained did occur and to this day, I really don't know what it was and therefore cant conclude anything, other than the fact our modern day history seems full of it!

Woodbridge Reporter – Entities were seen!

What a load of rubbish published by the *Woodbridge Reporter* claiming that entities were seen! Well words fail me. I presume their information was drawn from *Sky Crash* – which, as you all know, was based on disinformation – never mind utter fabrication by Larry Warren.

Another sighting brought to my attention involved two women from Birmingham England, who encountered something completely outside of everyday life, when after sighting a UFO, they sustained injuries involving **blistering on the skin and arms** – worse – **some of the hair had been removed**. How on earth can you apply any logic to incidents like this that fortunately only appears to happen to a small number of people rather than anything full scale?

Below is a photo of me and my wife taken in that year; as John knows, Yong Ho isn't keen on her photo being shown. But I'm sure she won't mind! (We hope).

Selected UFO report from

1987

British Police Officer witnesses, Flying Saucer hovering over farmer's field!

An unusual sighting was brought to my notice by John, from West Mercia Police officer Pat Rollason who he interviewed some years ago. Pat asked him not to divulge his name until he had passed away, which happened in 2010. It involved a saucer-shaped object seen hovering over a farmer's field followed by a burnt area found afterwards. Here are the details of what happened . . . as outstanding incidents like this shouldn't be forgotten.

THE HALT PERSPECTIVE 2

In May 1987, Pat was stationed at Bridgnorth Police Station, Shropshire, when he received a telephone call from Captain Robbie Evans, owner of the Wyken Estate who reported a strange red glow in the sky over Chempshill Coppice near Worfield – an area of mature woodland forming part of the Davenport estate.

Pat: *"As I was about to get into the police car, I was aware of a loud humming noise resonating in the air – like an electrical buzzing – but thought no more of it at the time. I made my way to high ground overlooking the area concerned, close to Rindleford – a tiny hamlet, near Worfield – and was shocked to see a **grey saucer-shaped object**, making a quiet humming noise similar to what I had heard when leaving the Police Station, estimated to be 100-200 feet across, with a dome on top, hovering over a field. Projecting from underneath the 'saucer'* **were three beams of orange light** *– diffused, rather than bright. I stood watching for a few minutes, feeling the hairs standing up on the back of my neck – then the humming noise increased in pitch to a droning noise. The next thing that happened was that it shot off at terrific speed and out of sight."*

The officer returned to the scene the next day and found a huge area of dried grass formed in a big circle, created not through the application of any heat but as if all the moisture had been sucked out of the ground only on the inside of the circle, in complete contrast to untouched plant growth on the outside.

He submitted a report to the MOD and it's a safe bet that the report was later destroyed or lost as John was unable to track it down. I'm sorry for his passing but feel that I should highlight incidents like this which need to be preserved and available for the public to read rather than hunting about in Government files trying to find reports which are no longer available. It's odd that reports like this are comparatively unknown yet most people know of the PC Alan Godfrey sighting in Todmorden, Yorkshire. I know Alan and have met him while over here lecturing. I hope he's well. These things are dangerous, look what 'they or it' did to a Staffordshire man's car, in September of the same year – wrecking the electrics to such a degree the car had to be scrapped later. More victims to the plague of sightings that took place in the same year was the now long forgotten incident which took place at the Devon coast when members of the fire service were staggered to see **a huge craft, 'diamond' in shape, made up of what appears to have been three lights, above their heads with objects moving in and out of it.** John tells me that during the interviews held with some of the men that they were not only bewildered but extremely frightened. Flashing blue lights on the emergency vehicles were switched off as it was thought they might have attracted more attention.

During a talk at the Smithsonian-affiliated National Atomic Testing Museum, Las Vegas, I accused the government of a UFO cover-up that involves a secret agency to deal with what *might* be extraterrestrial visitations. Telling the audience that there is an agency, a very close-held, compartmentalized agency that's been investigating this for years, and there's a very active role played by many of our intelligence agencies that probably don't even know the details of what happens once they collect the data and forward it. It's kind of scary, isn't it?

Selected UFO report from 1988

Another example of how these objects change peoples' lives forever

On the 6th of March Pauline Godbold (now Emerson) (aged 14) was attending to her horse, 'Charlie', at the family home (the old Railway Station house originally sited next to the railway lines removed after the A14 road was built) in Godmanchester, Cambridgeshire. *"At 7.20pm I heard a faint noise, which I took to be an aircraft approaching. When I glanced casually upwards, I saw a dense black square object, making a terrible noise as it passed overhead, followed by the most disgusting smell. It looked about one-and-a-half metres long and twenty millimetres thick. It was covered with perforations and had a small 'bump' set into the middle of the craft – like half a football, with something resembling antennas sticking out from each corner. I was very frightened and ran into the house, screaming. My mother and father, who hadn't seen the UFO, told me they had heard a loud vibrating noise, followed by the air being sucked out of the room, and then an awful smell."*

Enquiries made with RAF Alconbury, and other surrounding air bases, revealed that no aircraft or Exercises had been carried out over Godmanchester on that day. Ron West – an Investigator for the East Anglian Paranormal Research Association, visited Pauline at her home address, in April 1988, and found she was being treated for blurred eyesight – a condition described by her local doctor as *'enlarged pupils, somewhat sluggish'*. For her courage in reporting the matter to the local newspaper, who featured the story alongside headlines, such as, **'Smelly Spaceship'**, together with an illustration of an 'alien', piloting a teabag, Pauline was subjected to both verbal and physical abuse from the children at the school she attended. According to Mr. West, the matter was discussed with the Education Welfare Officer, who told him that Pauline was highly regarded at the school and was considered truthful. Unfortunately, because of the unwarranted attention she was receiving, Pauline would have to be moved to another school. As a result of a newspaper appeal by Mr. West, two other people came forward to report having seen a similar object but on different dates. We spoke to Pauline, now married and living in the Lincoln area. **She told us she still suffers from eyesight problems,** despite many visits to various opticians over the years her vision appears to actually improve with age, rather than deteriorate.

THE HALT PERSPECTIVE 2

Charles: This was a distressing incident which happened outside the family home at Godmanchester, a place that I know well as it's off the A14 road just into the adjoining county of Cambridgeshire which I used to drive along. Pauline was herself the butt of humour and forced to leave school, especially after the Press blew it out of all proportion with their article full of silliness and cartoon depicting the UFO seen. I understand she still suffers from eye problems to this present day. John invited her to come and see me at the 2019 Woodbridge Conference – but she expressed a great reluctance to talk about something which still upsets her now, all these years later, and declined to do so.

Other items of interest brought to my attention by John Hanson includes a letter sent to then Editor of *Flying Saucer Review,* Gordon Creighton, by a lady who lived near a Strategic Air Command base in California; long gone now. She had the courage to report something so out of this world! Then suffered afterwards from various physical ailments, which have a familiar ring to them judging from the other many reports involving similar complaints! This is serious and no answer is forthcoming. Despite our best efforts we remain not only baffled but unable to defend our citizens of this scourge. Another strange tale from the guy and his family living near the Thames, London; they actually filmed the object and contacted the local TV Station hoping that they might show some interest . . . guess what? They declined to have anything to do with him. Why? And on whose orders?

1988 – *Suffolk Advertiser* covers story on The East Anglian UFO & Paranormal Network

The *Suffolk Advertiser* carried a story on the front page of their newspaper on the 16th of September 1988: **'East Suffolk set for 'Close Encounters'.** They told of the work carried out by The East Anglian UFO & Paranormal Network, run by Ron West in Essex and Brenda Butler in Leiston, Suffolk, who had been

THE HALT PERSPECTIVE 2

investigating reports of a flurry of reports involving unusual craft seen in the sky over Ipswich and the Woodbridge area. Importantly and not surprisingly some of these UFOs had been plotted moving from Belgium over the sea, then to Kent all the way along the Essex coast to Suffolk. **Brenda also spoke of incidents she had investigated involving impressions left in the ground, after objects had been seen to land**. Brenda has been involved in researching and investigating all manner of strange UFO/paranormal reports since 1963. Calls for a public enquiry were made in December of this year, based on what exactly? The mind boggles with the failure to question the veracity of something that had whipped up the imagination, and was hardly based on fact!

1989

UFOs plotted on Radar heading towards East Anglia!

Charles: In November 1989, unidentified flying objects were tracked on radar moving over the East Anglian coast from the Belgium area, which was, by the way, the centre of media attention following the Belgium Air Force being scrambled after many witnesses described seeing a flying object which was flat, triangular in shape, with lights underneath, which I have commented on previously, taking into consideration the similarities between what was being reported in the 1950's. We weren't the only ones! A huge number of similarly described triangular objects were reported by residents from around the East Anglia area during the same period from the archives of the late UFO researcher, Ron West – some of which I've looked at personally. I can't say if there is any connection with what we saw, but logically I wouldn't be surprised if there was.

1990

John: At 1.20am **2nd January 1990**, Peter John Maddocks (21) of Woodbridge, Suffolk – an RAF serviceman – was walking home near Woodbridge, when: "*I noticed two cigar-shaped objects in the sky, heading in a North-South direction towards Essex. They were below a cloud bank and completely silent. A cigarette, at arm's length, would have covered them. Ten seconds later, they were gone from sight.*" At 1.30am, Anthony Weldon (49) was driving home with his wife, daughter, and her boyfriend, along the A12 between Chelmsford and Ingatestone, after having celebrated New Year's Eve, when they saw two objects, side by side, heading across the sky towards the direction of Brentwood, some 1,500ft up in the air. Five seconds later, they were lost from view. Others that saw something highly unusual on this date were George T. Brown (26) of Sir Francis Way, Brentwood, Essex. He was standing outside his girlfriend's house in Park Road with his girlfriend, Susan Watson (20), at 1.30am, when they noticed: "*...**two very large silver-grey in colour oval-shaped objects,** moving at speed across the sky. They were at a height of about 2,000ft, moving at 2,000mph. The ends of the objects were pointed and the fronts rounded. I last saw them heading towards the coast. Susan was so petrified, she ran indoors.*"

Three yellow 'lights' over Suffolk

Linda Shotbolt of Bury Road, Cockfield, Burry St Edmunds, was preparing the family tea, on the 2nd of March, when she was called outside by her husband, John, who told her about something strange in the sky: "*We stood and watched these **three yellow 'lights'** hovering above ground level over Cockfield Green. One was bigger than the rest; it looked like a triangle. The left one moved to the left, so did the right-hand one. The third one then took off across the sky, at speed.*" **(Source: Personal Interview)**

THE HALT PERSPECTIVE 2

Belgium fighter Aircraft scrambled

In a letter declassified by the MOD in February 2010 sent to the MOD by the Public relations officer at the Belgium Air Force, we learn that quote: *"Relating to your questions I can confirm that two F-16s have been scrambled on March 30, 1990, as a reaction to both visual and radar observations. The scramble was co-coordinated with, and authorized by, the Sector Commander of the NATO Air Defence System".*
(Source: Declassified Defence Documents, exact date not ascertained)

1991

On December 27th I wrote to Jacques Vallee

*"Dear Mr Vallee, I recently read your book **Revelations** and am extremely disappointed. I found your research of the 'Bentwaters' incident to be slim to nonexistent. It appears that you used the book **'Sky Crash'** and **'Out of the Blue'** as gospel. Both books, although I'm sure well intended, miss many important facts and are very misleading, especially the former. I can sincerely say I honestly tried to assist Dot Street and Brenda Butler, but to no avail. I have never been contacted by Jenny Randles so I can't comment on her. I do know they were all 'fed by numerous individuals' with their own motives. However, I agree with many parts of your book but am concerned if all your research was similar to the Bentwaters portion. I have never sought the limelight, nor have I hidden. The fact that you never contacted me or the other main participants causes me concern as to your motivation (every other researcher worth his salt has found me and discovered me reasonable within proper bounds). I believe the story should be told but without sensationalism. I can tell you with great certainty, Bentwaters was not an experiment. I am sorry, but it is not wise to put all the facts in this letter as I have no idea where it may end up. I can say this – I was on the inside of the organisation and can prove beyond a shadow of doubt that the US Air force was not conducting an 'experiment'. I can further guarantee you there was no US effort to cover up the incident – those that were involved just got tired of constant intrusions into their personal lives. If you'd like a small sample ask Dot Street and Brenda Butler about how they literally kidnapped my teenage son and plied him with drinks to learn more 'facts'. Yes I am aware we have some amazing capabilities. In fact I suspect one or more government agency has more than a passing interest in the 'unexplained', if so it's beyond normal classifications and something you and other outsiders will never be given access to. I look forward to meeting you and potential discussion."*

1994

The Colonel speaks at Leeds

Charles: Over the years I've been a fairy regular visitor to the United Kingdom. In 1994, I was over in the UK to record an interview with *London Weekend Television*. I found time from my busy schedule to deliver a lecture to an audience of UFO enthusiasts on the 31st of July 1994 at a hastily arranged venue at Leeds by Graham Birdsall of UFO magazine. Speaking publicly about my role on the nights in question left me feeling a touch uncomfortable, I didn't wish to appear as some kind of UFO expert, but merely a private citizen who had with some reluctance agreed to participate in a number of TV programs that dealt with the extraordinary incidents that had taken place at RAF Woodbridge. Interestingly Larry Warren, who was also scheduled to appear on *London Weekend* TV, later claimed in an interview published in *UFO Magazine* **that he had been banned.**

THE HALT PERSPECTIVE 2

This is what he had to say: *"I could have got very angry about that but I do feel perturbed because I feel that Mr. Halt believes that he has to minimize the importance of the events. The long and short of it is, still that he is taking the 'pro' side. He is on the right side and so I have told everybody to support him! His point of view is that I couldn't have been working at Bentwaters when I said that I was. He says that the Security Police came over to the Bases and just sat round for ten weeks being put on 'flight' which is totally ridiculous. Air Force people would just laugh at that! Its two weeks training, and then just OJT. I have all the documentation putting me on duty that night and he knows that! On the other side he comes out and says that I and others were meddled with. He is an enigma in himself. I wish him well. This isn't personal, but like I said, he's doing his job and I'm doing mine. We are both working towards the same end."*

Larry Warren has the temerity to question my truthfulness, maybe the best line of defence is to go on the offensive and that guy sure has done that for many years until he was found out in so many ways, looking back now in 2020, it's incredible to believe that this nonsense went on for so many years. Probably because so many people wanted to believe that this version of events actually took place. Matters which I have no understanding about but clearly what Warren reported has now been shown to be fabrication.

1995

Charles: Following on from what appeared to be anger management issues, I received a letter in June of this year (1995) from Larry Warren's legal agent in the States, warning me against making false statements. In July of that year he wrote to the BUFORA in England, a copy of which is attached.

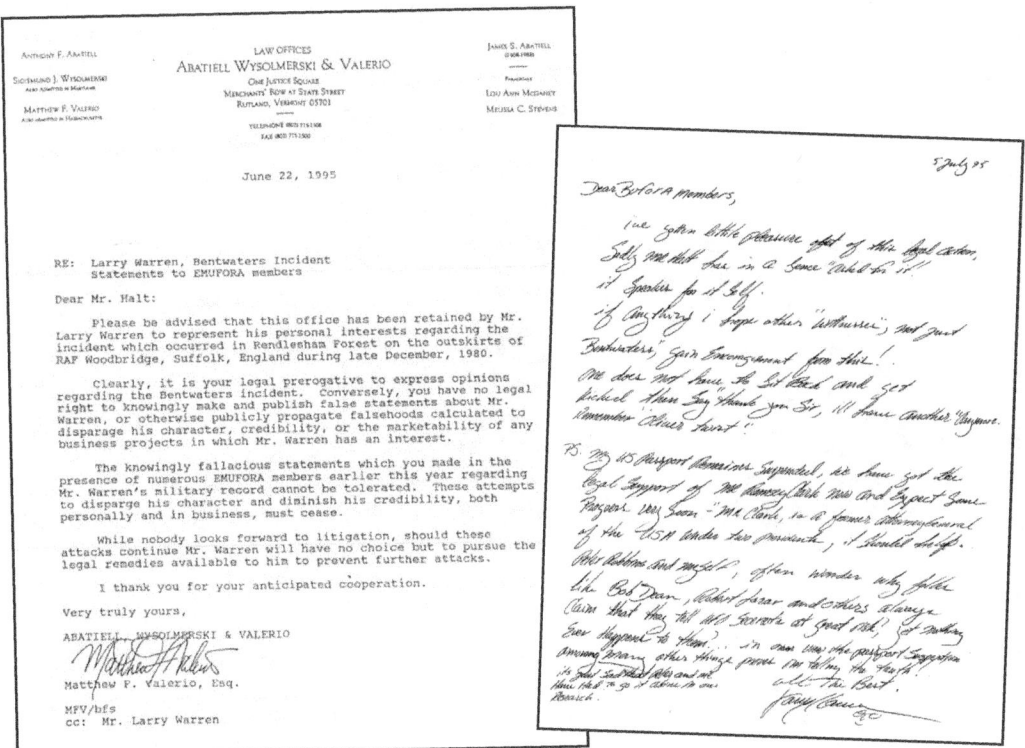

THE HALT PERSPECTIVE 2

John: A special year for me, as the reader can see....

John Hanson: keeping an eye on time travellers dropping in on the Midlands.

A young woman in her 20s was driving home from work to Netherton shortly before midnight early in July.

Helen Smith had made the journey dozens of times before and knew the route so well she could almost have driven it blindfold.

Along the dual carriageway to Bromsgrove, then north-west towards Hagley, Stourbridge and the glittering Black Country skyline.

But the details of this particular journey are indelibly etched on her memory. During it, she witnessed something she had never seen before in her life - and has never seen since.

Diamond shaped object spinning round and round

Helen was approaching Clent when blue lights flashing above the hills drew her eye. To her astonishment, she saw a strange, black diamond-shaped object spinning round and round in the sky.

Never letting it out of sight she sped back to Netherton where she climbed with her father up a nearby church tower to get a better look.

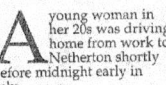

At first he was incredulous but his scepticism swiftly evaporated when he, too, spotted the craft hovering overhead.

Even after studying it he was unable to identify the object before it disappeared into the darkness as suddenly as it had appeared.

Following stories in local newspapers three other witnesses confirmed they had also seen the object. No logical explanation for it has ever been found.

In January, a disc-shaped object with red pulsing lights was seen in the sky above Stirchley. It vanished and reappeared in Cumbria only minutes afterwards.

And on another night in May this year a woman reported seeing a pulsating scallop-shaped craft in the sky above Longbridge.

Visible for about ten minutes, it was seen by someone else at Crabbs Cross, Redditch.

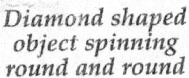

Until recently, these and many other similar unexplained incidents might have been put down to overactive imagination or a few too many pints at the local.

People have always been fascinated by outer space. The idea of little green men visiting Earth in spaceships is nothing new.

From H G Wells' War of the Worlds to Dr Who, 1001: A space Odyssey, Star Trek, E.T. and more recent sci-fi box office hits such as ... evidence shows

preoccupation with time travel is eternal.

Understandably, given the derision with which many such claims have been greeted in the past, those who see UFO's tend to

Retired police officer 'on another planet' with UFO's!

be reticent about going public.

But modern technological advances have made "flying saucers" seem less of a fantasy, more a genuine possibility.

Retired West Midlands Police officer John Hanson treats all reports of sightings seriously. He keeps an open mind about UFO's, neither believing nor disbelieving in them.

In his role as Worcestershire agent for Quest International, he is setting out to build a comprehensive record of UFO sightings. It will help establish whether there really is life on other planets.

Quest International is an independent organisation which

John's son Keith, graphically illustrates each reported sighting in the Worcestershire area. As you can see from this illustration and the one opposite, shapes vary quite considerably.

gathers and collates information about unexplained phenomena.

Father-of-three John, aged 49, is the point of contact for anyone who sees or wants to discuss a sighting which cannot be explained logically.

By collecting all the details at his Alvechurch home, studying and comparing them with other reported sightings, he aims to compile a vast library of information.

He also links up with other Quest agents in Worcester and Shrewsbury to create a wider picture of possible alien activity.

"I am not a science fiction fan, I have both feet on the ground. But I finally believe there is a need for investigation of UFO sightings," says John.

"Too often, people have no chance to discuss what they have seen for fear of ridicule.

"They cannot talk about it, yet some stay traumatised for years. It has an impact on their lives.

"You've got to look at things scientifically. About 50 per cent of sightings can be explained.

"But there are others which don't resemble terrestrial craft. No one ever comes forward to say this is one of their new research aircraft, or that is one of their advertising balloons.

"Such craft conform to certain patterns. They never make any noise.

All move at a colossal speed

"All move at colossal speed and change their shape. Witnesses agree about this and there's no reason to dispute what they say.

"One man was with about 15 others on a pub car park in Yardley when he saw a disc-shaped craft. It happened in the 1970s and he still has nightmares about it today."

John's curiosity about UFO's was awakened by two police colleagues who personally experienced unexplained sightings. He says he has never seen anything himself.

Thorough investigation of circumstances

"I read about Quest International in a science journal. It was founded by an ex-policeman 15 years ago. Its headquarters are in Yorkshire.

"The idea is to communicate information via a nationwide network. We carry out a thorough investigation of circumstances surrounding a sighting and the object." John showed me a short clip from an amateur video of the UFO filmed near Longbridge. It showed a bright flashing light which darted around the screen, apparently following no direct flight path.

THE HALT PERSPECTIVE 2

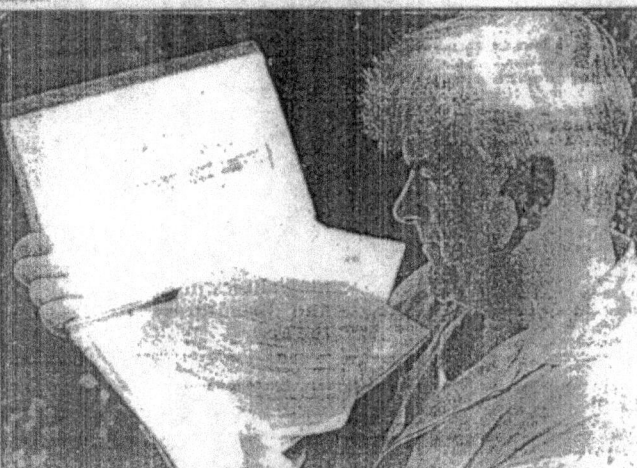

REDDITCH ADVERTISER - 7 NOV 1995

John is reaching for the stars

by PAT GRIFFITHS

STUDENTS enrolling for evening classes at Redditch NEW College may have noticed an unusual subject on the timetable.

For retired West Midlands policeman John Hanson is launching a series of lectures on unidentified flying objects.

John is the Worcestershire agent for Quest International, an organisation set up to monitor sightings of unexplained phenomena in the sky.

Now he plans to share some of the information he has gathered with students.

Among recent case histories he will be relating is that of a young woman who was driving to Netherton shortly before midnight last July.

Blue lights

Sarah Kelly drove along the dual carriageway to Bromsgrove, then north west towards Hagley, Stourbridge and the Black Country.

She claims she was approaching Clent when blue lights flashing above the hills drew her eye. To her astonishment, she saw a black diamond-shaped object spinning round in the sky.

She sped back to Netherton where she climbed with her father up a nearby church tower to get a better look. His scepticism evaporated when he, too, spotted the craft hovering overhead.

Three other witnesses confirmed they had also seen the object.

In May a woman reported a pulsating scallop-shaped craft in the sky over Longbridge.

Visible for about ten minutes, it was seen at Crabbs Cross, Redditch.

And on a night in January, a disc-shaped object with red pulsing lights was seen in the sky above Stirchley. It vanished and re-appeared in Cumbria minutes later.

John, aged 49, treats all reports of sightings as genuine. He keeps an open mind about UFOs.

He is setting out to build a comprehensive record of UFO sightings. By collecting all the details at his home near Barnt Green, studying and comparing them with other reported sightings, he aims to compile a vast library of information.

He also links up with other Quest agents in Worcester and Shrewsbury. He said: "Too often, people have no chance to discuss what they have seen for fear of ridicule.

"One man was with about 15 others on a pub car park in Yardley when he saw a disc-shaped craft. It happened in the 1970s and he still has nightmares about it today."

● UFO spotters can talk to John on 0121 447 7091.

● *John holds an official report form for UFO sightings (c27343).*

Further sightings of UFOs over Rendlesham, Suffolk area!

Mike Hall was out walking his dog near the runway at RAF Woodbridge on the 31st December 1995 at 10.45pm when he saw a Triangular-shaped object hovering over the airbase.

Paul Pittock was driving from Woodbridge to Melton, Suffolk, one evening in January 1995, when he saw a bright light hovering in the sky above the now closed RAF Woodbridge/Bentwaters Air base. Curious he stopped the car by the side of the road and watched with surprise as the 'light' began to move from side to side in the sky. Rushing home he picked up his telescopic sight and accompanied by neighbour Richard Warnock drove back to the airbase just in time to see whatever it was drop down towards the flight line and disappear. *"As we stood by the entrance gate to the Base, wondering what was going on, over thirty military vehicles drove up; they included a military ambulance and a larger white vehicle covered in aerials, after unlocking the gate drive then drove onto the Bentwater's Airbase, closed some 16 months ago. With tyres screaming and lights flashing the vehicles drove around the air base pointing searchlights into the sky as if looking for something; there were even helicopters hovering overhead. We saw an orange red glow emanating from the flight line, then a glowing **triangular-shaped object appeared**. It had a distinct outline and could be seen clearing the slope. It stayed for a while and then left."* (**Source: Personal Interview**)

1996

Vehicular Unidentifiable Flying Objects – Celebrating the work of Mr T. R. Dutton. RIP

John: In October 1996, *Contact International* conference opened its door to the public. Its speakers included, Nick Pope, Roy Lake, Brian James, Mathew Williams, and Terrence Roy Dutton. Roy had spent 37 years in the aerospace industry, including involvement in the Britain's short lived space programme. He retired from the Future Projects Department of British Aerospace PLC, Manchester in 1991. His interest in the UFO enigma was triggered by sightings from the south Manchester area in 1967, when he began 29 years of technical research in into the nature of the phenomenon.

Rendlesham Forest, Suffolk

Roy: *"Throughout the course of more than 40 years research, much attention has been given by the media and authors, to the probability of an official cover up. The drip feed release of Ministry of Defence UFO files in Britain and the public disclosures of ex-US Military personnel, now released from security restrictions over there, have refuelled the clamour for official announcements. This book [UFOs in Reality – Programmed Aerospace monitors of our species T.R Dutton, 2010] provides good reason for official cover ups and denials. There is little room for doubt that Defence and intelligence agencies throughout the world will have carried out work similar to mine and concluded in a similar way – that human activity **is being constantly monitored by very advanced technology, originating from somewhere out there in space.**"*

John: Some years ago I realised that many UFO sightings occurred close to ancient sites. Initially the very idea seemed incongruous, to say the least, in a society where to suggest even such a thing would attract harsh comments from those who would reject the idea out of hand. After all, what on earth could these

THE HALT PERSPECTIVE 2

'machines' from the perceived future, with their advanced technology, have to do with ancient sites? The idea seemed preposterous! The more I researched into this, the more I realised **there was an association** between such locations and sightings of UFOs. Why should they come from the future – how about from the past? If so, what is the purpose of these continuing incursions into our airspace? Roy was able to prove to his satisfaction that nearly 80% of sightings took place near historical sites. 50% had human links and 67% took place near major roads (many of which, no doubt had associations with original Roman roads). He drew up charts for expected UFO arrival times defining 'delivery tracks' and 'retrieval tracks' he was able to show that the UFO activity around Warminster during the mid 60's correlated well, and that the Valentich aircraft disappearance off the south coast of Australia in 1978 was also explained by the timing of the UFO at that point. Further events that fitted into the 'Dutton model' of analysis and evaluation, which also took in the relationships of the sun, planets and fixed stars – he was able to confirm from the graphs prepared that this correlation of behaviours also fitted the Captain Mantle crash of 1948, the **Rendlesham Forest Incident**, and a recent sighting that took place in 1995 when a Triangular UFO was reported by Boeing 737 pilots at Manchester Airport. For years I pored over maps of the Suffolk area attempting to locate the presence of ancient sites in Rendlesham Forest and found evidence of a tumulus and what appeared to have been the remains of a mound like Silbury Hill in Wiltshire, not forgetting the close locality of Butley Abbey. In 2018 we learnt of the death of Terence Roy Dutton, a pleasant man whom we had met on a few occasions over the years. He published a book '**Terence Roy Dutton, and his hypothesis [***UFOs in Reality – Programmed Aerospace monitors of our species***'.]**

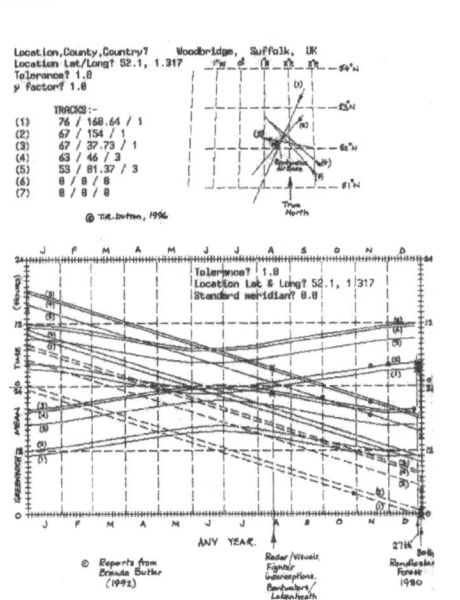

1997

Letter sent to the Prime Minister and MPs

We have included a newspaper article published in June 1997, from *The People* that relates to former Corporal Larry Warren, who describes seeing, three non human beings, one foot off the ground …ghost white faces, dressed arms no legs…baloney…what sort of description is this?

THE HALT PERSPECTIVE 2

On the 27th of June 1997, Ron West, head of the Essex UFO Society wrote to Kerry Philpott at the MOD in London advising her he had written a letter to the following MPs: **Prime Minister Tony Blair, William Hague MP, Paddy Ashdown MP, Ieuan Wyn Jones MP, Ivan Henderson** [who had previously put a question to the House on the subject of UFOs] and **George Robertson MP**, Minister of Defence. This letter included a typed-up copy of my memo plus, a typed two-page statement containing a brief account of what Larry Warren had witnessed, rather than the full version of events published in *Left At East Gate* in 1997. Ron had met with Larry at Ipswich during the same year after having written to him hoping to see him later at the Sheffield Conference. One wonders *now* how Ron West, a veteran of UFO research and others could have been so gullible to believe without any evidence the fantastic story from Warren . . . but people did and continued to accept it as genuine for many years to come, which illustrates the dangers of blandly accepting wild stories that fit into one's own belief system! One such example and it's an important one was the information supplied by Airman Steve Roberts (John 'Davey' Engals) who was not out in the forest during December 1980, but worked in the offices with Jim Penniston. 'Steve' picked up the story from him and others, and like some viral infection disseminated it accordingly. Jim will confirm that, at least we agree on something!

Ron West writes to Kerry Philpott at the MOD in London

John: On the 12th of September 1997, Ron West again wrote to Kerry Philpott at the MOD in London with regard to his previous letter sent to her on the **28th of August 1997.**

He told her he was "*Extremely vexed that you have excluded a response to enquiries made regarding the documents of: 1. Colonel Halt USAF, documents to the RAF/CC Unexplained lights. 2.**The document, 'UK Eyes 'B'. 3. The statement by USAF security policeman, Larry Warren. 4. No answer to any of the nine questions that I asked you at the end of my letter which I state again, in case that you have misplaced my original letter of the 27th July 1997. With regard to your reply, paragraph 4, I should be grateful if you would forward me a* *copy of the substantiated evidence that was gathered as well as a copy of the original assessment. I now list the questions that I originally asked you.*

1 - Could I please have your comments re the two printed documents? **A** - Col Halt's letter to the RAF/CC. **B** - MOD letter, '**UK eyes only**' and **C** - the statement by the USAF Patrolman.

2 - **Now that the book** *Left At East Gate* **has been published and members of the USAF have admitted that an incident (UFO) took place in Rendlesham Forest.**

3 - I think it is about time that the truth about the incident in Rendlesham Forest was released.

4 - I feel that is about time the British Government admitted that UFOs do exist and that they are visiting the British Isles?

5 - **Will you also admit that there is a vast underground base beneath RAF Bentwaters?**

6 - Why do the MOD still state that they have no documents re the Rendlesham Forest incident, when the Freedom of Information Act in the USA has produced the Halt Document?

7 - What is the British Government doing about the Flying Triangle that is now penetrating our skies, visiting military Bases, Nuclear Power Stations and other nuclear sites?

8 - Will the MOD admit that the **Flying Triangle** is not of Earth origin?

9 - Can you expand upon the rumours about the **PHOENIX AGREEMENT?**

This was a document endorsed on MOD notepaper purportedly submitted by the OSI following their investigation into the incident mentioning entities one and a half meters tall wearing nylon coated pressure suits but no helmets claw like hands with three digits and opposable thumbs – Landed deliberately as part of a series of visits to SAC bases in USA and Europe... This document is obviously faked, to either raise interest on the event or another example of disinformation.

On the 20th of September 1997 Deborah Ailes assistant Private Secretary to Tony Blair wrote to MP Martin Cave thanking him on behalf of the PM for the letter of the 20th of August 1997, '*regretting that the Prime Minister has not yet had the opportunity to read Left At East Gate."*

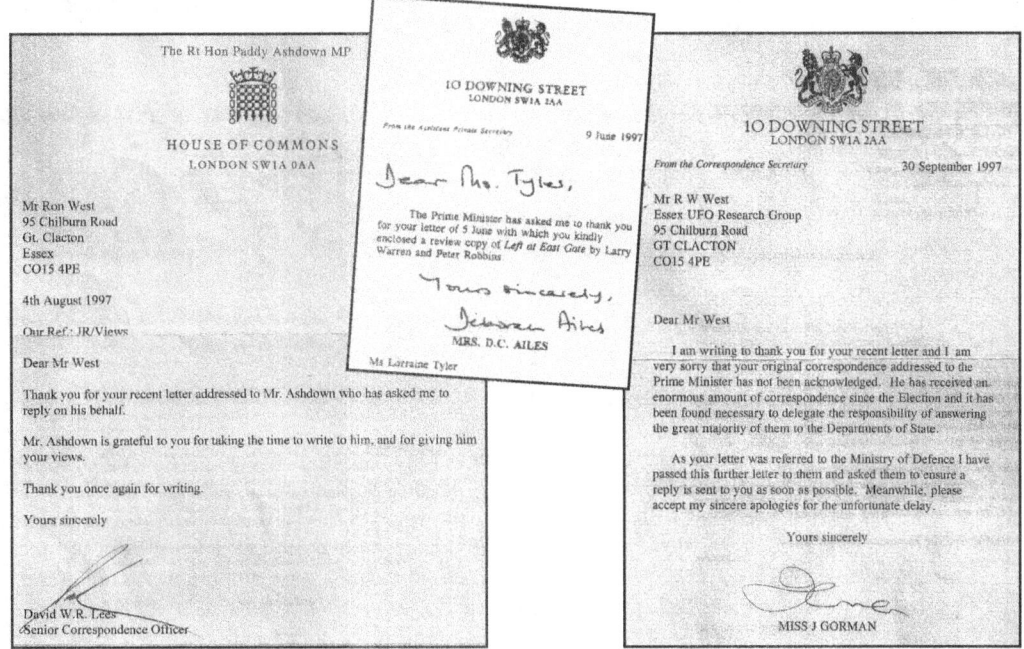

THE HALT PERSPECTIVE 2

Lord Peter Hill-Norton-Asks Questions in the House of Lords

John: The Lord Peter Hill-Norton (and his son) who I had the pleasure of corresponding with some years ago was also taken in by the Larry Warren story. On the **28th of October 1997** he asked Lord Gilbert the then Secretary for Defence a series of questions in an open session of the House of Lords some of which had been taken directly from the *Left At East Gate* book. Lord Gilbert's answers were of course non committal. On the same day America's Tabloid *the National Enquirer* published a feature article entitled '**US Airman Shocking Book Blows Lid off INTERNATIONAL COVER UP'** brought news of the incident to several million readers that week.

UFO/Aircraft Encounters File – 852 reports!

Charles: John Hanson brought my attention to a document endorsed (**Not for Sale**) that had been sent to him which caught my attention. *UFO/AIRCRAFT ENCOUNTERS FILE* 'to Major Donald Keyhoe and Dr James Macdonald' published by *Dominque* in February 1997 with acknowledgements to the following personnel – Jan Aldrich and his Project 1947, Barry Greenwood, Loren Gross, Dr Richard Haines, Richard Hall, Larry Hath (*U* UFO Database, Joel Mesnard (Lumieries Dans La Nuit), Perry Petrakis (SOS OVNI/Phenomena and Jean –Jacques Velasco, Sepra)

This is a catalogue of sightings involving reports from pilots which numbers 852 reports! It includes destinations from France, Australia, USA, Germany, and Tokyo. It's frightening in its implications or at least it should be. Most people believe that the first UFO sighting report was from Kenneth Arnold on the 24th of June 1947. Not so – in fact sightings of similar objects can be tracked five years before this, beginning with reports of orange discs, black cigar-shaped objects, 'V'-shaped formations and pulsating lights to name just a few. This sort of information you won't find in Wikipedia! It's staggering that nearly a thousand reports from pilots were made available and this catalogue was only up to 1997, this list has increased substantially to the current date. So what the hell is going on? How anyone can remain sceptical is beyond me!

Fortunately the bastion of British newspapers, ***The Times*** also made a reference to the incident! Words fail us!

1998

MOD and 'the little green men'!

At 10.30pm, **15th January 1998**, an object – described as being "*a long, dark object, with two bright lights at either end and several red ones in the middle*" – was sighted in the sky, between Badingham and Laxfield, in Suffolk. The matter was brought to the attention of the Station Staff Officer Lt. Col. (sec 40) at Wattisham Airfield, as a complaint of a low flying aircraft, who wrote to the couple about the incident, in which he advised them: "*None of the helicopters from the base were out that night, but as the sighting was made outside their airspace for which they had any responsibility, we would not have been aware of any aircraft flying between Laxfield and Badingham*". Another document, endorsed '*Flying complaints*

progress report', submitted to the MOD in respect of enquiries carried out into the allegation, contains the following written note: *"To the best of our knowledge, this is not any aircraft from Wattisham – possibly a Lakenheath M3, or maybe a Puma from Odiham; other than this, **'the little green men have it'**."*
(Source: MOD declassified documents, February 2010 defe-24-1990)

My E-mail to Brenda Butler, 25th of September

Charles: *Your wild experiences really sound like something is heating up at East Gate. It's hard enough to believe what happened to us back in 1980, let alone what's going on now. I would suggest you try hard to establish a dialogue with whatever you have come in contact with. I would be most interested in hearing the results. If you do establish a dialogue and I can help, I am willing. When I warned you to be careful, I was not talking about something beyond us. My concern was that an agency with secretive powers might do something. You be the judge of that. I do know that several of the airmen were hypnotized, drugged, and then threatened. I have to assume now that you realise, when I gave up on your original* Sky Crash *trio, I have been telling the truth. Keep in touch and be careful.*

Most people still reject out of hand that such things (UFOs) could exist in a 21st Century world of technology where fairy stories and sightings of unidentified flying objects *should* have no place. I have never been officially approached, although people from Kirtland and various sundry agencies have invited me to lunch that had an interest in this subject and things, and I played games with them, like they did with me. I think the only thing that has kept me out of, out of the middle of it, so to speak, is that I have some very, very high contacts, including probably the most senior Senator in Washington, and, uh, my last position as the Director of Inspections, Director for the DOD IG, where I had total inspection oversight for the whole Department of Defence, and had some very good contacts there. It's probably protected me, but some of the other people have been bothered and meddled with and, unfortunately, it's caused a lot of personal problems for them.

Sadly, Ron West passed away this year (1998). This photograph of a wreath laid epitomises the passion that he felt about the UFO subject.

2000

Newspaper coverages for this year included *Evening Star* **14th of March 'New Twist in UFO Mystery'** with a reference to Orford Ness.

THE HALT PERSPECTIVE 2

UFO Film taken of UFO over Woodbridge area 27th December

John: A group of us – including Brenda Butler, Jack Solomon (then head of the Norwich UFO Group), and members of the Essex UFO Branch (not forgetting the dog, Mason) – were stood talking on an elevated section of the forest, near to the end of track 10, opposite to the field nominated by Larry Warren (who was himself in the forest that night) as being the one where he saw the UFO land, 20 years ago. A yellow 'light' was seen just above the horizon, towards the direction of Orford Ness Lighthouse. This was followed by a number of others which appeared in the sky, forming a horizontal line, approximately four to five miles away, apparently over the coast or out at sea. We do not maintain that this was any 'alien craft' – all we can say is that we have never seen any strange 'light' like this over the forest before, at this particular location. Fortunately, we managed to video the effect by using a Sony Handycam video camera; with night light 72x digital zoom.

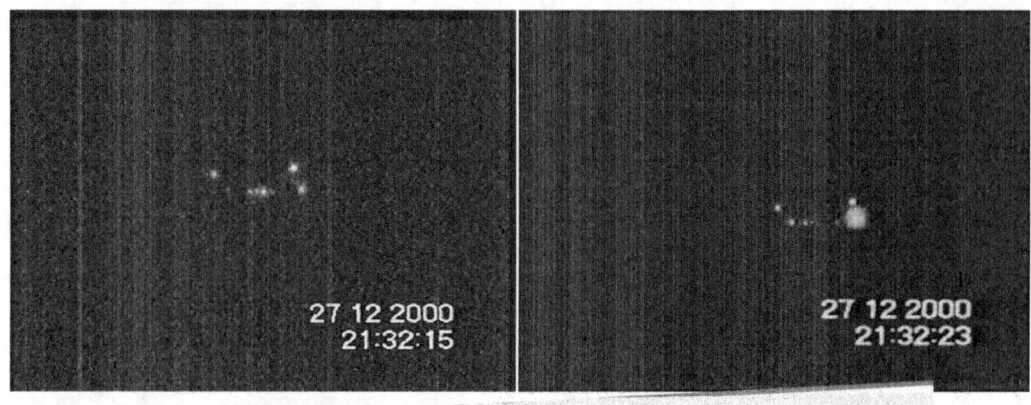

THE HALT PERSPECTIVE 2

The following day we were interviewed by the local TV Station, *Look East*, and *Suffolk Advertiser*, but it was not until many months later, that we discovered we were not the only ones to have witnessed something unusual occurring in the forest, at that time, during that evening – one of whom was Mark Doulton and members of the Southend UFO Group.

Mark Doulton: "We arrived in the forest at about 8pm, and were immediately struck by the intense cold (some 15 degrees below freezing). We walked down track 12 but, finding nobody about, decided to look down track 10. Following consultation with Chris Martin, who was in our group and had been successful in capturing UFOs previously on film, we decided to meditate as part of an experiment. Much to our surprise, some 20 minutes later, we were rewarded by the sight of a strange flashing in the sky above our heads. This 'flashing', whatever it was, had certainly not been visible before – apart from this, the sky was relatively clear. We watched this strange 'flashing' for some minutes, before deciding to move to track 12, in order to meet up with other groups. We noticed the 'flashing' seemed to be concentrated in one area of the sky only. Not being experts on weather phenomena, we cannot say what this was, but having been to many countries and experienced severe storms I have to say this was nothing like what we saw that night."

Other witnesses. Following the publicity, people reported having seen strange lights over Woo Way, Orford, at about 8pm, along with a report of an orange 'ball of light' seen hovering over the sea, at 10.45pm, accompanied by the arrival of a helicopter – which appeared to be looking for something. Whether it was a UFO could only be speculation.

Butley Abbey – is there a connection?

The images are interesting and show, if nothing else, that this was no refuelling aircraft – what an amazing coincidence that it was filmed on the 27th December 2000. There were many witnesses to this object's appearance over the same direction where we saw the UFO now under 40 years ago, looking eastwards towards the coast. People have wondered if there was any connection between the UFO activity and Butley Abby which lies in a short distance away, understanding the alleged association between UFOs and ancient sites. If you look at a Google Map you will see where it is. Now if you project an imaginary line along Church road, which converges onto the Abby – westwards it lines up with the East Gate track. Along this line about halfway along Google endorses the following information, 'Rendlesham Forest UFO landing'. A look at a Victorian map of the location, shows the existence of a road/track way which runs from Butley Abby to Folly Farm, then a large area of farmland. After the airfield was constructed, much of that farm land was lost. All that remains is Folly House, situated next, to the runway lights. Brenda told John that when Butley Abby was a Bed and Breakfast, they charged over £200 for people to stay in the ghost room. In the 1800s, when the 14th century gatehouse of Butley Priory was being used as a vicarage, one of the rooms was kept constantly sealed and known as the 'Ghost Room'. The phantom was thought to be the spirit of Robert Brommer (or Browner), prior of Butley in the early 16th century.

Book: *'UFOs That Never Were'*

During this year The Suffolk based newspaper, *The Evening Star* carried an article about Jenny Randles new book, '**UFOs That Never Were**' in which she stated, "This case has become such a confusing mess of claim and counter claim, sifting fact from fiction has long dogged this case." She concluded that no unearthly craft was seen in the forest, and advances the theory that there is a connection between UFO sightings and the nearby Orford Ness secret military site. Interestingly she mentions about the discovery that a "US scientist who worked on Cobra Mist dropped a sheaf of secret documents by accident while leaving Heathrow Airport. These discussed the location of a new experiment to be named 'COLD WITNESS'. Orford Ness was cited along with the involvement of the NSA, physicists and MOD scientists in strict secrecy. Jenny tells the readers that Colonel Halt told her *'That there was secret research on the 'Ness' and that sometimes his men were asked to clear up after some sort of incident. They were not allowed to discuss the incident.'* She believes that a covert experiment occurred there after Christmas 1980 which created glows in the atmosphere as a side effect of the energy beam. (Colonel Halt told me the same but could not comment anymore because of the restrictions place on him. However he was adamant that what he saw was no experiment.) He is also suspicious of any 'accidental dropping' of top secret documents; like me he wonders if this was deliberate!

2001

Lord Hill Norton asks questions in Parliament!

On the **25th of January 2001** Lord Peter Hill-Norton asked Her Majesty's Government: – Whether they were aware of any involvement by Special Branch personnel in the investigation of the 1980 Rendlesham Forest incident.

Reply: Baroness Vernham Dean:- Special Branch may have been aware of the incident but would not have shown any interest, unless there was evidence of a potential threat to national security. No such interest appears to have been shown.

Lord Hill-Norton asked Her Majesty's Government:- Whether personnel from Porton Down visited Rendlesham Forest or the area surrounding RAF Walton (presume this should be RAF Waton) in December 1980 or January 1981; and whether they are aware of any tests carried out in either of those two areas aimed at assessing any nuclear, biological or chemical hazard.

Reply: Baroness Symons of Vernham Dean:- The staff at the Defence Evaluation and Research Agency (DERA) Chemical and Biological Defence (CBD) laboratories at Porton Down have made a thorough search of their archives and have found no record of any such visits.

Lord Hill-Norton asked Her Majesty's Government:- Whether they are aware of any uncorrelated targets tracked on radar in November or December 1980; and whether they will give details of any such incidents.

Reply: Baroness Symons of Vernham Dean:- Records dating from 1980 no longer exists. Paper records are retained for a period of three years before being destroyed. Recordings of radar data are retained for a period of thirty days prior to re-use of the recording medium.

Lord Hill-Norton, asked Her Majesty's Government:- What is the highest classification that has been applied to any Ministry of Defence document concerning Unidentified Flying Objects.

Reply: Baroness Symons of Vernham Dean:- A limited search through available files has identified a number of documents graded Secret. The overall classification of the documents was not dictated by details of specific sightings of UFOs.

Lord Hill-Norton asked Her Majesty's Government:- Whether they will detail the underground facilities at the former RAF Bentwaters installation; and what is the purpose of these facilities.

Reply: The Minister of State, Baroness Symons of Vernham Dean:- There are no underground facilities at the former RAF Bentwaters.

Lord Hill-Norton asked Her Majesty's Government:- Whether they are aware of any involvement in the 1980 Rendlesham Forest incident by either Ministry of Defence Policy or personnel from the Suffolk Constabulary.

Reply: Baroness Symons of Vernham Dean:- The Minister of Defence is not aware of any involvement by the Ministry of Defence Police in the alleged incident. The Ministry of Defence's knowledge of involvement by the Suffolk Police is limited to a letter dated 28 July 1999 from the Suffolk Constabulary to Georgina Bruni that is contained in the recent book.

Lord Hill-Norton asked Her Majesty's Government:- Whether they are aware of any investigation of the 1980 Rendlesham Forest incident carried out by the United States Air force, the Air Force Office of Special Investigations or any other United States agency.

Reply: Baroness Symons of Vernham Dean:- The Ministry of Defence's knowledge of an investigation by the US authorities into the alleged incident in Rendlesham Forest in 1980 is limited to the information contained in the memorandum sent by Lt Col Halt USAF, Deputy Base Commander at RAF Woodbridge, to the RAF Liaison Officer at RAF Bentwaters on 13th January 1981.

Lord Hill-Norton asked Her Majesty's Government:- Whether, in the light of the new information contained in Georgina Bruni's book 'You Can't Tell The People', they will now launch an investigation into the Rendlesham Forest incident and the response to this incident by the United States Air Force and the Ministry of Defence.

Reply: Baroness Symons of Vernham Dean:- No additional information has come to light over the last 20 years to call into question the original judgment by the Ministry of Defence that nothing of defence significance occurred in the location of Rendlesham Forest in 1980. Accordingly there is no reason to hold an investigation now.

Lord Hill-Norton asked Her Majesty's Government:- Whether they have made any approach to, or received any approach from, any United States government or military agency concerning Georgina Bruni's book 'You Can't Tell The People'; and, if so, whether they will give details of any such approach.

Reply: Baroness Symons of Vernham Dean:- As a matter of courtesy, the Ministry of Defence informed Headquarters 3rd Air Force at RAF Mildenhall about the book. The US authorities have not subsequently approached the Ministry of Defence on the issue.

Lord Hill-Norton now asked Her Majesty's Government:- Whether they now agree with the analysis of the basic facts of the Rendlesham Forest/RAF Bentwaters incident in the fourth paragraph of Lord Hill-Norton's letter to Lord Gilbert of 22nd October 1997, reported on page 429 of Georgina Bruni's book 'You Can't Tell The People'; or, if not, in what respect they disagree.

Reply: Baroness Symons of Vernham Dean:- The Ministry of Defence's position regarding this alleged sighting remains as it did at the time of Lord Gilbert's reply to the noble Lord's letter of 22nd October 1997. From surviving departmental records, we remain satisfied that nothing of defence significance occurred on the nights in question.

Numerous Newspaper coverage – following the 20th year anniversary

Eastern Daily Press – 20th August 2001: Secret report on UFO opened MOD files reveal UFO military enquiry into East Anglian sighting, etc…

The *Daily Star* in their edition of the 30th August 2001 carried a story titled **'DON'T TELL ANYONE BUT THE ALIENS HAVE LANDED'** – in this article accompanied by drawings of galactic spacecraft and lovable. ET, Dr David Clarke claimed he had discovered five top secret documents which could prove that Aliens had landed on English soil, but had been blocked in his attempts to get them published by worried Defence top brass!

Other newspaper accounts relating to the same incident were **East Anglian Daily Times** 5.9.2001 **'Probe urged over MOD Memo on UFO mystery'** bullet points' included: reference to Georgina Bruni and her new book, and mystery object seen near East Gate, etc…

Meeting Georgina Bruni – a treasured conversation © David Price

David Price: *"I first met Georgina at a B.U.F.O.R.A. conference in Hampton Court in 2001 at her book launch of 'You Can't Tell The People'. She was very nice, polite and knew her subject. We became friends and kept in touch until we met again in Leeds at the U.F.O. Conference a further three times over the years up until her death which I still find very sad."* The photos taken by him of Georgina Bruni who we met in 2001 are published for the first time and are much appreciated.

David: *"I met Georgina twice in Rendlesham Forest Suffolk some years back and treasured the conversation held with her about UFOs while accompanied by Brenda Butler."*

Our condolences to the family of Georgina Bruni (who passed away in 2008).

John Hanson: I had the pleasure of meeting and sharing a glass of wine with Georgina at the *Cherry Tree* public House – during a walk around Rendlesham Forest chatting with her and Brenda Butler on two occasions. She made a brief reference to me in her book *'You Can't Tell The People.'* Georgina told me **she had some very traumatic experiences with UFO interactions going back many years.** I felt it wasn't right to intrude by

THE HALT PERSPECTIVE 2

GEORGINA BRUNI
PO BOX 697, CHELSEA
LONDON SW3 2BL
E-mail: georgina@easynet.co.uk

26 August 2001

David Price
37 Gun Lane
Knebworth
Herts SG3 6BJ

Dear David

I must apologise for the delay in sending this reply, I have had so much mail regarding my book and can only find time to reply at the weekends.

I sincerely want to thank you for your kind letter and the photograph you sent which was taken at the BUFORA talk. It was a pleasure to meet you and your friends and I look forward to meeting you all again at Leeds in September.

I'm not sure if you are have heard the latest news regarding the Rendlesham case, but please read the September issue of UFO Magazine (published on 30 August). We now have the MOD Rendlesham file. It's really good news.

Malcolm Robinson sent me a review of the Rendlesham Sky Watch, it looks like you all had a good time. I would like to take up your offer of seeing a copy of the film that you made with your camcorder, if that is OK. Please let me know the cost and I will reimburse you.

Best wishes

Georgina Bruni

P.S. Enclosed front cover copy of MOD Rendlesham file.

THE HALT PERSPECTIVE 2

asking her what had taken place – and still wonder whether this was one of the reasons why she had embarked on her own personal journey to write the book? Whatever the reasons she did an excellent job and I would have been pleased to have worked alongside her as a Detective. She had the right qualifications for that! RIP.

Larry Warren puts some questions to Georgina Bruni – Her answers!

It is worth bringing to the reader's attention a number of questions put to Georgina Bruni by Larry Warren who, from the outset, questions her integrity after publication of her book. "**You Can't Tell The People"** in November 2001. We don't have the room to include this very lengthy document spanning 10 pages…but we felt we should, out of respect for Georgina, bring some of the 'highlights' to the reader's attention.

Larry: *"Why do you write that I saw a "huge machine land"? I've never said that, and it wasn't "huge", I also never saw the machine land! So what is your purpose for attributing that description to me as if you are quoting me?"*

Georgina: "This is not a direct quote: On page 45 of your book *Left At East Gate*, you say there was an explosion and then you saw a machine on the ground, it was big and almost the shape of a pyramid. On page 46 you say as you stood in front of the thing, you walked ten paces to the left and ten paces to the right and could see your shadows in it. Now please turn to page 385 in your book, where you are quoted as saying: *"There was a burst of intense bright light. After that, a massive structured object could be seen on the ground where the fog had been."* In your video interview (as above) with Anthony James you stated that the object was 30 feet across and rose to 25 feet at a sharp angle. Now, was that big or not, and did you see it land or not?"

Larry: *"Again, I ask did you really read,* "Left At East Gate"?

Georgina: "Yes, I really did read it but did not necessarily take everything in it at face value. Would you like a list of errors from that book Larry?"

Larry: *"Have you watched the 3-part CNN broadcast from 1985? If so, why did you mention it only in passing in your book, and on top of this describe it inaccurately. Example, "Capt Mike Verrano doesn't just "claim" to have driven Williams to a jet with film of the UFO," He did! You also write that Larry Warren was "surprised to recognize Verrano on the show," How do you conclude this? I worked with Chuck Decaro from beginning to end on that program and had spoken to most of the participants before it was broadcast in February 1985. Why the surprise? I was the first person interviewed by CNN in September 1984 as well."*

Georgina: "I did not use the word "surprised". What I wrote on page 72 is as follows:' In Left at East Gate he [Larry] refers to the CNN documentary, stating that although the faces of the witnesses were blacked out he recognized Captain Mike Verrano.' Now, please turn to page 178 of *Left At East Gate* where it reads as follows: 'Though their faces were obscured and, in one case, a voice disguised, I recognized Master Sergeant Ball, Sergeant Gulyas and Captain Verrano'. Who exactly did you speak to? I ask this because according to De Caro, these witnesses were interviewed separately and discretely and did not want to be named. In fact, all their faces are blacked out on the film. Isn't it true that you did not speak to most of the participants? After all, two of them were NCOs and one was a captain. All were still serving in the service and I doubt they would have wanted to talk to you at that time. Besides, De Caro would not even reveal their names 20 years later because he gave them his word. I did not just mention it in passing, please re-read my book. Yes, I have seen a copy of that film and Verrano's face is clearly blacked out and his name is not used in that segment. You are wrong about Verrano mentioning Williams, he does not. Only De Caro mentions the "base commander" The base commander was Colonel Ted Conrad, Gordon

THE HALT PERSPECTIVE 2

Williams was the Wing Commander, and there is a big difference. Isn't it time you got your facts right!"

Larry: "On page 73 of your book, you write that "I was convinced Gordon Williams communicated with the crew of an "Alien Spaceship". Again on page 73, you state that "No one else puts Williams at the landing sites"! On the first point, (Again) I've never in 20 years described the phenomena we saw as one "Alien" nor have I ever described the machine we saw on Capel Green, as a "Spaceship"! (I mean how would I know?) If you had read "Left At East Gate" you would have noticed that I do not believe the object came from "Space" at all. I believe it was from the future! I also expressed this opinion to you on the phone as well (Check your "research tapes") on the first point again, I never said that "definite" communication with the "crew" (Another description I've never ever used!) Took place with Williams, I say, some form of communication could have taken place, with Williams. Once again, please describe your research methods on these points, if any were used? As for others placing Williams on site, you write that "no one else does!" Halt has, the interviews with participants conducted by Ray Bouche confirms that "fact" as well, and was published in a MUFON journal and "Left At East Gate! Your book goes to great lengths to remove Williams from the incident, however you're writing, and the man's own actions and words indict him as having been involved."

Georgina: "Ray did not confirm that fact. During a conversation I had with him, he explained that Colonel Halt had told him that Williams had taken the film canister to a waiting aircraft. That does not mean it was that night, in fact the canister was taken to the aircraft a few days later and according to all the people I have interviewed, Williams was not involved. Halt has denied he said that to Ray Bouche and claims there was a misunderstanding. This is confirmed in a tape recorded interview that Peter Robbins did with Halt, which is included in your book and is available on your website at www.leftateastgate.com"

Larry: "He was! This is a bit more complex than the previous questions, but do give it the old college try. I will simplify it, why did you ignore established facts? (And please, no Spin!)

Georgina: "Larry please these are not direct quotes. Turn to page 490 (index) in *Left At East Gate*, where it states: Warren, communication with alien entity, page 61-62. Now, am I correct in saying that the alleged alien contact in the underground was connected with the incident that took place earlier? On page 47 of your book you state, "They had large heads with catlike eyes. I could not see other facial features. They were not human at all, but I was not frightened." So, you think that those from the future are not human? Well, if they are not human, then they must be alien! You only ever told me that you thought they were from our future after I told you that other witnesses were of this opinion. You ask how you would know it was a spacecraft. Why don't you turn to page 52 of your book where you say that a Naval officer told you the day after the incident that what you had seen in the forest represented a technology far advanced to our own and that numerous civilizations visit this planet from time to time. And recall you told Anthony James that Williams had interaction with another life form. Anyway, we've already covered the Williams saga."

Larry: "In your book you claim the following (false) information. Larry Warren was never cleared to work in the WSA." Did you really and truly read my book?" Did you review my existing military records, (published in the appendix) or did we make these records up as well? Had you done so, you knew before you published your book that on 11th Dec 80, I was posted to D flight with my security clearance (intact), on the 15th Dec 80, I received my (PRP) which is clearance to work with nuclear weapons, (in the WSA). I did so twice before the UFO incident. I believe that you knew that too! From where I stand, I don't see a hint of "investigative journalism" skills on your part!" Please explain why you make blanket statements that are clearly false?

Georgina: "According to my military sources and those who actually worked in the weapons storage area, you had to have special clearance to guard nuclear weapons. You claim in your video interview with Anthony James that you had *"Secret clearance to work around nuclear weapons"*, but you had only been on guard duty for approximately one month at Bentwaters, so I am not convinced that you would have had this clearance. Apart from a couple of TDYs you spent the remainder of your service in the supply hut waiting for your discharge. It stands to reason that a newbie would not be put in charge of guarding nuclear weapons. I would be very surprised if the Air Force allowed this. The records you produced are standard training procedure. One day training for the WSA does not guarantee that you would have guarded nuclear weapons. You might have been on guard on the perimeter fence but I am not convinced you would have been inside, unless of course you can prove otherwise. Please read page 31 in your own book, as follows: 'I was now assigned to D Flight and spent the first week in the weapons storage area, mainly checking access badges – not very exciting work.' The nuclear weapons area was a separate area, I know because I had access to it when I visited the installation after its closure. I also have the DOE map of Bentwaters. You would have only been on the gate checking badges at the entrance to the weapons (not nuclear) area and not inside the gates."

Larry: "To all that have read this, I'm not the sort that likes to put people on the spot, nor do I like to be perceived as a bully. Ms. Bruni has chosen to include information in her book that she knows is false, she also spun statements about me to fit her agenda, never in 20 years has anyone done this, (Not even the debunkers!) I wanted to take legal action but reminded myself that the many thousands of intelligent people the world over, who have read my book will find the problems that I have with Ms. Bruni's book to be self-evident. Read her book by all means, but you won't find anything to be "Definitive" or with regard to Larry Warren, "True" at all."

Georgina: "I think what you mean Larry, is that in 20 years nobody has dug deep enough with regard to your claims. In fact, when anybody tried to, you had a fall out with them or became very defensive, as you did with me. I know Peter Robbins did his best and I respect his research and it could not have been easy working with you. As I explain in my book, I only worked on a chapter of the Larry Warren story and it completely drained me. I know you liked the attention but there had to be a cut off point because the book concerned the Rendlesham Forest incident and although you were a player, there was much more work to do and more witnesses to interview. I was very thorough when it came to investigating the incident and all those who claim to have been involved. I am confident that my book and indeed these answers show who is telling the truth. I feel my book does more than other books have done to prove the lighthouse theory is a joke. It offers proper evidence, not just theory. It features actual USAF pictures of the landing site and evidence of ground indentations that could not have been caused by animals. It also features Adrian Bustinza's testimony revealing that he was forced under pressure to say that it was the lighthouse. It also reveals that two other witnesses were not responsible for typing the alleged statements, which the skeptic's claims are proof that the lighthouse was responsible. I do cover the skeptic's theories including Ian Ridpath's, but I refuse to waste precious space on debunkers who have no case. I believe I have been very fair to the witnesses, there have been no complaints from them, in fact it is the opposite, and they have congratulated me on my research. You are the only person to make complaints regarding your alleged involvement."

Charles: It's clear that, irrespective for whatever reason, Mr Warren has completely lost focus on the truth, whatever that is. Anyone with a grain of common sense and rationality can now see behind the cloak of subterfuge which fooled so many people over the years who desperately wanted to believe that aliens swung down from the landed craft in the forest and conversed with senior officers!

Tells you much about the people, who swallowed it down, hook line and sinker without daring to question the word of a guy who was at one stage considered a celebrity even if they had misgivings – a trait of human behaviour, because they wanted to believe that aliens were seen! The UFO business seems to be riddled with pack mentality, in itself phenomenon where people make decisions based on the actions of others, without even realizing it, stemming from man animalistic drive to want to fit in!

THE HALT PERSPECTIVE 2

The fact that within this business which is built on a need by many 'hopefuls' to force Governments to disclose what they really know about the UFO subject, ultimately gets us nowhere. I should know I've also tried to get Senators to get up and take notice. I'm not saying anybody should give up, far from it what I am saying is that we will never get anywhere if we blindly accept without any scrutiny stories like this which for whatever reason are not built on facts but fabrication. Problem is as I have said before if one was given a cocktail of drugs to induce a false memory . . . then we should take that into consideration but the damage is done. As for the version of events given by Larry hang on this sounds familiar, bright lights, pyramidal object seen, then aliens;s heard that before! I think Georgina has covered the situation adequately, and shown exactly where Warren is coming from! No wonder they pulled the book! But he's not the only one! For example, look at RAF Watton and what happened there, with sensational claims of aliens seen outside the perimeter fence! Which has been covered in depth, blandly accepted by those without any questioning, who believed that wild tales were corroboration of what exactly? Someone also claimed that the object that came to earth in Rendlesham Forest seen by Jim Penniston was the crash landing of Lockheed F-19 Stealth fighter. This small triangular shaped aircraft according to *Jaynes* was not in existence till 1982!

However according to UFO researcher Robert Moore, in May 1987 the 'culprit' may have been the XST plane (Experimental Stealth Technology) which was in existence from 1977 onwards. According to *Jaynes,* five of these were built and two crashed, one of which was rumoured to have attempted to land at Woodbridge but missed the runway and came to rest in the woods with a one/two man crew! This rumour by way of a change came from, it is said, by an American on tour of the airbase, following conversation about the incident in 1980. Robert who is known to John wrote a letter to the *Sunday Mirror* castigating the authors of what he referred to as a **'miss match of lies misperception and misinformation'** following the release of a new book the **UFO Book Conspiracy** which was the subject of newspaper publicity on the 24th May 1987. This was in 1987, only seven years after the event! Seems nothing changes!

Charles: Here is a copy of the email (right) I sent to Brenda Butler during this year which gives you an idea of my views at the time.

July 3, 2002

Dear Brenda:

It was good to hear from you. I don't remember telling Georgina I did not want to be contacted. It sounds like you are really on to something. You are seeing and experiencing a lot more than we did. I seriously doubt the military has anything to do with it.

When I went out with the police we went from Bentwaters to Woodbridge (as I remember) by way of the public road (through Eyke) onto Woodbridge and then out the East Gate down the road. We turned right on the Forest service road for a hundred or more feet then left on the dirt road toward the sea. After several hundred yards we turned left on a trail and continued for several hundred feet. From there we went right into the trees toward the fence line. The "landing site" was about 200-300 feet from the fence. Ahead and to the left was the Boast home. Hope this helps.

The marks on the trees in the pictures are much larger than we noted on the infamous night. I also think you have mislocated the site in the picture of a map you sent. The map is not large enough and does not have enough clear references to say for sure. As far as posts. I did not see any and do not remember seeing any at later dates (1989 and when I did the filming).

Have you tried to catch some of the happenings on film? Infrared film?

Good luck- win the lottery and I'll join you for a party at the site.

Chuck

July 25, 2000

Brenda Butler 1 Mafking Place
Leiston, Suffolk IP164EN
England

Dear Brenda:

Thank you for updating me on happenings in Rendlesham Forest. I was sorry to hear you received what sounds like radiation burns. I hope you are ok. In several similar cases in the States the victims suffered badly. I suspect you now believe me and the fact that I was not trying to hide anything or part of a cover up. I'm convinced now that certain agencies left me out there to take the heat and look foolish.

I am also convinced that whatever is going on is much more than mind control although that appears to factor for some of the participants. Be careful, as there could be some real danger in what you are doing.

Keep me posted, as your experience sounds so familiar.

Chuck

THE HALT PERSPECTIVE 2

2003

Lies, distortion and silly stories – fodder for the Press!

The *Daily Mail* **30th June 2003**, published details relating to yet another possible explanation for what took place in Rendlesham Forest, as reported by the airmen concerned. The *BBC Inside Out*, Rendlesham Forest Incident case revealed the following:–

> 'It was a hoax! Not only can we tell you that most of it was a hoax, but also how it was done. They included that a puzzled Halt referred on the tape-recording to: "*The red, white, and blue lights of the UFO are still hovering over Woodbridge*". However, former USAF Security Policemen – Kevin Conde, has exclusively revealed that these lights were the result of a practical joke he played on the gullible airman. "*I drove my patrol car out of sight from the gatehouse, turned on the red and blue emergency lights, and pointed white flashlights through the mist into the air. The bottom line is that, that was not a UFO – it was a 1979 Plymouth Volare!*", explains a bemused Conde.'

In a similar vein **The *East Anglia Daily Times*,** 'TV Probe pledging to solve UFO puzzle-special extended documentary, told their readers that the BBC series '***Inside out***' would finally explain the mysteries of the UFO sighting in the forest. This had been put together by James Easton who had been contacted by former sergeant Kevin Conde, who told him, *"The only UFO incident that occurred during my tour were hoaxes I participated in and the only alien that landed was Mrs Conde's little boy Kevin."*

This was followed by another 'scoop' on the **2nd of July 2003**, when journalist Michael Hanlon of the same newspaper, **UFO-OLED!** reiterated at some length the incident involving what the airmen had seen, along with Colonel Halt and his version of events [which has never altered in 40 years] explaining it away as a hoax perpetrated by Kevin Conde, who attributed the three landing marks found in the forest as being the impressions made in the ground by a landed helicopter three large skids.

Charles: What a load of rubbish anybody with an ounce of common sense can see what is happening here. For a start you couldn't drive a car through the forest there were hardly any tracks which would have facilitated the passage of a saloon car never mind much larger off road vehicles. It should be of concern to all of us as to why it is that the media will always take so much interest in matters which denigrate the true picture of what is and has been going on for many years, rather than having the courage to confront something for which for all we know may have a scientific explanation.

If you knew the scene then you would know how ridiculous the suggestion was made that it was a helicopter!

Unfortunately that wouldn't sell newspapers! Yet another claim that the documentary makers have solved the enigmatic puzzle of the UFO was trotted out by the BBC in their series of *Inside Out*…. explanation Lighthouse! I'm not surprised that the BBC would run with wild stories like this borne from figments of fantasy and vivid imagination rather than anything sensible. [**This wild accusation was again resurrected** in 2009 by the newspapers].

Unexplained sightings – now forgotten

Common sense dictates this wasn't the answer for what was seen by the airmen concerned. To those that believe it was then who was **responsible for the massive number of UFO sightings** which occurred in East Anglia, during the 1980-1990s, which appear to have been deliberately ignored by the media? We treat Conde's explanation as having no substance whatsoever. Even as this book was being compiled, John received an email from a former airman on the base in December 1980, **who claimed he had fired up rockets over the forest as he was bored!** Needless to say he didn't give his name … yet another 'red herring'!

Georgina Bruni commented: *"You've been fooled! Your consultant James Easton no doubt forgot to mention that he had previously interviewed Kevin Conde for his debunking on-line newsletter, who said: "This incident [hoax] occurred* **after Christmas.** *For reasons that are hard to explain, it is my impression that I pulled my stunt during an exercise. We would not have had an exercise during the Christmas holiday. That is a strong indication that my stunt is not the source of this specific incident."*

John: Here are further photos of Georgina, a lady that was well thought of and respected. Many people over the last few years have emailed us wanting to see more photos of her. It's the least we can do. Photos shown are of her, Brenda and Chris Pennington in London during the release of the book '**You Can't Tell The People',** the second is my favourite, *"With the girls"* and lastly one I took of her and Brenda while 'traipsing through the woods'; … thanks Georgina for your friendship.

THE HALT PERSPECTIVE 2

PART 5

THE COLONEL FIGHTS BACK

2009

More Cow Pies – Caught with a finger in one by the look of it!

ON the **6th January 2009**, scientific skeptic author **Brian Dunning** published his own book on the Rendlesham Forest UFO; also a podcast episode titled **'*The Rendlesham Forest UFO'***, in which he evaluated the original eye-witness reports as well as audio recordings, and the resulting media reporting of this incident. After a lengthy analysis Dunning concluded: *"Col. Halt's thoroughness was commendable, but even he can be mistaken. **Without exception, everything he reported on his audiotape and in his written memo has a perfectly rational and unremarkable explanation** . . . All that remains is the tale that the men were debriefed and ordered never to mention the event, and warned that "bullets are cheap".*

*Well, as we've seen on television, the men all talk quite freely about it and even Col. Halt says that to this day nobody has ever debriefed him. So this appears to be just another dramatic invention for television, perhaps from one of the men who have expanded their stories over the years. When you examine each piece of evidence separately on its own merit, you avoid the trap of pattern matching and finding correlations where none exist. The meteors had nothing to do with the lighthouse or the rabbit diggings, but when you hear all three stories told together, it's easy to conclude (as did the airmen) that the light overhead became an alien spacecraft in the forest. Always remember: Separate pieces of poor evidence don't aggregate together into a single piece of good evidence. **You can stack cow pies as high as you want, but they won't turn into a bar of gold."***

Charles: Brian Andrew Dunning is an American writer and producer whose focus is on scepticism. He has hosted a weekly podcast, *Skeptoid*, since 2006 and is an author of five books on the subject of scientific scepticism. The *Skeptoid* podcast has been the recipient of **several podcast awards including the Parsec Award and Stitcher award.** *Skeptoid*, in May 2014, attracted **161,000 listeners** weekly!

Dunning also created a spin-off video series and has written several books based on the podcast. Dunning co-founded *Buylink*, a business-to-business service provider, in 1996, and served at the company until 2002. He later became eBay's second biggest affiliate; **but has since been convicted of wire fraud through a cookie stuffing scheme**. In August 2014, he was sentenced to 15 months in prison, to be followed by three years of supervised release for the company obtaining between $200,000 and $400,000 through wire fraud **(Source: Wikipedia).** As far as Dunning is concerned – well, cow pies to him! He is typical of so many people that can't bother to check up on the facts; one might have thought he would have asked me what I thought? A look at the *Amazon* website, where this book is on offer, shows very few reviews and a complaint how thin the book is without any new information. I was only Deputy Base Commander at the Airbase – what would I know?! It would be funny but you know it's tragic when idiotic statements like this are put out by people who can caste judgements based on superficial knowledge of what they know, which in this case is none at all!

2010

In 2010, Jenny Randles – one of the co-authors of the 1984 book *Sky Crash: A Cosmic Conspiracy* – eventually voiced her doubts that the incident had ever had anything to do with extraterrestrial visitors. Jenny: *"Whilst some puzzles remain, we can probably say that no unearthly craft were seen in Rendlesham Forest. We can also argue with confidence that the main focus of the events was a series of misperceptions of everyday things encountered in less than everyday circumstances."* Wish I had the same confidence Jenny! Sorry I never got round to reading the other book you published for the American market, *Out Of The Blue,* which appears to have two covers?

UFO Matrix – Claim that General Gabriel took possession of tape recording?

Philip Mantle, editor of *UFO Matrix*, published *Issue 3 Volume* 1 in **2010**, which contained various articles about the Rendlesham Forest Incident. It began with a contribution by **Nick Pope** who outlined the sequence of events that are now so well known to most of us, and told the readers that shortly after the event **General Gabriel Commander in Chief, United States Air force in Europe** visited the bases and took possession of the tape recording made by Charles Halt, which according to Nick was confirmed in a MoD Document.

Nick: *"Although it is not known if other material relating to the incident was involved or what further action was taken – in 1994 I undertook what police would call a cold case review of the incident. What I found shocked me. It was soon clear that the original investigation had been fundamentally flawed by procedural errors, delay and poor information sharing. The USAF had not cordoned off the landing site, taken soil samples or used a metal detector to search the area. The incident was not reported to the MOD until nearly three weeks after the event. When it was, the dates in the official US report were incorrect. The USAF didn't pass the witness statements **(including Jim Penniston's sketch which would have made it abundantly clear that a structured craft was involved.)**"*

THE HALT PERSPECTIVE 2

Charles: First of all I'm not prepared to accept Jenny's hypothesis made on the basis of limited evidence as a starting point for further investigation; correct me if I'm wrong but if that was the case then why did *Sky Crash* ever come into being? There are more than enough witnesses in this book, who have seen things in the sky and also on the ground that won't fit into this parameter of 'everyday things encountered in less that everyday circumstances'. Sorry Jenny – it sounds like Gobbledegook!

I would say taking Nick's comments into consideration, and my comments about this previously on page 284, one might feel that jurisdiction for any investigation would lie with the MOD, as the incident took place on UK territory. It's clear the MOD could have launched some investigation, but chose not to do so primarily because of a number of reasons, notwithstanding that time has shown us the vagaries of accepting the deceptive testimonials of some of the men involved, which is tainted with suspicion – and downright lies!

Where is the evidence of any structured craft? Searching an area the size of the forest would not have been physically possible – for what purpose? The only film from either night was Penniston's and Nevels'. I never handled any film.

A plane did go Germany soon after the event but it was supposedly to take some late promotion papers to a board. What I said, was that I was told, by others that Gordon Williams received something while in the cockpit of an A-10 bound for Germany. Mike Verano claimed it was film of the UFO. I think it was Mel Zicklers efficiency report that was late and they wanted it to get into his file before the promotion board. I remember talk of that happening. This was well after the event in the forest. I could be wrong but I don't think so. The only related film it could possibly have been, is Neville's 35mm film. To have acquired it, someone would have to have broken into his home and produced a copy . . . **not likely! Williams was never at the site – ask him**. This wild tale is based on something Mike Verano remembered. We all know there was no video, only Monroe's 35mm film. If Williams told Mike that it was a cover for flying Zickler's late evaluation to the CINC for an endorsement so it could get into his promotion file – a video is wishful thinking.

At the Washington Press Club, I and five other US officers that included Captain Robert Salas and Robert Hastings, discussed the implications of what took place, not only there but at other sites where UFOs had been reported. Accordingly, an article appeared in one newspaper by journalist Gemma Wheatley that included the banner-grabbing headline: **'US Colonel's proof of alien cover up'**, with, once again, the misleading statement that **'beams were shone into the nuclear weapon store'**, which I refute.

On **August 5th 2010,** *The Daily Star,* launched their article **'Top Secret UFO reports are released 30 years later'.** The *East Anglia Daily Times,* in their edition of the 20th of September 2010, also told their readers about the Press Club Conference in Washington, quote: **UFOs HAD TAMPERED WITH NUCLEAR MSSILES IN THE US AND THE UK** – Followed by my version of events. *Interesting to see that when Jim was interviewed about what he saw, well there **is nothing about <u>him getting that close to the 'Triangular UFO' or seeing any hieroglyphics?</u>**

The *Daily Star,* on the 28th of September, 2010, went to town with banner grabbing headlines and illustration of a triangular UFO. In November, Brenda Butler, now a friend since the early days when she and Dot plagued me, organised a talk in the forest, over camp fires burning and a hot dog van parked nearby! Brenda erected a marquee which contained many intriguing photographs of strange things captured by her on film in Rendlesham Forest over many years standing; what they are and what they represent I don't have a clue, other than to say strange things were seen in that Forest over the years! Other celebrations included the Woodbridge Conference, which we have made a previous reference to, but we thought the reader might like to see some of the memorabilia associated with that event, not ten years ago…[According to Donald Moreland, the tape-recording made by Colonel Halt was handed over to General Gabriel, during a visit to the airbase.]

THE HALT PERSPECTIVE 2

THE HALT PERSPECTIVE 2

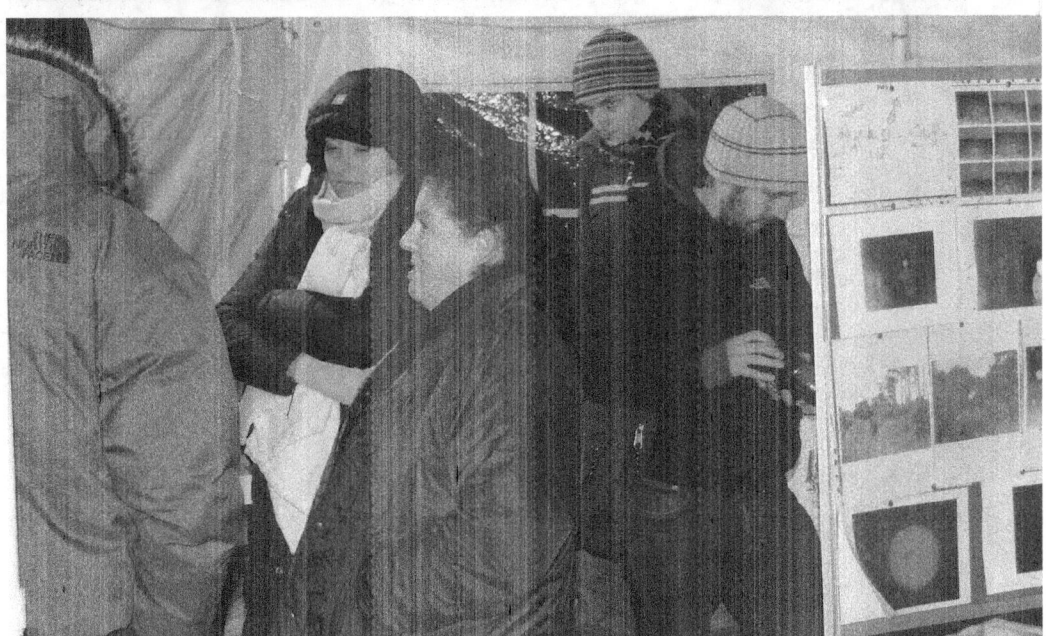

THE HALT PERSPECTIVE 2

BBC article: Brenda "We will never know"

The (On line) *BBC* article, 15th December 2010 – 'UFO investigator Brenda Butler says we will never know the full details of what happened in Rendlesham Forest 30 years ago'.

Quote: In December 1980 there were reports of unidentified flying objects over the forest near Woodbridge, Suffolk. Orford Ness Lighthouse, a crashed satellite and a hoax are amongst the explanations still being debated. *"There was something in the forest,"* said Ms Butler. *"I think it came from another dimension."* BBC Suffolk marked the 30th anniversary of the sightings, with a special two-hour broadcast live from Bentwaters Cold War Museum on Friday, 17 December, 7-9pm. *Mark Murphy is presenting the show. Ms Butler, from Leiston, has been at the forefront of discussions about what happened in Rendlesham and spoke to Mark at an anniversary event in November 2010. Key to the discussions are recordings made by US Colonel Halt, the deputy commanding officer of RAF Woodbridge at the time. *"They chased the lights and saw a craft,"* said Ms Butler. *"We've seen craft down here;* **we've seen ETs (extra terrestrials) down here,** *so yes, they definitely saw something."* But 30 years on, Ms Butler believes the discussions will continue. **"In Colonel Halt's own words, if it ever came out what happened, governments would topple, they will never, ever, be allowed to tell us what really happened."** A Ministry of Defence memo reads: *"No evidence was found of any threat to the defence of the United Kingdom, in the absence of any hard evidence, the MOD remains open minded."*

Extraterrestrial sightings!

Ms Butler said she had visited the forest at least once a week for the last 30 years, and has made regular contact with extraterrestrials. *"We've seen different beings in the forest,"* she said. *"We've seen the black cat, we've seen the little brown monks which float around, we've seen disks, we've seen the craft in the sky, we've seen shadow man, and we've seen ghosts. We see all kinds of stuff in the forest."*

2011

Daily Mail & Telegraph – take with a pinch of salt!

On **Saturday 6th August 2011**, *The Daily Telegraph* published Jasper Copping's article '***Rendlesham Incident: US Commander speaks for the first time about The Suffolk UFO'***. The article centred on Colonel Ted Conrad – ex-base Commander of the twin airfields of RAF Woodbridge/Bentwaters – and his views on the Rendlesham Incident. Copping writes in his article: *"Just after Christmas (1980), mysterious lights were seen in the sky above nearby Rendlesham Forest, and after a second night of reports from his men, Colonel Conrad investigated himself."* Colonel Conrad said: *"The search for an explanation could go many places, including the perpetration of a clever hoax. Natural phenomena such as the very clear cold air having a theoretical ability to guide and reflect light across great distances or even the presence of an alien spacecraft. If someone had the time, money and technical resources to determine the exact cause of the reported Rendlesham Forest lights, I think it could be done. I also think the odds are way high against there being an ET spacecraft involved and almost equally high against it being an intrusion of hostile earthly craft."*

*****John**: I met BBC presenter Mark Murphy during the 2012 celebrations in the forest and asked him if he might consider inviting me to talk about the UFO subject, taking into consideration my background as a police officer, and having spent the last (then) 17 years researching into British UFO history – having been a regular speaker, on *BBC Midlands/Coventry and Warwickshire*. I'm still waiting to hear from him! But of course I've had many rebuffs from the BBC over the years, following publication of the *Haunted Skies* books. As my National Newspaper colleagues tell me, *"They don't want serious researchers."*

THE HALT PERSPECTIVE 2

Charles: For me this year held some importance with regard to the events that had befell me, following an affidavit made in my home county Virginia, on the 30th April 2011.

AFFIDAVIT OF CHARLES I. HALT

(1) My name is Charles I. Halt

(2) I was born on

(3) My address is

(4) I served in the U.S. Air Force for 28 years, retiring in 1991 with the rank of Colonel. In December 1980, I was the Deputy Base Commander at the Anglo-American base, RAF Bentwaters, in Suffolk, England.

(5) Late in the evening on December 27th, and continuing into the pre-dawn hours of December 28th, in response to reports of unusual lights in nearby Rendlesham Forest, I led a team of USAF Security Policemen into the woods to investigate. This was the second such incident in as many days and rumors of UFO activity were rife on base. By going into the forest, my intention was find a logical explanation for the mysterious lights.

(6) While in Rendlesham Forest, our security team observed a light that looked like a large eye, red in color, moving through the trees. After a few minutes this object began dripping something that looked like molten metal. A short while later it broke into several smaller, white-colored objects which flew away in all directions. Claims by skeptics that this was merely a sweeping beam from a distant lighthouse are unfounded; we could see the unknown light and the lighthouse simultaneously. The latter was 35 to 40-degrees off where all of this was happening.

(7) Upon leaving the forest, our team crossed a farmer's field. As we did so, someone pointed out three objects in the northern sky. They were white and had multiple-colored lights on them. At first, the objects appeared elliptical but, as they maneuvered, turned full round. They were stationary for awhile and then they started to move at high speed in sharp angular patterns as though they were doing a grid search.

(8) About that same time, someone noticed a similar object in the southern sky. It was round and, at one point, it came toward us at a very high speed. It stopped overhead and sent down a small pencil-like beam, sort of like a laser beam. That illuminated the ground about ten feet from us and we just stood there in awe, wondering whether it was a signal, a warning, or what it was. It clicked-off as though someone threw a switch, and then the object receded back up into the sky.

(9) This object then moved back toward Bentwaters, and continued to send down beams of light, at one point near the Weapons Storage Area. We knew that because we could hear the chatter on the two-way radio. Several airmen present later told me that they saw the beams. I don't remember any names at this point. From my position in the forest, it appeared that one or more beams came down near the WSA. At the time, the object was just to the north of the facility. I had great concern about the purpose of the beams.

(10) In keeping with official U.S. Air Force policy, I can neither confirm nor deny that the Weapons Storage Area held nuclear weapons. However, I am aware that other former or retired USAF Security Police who worked there at the time of the incident are now on-the-record confirming the presence of tactical nuclear bombs at the WSA.

(11) I believe the objects that I saw at close quarter were extraterrestrial in origin and that the security services of both the United States and the United Kingdom have attempted—both then and now—to subvert the significance of what occurred at Rendlesham Forest and RAF Bentwaters by the use of well-practiced methods of disinformation.

(12) I have not been paid nor given anything of value to make this statement and it is the truth to the best of my recollection.

Signed:

Date: 6/17/10

Signature witnessed by: Katherine C. Shaw

Notary: KC   My commission expires April 30, 2011

I emailed Jasper Copping wishing to put the record straight. *"Another good reason to take anything you read in the media with a grain of salt. Remember their goal is to sell their publication – the truth is damned. The only investigating Conrad did was to listen to the participants when I took them to him after interviewing them and taking statements. His only trip to the site was when I took him and his family out to look. Apparently he's not aware, or ignoring, all the witnesses such as the Air Traffic Controllers, cops and civilians. You might want to talk to Tony Cossa, the then Communications Group Commander, who ordered his two repairmen, that also witnessed the event, to keep quiet.* **Apparently the spooks took it seriously when they used hypnosis and drugs on the airmen** *to get the whole story to apparently 'plant' false memories. Conrad's such a coward – he didn't want his name involved; hence I was told to do the memo, which he read and approved. I was then hung out to dry when it hit the Press. Everybody above me hid when it hit the Press. Disappointing! What you're seeing is some very skilful disinformation. You have no idea the ends some agencies will go to discredit this."*

Dr. David Clarke – The subject is dead!

Sheffield Hallam University academic and the UFO adviser to the National Archives – said in 2011: *"The subject is dead in that no one is seeing anything evidential. Look at all the people who now have personal cameras. If there was something flying around that was a structured object from somewhere else, you would have thought that someone would have come up with some convincing footage by now – but they haven't. The reason why nothing is going on is because of the internet. If something happens now, the internet is there to help people get to the bottom of it and find an explanation. Before then, you had to send letters to people who wouldn't respond, and you got this element of mystery and secrecy that means things were not explained. The classic cases like Roswell and Rendlesham are only classic cases because they were not investigated properly at the time."*

Charles: So let me get this clear in my mind. First of all, I would love to know what was the nature of what was seen – not only by me – but by other service personnel at the end of December 1980, not forgetting the evidence previously submitted, outlining countess other UFO incidents for that year.

Also if one takes into consideration other sightings of strange airborne objects over the forest and Air Base throughout the years, and hundreds, if not thousands, of others which were reported around the East Anglia area between the 1980-1996 period, do we apply the same line of reasoning towards these? If one relied on the Internet to come up with the answers then God help us! Blinkered vision here David; from a man that used to work for BUFORA and investigated sightings brought to his attention. Now presumably with the hindsight of experience, you will be able to explain away these – as what, exactly?

Colonel Conrad goes on the attack!

The *Daily Mail* Monday 8.2011 'Suffolk UFO sighting could have been a hoax: U.S. commander talks about Rendlesham Forest incident for first time in 30 years.'

Quote: US Air Force Colonel Ted Conrad was base commander of the airfields at Woodbridge and Bentwaters, near Ipswich. At the time the base is believed to have stored nuclear weapons. After spotting some strange lights in the sky, two nights in a row, **Colonel Conrad** went to investigate and, after clearing some bushes, found some strange markings on trees which he believed could have indicated a spacecraft landing. He then picked a group of his own men and sent them into the forest that evening. Armed with night vision goggles and a camera, they searched the area and, after seeing nothing suspicious, some of the men returned to base. However, Colonel Conrad's deputy – Lieutenant Colonel Halt – stayed behind and kept in touch with his superior via radio. Lt. Colonel Halt then reported he saw more lights on the ground and in the sky. Other senior officers on the base went outside to see if they could see the lights but nobody was able to, despite it being a perfectly clear evening. Speaking to Dr David Clarke – UFO adviser to the National Archives – Conrad said: "*He* **(HALT)** *should be ashamed and embarrassed by his allegation that his country and England both conspired to deceive their citizens over this issue. He knows better."* The former Commander has also dismissed Sergeant Jim Penniston's claims that he had gone into the woods on the first night of the sightings and touched an alien aircraft.

*Colonel Conrad said he interviewed Penniston, **who did not say that he had touched the aircraft but did say he saw lights in the distance, and that** "we saw nothing that resembled Lt. Colonel Halt's descriptions either in the sky, or on the ground".* (The reporter is not identified in this article.)

Setting the record straight with the *Daily Telegraph*

Charles: I asked John to check this out again in view of the fact that whoever the unidentified journalist was that wrote this article he couldn't have got it more wrong? I presume they mixed him up with me? Conrad out in the forest finding traces of possible evidence of a spaceship landing – what a load of rubbish. Then I am attacked by Conrad…whose he working for?

It's strange that when a National newspaper publishes anything about the UFO incidents at Rendlesham Forest, it's immediately seized on by the others, and is then the subject of further Press attention. Whether there is any truth, is of course a commodity that appears very scarce, as we have seen in the write ups so far

Jasper Copping

The *Daily Telegraph* picked up on it and ran the story…So I again emailed journalist Jasper Copping, of *The Daily Telegraph*, in August 2011, Subject: **Re: Press query,** *Sunday Telegraph***, London. Date: Tuesday 9th August 2011.** Jasper: I will have to assume you're looking to print the truth, not 'sell' a sensational story. Ted Conrad is having memory problems, has his head in the sand or continuing the cover-up. Even his son has admitted to family talk substantiating the incident. Let's start with his investigation. I interviewed the witnesses, collected their statements (I still have them) and then took the witnesses to Conrad to tell their account. I took Ted Conrad and his family to the site in the forest and showed him the depressions. When talked with Gordon Williams, neither he nor Conrad wanted their name mentioned with the incident. Thus, I was directed to get with Don Moreland (RAF) and see what he wanted as it was to become a British affair. I did so and he asked for a memo. I wrote it and it was typed by Conrad's secretary. Conrad read it, showed it to Williams and both approved. It was never meant for public dissemination. Conrad has his chronology mixed up but that is understandable.

Through the years Conrad has made conflicting statements about the events. First he stated he never went out to look in the sky. Then stated he never saw anything. Apparently he doesn't remember talking to me on his radio [about seeing a UFO sending down beams of light onto the Base]. You need to read Robert Hastings book *UFOs And Nukes*.

Hastings has gotten confirmation from the Air Traffic Controllers on duty that saw the object flash by and go into the forest

THE HALT PERSPECTIVE 2

and even observed it on their scope; he's gotten statements from SP's as well as a Communications man working in the WSA stating their sightings. He's even dug up the RAF Controller that picked up something on his scope. Remind Conrad of his article in the *OMNI* Magazine, dated March 1983. It's on page 115 and titled UFO Update. In the article he describes the first incident in detail and concludes, 'those lads saw something, but I don't know what it was'. Now he's smearing those involved. It's pretty clear there was a very intense confrontation with something in the forest. Does Conrad want to talk about how the airmen were then subjected to mind control efforts using drugs and hypnosis by British and American authorities? **NO REPLY!**

2019 *The New European* has appointed **Jasper Copping** as editor. Jasper was previously news editor for the newspaper and also previously served as deputy news editor and reporter over ten years at **The** *Daily Telegraph* and *The Sunday Telegraph*.

Now they say I sketched alien spacecraft – rubbish!

The same newspaper *Daily Mail*, used the UFO illustration from *Sky Crash* and labelled underneath it: '*Sighting: 'Lieutenant* **Colonel Halt's sketch of the alien spacecraft he claims to have seen in Rendlesham Forest'** .The illustration is endorsed with © *Corbis*. The article also includes a photograph of me (on the left) and Kevin Conde, titled '**Lt. Colonel Halt (on the left) filed a report to the MOD and said he believed the lights were extraterrestrial**, *while Kevin Conde (right) admitted to the BBC that he had played a prank on a colleague, while he was working at the base*'. To add insult to injury metaphorically of course, was the misleading text attributed to me: '**My Sketch of an alien spacecraft I saw in the forest!**' Baloney! Surely that image is more or less identical to one that was originally published in *Sky Crash?*

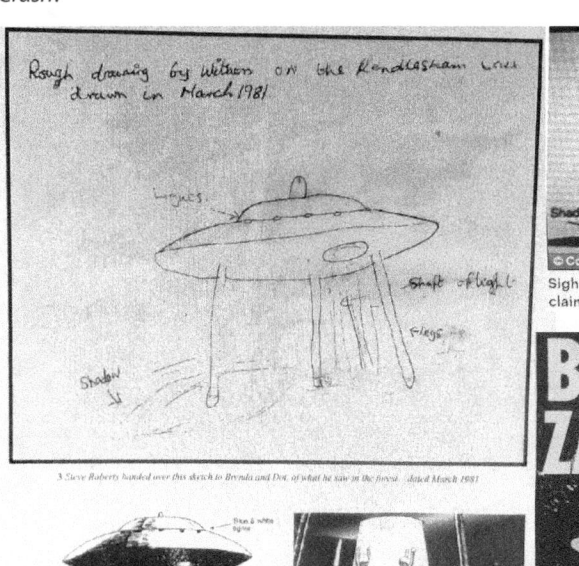
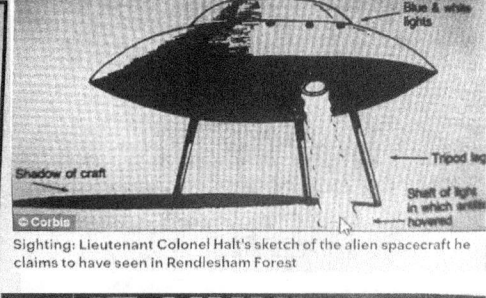
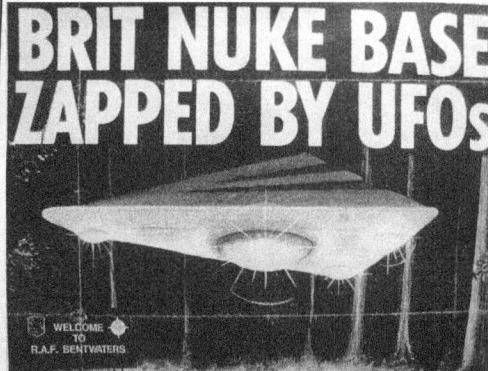

THE HALT PERSPECTIVE 2

Once again, further inaccuracies! We were intrigued about the copyright. John searched the *Corbis* website for this image, but found no trace of it – so he emailed *Corbis Images* at 111, Salisbury Road, London NW6 6RG, United Kingdom, asking them if they had any images pertaining to the Rendlesham Forest UFO incident of 1980. On the 14th February 2013, Yuliya Stuart from *Orbis* replied: "*Unfortunately we do not have any images matching that description.*" In another email, she responded: "*I tried to find an image of a UFO in Rendlesham Forest, but there wasn't any on our website.*" We then sent her the original image and asked if they could explain why their corporate copyright was affixed to the image. Yuliya Stuart stated: "*Not sure about the image, as I couldn't find it. Perhaps it is on our site but has a different keyword.*" One might think that they would know where this image was on their website, understanding its importance. The firm quoted us approximately £70 for copyright fee to use any of their UFO images. Had they purchased the image? If so from whom, and why weren't they more forthcoming with the details of the person acknowledged as the original copyright holder? [John had originally obtained permission and paid a copyright fee to the owner for this]. One presumes that they charged the *Daily Mail* a fee?

Larry Warren and I will be on stage together!

Talking about setting the record straight here is another 'anomaly', as you can see from the newspaper article written by reporter Tom Potter of the *East Anglia Daily Times*, who has been very helpful and unbiased, a man whom John and I learned to trust – a rare commodity in this business when it comes to dealing with journalists! According to the article published in late 2010, (not sure of the exact date) the readers are told by local UFO organiser Gordy Goodger, (who has staged other conferences at Woodbridge Community Hall) about a forthcoming a conference planned for June 2011, which would be attended by a number of guest speakers that would include, **Jim and John, Larry Warren and myself**! **NO way!** Despite the fact that Tickets were on sale advertising that I was going to be talking... Wishful thinking!

'Historic' conference promises UFO truths

WOODBRIDGE: Leading lights descend for close encounter convention

By Tom Potter

THE main players in an unsolved paranormal saga are set to return to the scene of a 30 year mystery.

The infamous Rendlesham UFO incident has become the stuff of legend, dividing sceptics and believers worldwide since December 1980, when strange lights were seen by US airmen at RAF Bentwaters and Woodbridge.

Last December, Woodbridge Community Hall hosted the 30th anniversary Rendlesham Forest UFO conference, followed this September by a forum for local witnesses to share their tales.

Now, organisers of both events are inviting back past speakers and introducing more characters to the debate for another conference next June, including Colonel Charles Halt, former Deputy Base Commander and subject of the fabled Halt Tape, on which the Colonel and his patrol are heard investigating the forest sighting.

For the first time since the notorious incident, he will be joined Sergeant Monroe Nevels, who can also be heard on the famous tape operating a Geiger counter at the investigation scene.

Former US airman Larry Warren will join old colleagues John Burroughs and Jim Penniston, returning with their accounts of events and presenting the "most comprehensive and accurate overview of the incident".

Also appearing is Peter Robbins, co-author of *Left at East Gate: A First-Hand Account of the Rendlesham Forest UFO Incident, Its Cover-Up and Investigation*.

Another special guest on the night will be Travis Walton, an American logger who vanished in Arizona for five days in 1975 and returned claiming he had been abducted by a UFO. His story remains one of the best-known cases of alleged alien abduction.

Organiser George Goodger promises new evidence will be revealed at the two day conference on June 16 and 17. He said: "This event is nothing short of historic. John and Jim will be back in Woodbridge to present world exclusive findings of their recent investigations.

"Charles Halt will deliver a talk on the events of December 1980 and, for the first time ever together since those actual events, will appear with Monroe Nevels.

"Travis Walton will tell the amazing story of being abducted by extraterrestrials and held captive for five days. His appearance is an extremely rare opportunity to hear first-hand the inside details of one of the most thrilling UFO abduction cases in history.

"Larry Warren is recognised as the Rendlesham Forest UFO incident whistle-blower and the one who first got this story out."

Weekend tickets, costing £40 each, can be booked by sending an SAE with payment by cheque or postal order to Mr G Goodger, 108 Spring Road, Ipswich, IP4 2RR.

Paypal payments of £40, plus £2 to cover costs, should be sent to paypal@spaceportuk.com. For more information call 07811 021230 or 01473 423143, e-mail info@spaceportuk or visit www.spaceportuk.com/events.html.

tom.potter@eadt.co.uk

THE HALT PERSPECTIVE 2

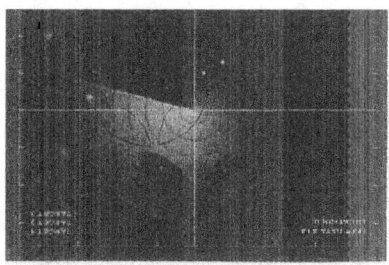

Subj: Bentwaters
Date: 3/10/2011 3:08:19 P.M. Eastern Standard Time
From:
To: gowill57@comcast.net

General Williams:

I feel that I owe you an explanation for many things that have made the press for the last few years. First I would like to thank you for the example you set and the leadership displayed as the 81st Commander. It made a lasting impression.

After you left Bentwaters Sam Morgan began playing a copy of the tape I made in DEC 1980 at cocktail parties and for various British groups unbeknownst to me. He gave out copies of the tape and even mentioned my memo concerning the event. I was shocked as I was content to let the event die. An American writer named Larry Fawcett came in under the Freedom of Information Act for the memo. We didn't have an official copy so he went to 3rd AF. Pete Bent (acting 3rd AF CC) called me and told me he was going to release the memo. I pleaded with him to destroy it. My words were "if you release it your life and mine will never be the same". He released it and you know what happened after that. I was hounded to death. Finally, since there was so much disinformation and my name was out there I started telling the truth.

One result is many people came forward that knew part of what happened. Were you aware 4-5 or more of our airmen were drugged and hypnotized? One or more were given false memories. Not long after the incident General Gabriel came to visit. Recently released British files state he was given a copy of my tape. Nearby British residents as well as the Forest Service Staff all claim the were visited by strange men in trench coats asking questions about the nights in question. Everyone I asked, including the OSI, told me at the time they had no interest and we were not going to investigate. Last week the British Government released the remaining files. Strange but the files of our incident have gone missing. Just like both Sgt. Penniston and Sgt Nevilles 35mm film's. Even two of the plaster casts Penniston took of the indentations of the craft landing pads disappeared. To say nothing of the British radar tapes. Captain Verano has gone on record saying he delivered a package to you plane side which you stated was the UFO pictures bound for Germany. I know you must know something as Al Brown was in the B/W Control tower the night I was out. We weren't flying so his presence there is strange. The B/W Controllers have now come forward and confirm they all saw a glowing object, saw it streak at high speed across their scope and go into the forest at W/B. The WSA Tower Operator and a Comm man working there also saw something. A friend chased down the British Air Traffic Controller and he too says he saw something despite the tape disappearing.

When I retired I was debriefed. I asked if I could talk about the incident and was told yes. I would be interested in your comments. If you are not at liberty to talk could you at least admit there was an investigation. It really doesn't matter much to me but it may enable several of the involved airmen to finally put the issue to rest. What happened has really ruined their lives.

Chuck Halt

In this year I sent an email to General Gordon Williams, which is attached. Little did I know that I was to end up in a quandary, many years later following the death of the General, which is discussed towards the end of the book, as it may be of relevance – or of course it may not be. **Did the General have a message for me?** Sadly I don't know…more on that in due course.

THE HALT PERSPECTIVE 2

27th December. Book: *The UFO Files*. Four out of five stars!

The Mail on Sunday published an article – awarding David Clarke's book '**The UFO Files**' – 4 out of 5 stars. Reviewer Harry Ritchie compared the results of his "expert rummaging" through the MoD archives with the breaking of the MPs expenses scandal earlier that year. Both breakthroughs were achieved as a result of investigative campaigns using the Freedom of Information Act. He wrote: *"UFOlogists believe aliens are among us and the military and political establishment are either blind to this dramatic fact or have covered it up. This book proves decisively that both beliefs are nonsense. The reality is both reassuring and un-thrilling. First,* **there are no flying saucers and little green men,** *hence the lack of even the most microscopic piece of hard evidence. Second, the MoD has neither covered anything up nor been blindly dismissive. In fact, until finally closing its UFO investigations unit earlier this month, the MoD has often taken UFOs seriously, even commissioning secret reports. In 2000 its Condign report concluded: 'That UFOs exist is indisputable' Eh? Yes, UFOs are real [but] they are not extraterrestrial spacecraft...they're natural phenomena which we don't really understand yet....The only remaining mystery is this: why would the MoD want to keep things top secret? It's not because there's any conspiracy but because it has held us, the public it is supposed to be serving, in a mixture of fear and contempt. All that the MoD's secrecy achieved was to encourage dark rumours and daft fantasies."*

The UFO Files had also been the previous subject of leading news stories published by *The Sunday Times* and *The Sunday Telegraph* on **20th September 2009.** These concentrated upon the contents of the Defence Intelligence Staff documents from the '90s that are featured in the final chapter of the book. *The UFO Files* were also reviewed by Neil Chandler in *The Daily Star on Sunday.* Who, to be fair commented, **"Yes, but where is the evidence proving that they are natural phenomena, if so, shouldn't there be a governmental health warning, and why the cover-up?"**

2012

Simon Sharman writes to the *Daily Telegraph*

Charles: Simon Sharman – with background media experience, and member of the on-line Manchester UFO Truth Group a Political Campaign (whom I met at my talk, in July 2015) wrote the following email to Mr. Tony Gallagher – Editor of the *Daily Telegraph*:

"I want to bring to your attention Jasper Copping's piece on the end of ufology, dated **4th November 2012.** *Having covered my main issues with his shoddy journalism in my on-line response found here, I must inform you of my concerns. It would appear that his entire article was based upon a statement made by Dave Wood, Chairman of something called the Association for the Scientific Study of Anomalous Phenomena (ASSAP). Considering this organisation, if it can even be called that, what was the centre of Copping's argument – one would assume that we were hearing from 'experts' in the field. Unfortunately for your night editor, this couldn't be further from the truth.*

Here's why...

1) The group hold their meetings in pubs.

2) They publish reports on anything from vampires to fairies.

Simon Sharman (centre) with Charles Halt

3) They have NO coverage of UFOs to be found in their on-line literature barring the most mundane of generic pieces, the most recent dated 2010. To publish statements on matters of the state of UFOlogy from a group such as this can only be described as 'Page 1 Google Journalism'. It simply isn't good enough for someone who's job description is Night news editor, as I see no editorial skill on display. On top of that, Copping also wrongly cites a previous incorrect Telegraph 'report' concerning the date that the government UFO hotline was shut down (and clearly more page 1 Google investigation). A two minute effort would have ascertained that this occurred in 2009. The reality is that ufology is far from dead and there needed to be more balanced input from active and more qualified experts in the field.

Dr. David Clarke does not come under this category as, although he may be qualified, he is well-known for his sceptical and debunking views. All in all, to put out such badly researched and incorrect content, to a global audience, is nowhere near the mark. Having been a broadcaster myself for many years I would never get away with such lacklustre efforts in my films or programs, and the printed word is often much more powerful (and therefore damaging) being far less transient. I hope you take this criticism in the tone that it is intended, which is that I would like to believe some form of internal follow up action will be taken. I look forward to your reply." Sincerely, Simon Sharman,(*Truspiracy* blog, 2012), a member of the *Manchester UFO Truth Group*.

A reply came from Assistant Editor – Hugh Dougherty, a few hours later, in which he thanked Simon for the email but defended what **Jasper had written as a fair and balanced piece of journalism.**

Simon wrote to him….

"Dear Hugh, Firstly I would like to thank you for taking the time to respond to my concerns so promptly, and for considering my issues with what appears to be some degree of thought. Unfortunately, I believe that when one considers the title of the article was **"UFO enthusiasts admit the truth may not be out there after all,** *and the sub-heading being,* **'Declining numbers of 'flying saucer' sightings and failure to establish proof of alien existence has led UFO enthusiasts to admit they might not exist after all.'** *I think it's safe to assume that the general premise of Copping's piece is quite clear. The story is quite literally based upon the words of Mr. Wood as I have previously said. If there was another basis for the piece which I somehow missed I would very much like to know what it was. Although I thank you for pointing out the full name attributed to ASSAP, I am completely aware of what it stands for and, in fact, it is their wide area of interest that concerns me the most. To suggest the state of ufology is dead, based on comments made by an organisation that discusses the nature of fantasy figures such as vampires and fairies, is utterly incongruous if one knows anything about the nature of some UFO incidents, which are not mere 'fairy tales'. I'm not talking about the 90% of explainable cases that are misidentifications, natural phenomena or hoaxes.*

RAF Woodbridge case of 1980

I'm referring to the very serious incidents such as the RAF Woodbridge case of 1980, which was definitively a real event that even the late Hill-Norton, Admiral of the Fleet, became involved with. So concerned was he about the reality of the incident and its significance to our national security that he repeatedly made a fuss in parliament in search of answers. Of course there are many more real incidents I could make reference to, where corroborative evidence exists, such as radar confirmation etc., which definitely takes the subject well out of the 'ghosts and paranormal' arena.

With reference to your question of relevance regarding their meeting spot being a public house, and your comparison to literary greats such as Tolkien and CS Lewis, I feel it necessary to point out just one thing. Those creative geniuses were famous for precisely that – creating incredible works of fiction and fantasy, a process which is undoubtedly assisted by varying degrees of intoxication of some sorts or another. I, for one, am very grateful for their time spent in the pub if it helped them write those amazing books. On the contrary, any organisation which makes use of the words 'Scientific Study' in its very title cannot be expected to be taken seriously or 'scientifically' by conducting meetings in houses of intoxication. Also, as I pointed out previously, there appears to be no evidence of any scientific thought, work, or papers on UFOs, published anywhere on their website that I could find (there are a total of three very old pages on UFOs on their entire website, none of which have any real substance). This does not constitute a body that can legitimately call itself a scientific UFO body, and therefore could never be cited as a credible voice for ufologists across the UK."

Sincerely, Simon Sharman.

Daily Telegraph on the existence of UFOs: 'UFO Enthusiasts Admit The Truth May Not Be Out There After All – Declining numbers of "flying saucer" sightings and failure to establish proof of alien existence has led UFO enthusiasts to admit they might not exist after all'.

Jasper Copping of the *Daily Telegraph* (4.11.2012) published another story on the UFO subject: 'Having failed to establish any evidence for the existence of extraterrestrial life, Britain's UFO watchers are reaching the conclusion that the truth might not be out there after all. Enthusiasts admit that a continued failure to provide proof and a decline in the number of "flying saucer" sightings suggests that aliens do not exist after all and could mean the end of "Ufology" – the study of UFOs – within the next decade. Dozens of groups interested in the flying saucers and other unidentified craft have already closed because of lack of interest and next week one of the country's foremost organisations involved in UFO research is holding a conference to discuss whether the subject has any future. Dave Wood, chairman of the Association for the Scientific Study of Anomalous Phenomena (ASSAP), said the meeting had been called to address the crisis in the subject and see if UFOs were a thing of the past. "**It is certainly a possibility that in ten years time, it will be a dead subject**," he added. "We look at these things on the balance of probabilities and this area of study has been ongoing for many decades. The lack of compelling evidence beyond the pure anecdotal suggests that on the **balance of probabilities that nothing is out there.**" "**I think that any UFO researcher would tell you that 98 percent of sightings that happen are very easily explainable.** One of the conclusions to draw from that is that perhaps there isn't anything there. The days of compelling eyewitness sightings seem to be over."

He said that far from leading to an increase in UFO sightings and research, the advent of the internet had coincided with a decline. ASSAP's UFO cases have dropped by 96 per cent since 1988, while the number of other groups involved in UFO research has fallen from well over 100 in the 1990s to around 30 now. Among those to have closed are the ***British Flying Saucer Bureau**, the **Northern UFO Network,** and the **Northern Anomalies Research Organisation**, as well as a fall in sightings and lack of proof. Mr Wood said the lack of new developments meant that the main focus for the dwindling numbers of enthusiasts was supposed UFO encounters that took place several decades ago and conspiracy theories that surround them. In particular, he cited the Roswell incident, in 1947, when an alien spaceship is said to have crashed in New Mexico, and the Rendlesham incident, in 1980 – often described as the British equivalent, when airmen from a US airbase in Suffolk reported a spaceship landing. Mr Wood added: "When you go to UFO conferences it is mainly people going over these old cases, rather than bringing new ones to the fore. There is a trend where a large proportion of UFO studies are tending towards conspiracy theories, which I don't think is particularly helpful. The issue is to be debated at a summit at the University of Worcester on *November 17th and the conclusions reported in the next edition of the association's journal, Anomaly."

The organisation, which describes itself as an education and research charity, was established in 1981.

---

*Denis Plunkett of the British Flying Saucer Bureau – An inspiration to all!

THE HALT PERSPECTIVE 2

John: I don't accept any of this as having any validity whatsoever. I've traced hundreds of people, some of whom were high ranking Police/RAF officers, who have not the faintest idea what these things are and where they come from! Denis Plunkett was Head of the International Flying Saucer Bureau, (UK) formed by Albert K. Bender (USA) in 1952, from which the Bristol-based British Flying Saucer Bureau was formed in 1953 (an amalgamation of the British Flying Saucer Bureau and Flying Saucer Club.) When Denis left for National Service with the RAF, in October1952, his father, Captain Plunkett, took over the running of the organisation until Denis returned, and was actively involved until his father's death in 1992.

Denis was still very much involved with the running of the group until, he too, passed away some years ago. In April 1954, Dennis was still serving at RAF Church Lawford, when he saw a *"mysterious black sphere moving in and out of cloud over the airbase, one day, and of a security notice posted on the wall of RAF Church Lawford, reminding the service personnel of the Official Secrets Act and the dire consequences of failing to keep quiet about any unusual airborne activity seen by the service personnel."* He was a real gentleman, and gave me much encouragement and assistance with regard to his own specialised knowledge of the subject going back many years. In 2009, at 79 years of age, he celebrated 58 years of marriage and was a real pleasure to know.

He and his wife Maureen were a lovely couple to talk to and I have nothing but praise for Denis. He had to endure a nasty smear in the press about the organization having closed down in 2001.

Denis: *"How can I say how much I was shocked when I opened the **June issue of UFO Magazine**, and discovered that a local reporter, mentioned the **suspension of UFO conferences during the summer by the British Flying Saucer Bureau,** was then transformed in a theatrical performance by the correspondent of a national newspaper into the shutdown of the BFSB – news which then went round the world and caused such a hullabaloo. I must categorically state that at no time, to no local or nationwide newspaper reporter, and in no television or broadcasted interview, I ever said anything that could lead to confusion and be interpreted as meaning the shutdown of the oldest UFO organization established in the world."*

Denis has been involved in researching the UFO subject since 1945. Now let's look at what he and Maureen saw in **June 1966**. *"Maureen and I were preparing for bed. I went to pull the curtains and couldn't believe my eyes. For a moment I thought I was seeing things, but then realised it was **nine brilliant white*** *lights dancing in the sky*. I shouted to Maureen to come and look, and for an hour we stared in wonderment, transfixed by the lights, which flashed on and off like lights on a Christmas tree. Initially, I assumed it was an aircraft, but I soon dismissed this theory because the patterns they were making were too irregular. **Suddenly, one light left the group and remained in the same position for ten minutes before rejoining the main pattern,** which was a loose formation, with the lights constantly changing positions. Then they disappeared, never to be seen again. Maureen and I tried to explain away what we'd seen. We ruled out about ten possibilities, including helicopters, as there wasn't a sound disturbing the balmy night air. We had no explanation and struggled to sleep that night. Where had they come from? Why were they here? Where had they gone?

I presumed that the other two UFO organisations, Northern UFO Network, and the Northern Anomalies Research Organisation, had suffered the same fate, as the countless others as time passed, with people moving on to open other groups and organisations, that were numerous in the mid to the late 20th Century, or sadly had passed away.

A look on the Internet (2020) for Northern Anomalies Research Association, comes up with **NARO,** and identifies at least 20 separate organisations that have nothing to do with UFOs! But on that page it shows this: [Steve Mera. Biography; (**Northern Anomalies Research Organisation**) ran by Peter Hough & Jenny Randles; Steve is Co-Host of Planet X Radio. Have UFOs Disappeared? August 16, 2013; **Northern Anomalies Research Organisation**, and recently, the **High Frequency Active Auroral Research Program** . . . Among those to have closed are the British Flying Saucer Bureau, the Northern UFO Network, and the **Northern Anomalies Research Organisation**.]

I then looked up the High Frequency Active Auroral network which is, **High-frequency Active Auroral Research Program (HAARP)** initiated as an ionospheric research program jointly funded by the U.S. Air Force, the U.S. Navy, the University of Alaska Fairbanks, and the Defense Advanced Research Projects Agency (DARPA. It was designed and built by BAE Advanced Technologies. Its original purpose was to analyze the ionosphere and investigate the potential for developing ionospheric enhancement technology for radio communications and surveillance. As a university-owned facility, HAARP is a high-power, high-frequency transmitter used for study of the ionosphere. **(Source: Wikipedia)**

Deliberate Deception – A Case of Disinformation in the UFO Research Community

Charles: This was a 100 page publication – also available to download – By Peter Robbins – loyalties for Larry! In May 2014, [seventeen years after the publication of *Left At East Gate*,] Peter Robbins found himself having to set the record straight regarding a new accounting of those events published by Nick Pope, Jim Penniston and John Burroughs in their book **Encounter in Rendlesham Forest: The Inside Story of the World's Best-Documented UFO Incident**.

Peter continues his criticism of the way that Larry has been treated and takes Nick to task on the one hand, while praising him on the other – a course of literary action echoed in a later response of his – this time in a hard copy book published as response to the lecture given by me.

One thing you can't criticize Peter Robbins for is his loyalties for Larry. He has fought tooth and nail for Larry despite many criticisms about Larry and his role over the years but of course time has moved on and shown many flaws in a structure that has been falling apart. This has nothing to do with Larry being there, or was he the first whistle-blower? Admittedly time has shown that Peter eventually found the courage to dissociate himself from Larry Warren – but history should record the facts rather than conveniently taking chunks out of it out to suit individuals' own agendas, changing moods, and belief systems – the damage has been done.

Huffington Post USA

Charles Halt, Former Air Force Colonel, Accuses U.S. Of UFO Cover-Up!

WEIRD NEWS, 24/09/2012 19:07 BST | **Updated** 07/12/2017 03:01 GMT

LAS VEGAS – Former Air Force Col. Charles Halt accused the federal government of a UFO cover-up that involves a secret agency to deal with what might be extraterrestrial visitations. *"I'm firmly convinced there's an agency, and there is an effort to suppress,"* Halt told an audience of 200 people Saturday night at the Smithsonian-affiliated Museum. Two former Air Force officers who were part of the infamous *Project Blue Book* – the military's official UFO investigation in the 1950s and '60s – and a former investigator with Britain's Ministry of Defense were among the panel of speakers for a program entitled 'Military UFOs: Secrets Revealed.'

Halt, pictured above, was the deputy base commander of the RAF Bentwaters military base in England and one of numerous eyewitnesses to **several UFO-related events** at Rendlesham Forest in December 1980. He believes the observed UFOs were either extraterrestrial or extradimensional in origin. *"I've heard many people say that it's time for the government to appoint an agency to investigate, there is an agency, a very close-held, compartmentalized agency that's been investigating this for years, and there's a very active role played by many of our intelligence agencies that probably don't even know the details of what happens once they collect the data and forward it. It's kind of scary, isn't it? In the last couple of years, the British have released a ton of information, but has anybody ever seen what their conclusions were or heard anything about Bentwaters officially? When the documents were released, the timeframe when I was involved in the incident is missing – it's gone missing. Nothing else is missing,"* Halt added that he's never been harassed over the reports he made about the Bentwaters UFO incidents. *"Probably for a couple of good reasons, number one, my rank and some of the jobs I've held, but also very early on, I sat down and made a very detailed tape and made several copies of everything I know about it and they're secluded away. Maybe I'm paranoid. I don't know, but I think it was time well spent when I made the tapes."*

THE HALT PERSPECTIVE 2

2013

MOD declassifies their UFO files

John: Declassified files, released by the National Archives in late June 2013, reveal that the MOD closed its UFO Desk in 2009, claiming any investigation into sightings *"would be an inappropriate use of defence resources"*. The 25 files included 4,400 pages and cover the work carried out in the final two years of the MOD UFO Desk – from late 2007 until November 2009. Officials decided to close the 'UFO hotline', as it was deemed to have *'no defence benefit'*, and resources devoted to it were taking staff away from *'more valuable defence-related activities'*. They include accounts of alleged abductions and contact with aliens, as well as UFO sightings near UK landmarks, including the Houses of Parliament. In a briefing to the then Defence Secretary – Bob Ainsworth – in November 2009, Carl Mantell, of the RAF Air Command, suggested the MOD *"should reduce the UFO desk, which is consuming increasing resources, but produces no valuable defence output"*. He said that, in more than 50 years, *"No UFO sighting reported to (MOD) has ever revealed anything to suggest an extraterrestrial presence or military threat to the UK"*. An official MoD statement declared, *"The Ministry of Defence has no opinion on the existence, or otherwise, of extraterrestrial life. However, in over 50 years, no UFO report has revealed any evidence of a potential threat to the United Kingdom."*

2014

Encounter in Rendlesham Forest, Nick Pope, Jim Penniston & John Burroughs

Charles: In this book published on the 1st of April 2014 co-author Jim Penniston had this to say about the UFO subject and his commanding officer bearing in mind over the years the two of us had appeared together in various films and documentaries. Jim: *"***I believe that 99 percent of UFO sightings** *can be explained, as natural occurring phenomena, or people who have psychological issues which manifest exponentially when they see things they can't explain. My experience falls into the remaining one percent!"*

Well I can't accept those contradictory statistics which are trotted out to us by those that have decided to completely ignore the weight of evidence much of which is documented in this book! If you look at British UFO sightings for the whole of 1980, over a 100 sightings (some have been left out) it's hard to imagine why the media would constantly seek to dismiss what we saw all those years ago, as having no foundation. But they do! **How convenient that Jim's encounter falls into the one per cent**! This means then that all of these hundreds of people, this book their accounts can be explained away rationally as what? I challenge Jim to put his money where his mouth is!

We grow weary of so many daft explanations put forward to explain what was witnessed in Rendlesham Forest, Suffolk now 40years ago. Ranging from misidentification, atmospheric phenomena, balloons, drones, covert technology, or now what appears to in vogue, **'testing of New weapons' using hallucinogens by scientists or engineers from top secret laboratories, on troops on the ground.** Not forgetting the SAS or Porton Down scientists…what next? Fairies or even the Loch Ness Monster!

Leopards do change their spots!

Jim then praises me referring to me as an *"enlisted man's Colonel who valued the NCO's that he commanded. He valued their knowledge, skills, assessments, opinions, judgements and the people themselves, as a valuable and key part of the USA mission. Colonel Halt is an officer who truly believes you are only as good as people you command. The Colonel believes it was the NCO corps that made it all happen. Then his conduct in regards to the Rendlesham Forest incident, well he was only following orders and he stretched those orders as far as he could without jeopardising his career."* As the reader will see in due course, something inexplicable took place five years later, with the release of a new book by Jim and Gary Osborn which includes some very nasty verbal attacks on my integrity and character – completely unwarranted and not the sort of behaviour I would have expected from a gentlemen who I had regarded with great respect! Much more on that further along!

Phenomena Magazine – Claims of disinformation campaign against Larry Warren!

Published by Steve Mera and Brian Allan of *Phenomena Magazine* in August **2014** as a free download on their site and in *UFO Truth*. **Steve Mera:** *"More recently we became aware of a new publication entitled 'Encounter in Rendlesham Forest: The Inside Story of the World's Best-Documented UFO Incident', co-written by the former intelligence officer for the Ministry of Defence – Nick Pope, and former US Air Force personnel Jim Penniston and John Burroughs. Surprised at learning there was enough new data on the Rendlesham incident to produce another book on the incident, we obtained a copy and settled down to digest the contents. However, as we worked our way through the events described in the book, we became aware of the absence of critical material which appeared in* **'Left At East Gate.'** *This even ignored the rightly deserved recognition Larry and Peter should have for their years of investigative research. How very odd. We were aware that, not only did Peter respect Nick Pope, but considered him a good friend. It had to have been impossible for Nick to have done this accidentally. Suddenly, it occurred to us that here was the start of a disinformation campaign along with conspiratorial issues concealing a veiled vendetta. What on earth were we seeing here? Was the Rendlesham Forest incident to take a new direction, a direction that could possibly be leading us away from the truth? 'Encounters in Rendlesham Forest,' also assisted in creating confusion over statements Charles Halt had made. Had he also moved the goalposts?*

Steve Mera: *…To be fair, the book did keep our interest, but probably for the wrong reasons and we were left confused and ill at ease. Not only must Nick have left Larry and Peter perplexed, but also many in the UFO community. A week later we received a document from Peter Robbins entitled* **"Deception: A Review and Critical Analysis of the book, Encounters in Rendlesham Forest",** *and that was exactly what it was. It has been re-titled to differentiate that manuscript from the completed work you are about to read. This document represents a thorough and yet a fairly conducted in-depth investigation, which is surprisingly objective and at the same time, it has the all the precision of a surgical procedure. We believe that* **"Deliberate Deception: "A Case of Disinformation in the UFO Research Community"** *has huge implications, not only for the Rendlesham Forest incident but Ufology in general."* [Authors': time was to show just how huge those implications were for the parties concerned!

THE HALT PERSPECTIVE 2

Peter Robbins' Review of *Encounter In Rendlesham Forest*

Peter: "*Last autumn my friend and colleague Gary Heseltine, who is also publisher of* UFO Truth Magazine *in beautiful West Yorkshire, asked if I'd be willing to use one of my regular magazine columns to review a new book due for publication in late April 2014. Issue number six of* UFO Truth *would be going out to subscribers early that May so it was imperative that I locate, read, then write my review as soon as possible, then make my deadline, something I regularly excelled at failing to do. Keenly aware of my adversarial history with its two authors, Gary just wanted to make sure I was up for the assignment. He knew I would write an objective, even-handed review if I accepted the assignment.*"

In the book Peter tells of requesting a copy of the book to review a month or so before it was published, and then when this didn't take place, he found a copy in a New York book store. Reading it he says, "*The pattern, for there was no other term for it, was subtle at first, then more apparent. It emerged from just below the surface of the key author's words, and if my imagination wasn't running away with me, it was a pattern of deceptive writing that seemed to have been deliberately undertaken in an intentional manner, and calculated only to manifest negative intent. The more I observed it come into play, the more uncomfortable it made me. This feeling was soon replaced by one of anger, and finally one of serious concern. More, it was clear to me that this was something very few readers would ever pick up on or even look for. The reason for this was that each separate element in the overall pattern was a specific piece of information that could have only been found in one source: the book* Left At East Gate, *which I had co-authored with Larry Warren on the Rendlesham Forest UFO incident published seventeen years earlier in both the United States and the United Kingdom. Each data point in the pattern was presented respectfully and authoritatively by Nick Pope, but always in an incomplete, misleading or reconfigured form, and always – always with the seeming intent of leading readers to doubt Larry Warren's account, credibility and motivations regarding his involvement in the events of December 1980, and in the process, to reflect poorly on my professionalism, research and investigation skills, and reputation as well.*"

Charles Halt is a manipulator

For me, Charles Halt long ago emerged as the most enigmatic player among the witnesses. He is in the unique position of being both **witness/victim and manipulator,** *especially with regard to the influence he had over Jim and John for most of their adult lives – and in that respect he has successfully played the pair off against Warren for several decades now. It's both interesting and depressing and not without some irony, to observe that the kind of critical undermining which Halt has used against Warren for so long he now applies to undermine the credibility of Burroughs and Penniston. The book carried on highlighting various inaccuracies and praising while at the same time criticizing Nick's style and some of the written text for example...*

(1) Peter – *The following day's debriefing, the one that Warren was involved in, is then discussed with the addition of several new inaccuracies. We are told that two de-briefers presided when Larry has only and always maintained that there were three. Nick accurately reports that at the end of the debriefing it is Warren who asked the question, "'What would happen if they talked about the UFO?" "Bullets are cheap," he said with a smile.'" However we are then told that this was followed by the remark, "Yeah, they're a dime a dozen." Where did Nick come up with these patent inaccuracies? I'd never heard of either before reading them in this book and Larry Warren has never said or written them. Am I splitting hairs here?*"

(2) *Charles Halt is quoted as saying "I never told [Left At East Gate author] Peter Robbins any structure was penetrated by beams. I was several miles away. From my view, a beam or more came down near the WSA. I don't know for a fact that the beams landed there. I know they were in the area. I was too far away but relied on the radio chatter which indicated the beams had landed there." This passage is memorable for me not only for the obvious reason, but because to the best of my knowledge it marks the only time that anyone has*

ever deliberately lied about me in a book in my more than thirty years in the field of UFO studies. Larry Warren and, at the time, UFO researcher Bob Oechsler (who had driven us to the meeting), were also present when Halt made the statement, should this be of significance to the reader. **I understand the Colonel has since stated he was aware of the beams having penetrated the bunkers,** *but not as a witness, though I am not absolutely certain of this."*

John: I would be the first to appreciate that as time moves on people's attitudes change. An example being melting support for Larry Warren, following the realisation his account(s) can't be trusted. The problem is that so much of this information is still available on the Internet, and it provides a springboard for people to comment on unaware of recent developments.

In **October 2014,** The *East Anglian Daily Times* gave some publicity to a film which was produced by Daniel Simpson, **'Rendlesham UFO incident'.** (For the US the film was titled **'Hanger 10').** Its premiere was at the Colchester Film Festival on the 22nd of October 2014, with release on the 9th of February 2015. Brenda Butler was one of the dignitaries to be invited along with Gary Heseltine. The film, the first it is claimed to have been made about the UFO incident, centres around three metal detectors looking for Saxon gold in the forest. What they find is a terrifying encounter with an 'unforgiving alien presence'. Brenda thought the film was a load of rubbish. She asked the producer what he thought. He replied the same according to Brenda! The paper also showed Larry and Gary discussing the letter sent to Warren from his mother. It was of interest to find out that Gary and Daniel were interviewed by the *BBC* about the forthcoming film.

THE HALT PERSPECTIVE 2

Brenda preparing posters for delivery around the Forest for the forthcoming conference

PART 6

THE WOODBRIDGE CONFERENCE – GOOD AND BAD!

2015

Gary Heseltine – forthcoming visit by Charles Halt

IT may be of relevance to include a comment published on *Facebook* by Gary Heseltine in **July 2015**, just before the conference took place. This epitomized the then current feeling towards the presence of Charles Halt who had merely accepted an invitation to come over to England and deliver a talk, who was found guilty in the court of **Facebook** law. Then having to prove his innocence rather than the other way round!

Gary:*"A number of people have asked whether I will be attending the Charles Halt lecture today in Woodbridge and sadly the answer is no, I will not be attending. That is because I have <u>ended my association with Col Halt after seven years</u> in late 2014, following his sustained and continued attacks on the original Rendlesham whistleblower, Larry Warren, which I find unfair and totally unwarranted. Whilst Halt is an extremely important witness to the events at Rendlesham and the Halt Memo is one of the top 10 UFO documents in the world, I believe that with his high rank that he should be trying to bring the witnesses together, however, over time, I found that this was not the case, far from it. Whilst Larry is many things I don't believe that he is the 'wannabe' and liar that Halt paints him to be and that he is an integral part of the Rendlesham jigsaw. In private emails he was very critical of me for my continued friendship with Larry. This I found unacceptable and with his continued verbal attacks on Larry his actions caused me to bring an end to our association. As a result I have withdrawn our 'collaborative' film script **'Three Nights in December.'** However I intend to draft a completely new script told from different perspectives."*

This Morning TV contacts me! Hopes dashed away! No surprise there!

John: On the **1st of July, 2015,** I received a telephone call from Matthew Claydon, who was Day Researcher for **This Morning TV Studios**, London Television Studios, Upper Ground, SE1 9LT, Tel: 0207 157 4777, who

THE HALT PERSPECTIVE 2

spent a short time discussing the UFO subject and then asked me about a piece of film which I had taken in Rendlesham Forest on the 27th December 2000, which they wanted to use on the show that included an appearance by Malcolm Robinson on the morning of the 2nd of July 2015. In an email to me he (Matthew) said: *Hi John, thanks so much for chatting to me just now. If you could send me over the footage and a brief description of the event, I'd be very grateful. Thanks, Matt.* I thought wow, they are going to make some reference to the unique film and show maybe just a few frames.

Pooed her pants!

Instead it was the usual load of old rubbish which stereotypes the media's attempts to relegate such subject material to the crackpot elements, hardly helped by an inane comment made by Philip Schofield who asked a caller that bothered to ring in about her experience in Rendlesham Forest, whether it was **"enough to have pooed her pants", amidst general laughter**. I appreciate that this was never going to be a serious discussion on the UFO subject, what I did expect was the courtesy of at least informing me that although I had gone to a great deal of bother to send Matthew **a clip of film, the stills, a copy of Volume 8 on PDF**, and the newspaper cutting which accompanied it, **nothing was actually said about this material!**

Malcolm had this to say afterwards: *"Prior to going live, I was told by a chap from the show that he wanted me to speak about a number of Scottish UFO sightings, so I knew they would be coming up. Sadly they only got round to one of those Scottish incidents as time was against us. Then all too soon (about 10 minutes) it was over, they cut to the commercials and that was it. Now I was a wee bit cheeky at this point, as I said to Amanda Holden, Right Amanda and Phil, let's have you, let's get a group photo to which thankfully they were more than happy to do so and we all grouped together for a shot of the four of us. One of the studio guys used my camera but there were at least another four photographers from the floor all taking photographs as well for their web site. And with that it was back to the green room, however before I left the studio, I was asked if I would like to go back and do another live piece in about 45 minutes, this would be a live on air phone in. I didn't need to be asked twice, this would give me another chance to present to the public the reality of this subject. And so once more, with a wee bit of extra blusher applied – I was again ushered back to the couch where I was joined by Amanda Holden and Philip Schofield. There were a few technical hic ups at the start of this segment where they lost the caller's voice but after that we took a few calls from the general public and I was asked to give my thoughts as to what they saw."*

THE HALT PERSPECTIVE 2

14th July 2015 – *Daily Express* newspaper – contacts John – not credited!

Charles: Jon Austin published an extensive interview made with Brenda Butler, which included references to MIB etc., on the **14th July 2015,** and in my opinion, denigrated the UFO subject.

On the afternoon of the same day John Hanson was contacted by Mr. Austin, who asked him for any information pertaining to the radar tapes. He sent him a PDF, along with requested photos and other information, and also spoke to him at length about my part in all of this. John was disappointed that once again **no references or credits** were included in that on-line article during my visit to Suffolk.

14th July 2015 – *The Independent*. 'Former Air Force Colonel claims he has new evidence that aliens visited Rendlesham Forest in Suffolk in 1980' under a large delightful photograph of a man polishing his flying saucer! Next to it are photos of teenagers in Rendlesham Forest and a photo of the tacky flying saucer situated by the Forestry Commission! Glad to see nothing changes!

Colonel Charles Irwin Halt talks at Woodbridge, Suffolk

John: A few days before the **11th of July 2015,** I was contacted by Christopher Clark, who described himself as a surveyor, currently living in Woodbridge. Mr. Clark told me that he knew Charles Halt very well and that he had dined with him and his family during his time as Deputy Base Commander. Christopher, well-spoken and articulate, was in-sistent that he meet up with Charles Halt for dinner, but I had to tell him that this was not possible, owing to the Colonel's commitments. Chris told me that a few days after the UFO event he had asked Charles, during a visit to the Officers mess on the Base in December 1980 if he could take him to where it had happened. Charles took him to the location – which was, according to Chris: "…*a cleared area, where some Americans were busy cleaning up.* **I checked the ground with my Geiger counter** *and found some radiation. I then helped Charles to obtain a plaster cast of one of the impressions in the ground, and asked him if he would allow me to interview the three men who had reported the incident. He declined, saying that this wasn't possible. I* **then took a roll of film***, which I still have in my possession, which has never been processed*"...

Charles: John told me about a guy that had been pestering the staff at the *Bull Pub* in Woodbridge a few days before I was due to talk in July 2015. He introduced himself as Chris Clarke, a surveyor by profession living in Woodbridge.

John asked him how he knew me and he told him of having invited me round for lunch with his wife during 1980, and that he was (or is) a friend of Colonel Bayer and that he had been into the forest and examined the 'landing spot' and also claimed he had taken measurements of the site. Then took a roll of film of the area, which he has put somewhere in the house but never processed! He claimed he kept quiet because I had asked him to do so! I have not the faintest idea of what this man is on about. John asked him about the film which he then claimed he had lost. He never mentioned any of this when he spoke to me in the hall!

Now over nearly 40 years later there appears to be an endless chain of people who seek to gain financially through the production of films, plays and TV series, what 'they' believe took place in Rendlesham Forest, Suffolk, England. Some are well meaning others involve a multitude of explanations based on individual beliefs knowing that the focus of media attention – like its Roswell counterpart –caters to a public who have a stereotyped impression of what UFOs are –offering scenarios, involving aliens meeting with Base commanders and goodness knows what, drawn from the product of overactive imaginations and failure to research the subject properly.

John: We would like to thank everyone who was involved, Retired **Colonel Charles Irwin Halt, Brenda Butler, David Bryant** (Master of Ceremonies) **Steve Wills,** and **Lionel Beer,** at Woodbridge Community Hall, Suffolk, on the evening of the 11th July 2015, which was a success, judging from the full house.

When this matter was first proposed, some months ago, I was subjected to a barrage of veiled threats made against me on-line, by a number of people who clearly felt that their procrastinations would derail the forthcoming talk and persuade me and my co-organiser, Brenda Butler, to withdraw.

History will record the opposite! Special thanks should go to **Tom Potter** and the Editor of the *East Anglian Daily Times,* for their support and subsequent newspaper publicity advertising the forthcoming visit by Colonel Charles Halt. We would also like to thank James Hazel, of *BBC Radio Suffolk* (who attended and interviewed Charles Halt), and the same TV station for an interview conducted with Brenda Butler, although I was disappointed by the total lack of any acknowledgement made of my personal commitment towards organising this venue or of my knowledge of the subject.

David Bryant, Master of Ceremonies/Author/Space Rocks

David: On Saturday, Linda and I, together with friends Jason & Thomas, spent a day with Colonel Charles Halt (Commander of RAF Bentwaters at the time of the Rendlesham Forest UFO incident). The forest was full of dragonflies, despite a total absence of nearby water! There were Emperors, Brown Hawkers and Common Darters, as well as lots of newly-emerged Graylings.

The day started with a small group accompanying the Colonel around the forest, where he pointed out the sites of the major events of December 1980. The Press was in attendance, so it was pleasantly surprising how forthright the Colonel was with his reminiscences, particularly in regard to the accounts of some of the other alleged witnesses . . . I have to say: the Colonel and his son Clifford were the most delightful people and it was an absolute pleasure to spend the day with them. Needless to say he declined to visit the 'UFO Sculpture 'on the grounds that it wasn't in the right place. Now it's very much a tourist attraction, bruised and battered!

After lunch we moved on to Woodbridge Community Centre to set up the hall for six hours of talks and discussion: I MC'd the event and (despite the lack of decent mikes) received much very gratifying

THE HALT PERSPECTIVE 2

feedback: thanks to all for that! I enjoyed my one hour lecture and, again, there were plenty of positive comments (and book sales! LOL!) Hopefully I might be sent some photos with me in! I enjoyed delivering my forty minute lecture and, again, there were plenty of positive comments. The Colonel spoke for around 80 minutes and mingled with attendees throughout the event, signing autographs and posing for photographs.

Bearing in mind that I attended the conference as an unpaid guest speaker, talking on an entirely unrelated topic to the Colonel, – **within hours of the event, I began to receive abuse from all sides of the Warren – Halt – Penniston – Burroughs debate.** Now personally speaking, face to face I have always found Larry Warren a pleasant enough person: I knew he had an ongoing conflict with Colonel Halt, but hadn't realised that everyone is supposed to take sides! Larry has often been 'frank' when discussing the Colonel, but apparently his supporters don't feel Charles Halt is entitled to respond. The online 'dialogue' has polarized the UFO fraternity, attracted comment from people who didn't even attend the event and unfairly heaped invective on totally neutral pundits such as Nick Pope. The festering sore between Larry Warren & Charles Halt and the two most credible other witnesses – Jim Penniston and John Burroughs – **does nothing to further the cause of disclosure and adds fuel to those who seek to dismiss the entire incident. Astronomer and UFO debunker Ian Ridpath must be laughing himself sick!**

After ten years trying to help raise the profile and credibility of the event in lectures, websites, articles and, latterly, books, I'm done with the RFI: it seems unlikely that, after 35 years, any resolution will ever occur and, having met most of the major characters, I have been able to draw my own conclusions, and these are the books that I written and published.

THE HALT PERSPECTIVE 2

THE HALT PERSPECTIVE 2

David Bryant

Dishonoured Promises

Charles: I still feel, now five years later, let down badly by ex-hospital porter – podcaster Ben Emlyn Jones, who has never had the common decency to apologize to us personally after reneging on a 'gentlemen's promise' with regard to the film taken privately in Rendlesham forest Suffolk by him in July 2015.This was supposedly to have been given free gratis to the Forestry Commission, following my suggestion that any money made from the film was to be 'ploughed back' into forest preservation. Instead he scrounged £60 from John to get home and then promptly uploaded the films to *You Tube* against our verbal wishes and agreement made. What I also found dishonourable was that when I asked Jones to switch the camera off while I made an off-the-record statement, he switched the camera off and then on, unknown to me. What a cad! The crazy thing is that Jones, who says he used to respect John Hanson and his work can't <u>understand what he's done wrong!</u>

Ben Emlyn Jones

THE HALT PERSPECTIVE 2

Fighting for the cause of truth!

There is an irony here – if I hadn't addressed my long-held suspicions about the validity of the version of events given by Larry as to what took place over those few night at the end of December 1980 during the evening of the conference, then one may presume that the reputation of Mr Larry Warren would have remained intact for even longer. The majority of the guests had the opportunity to meet me personally and spend a few minutes talking to me and shaking my hand. Larry and Peter Robbins were banned by John and Brenda Butler following discussion after a number of inappropriate cartoons were made available on the internet showing myself in jail with Larry and Peter Robbins stood outside in the role of prison guards.

Initially it was thought this had been sanctioned by Peter and Larry – this proved not to be the case. John then persuaded me to let Peter attend – Peter then declined.

In a way this was the 'straw' that ultimately broke the Camel's back and was the beginning of the end for Larry and his book *Left At East Gate*. Unfortunately this period of 'transition' was too spark off further threats made against Sacha Christie, John Hanson and others, who have supported me – for at least 18 months – two years, before Larry finally was brought to task by Sacha following an investigation into allegations of large-scale fraud – which was reported to the Police . . . including complaints made of criminal malicious communications to the Police by Sacha Christie and James Welsh following painstaking investigations over the last few years into the truthfulness of the claims made by Larry Warren as published in *Left At East Gate,* as to the role played by him during the end of December 1980.

In addition there is much suspicion on signed documents produced by Warren which are claimed to be bogus…and not unnaturally raise great suspicion as to their authenticity. Some have been allocated crime reference numbers but little police action has been taken so far. If they (Warren and Ben Emlyn Jones) have the right to attack our characters then we have the legal right of reply if only to set the record straight and ensure fairness.

John: It's difficult to know where to start and where to finish with the vicious attacks made on myself and Colonel Halt after publicizing details of the forthcoming conference 18 months beforehand. A situation which became worse following what Colonel Halt had to say about Larry Warren at the Woodbridge Conference which took place on the **11th of July 2015.** This upset many of his 'followers' at the time, and led to verbal and written procrastinations on Facebook that are too graphic to publish here, with hatred and obscenity, that show us much about the character of the persons involved.

Incredible now, five years later, one Scottish researcher – David Colman – still moans about me on the **Rendlesham Lone Rangers website** years later after having forgotten his verbal attacks on me, in which he accused me **of theft** and ripping people off – **why, because I charged £20 a ticket!** No apologies! As Colonel Halt has said many times – we have the right to defend ourselves!

Fortunately I received a large number of emails and personal telephone calls, thanking me and Brenda for having arranged the venue. However I was unprepared to enter into any discussion on *Facebook* with some people who strongly attacked, sometimes with profanity, my part as a co-organiser, feeling I was to blame for allowing Colonel Halt to criticise the part played by Larry Warren.

Herd mentality and egos reign!

This emphasizes the 'herd mentality' of those in the UFO community that, instead of ringing me up to openly discuss their grievances, dashed off reams of text on Facebook, which included criticising Colonel Halt's talk being shorter than was proposed – along with allegations of suspicious activity taking place behind stage, involving interference with the microphone and shuffling of Colonel Halt's papers, along with a reference from a colleague to the effect, i.e. '*John was only partly to blame*', is it no wonder that I will not engage in never-ending pointless discussions on Facebook.

I was also disappointed about the criticisms, directed by various people on Facebook who were there at the meeting after the event, some of whom were so-called friends, about the part played by David Bryant, who graciously offered his services free to act as Master of Ceremonies. This is totally unfair and without substance. What is astonishing is that these people also lacked the courage to speak to him face-to-face, but instead chose to make defamatory claims about his character on the Internet!

Threatened by Peter Robbins!

This talk led to a book being published by someone who I had regarded as a friend – Peter Robbins. He threatened me with all manner of legal actions. He had assisted me with some of the content of *Haunted Skies*, and I was shocked that he chose to do this in a knee jerk reaction, without at least bothering to contact me.

HE HAS NEVER PERSONALLY APOLOGISED TO ME.

When Colonel Charles Halt came over to the UK in July 2015, there were some interviews conducted by the *BBC* on site and at the Woodbridge Community Centre.

Media's apparent blackout on John Hanson – one of the organisers!

Bob Tibbitts: *"I have just listened to the BBC Radio Suffolk broadcast by Mark Murphy, in its "listen again" facility on the website. I would like to mention that the feature about Rendlesham Forest and the upcoming talk by Col Charles Halt was produced in a fairly well-balanced way and refreshing in that the usual 'tongue-in-cheek' attitude usually applied to this subject matter, was absent. However, I was a little surprised to say the least that the presenters did not include information about who organised and paid for it to take place.*

John Hanson put this event together with Brenda Butler and paid for Colonel Halt to come to Suffolk to give the talk. John has also gone to great lengths to arrange for other speakers to talk at the gathering in Woodbridge. It seems discourteous of the presenters at BBC Suffolk, not to ensure that John Hanson was given kudos and recognition for his efforts. They could have at least made mention of his extensive investigations into the UFO subject over many years and authorship of eleven volumes of 'Haunted Skies', *Volume 8 of which showcases over two hundred or so pages devoted to the Rendlesham Forest Incident. Perhaps the BBC could rectify this omission by featuring John's works on a future occasion"*

John: Bob is the designer and typesetter for the *Haunted Skies* books, a role he has been carrying out since the early days. Bob has been interested in UFOs since the late 1960's and was head of Coventry UFO Research Group. He produced a magazine titled '*SYNTONIC*', and we thought it would be nice to show the readers a photograph of him and a cutting from the early days. He has always been there for the *Haunted Skies* books both as a friend and adviser.

THE HALT PERSPECTIVE 2

'UFOs may date back to the Bible'

Evening Telegraph Reporter

LIKE many lads of his age, Bob Tibbitts likes girls, pop music and psychedelic paintings. But he has a passionate interest in enigmatic objects which, like the Loch Ness Monster, have kept people guessing for years — and the mystery of U.F.Os.

"I want to collect as much information about U.F.O.'s as I can, before I am old and wrinkled, so in a few years time I hope to be something of an expert," he said.

Bob is 17, and lives at 43, Tanners Lane, Tile Hill, Coventry, bungalow with an essential ingredient — a big living room window from which he can stargaze.

For Bob, it is a case of believing is not necessarily seeing. It's a long time now since he saw what he thought was a U.F.O. That doesn't bother him, for he is convinced that these alien bodies are very real and have a purpose in their existence.

Gawped

Real or not, people from Cheylesmore to Chile, from Brazil back to Bell Green, have gawped at these weird and wonderful phenomenons.

Coventry and Warwickshire have had their share of UFOs. "Cigar-like UFO over Leamington"; "Invaders, or the moon?" "Stupendous sight near Banbury". "Lights in sky like car headlamps"; and "Councillor and his family see seven UFOs at Stratford". These are but a few of the colourful headlines that have wrestled with readers' imaginations.

Bob, an apprentice compositor with the "Evening Telegraph", became interested in UFOs three years ago.

Know how

He is trying to assimilate a fundamental knowledge of astronomy to help his UFO know-how. "Knowledge of basic astronomy is important," he said. "With it, you can say at once whether a sighting is a UFO or a meteorite."

As Bob's fascination for UFO's has grown, so has his interest in the Bible, "because I think there is a connection."

The Bible, he told me, indicated that some form of spacecraft, operated by beings similar to humans, visited certain people and places of the Old Testament.

Could it be, he reasoned, that just as Christ was sent to the earth with a message, so were the strange objects that were puzzling thousands?

"The fact that so many have been seen in daytime strengthens the existence of UFO's," said Bob. He has one main ambition — the furthering of his hobby. "I'd love to have a go with the telescope at Jodrell Bank."

Bob Tibbitts

UFOs AND THE BIBLE MIRACLES

THE suggestion, in a recent article in the "Evening Telegraph" that U.F.Os may date back to the Bible is well known in U.F.O. research circles.

Many of the miracles mentioned in the Bible, can probably be attributed to U.F.O.s, and it is possible that Jesus himself was a spaceman.

Many people who might otherwise turn to Christ must have visual proof first. The same applies to U.F.O.s. Only seeing is believing to a great many.

May not the increasing unrest in the world be due to lack of faith and a disinterested outlook in general.

D. Speed.
(Coventry U.F.O. Research Group).
Bell Green.

★ ★

IN reply to Mr. Bob Tibbitts, I, too, have studied astronomy rather extensively, and have my own 8in. refracting telescope. I am also a member of the British Astronomical Association.

I entirely agree that some aspects of astronomy are connected with the Bible and religion, and sometimes the two do not mix, but I was surprised at the suggestion that most people, who have virtually no knowledge of astronomy, could take a meteorite for a U.F.O.

A lot of people do not recognise meteorites as such, but m usually as "shooting stars," although they may not have idea what they really are sight of a meteorite, or a sh of them is so familiar, such as the Geminid, or better kno Leonid shower is taken rat for granted and thought little of.

More often weather ballo and artificial satellites are taken for U.F.O.s, because course they take in the sky gests that they are manned in ligently and with purpose. of changing course or direction the wind. This is especially so weather balloons, being made a light aluminium alloy.

Both, incidentally, are m of the same sort of material that when they reflect the s light, they make quite convincing sight as a U.F in the night sky to people see them.

As for "loving to have a with the telescope at Jod Bank," this is a radio teles and not an optical one, and information is gained lar from computers. Incident some of these can be seen various times when Jodrell B is open to the public.

Brenda Qu
(19 years)
Wyken.

Boys' red UFOs may have been planes

MULTI-COLOURED globular objects flying through the night sky above Coventry — this is the latest report of unidentified flying objects over the city.

It comes from two Canley schoolboys who said they stayed up long after their bed-time to watch the "strange sight" through binoculars.

Brian Underhill, aged 14, of 3, Hancock Green, said an object appeared glowing red over the Earlsdon area at 9.30 p.m. on Monday. It was joined by another of similar appearance at 11.30 p.m., and they both disappeared at midnight.

Watching with him was Derrick Arnold (12), of 1, Hancock Green, who said the U.F.O.s were "circling very fast, then stopping and changing colour". They went green, blue and white, and then back to red again and moved off.

Brian said he saw them while he was on holiday at Skegness a few weeks ago. The objects he claims to have seen on the previous occasion were "like the same colour and shape and moved in the same way."

Last month several people reported seeing U.F.O.s over Coventry. Three people described what they saw as being red, but the shape and behaviour of the objects were varied.

A spokesman at Baginton Airport said that the two boys might have seen aircraft, bearing red flying south of the city between 9 p.m. and midnight.

'The Colonel Returns' by Gillian Maddison, issue 78, *Phenomena Magazine*

John Hanson: I am the sort of person who doesn't attack people, and can't understand why people do – in a business, frankly, that I regret ever having got involved.

Conferences should in my opinion be about discussion between the speakers and audience sat around huge tables, rather than to some degree paying homage to some one's ego! Been there done that, too many times. Cynicism has taken over I'm afraid. So the fact that I have been the target of hatred and attacks, by people like Larry Warren, Peter Robbins, and Maddison, allows me to exercise the right to answer the allegations, particularly when they have been published in a magazine.

Gilly Maddison contacted me asking if she could attend the day before and interview Charles Halt. She said she was a friend of Brenda Butler, and I agreed.

I met her outside the *Bull Public House*, Woodbridge, Suffolk which was where Colonel Halt was staying. The first time I met the lady I had no reason to suspect what lay in store for me – and up to now (2020) wasn't even aware of the contents of what she had written in the *Phenomena Magazine* article . . . until recently .

However, before I outline what (or wasn't published), it may be of relevance to remind the reader of what the lady had to say in her post on *Messenger* on the day before the meeting (**10th July**) [when photos of myself and Dawn were posted up]. **These were most offensive, in that the facial features of us had been blocked out?**

Text from that post . . .

Gillian – 10th July 2015: *"Spent a couple of hours with USAF retired Colonel Charles Halt today. He returned to his old stomping ground in Woodbridge yesterday ahead of the conference, he is headlining tomorrow, **July 11th (2015)** on the Rendlesham Forest Incident of 1980. When it comes to the incident – the jury is still out as far as I am concerned. I have spent hours interviewing some of the key players and I remain as baffled as ever. **Unidentified Flying Objects or Unbelievably Fucking Obvious?** Who knows? But one thing is for sure-Colonel Halt is a hugely entertaining and witty man of great intelligence and character. After hearing what he had to say during our interview today I feel sure this conference is going to be a mind blower for many attending. I also met up with long time friends of the Colonel authors **Brenda Butler and John Hanson**, who brought Colonel Halt over for the conference. Whatever your take on the RFI tomorrow night is shaping up to be an interesting one as no one is quite sure what Colonel Halt is going to reveal. I am not sure if tickets that have been on sale for £20 are still available. Derek Savory, also a friend of Charles Halt, may know if there are any available on the door. The event is to be held at Woodbridge Community Centre – doors open at 5pm."*

"In May this year, I met up with Larry Warren who is known and loved worldwide."

Gilly: *"In May this year, I met up with Larry Warren who is known and loved worldwide for speaking out about his RFI experience. I spent a few hours with him and recorded interviews. From that experience, I* found Larry to be a hugely entertaining, warm, complex and interesting person. At the time of the RFI, he was a 19 year old Security Police Officer in the USAF based at Bentwaters, home of the 81st Tactical Fighter Wing during the Cold War. As someone who was there in 1980, Larry has a story to tell. His story cannot and should not, be taken away from him. For better or worse, it has had a profound effect on his life. And make no mistake, whatever anyone thinks of Larry Warren, he has a legion of fans across the world who will stick by him no matter what. Many people it seems are fiercely protective of Larry. Their loyalty should not be underestimated; this is a man who is loved by many. He is quick to point out he is probably disliked by just as many too – but that is Larry.

In life, it is the easiest thing in the world to have an ill-informed opinion on absolutely anything. Talk after all, is cheap. However, having an informed opinion is a little harder because it requires work and research or better still – first-hand experience of the subject. How many of the non-local people who claim to be authorities on the RFI or have strong opinions one way or the other were living in Suffolk at the time and have any genuine first-hand knowledge of it? I mean knowledge that has not come via someone else or from a book. Only a very few civilian RFI researchers come directly from the area and actually remember the events of December1980. On the military side, Larry Warren was living and working smack bang in the middle of it all at the time and therefore has first-hand knowledge that other people coming into the saga years later do not have. Like it or not, he is on a list of participants in certain aspects of the RFI. Regardless of whether you believe him or whether you don't, Larry Warren has something most other people do not have – that is, actual knowledge and experience of the RFI at the time it happened. In whatever capacity and on whatever day, Larry Warren was there. We should not forget that."

"One of the talks [David Bryant] was practically impossible to hear."

"Another one, in my opinion, was illustrated with some very odd-looking pictures and seemed to consist of regurgitated information about astronauts and the possible moon-landing hoax that we all know about anyway. We also learned that astronauts have supposedly seen many UFOs while zipping about in space. However, as some of the Apollo astronauts (some of America's biggest heroes) were then referred to by the speaker as 'recovering alcoholics', (some of whom, apparently still like a drink –according to the same speaker), it did leave us wondering what to believe. The speaker intimated that he has spent years meeting with the said astronauts. He implied he had great fun plying one astronaut in particular with 'jugs of Margaritas'. Alcohol, apparently, made former astronauts loose-lipped in the company of the speaker and tell him stuff. Ok… sure…moving swiftly on… How happy would you be to be called a recovering alcoholic in public? Not nice and not professional – in my opinion."

John: 'Gilly' points out that Derek Savory, along with three others, were <u>unpaid volunteers</u> to help facilitate local RFI events put on by a **UK publisher.** *"Brenda and her group of friends help make these events happen for the publisher, who is not local and may find it hard to stage events without local assistance."* **Is she referring to me? I'm not local but have spent nearly 20 years visiting the Rendlesham Forest and tracing many witnesses. I later sent a cheque made out to Derek Savory for £250 – £50 for him, £50 each had already been paid to his two sons who were on the door (paid out of the ticket money from their sales), £50 to Brenda Butler, Joe Laming £50. £50 pounds to Bernie (Brenda's boyfriend), £50 I believe to Derek's wife who was selling tea and sandwiches, which is neither here nor there but at the end of the day they didn't have to pay a penny for the hire of the hall.** So as you can see they certainly weren't *'unpaid volunteers'* as stated by Gillian Maddison. Let's get the record straight!

At that time I had no idea that, like many others around that period of time, 'Gilly' was fully supportive of Larry Warren (and no doubt still is), not that that this was a problem but in hindsight, looking back, its clear there may have been some agenda to her request.

THE HALT PERSPECTIVE 2

What an awful, overbearing statement, by an alleged 'journalist' – attacking the character of someone who is very professional and well respected within the UFO Community, in much demand by the BBC as an authority on astronomy, not forgetting his knowledge of space rocks! He has also written three excellent books, one of which addresses the issue on whether the moon landings took place. Couldn't she have brought these complaints to our attention rather than trotting out her criticisms in a UFO magazine which we had no knowledge about? Why didn't the editor contact us for comment?

In addition, I was approached by one man who told me that he had seen someone throw a roll of dollars into the holdall belonging to Clifford Halt, the son of Chuck, who had come over here with him. This was another attempt to smear the reputation of not only Colonel Charles Halt but also his son. In addition, one of the problems was the sound equipment which was rubbish. This was not due to our fault. There are so many criticisms I could make of this woman and her cohorts.

David Bryant – I'd like to put the record straight!

David: The fact that Charlie Duke is a recovering alcoholic is public knowledge and he wrote about the fact at some length in his book 'Moonwalker'. He is just one of the Apollo astronauts who have had problems with alcohol and mental and physical health issues. **As you know, the fact that I have corresponded and spent time with most of the Moonwalkers** (and countless other space travellers) is indisputable. Most of the events where I met them were held in hotels with late night drinking sessions being the norm. It is, in my opinion, hardly surprising that, with the celebrities lubricated by alcohol, I have been fortunate enough to hear some first-hand UFO accounts from the likes of Bean, Mitchell, Carpenter, McDivitt and so on. I suspect they enjoyed these events in the UK as an opportunity to talk outside the official 'box'. Unlike the writer of the piece, I can absolutely prove that I have met and corresponded with these guys: if she had been at the meeting (or had paid more attention to the video) she'd have heard me say repeatedly that I consider them all to be brave, extremely patriotic and incredible aviators. I have NEVER criticized any of them as men!

My talk included a slide that made it plain that I repudiate the statement by Peter Paget in 'UFO Matrix' magazine: "Have you noticed that most men after their return (from the Moon took to the bottle, got religion or just went mad?" 'Gilly' has obviously decided to omit that detail from her account of events. The whole thrust of my argument was to show that, if the Apollo landings were filmed in a studio on Earth, surprisingly few people would need to know about it: furthermore, I repeatedly stated that, if this were the case, in participating in the simulation and maintaining the official story for sixty years, the Astronauts reveal themselves to be even more patriotic and self-effacing than generally accepted.

Before the afternoon of the RFI conference, I had been fortunate enough never to have met or heard of the 'video journalist' Ben Emlyn Jones. The first contact I had with him was when he tagged along on the forest walk: several people were taking video or still photos (me included!) and I was absolutely unaware of his intention to use his material online. He foisted himself on me and my friends to obtain a lift (uninvited!) back to Woodbridge for lunch: at no time did he declare that he was going to use the video online.

At the meeting, several other people were taking video on cameras and phones. I was aware of Mr. Ben Jones' presence to the left of the stage while I was introducing the event and giving my talk, but assumed he'd been invited by organizers John Hanson and Brenda Butler to make a record of the evening for the organizers' private use. When I was advised that the video had turned up on *YouTube*, I was more than somewhat concerned, because I had given my word to a friend (and customer) of mine that his son's image would not appear in any public forum without his permission. Furthermore, I am certain that Col. Halt, like me, would never have given permission for the video of our talks to be used unchecked and without explicit permission. These are the reasons I requested the video be taken down from *YouTube*.

THE HALT PERSPECTIVE 2

Photograph taken by David Bryant in Rendlesham Forest (enhanced) that depicts a 'figure' standing in the darkness

THE HALT PERSPECTIVE 2

PART 7

ASTRONAUTS AND OTHER WORLDS!

Astronauts and UFOs

DAVID Bryant: Even after more than 60 years of investigation and debate, the fundamental question remains unresolved: what exactly are UFOs? Each of the many theories seems to explain one or more aspects of the phenomenon. Setting aside deliberate hoaxing, these, and the main points they address, can be summarized as follows: • Natural or meteorological: explains the absence of widely-acceptable physical evidence • Inter dimensional travel/time travel/worm-holes: all take into account the vast size of interstellar space and the velocity limits imposed by the General Theory of Relativity • Advanced human technology: the secrecy maintained by many governments and their apparent lack of interest in researching UFOs is understandable if they are their operators! • Hallucination &

David Bryant and his wife, Linda

psychological pathology: all of the above points, together with the abduction phenomenon and very close encounters, are explicable if we assume that the events occurred in the witnesses own minds.

There is also, of course, the explanation that was widely accepted at the start of the 'Flying Saucer' era: that UFOs are spacecraft operated by extra-terrestrial biological entities (EBEs) To many people – particularly those who grew up during the heady years of the 'Space Age' between 1957 and 1972 – this seems by far the most logical and credible explanation: we were making our first stumbling steps into Space: surely the ultimate expression of this 'outward urge' would be to visit other star-systems and contact other intelligent life forms. If our species, then why not others?

But, ironically, it is the exploration of near-Earth space that has caused many people to doubt the extra-terrestrial hypothesis: *"If UFOs are spacecraft operated by alien astronauts,* (the argument runs) *then why don't our astronauts encounter them in Space or on the Moon?"* So, in the final analysis, the 'ET Hypothesis' largely stands or falls upon this question: do US Astronauts and Soviet Cosmonauts believe in an extra-terrestrial origin for UFOs and have they encountered them during their missions? If the answer is 'No!' then it becomes almost impossible to support the 'alien spacecraft' identification.

Having been born in 1951, I have watched the beginning and the sad decline of human space exploration: from the age of six I was fascinated by rockets. I constructed my own increasingly complex devices, culminating in a liquid-fuelled missile when I was seventeen. Starting in 1961, I kept a diary of every manned mission and, so determined was I to become an astronaut, that ultimately I joined the Royal Navy as a pilot. Four decades later, as the owner of an aviation and space collectibles company, I have been privileged to meet many of my childhood heroes both professionally and socially. The space travellers and pilots I have met, particularly those from the United States, are very patriotic. Although occasionally critical of the way some recent administrations have marginalized the space program, they generally support the official NASA line when discussing UFOs and other contentious issues in public. However, a few late-night sessions with a pitcher of margaritas or Tanqueray martinis have revealed some fascinating insights. The conclusion I have reached is that, during their missions many astronauts and cosmonauts have witnessed objects that defy immediate explanation. Furthermore, since most of the pre-Shuttle spacemen have thousands of hours experience as test pilots or military aviators, it is perhaps unsurprising that a number have reported encountering UFOs in the atmosphere. Some intriguing (non-verbatim!) quotes:

James McDivitt, Gemini IV – In 1965, McDivitt witnessed an apparently **metallic cylinder with antenna-like structures,** which he attempted to photograph. When I asked why he didn't wake his fellow crew-member, Edward White, he replied that *"...it wasn't in the mission profile. I was on watch; Ed was scheduled for a sleep period. You have to understand the military way of things: you do what's in the profile!"* **Later, however, both astronauts reported two egg-shaped objects leaving glowing trails.** McDivitt told me that the photographs of these on many websites are either fakes or merely show reflections in Gemini IV's window: he has never seen prints of the exposures he made, and feels it is likely they were over exposed due to the UFO's proximity to the Sun.

Scott Carpenter, Mercury 'Aurora 7' – asked if it was true that he had reportedly stated: *"At no time, when the astronauts were in space were they alone: there was a constant surveillance by UFOs."* Carpenter replied that he had said *"..."***something like that".** I asked if he was referring to the 'fire-flies' he and John Glenn had observed during their Mercury missions: these he dismissed as ice crystals or frozen urine. I spent time with Carpenter on three separate occasions and asked for clarification: other than to confirm the quote above, he would not comment further, other than to explain that he had *'**no wish to get myself in trouble again!**'*

James Lovell, Gemini VII, Gemini XII, Apollo 8, Apollo 13 – I asked Lovell about the 'bogies' that were reported on his Gemini VII mission. He stands by the original statement that he and Frank Borman were not looking at the top stage of their Titan II launch vehicle, which they could distantly see at the same time. **He also confirmed that he and Buzz Aldrin observed two 'bright unknowns' during their Gemini XII mission.** Lovell laughs at the interpretation of his Apollo 8 communication about Santa Claus, remarking that the tongue-in-cheek comment was, after all, made on Christmas Day!

Gene Cernan: Gemini IX, Apollo 10, Apollo 17 – When asked to confirm the reported sightings of UFOs during his three space missions, Cernan freely did so, and (paraphrasing his widely-published quote) said: *"Look: I've publicly said that I believe they (UFOs) are real and that they come from someplace else: from some other technological civilization. There is too much evidence not to (believe that)"*

Richard Gordon: Gemini XI, Apollo 12 – I asked Gordon about the reported encounter with a UFO during the Gemini XI mission. He confirmed that both he and Pete Conrad had seen a bright, solid object, which Conrad had photographed. Gordon stated that this had been identified by NASA as the Soviet Proton 3 satellite: he felt this was unlikely, since the object had visible length, which would not have been the case with a 3 metre long spacecraft 450 km away.

Dr 'Buzz' Aldrin – Dr Aldrin was at pains to deny the various online reports that he and Neil Armstrong observed landed alien craft on the Moon's surface, dismissing these accounts in the most colorful language! However, he was happy to confirm that the A11 crew did encounter an apparently ***intelligently-guided object in lunar space*** which they elected to ignore in case reporting it caused the mission to be aborted. He was adamant that the object was *not* the S4-B stage of the Saturn launch-rocket, which was too far away by that point. Aldrin surprised me by stating that an apparently artificial structure 'somewhat like the obelisk in the movie 2001' had been photographed by the Mars Global Surveyor as it orbited the small satellite Phobos and that another had been similarly imaged on Mars itself.

THE HALT PERSPECTIVE 2

Dr Edgar Mitchell: Apollo 14 moonwalker. I have met Dr Mitchell a number of times and discussed the UFO phenomenon with him in a general way: he famously grew up in Roswell, NM, in October 2011. **He amazed me by casually mentioning that he had been briefed that US intelligence agencies are actively working with four alien species, which he went on to describe! I asked if he would include this information in the next day's lecture: he agreed and did so!** During his time on the surface of the Moon, Dr Mitchell undertook an experiment to communicate telepathically with extraterrestrial entities.

Pavel Popovich – In email exchanges with Marina, test pilot and ex-wife of this legendary Cosmonaut, **I was informed that her former husband had personally witnessed a triangular UFO from an airliner on which he was travelling. She also told me that Russian scientists were in possession of debris from five crashed UFOs** and that cosmonaut and military pilots had logged over 3000 credible sightings since 1945. My conclusions: Having broached the subject of extraterrestrial life and UFOs with a number of Astronauts, I personally believe that they have more to say on the subject than they feel comfortable about disclosing. Their natural reluctance to say or do anything controversial, or that would expose the Astronaut Corps to ridicule, prevents them from making speculative statements. This, in my view, makes the disclosures of space travellers such as Popovich, Mitchell, Cooper and Slayton that much more credible.

Astronauts/Cosmonauts who have confirmed a belief in the reality of the UFO phenomenon: The internet is crowded with alleged accounts of UFO encounters by space travellers from the US and former Soviet Union, the great majority of these are complete fabrications. The reticence shown by many of the Astronauts to discuss the subject is generally either because they have nothing to discuss or because they have grown weary of being misquoted. Occasionally, however, someone will confirm a belief in extraterrestrial life or even admit to having personally witnessed a UFO. Here is a partial list: **Dr Edgar Mitchell, Gordon Cooper, Donald 'Deke' Slayton, Charles 'Pete' Conrad, Pavel Popovich, Story Musgrave, Eugene Cernan, John Glenn, Joseph Walker, Robert White, Buzz Aldrin, Jim Mcdivitt.**

John: Professor Brian Cox – States UFOs are a load of bollocks!

Ironically, Professor Brian Cox was asked about UFOs, by someone during a live *BBC* broadcast. He replied they were "*a load of bollocks!*" Very strange reply, presumably based on total indifference to even conducting his own research into the subject; of course he's not on his own. We should also take into consideration that there have been many instances of **UFOs seen hovering in the sky over the BBC transmission masts brought to our attention over the years**. Many of them were no doubt subject to some investigation, although the chances of any paper trail are remote.

In 2012 Professor Brian Cox was with comedian Dara O'Brian during a radio broadcast and said he had hoped to point the Jodrell Bank telescope at the planet Threapleton Holmes B, after it was discovered, live on air last year and listen for signs of life. But he claimed he was prevented from doing so because the Corporation was concerned that **a discovery of aliens could violate BBC regulations**. Speaking on the *BBC Radio 6 Music* breakfast show on Wednesday, **Professor Cox said: "*The BBC actually said 'You can't do that. We need to go through the regulations and health and safety and everything in case we discover a signal from an alien civilization'. [I said], you mean we would discover the first hint that there is other intelligent life in the universe beyond Earth, live on air, and you're worried about the health and safety of it? It was incredible. They did have guidelines, compliance!*"

Is this FINAL evidence of 'alien' intelligence?

David: For twenty years my wife Linda and I have maintained the UK's only full-time meteorite dealership, *Spacerocks* UK. We both have university qualifications in Astronomy and have lectured widely at many of the country's most august institutions. At any moment we have several thousand meteorites of all types in our inventory and are, therefore, completely familiar with their appearance. Despite the present 'lockdown' situation, we are still supplying meteorites and bringing in new stock.

On Friday, April 17th I received a parcel of meteorites I had ordered from a dependable regular source. These were twenty examples of a very well-known and popular common chondrite known as NWA 869. At this point, it's worth giving a brief explanation about what meteorites are and where they come from. The Solar System (the Sun, planets, asteroids and comets) condensed from a cloud of dust and gas (the solar nebula) around five billion years ago. The first solid objects were millimetric spheres called chondrules. These joined together over a few million years to form increasingly large chunks.

Eventually, by collision, these accreted to form planetesimals and finally, around 4.5 billion years ago, the eight large planets and other, smaller bodies that make up the Solar System. The vast gaps between the orbits of the eight major planets are full of debris from these early days: additionally a region between Mars and Jupiter holds many thousands of smaller planetary objects known as Asteroids. These occasionally collide (more so in the past) launching more rocky and metallic debris into the Solar System. If one of these fragments collides with the Earth on its passage around the Sun it will heat up to over 6000 degrees because of friction with the atmosphere: this is the cause of the familiar shooting stars (meteors) we may see at night. If a chunk is large enough, it may survive and reach the surface of the Earth: this is a *meteorite*. There are, broadly speaking, three types of meteorite:

1) Chondrites: fragments of the original ancient stones that remain from the start of the Solar System. These often contain chondrules, the small spheres mentioned earlier. Chondrites are all around 4.5 billion years old. 2) Achondrites: stony material blasted off the surface of a planet, asteroid or satellite by the impact of another object. Achondrite meteorites have been proven to have originated on many bodies, including Mars, the Moon and asteroids such as Vesta. 3) Irons and stony irons are fragments of the cores of fully-formed small planets that were disrupted during collisions billions of years ago. (As the first planets grew in size, heavy elements such as nickel and iron sank to their centre's to form metallic cores, such as the Earth's).

Generally speaking, meteorites are named after the place where they fell or were found: hence the iron meteorite that made the Arizona Meteor Crater is called Canyon Diablo and that which exploded over Russia in 1947 is known as Sikhote-Alin. The meteorite we are discussing here, **NWA 869**, comes from a large strewn field which was the 869th such to be discovered in North West Africa: hence its name! Why 869 are so prized by collectors is that most of meteorites from this field are small, complete examples, rather than fragments of larger bodies that exploded as they passed through the atmosphere (See photos!). The majority has an attractive blue-grey fusion crust (melted surfaced) and their shape reflects their attitude as they streaked downwards. (This is known as 'orientation': a bit like the way spacecraft enter the atmosphere heat-shield first!) OK: that's the technical stuff out of the way!

When I was processing the parcel of newly-arrived 869s, I suddenly noticed a metallic glint from one of them, this isn't unusual: all chondrites contain nickel-iron and some display quite obvious metallic flecks. This was different: in this case, the shiny region could be seen to be a small cylindrical feature around 6mm in diameter. It was protruding at an angle from a region of glassy fusion crust, which, in places, could be seen to flow away from the object. Another interesting feature is that the cylinder has a small impact crater on its surface: something not uncommonly seen on iron meteorites or, indeed, spacecraft on their return from orbit! I have no doubt at all that the object embedded in the NWA 869 meteorite was in place as the stone entered the Earth's atmosphere sometime in the past. Since the meteorite itself was formed several hundred millions of years before the planets, it begs the question: who made it, and where did it originate before becoming part of the Solar Nebula? 4.52billion years old!

THE HALT PERSPECTIVE 2

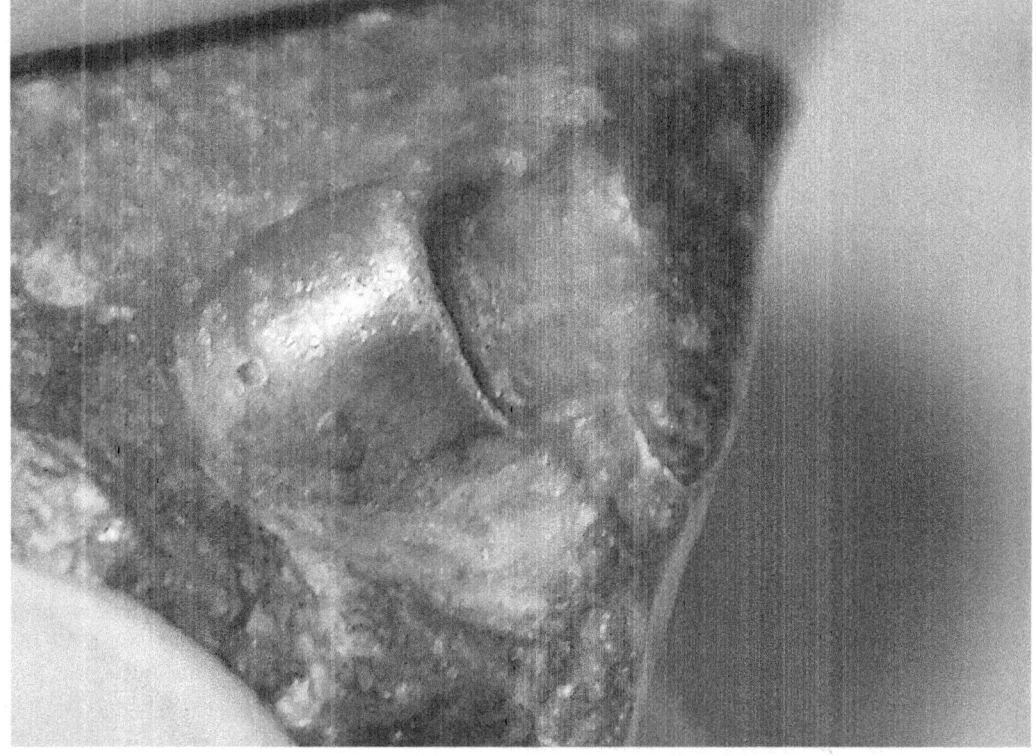

THE HALT PERSPECTIVE 2

Charles: Very interesting; certainly provides much food for thought! David Bryant, a retired Royal Navy Pilot from Norfolk is an authority on space rocks/meteorites and knows many of the astronauts both US and Russian. He is often in demand by the BBC for his knowledge of astronomy. I know David and have much respect for him, as he was our MC at the Woodbridge Suffolk UFO conference held in 2015. I met him again on September 8th 2019 at Woodbridge Community Hall.

You can't ignore the evidence from our own astronauts of inexplicable objects seen by them while out in space, very interesting information that isn't generally known about. It's peculiar that matters like this are ignored by the media, probably because it's difficult to fault their accounts, but I suppose the media would be limited in what they could throw at them by way of silly explanations. Down on the ground now that's a different ballgame!

One might think that the intriguing photos of something, that may for all I know, was **produced by an intelligence not of this planet** should be phenomenal in its implications, but like the UFO subject, has shown a lack of interest following some initial publicity about the matter. This seems odd taking into account David's professional reputation and knowledge of astronomy. David has also written a number of books, in one of them, he claims that the astronauts never went to the Moon! If it was anybody else I would take this claim with a pinch of salt! But he knows the astronauts, both Russian and American – food for thought indeed! Many years ago in the 1970's David sighted **three globes flashing through the sky followed by the arrival of RAF jets** – coincidence or another example of the Air Force responding after the objects were picked up on radar, or sheer coincidence?

THE HALT PERSPECTIVE 2

PART 8

DOWN TO EARTH... THE ATTACKS BEGIN!

IN September 2015, Peter Robbins published '**Halt In Woodbridge: An Air Force Colonel's Thirty-Year Fight To Silence An Authentic UFO Whistle-Blower'** drawn from a need to defend his friend and co-author Larry Warren. This book, while withdrawn, is still for sale on Amazon (2020) with second hand copies accompanied by **37 reviews mostly in support of Peter and condemning me**, despite the fact that Mr Robbins later dissociated himself from Warren. Here is what it said, in the damning statement below, on the *Amazon* page bearing in mind that people who know little about this incident, may well believe the downright lies, and the harm that they have done personally.

Quote: "One of the most fascinating and intriguing UFO cases of all time occurred in December 1980 in the United Kingdom, near the U.S.-operated military base of RAF Bentwaters, within the Rendlesham Forest. For thirty-five years, it has stood the test of time as something truly extraordinary. Moreover, it has been subject to more controversy than any other UFO case in history, rivalled only by Roswell. **One element of this controversy concerns one of the key witnesses of this case, a U.S. airman named Larry Warren, who has been attacked repeatedly by the base's Deputy Commander, Lt. Colonel (later full Colonel) Charles Halt. These attacks have become so misleading and vicious, that they have not only caused serious confusion about what actually happened during the Rendlesham Forest Incident (RFI), but have triggered speculation about**

Mr. Halt's motives

Peter Robbins is one of the leading experts on the RFI, and is the co-author (with Larry Warren) of *Left At East Gate*, one of the most important studies of the RFI. Here, Mr. Robbins has not only written a definitive refutation of Mr. Halt's attacks on Larry Warren, but has made the definitive defence of Mr. Warren, proving conclusively that Warren was there, and was truthful in his testimony about what transpired.'

Glowing recommendations

The glowing commendations on the back of this book, from Nick Redfern, Budd Hopkins, Tim Good and a quote from John. E Mack, identifies a real problem with this business, where belief systems and egos override common sense and rationality. Whilst the passing of time shows that the lies were not from me, but from Warren, it is fair to say that that my reputation has been vindicated.

Captain Robert Salas also wrote comments in Peter's book

Robert and Stanton Friedman wrote a book titled **Unidentified The UFO Phenomenon.** This is what they had to say, about the book on the *Amazon* website. "*There are two things I know about the UFO*

THE HALT PERSPECTIVE 2

phenomenon. One is that real objects of unearthly origin are visiting our planet. [The other] is that the phenomenon of people being abducted is a reality. Robert Salas. In 1969 the U.S. Air Force issued a statement that read – No UFO reported, investigated and evaluated by the Air Force was ever an indication of threat to our national security. This statement is patently false. It has been proven untrue by the testimony of many military officers and airmen and documentation of incidents involving UFOs and nuclear weapons, testimonies of which the U.S. Air Force was fully aware. UNIDENTIFIED includes details many of these testimonies – some for the first time. As partial justification for its position, the Air Force cites a University of Colorado study that was contracted and paid for by US government funds. UNIDENTIFIED, reveals how this study was actually, just another part of the plan,

Robert Salas

to cover up the reality of the UFO phenomenon. For the first time, UNIDENTIFIED publishes evidence that the investigators for the Colorado study knew about the UFO-related missile shutdown incidents but did not investigate them or include them in their final report."

Best of luck to the both of them, as you can see Robert has a copy of one of the *Haunted Skies* books in his hand after meeting up with Sacha Christie, while over here to lecture. He and John know each other to speak to.

Putting the record straight again!

Well not many folks are aware that I do have a quite a large amount of accumulated documents, emails and letters from people over the last 40 years, as the example in the image opposite shows. This enables me to check out any relevant material requested from various film companies, journalists, etc., if required.

One letter very supportive of my role, was from **Ralph Noyes, who was head of the MOD;** he admits that they were embarrassed with the way the MOD handled reports from the public, even impeccable sources.

9, Oakley Street,
London SW3 5NN
01-351 6659
England, UK

12th April, 1989

Col. Charles I. Halt,
485th TMW/MB,
ATO,
New York 09188

Dear Colonel,

    Please forgive a letter out of the blue. I am writing to you as a former member of the British Ministry of Defence, from which I had retired to pursue a second career as a freelance writer shortly before those remarkable events took place near the USAF Base at Woodbridge in Suffolk in late December 1980.

    I wish I had been in post in the Ministry of Defence at the time when your remarkable report of 13 January 1981 reached the Department ! Former colleagues have told me very little about the manner in which they handled this matter despite my attempts to secure some statement from them. (I can't say that I'm too surprised by their prevarications when I recall my own days in the Department and the unease and embarrassment with which we treated reports of alleged UFOs, even when reaching us from impeccable sources). I assume, however, that a good deal more took place as a result of your report than has ever appeared on the public record.

    As an ex-member of the British MOD, I am now in the same position as any other citizen - viz. looking in from the outside. But I continue to feel that your 'encounter' of 29 December 1980 is one of the most important on record and that it contains many clues to the real nature of the UFO phenomenon. I have recently (after careful thought) chanced my arm on the enclosed paper, which I hope to see published later this year under the editorship of Timothy Good, to whom you gave some useful information when he was researching for his book, ABOVE TOP SECRET.

    I am only too well aware that you have had a great deal of ill-informed hassle from other quite unqualified people (and the enclosed paper expresses my sympathy to you for this !). But I wonder whether - after this lapse of time - you might feel able to comment on the enclosed. I recognise the potential difficulties for you as a serving officer (indeed, I partly share them as a former Defence official). But I believe that you would be contributing greatly to our understanding of an important and puzzling phenomenon if you felt able to give me a considered response to the paper. I hope you will accept my assurance that I would not ascribe any statement to you in any further publication without your permission, and that I would therefore treat your reply as confidential unless and until you authorised me to place any part of it on the public record.

    Yours sincerely,

(Ralph Noyes)

THE HALT PERSPECTIVE 2

I was shocked to see what I considered a deplorable breach of conduct from Robert, a man who is well respected throughout the UFO Community on both sides of the Atlantic, and someone whom I had previously I regarded as a colleague. He attacked me viciously in Peter Robbin's book, which is difficult to understand never mind forgive. Why didn't Robert contact me about this personally? We've sat on panels discussing the UFO problem, so it's not as if we don't know each other. Robert was someone that I thought was a friend, but I am at a loss to understand why he sided with Larry Warren and attacked me publicly, with vicious comments made in that now defunct book, which is a knee jerk reaction to comments made by me against Larry Warren at the 2015 Woodbridge UFO Conference.

I would also like to point out that I was surprised to see coverage of this in the **Phenomena Magazine**, and disappointed that nobody in charge there contacted John or myself, if only to put the record straight. People should stand together rather than attacking each other? Surely there's been enough of that? Peter, by the way hadn't even been there to the Conference, but felt qualified to write what he did, even after John Hanson had emailed him to put the record straight following the visit by me. This is not the way that I conduct business – why couldn't he have emailed me or spoken to me on the telephone? But this isn't about Peter Robbins, who later apologised, it's about the fact that Robert called the *Travel Channel* asking how much the *Travel Channel* folks paid me. I think he wanted to know how much to ask as they had asked him about a possible program. I told him I only got expenses. I think he was shocked. Robert asked me for some advice on dealing with the film crew. Apparently they're going to do a program with him. I telephoned him and basically told him how shocked and disappointed I was when he fell in with Robbins/Warren and company and posted all the nasty comments about me. **He claimed not to remember.**

Obviously he's become another entertainer that makes the circuit. He told me he doesn't trust some of the most honest and reliable speakers in the field. This book, although withdrawn from sale, is now still available to purchase on the Internet albeit as second-hand copies…But the damage is done! I feel that I have the right to put things straight. Whilst I appreciate that we covered this matter in the previous book, many folk are apparently still unaware of what he alleged against me. But you know the problem isn't just about Robert – who should have known better given his rank and well respected public image. It's about the way in which some people can be 'played' by others, to allow themselves, without any moral justification, to attack the character of a third party, based not on evidence, but their friendship with someone else whose grievances, adopted from another party were a contributing factor. We have seen through the medium of *Facebook* how bullying and intimidation can affect thoughts and behaviour of others. As we have seen over the years those that oppose or question other people's behaviour are driven away by the herd instincts of those often in the majority that cannot believe they are wrong! An example of this is of course the way in which Warren influenced people who were trying to gain his trust and friendship…We all now know the truth and have hopefully learned a lesson!

These are the quotes made by Robert, followed by my answers

Robert Salas: Halt has stated that he went out in the field the third night (December 27 and 28) with four others (Zickler, Nevels, Englund, Bustinza) after Englund comes to him and says 'It's Back!' Presumably because of the second night incident involving Bonnie Tamplin and Ball. Ball was there already or joined them. Halt said that Bustinza was at his side the entire time. Halt states that he was in radio contact with Colonel Williams (Wing Commander), who was back at the Command Post. (Reference: 'The Jimmy Church Show' – 2014). At some point in the evening/early morning, some twenty or twenty-five others, airmen and civilian police came out to Capel Green, including Burroughs and Warren. Recently, Burroughs has confirmed that he saw Warren out there. Both he and Warren encountered a yellow coloured mist near ground level. He also confirmed that lights came from this mist and seemed to form some type of being, confirming a similar statement that Larry Warren has made. (Reference: KGRA radio show, 8/27/15).

WHY HAS HALT REPEATEDLY STATED THAT WARREN WAS NOT OUT THERE THAT NIGHT, WHEN OTHER WITNESSES HAVE VERIFIED IT?

Charles: There are two supposed witnesses, Greg Bartram and Adrian Bustinza. Greg has contradicted himself on at least two occasions and Adrian was with me the whole time I was out there. John Burroughs did not even know Warren at that time. Adrian's voice even appears on my tape. After I sent the 15 or so cops back to the base, John Burroughs remained and I briefly talked with him. He asked if he and Adrian could go forward for a look. They briefly did, returned, and said nothing about any confrontation with any object or beings.

WHY HAS HALT FREQUENTLY MADE DEROGATORY STATEMENTS ABOUT WARREN'S TESTIMONY ABOUT THE EVENTS OF THAT NIGHT WHEN BUSTINZA, FOR ONE, HAS VALIDATED SOME OF HIS STATEMENTS?

Charles: Adrian was with me the whole time. Keep in mind he was subjected to a 'debriefing' soon after that could have influenced his memory.

Robert Salas: Who ordered these other people to come out there and why? Halt was the senior officer in the field. He either gave the order, or Colonel Williams gave the order. Either way, Halt should have known about it. But what was the reason to have these other people out there? Halt had already reported strange lights all over the forest. There would have to be a specific purpose to have the others out there. And, since Halt would have known of their presence, he would have been involved in organizing their activities, since he would have been the senior officer.

HALT HAS NEVER OFFERED A DETAILED EXPLANATION AS TO WHY SO MANY PEOPLE WERE IN THE FIELD AND PREPARING FOR SOME INCIDENT. SINCE HE WAS THE SENIOR OFFICER IN THE FIELD, HOW DOES HE EXPLAIN THIS?

Charles: The 15 or so cops were already out there when I arrived. I was shocked and quite upset knowing the potential for an embarrassing public relations incident. Obviously, Bruce Englund took it upon himself to take the 'team' out.

Robert Salas: In a recent radio interview, Adrian Bustinza admitted he was interrogated by US intelligence agents about the RFI. Halt has always claimed he was never interrogated by USAF intelligence agents or any other agency about the RFI.

SINCE EVERY OTHER WITNESS TO THE RFI WAS INTERROGATED (SOME BY EXTRAORDINARY TECHNIQUES), HOW DOES HALT EXPLAIN HIS CLAIM THAT HE WAS NOT INTERROGATED? HE WAS ONE OF THE PRIMARY WITNESSES. IF GOVERNMENT AGENCIES WANTED TO OBTAIN AS MUCH TESTIMONY AS POSSIBLE TO EXPLAIN THE EVENTS, HIS TESTIMONY WOULD HAVE BEEN IMPORTANT. THIS RAISES THE QUESTION AS TO WHETHER OR NOT HALT COULD HAVE BEEN IN COLLUSION WITH THOSE AGENCIES.

Charles: You obviously do not understand how the OSI and their counterparts operate. They do not report to anyone on the Base and only notify the senior leadership when they feel it necessary. I personally confronted the OSI Commander, Chuck Matthews, and told him of the encounter. His reply was they were not interested – an obvious lie, as I later learned of the 'debriefings' and that they took place in his building. I am convinced I was left out, as they had already done a good job of using Warren and others with a planted story that would make the incident, if it ever got out, as unbelievable. Disinformation is an 'agency' speciality. Perhaps you didn't know that?

Robert Salas: Major Zickler was in charge of base security, but he worked for Halt and was with Halt on the third night. Halt claims he never knew about the interrogations, even though it was Zickler who ordered the men to report for the interrogations.

Charles: Major Zickler was not with me. He stayed at the party, as did all the other police officers. Zickler did not want to be involved publicly. He certainly got involved later behind the scenes.

AS DEPUTY BASE COMMANDER, ONE OF HALT'S RESPONSIBILITIES WAS BASE SECURITY. WHY WAS HE NOT TOLD THAT THE MEN UNDER HIM WERE BEING INTERROGATED?

Charles: I already covered this earlier. When the OSI and their counterparts do things, they don't usually tell the Base leaders.

Robert Salas: In a recent statement, Adrian Bustinza said that Colonel Halt ordered him to confiscate all cameras and recorders in the field on the third night.

Charles: I did not confiscate any cameras or recorders. The only recorder was my pocket cassette recorder and the only camera was the 35mm camera Nevels had.

Robert Salas: WHY DID HE ORDER THAT ALL CAMERAS AND RECORDERS BE CONFISCATED? THIS WAS SUPPOSED TO BE AN INVESTIGATION. MORE PHOTOS WOULD HAVE HELPED IN SUCH AN INVESTIGATION.

THE HALT PERSPECTIVE 2

Charles: I did not order or have any equipment confiscated. There were no other cameras or recorders. Warren's claim of tripod mounted cameras and British police is nonsense. I have statements from the Suffolk Police that deny any British participation while I was out. The police constables did make a daytime visit and wrote the incident off.

Robert Salas: Halt has only released nineteen minutes of the tape recording he did that night. **HE WAS OUT THERE FOR ABOUT THREE HOURS. WHY HAS HE NOT RELEASED THE ENTIRE TAPE?**

Charles: I only had one tape and no spare batteries, so I only recorded when I thought it important. I never expected to be out that long or to have such an experience.

Robert Salas: He has told me (and others) that he is withholding some key information/evidence about the incident as a way to protect himself. **WHY OR FROM WHOM DOES HE FEEL THE NEED TO PROTECT HIMSELF?**

Charles: When it became public, I realized there was potential for an effort to silence me.

Robert Salas: IF WHAT HE IS WITHHOLDING WILL BRING SOME CLARITY TO THIS CASE, ISN'T HE DOING A DISSERVICE TO THE CAUSE OF TRUTH IN THIS MATTER?

Charles: What I have kept for safekeeping is a recording I later made that details what happened. It does not contain any new information. I did send a copy to Larry Facwett and Barry Greenwood as they were working with Warren at the time. They quickly discovered Warren to have lied to them and dropped the idea of a book. Warren even admitted to them he lied about his involvement. Read the new book when it's available early next year as its detailed.

Robert Salas: Halt claims there was no underground facility at Bentwaters. He certainly should have known. He has claimed, as Deputy Base Commander, he knew everything about the base. **IT IS MY UNDERSTANDING THAT IT HAS RECENTLY BEEN DETERMINED THAT THERE WAS INDEED AN UNDERGROUND FACILITY. HOW DOES COL. HALT EXPLAIN THIS DISCREPANCY IN HIS TESTIMONY?**

Charles: Who says there is an underground facility? Warren's book shows a picture of the command post and says that's where he entered an underground facility by way of an elevator. Go visit the command post, as it's a museum and open. This whole claim is so far out that I'm surprised it's in their book. Warren initially claimed he was kidnapped and taken underground. Later he says it was Adrian. Warren's mother sums it up well when she says Larry was always a good liar.

Major/Colonel Malcolm Zickler

Malcolm knew a lot more than he was ever willing to say. He was very much a guy that worked in the background at the Base and I believed he would have liaised with the AFOSI and other British and American agents to **provide a cover story to explain what had taken place**. He had to know that John, Larry, Jim, and Adrian, were messed with during the investigation held after the events. Lt. Colonel Malcolm S. Zickler was in charge of security for both Bases. Both Bases operated together within the same chain of command. If we were simply talking about a report of unexplained lights; that in itself would not be reason enough to call out a Disaster Preparedness Team. Indeed, no such team was sent to the area. Captain McCollom was the Public Affairs Officer at the time. Yes, we regularly had Base exercises at least once a month.

We did not have any in the week between Christmas and New Year. After departing RAF Bentwaters Malcolm moved to Eglin AFB Florida where there was then reported numerous UFO events. He then moved on to become head of System Security Engineering and Chief of Operation Security at GE Aerospace to include going to extensive lengths to test and create realistic scenarios on an Air Base. How does a Squadron Commander in charge of Security Police and Law Enforcement, ascend to working with the **US Special Forces Counter Intelligence Deception Unit?**

Captain Robert L. Salas graduated from the U.S. Air Force Academy and spent seven years in active duty from 1964 to 1971. He also held positions at Martin Marietta and Rockwell and spent 21 years at the FAA. In the Air Force, he was an air traffic controller and a missile launch officer as well as an engineer on the Titan 3 missiles. Capt. Salas testified about a UFO incident in March of 1967, where he states that 16 nuclear missiles became non-operational at two different launch facilities immediately after guards saw UFOs hovering above. The guards could not identify these objects even though they were only about 30 feet away.

2016

May 2016 – UFO expert claims RAF Bentwaters encounter was aliens searching for nuclear weapons!

Scholes UFO expert claims RAF Bentwaters encounter was aliens searching for nuclear weapons. Revelations from Gary Heseltine come 36 years after UFOs were spotted at a Suffolk RAF Base. From **SUSIE BEEVER** Breaking News Reporter.

A UFO expert has made a shocking revelation about a famous British extraterrestrial encounter. Gary Heseltine, from Scholes, Holmfirth, **claims aliens who visited RAF Bentwater in Suffolk in 1980 were interested in a "secret stash" of nuclear weapons!** Dubbed as the "British Roswell", the site was claimed to have been visited by UFOs over three nights that December. Gary was at the airbase while making a documentary, who himself has served in the RAF, says witness Colonel Charles Halt told him at the scene that he (Halt) said a UFO had *"shone a beam on the weapons storage area (WSA); the site had more nuclear missiles than anywhere else in Europe".* He claims he was told the secret while touring at the site for a documentary which was never finished. [Strenuously denied by Charles Halt].

Charles: They say there is nothing like a woman scorned, well in this case Gary clearly feels umbrage that he and I discontinued working together. The fact that alleged conversations, confidential or not, were released into the public sector shows the character of a man – himself an ex RAF employee who would have signed the **BRITISH OFFICIAL SECRETS ACT**.

No doubt one of the reasons why he contacted the newspapers with what I see as nonsensical comments made about alien species interested in a stash of nuclear weapons. Who are the alien species, where do they come from, where is the evidence – just pure speculation based on what? Prove it Gary! None of this makes common sense in my opinion, others will disagree. This 'story' was, of course, picked up by the usual journalists desperate for any story especially ones based on outlandish claims…here it is… stuff like this spreads like wildfire.

THE HALT PERSPECTIVE 2

In **April 2016**, I lectured in Los Angeles, alongside Nick Pope, for CERO International, the host being Yvonne Smith.

RENDLESHAM UFO Aliens that 'visited' RAF Base were 'after nuclear weapons',

On the **24th May 2016** – Jon Austin *Daily Mirror Online* – "**RENDLESHAM UFO Aliens that 'visited' RAF Base were 'after nuclear weapons',** says ex cop. ALIENS suspected of visiting a US air base in the UK in the 1980s may have been interested in its nuclear weapons stockpile, new researchers including an ex-police officer have claimed.

Quote: The Rendlesham mystery remains the UK's most puzzling UFO case and has been called Britain's Roswell after the infamous alleged flying saucer crashed in the New Mexico desert in July 1947. Now, former police officer, Gary Heseltine, 56, claims to have gathered new evidence which could prove aliens did visit Rendlesham in 1980 – and why. The UK alien sighting happened when three US officers based at RAF Bentwaters claimed a "*triangular-shaped craft*" landed in neighbouring woods in the early hours of December 26, 1980.

Retired Colonel Charles Halt, 76, who was Base Deputy Commander at the time, claimed the officers who first saw the lights, and then a UFO 'on the floor', **could not account for a 40 minute period** while searching in the woods when their communication systems went 'off air'. The three officers – John Burroughs, Bud Steffens and James Penniston, later told of feeling 'static' as they observed the object's flashing lights and hieroglyphic-like markings.

Mr. Halt then said on the evening of December 27th 1980 that officers had shouted: "*It's back, the UFO's back*". He went to investigate with a team who found three 1.5inch 'impact holes,' damage to the canopies of trees and 'higher radiation levels' in the 'landing' area. He said soon after they saw a mysterious object in a field between the woods and a farmhouse with '*a red light moving*'. The case was later investigated by the UK Ministry of Defence (MoD), but it concluded there was no evidence **of alien visitations or any national security risk**, **and the sightings were most likely the result of beams of light from a nearby coastal lighthouse.**

Mr Heseletine says new research has uncovered the fact that there was a huge stash of nuclear armaments stored at RAF Bentwaters at the time of the mass sightings. Theories about the case have re-exploded since a special conference to mark the 35 year anniversary held in the area last July. Then, top speaker Rendlesham witness Colonel Charles Halt, who was Deputy Base Commander at the time, revealed details of new radar evidence.

Mr Hestletine, a British Transport Police officer for 24 years before becoming a UFO sleuth, said Mr. Halt had revealed to him about the Suffolk air base holding the largest nuclear weapons arsenal in Europe. He said: "**Col Halt told me RAF Bentwaters had 'more nuclear missiles in the weapons storage area (WSA) than anywhere else in Europe'**". In his account of the sighting Col Halt said the **UFO had fired beams of light into the weapons storage area of the base.** Mr Hestletine said Col Halt made the admission during a visit to the base: "*As my wife Lynn and I walked with Colonel Halt through Rendlesham Forest I clearly remember him saying 'that there were more nuclear weapons in the WSA at Bentwaters than* *anywhere else in the whole of Europe' and he laughed that the peace protesters who were just up the road camped outside Greenham Common were oblivious as to where they really were."* Lynn added: *"It has always stayed with me because of the fact that the peace protesters at Greenham Common had been duped."*

But Col Halt has been reluctant to confirm the nuclear element to his alleged admission. He told *Mirror. co.uk* **"My comment to Gary was: 'It appears the beam was in or near the weapons storage area'. Keep in mind I was a mile or more away. I never made such a statement about weapons to Gary. Those are his conclusions."** The UK and US governments will not confirm or deny where nuclear weapons are stored. But Mr. Heseltine, who edits the *UFO Truth* internet magazine, is convinced of the theory. He pointed to the Base being on high alert in December 1980 because Soviet troops were massing on the border of Poland. He added: *"This information now provides for the first time a genuine motive as to why UFOs turn up at the Base in late December 1980 at a time of world crisis and clearly implies to me that a huge cache of illegal nuclear weapons posed a potential destabilizing threat to the Earth. Just weeks ago two former radar operatives came forward to claim they saw the UFO on radar at the time."*

Charles: Gary Heseltine forgets that I have all the correspondence from him. I emailed him a few months ago and asked him for a comment. No response. If anyone was critical of Warren it was Gary. He gave in to Peter, because he and Larry promised to support his new magazine. Maybe we should consider putting some of Gary's correspondence in a revised book, it would make interesting reading. This is the guy that gave Larry Warren a *bravery award* – what a load of rubbish. Events have shown me that I could never trust Gary Hesletine – he has allied himself with a man that has attacked me viciously, never mind making physical threats to those that don't support him. I can't be and won't be involved with these people ever. Here is a perfect example of what I've just spoken about….

John: Over the years I've heard so many conflicting statements made about the radiation detected at the location nominated by Colonel Halt

'A Little Statement to John Hanson'!

21st July 2016 – Ben Emlyn Jones Podcast 197 *"LARRY WARREN SPEAKS"*

QUOTE: from Jones: *"This week on the HPANWO show: Larry Warren, one of the principal witnesses to the Rendlesham Forest incident of 1980 and co-author of Left At East Gate, one of the oldest and most popular books on the subject. Larry has been subjected to some very harsh personal criticism in recent months causing trouble that has spilled over into the lives of people and even entire organisations. In this programme he responds to the most serious allegations made against him."*

Transcription starting at 00:59:00 (extract from main conversation)

John: This was taken in 1995, when we met Larry and Peter at Cheltenham. I asked Peter about why he and Larry had included in the book **Left At East Gate** the fact that 'Cloud busting' went on in the Forest? When rain was not in short supply, he told me that it was journalistic licence.

I checked out the background to much of the information in the book with regard to UFO references and found that

THE HALT PERSPECTIVE 2

some of them didn't exist. If I had mentioned my misgivings I would have been singled out for attack by his cronies. So I kept my mouth shut and I'm not proud of myself.

01:50:13 **Warren:** "And umm but I do want to make a little statement to John Hanson, who is publishing the new Halt Book called *The Halt Perspective*. Is that correct?".... (Jones: "It is, yes it's in the final stages now I think.") "Isn't that joyous! Well, I would like to say to John Hanson who promoted the conference that allowed Halt to slander me: John! And let me say this because I know you'll hear this! You really should read *Halt In Woodbridge* but you won't but you really should listen to this programme that I'm doing right now but you won't at your peril.

Because, my friend, I look forward to reading about Colonel Halt's life. I think it'll be interesting."

01:50:56 **Warren:** "**I absolutely hope you're smart as an ex-cop should be to not use any of this slanderous, defamatory, second and third hand, false information the internet girl is posting and sending to you because if you think you're gonna put that in your book and get away without a lawsuit I need you to be aware of the slander and libel laws in THIS country!**"

01:51:25 **Warren:** "<u>Because I won't go after Colonel Halt.</u> I will go after you, John, and I will have you in court, your publisher and everything you own my friend because you were warned and that's all I can say. Otherwise I wish you luck. I'm gonna read the book. I look forward to it. I hope Halt's smart enough to, you know; just leave me out of it! You don't need to put me in it."

01:51:46 **Jones:** "Hopefully he will yeah...."

01:51:49 **Warren:** "But John, listen! You know, we **don't have to like each other but I tell you what my friend if you put in YOUR book any of these spurious, untrue, false, misleading, defamatory statements made by that woman – you know who I mean – I will see you in court!** Otherwise, good luck with the book. I look forward to reading it. So does my lawyer. His name is Steven."

(Ben Emlyn Jones goes on about how <u>much he used</u> to respect John Hanson and how he – Jones – was involved with the recording of the Halt presentation at Woodbridge and how he was so much looking forward to the day in Woodbridge. *Jones feels that John Hanson blames him for something, although all Jones was asked to do was record the event.)

Banned From That Conference Too!

01:52:54 **Warren:** "I think John has a tendency to blame anyone else uhhh you know I've been very clear with him from day one even before that conference. Oh I think we were banned from this. Sorry I was banned from THAT conference too." (Jones states that Peter Robbins was banned as well as Warren.)

Warren: "Oh Peter too! Oh well. I wouldn't have even you know... gone......"

01:53:11 **Jones:** "Halt basically said that was one of the provisos I think when Halt came over he says I don't want these two guys anywhere near me."

01:53:19 **Warren** (hard to hear with Jones talking at the same time): "**It must be a sexual thing...a fucking man... I have to tell you. I know Halt and you know and you know people think we're ...and I've met with him years ago and ummmm..I served...a nice guy on the Base...**"

01:53:36 **Warren:** "But ummm...I.. my thing with Hanson uhhh I have a different view and uhh yeah you know his books are interesting. I've gone through them and he... I hate to say...now, hey there's some mistakes in my book – my tactical technical errors in uhh East Gate no doubt – but when you have a picture of Jim Penniston and and have a caption under it that says 'A young Larry Warren' of ALL people under Jim Penniston I'm thinking you know was that a publisher thing or was that YOU just puttin' stuff out. I don't know!" (Jones comments that it was most likely a typo and Warren agrees that it was possible.)

01:54:17 **Warren:** "I mean I had umm Ronald Reagan in the Presidency in our book uhh when the incidents happened and in reality it was Jimmy Carter who was the outgoing.... Reagan was coming in January or February." (That's hardly a typo, just incorrect information) **[END]**

Ranting and ravings – no wonder the subject isn't taken seriously!

Charles: Nothing changes, I thought this was about UFO research and instead it's about dire warnings, threats and procrastinations from two people who do more harm to the chosen subject, never mind the filth that pours out of their lips. Well suffice to say; despite the empty threats of court action by Warren, who feels aggrieved by the content of the then, forthcoming book, nothing has happened yet! All it does is to once again show the sort of ranting and raving from a man, whose reputation precedes him. Hope he enjoys reading this one as well!

John: On the 20th of April 2012 Ben, a hospital porter for 22 years with an exemplary record, was suddenly suspended last year and told to go home without being given an explanation. After a week of confusion he was asked to return to a meeting where his employers told him he had been suspended because of material posted on his blog website. Ben is described as a very enthusiastic blogger on controversial subjects such as 9/11, UFOs and other subjects – his blog website HPANWO (Hospital Porters Against The New World Order) claimed to have thousands of readers – was interviewed by Richard D Hall. During that interview a clip of film was shown in which at a *Probe* conference Ben was filmed burning his census form. I hadn't realised that he was so paranoid, and realise now I made a bad mistake in asking him to get involved. No wonder he was sacked! He has the temerity to still advertise himself photographed in **NHS porters uniform** with nursing staff on his Facebook page.

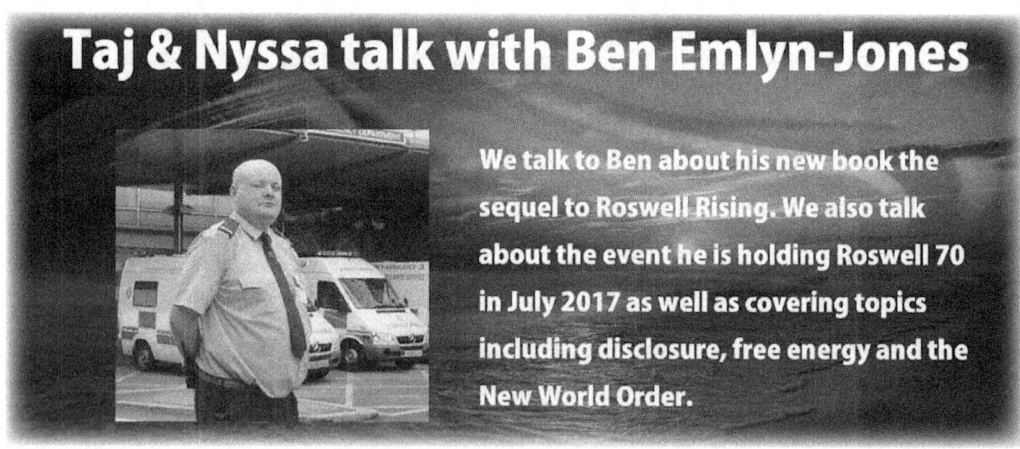

PART 9

THE MEDIA'S TWISTS AND TURNS!

Big let-down journalist Jasper Hamill – reneged on his promise!

JOHN: Another example was the despicable treatment I received from *Mirror* journalist Jasper Hamill, who invited me to London (at my own expense) in 2016, offering to write a story about the *Haunted Skies* books and also the forthcoming *Halt Perspective*. After having made my way into the very impressive building, I asked the receptionist on the desk to call him, expecting that I would be interviewed in his office. Eventually he arrived and then took me to a back street café, where I was served with a black coffee and beer. We spoke but the recording device he was in possession of packed up. He told me the interview was over and apologised for not taking me to the station as he was going in the opposite direction. I never heard any more, despite emails and letters sent recorded delivery to Jasper Hamill at web@mirror.co.uk asking him if he was going to publish anything about my visit. Here is one I sent to him on **Friday, September 16, 2016** 3:08 pm. **Subject:** Please forward to Jasper Hamill – *Hi Jasper, your **email address that I have here is now defunct.** Did you ever get round to publishing anything on the Haunted Skies books please following my personal visit to see you in London last year? Regards John Hanson retired Police Officer UK. Now four years later I have still not heard from you – an apology would have been acceptable…*

Open letter – *WHO IS THE RENDLESHAM FOREST WHISTLEBLOWER?*

2016 – Retired USA Police Officer Steven Longero comes forward!

Philip Mantle: Steve Longero, previously employed as a Police Officer for the Dept of Veterans Affairs 1986-1989 at the County of Santa Clara Dept of Correction in 1988 and also a Reserve Police Officer for the city of Manteca, until he retired in 2012, contacted Philip Mantle, former Director of Investigations for the British UFO Research Association, proprietor of FLYING DISK PRESS.

In December 2016 Philip Mantle, said *"This year we have the new book 'THE HALT PERSPECTIVE' co-authored by Colonel Halt and John Hanson and published by 'Haunted Skies'. To some, the RFI is THE case that can change ufology forever, while others dismiss it, offering a variety of natural explanations to account for the observations in question. For those who do*

Steve Longero

not know who Colonel Halt is, he was the Deputy Base Commander at RAF Woodbridge in 1980 and was an eyewitness to some of the UFO events observed in December 1980.

I am not going to go over old ground and my own opinion on the R.F.I remains open but I am not convinced with a lot of the sceptical arguments against it. So, with all this in mind, I have recently taken the opportunity to interview one of the US Airmen that was on duty on one of the nights in question.

To the best of my knowledge he has not gone on the record before and his name is Steve Longero. I spoke with Steve twice on the telephone on October 29th & 30th 2016."

Steve: "*I am a Former USAF security Police officer with an Honourable Discharge having served from 1980 to 1984. Yes, I was in the forest, I saw the lights, heard the conversations, talked about it and was told to be quiet! My roommate was Ed Cabansag! I really never talked about it to Penniston and Burroughs but I was there! Warren can tell you! Yes, we were debriefed and told to keep quiet!*" [Some of the following interview will be paraphrased while other parts will be verbatim.]

Philip Mantle (PM): Can you tell us when you joined the USAF?

Steve Longero (SL): "*Yes, it's been a long time. I joined in July, no June 1980.*"

PM: Were you stationed anywhere else before you went to Bentwaters?

SL: *No, that was my first duty. I was a security policeman. You know my job was patrolling the flight line and the weapons storage area (WSA)*

PM: Do you remember the nights in question in <u>late December 1980</u>?

SL: "*Yes I sure do. I went on duty, what I remember is that on one of those nights I was guarding the Weapons Storage Area (WSA). While on duty that night, we had a very sophisticated alarm system and everything just went off. And then you know, I could see these lights over the treetops, and I was thinking, what's going on. Then they started sending people out there and at first you know it was hard to believe, you know, all these bright lights. It's hard to take in. Well from what I remember the lights, fluorescent lights, kind of a glow, like a reddish glow. I remember going out there.*"

Steve went on to add that he went out into Rendlesham Forest and there were a lot of other people already there. The forest wasn't that far from the perimeter. He was only a few hundred yards into the forest. He could not remember who ordered him to go out there. He remembered the flight chief being out there. He saw the lights in the forest.

According to him there were a number of others out there including **Larry Warren and Jim Penniston and Cabansag**. He was out in the forest from between one to two hours. A few days later they were told not to talk about it. Steve went on to confirm that <u>AFOSI agents were there</u>, he was asked to sign something and told not to talk about it. He confirms that '*light-alls*' (portable lights) were taken into the area and that Larry Warren was there also John Burroughs and others and they discussed what they were going to do.

SL: "*I can't remember verbatim what I saw that night but I was there.*"

PM: What I'd like to ask you again Steve is when you went out into the forest you could see the lights over the trees. Could you tell me what those lights looked like please?

SL: "*They looked like fluorescent coloured lights, like red and green, glowing lights and that's what they looked like.*"

PM: How long did you view them for do you reckon?

SL: *"I'd say ten to fifteen minutes, and I could see them hovering over the treetops and it was just hovering over the treetops and it was just, **like an eye** that was almost following everybody."*

PM: When you went into the forest you mentioned others, can you remember anyone else who was there?

SL: *"**Yes, Penniston and Burroughs and Cabansag and, I remember others starting coming, we all kind of got dispatched there, if I remember Larry was out there. Because if I remember right Larry was working at a gate and he got picked up by a want to say a Lt Englund, I remember, he was at the East Gate and I remember he, they transported people from there, like I said they sent a lot of people out there**."*

PM: So when you were in the forest, can you explain to me what you saw and what it was like there?

SL: *"It was real kind of quiet and, you know, this thing hovering over the trees, and you were like, kind of tracking it and like 'what is this?' you know, and it was like following, it was like watching us, that's what it looked like to us. It seemed like something watching us."*

PM: What colour was it?

SL: *"From what I remember it was like aglow, it was really glowing like a reddish, greenish light. It was a, like, it was really glowing. You know what it looked like, like something was really hot and it was just glowing."*

PM: Did you see Col Halt, was he there?

SL: *"**Col Halt came afterwards, yes; he came afterwards, after all that was called in. I remember him turning up,** that's when they kind of gathered everyone around and said this is what we are going to do, and everybody kind of dispersed and did what they were told to do, I remember we had like a little briefing right there and everybody was just like, we just could not believe what we were seeing. Your adrenalin was flowing and I remember people saying like 'what is that?' you know."*

PM: Now I know I have asked you this question before Steve but some people believe that you misidentified the lighthouse. What do you say to that?

SL: (laughs) *"I don't think so."*

PM: Could you see the lighthouse at the same time?

SL: *"I won't say it was the lighthouse; no it was not the lighthouse. Not unless the lighthouse could move (laughs) unless they could float that thing in the air. And then, you know as we got, as people were getting close to this thing it kind of came nearer to us and then it would go forward and then go back and all of a sudden it just disappeared, like something out of Star Trek, it was like warp speed and we were all 'what was that?' it was gone and then that's when they started doing all their investigations and I was just a, after we secured the area they said okay, you're gone, get out of here."*

After the event!

PM: Was there a lot of talk about it back at Base afterwards?

SL: *"Oh yes, it was all over the base, it was a big topic."*

PM: You said that you were debriefed a few days later, is that right?

THE HALT PERSPECTIVE 2

SL: *"Yes, I want to say a day or two later, I remember that night we all used to go and eat at the chow hall and everybody was talking about it and I remember, in fact I want to say I was sitting at the table where* ***Penniston was sitting and he was a Staff Sergeant and he told all of us to stop talking about, it. I remember that, you know, stop talking about it."**

PM: You said also that Larry Warren was also involved in helping set up the *light-alls* is that correct?

SL: *"He was, yes that's true".*

PM: So who debriefed you Steve?

SL: *"You know Philip, I remember going in, they called us in individually and I want to say that it was security police investigations and I do believe that there was an OSI agent in there. I remember this OSI gentleman with a beard, I remember getting pulled in I remember getting talked to by Major Zickler; I remember getting called into his office for something like that."*

PM: Can you remember what the conversation was (with Major Zickler)?

SL: *"Well, you know, what you saw, remember where you work in the weapons storage area (WSA). It was like you don't need to talk about this you don't need to make a big deal out of this".*

PM: And we are talking about nuclear weapons here aren't we?

SL: *"Yes sir."*

PM: So there was a lot of talk, was there, on consensus about what this thing was?

SL: *"Yes, it was like 'what did we see?' was this, was this an experimental aircraft? I remember that was one of the things, you know, 'what was that?'"*

PM: What do you think it was?

SL: *"I think it was something not from this world. Just because the way it hovered and just the way it disappeared. That's what I think, that's what I've always thought."*

PM: You know Larry Warren has been criticized quite a bit. What do you have to say in answer to that?

SL: *"I think there were a lot of haters out there who just didn't like Larry Warren. I liked Larry, I went to tech school with him and I never had a problem Larry, but I know there were people in that unit that didn't like him for whatever reason, maybe they didn't like his personality but I never had any issue with Larry."*

PM: But you definitely remember seeing him there don't you?

SL: *"I remember, what I remember is that we had something to do with these light-all things, I remember yes. And that was out there, yes."*

PM: Did you get to know any of the civilians in the area at the time?

SL: *"No. After that I just kind of kept to myself and kind of thought I'll do my bit and get out of here."*

Phil Mantle: I thanked Steve Longero for speaking to me and for going on the record for the very first time.

---

*John – Larry also said, *"The next morning I was back at Bentwaters, having coffee with a number of other guys who had been there at the incident. I noticed that my eyes were watering profusely and I had a metallic taste in my mouth. My buddy looked at me across the table and said, 'What the hell happened to us?'* **I started to talk, but <u>Sgt. Penniston</u> told me to shut up."**

Fox News 7. 12. 2016. The *Sun* (Writer not identified)

(Accompanied by an illustration of a four fingered alien grey, replete with an Area 51 badge walking about in a public enclosure) – 'It was not from this world': Witness to 'Britain's Roswell' UFO incident breaks 36-year silence.

"A new witness has broken his 36-year silence to speak out about Britain's most famous UFO incident. Steve Longero was told to keep quiet by his superiors following the infamous Rendlesham Forest incident in Suffolk. But now the retired U.S. Air Force police officer has gone on the record for the first time and said: "I think it was something not from this world." The incident – dubbed the British Roswell – took place over three nights between 26 and 28 December, in 1980. Military personnel from nearby RAF Bentwaters and RAF Woodbridge, including the Deputy Base Commander, witnessed strange lights in the forest and hovering above the twin NATO airbases which were on high alert as the Cold War was at its peak.

Steve, who served as a police sergeant in the USAF, was guarding the weapons storage area when the alarms started going off. He said: 'While on duty that night, we had a very sophisticated alarm system and everything just went off. Then I could see these lights over the treetops, and I was thinking, what's going on? Then they started sending people out there and at first it was hard to believe, all these bright lights. It was hard to take in. Well from what I remember the lights, fluorescent lights, kind of a glow, like a reddish glow. I remember going out there.' Steve went out into the forest where he remembers seeing a large group of other military personnel had already gathered including Staff **Sgt Jim Burroughs, Airman First Class Edward Cabansag and Airman First Class Larry Warren**. Describing the UFOs, he said: 'They looked like fluorescent coloured lights, like red and green, glowing lights and that's what they looked like. I could see them hovering over the treetops like an eye that was almost following everybody.' He added: 'It was real kind of quiet and this thing hovering over the trees, and you were like kind of tracking it and like 'what is this?'. And it was like following, it was like watching us, that's what it looked like to us. It seemed like something watching us. From what I remember it was like aglow, it was really glowing like a reddish, greenish light. It was really glowing, like something was really hot and it was just glowing.' **He also recalled seeing Colonel Charles Halt there, who made a tape recording describing how beams of light were being shone down by the UFO. He has written an explosive new book called *The Halt Perspective* describing his close encounter.** Mr Longero said: **'Col Halt came afterwards,** after all that was called in. I remember him turning up, that's when they kind of gathered everyone around and said this is what we are going to do, and everybody kind of dispersed and did what they were told to do. I remember we had a little briefing right there and everybody was just like, we just could not believe what we were seeing. Your adrenalin was flowing and I remember people saying like 'what is that?''. Rubbishing theories that the lights in the woods were caused by a lighthouse on the east coast, he laughed: 'I don't think so. Not unless the lighthouse could move. Unless they could float that thing in the air. And then, as people were getting close to this thing it kind of came nearer to us and then it would go forward and then go back and all of a sudden it just disappeared, like something out of Star Trek, it was like warp speed and we were all 'what was that?', it was gone and then that's when they started doing all their investigations. After we secured the area they said okay, you're gone, get out of here.' Steve said he was debriefed a few days later and was told not to talk about what he saw as the base had nuclear weapons on site.

Philip Mantle, interviewed Steve for *Outer Limits Magazine*, and said: 'Steve does not claim to be anything special but he wanted to emphasise that there were a lot of others involved who were witness to the events in question, many of whom have yet to add their voice to these events. Steve has confirmed the open secret that nuclear weapons were stored at RAF Bentwaters at the time although he did not personally witness any lights being shone onto the WSA. He has confirmed much of what Colonel Halt

THE HALT PERSPECTIVE 2

has already said on the record and he is in no doubt that Larry Warren was there. What is clear is that despite the best efforts of some this case will continue to be hotly debated for many years to come."

The story originally appeared in The *Sun*.

Another interview…

In an extraordinary interview with ***theanalysis.net***, Steve said: "A month before the Base was put on alert I was called out and I got onto a bunker by one of the gates. "**I was having a pee outside when I saw an orange glowing light in the woods – it was a reddish ball.**" It stopped right in front of me – it just stayed there and hovered two feet off the ground and I called for reinforcements I was scared to death." [**Would this be November 1980? No mention of other witnesses?**]

Following on from the account given to us by Ken Kern, relating to a mysterious event that took place in the forest, involving Airman Steven Wagner and Charles Campbell, I couldn't shake off the suspicion that what **Steve Longero had witnessed took place in either June or November 1980,** taking into consideration, that Steve had himself said it took place a month before the end of December, of course I may be wrong at the end of the day it's up to the reader to make their own minds up on the validity of the interview statements presented here. For all we know there might have been another incident he was involved in earlier than the end of December 1980?

This news first broke in August 2020; reports in the media were devoid of details of associates straightforward and simple.

As time went by particularly nearing the 40th Anniversary in December 2020, the story appears to have grown and sprouted all manner of information, dragging in anybody and everybody. Oddly *Nexus Newsletter* covered the story, but referred to Colonel Halt as **HOLT** on a number of occasions… so much for the eye on detail here!

Another interview…

Jon Austin @ Daily Express: 7.12.2016. RENDLESHAM MYSTERY: UFO key witness speaks for FIRST TIME and says object WAS alien

He said: "I think it was something not from this world." Mr. Longero was guarding the weapons storage area when the alarms started going off. He said: "While on duty that night we had a very sophisticated alarm system and everything just went off. And then I could see these lights over the treetops, and I was thinking, what's going on? Then they started sending people out there and at first it was hard to believe, all these bright lights. It was hard to take in." When Mr. Longero went into the forest it was swamped with other military personnel. He described seeing UFOs looking like "fluorescent coloured lights, like red and green, glowing lights and that's what they looked like".

Steve told **Outer Limits Magazine:** "I could see them hovering over the treetops **like an eye** that almost following everybody." At a debriefing afterwards the witnesses were sworn to secrecy as the Base had nuclear weapons on site. "It came towards us into the forest, moving, bobbing up and down in the trees. It was oval, about 100 to 150 yards away, with a **dark centre and red around it.**" He claimed there were "sparks" coming from it and after a minute it "exploded and disappeared." They then spotted objects in the sky, 3,000 to 4,000ft up.

Another interview...

"It was real kind of quiet and this thing hovering over the trees, and you were like kind of tracking it and like 'what is this?'. And it was like following, it was like watching us, that's what it looked like to us. It seemed like something watching us. **Soldiers investigated what the lights were**, *including Staff Sgt Jim Burroughs, Airman First Class Edward Cabansag and Airman First Class* **Larry Warren."** Mr Longero said the UFOs looked like red and green fluorescent lights hovering over treetops. He also dismissed one theory that the lights had been caused by a lighthouse.

Another interview...

Longero, now retired from the Santa Clara County Sheriff's Office since 2012, recounted that his stint at Bentwaters Air Force Base was his first duty posting and after the UFO incident, it was the talk of the base. *"Yes. I was in the forest, I saw the lights, heard the conversations, talked about it and was told to be quiet! My roommate was Ed Cabansag! I really never talked about it to Penniston and Burroughs but I was there! Warren can tell you! Yes we were debriefed and told to keep quiet!"* Longero said he was pulled from his assignment, **"patrolling the flight line and the weapons storage area,"** the night of the incident (December 26, 1980) after alarms went off on the Base. He remembered seeing: *"all these bright lights"* above the tree tops. *"It was hard to take in. Well, from what I remember, the lights, fluorescent lights, kind of a glow, like a reddish glow."* He said that he was transported out to the forest and would remain there for one or two hours.

Gut instinct

John: As someone who worked in the police for a number of years then transferred to the CID as a Detective having worked on many murder enquires and serious incidents at the time of the Birmingham Pub Bombings and IRA threats…I would like to think that I am a good judge of human character, and can tell if someone is '*spinning a yarn*'. I'm not suggesting that Steve is lying, far from it, but there are discrepancies here and gut instinct flags caution. It was a long time ago; I think he's got things mixed up. There is a 'thread' in the backcloth of at least 50 interviews made with the media that leaves me uncomfortable. The inclusion of similarities with other reports and the Larry Warren story leaves me suspicious…. Why didn't Steve contact Colonel Halt and discuss the matter with him…I wasn't there but Colonel Halt was, and this is what he had to say…

Comment made to Philip Mantle from Steve Longero

Charles: In an article in *Open Minds* written by Alejandro Rojas, I commented on the interview Philip did a few weeks ago with Steve Longero. http://www.openminds.tv/usaf-police-officers-ufo-claims-refuted-by-deputy-base-commander. I dismissed the claims made by Steve Longero.

Philip took the liberty of showing the above article to Steve Longero and asked him if he would like to respond. This is what he said:

"Now Halt is trying to say I wasn't there? Lol. Philip on my kids (life) I was there! That's how I remember the events. These guys are incredible! At this point Philip he is questioning my integrity! It was a long time ago but that's how I remember the events! Why hasn't anybody else come forward to dispute what I said? That's what I remember! I don't want to get bitter or in a pissing match! Really! This is getting out of hand! Lol. My opinion is the less of us that come forward the better it is for those who want to write books! Just saying! Halt can also contact me!"

THE HALT PERSPECTIVE 2

My comments ignored by *Open Minds*!

I read the latest *Open Minds* posting and was shocked. A major posting was the report made public by Steve Longero. **Earlier I sent enough information so that the program makers would know there was something really wrong here.** I am really disappointed. I thought they wanted to stick to facts. Either Steve Longero has been compromised by Warren, the 'spooks' have gotten to him or he wants attention. **The least you could have done is let me post the truth.** To say I'm disappointed is to say the least! [On page 28 of *Left At East Gate* there is only a brief reference to a Steve **Longaro.** (Longero)]

MUFON picked up and published Steve Longero's wild tale in their January Journal. Steve was Larry Warren's drinking and whatever buddy. He was on duty the first night only **but miles away guarding the WSA.** I recently learned that Warren has been in touch with him to support his involvement. **There are more holes in Steve's story than you can believe.** I am truly disappointed in MUFON for publishing what they did. Doesn't anybody do due diligence anymore? Steve's unsubstantiated story does nothing but muddies the waters and certainly does not do anything for the MUFON reputation let alone for disclosure. I contacted the individual that first picked up and published the story in the UK. His response to me was *"let the reader sort it out as to the other tale about it being a black project"*, I have no idea what this man is talking about! Former Bentwaters cop Steve Longero tells us now of being involved in the event. We know he was on duty the first night but definitely not in the forest. The third night he was on break. His tale is all screwed up but he says Warren was there. We know Steve was one of Warren's friends.

I suspect Warren or Heseltine asked him to lie about Larry to support them. Why would he wait 36 years to speak up and then speak to Philip in England? You will notice from the interview conducted with Philip, **Longero was not asked 'on what date did this happen?' Instead he was 'led'** by Phil asking him do you remember the nights in question in **late December 1980**? This is bearing in mind that Phil had previously interviewed him twice on the phone, and I am guessing the above conversation was from the second interview.

There seems to be something strange going on here. I'm tired of all the disinformation out there. It seems that every time I turn around I hear more nonsense or am accused of something. Contrary to some recent speculation in the social media I was never told I didn't have a need to know. I don't know anything about this. I do know I did not go to the doctor after the event.

As far as Steve's involvement – he was a low-ranking cop on duty the first night (25-26 December).

Not on duty that night!

He was not on duty the night I was in the forest (27-28 December) but on December 25-26.

Steve was posted at the Bentwaters Weapons Storage Area (WSA), which was more than a mile away. Unless he was in the WSA tower, which he was not, one could not even see the forest. He could not have left that critical guard post. He states all the alarms in the WSA went off. That didn't happen. Such an occurrence would have provoked a response to behold. All available cops would have been recalled, armed and dispatched. The incident would have immediately been up-channelled all the way to the Pentagon, Senior Officers called and a police blotter entry made. None of this happened. Even without the alarm, Steve could not have left his post. He claims that he went into the forest and saw Warren, Penniston, Burroughs, Cabansag and me. The only cops that went into the forest the first night were Penniston, Burroughs and Cabansag.

The Senior NCO cop on duty that night was MSGT. J. D. Chandler, who stayed at the East Gate of Woodbridge Base, the first night, and did not let anyone else go outside.

THE HALT PERSPECTIVE 2

Obviously, Steve has the first and third nights co-mingled. I definitely was not there the first night as my family and I were dinner guests of the Base Commander and stayed very late.

The first night Warren initially claimed he was in Germany *(see Left At East Gate)*. It was later learned from his girlfriend 'Cookie' and others he was actually in the 'cop' dormitory drinking and lied about being in Germany.

Steve is not the first fellow officer that was asked to lie to support Warren's involvement. I have written documentation from another of Larry's drinking buddies from Bentwaters asking him to lie about his involvement in the incident, in addition to what Barry Greenwood, told me (on page 254)

I tracked down the source of Steve's recent tale and discovered it to be a less than respected UK UFO follower who was obviously being used. I contacted him and asked why he didn't verify the story. His comment was *"I just report and let the reader sort it out."*

Like John, I'm starting to see a pattern here as if additional information is being 'fed in' from other sources as time goes by which confuses rather than clarifies, of course we might be wrong, but that's the overall feeling.

Longero reported, *"I was having a pee outside when I saw an orange glowing light in the woods it was a reddish ball."* Someone else who responded to a call of nature, in the same forest and then saw something unusual six months previously, was, airman **Steven Wagner**, who had this to say:

"I can't tell you if this ever made the blotter. I think CSC and everyone else was laughing too hard to take it seriously. Typically weekend mid shifts were a boring affair; if you were lucky enough to be assigned post with someone you were friends with then you could pass the night enjoyably. Saturdays were tolerable due to some limited flight line activity, but Sundays were miserable.

This particular Sunday the **15th of June 1980**, *was pretty eventful. Shift started with guard mount. Guard mount is a pre-shift formation where the flight chief and flight commander gauge each Security Patrolman's fitness for duty that day, share any pertinent security updates, and to give out post assignments. This night, myself and Charles M. Campbell, both A1C at the time, were assigned to Alpha2 ART (area response team). Alpha2 is a roving vehicle patrol within the Alpha 2 alert parking area for A10 Warthog aircraft.*

Airman Michael LaBrucherie was assigned Alpha1, which is the gatepost. Although not close friends with Mike, all of us had little cliques we ran with; he was a nice enough guy. Chas and I made sure to look out for him, as gate duty on the weekends was brutal. Mitch Petersen delivered our meals at around 0145 and Chas, Mike and I, ate on the tailgate of the pick-up and chatted away generally.

The specific time frame of the occurrence I can't pinpoint for you (it's been 35 years!) sorry. I can't tell you it started sometime around 0230-0300. I stepped out of the patrol vehicle and went to the side of the maintenance buildings to have a pee there was a berm that ran behind the buildings and the entire length of them."

Ken Kern – then a member of the Security Police, posted to 'B' Flight, confirms this account:

*"The exact words off my index card 'diary' were '***15th June 80*** – Interesting night – it's our 2nd mid and Steve Wagner & Campbell have A-2. They saw a* **UFO on five different occasions** *that night, described as a* **red globe 20ft in diameter**. *It hovered at times over aircraft pads/structures. Labrucherie also sighted the UFO; he had A-1. At one time they said the* **UFO glided over the trees to a meadow, where it suddenly disappeared into a white flash** *and then nothing; except two deer which they say we're not there previously. I believe this story to be authentic'."*

Introducing Gary Heseltine

Former detective Gary Heseltine, born in 1960, worked for the RAF Police from 1983 to 1989 and the British Transport Police from 1989 to 2013. He was entrusted with the investigation of all kinds of offenses, including murder, manslaughter and rape, and specialized in questioning witnesses and suspects.

After the terrorist attacks in London in July 2005, he was one of the first detectives to question witnesses. After the pressure on him because of his UFO activities had increased, Heseltine resigned from active police service and founded a new two-month magazine in April 2013 entitled **UFO TRUTH MAGAZINE**. In it he regularly publishes articles by recognised experts in the field.

PART 10

GARY HESELTINE JOINS IN!

2017

2nd January 2017: Posted on *Facebook* by Gary Heseltine

THIS was a very lengthy overview of the UFO events which had taken place in Rendlesham Forest during the end of December 1980. In order to save space we decided to include the salient points. First of all Gary acknowledges that Brenda and Dot were the original investigators, but questions whether they were the original 'whistle-blowers'? He then refers to a Sergeant in the Reports and Analysis section of the **81st Security Police Squadron Steve Roberts aka 'J.D INGLES'** and describes his role at the Base referring to Ingles [which should be John 'Davy' Engalls].

Gary draws the reader's attention to the fact that in January, 1981 Ingles told Brenda that he had witnessed a landed craft with alien beings and of having seen **Colonel Gordon Williams 'communicating' with the aliens!** However, by 1987 he had changed his story to say that the incident was a hoax perpetrated by the USAF? Georgina Bruni ultimately said this of Roberts who she interviewed: "**Steve Roberts' story is so inconsistent that if he decided to stand up and tell the truth today, would anyone really believe him?"** (Page 59 *'You Can't Tell the People'*) Gary then runs through a number of others that might have earned the accolade of 'Whistle-blowers' which included, Jim Penniston, John Burroughs, Sergeant Adrian Bustinza; *". . . Colonel Charles Halt – The Deputy Base Commander, the man named in the famous document produced in the 'News of the World' article on 2nd October 1983."* Fact: he fought not to have the Halt Memo released. He did not want to go public. At the time of the article he was still a serving officer and feared that the release of the memo would affect his career, so Halt is certainly not the whistle-blower.

Gary Heseltine: Larry Warren has for many years provoked much controversy with regards to his 'Capel Green' scenario but significantly not in October 1983 when the case first made national and international headlines. He was not the source of major controversy that it became in subsequent years, simply because none of the principal witnesses were in a position to speak publicly about their involvement because they were still 'serving' in the USAF. So, let's examine Larry Warren's actual witness whistle-blower credentials. His involvement in the case began in late 1982 when rumours of a significant new military witness began to circulate within the environs of the case. As time went on the pseudonym of 'Art Wallace' was given to him (by Larry Fawcett) and his account began to emerge. He had been a direct witness to an incident involving a *****strange ground-hugging mist**, with a large number of

---

*****John:** Ground fog & Holiday period was one of the reasons why helicopters weren't up in the air.

fellow airmen stood around it in a circle, that a red light had come from the sky, stopping over the mist, then there was an explosion of light that hurt his eyes and after the light had diminished he **saw a translucent type of shimmering craft on/near to the ground where the mist had been, and that at one point he had seen three child-like 'entities/aliens' appear like bubbles from the edge of the craft.** Whilst there is some debate as to all of the actual steps that led to the unearthing and disclosure of the 'Halt Memo' what is clear by most respected authors/researchers is that Art Wallace/Larry Warren had been involved in some capacity during that process.

On 9th October, 1983 a newspaper article stated that John Burroughs had confirmed to Larry Fawcett, a Deputy police chief in Connecticut that the story outlined by '**Art Wallace' (Larry Warren)** was **correct.** (Page 118 *Left At East Gate*)' On **21st November, 1983** in Beverly, Massachusetts 'Art Wallace' made his first public appearance to a number of people which included a member of the Press, Andrea Atkins of the *Beverly Times*. At that point he is now facing the media in the flesh, albeit still under the pseudonym name but his face was now out there in the public domain so there can be no doubt in my mind that this is the point at which he was the first actual witness to go public. So, from the original whistle-blower point of view there can be no doubt that by late **November 1983 the first original witness to UFO activity during the Xmas period December 1980 to face the media in public was LARRY WARREN using the pseudonym name Art Wallace**.

The controversy surrounding Larry Warren's account was always there but as the years passed it began to intensify. During that time, a period of 10 years he had become the public face of the RFI and appeared in many TV interviews. As time went by several of the key witnesses began to leave military service and began to be interviewed on camera in documentaries. Penniston and Burroughs come forward on camera and were dismissive of the Warren account because it does not match their own recollections of the incident. **Halt finally came forward and was totally dismissive of the Warren account. He said he wasn't there at all, not in the forest and had not completed his training so couldn't have been assigned to a shift.** Many of the now accepted witnesses felt that Warren's account was 'unhelpful' to the case as it seemed at odds with the others and contained some 'outrageous' details. So, despite the fact that Warren had been in the public domain for many years on his own dealing with the media, the 'main witnesses' were coming forward to pour scorn on Warren's account.

A major book was published in 1997, *Left At East Gate*, which centered on the story of his involvement in the Capel Green scenario. The book was very well received and was on the ***Times* bestseller list for several weeks**. **Nick Pope**, the former MOD officer who had been at the UFO desk between, 1991-1994 wrote a glowing endorsement of the book at that time. The book essentially told Warren's life story and his involvement with the Rendlesham case. Significantly the book outlined two specific events that would gain more importance over time – **he allegedly made a phone call** to his mother in the States within hours of his involvement in the incident where he alerted her that he'd seen a UFO and it had involved aliens. The call was made on the base and it was terminated abruptly by station staff. Within **a few days he then wrote a letter to her** where he makes reference to the phone call days earlier. The letter was dated 6th January 1981, seven days before Lt Col Halt wrote his one page memo to Squadron Leader Moreland, the RAF liaison officer. The significance of the phone call and the letter would not be fully appreciated until 2014. The book is also significant because it shows transcripts of calls made by Larry Fawcett, the Connecticut police officer, to Adrian Bustinza and Greg Battram. 20th April 1984 **an interview with Adrian Bustinza confirms much of Warren's account**. (P139-154 LAEG) 7th February 1984 Larry Fawcett interview with Greg Bartram that confirms that he was present when Larry Warren had made a phone call from on the Base to his mother that was abruptly terminated. (P134-138 LAEG).

*****Authors**: a cursory look on the Internet in December 2020 **fails to reveal any trace**. We tried the *New York Times* and the *Times* covering the initial publication in 1997 up to 2017 but were unsuccessful. If we have missed it, we apologise.

THE HALT PERSPECTIVE 2

Gary Heseltine: For a seven year period between late December 2007 and summer 2015, I had research/writing corroboration with retired Colonel Halt regarding a proposed film script about the whole incident. During the early days of piecing together the main story it soon became clear to me that the final member of Halt's team out in the forest on the 3rd night of activity was Sergeant Adrian Bustinza, however, the reason why I mention this is that Halt seemed always reluctant to confirm this fact and that he had been at best strangely vague to me about who had been the fifth person with him i.e. Halt, Englund, Ball and Nevels. Given that Bustinza was named on Halt's audio tape and is in the written transcript he was reluctant to confirm that Bustinza was with him on the 3rd night of activity. It should have been an easy thing for him to recall given the tape and the transcript. I suspect the reason why that was so was because of what Bustinza had said in an interview with Bruni in her book that highlighted disturbing aspects that closely mirrored the original account given by Larry Warren, something he had always rejected claiming that Warren had been 'messed with' and that if anything Warren had been implanted with a false memory of a fanciful tale.

Gary Heseltine: Salas then makes some observations about the points made by Bustinza which included that Bustinza has confirmed much of what Larry Warren and John Burroughs had said over the years. In addition he also highlighted that **Bustinza's testimony raised serious questions about Halt's account of what had happened on the 3rd night. Salas had formed the opinion of a number of years that Col Halt had not been completely forthcoming about the facts involved in the RFI and of his involvement**. (Page 140/141 *Halt In Woodbridge* by Peter Robbins)

Gary Heseltine: That too had been my conclusion following our seven year collaboration period which I ended in 2015 due to his (Halt's) repeated personal and uncorroborated attacks on Larry Warren. One aspect that he referred to was Halt's often declaration that Larry Warren was not involved in the 3rd night of the incident and that Salas believed that Halt had made a 'concerted' effort to discredit Warren's testimony over the years. Sadly I have to agree with Salas.

Without a shadow of doubt Larry Warren was there on the 3rd night of activity and many aspects of his original account had been correct from the start when he went public in 1983. It also confirmed John Burroughs second UFO event that Halt has always denied i.e. that after being denied a request to move forward to join Halt's team Burroughs and Bustinza eventually did get ahead of Halt and that Burroughs had a UFO encounter with Bustinza on the 3rd night. If Bustinza and Burroughs are correct with their 3rd night experiences then **Halt's account is woefully incomplete and flawed and real questions should be asked to find out why that is**.

Charles: Who really cares who the original whistle blower was? I don't see the relevance here. As far as fighting to ensure that the *Memo* was not released, this is rubbish; if that was the case then why bother submitting a memo at all? At the end of the day I wrote a faithful account of what I witnessed along with other colleagues, taking into consideration I had no idea how widespread this activity was or what I was witnessing. For those that suggest all manner of inane explanations for what took place I suggest you read this book and its background and you may feel that we weren't on our own. My job

THE HALT PERSPECTIVE 2

isn't to determine what these things are and where they come from, just to carry out my duty and I think that I did that to the best of my ability.

Further mention of the claim by Larry that he saw a translucent type of shimmering craft on/near to the ground where the mist had been, and that at one point he had seen three child-like 'entities/aliens' appear like bubbles from the edge of the craft. More rubbish! For the information of those who haven't yet read it. I can only tell you that at no stage when I was out there in the Forest conducting investigations did I see Airman Warren. Nobody else mentioned his name until later. Common sense which appears to be prevailing now about his wild version of events indicates otherwise. I accept that he may have been there but I wasn't aware of this and can only tell what I witnessed. I interviewed everyone involved in the incident and took statements. Not one person mentioned anything about Warren being involved. In fact, his name never came up until years later. At that point he was working with Larry Facwett and Barry Greenwood on a possible book. **When they discovered he was lying about the incident they dropped him.** As for the so called UFO sketch of the 'turtle/tile' shaped object provided by Larry, he told John Hanson in 2006 while out in the forest, this sketch was drawn from spiritual direction with Betty Luca and that the UFO photograph shown to him by John taken in November over the Leiston area was identical to what he had seen.

What's important is the truth of what happened needs to get out, versus all the false stories and wannabe witnesses. If I had wanted to cover anything up why would I have submitted the memo to Donald Moreland. I could have easily explained away what we saw as being natural phenomena even the darned lighthouse. Instead I chose to report to the best of my ability what had taken place. It appears you can't do right for wrong. I would be failing in my duty as Deputy Base Commander if I hadn't done anything at all. That's not the way I work. Since then I have realized that we weren't the only ones to sight something completely, for me, out of the normal. What it was we saw I don't know to this present day.

I appreciate that once again there has been speculation about this *'alleged'* (Gary's word) letter written by Warren to his mother and have noted the comments made with regard to its claimed authenticity. But let's make one thing clear this was an American Air Base, on loan from the British, charged ultimately with the Defence of the Realm. That's why we were there. Warren rang his mother using reverse charges to the States, and he was in breach of Air Force Regulations. Behaviour like this could cause serious implications. I am reminded of the expression used over there 'Careless talk costs lives' Don't get me wrong – guys called home, but spreading unsubstantiated information like this was not, at the end of the day, his to do. There is a chain of command in the Air Force and it would be dereliction of my duty if I had allowed behaviour like this to go on unchecked.

Gary, you have got it wrong – I never played down Bustinza's involvement. Where did that come from? Bustinza was at my side, so close I could have touched him. He only left me when he and Burroughs went forward at the end for a brief period. Gary quit responding several years before I came to talk last year. He fell into the clutches of Peter as he couldn't sell the screenplay and Peter looked like he could help more with the new magazine. What a cad!

I never told you, or your then girlfriend, anything about any weapons at RAF Bentwaters. You made an assumption and I did not comment. You also quote me as saying Bentwaters had the largest stockpile of --- in Europe. Again another lie, as I had no idea what was stored elsewhere. I trusted you as you know the truth, but I guess selling a magazine and publicity is your focus. Do remember, I have all the correspondence with you. Makes interesting reading! I'll bet you don't remember all of what you said. Care to respond? Two can play the game with the Press.

When we returned to the vehicles/*light alls* – John Burroughs was still there. He was insistent on going forward to look again at the landing site. I reluctantly agreed. He took Adrian with him. They were visible

THE HALT PERSPECTIVE 2

the whole time and quickly returned without saying anything occurred. That's why I never made an issue about it. John now says something happened. If it did, the four of us plus a few cops never saw anything and they were in view the whole time. Somewhere we need to inject the fact that Adrian never left my side the whole time until he briefly went with Burroughs to again look at the site. Adrian did go back for *light-alls* but that was before I arrived.

Larry clearly gives the impression that he was not directly involved, but "thinks he may have" seen the same thing. Nothing like the version of events we read in his book involving seeing a pyramidal object land and claims of English police officers taking photographs, the arrival of Colonel Williams and 'beings entering into some form of perceived communication with the officer.' He'll say it was the first night. Who knows as at one point he says he was in Germany but associates, including Cookie, say he was drinking in the dorm. Too many stories! He says he was in the same place as the UFO. Guess what? That would have been miles away from the road to the Base. He also mentions something was left behind – nonsense!

Gary, we met many years ago when you cornered me during a visit to the UK. I had a gut feeling not to trust you but you kept telling me how important it was to get the truth out and you could put together a bestselling screenplay and perhaps a movie. I reluctantly agreed.

You intimated to me that you were convinced that Larry Warren was using what he learned from others to paint himself into the event. We both agreed that because of his actions at the time he was "Debriefed" and probably had either had false memories implanted or was just a 'wannabe', perhaps some combination of the two.

You proceeded with 3-4 versions of a potential play (of which I still have copies) but came to realize with starting a **new magazine it would be more profitable to throw your lot in with Peter Robbins and Larry Warren. Little did you know that Larry would implode and be caught in lies, photo shopping, and claims of falsifying documents and memorabilia, to say nothing of threatening the lives of others?** I was shocked to discover you gave Larry a bravery award. You are either the slowest whitted cop ever on the force, or a cowardly fraud. It's time to wake up to the facts. Larry has a problem with drink and substance abuse and has been using others for years. I'll bet he's even given you a sad tale and borrowed money as he's done to so many others. Don't tell me he has Post Traumatic Stress. His only stress is from fear of being caught in his lies. I keep hearing he's an honorably discharged vet. He was discharged under the provisions of AFR 35-10 (Unsuitable or undesirable for the convenience of the Government with a coded discharge that would not allow him to re-enlist or ever get a government security clearance.) All of this after the US Government spent $10,000+ on his training and travel. Most of the book *Left At East Gate* is just plain fraud. The worst case worked on the UFO community since Roswell. The longer you wait to admit the truth, the deeper the hole. All your rebuttals to critics have ignored the truth. You spent multiple pages discussing who was the original whistle blower? Who really cares? The facts and truth of the incident are what people care about. It's time to wake up! You have done a great disservice to the UFO community.

The role of the OSI according to a retired Suffolk Constabulary Detective Inspector

In **January 2017**, following the publication of the article in the *East Anglian Daily Times*, a number of other replies were posted up, one was from James (who supplied his full name and address to me), asking that Colonel Charles Halt be informed, saying: "*First can I say that I had no involvement in this incident. At the time I was a Det. Insp. at Ipswich Division that also covered the Base areas... This incident did not have any CID attention. However I worked with the OSI in the early 70's when I was with the Drug Squad* and later on general crime involving US personnel. My good AFOSI friend was at Bentwaters/Woodbridge all of this time. **I haven't named him as I do not have his permission**. He resides in Nevada and is currently holidaying in California. I will speak with him on Skype in a week or so. In discussing the various headlines over the years **he has told me that there was no basement at the AFOSI office**. I can verify that. However the Security Police had offices in a new block further towards the flight line. I understand it's alleged by personnel, that during interviews they described one of the AFOSI officers as having a beard. He states that under no circumstances were USAF military including Special Agents allowed to grow beards. **In his training they were strongly lectured that the <u>USAF does not administer sodium pentothal or any similar drug</u>. He states that having regard to the circumstances, the AFOSI would not have had a deep involvement and would have left any possible investigation to the Base Security Police.** As far as I'm aware two experienced Suffolk Constabulary constables attended the scene and formed their conclusions. These were included in a report by Woodbridge Inspector Mike Topliss. I take it you have had sight of the text. Finally, like you I have an open mind on the matter. It all depends where an independent balance of probabilities rests."

Charles: John contacted retired Police Inspector Mike Topliss, who was in the Suffolk Constabulary Police Force, and responsible for answering members of the public questions about the Police presence in the forest during the end of 1980, and other matters pertaining to the Air Base. He was to encounter a **UFO** while driving near Saxmundham some years later! (Full details in ***The Halt Perspective***)

Mike: "Personally I do not recall any D.I. at Ipswich called 'James' over the relevant period. However, the Suffolk branch of NARPO will be able to identify the officer. Regarding the Security Police, it is correct that they would not be competent to investigate anything of this nature and I also knew members of the AFOSI at the time who gave no indication that they were involved. As the CIA was actively promulgating the UFO phenomenon as a 'cold war' misinformation tool it would not be surprising if they were involved in this incident and any subsequent debriefings. The AFOSI agent described by James as currently living in Nevada was long gone from the area and retired at the relevant time. He would therefore not have any significant knowledge of what went on. Just a minor correction on the final reference to my report: I was never an Inspector at Woodbridge but dealt with Emergency Planning and Counter Terrorist Planning at the Suffolk Police HQ. I worked in close liaison with Special Branch and had previously been the local police liaison officer for **Sir Patrick Walker, head of Homeland Security (MI5),** with whom I occasionally met at his home address and discussed topical issues on an informal basis. There was no indication of the involvement of either of these two agencies in the debriefings. I did not know the officer (full name released) when I was in the job but, from his comments, he appears to think that the AFOSI did not have much involvement in the subsequent investigation which accords with my own information. As I mentioned before, and given recent media revelations by ex CIA members of an orchestrated campaign of disinformation about UFO sightings post Roswell, I would find it hard to believe that they were not involved in such an intelligence gathering opportunity at that time. If they were involved then it would be likely that UK SIS would also be there to monitor developments. Both organisations, by their very nature, would have no particular aversion to beards or even masquerading as AFOSI agents. Given my position and contacts at the time of writing the 'report' (letter) referred to by James I am confident that the only significant UK police involvement was the routine initial attendance of local uniformed officers."

Facebook blogger, Sacha Claire Christie

On the **6th January 2017** – Facebook Blogger Sacha Claire Christie made an appeal asking if anyone would like to help end the debate with regard to the alleged fraudulent claims involving 'Art Wallace' by contributing towards paying a handwriting expert to conduct an examination of the documents.

She asked one of many questions regarding the validity of Mr. Warren '*Why would a medical form have parts tippexed out and written over?* The only thing I can say at first glance they may look genuine but

I was in no position to authenticate them as he (Warren) briefly flashed them in front of me. The Eye Doctor at Bentwaters at that time was Lester Sharpton. I knew him well as we both were Boy Scout Leaders. If Larry had an eye problem, that's who he would have seen. Never heard of the other supposed Doctor he claims saw him. I suspect the appointment slip he shows was for his discharge physical and he altered it. If he had a cornea burn there should have been follow-up and perhaps a disability rating. More lies!

Another area that is now very suspect is his multiple medical claims resulting from his supposed encounter. If he had all the issues he claimed, where's the documentation? How could anyone just take his word? He should have had a discharge medical examination with potential for a disability rating. Nothing, that tells me something. He has shown what appears to be a forged medical appointment slip. He claims he saw doctors after his discharge for supposed related issues. Where are the results? Sure looks like more fraud here. I have no idea what on earth this man is talking about. I was Deputy Base Commander at that time and regard statements like this as having absolutely no basis at all. This is the ramblings of imagination to say the least – what will they keep coming up with next?

Paranormal Researcher Sacha Christie with Kelli Hollis (left)

Kelli Hollis is a British actress, best known for playing Tina Crabtree in the three Channel 4 related films, shop owner Yvonne Karib in Channel 4's popular comedy drama *Shameless* and Ali Spencer in ITV soap opera, *Emmerdale*. Wikipedia: Born June 29, 1976, Leeds, West Yorkshire, England. Occupation: Actress, Director. Years active:1999 to present.

THE HALT PERSPECTIVE 2

On loan from Donald Moreland

PART 11

COLONEL HALT RETURNS TO WOODBRIDGE, SUFFOLK!

2017

May 2017: Re Josh Gates *Expedition Unknown* – visit to Suffolk

JOHN: Following a number of emails made between myself and Los Angeles-based Karin McEvoy, a representative employed on the team of the highly praised TV series **Expedition Unknown**, she had this to say to me. Dear John: *"Our story team has enjoyed going through 'The Halt Perspective' since we last spoke. Congratulations on authoring such a comprehensive coverage of everything leading up to this event. If you have the original copies of any of the documents from THP listed below and can bring them it would bring a lot to the retelling of this story. Also, and more importantly – if you have any new documents, particularly letters and reports on from police or military personnel or on government letterhead from your upcoming book that you can bring that would make our Rendlesham scene fresher (our series won't actually be airing until October). Feel free to let me know if you have any questions or concerns. We can take some still photos of our shoot at the Bentwaters Base with you there to include in your new book too if you'd like."* Sincerely, Karin McEvoy.

The visit had been arranged by the *Travel Channel Shows* film company from Los Angeles, a company that present popular features for Travel Channel.com entertaining their viewers with subjects ranging from American Mobster, Bizarre foods, extreme Hotels, Booze traveller, Manhattan project, Stonehenge, even the Lincoln assassination, and many more including their forthcoming visit to Suffolk to interview Charles Halt and Gary Baker who met up with Tom Potter of the **East Anglia Daily Times** during May 2017.

The Colonel arrives in England

We met Colonel Charles Halt on the Saturday afternoon after he had flown in to London Heathrow Airport, following a gruelling overnight flight journey – then having to find a hire vehicle and make his own way up to Suffolk! Never mind driving on the left hand side of the road. Along with a colleague, I met him at the Bull Public House, Woodbridge Suffolk. Although the Colonel was tired after the drive we were soon ensconced in comfortable chairs outside and drinking beer! The next morning we all met up at the Cold War Museum and were introduced to **Josh Gates** and his film crew who had hired some actors to dress up as US service personnel who were to set the scene of what took place. Colonel Halt pointed out they weren't wearing the right uniform! Later Colonel Halt gave an impromptu talk at the *Bull Pub* which attracted the attention of a number of people who came over to shake his hand.

THE HALT PERSPECTIVE 2

Tom Potter

Josh Gates

Gary Baker

THE HALT PERSPECTIVE 2

The program '**Hunt tor Extraterrestrials'** premiered live on air on the **4th of October 2017.**

Charles: In May 2017, while over here in the UK at the invitation of **Josh Gates** from *Expedition Unknown* the LA based Company, I met and talked with Tom Potter from the *East Anglian Daily Times* who takes the subject seriously, and had the pleasure of also meeting Gary Baker; one of the guys that worked at RAF Neatishead on the radar in 1980. (See page 261 for our conversation)

I later found out that Nigel Kerr who was on duty at RAF Watton confirmed that an object had been tracked which disappeared into the forest after being telephoned by Sergeant John Coffey.

During this year I was a speaker at the 'Philly' Philadelphia Mufon Conference on the 27th/28th of October, held at the Sheraton Bucks County Hotel, Langholme, Pennsylvania. On the Sunday I spoke about what had taken place in Suffolk, when Deputy Base Commander. Other speakers included Ben Moss, Tony Angiola, and Ray Stanford, Steve Mera and Travis Walton to name just a few who lectured on their chosen subject.

July 2017 – A visit to see retired RAF Squadron Leader Donald Moreland

John Hanson: In July 2017 we visited Donald Moreland and after presenting the Colonels compliments, he agreed to speak to us about his albeit brief involvement in what had taken place, following the report submitted by Charles Halt, summarizing the most extraordinary events that had taken place a few weeks previously. He and his wife Gwen made us welcome at their home in Anglesey and after introductions we presented him with a copy of the *Halt Perspective* which he glanced through and said he was looking forward to reading. He told us that this was the second visit to him about what had taken

THE HALT PERSPECTIVE 2

place and that he had enjoyed meeting Dr David Clarke some years ago. Donald, although sceptical of the existence of UFOs per se, was adamant that he had no reason whatsoever **not to believe the contents of the report submitted to him by Colonel Halt whom he had every respect for**. The fact that he had titled the covering letter *Unidentified Flying Objects* were neither here nor there. *"That's what Colonel Halt said they were, he called them UFOs. I wrote the covering letter (dated 15th January 1981) after receiving his letter dated the 13th of January 1981. I do recall discussing it with Sam Morgan and the police officer Major Malcolm Zickler.*

On 30th November 1983, while still serving at RAF Woodbridge as RAF Liaison Officer, no doubt engulfed with a never ending chain of enquiries/letters sent to him by enthusiastic researchers wishing to gain further insight into what happened. He wrote to Pam Titchmarsh, Defence Secretariat Div 8a MOD London, he wrote this: *"The enclosed letter was sent to the Base Commander here, and I forward it on for any action you consider necessary. They didn't teach me about the Sub-dwarfs Solar system when I studied Astro Navigation at Navigation School!"*

Lingering memories!

John: As we leave this year my memories linger on the visit to see Charles Halt and his family, in the States, The Smithsonian Institute, Washington, The White House, West Virginia, and the Blue Ridge Mountains. Time slides by so quickly. Closer home, we met up with Donald Moreland and his lovely wife Gwen. Then meeting up with the Colonel, again when he came over for the OLM Conference in Hill arranged by Chris Evers, and a visit to Rendlesham Forest, arranged by Josh Gates, from the L.A based Travel Company. Not forgetting his talk at **The International Congress UFO Conference.**

Trained killer!

Here is one of many examples from a man who describes himself as a trained killer! This relates to a photo taken showing a UFO hovering over an A10. Excuse the mistakes – they are his.

2017 – Larry Warren posts this on Facebook – adamant the photo he took shows a UFO

Re- A10. Unknown craft-Photo......some facts for those concerned if I may, **The photo in question was taken by me......yes me mid day December 28th 1980 from out of fellow sps car window (Jim Harper) was the sps name**..........D flight was going back on rotation that night, so I and a few other guys decided to head to Ipswich for the day.....as I wrote in our book (I did you know) I was on the hunt for an amplifier at axe music......sadly I didn't know that EVERYTHING in the UK shut down on Sundays............ and I mean everything for folks too young to remember. I talked old Harper into giving us a lift to the bus stop on the main gate of RAF WOODBRIDGE........and before we left I stopped into the Bentwaters PX (NAAFI for you Brits) and bought a keystone 110 as a camera...perhaps for 10 Yankee bucks (I read from the lynch mob this was 35 mm speed film........like on so many counts spurred by that bunch of yapping dogs, WRONG) I took my first test shot of Bentwaters Main gate.......That's the famous ALERT photo as seen in the very famous book I co-authored with the delightful Mr. Peter Robbins! See you had to crank the film forward with each shot in those days. Mind you. and I do mean YOU.......this was already **2 days into what YOU folks call the RFI**..........(we that lived it call it other things) so off we drove to Woody. (RAF WOODBRIDGE,) we so loved them nicknames we did !)......now heading for the start of Woody's fence line I rolled old Jim's window down, turned to my left and took another shot**.......I didn't notice the A10 but it would have been heading to Bentwaters from the flight level and direction in the picture.....**A10s were not a big deal for us.......see we baby sat them 24-7..........we then headed down Woody's back gate road,,,(NOT known **as EAST GATE road back then........That's another ufology add on**) caught the bus and the rest is recounted in that Famous book called......well you know that part. Now like all good airmen we took pics to send home to our families........UFOs were not our focus.......... and we were not green boys ...**I'd already lived in the UK before the USAF.........and by the time we in Security forces .(not beat cops like JB and JP) we were highly trained combatants.** Killers if you will.......it's a fact that seems lost on the "gentile souls" within so called ufology...........in fact alpha team spitz naz was our target, 24 7.....and I'm certain we if needed would have put a hurt all over them if attacked. back to the picture........it meant nothing to me just an A10 with what I thought was a little speck of dust above it..............and it meant nothing for another 34 years ...until Mick Sayer blew it up..... and saw what I'd never seen! The photo is a color photo and not black n white as it looks on FB.......about 4 years ago my pal Lindsey scanned all my service related photos into my original LARRY WARREN FB page under the album title BENTWATERS BACK in THE DAY. I must say after Mick Sayer brought it to my attention after HE reviewed my photo section was stunned! then others got involved in the process.......... much smarter folks than myself.....the object thing craft whatever matches to a 'T' what I'd tried to describe over the previous 34 years........Then Dr Bruce Maccaby...an optical Physicist (spelling still sucks) whom the US navy trusted for years did his own review of the photo...in brief he said "object is above and beyond the A10, object is tens of metres wide...the two anomalies above the A10 have NOT been added to the photo as it would be impossible to do so " i.e. the unknown object only defines itself with enlargement...........and can NOT happen with Photoshop........Being that the photo is 110 as it makes trickery beyond any odds......I wish you ALL could read the very important dialog the photo generated a few years back. But sadly a fella called Dave Kelly hacked my account. (This we know for fact.).......... Like I always have said. I'm not, nor have I ever been in the believe me Biz............but this small pack of deer ticks are well and truly making the subject look like a day at the circus.......and worse still are the in educated shills riding along over the cliff with them. I shall be around long after they become a small RFI foot note......Cheers to the thinkers Larry Warren ex 81st SPS.

THE HALT PERSPECTIVE 2

Another tall story dashed on the rocks of fabrication!

Charles: The *UFO Truth Magazine* shows the Larry Warren A10 photo replete with a UFO – now that's odd because I have in my possession the **original photos taken by Larry which show nothing of the sort**.

In addition to this I know a lot of work has gone into checking out this photo and that it has been established through careful scrutiny and computer examination that the 'UFO' has been added to it. Such fakes don't help the UFO cause rather they retard it and make us look like fools. I am satisfied that this photograph which claims to have been taken by Larry and showing a UFO on it has been proved to my satisfaction to be a fake; yet another attempt to confuse people drawn from an insatiable desire to perpetuate one man's flights of fancy and imagination into the pages of history – which cannot be allowed to happen. Many people out there are no longer willing to accept unsubstantiated claims like this as having any bearing on what took place in and around Rendlesham Forest in December 1980, especially taking into consideration the number of people who have decided to come forward years later to speak of what they did or didn't see, or presenting UFO photos as genuine when in fact the opposite prevails.

Of course he's not the only one. Brenda was contacted by a Mr Williams on the 30th of June 2000, who told her he was a security officer in the area and about having sighted **an orange dome shaped object over the Forest on the 25th of June of that year**, last seen heading towards the Airbase. During a second visit to the locality with friends they witnessed near to the runway at Woodbridge a cluster of coloured lights in the trees near to east Gate entrance. This is ok so far, let's be fair we've heard many accounts of strange lights seen in and around the sky over the Bases from apparent genuine witnesses. However, like John, I do wonder about the validity of what he then told Brenda Butler, involving an admission that he had belonged to the 'Secret Police' – whatever that means. Mr Williams then spoke of having heard of reports of tall thin people disappearing into the ground, secret tunnels under the forest, and mind control experiments carried out on young soldiers! Well my only comment is that it's nonsense and yet another attempt by someone to 'muddy the waters' of what actually took place!

PART 12

EXPLANATIONS FOR WHAT WAS SEEN BY US!

2017

Book: *THE RENDLESHAM FILE* – BRITAIN'S ROSWELL?

THIS was a lengthy book published by Philip Mantle of *Flying Disc Press,* on the 29th of October 2017 – written by Andrew Pike.

Amazon had this to say about it. Quote: The Rendlesham File: Britain's Roswell? Is a scientific investigation into the possible cause of the Rendlesham Forest Incident of December 1980 involving UFO sightings in and around Rendlesham Forest between the twin airbases of RAF Bentwaters and RAF Woodbridge in Suffolk, England? **It examines the likely cause of balls of light and a triangular craft that appeared in and around the area seen by the airmen of the twin bases and local civilians.** Following a review of the 1974 Berwyn Mountains incident in the summer of 1980 attention was drawn to strange plasma-like balls of light seen at Rendlesham Forest during the following Christmas. What at first appeared to be a simple case of possible earthlights, meteorological and aerial plasma phenomena developed into an investigation which included microwave technology, radar, electromagnetic influences on the human body including the brain, black budget advances in mind control and exotic aviation including stealth and anti-gravity technologies. Many of the black projects examined held answers to the causes with developments in the investigation coming as a result of FBI and CIA files. There was also evidence from astronomical, geophysical and electromagnetic research going back to the late 1800s. This led to significant clues from scientific advances during World War Two with further answers also coming from the 1950s in plasma physics and astronomy, especially plasma cosmology right up to the present day. Some of these advances were also made by scientists working alone away from mainstream science as a result of the taboo nature

Andrew Pike

of their research. This book gathers together these diverse areas of research to show that more than just earthlights occurred that Christmas and in doing so **highlights black projects** and mainstream scientific research that are significant to many other areas of ufology and other paranormal subjects. **It was discovered that everything witnessed during the Rendlesham Forest Incident was seen before, either in and around the forest, or around the world before and since the event**. This allowed the scientific investigation to follow the science through to possible answers. In doing so it became obvious that something had heightened and brought together many phenomena that Christmas which would otherwise be seen separately or to a much reduced intensity. Military secrecy and a general view by the Ministry of Defence that this was of no defence significance **proved to be wrong and through the black projects and declassified paperwork** it was shown that this view by the powers-that-be might be part of the cover. Although much of the scientific conclusions were in place by 1989 developments and further research unfolded over the following decades appearing with an eerie habit of serendipity. These added strength to the conclusions already established. **To date this is the only extensive civilian investigation into the science of arguably the most famous sightings in UFO history.**

The Rendlesham File is the first book written about these events by a UK academic. Andrew Pike is a qualified astrophysicist and a Fellow of the Royal Astronomical Society. The Rendlesham File takes an unbiased scientific look at the UFO sightings in question and outputs all of the information under the microscope. Is there a scientific explanation for these UFO sightings or are they truly the result of something that is yet beyond our scientific capabilities? Open The Rendlesham File and discover the answers for yourself.

Nick Pope: This well-researched and eminently readable book significantly enhances our knowledge of the UK's best-known and most compelling UFO incident. Pike comes at the story from the perspective of being an astrophysicist, and his scientific approach is a welcome one, and one that's far too seldom seen in ufology. His academic approach, coupled with his boots-on-the-ground research, makes this a fascinating read. For anyone expecting that Pike, as a scientist, might produce a somewhat dry account, think again! He frequently wears his heart on his sleeve, and pulls no punches in some of his criticisms, most of which are well-deserved. Given Pike's specific areas of expertise – which include plasma physics – I was particularly interested in his insightful analysis of the MoD intelligence assessment of the UFO phenomenon that's colloquially known as **Project Condign**. Ironically, both he and I have been (wrongly) suspected of being the anonymous author of the study's final report. Pike is accurate if somewhat harsh when he describes the author as being the "wrong man for the wrong job", but perhaps the most important point he makes about Condign is just how dated the study is. Given that the final report was published in 2000, the science (and associated technology) being discussed is now nearly twenty years old, in a particularly fast-moving field. Two minor quibbles. Firstly, Pike suggests – citing a 1994 interview that I gave to ufologist Nick Redfern – that the MoD was "muddled" over the case, when any apparent inconsistencies simply reflected the difference between the MoD's public and private position. Secondly, I think Pike underestimates the effect that the exposure of the **Larry Warren fraud** has had on people's understanding of the Rendlesham Forest incident. He argues that some of Warren's information might nonetheless be useful, when in strictly evidential terms it's utterly discredited and, thus, worthless. However, these are comparatively minor points, and shouldn't serve to detract from what's unquestionably a fine piece of scholarship.

Recommendation to buy the *Halt Perspective*

Andrew makes a reference to the *Halt Perspective* book. *"**The other big book, literally at 800pages is The Halt Perspective. As the name suggests this is Halt's take on things compiled with John Hanson, however it is much more containing a wealth of sighting reports from the area, background information and hundreds of pictures and illustrations. I can also highly recommend this book. It is not possible to put everything in any Rendlesham book because of the size and complexity of the case, so this book serves as a good source of additional information."*

THE HALT PERSPECTIVE 2

Charles: The claims of police and military personnel attending and burn marks found in the ground never mind allegations of radiation found make interesting reading, especially in view of what we recorded on a Geiger counter at the scene of our UFO incident in Rendlesham Forest.

Of course incidents like what we experienced attract worldwide attention, but behind the apparently often perceived occasional singularity of incidents like this there are many other strange sightings that don't attract attention – this in itself is disturbing as it offers further evidence that we are definitely not alone, they defy present understandings and should not be ignored. People continue to ask me about the radiation found at the scene in Rendlesham Forest. In my tape recorded memo which was taken at the time we describe the readings at the site as "minor clicks" and "three to four units", [i.e. 0.03 to 0.04 mR/h.] We picked up these readings as we approached the site and then checked each of the landing marks. The highest reading mentioned on the tape is "seven tenths", i.e. 0.07 mR/h; a 'spike' obtained briefly at the centre of the site, not a steady level. Others of course have been dismissive of this evidence and suggest this was only background radiation. Have you recorded any other incidents involving UFOs and the presence of radiation found afterwards? I recently learned of the publication of Andrews Pike's latest book. I contacted Andrew and offered to comment and suggested he read the book John and I had published. I haven't heard back. I guess it's nice to sit in an armchair and solve what was a significant unexplained event. Especially if you weren't there! If you are a friend of his ask him some of the following:

1- **How could ball lightning linger for about 5-10 minutes?** Move through the forest bobbing up and down avoiding trees and back into the fields apparently because we tried to approach it all the while sort of blinking and then explode into multiple white objects.

2 - **How does he explain the Bentwaters Air Traffic Controllers** seeing the object go across their radar scope twice at greater than 1000 MPH and then go into the forest where we were?

3 - **How does he explain the radiation readings?**

4 - **What about the WSA cops** that looked at the bright objects we saw in the sky with 10X binoculars and saw triangular objects.

5 - **What sends down white laser like beams?**

6 - **Does ball lighting do the above?**

7 - **How does he explain several multiple colored objects** in the sky moving in a synchronized pattern and seeming to change shape? Numerous civilians also saw strange objects in the sky.

8 - If we had some classified stealth object why did it show up on radar? Do you really think we would have had such a craft then and flown it in the local forest at Christmas?

9 - **Why did the CIA UFO advisor to the White House suddenly appear at Bentwaters and get involved in debriefing 5-7 witnesses with drugs and hypnosis?**

10 - Does he seek to explain away a huge number of UFO sightings that occurred around the East Anglia area involving similar objects sighted before and long after 1980 as investigated by John Hanson? Only today John sent me another great swathe of files many of which contain original illustrations depicted by the witnesses . . . I accept I can't give you an answer but clearly those illustrations don't resemble ball lightning or plasma energy?

11 - Also I would like to clarify something that Andrew has made references to in his book about a 'military Deep Throat' source On page 150 he cites a description supplied by John Burroughs of a 'strange light on the first night and a drawing of a spiky orange ball on top a cone of light rays beaming down to the ground like a skirt.' He (Burroughs) says: *"Within the cone were lights with other lights outside it. The object was illuminating nearby trees as it sat in the forest. The drawing and details were 'leaked' via deep throat although I have my doubts about using the word 'leaked' in this situation."* He (Andrew) then refers to the 'Deep throat' drawing in *Sky Crash* and says *"It intrigued me because it looked very much like charged plasma sphere discharging to earth, or possibly being powered from the ground by some means, that power might have been artificial or natural (as we will see later) It showed remarkable similarity to*

standard charges drawn in many physics text books and might have been natures version of something we can explain in the laboratory. Later we will also see a similar UFO encountered in 1992 which revealed more, finer details involving the structure of this type of phenomenon."

12 - The illustration as shown in *Sky Crash* which resembles a 'wigwam with a light on top' and endorsed 'from a deep throat' **was actually drawn later as an artist's impression** by Mike Sacks who was accompanied by Manchester Solicitor Harry Harris following an interview with me at the Airbase. It was about 1982 and we all agreed not to reveal the 'meeting', although I would refute any arrangement was made with General Gordon Williams. I was very disappointed when the gang – Brenda, Dot, Jenny, Harry and Mike sold the story to the *News of the World*. There's more but that's a start. I would classify Andrew with the other de-bunkers, such as my friend Ian Ridpath, as either looking for attention or being paid to muddy the 'waters.' I suspect the latter.

November 2017: CASE CLOSED? Has the Rendlesham 'alien UFO' mystery finally been SOLVED? EXCLUSIVE: Britain's most perplexing UFO mystery may finally have been solved after an astrophysicist investigated the 37-year-old unsolved case. By *Daily Mirror* journalist Jon Austin on the 8th of November 2017 who told the online readers excitedly of yet another explanation with banner grabbing headlines for what occurred during December 1980! [I met Jon at the Woodbridge UFO Conference I recall and he seemed very disinterested in hearing of all the other evidence in my possession relating to this incident. Like so many other journalists – entertainment and titillation is sadly what they tell me the readers want!

The Rendlesham File is the first book written about these events by a UK academic. *"It takes an unbiased scientific look at the UFO sightings in question and puts all of the information under the microscope. Is there a scientific explanation for these UFO sightings or are they truly the result of something that is yet beyond our scientific capabilities?"* In September, researcher Russ Callaghan shocked the UFO community with a new theory that the Rendlesham UFO could have actually been a **top-secret US Air Force training capsule, used as a dummy run** for missions to pick up satellites that re-entered earth, as exclusively revealed by Express.co.uk…etc, etc.

John: Nigel Mortimer author of several books on the UFO subject who has been actively involved in UFO investigations since 1980, took an interest in Rendlesham Forest and met up with Brenda Butler, and others in 2016. Nigel, **who says he saw four aliens in the forest,** also sells spirit boxes to communicate with the dead, and other worldly intelligences, one whom is named Sharlkek. He was putting on a conference in November of this year but as far as I know it never transpired. Sorry, but crazy stuff involving all manner of weird allegations…Amazing how the UFO sighting that took place now 40 years ago in a forest still, and always will attract publicity – sadly it's not about any truths!

17th December 2017: Peter Robbins Statement of separation!

"Following months of escalating disagreements, some on matters related to our work together over the years, some regarding other issues, I am separating myself from my co-author of "Left At East Gate," Larry Warren, until or unless these matters can be resolved between us. It gives me no pleasure to do this but it's what I have decided I have to do. I've no wish to engage anyone in dialogue on this at this time." Peter Robbins.

THE HALT PERSPECTIVE 2

PART 13

THE NEVER-ENDING STORIES CONTINUE!

2018

CHARLES: The front cover for *UFO truth magazine* dated 2013, shown with the eloquent paragraph of praise for its Editor by Robert Salas may for all I know, be a contributory factor which led him to attack me two years later!

Official – AIRMEN TAKEN BY ALIENS IN SUFFOLK – Colonel's new UFO claim!

16th January – *The Sun* newspaper – by Rob Pattison and Emma Parry – former staff reporter at *The Sun* newspaper and the Press Association, published a misleading article on page 3 with its banner-grabbing headlines as above – next to a photograph of Ice Queen Brianne Delcourt wearing skimpy underwear with a comment by Nick Pope… "**This is a bombshell**". Gary Heseltine of *UFO Truth* website claimed that Colonel Halt said "**Burroughs may have been abducted**" in a video recording made in 2010.

On her website page Emma asked: "*In the interests of fair and accurate reporting I would obviously like to give you a full right of reply. Did you ever make these comments? Have you been giving false or **misleading information** to researchers/ the public? Should you wish to comment you can call me on 646 544 6515 (I'm based in Los Angeles) or you can email me here? Thank you in advance, Emma.*"

THE HALT PERSPECTIVE 2

John: I emailed her. *"Dear Emma, My friend and co author Colonel Charles Halt was good enough to share your email to me regarding your enquiry to him about a video recording in which, once again, it is wrongly claimed **aliens were seen** during the Rendlesham Forest Suffolk incident(s) in December 1980! I'm a retired CID Officer from the West Midlands Force and have been involved since 1995 in writing 16 books chronicling exactly to the best of my ability what took place, in and around the skies of Great Britain going back to the 1940s drawn from testimonials provided by hundreds, if not thousands, of witnesses proving that something unique and totally inexplicable has been – and will continue to manifest in our skies; the answers to which still appear to elude mankind, despite claims made by others! **With regard to your comment about Burroughs, I can assure you that Colonel Halt made no such claim!**"* No reply was ever received.

Another outlandish comment along similar lines was allegedly made by, of all people, Colonel Ted Conrad in a book published by John Burroughs and James Worrow *'Weaponisation Of An Unidentified Aerial Phenomenon'* in 2020. More on that in due course.

The online article attracted a single response from Neil M (surname withheld), which once again typifies the knee jerk reaction of so many who believe they know the answers – based on what exactly? Quote, Neil: *"I'm not sure why Katy Sandals wrote this article – it is just pure nonsense as no radiation readings were taken by Col Halt and his entire tape was just a sham to make it look like the accident involving the helicopter hitting the landing lights with the replica Apollo Command Module slung underneath was really a 'UFO incident'. Come on Katy – get real. You of all people know this was a prank that went wrong and as a result the USAF had to cover up this embarrassment with the usual UFO story. Col Halt willingly followed orders to make this silly tape recording, but he did so along the lines of the Orson Wells original play made for American radio audiences in which aliens are supposed to have landed."* In response to another article about the same subject he explained it away as, *"an accident which was extremely embarrassing for the 67th ARRS made worse by placing **Xmas lights on the replica command module**"*!

Charles: Neil, we have never met. Your comments put forward to explain away what took place in all probability before you were born, is now a familiar tune played on an old fiddle, pardon my pun! Obviously I can't spend my time fruitlessly seeking to correct every comment put forward with regard to what I was involved in as its never ending.

I have no illusions that in 50 years time the same old theories will abound, and continue to form what will be then, if it isn't already, an urban myth! John asked me to comment on what you wrote up. First of all you didn't bother contacting me about this. If you had, well I would have told you that you're way out! A never-ending story line of media inaccuracies, which confuses rather than clarifies, aggravated by someone who believes a chopper picked up a satellite from offshore then dropped it into the forest by mistake! I don't know about fairy lights on a command module but this sounds more like a fairytale.

If they did pick something up, I wasn't privy to this information, which would be odd as I was the Deputy Base Commander. Apart from that, due to the Christmas period and ground fog, they were grounded. In *UFO Magazine* 1996, Nick was interviewed about this very matter – he stated that he had presumed the radiation mentioned in the Halt letter was just normal background radiation. He asked the Defence Radiological Service what they thought, they replied: **"What the hell happened there?"** He asked them what they meant; they told him: **"They were ten times what they should have been in the area."** In 1997, Nick Pope wrote to Brenda Butler about the radiation level. He said: *"I was able to confirm with the Defence Radiological Protection service that the radiation readings taken by LT, Colonel Halt were* **TEN times normal, not 25** *as stated on* **Strange But True**. *I did check out the theory about nuclear material from a soviet satellite but found no evidence to support the hypotheses. I tried to get the investigation formally re-opened but was not successful."*

2018 – Forthcoming Capel Green film – *Indigo Transmit Films Ltd*

In the early part of this year there was considerable interest shown in the social media following news of another documentary under preparation about what had taken place in Rendlesham Forest during December 1980. In January 2021 there were, according to John Hanson, 75 individual posters/photos/adverts freely available on the internet under 'Capel Green', which shows true grit and determination, if nothing else!

On the 18th of January 2018, Film Producer Mr. Dion Johnson contacted me to advise me, that Larry Warren has recently undertaken and passed a stringent polygraph test facing a wide ranging series of questions which was conducted by one of Britain's foremost examiners (having completed over 2000

THE HALT PERSPECTIVE 2

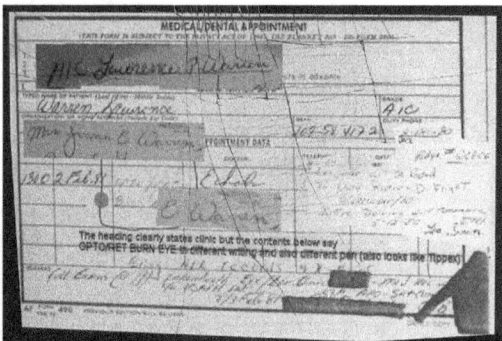

tests) and presumably wanted me to comment, or at least volunteer to take part in the film? Who knows? What's the betting that one of those images showing the machine gun toting hero, on one of your adverting posters on the internet, characterises the part played by Michael Stacy Smith? *Of course I may be wrong?*

This is what I had to say in return:

Dion: I hate to tell you, but you are being had. Suggest you read "*The Halt Perspective*" before getting egg on your face. For starters Mr. Warren has lied about his involvement on the first night (the events unfolded over three nights). He was not present with us at the site on the third night. There were no entities or a physical craft on the ground. The event on the first night occurred in the forest. The night I was out with a team and what we witnessed was not at the site that Mr. Warren claims.

Mr. Warren was separated from the AF as unsuitable/undesirable for the convenience of the government. In other words he was kicked out. His testimony has changed through the years as he's learned details from real participants. He's asked several of his former associates to lie to support him (this is documented) every serious researcher has written him off as a very convincing liar – even his mother made a comment to that effect. Talk to any other serious researcher (I can give you many names), other than Gary Heseltine, who is using him, and you'll get the truth. Even Peter Robbins, who really wrote the book *Left At East Gate,* will verify the facts. His antics have even been the subject of media interests, here is an example….

Several years ago Mr. Warren claimed to have passed a voice stress analysis. Guess what? I have documented proof he failed. He may have passed a polygraph session but do your homework; there are multiple ways to beat the test. You might ask Mr. Robbins about his fraud activity and association with ***Operation Bullpen**. Please do not use my name, memo or tape. By the way the original whistle blower was a cop named J. D. Engels who contacted the authors of *Sky Crash*. He later withdrew the claim.

Brenda Butler and J.D. Engels

---

*During the 1990s, the FBI identified a major problem threatening the entire sports and celebrity memorabilia market. In the mid-1990s, the Chicago Division of the FBI initiated a sports memorabilia fraud investigation targeting a group of individuals who forged, fraudulently authenticated, and distributed Chicago athletes' autographed memorabilia (including Michael Jordan). The case resulted in the conviction of fourteen individuals in five states involved with forging and distributing forged memorabilia. Information developed by the Chicago FBI's "Foul Ball" investigation suggested that the problem might be national in scope. Even though they didn't get the story right they started the ball rolling.

Do your own research. It shouldn't be hard as there's a ton of it out there about Mr. Warren. For starters read the book. Talk to the serious UK researchers as they all know the truth. Mr. Heseltine does too but is in it for the publicity for his magazine and potential money. Have you gone to the *OPEN MINDS* website? They have my talk from last February online. I only presented a bit of what I have about Mr. Warren. If you can't download it you can order it for a small fee. Have you talked to Sacha Christie? She was an ardent Larry supporter and even let him live in her home until she learned the truth. Larry made a big mistake in what he told her and left on her computer. There's no end of what's out there. Yes, Larry may have beaten the polygraph – but so did John Gracy (one of the greatest mass killers of our times). There are numerous ways to beat the test. Do your homework! By the way, I never said Mr. Warren was arrested or convicted! I rest my case. Ironically because of what I saw and my position within the command structure I am in frequent demand by many film companies who wish to interview me, often in situ in Rendlesham Forest. Hence my regular visits to the UK. But despite the numerous times I have spent over the years, putting the record straight, the inaccuracies continue to flourish. End of email to Dion.

Now, further FACTS!

Here is some additional information Dion – and it's damning – which corroborates the conversation held with Barry Greenwood on page 254 i.e. who told me that Larry Warren decided, as Bustinza was reluctant to go public, he would adopt Bustinza's story as his own. Well look at this…..

Email: **11th February 2014** Adrian Bustinza

Barry Greenwood

*"**I know what Larry wrote and where he got his information from, because I did convey to Larry, everything that happened that night,** and then what happened with me and John. We were young then and I needed to talk to someone, and Larry was the first person that I saw that I recognised, and I was scared at the time. I have forgiven Larry in my faith because of who I am. And yes, Larry has a lot of issues. I do know a lot more that I am saying, and will never come out because for the very reason that John is doing. The contact that I experienced was not only life threatening at the time, but has ever since been, always been a part of me and those involved .The most dramatic thing of the entire situation was what happened afterwards and the interrogations."*

Steve La Plume also told me in an email dated the **24th of August 2000**, "*I was pestered by associates of Warren who wanted him to back up his story. How am I supposed to do that I don't know as I wasn't there that night, I mostly tell them I was there , and yes he told me he saw something. He has even gotten me in some of his lies, and tried to manipulate me and such. He is such an amateur.*"

Where have I ever said that aliens were seen in the Forest or that Burroughs may have been abducted? More wishful thinking or flights of vivid imagination by Gary Heseltine!

Even Presidents have witnessed something highly unusual and unexplainable!

The more I learn the more I'm convinced there's a concerted behind-the-scenes effort to hide the real truths from us. Even some of our Presidents have witnessed something highly unusual and unexplainable. The problem is that so many of these incidents strike an accord with my understanding of what happened in December 1980. I was very sceptical and found what allegedly had taken place in the Forest and what the airmen reported having seen taking place hard to believe, because such things couldn't exist could they? I was really going to debunk it quite frankly; and as events unfolded I became more and more concerned that there may be something to this . . . I kept telling myself that there had to be some type of explanation for it, but I certainly couldn't find one and even to this day I can't give an answer.

John Burroughs accused me of trying to discredit those involved!

In 2018 John Burroughs accused me of trying to discredit those involved, including him and Adrian Bustinza. This is absolute rubbish, and lies! He accused me publicly of stating he and Adrian were tortured by intelligence agencies within our Government and asked me if I was willing to write a certified letter to the VA confirming that? I emailed him back on March 2nd 2018 at 3.24pm –

John Burroughs, it is interesting that you consistently write to me and take things out of context, and say things that may not be true. **You and the others involved on the first night never told me about your interrogations, until years later.** *If I had known at the time I would have raised the issue. As to your telling me about your debriefing at the AFOSI office just after the event, perhaps you are having memory problems. Several of your fellow cops saw you in uniform. Your commander was Zickler, and above him was Conrad and Williams, You stated that AFOSI overruled Williams which isn't true. It doesn't work that way if anyone did, it was the 3AF CCOR. CINC, get it right. If the VA or someone in the DOD wants to talk to me I would be happy*

Pope, Penniston and Burroughs

to cooperate, but I am not providing you with a letter to blab about it on another radio show. You need to get on with your life! What I have said is based on what you, Jim and Adrian told me, in recent times you seem to have forgotten. Additionally Warren also claims to have been debriefed. His claim is probably based on what Adrian told him. I thought you were getting help from the VA? What gives?

It seems pointless nit-picking on an incident that took place over 40 years ago. It seems to me that people continually try and muddy the waters of what happened there when I was Deputy Base Commander. I'm not perfect, but my interpretation of what happened is standard now. Most people appear to have accepted my version of events which is straightforward, unlike other participants who have woven monstrous claims of absurdity, now known to most people interested in the subject.

Chasing the lighthouse!

Sometimes you can't do right for doing wrong! Here is a reminder from Police Constable David King which is of interest. Admittedly, this doesn't answer what was seen initially, but John what did you end up chasing?

Could radiation readings be the key to understanding Rendlesham UFOs?

John: On the 17th of May 2018 the *East Anglian Daily Times* published an article entitled 'Could radiation readings be the key to understanding Rendlesham UFOs?' by reporter Katie Sandals.

Quote: Tim Acheson, measured the levels of radiation at locations around the site to see if they varied from other areas of the forest. *"There has been much debate about radiation readings from the 1980s,"* said Mr Acheson. He found that there were a number of radiation 'hot spots' at locations linked to the extraterrestrial sightings back in December 1980. *"As a scientist, I find all the debate without scientific evidence incredibly frustrating. I couldn't believe nobody has taken the time to do a thorough scientific study to settle the issue one way or another, so I took matters into my own hands."* For Mr Acheson the biggest question posed by these radiation readings is do the readings show the presence of UFO's or were the UFO's attracted by the high radiation levels? *"We can't qualify it,"* said Mr Acheson, *"but there is definitely a relationship."*

Nick Pope was the Ministry of Defence's UFO desk officer between 1991 and 1994 and led a review into the Rendlesham case." *This is a highly impressive and significant piece of work. The levels of radioactivity in Rendlesham Forest are an important piece of physical evidence, and a better understanding of this aspect of the story may prove critical when it comes to resolving the question of what took place back in 1980."*

Mr King was making a routine check with the law enforcement desk at RAF Bentwaters late on December 26 when a call came through from RAF Woodbridge to say that strange lights had been seen for the second consecutive night in the forest.

Mr King wanted to have a look – but he was diverted to an emergency at Otley Post Office and did not investigate the second sightings.

"I have said all along that it was the lights from Orford Ness, but no one wants to take notice of that as it doesn't fit in with what they want to believe," he added.

His crucial evidence comes a few weeks after the publication for the first time of original witness statements made by American officers a few days after the 1980 sightings.

The statements made by Staff Sergeant Jim Penniston and Airman First Class John Burroughs, of the 81st Security Police Squadron, were made to the Bentwaters air base deputy commander, Charles Halt. They admit that they 'chased a lighthouse.'

In the original Ministry of Defence investigation, the Defence Intelligence Staff assessed the levels of radioactivity documented in Lieutenant Colonel Halt's official report as being "significantly higher than the average background". This new radiation survey gives us considerably more data and is the sort of serious research and investigation that I wish more people in the UFO community, be they sceptics or believers, would undertake.

THE HALT PERSPECTIVE 2

An MOD spokesperson said: *"All our historic files which refer to UFOs, including Rendlesham Forest, have either been released, or are in the process of being released to the National Archives. The MOD continues to have no opinion on the existence, or otherwise, of extra-terrestrial life and **does not investigate reported unidentified flying object sightings."***

Meeting Tim and the others in the Forest

John: Following a walk and talk around Rendlelsham forest with EADT reporter Tom Potter, Colonel Charles Halt, Gary Baker and Tim Acheson, Tim told us *"There has been much debate about radiation readings from the 1980s, I found that there were a number of radiation 'hot spots' at locations. As a scientist, I find all the debate without scientific evidence incredibly frustrating. I couldn't believe nobody has taken the time to do a thorough scientific study to settle the issue one way or another, so I took matters into my own hands. The biggest question posed by these radiation readings is do the readings show the presence of UFO's or were the UFO's attracted by the high radiation levels? We can't qualify it, but there is definitely a relationship."* In light of some speculation that the evidence of what was plotted on Radar scopes by, servicemen over the nights in question, could not be relied on without proof of a military record. Gary Baker felt honour bound to show his certificate of military secondment.

John: Mr Tim Acheson and his wife Anicka, passionately interested in this incident, decided to conduct an examination of the local forest using equipment to test for radiation spikes, and after contacting the Forestry Commission was allowed to do so because *"I never mentioned the UFO word, if I had…they would probably have refused my request."*

Knowing that Colonel Halt was coming over to talk at the OLM Conference in Hull on the 1st of September 2018, Tim suggested a meeting could be arranged with the Colonel in the forest in order to identify the exact area where he had travelled through the forest, and the locations of any other sites that might yield any further results which could be contrasted to the many readings already taken by him over the many previous months spent in the forest, showing dedication to get at *"The truth as he told me"*

Tim: "*My greatest hope would be to spend a few minutes 'on site' with him in the area around the end of the gated track – beside the field. I've asked the Forestry Commission if they'd be kind enough to leave the gate open for me so we can drive there to save precious minutes which they have done before. If there's still time, I would then propose another couple of minutes on the road by the farmhouse to try to locate roughly where the beam was directed at the ground. I know the area like the back of my hand, and am very quick at getting locations, so you'll probably be surprised how quickly I can get the two main locations I need. I would not want to intrude on Chuck's time with his friends, and with that in mind perhaps you would want to join us on site?'*

Tim Acheson and his wife, Anicka

After meeting Tim – true to his word on the morning of the 4th September 2018, he allowed us vehicular access to the locked forestry gate leading onto the tracks into the woods after informing us during consultation with the Forestry Commission he had omitted to include the word UFO!

We followed Tim to the closest access point before needing to leave the vehicles and continued on foot to those historical locations, accompanied by Colonel Charles Halt. Tim proceeded to take a considerable amount of readings with us present and with Chuck's knowledge and memory of his experiences, even though he admitted himself it was 38 years ago at the time and the changes to the woods over the years have taken a toll. He used his recollection of an old oak tree that he had committed to his memory as a landmark. He was quite excited by some of the initial readings he made, saying there were definite anomalies in the places tested shown to him by Chuck.

Once Tim was satisfied that he had been shown locations for further investigation. He said this would take some considerable time, probably weeks, to continue taking further readings to obtain an accurate picture of 'today's' readings as possible despite the passing of the years. We drove back out of the wood

THE HALT PERSPECTIVE 2

416

trail and we followed Tim by road to the other side of Capel Green and we parked along the road, walking back to the location of the farmhouse where Colonel Halt and his team had followed the lights across Capel Green, then into the adjacent farmer's field and finally going off into the distance over Orford Ness.

Once Tim was satisfied that he had learned all he could by direct contact with Colonel Halt, he then produced The *'Halt Perspective'* and asked 'Chuck' to sign it for him. Which he did. Tim also produced Volume 8 of *'Haunted Skies',* which had much detail of the RFI, for signing.

It showed us that Tim was serious about his interest in the subject, and he promised that he would keep us up to date with his findings. Tim supplied to us an example of interesting preliminary isotope identification (by gamma-ray spectrometry) at one of the hotspots identified by the extensive radiation survey of the area performed in Nov 2017 to Apr 2018; telling us there is still a lot of interesting basic science work to be done here. Tim: *"In case you're interested, I've attached the early stages of our radiation maps of the field at Capel Green and the Bentwaters WSA. Each dot is a GPS-located average measurement, and more 'redder' means more radiation. When my work is complete we'll have complete high-res heat maps of these areas, clearly visualising any hotspots. We'll have thousands of measurements and absolutely conclusive data about the radiation landscape of any hotspots. The next step will be to identify the isotope(s) responsible for the radiation, including the natural background radiation in the area (which is exceptionally low).*

Thank you, for meeting me and for taking the time out of a very busy itinerary to meet me in situ to help me pinpoint the locations of the events of December 1980. I captured some accurate GPS locations, and noted useful landmarks and distances that will allow me to (1) reconstruct the route Chuck followed that night and (2) significantly narrow-down the areas of interest for my ongoing radiation survey – which means it will take less time to complete the work. It was also simply an enjoyable day, and I could easily have spent many hours discussing many things with all three of you. Thanks to Chuck, especially, for being so helpful and informative, patiently trekking all over the place with me, especially while still recovering from a serious operation a few weeks ago, not forgetting the long flight, drive and a conference. I would welcome any further opportunities to meet with any of you and continue our discussions. Apologies for being so focused on locations yesterday – I knew we had a limited time window to work within.

If you need anything else such as images or details of the instrumentation I used to survey the locations we identified, or if you have any other questions, just let me know. Primarily, I used the FLIR IdentiFinder R400 for gamma ray spectrometry (to identify the radioactive elements/isotopes/nuclides responsible for the radiation present) and a GMC 600+ to measure alpha, beta and X-Ray emissions. I hope within my lifetime somebody will perform spectroscopy on the plaster cast to investigate whether any residual radioisotopes match those found at the hotspot found in the area of the proposed landing site."

Charles: This was a busy time for me, during a visit to England. Irrespective of the passing of time little has changed in the locality, although of course there is vast difference, between what was a heavily forested area, in the time I was there and what happened after the Great Storm. After walking around the 'Capel Green' field, we looked over coastward to where we had continued our journey on that fateful night. Always brings back memories.

OLM Conference Hull – 1st of September, 2018

Then the drive up to Hull in Yorkshire, where I met, Sacha Christie, Chris Evers, Paul and Mary Sinclair, Steve Wills, Mary Rodwell, Philip and Christine Mantle, and many others not forgetting *'Alien Bill',* a guy that catches some amazing images on his camera. After my talk, John arranged for a Scottish Piper to come onto stage and play, *'The Blue Ridge Mountains of Virginia'* an area well known to me as it backs onto the family weekend retreat.

THE HALT PERSPECTIVE 2

Following my return to the Midlands I even watched a game of English Cricket, in rural Exhall Warwickshire, not forgetting the delights of the small bar! I was accompanied by 'Derek' the family Jack Russell's dog, Chris, Johns son whom I knew and John's granddaughter Holly – a time to enjoy the delights of the English countryside, opposite 'Tittys' Hill – kidding you not!

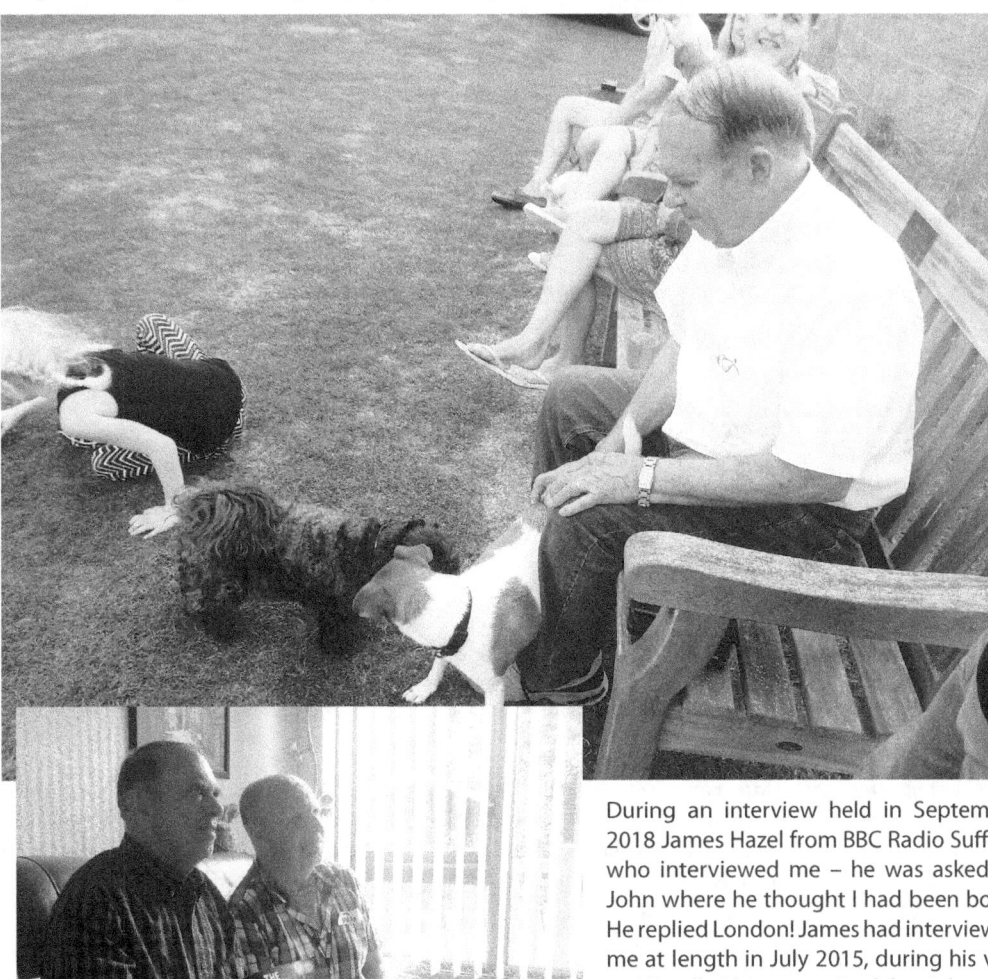

During an interview held in September 2018 James Hazel from BBC Radio Suffolk, who interviewed me – he was asked by John where he thought I had been born? He replied London! James had interviewed me at length in July 2015, during his visit to Woodbridge, organised by John and Brenda but didn't make any reference to the **Halt Perspective** book – no doubt because they have strict protocols on advertising.

Daily Express: UFO spotted in Rendlesham Forest confirms location as the 'UK's ROSWELL'. UFO hunters have returned to the UK's major alien hotspot and discovered that extraterrestrials are STILL targeting the site, according to paranormal

Charles with James Hazel

researchers. By Sean Martin, Thursday, October 25, 2018. *Quote:* On December 26, 1980, a patrol around RAF Woodbridge reported seeing lights, which appeared to land in the nearby Rendlesham Forest. They rushed to the site, thinking the lights might be a crashed human aircraft, however, they claimed to have found a round, glowing metal object with coloured lights that scared animals in a nearby farm. Now, paranormal investigators have returned to the scene of the crime and spotted more strange activity at a place dubbed the UK's Roswell.

Over the course of October 8th and 9th, a group known as *Ghostech Paranormal Investigations* spent time in the Rendlesham Forest searching for alien activity. To their surprise, they spotted what they believe was UFO and even obtained footage. As the bright lights of a UFO were seen in the distance, Jeff Young, lead investigator of *Ghostech Paranormal Investigations* told Express.co.uk: that their walkie-talkies stopped working and that "there was not one bird, squirrel, owl, no wildlife" seen during their investigation.

Mr. Young said: "**On the first night we managed to not only see the lights for ourselves, but we also captured them on film.** We were the only people in the forest and we had to walk three miles through the forest to reach the location so there are no roads or any other explanation for what we had witnessed.

Knowing where we had seen the UFO's moving within the trees, on the second night we positioned our cameras facing those areas but this time I would walk a half a mile to the opposite side so I could observe the whole area as well as my team being positioned at the landing site so we may get a better look at these objects. **This time we all saw the UFOs moving through the trees and again captured them on film but this time much clearer than before.**"

At this point, Mr Young says that Apache helicopters hovered above the investigators, seemingly tracking the bright lights in the forest. He continued: "*As we watched the UFO's there appeared an Apache Longbow helicopter above me, and it then made its way over to where the rest of my team were at the landing site; the helicopter circled us several times, then another joined it followed by a third. We then realised that they had also been tracking these UFOs as well as us with our cameras. The team then decided to leave the forest as they feared persecution and having our evidence removed.*"

John: No disrespect intended I've watched the film and all I have seen is a globe of light low down behind trees in the forest at about waist height. It moves slowly, and then disappears from view. Then at least two other Helicopters arrive overhead, one drops downwards. It's speculative to suggest that they were tracking the UFOs. We don't know that. The light could have been anything, but that didn't stop the newspapers from having a field day with over the top, ridiculous comments without any substance of truth. I know the forest well and have seen some amazing things I can't explain, including the film of a UFO hovering over the forest on 27th December 2000, still frames of which have already been shown. However, each and every incident should be taken on its individual merits.

Motorist sights UFO over Rendlesham Forest

Of course, the area is well known for UFO activity, I grant you that. An example which has not been published before occurred at 10.45pm, on the 31st of December 1995, when Doreen Howells (53) from Manningtree, Essex was driving home through Rendlesham Forest: "*Suddenly we noticed a white light and red light low down in the sky. We approached closer and when opposite the runway lights, which were not on, saw a massive* **great black shape** *moving across the roadway, level with the tops of trees, before disappearing from sight.*" Not surprisingly Doreen was later treated by her Doctor for a rash to her face and arms. She was also prescribed sleeping tablets after being unable to sleep for some time afterwards. Needless to say she was adamant that she would not drive through the forest again ever.

THE HALT PERSPECTIVE 2

Ron West of the now defunct East Anglian UFO and Paranormal Research Association, whose interest in the UFO subject was triggered off by what he saw in Malaya in the 1950's while serving in the British Army, interviewed her.

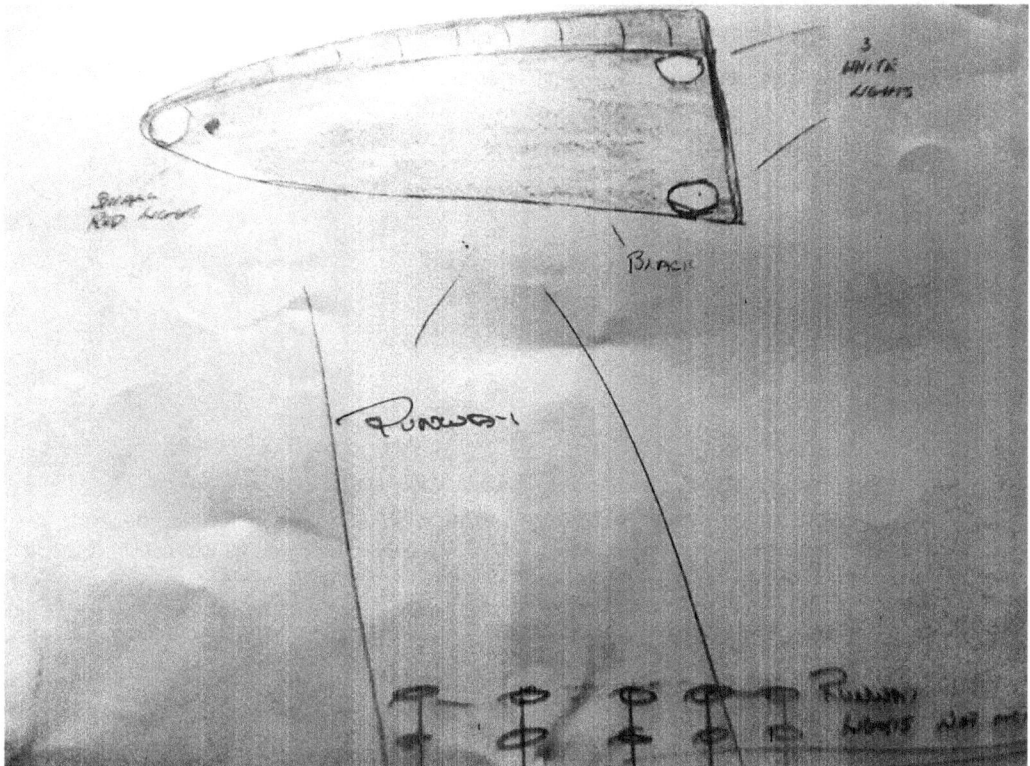

The *BBC One Show* – fact and fantasy! No surprise there

John Hanson: People continually ask me why this incident (important as it is) dominates the worldwide media stage of British UFO events. Why is it nearly always presented in 'isolation', rather than making the public aware of all of the other thousands of other UFO reports around the East Anglia area? The answer is of course that while it may not necessarily corroborate what Colonel Charles Halt and his men saw, it is a topic that has caught the public's attention, with more 'twists and turns than a snake's belly' as Colonel Halt would no doubt say. The problem is that while it attracts the attention of the Media in every shape and form, all other UFO sightings around the East Anglia area involving similar objects are apparently ignored deliberately. Probably because it would raise the public's awareness, that this is not a 'one off', but one of many thousands of inexplicable matters that have haunted the East Anglia area for many years

An example of this was an invitation by the *BBC One Show* to take part in a program during late 2018 to publicise the events that had taken place in December 1980 in Rendlesham. (This was the first time in 25 years of research and eight years of publishing 16 books!) After making my way down there (at personal cost again) to Rendlesham Forest, Suffolk, I met up with the film crew after having asked for and given permission by them I asked Katie Hole, the producer to show, a large number of previously unpublished files from the East Anglia area obtained from the late Ron West, head of the local UFO Society. Many of these depicted original illustrations of 'craft' and were signed by the witnesses. Suffice to say although initially being granted permission – I was prohibited from showing any of these files or mentioning The **Halt Perspective** or the *Haunted Skies* books during an interview with journalist Michael Douglas, whom I found a delight to talk with, accompanied by his small dog.

(A Skype call was conducted later with Charles Halt)

 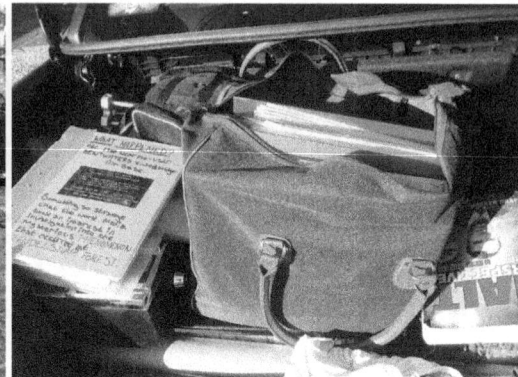

Michael Douglas with John Hanson

When the documentary film (https://aerialworx.co.uk/project/drone-filming-rendlesham-forest) was subsequently shown on *BBC* many people congratulated us – sadly the inclusion of UK comedian *Keith Lemon, talking about 'friendly ET spinning around the moon on his bike' – and other quips, no doubt considered an essential ingredient calculated to ridicule the subject, was shown to the viewers. UFOs don't exist surely?

Daily Mail Newspaper – 30th December 2018

Quote: Has the mystery of 'Britain's Roswell' finally been solved? Rendlesham Forest UFO 'landing' was a prank SAS tricksters played on US Airmen, insiders claim.

Dubbed 'Britain's Roswell', the Rendlesham Forest incident in Suffolk, has intrigued UFO enthusiasts since taking place in December 1980.

On three separate nights just before the New Year, military personnel said they saw lights flying in the sky and descending into the woodland – the group was convinced they had seen an alien spacecraft. Yet it has now been claimed that the extraterrestrial sighting was a hoax, played on the US air force by the SAS in revenge for capturing a squad and subjecting them to a brutal interrogation.

The SAS were said to have regularly tested US security by probing the perimeters of RAF Woodbridge in the English county, which allegedly stored Nuclear warheads and was believed to be a key target for Soviet agents. But when an SAS troop parachuted into the complex one night in August 1980 they were unaware the guards had upgraded their radar system. Their black parachutes were immediately detected and the British were hauled off for questioning. They claimed they were beaten up by their captors who refused to believe who they were and repeatedly referred to them as 'unidentified aliens', before being released 18 hours later after the British authorities intervened. Seething from the interrogation, SAS soldiers were

---

*Leigh Francis (born 30 April 1973) is an English comedian, actor, writer, director, and producer. He is best known for creating Channel 4's *Bo' Selecta!* (2002–2006) and portraying Keith Lemon in several *ITV* and *ITV2* shows including *Celebrity Juice* (2008–present), *Keith Lemon's Lemon Aid* (2012), *Through the Keyhole* (2013–present), and *The Keith Lemon Sketch Show* (2015–2016).

keen to take revenge. British X-Files expert Dr David Clarke, who has been researching the story for three years, revealed: 'After their release, the troopers made no complaint at their rough treatment but were determined to get their own back on the USAF for the beating that they had received. In particular, their repeated characterisation as "aliens" sowed the seeds of a plan. They said: "*They called us aliens. Right, we'll show them what aliens really look like."*'

As December approached, lights and coloured flares were rigged in Rendlesham Forest. Black helium balloons were also coupled to remote-controlled kites to carry suspended materials into the sky, activated by radio-controls.

Taking place over three nights between 26 and 28 December in 1980, military personnel from nearby RAF Bentwaters and RAF Woodbridge witnessed strange lights in the woods and hovering above the airbases which were on high alert as the Cold War was at its peak. A great deal of nocturnal Christmas fun was had at the expense of the USAF – and the matter should have ended there, according to a letter written to Dr Clarke by an alleged SAS source.' Unfortunately, a senior US officer (Lt Col Halt) led the US contingent out into the forest on the second night and took along his tape recorder. The hovering and whizzing lights were sufficiently impressive for him to send a report to the MoD. Someone in London recalled the events of the previous August and questions were asked. A few red faces – but also some satisfaction and amusement followed. The USAF was 'reassured' at a very senior level and no UK investigation was undertaken – for obvious reasons.' Dr Clarke said he was first contacted three years ago by 'Frank' who claimed to be a SAS insider. He had seen Dr Clarke talking about Rendlesham on a TV documentary and felt 'it was about time that the truth was revealed about the incident'. Dr Clarke, of the Centre for Contemporary Legend at Sheffield Hallam University, said: '*I investigated his incredible story by talking to trusted and open sources in the British military, including some high profile former SAS troopers. What happened in the forest, according to Frank, would be bread and butter for special operation soldiers trained to deceive and misinform whilst remaining invisible.*'

Charles: In December 2018 a claim that the SAS had allegedly flown into the forest was also made, according to the British Newspaper, *The Sun* (Emma Parry) and *Fortean Times Magazine* who printed the story as another explanation, for the events which took place. Other claims often involve talk of access into the forest by cars and small vehicles – which is rubbish; as a photo shows on page 10 of this book what it was like long before the Forestry commission laid their tracks – another myth tagged on to never ending tall stories by people who weren't even there.

When I initially saw the story, I thought it was a joke. Surely an SAS officer would be smart enough not to be drawn into such a silly story. That is, unless he was helping the MOD to deliberately confuse the situation. Common sense dictates that this is all another silly story!

The 33th ARRS would never have weapons on the Base. Yes, they had interesting weapons, but they were only issued when loading up for a covert mission. Until then they were kept in the armoury. The 81TFW Security Police had exclusive responsibility for the security of the Base. Stop and think. Ask any cop stationed on the Base at the time. If they saw a 33ARRS member with a weapon they would have been taken into custody – period. I've met so many people over the years who have laboured long and hard to raise the flag on the UFO subject – some are sensible but most perpetuate the craziest of theories.

This is another example, who the hell 'Frank' the informant is, is anybody's guess. I've discussed this with John, like myself, how can any person accept evidence of a wild unsubstantiated story like this, from an alleged ex SAS 'insider' whatever that refers to, for all I know he could have been the cleaner? The more weirder, the more such 'comic' book stories attract the attention of the newspapers.

It's obvious that any action such as this would not have happened; if it had – we wouldn't have known about it. In addition of course why would the US Air Force beat up the intruders…If in fact people had been detained parachuting into the airbase I would have known. I was the Deputy Base Commander, and can categorically tell you, no such thing happened.

This story formed part of Dr David Clarke's on-line blog (some two years previously).

Colonel 'Ted' Conrad

He brought 'Frank's' report to the US Base Commander *at the time of the UFO incidents, Colonel Ted Conrad who agreed that Frank's story simply did not stack up*. "**US Bases are not on US soil, rather all of them remain on sovereign British soil…US citizens who are stationed and work there are the 'aliens'. The SSA was guarded 24/7/365 by armed, trained security personnel who were instructed to shoot to kill, if necessary to prevent a breach.**"

Surely we aren't expected to believe this whole event was a prank played by members of the British army's elite Special Air Service (SAS) in revenge for their rough treatment at the hands of the US guards at the twin-base complex! This 'story' is still doing the rounds and was recently resurrected by *BBC* filmmaker Simon Holland in a new *YouTube* series on Rendlesham.

I looked at the two *YouTube* videos produced on the 26th of January 2020 and 11th of December 2020 by *Professor (nickname) Simon Holland, who says he, joined the RAF in 1976 and was employed in the weapons engineering branch.

Mr Holland doesn't mention, to our knowledge, anything about the allegation of SAS men parachuting into the forest, as an explanation, for what was witnessed but speaks of being contacted by an RAF Officer who told him what really happened – from 'someone of the highest authority', (unnamed of course) who was there on the December night it happened.

He admitted it was the space module capsule which landed on its three legs and was just part of an elaborate exercise!

In conclusion, it is apparent that the media obtained sight of this claim and decided to publish something that would catch the attention of the public rather than actually publishing the full FACTS which would have shown this allegation for what it was – a load of old rubbish. Yet again another example of the way in which the newspapers are not interested in the truth but only spurious stories which have not stood up to scrutiny; if the reader had been aware of the whole story . . . As for the honourable 'professor' who wound up his assessment of the incident as *"That's what it was – the chance of it being from fucking Zog is zero."*

I rest my case and remind the reader to ignore his hypotheses! He wasn't there but further states that he visited the Base in 1981, and that any discussion of the UFO incident was discouraged! Another tall story no doubt! Why did he visit the Base? Who discouraged him about discussing the UFO incident, was it a senior officer or one of the lower ranks? How did he know of what had taken place? How did he get onto the Base?

Capsule Wasn't There – *WATCH MY LIPS!*

For a start the capsule wasn't there, no planes or helicopters were flying, due to ground fog and the holiday period. Never heard of him, and I was there. This was an American airbase, not a drop in centre!

*Simon edits for BBC, Nat Geo, Discovery, Smithsonian TV, Ch4 and Ch5. Produced films for University of Hawaii NASA funded program, finding earth-killer asteroids. French recorded history project. He is a private pilot and keen gardener. He lives with his partner Dorothy Faison in a water mill in SW France.

THE HALT PERSPECTIVE 2

December 2018: Drones abound – they even shut down major airports in the UK!

In December 2018 I made my way to Woodbridge, England after having been invited by a US travel company, to take part in interviews conducted at the, now private, Bentwaters Air Base.

On this occasion an impressive drone was used which proved most helpful in securing footage from the air. Can you imagine the feelings that ran through me while aloft the old Control Tower, and walking down the Weapons Storage Area, reflecting on memories once again from nearly 40 years ago? Those memories were further influenced by a walk around the Cold War Museum, sharing stories with the staff and being impressed with the wealth of memorabilia that adorns the walls.

THE HALT PERSPECTIVE 2

Gatwick London airport shut down!

The next day the papers were full of a security scare at Gatwick Airport London when flights were closed down – leading to *hundreds of flights being cancelled, following reports of drone sightings close to the runway. The reports caused major disruption, affecting approximately 140,000 passengers and 1,000 flights.* There have been previous sightings of UFOs in that locality, why Gatwick, why Heathrow, why any airport? I don't know. That was a hell of a coincidence.

John wrote emails to the press about these incidents but never had the courtesy of a reply!

THE HALT PERSPECTIVE 2

On the 19th of December 2018 an unidentified person posted up a clip of film purporting to show a UFO moving over a taxiing aircraft at Gatwick. To this present day, despite an arrest of a couple who were later released, the explanation for what it was is still unknown. From his archives we learn of the following interesting reports – note the similarities.

In August 1978 a black cigar-shaped object was reported by motorists in the sky near the airport, one of a number of reports John has told me about at this location and other airports. On another occasion a triangular shaped object was seen 12 miles from Gatwick. Interesting and no doubt more than coincidence at least two of these sightings took place near to, or over, the *Pound Hill* ancient earthworks/site, not far from Gatwick – which often figures in the background of reported UFO activity. Apart from that, John has a number of reports over the years of other strange objects seen hovering over Gatwick airport. One is from Ursula Scratchley, whose account is shown. Contrast this with a sighting on or about the 20th August 1958. Gilbert Wilkinson – (then aged 12 at the time), living in Crawley, West Sussex – was out roller skating at the back of his house, just after the sun had set, when he happened to glance into the sky to his left, and saw a huge 'disc'-shaped object flash across his field of vision between the houses in the close. *"I probably had it in view for no more than two seconds, because of the tremendous speed.* **It was golden-yellow in colour, and travelling on its edge – like viewing a bicycle wheel from its side – showing a small flame flowing from the bottom of its circumference.** *It was larger than a full moon in size, completely silent, showing no condensation trail or sonic boom, etc. Unfortunately, there was no-one else with me at the time. I rushed in to tell my parents, but they did not report it to the police. I knew straightaway this was a UFO, as the only man-made object in the skies at the time was the Russian Sputnik. The course the object was flying on would have brought it right across the western end of Gatwick Airport – surely someone must have seen it? The sighting was truly awesome. I wasn't frightened, but completely taken aback by the marvellous beauty of what I saw."*

In 1986 Ursula Scratchly was entertaining a friend at dinner. It had been a relaxing soirée at the Forest Row house in Gatwick Airport's periphery.

Mrs Scratchly's guest Penny Crowder thanked her host and walked out into the warm September air towards her car parked in front of the house, in Post Horn Lane.

Before opening the driver door, she and Mrs Scratchly looked skyward, where they witnessed a celestial spectacle in the clear night sky that would change their view of the world and the universe forever.

The two women saw a glowing, orange ball with a pale, orange aura surrounding it, moving slowly across the sky from east to west.

Mrs Scratchly, now 54, remembers the shocking events vividly. She told the News this week: "It had a construction around it, like frame. It was very strange and very shocking. I couldn't speak.

"The thing was moving very slowly away and suddenly it disappeared into a tiny dot in the sky then vanished completely."

They phoned flight control at Gatwick Airport but officers said nothing had shown up on their radars.

Reports are still trickling in about sightings in the area, the last one logged just six weeks ago.

THE HALT PERSPECTIVE

Tim, Thanks for all your info and help. Enjoy

Hope you enjoy. John Hanson 4.1.18 12.50am

Colonel Charles Irwin Halt
USAF Retired

in collaboration with

Retired UK West Midlands Police Detective
John Hanson

THE HALT PERSPECTIVE 2

PART 14

THE TRUTH, THE WHOLE TRUTH AND NOTHING BUT THE TRUTH

2019

CHARLES: In 2019, I emailed author **John Steiger,** living in the United States, then in the throes of publishing three plays by UK Publisher, ***Flying Disk Press***, entitled *'**The UFO Trilogy: Dramas For The Stage',*** based on three hypothetical trials before a hypothetical 'Judge in a Court of Law', to determine from evidence offered by the 'Defence and Prosecution' witnesses the most likely 'verdict' for what happened in Rendlesham Forest all those years ago.

I suggested the playwright contact me after pointing out the omission to the 'Court' in this proposed production, or should I say 'trial', to include evidence given by (1) witnesses who were in the Weapons Support Area who saw what appeared to be a **'mother ship'** in the sky. Through 12X binoculars triangular objects were then observed.

(2) Then, what about the testimonials of the local civilians, who also saw UFOs, and evidence from Air Traffic Controllers in the Bentwaters Tower, who physically saw the glowing object and watched it descend into the forest where we were. This was after it twice went across their radar scope at more than 2,000 MPH.

(3) There's also the issue of the RAF Wattisham radar logs being confiscated and both radars out of use at the time (nonsense as they were the primary air defence for the whole section of the country) and to remain silent. I could go on! John Hanson contacted the publisher, Philip Mantle, who apologised but told him that the three plays published in book format were completed and that it was too late to include the comments made by me!

THE HALT PERSPECTIVE 2

New book – 2019

The Rendlesham Enigma by **Jim Penniston & Gary Osborne**, was published on the **22nd July 2019.** *Amazon* blurb for the book contained the following – Rendlesham Forest Incident of December 1980 is considered by far the most significant event in UFO history. It was also a unique military-related event, having taken place in Rendlesham Forest just outside the twin bases of RAF Bentwaters and RAF Woodbridge in Suffolk, England – both of which had been transferred to the United States Air Force in 1951 by the British MOD (Ministry of Defence), becoming one of the largest and most important NATO complexes in Europe during the Cold War.

The account given in this book is that of James W. Penniston, a Staff Sergeant at the time of the incident, who was the primary witness who led the investigation in the beginning and had 'Top-Secret clearance' – one of only eight people with Top-Secret clearance working Security at the twin bases. **His credibility and honesty were highly respected throughout his years in the USAF**.

Jim Penniston has teamed-up with author Gary Osborn to present the **definitive account of the Rendlesham Forest Incident** and the aftermath of events, just as he witnessed and experienced them from the incident itself, which began during the early morning hours of Boxing Day, December 26th, 1980.

About the Co-Author Jim Penniston

USAF Security Forces/retired. He entered the Air Force in 1973, and served over twenty years active duty in the US Air Force. He was assigned to the Strategic Air Command Elite Guard in Omaha Nebraska, providing security for General Officers, Congressmen, Foreign Heads of States, and the President and members of his Cabinet. Penniston held key assignments throughout the world, including service in *Desert Shield* and *Desert Storm*.

He wrote defense, security, counter-terrorism, and contingency plans for the USAF and NATO. Additionally, he provided security support for **Air Force One,** and other classified aircraft weapon systems. Penniston held for the majority of his twenty year career, a **U.S. TOP SECRET/BI/SCI** and a **NATO TOP SECRET COSMIC/ATOMAL** security clearance. Sergeant Penniston and his team were "First Responders" to a security investigation of a craft-of-unknown-origin, located just outside RAF Woodbridge, England. In December 1980 that case, is known as the Rendlesham Forest Incident, and is the most documented account in military history.

Jim is a frequent lecturer and presenter at numerous MUFON and other related events and conferences of similar subject matter. A speaker at two *National Press Club* events; His first responder's account of the Rendlesham Forest Incident has been featured worldwide on numerous television and radio programs. In addition, Penniston has been a contributor to other books. He is co-author of *Encounter In Rendlesham Forest*. End of blurb.

New book – 2020

Weaponisation Of An Unidentified Aerial Phenomenon, The Rendlesham Forest UAP Incident 40 Years Later. Authors: John F Burroughs & James Worrow published 15th December 2020.

KDP *Amazon* blurb – The famous UAP sightings in Rendlesham Forest during Christmas of 1980 have been very well documented over the last 40 years and several books have been written on the subject. The spin stops here, boring as it might be! The *Condign Report,* released in 2006 confirms that a Phenomenon exists and should be studied further for weaponisation! Everyone within the UAP community is waiting for confirmation. Well, guess what, confirmation has happened because the military have figured out how to weaponise UAP technology. This book exposes how certain players manipulated witnesses and used the encounters to further their own goals and to cover up the truth of what really happened during those three nights in 1980.

John Burroughs has written a very personal account and reveals details never published before of how the incident and events since have impacted his life. His co-author James Worrow has conducted in depth research of the Phenomenon and of military applications developed over the last 70 years that may have played a part in the events and how the event itself may have led to some of these developments. There are several contributors, including Ronnie Dugdale, who has provided a detailed timeline of the events as they happened, Dr David Clarke who, via Freedom of Information Act requests, was instrumental in getting the *Condign Report* released, Winston Keech, investigator of *Earth Mysteries* and UAP, who has visited the site on several occasions and found anomalies, and Larry Lowe who has been investigating UAP's for 50 years. There are also personal accounts from those who helped John with his VA settlement and Adrian Bustinza, who was with John on the third night of the encounters. This book is about one man's journey to seek the truth about an event that changed his life and the lives of his fellow servicemen. End of blurb.

Charles Irwin Halt comments – Bringing people to book!

Vicious attacks by Monroe Nevels on my character in Jim's book and to a much lesser degree in John's book!

I just finished reading John's book ***Weaponisation Of An Unidentified Aerial Phenomenon***. Pretty crazy, as expected. He admits he really doesn't know what happened in the forest and then goes on to say all he saw were lights and on to describe a triangular craft. Well what is true? He states Jim's code tale is not true. From there he surrenders himself to several, with way-out explanations, without any substantial proof. Somewhat like Jim's done. Just more mudding of the RFI waters. Along the way he gets Ronnie Dugdale to do a timeline that's partly correct. I'm glad someone gave me the book as it's a waste of money.

I asked David Boardman – a friend of John Hanson, who has spent time with his wife Julie, in the States visiting us – to look through Jim's book and identify the many contentious issues that need answering, as they form the **basis of many astonishing and 'unprovoked' attacks on my character.** In addition, taking into consideration similar grievances expressed by John Burroughs and his co author, with regard to my part in the proceedings, which to be fair were not as contentious but still need addressing if only to put the record straight from my point of view.

THE HALT PERSPECTIVE 2

So I will answer the criticisms and attacks on my character as they appear in both of these books, trying not to duplicate the answers – you will see what I mean. I've never attacked them or queried their part in all of this so why, suddenly 40 years later, does this campaign of hate begin? Basically down to one man – Monroe Nevels. What's so sad is that when you look back at the number of books written by so many popular authors who tried to raise the awareness bar on the UFO subject, we end up with publications like this…different times I'm afraid.

THE HALT PERSPECTIVE 2

First, let's look at what he said about the event, in 2013

Monroe: As the men crossed a farmer's field, the object seemed to head straight for them – then disappeared. The sky above was a gray-white and **three crafts** were visible. *"There were **three objects or lights**. The largest light was the leading or command vessel. The lights were three vessels that moved independently of each other. They were moving and were able to jump from Woodbridge and show up over Bentwaters in less than a second. **While the craft was on the ground,** pieces of flying debris were being shed, which appeared to be like molten steel in a boiler pot. It seemed to get hotter as the object was approached. I took photos with a Nikon F3 and a 105mm f/2.8 lens, with TriX @ ASA 400. I processed them myself in my home photo lab. They were fogged, and after a few years I realized the reason: Radiation detected around the sight and on the trees. This is why none of the photographs could be viewed. By the way, I was and am a Professional Photographer. I was methodical with my work, and as a Disaster Preparedness Tech., I knew and did my job professionally. I KNOW WHAT I SAW!"*

Monroe also took numerous photographs of the lights and object; unfortunately these photographs, when developed by Monroe himself were found to be fogged.

Colonel Conrad directed Monroe to scan the skies for several days after the incident. *"Col. Halt and myself, along with the others on that night, saw, over to the left of the farmer's field, a yellowish object from a distance that looked as though it might be a very hot metal, or steel, burning at very high temperatures. It seemed to get brighter as we went over the fence, but suddenly was gone. As I looked up, I pointed out to Col. Halt they were in the sky. As I know how brightness can make the eye/brain think all sorts of things, I saw them moving, so to make sure my statement was accurate I lay down on my back, closed my eyes and opened them again, several times. They were indeed moving. There were three of them. And, as sure as they were there, they were gone; they were also seen overhead by an excited group at RAF Bentwaters"*

John Burrough's book, with an input by David Clarke, has some muddled chapters, including confusing references to Rendlesham Radar and reality. It appears to follow along the lines of Nick Redfern's book, published in 2020, which suggests that the answer lies heavily in the use of weaponising UAP technology – hard to disseminate!

Who knows what happened? If it was some sort of exercise conducted over the Christmas period, well then how do you explain the similarities with other sightings of inexplicable airborne objects that took place in the East Anglia area over the last 70 years?

Ronnie heard of the incident following conversation in a local nightclub!

Interesting that Ronnie Dugdale Jnr has finally admitted knowledge of what happened very soon after the incident, when young airmen at the night club he frequented in Ipswich talked about **unusual lights and craft** seen in the Rendlesham Forest. First I've heard of this – John asked Brenda Butler about this in 2021, she said this was also news to her! Maybe Ronnie can let us have further details?

I've never, met the guy? I'm told that he is also writing his own book on the events that took place over the Christmas period of 1980 – has he ever contacted me? No.

Jim Penniston and Ronnie Dugdale

THE HALT PERSPECTIVE 2

Time line and aftermath of the 1980 Rendlesham Forest Incident

Ronnie wrote up a comprehensive **Time line and aftermath** of the 1980 Rendlesham Forest incidents in John's book. At first glance, good going, nothing contentious here, other than Ronnie queries why I would contact Captain Sue Jones to ask her who was available, when LT Englund and Monroe Nevels were next to me at the Base dinner? Answer – Captain Sue Jones was at the dinner at the Woodie Bar. Bruce Englund **was not there** and only turned up to notify of the object's return. **Nevels was never at the party.**

As I have said before, I wasn't aware of the two men having been out earlier. There are other issues I would like to comment on published in this book, as I want to put the record straight. One of them, which falls short of expectation is found on **page 77** when Ronnie, who has himself suffered from vicious attacks from Larry Warren in the past after befriending him, outlines Larry Warren's version of the events that took place.

Ronnie Jury is out for Larry!

But, what on earth would prompt him, knowing exactly what has occurred over the last five years following death threats from Warren against people like Sacha Christie and others, to make the following comments: "*Larry Warren is the most controversial of all the Rendlelsham Forest incident witnesses, because his story has never been consistent. Authors and researchers have been frustrated by the different versions of the his story he has told and left <u>wondering which version, if any to believe</u>. However Adrian Bustinza has stated on more than one occasion he saw Larry in the Forest at least at some stage and airman Steve Longero has also recently said he had seen him in the forest. Just where and when has never been made clear,* **so until more witnesses come forward we will just have to say the Jury is out**.

Followed by another strange comment about the book **Left At East Gate**, in which Ronnie says "*Larry Warren had 20 years before this book was published to get his story straight…it is for the reader to decide if he is describing his story the way he believes it occurred or has he sensationalised details told him by Adrian Bustinza and others?"*

Sounds like he is giving him the benefit of the doubt and why hasn't Ronnie explained to the readers **that the book was taken off the market by his co-author**, and more importantly for what reason?

Why have pertinent important details been omitted? For what purpose? Surely the reader, and there are no doubt some who aren't aware of the background on this incident, should have **all of the facts** not just some. I've outlined my opinions on the credibility of Longero – who wasn't there!

To give you an idea of just how convoluted Larry's story is, here is yet another example of the way in which the 'fish gets bigger' with each telling! If you're not sure, go on to **Google** and punch in **Larry Warren LIES** . . . see what you catch!

New *BUFORA Journal* Issue 15th April, 2005

Here is an article from Doreen Jenkinson, who tells of joining a group of people in the forest on the 14th August 2004, led by Larry Warren. Doreen tells us of a conversation with Larry, who talked about **top secret nuclear weapons** being housed at RAF Woodbridge and Bentwaters, and an event on the 27th of December 1980. This involved 40 witnesses. Apparently an alert went out to military personnel, who were ordered to investigate after a UFO had crashed, taking off part of a tall pine tree. **Three creatures were seen leaving a craft.** Over three nights UFO lights were observed. On one occasion a 'laser beam' was directed from the UFO into the storeroom which **later revealed TEN nuclear missiles were disabled.** I rest my case. You know my thoughts on this!

THE HALT PERSPECTIVE 2

I was asked about the date of the first UFO incident (involving Penniston and Burroughs) by Robert Hastings, and confirmed the morning of 26th December as now being correct. As I said to you, the reader, before – there is no evidence to support the claims made that an alien craft landed and <u>that Gordon Williams entered into some sort of a dialogue with the entities. This is completely untrue.</u> I also have no idea about any UFO on the ground, seen by me or members of my party.

While we are on the subject, I would like to discuss 'Cookie' – who is known to me personally.

Cookies anyone? Or a CIA Head Doctor?

Lindy 'Cookie' Vaughan, referred to as Airman 'Cookie'/Airman Belinda 'Cookie' Green, who is mentioned on **page 41/49/69** of John's book, claimed that she collected the 'men' and drove them back to the Bentwaters Airbase, where they were met by a man in a white coat and his team, the person whom Colonel Halt recently claimed was a CIA 'clean-up doctor'.

On **page 69-70**, 'Cookie', who's been in touch during recent years, says that, *"I was led away by a man in a white coat following the incident, while reassuring the other airmen that 'everything was going to be ok', followed by the man with the white coat putting his arm round me, as I was in a shocked condition then leading me away."* 'Cookie', says she heard me say **"No, not me"**, then the man with the white coat said, **"Yes, you as well, you must come also".**

'Cookie' surfaces again on **page 85**, when following an interview on *Phenomenon Radio* she alleges that she was tasked to pick up dazed and confused airmen on more than one occasion on different nights and driving them to the CIA 'clean-up doctor' and his team at Bentwaters. It's claimed that she was also harshly debriefed, but she has **trouble separating what was real and what was not**. She says she was put under hypnosis and they tried to get her to lie. They failed. The de-briefers agreed they couldn't get 'Cookie' to lie.

Look, I'm not coming this way again in another book, so this will be the definitive ANSWERS to nonsense such as this. For a start I wasn't shocked, why I should be? Intrigued, excited . . . yes, of course. Why wouldn't anyone under those circumstances – odd that I was able to tape record my comments as I went along without any sign of abnormal stress!

'Cookie' worked in the supply depot at the Airbase. On occasion she also delivered food packs to the on-duty security guards when, during these visits, she too saw strange *'craft'* in the sky, which she maintained were neither examples of any flying lighthouse or aircraft. According to her *"I'm sure someone was watching us. I saw several 'crafts' and each time I did so they would seem to separate into, maybe, three or five smaller completely silent objects. Not only would I not hear them but also there was an absence of birds and animals until they were gone. I had the strongest impression that the locals also saw these 'craft' on a regular basis and just accepted it."*

Sacha Claire Christie, also interviewed 'Cookie', daughter of a former marine, on a number of occasions in 2016, following consultation with me. During those conversations 'Cookie', from Queens, Long Island, New York, told of being posted to RAF Bentwaters at the age of 18 following basic training, which is when she met Larry. *"He told me he took Adrian's story, he told me the craft wasn't on Capel Green it was at the other side, he got mixed up. I said something about his training days, finishing, going to Germany . . . I said you must have only been on your first shift*

Lindy 'Cookie' Vaughan

then? He said far too enthusiastically, 'yes it was my first shift'. Then he told me vans were outside his mum's house when he rang her. I had never heard that in nine years! Then I listened to Adrian's last show and I realized. His story is a combination of Adrian's and Johns. All the things he said and changed were because of what Busty said. Larry being the total narcissist that he is, assumed I would adjust the story for him and carry it forward, explain away his memories as mind control or whatever. Or he must have thought I would lie for him. **His biggest fear, he claims he was there the 1st night it started, he was NOT on duty, and he even named his book wrong. Left?...nope it was Right, at East Gate.** When I started having my experiences, and a few other people, we went to the bar that was in a dorm. Larry got all kind-of jealous that he had not been involved as yet. The next day friends are telling me he has run around telling the tales and wrote himself into it, what?? Crazy then, he knows I can out him and he freaks. Strange that, I saw somewhere he kept saying, about me, when my name was brought up, but she was not a cop like me, not security.

Worked with the OSI on undercover operations!

I actually worked with OSI, on an unrelated case out of my job in supply, then was cross-trained into the new job they formed, security/supply and was over the pilferage cage, that's how I got hired on so quickly at the jail as a corrections officer . . . anyway, he wanted to use me as a witness for his stories, just didn't want me to ever tell the truth.

I also worked in supply, while cross-training into Security augmented . . . due to the huge theft problem. Yes, I found out about it as soon as I got there and had it figured out in less than a week, unfortunately my work mates, a few who also were roommates in an apartment in the 'switch', were involved. The top guys were like um . . . well, when the shipment left Germany it was all counted and checked out, but when I am checking it in . . . Not so . . . this and that missing, back then you know, not much in the way of cameras and tech . . . so I watched and listened, and sure . . . enough . . . they are just taking what they want as they unload, so technically it never made it into the warehouse.

Yes, I snitched, I was raised right, and a thief is a thief . . . the guys lost a stripe or two and laughed it off. My Base Commander allowed me to get it all set up and have them taken down where no one got hurt and lesser charges for some of them, I was even taken to your British jail and sat for a while to look like I was in trouble too. Then they snuck me out and I watched them strip our apartment down and find all the hidden goodies, ugh, ugh, ugh!! I think it was **Colonel Halt** *that gave me a fatherly speech about staying a good girl and choosing my friends better but how I had a great future ahead of me, etc. I was called 'cookie'. As that was my nickname since basic, but the asses in the agencies called me 'Bambi Eyes' and said I couldn't lie if my life depended on it, made me so mad.*

This is where I wish I could give you specific names and jobs and all that but like I said, at that point in time, you're 18 and you're told . . . 'we own you, we can make you disappear, ammo is very cheap, we can get to your family', etc. Made to sign papers of non-disclosure, told 'you will lose your job at the very least, never ever tell anyone, anything, anytime, ever'. You believe them . . . they are the authority, period . . . and I am from an all- military family, so double the power play there. I will tell you there is a basement-type room, on BW or WB. Not sure any more, as I was so disoriented. I was shot up with what they said was sodium pent. That is when I got the name 'Bambi Eyes'. I was apparently very entertaining under that drug."

As many people will know, Sacha was to suffer some hideous, indescribable verbal attacks on her character by Warren who, during a *Facebook* rant, accused her of associating with terrorists! On another occasion he made a death threat against her, saying he would force her windpipe down her neck and kill her. Why he wasn't prosecuted after she reported it to the Police beggars belief!!

I contacted Sacha Claire Christie in February 2021, who had 'blown the whistle' in more recent years on Warren's extensive list of criminal wrong doings involving, in the main, all manner of forgery – details of which can be found on the following Internet link: https://sacha-christie-infomaniachousewife. blogspot.com/2016/06/fake-john-lennon-ufo-sketch-mystery.html?fbclid=IwAR3ZOeJ39zRWpegcCsa wO4nmf5ntlvPfkiPo4-9tFxrql9IviR_RmTl19F0

With regard to another very nasty verbal attack made on her and another *lady some years ago, not from Larry but from Jim and John, during a debate, on *Facebook*, in which veiled threats were made of a visit to the 'persons house' and that they lamented the fact that *'It was a shame she hadn't had a visit from **Mr Cancer cell'**.

Sacha: "*It is important that you have the context of my reaction to them. I am just not sure who actually said it but it was said. I also find it interesting that my comments are the only ones available and that there is no sign of the comments John and Jim made that day. This is what I had to say in response, John Burroughs and Jim Penniston: You should be banned from* Facebook *for your aggressive and threatening behaviour towards two women on* Facebook *who simply asked you some questions. You called Hilary a dumb dog and threatened (another woman) with **a visit to teach her a lesson!!!***

Have you lost your minds completely? Who the hell do you think you are? You are a pair of disgusting self-obsessed bullies. How dare you talk to people like that? Now you really have shown yourselves to be completely unhinged and beyond reason and you had the audacity and temerity to say that I'M UNHINGED. You look like a pair of total idiots. GET A GRIP AND GET OVER YOURSELVES. YOU'RE NOBODIES. MADE OF CLAY – JUST LIKE THE REST OF US. Carry on like this and you will find yourself either getting arrested or banned from Facebook. *It's an arrestable offence to threaten a person with a visit to teach them a lesson; it's called online bullying . . . Did you know that because you are NOT minor deities, you are not above the law?*

All messages can be retrieved even if you have deleted them and I am recommending to the offended that they report you to both Facebook *and the Police. Somebody pass this on because they have blocked me in every direction, pathetic childish playground behaviour. I feel sickened to my stomach."*

In Jim's book Page 399 (15) – He refers to Col Halt's alleged comments regarding himself and his men surrounding the object. Quotes Jim Penniston saying 'Halt does have people scratching their heads with the things he has said over the years . . .

Major Zickler was not present, as he stayed at the party with Conrad, as he didn't want his name in it. Verano, Palmer, Combs and Thompson were not there and John Burroughs was held back and ordered to stay back on the service road. Now he talks about all kinds of things that I know didn't happen.

There were no 'Bobbies' there. No-one, to my knowledge, was taking pictures (other than Nevels) and no film was confiscated. It appears from this version of events that Larry may not have been present. You have no idea how skilled these people are in fabricating disinformation.

My advice is to be very cautious with regard to claims made of this nature, as they are untruthful. Carl Thompson was one of the Air Traffic Controllers on duty that night (he and his partner saw the object, both on the screen and visually). There's no way Bustinza could have known his name, as he didn't come forward until recently and their duty roster is not known generally – just further evidence that someone messed with Adrian. The plot thickens! I can only recommend that you proceed with caution.

Well here we go . . . my thoughts, my opinions and comments defending my character against an onslaught of verbal attacks by those that I thought I could trust!

---

*The other lady is known to me. I spoke to her recently, she informed me that as time has gone on she has sorted out things with John but hasn't forgiven John Burroughs.

THE HALT PERSPECTIVE 2

Jim's Book: The *Rendlesham Enigma*

Page 19 – Cites inconsistencies – 'One witness (John Burroughs) presenting very different details of his accounts from previous years'

Charles: Well he's not on his own; this has been covered, in what will be the two books, but who knows what was pumped into him by those that wanted to create false stories. Same with Warren and others, I've expressed my feelings on this.

Page 23 – Questions, within the context of protocol: what is more likely to be true regarding John Burroughs accounts relating to his contact with Central Security Control and the reporting of lights in Rendlesham Forest.

Page 24 – Notable – an extract from a hypnosis session is used to support a record of facts.

Charles: Can 'recall' during a hypnosis session be relied upon to represent a true record of facts?

Pages 32, 33, 39 – Critical references about John Burroughs behaviour – unfair bearing in mind that John was not consulted with regard to any comment he may have liked to add, if only to defend himself, something about people that live in glass houses shouldn't throw stones!

Pages 122/123 (10) – Questions regarding Colonel Halt's whereabouts and timings – following the initial event.

Charles: I've said what I want to say on that; haven't a clue what the guy is on about, apart from that it's none of his darned business!

Page 124 (15) – Suggests that it could be said that Col. Halt compromised Security Police protocols.

Charles: Not sure what he means. I was ordered to go and investigate and determine the nature of any possible threat to our Airbase after strange lights were seen over the Forest, which could have been anything; better safe than sorry, not forgetting this was an Air Force Base, for all I knew they could have been terrorists.

Page 124 (16) – Suggests mistake made by Col. Halt or Co-Author (John Hanson) regarding the date of Adrian Bustinza's attendance.

Charles: What the heck is going on here? Staff Sergeant McCabe told me just before 6am on the 26th December 1980, Boxing Day: *'Colonel, you're not going to believe this. Burroughs, Penniston and Bustinza were out in the woods last night, chasing a UFO'.* Technically that would mean the late night shift that would cover late night 25th December 1980/early morning 26th December 1980. Pointless question, as I can't see what they are getting at. If there was a mistake it would be a typographical error. This pales into mere insignificance compared to the avalanche of hostile questions directed at me in an attempt to usurp everything I've ever said over the years.

Page 130 (30) – Regarding the debriefing of Airman Cabansag, suggests that Col. Halt took matters into his own hands, and perhaps because of his own personal interests.

Charles: Rubbish! Matters that a Deputy Base Commander took into his own hands, I was fully entitled to make command decisions. What personal interests are they wittering on about?!

Pages 138/139 (46) – Highlights a comment from Linda Moulton Howe questioning whether Col. Halt knew a lot about the middle night and has never talked about it.

Charles: More rubbish! I have no idea what on earth she is talking about. I've said what I have said and that's the end of it . . . did she email me or try and contact me? – Of course not!

THE HALT PERSPECTIVE 2

Monroe Nevels testimony attacks Colonel Halt's account!

Page 152/153 – Col. Halt's view of the evening of the 'third night' contrasted with testimony of Monroe Nevels which presents an alternative perspective.

Page 153 – *'It's back'* – recounts allegedly different versions of comments made by Lt. Englund to Colonel Halt.

Page 154 – Munroe Nevels suggests that it is a waste of time analysing what Colonel Halt had said took place at the Officer's Club, after he (Nevels) and Englund arrived, as none of that happened – especially as Colonel Halt had always described it.

Page 154 – Colonel Halt refers to Lt. Englund's comments about taking Lightalls into the forest.

Page 155 – Suggests that Munroe Nevels never mentioned to the '*Rendlesham Enigma's*' authors that Lightalls or any heavy equipment had been taken into the forest when he was with Lt. Englund. Raises issues about the deployment of the Lightalls.

Weaponisation Of An Unidentified Aerial Phenomenon, **TOP SECRET, Monroe Nevels testimony-section from John and James's book. 'Airman abducted?**

His UFO sighting, admission of earlier visit to the forest!

Page 49-51 (summarized). It is claimed that, following reports of the UFO activity, Colonel Ted Conrad contacted Malcolm Zickler and then Lt Bruce Englund, who was ordered to call on Staff Sergeant Monroe Nevels. After doing so he informed Monroe that what he had to say was Top Secret. Nevels confirms the visit, and that he was told by LT Englund that they had been ordered to investigate the landing site that Penniston and Burroughs had identified to him earlier. LT Englund then told Monroe that *"One of the airmen had been taken, abducted into the space craft in Rendlesham Forest"*

A visit was made to the Forest at 4.30pm; subsequently a detailed examination was made of the landing site which had been pinpointed by Lt Englund. As they left the forest, now in darkness between 7-8pm, Monroe saw what looked like a bright green object through the night vision goggles, that resembled an eyeball like the pupil of an eye, pulsating slowly … The two men then made their way back to the Woodbridge Officers club, bar 'to report their findings to Colonel Conrad.

Page 52 –The two men speak to Colonel Halt and Conrad. LT Englund says the UFO is back! Colonel Halt ushers LT Bruce Englund into the cloakroom and speaks to him further. This isn't quite correct according to Monroe, who claims that quote: *"Colonel Conrad ushered us both into a side room. I saw Colonel Halt and Colonel Conrad. I believe Colonel Gordon Williams was there, I'm not sure but I think he was. Zickler was there, and in uniform …Colonel Conrad asked me if it warranted further investigation, which I agreed most definitely".*

Page 53 – Colonel Halt contacted the Disaster Preparedness Officer, Captain Sue Jones and asked her who their stand-by person was? She told Colonel Halt it was Monroe Nevels!

Charles: No date is given for when this was first brought out into the open, one imagines that the authors of the book are quoting from Monroe, when he had this 'rant and rave' on Facebook in late January 2021, when he had this to say:

Monroe: I was a Disaster Preparedness Instructor and taught many classes with gas chamber exercises, Disaster Preparedness Support Teams and worked exercises in the Command Post. I had direct contact with both the Base Commander (Col. Conrad) and Wing Commander (Col. Williams) because they TRUSTED my comments and keen eye around the Base. I will stand my ground with ANY of the distorters and lies. I KNOW WHAT I SAW! By the way, I am still in contact with Col. Conrad often and live only 86 miles from him. Read my story in "*The Rendlesham Enigma*".

There was a Paranormal Witness episode on the **Travel Channel** that re-enacted Englund visiting Nevels at his job location and their visit to the landing site before returning to Base and contacting Halt. The show added to the conflicting testimony of some, and dug up the old unproven story of beams of light being shined down from up above over the WSA.

Halt, Penniston, Burroughs and Nevels all participated in the show. Englund did not and his name isn't even mentioned but is described as something like a Security Officer or Shift Officer.

Any questions or answers will ONLY be the truth. Lt. England came to my home on RAF Woodbridge base housing on 27th Dec 1980. I was given a briefing ordered by Colonel Conrad. Col Halt is telling ALL sorts of lies about me, because he was involved ONLY because of me, and his story changes like the wind. I speak truth, and after 40 years, still live it and remember it like yesterday. I was trained oil Nuclear, Biological and chemical extensively and could spot a booby trap with a very keen eye. End of quote:

Book: *Rendlesham Enigma* criticism: – Discussion on who said '*It's back*' and who asked who, in the chain of command?

Page 156 – Asserts that Colonel Conrad did not want it known, especially by Lt. Col. Halt, that he had specifically sent Lt. Englund to pick up SSgt. Nevels and accompany him to the landing site. Munroe Nevels asserts that, as far as he is aware, no discussion took place between Lt. Englund and Lt. Col. Halt when they first entered neither the Officer's Club nor when they both entered the room.

Col. Halt had never mentioned being told by Englund that Conrad had specifically sent him to collect SSgt. Nevels to take him to the first night's landing site and investigate it.

Page 157 – Monroe Nevels denies ever hearing the words '*It's back*' mentioned to Lt. Englund, or anyone else for that matter.

Page 157/158 – States former Base Commander, Ted Conrad, told Dr. David Clarke (UFO sceptic) that the comment '*It's back*' had been relayed to him (Ted Conrad) by Col. Halt.

Page 158 – Acknowledges that '*It's back*' statement may have been said to Lt. Col. Halt by Lt. Englund without Munroe Nevels' knowledge. However, asserts that Col. Halt's account that Col. Conrad was present and heard the statement from Englund in various interviews was now certainly in doubt.

Page 158/159 – Asserts that at the Officer's Club, Lt. Col. Halt said *"Sergeant Nevels, do you mind if **I come along**"* Asserts that in all interviews Col. Halt has not mentioned asking for SSgt. Nevels if he could come along. Col. Halt had never publicly acknowledged Nevels being present at the Officer's Club. Monroe Nevels: – On the role played by Colonel Halt – who was ordered not to be involved, and that he didn't organise team into Forest, and lied!

Page 160 – Statement attributed to Munroe Nevels – "*Col. Halt has stated he went along to debunk this event, more as a sceptic. I did not observe this attitude with him. To me, it was an adventure for him and he wanted to be in on the action.*"

Page 160 – Col. Halt's claim that Col. Ted Conrad had ordered Lt. Col. Halt to assemble a team and investigate contradicted in the following note from Nevels – "*I later learned from Ted Conrad, and for his own reasons, not mine, that he did not want Col. Halt involved in this mission, and that he had actually ordered Halt not to get involved.*"

THE HALT PERSPECTIVE 2

Page 161 – In the light of comments from Munroe Nevels, doubt is cast on Col. Halt's comments that he assembled a team on Col. Conrad's orders.

Page 161 – Asserts that Munroe Nevels was not instructed by Lt. Col. Halt to calibrate and collect Geiger Counter equipment, etc., and that Lt. Englund could not have been ordered to pick up MSgt Ball by Lt. Col. Halt. Also, Lt. Englund did not collect Lt. Col. Halt with Msgt. Ball. States that Lt. Englund was with Nevels when he left the Officer's Club.

Page 162 – Questions timelines regarding MSgt. Ball collecting Lt. Col. Halt from his home.

Page 163 – Quote from Col. Halt indicates he was not aware that SSgt. Nevels was at the Officer's Club when discussing what should be done about the apparent 'UFO' related problem.

Page 164 – Asserts that it seems strange that Lt. Col. Halt would either call or go directly to the Disaster Preparedness Office to ask what NCO was on duty for the weekend.

Page 164 – Quote from Munroe Nevels – *"Colonel Halt said repeatedly that he visited or called Captain Sue Jones and asked who was on duty for the weekend. He also said I had a babysitting problem. These are both lies."*

Page 165 – Quote from Munro Nevels – *"At such times it seems everyone wants in on the 'action'. I didn't 'just fall into this' and neither was I taken along as an afterthought as Col. Halt would have people believe..."*

Page 166 – Quote from Munroe Nevels – *"Check the repeated stories of Halt's involvement. Halt has also made an issue of taking me to the Disaster Preparedness Office to pick up gear, but it was Lt. Englund who did that and took care of me while I again attended to the mission I was given, ordered by Col. Conrad"*

Page 166/167 – Cites an alleged discrepancy in the account regarding the choice of Geiger Counter.

Page 167 – Nevels states that he calibrated two Geiger Counters because one was found to be faulty. This was with Lt. Englund being present, not with Lt. Col. Halt or anyone else. When Nevels returned to the forest with Englund, Lt. Col. Halt was already out there.

Page 167/168 – Cites conflicting accounts of who collected Col. Halt in the Jeep.

Page 172 – Questions how Lt. Englund could have been driving the Jeep to pick up Lt. Col. Halt from his home if he was with SSgt. Nevels the whole time after leaving the Officer's Club.

Page 172 – States that it is fact that Nevels was known as a 'straight shooter' and continually makes the point that he is known for his integral honesty and that he would never lie or fabricate anything for any personal gain.

Book: *Rendlesham Enigma* criticism – questioning timings of Colonel Halt, regarding arrangements to enter the Forest. Squabbles about who picked who up!

Page 173 – Infers the reader will see that same things mentioned in different interviews with Col. Halt and Adrian Bustinza reveal that their accounts are not as straight forward or watertight as perceived when read side by side with comments from Munroe Nevels.

Charles: Surely the same logic could be applied to the veracity of all Munroe Nevel comments/ statements! I rest my case!

Page 173 – Sergeant Randy Smith recalls timings relating to permission for MSgt Ball to cross the Bentwaters Runway. Possibility of an hour and 15 minutes later than was arranged. Assertion that Col. Halt said that he was picked up 30 minutes after having arrived home to change and that he had simply altered his account to suit.

Page 174 – Alleges either Col. Halt or Malcolm Zickler (or both) have not been truthful regarding arrangements concerning the third night of events. Concludes it was only MSgt. Ball who picked Col. Halt up.

Page 175 – Questions Colonel Halt's recollection of, Adrian Bustinza's presence in the Jeep, which collected him on the third night.

Page 176 – Col. Halt said Adrian Bustinza was in the Jeep when he was picked up. Alleges Col. Halt does not really recall, so it is difficult to discard the possibility that he has given in to what people have said over the years.

Page 177 – Suggests that the most likely conclusion was that Col. Halt, was not the officer responsible for ordering Lightalls out into the forest initially.

Page 180/182 – Authors give their views on the timeline of events from the Officer's club to the forest. – (Notable that Munroe Nevels can't recall timeline anomaly – page 183 below).

Page 182 – Asserts that Col. Halt was the 'contentious senior officer' mentioned by Tony Brisciano (Motor Pool Attendant) when interviewed by Georgina Bruni.

Page 183 – Munroe Nevels cannot account for the anomaly in timeline of events regarding his arrival at the forest due to fading memory.

Page 187 (6) – Asserted that Munroe Nevels would never have agreed to take part in the TV documentary 'Paranormal Witness' had he known that Lt. Col. Halt was to be portrayed as discussing issues with him outside the Officer's Club and entering the Jeep with him to go straight to the forest.

Page 189/190 (29) – Asserts that it is wise to play 'Devil's advocate' when required and healthy to use counter-advocacy for just about everything you read, see or hear. Then links this statement to a quote in the 'Halt Perspective' book regarding Lt. Col. Halt attending the forest, with Munro Nevels, on the third night. Nevels asserts that it _appeared_ his words had been altered in the book by Halt and Hanson. Questions why did Col. Halt never mention Nevels being present at the Officer's Club.? (Assumptions being made as to the truthfulness of statements from Munroe Nevels?)

John Hanson to Monroe NEVELS: – Why didn't you contact me or Colonel Halt about this?

"I absolutely refute altering any words. I spoke to you personally on two occasions and we emailed each other. I had always regarded you as an officer, Christian in faith and gentleman up to now and you come out with this rubbish, conveniently waiting until John's/Jim's book comes out!

Let's remind the readers of what I said in the **Halt Perspective 1** *book..."I remained puzzled by the telephone conversation with Monroe Ruby Nevels about his admission of already having been into the forest and found the 'landing site' before he was even asked by Lt. Colonel Halt to accompany him into the forest."*

Sgt. Monroe Ruby Nevels – Three vessels or lights seen

As the men crossed a farmer's field, the object seemed to head straight for them – then disappeared. The sky above was a gray-white and three crafts were visible. *"There were three objects or lights. The largest light was the leading or command vessel. The lights were three vessels that moved independently of each other. They were moving and were able to jump from Woodbridge and show up over Bentwaters in less* than a second. While the craft was on the ground, pieces of flying debris were being shed, which appeared to be like molten steel in a boiler pot. It seemed to get hotter as the object was approached. I took photos with a Nikon F3 and a 105mm f/2.8 lens, with TriX @ ASA 400. I processed them myself in my home photo lab. They were fogged, and after a few years I realized the reason: Radiation detected around the sight and on the trees. This is why none of the photographs could be viewed. By the way, I was and am a Professional Photographer. I was methodical with my work, and as a Disaster Preparedness Tech., I knew and did my job professionally. I KNOW WHAT I SAW!"* Monroe also took numerous photographs of the lights and object; unfortunately these photographs, when developed by Monroe himself were found to be fogged.

In 2013 Monroe had this to say – *"Col. Halt and myself, along with the others on that night, saw, over to the left of the farmer's field, a yellowish object from a distance that looked as though it might be a very hot metal, or steel, burning at very high temperatures. It seemed to get brighter as we went over the fence, but suddenly was gone. As I looked up, I pointed out to Col. Halt they were in the sky. As I know how brightness can make the eye/brain think all sorts of things, I saw them moving, so to make sure."*

Charles: Well I'm not sure where to start, this seems to be a consolidated, continuing attack on my character by Monroe Nevels, in every shape, manner and form – not just in one book, but two books – questioning the whole of my involvement in what happened. My memo and tape recording are now under question, also what I did, what I said, and who I was with, even dispute over my orders. Monroe says the photos were fogged but one might think that he might have kept them for evidence, instead of binning them. Am I expected to take his word when he doesn't take mine! So why would he say the comment on **page 50** quote: *Col. Halt has stated he went along to debunk this event, more as a sceptic. I did not observe this attitude with him. To me, it was an adventure for him and he wanted to be in on the action."* Well what's wrong with that? I was the Deputy Base Commander – did he think that I would rush in chanting some sort of welcome to the aliens. Nuts! What next – a Dinosaur seen?

Why have these guys left it for near enough 40 years to mount a concerted assault on my integrity honesty and account? Someone even suggested I was part and parcel of some cover-up – if that was the case, why did I even write the darned thing?

On **page 87** of John's book, it is mentioned that on the 30th Anniversary of the incident held at Woodbridge, Jim twice claimed that I was part of the cover-up and working for the AFOSI! Nuts – if that was the case, why bother writing a darned memo!

Monroe Ruby Nevels has shown his true colours here. It's obvious he bears me much malice and I have found no reason why! …This all seems pointless. If the question is valid, out of courtesy, I will answer it but I shouldn't have to defend myself against these scurrilous allegations, which are published under the cover of Jim's book also in John's book, who have accepted carte blanche what Monroe has told them without at least emailing me to give me an opportunity to defend myself. Cowards!

Why and for what reason, to inflate their egos by personal attacks on me?

I've spoken many times over the years about what took place and haven't had any criticism directed at me with regard to my account. I thought this was about a UFO sighting which for me and others was a remarkable experience – and, like the thousands of others – still unexplainable; rather than scrutinising everything by those questionable people who served on the same Base, as I did, I have ever said with regard to my role as deputy commanding officer during the events that occurred at the end of December 1980.

THE HALT PERSPECTIVE 2

Why not have a go at Larry and Adrian if you want be pedantic? That would fill many books!

Where does one start and finish? His so called lie detector test, which I have commented on in an email to Dion previously, in my opinion there is now a real question as to the qualification of the examiner and her motivation? This is surely a biased – how can the statement considered to be persuasive when the person involved is giving a self-proclaimed positive character reference and it is not independently corroborated? I wonder if Munroe Nevels requested that the statement be included as a condition of him having an input into the book? The attacks are all coming from him rather than Jim – that is odd!

Clearly, Monroe needs to get some medical attention, as he's lost it completely . . . I'm not going to pander to him by defending all of the inane questions attacking me. I would refer him to the *Halt Perspective*, and the many times that I have stood and lectured before audiences both in the UK and the USA, some of which is on CDs and DVDs, stating my version of the events told so many times over the years. If Monroe had been to the landing site prior to our visit, he never mentioned it when we went out. In fact, he wasn't sure where the site was. His reaction when we found it was surprise. It certainly didn't happen the night we went out, although he (Monroe) says that he was at home at 4pm during the early afternoon with his three year old daughter when Bruce called around on the 27th of December. Nothing in the book about any babysitter, all I know is that Monroe was home babysitting, as his wife spent the evening at a chapel program. So taking into consideration that following Ted Conrad's orders to investigate on that afternoon, why is then a day or two later I took Conrad and his family out and Conrad had no idea where the site was and never mentioned being there prior or any knowledge of a previous visit by Monroe and co… Something doesn't sound right.

Several years ago, I challenged Monroe about his comment of having been there prior and he did not give me an acceptable answer. That all being said, Conrad may have been read in on the 'cover-up', but they would never have trusted Monroe.

Theodore 'Ted' Conrad was out there earlier, but that puts him in the middle of the cover-up. Conrad is not being honest. His wife and son have told John Burroughs there's more to the story. Undoubtedly there may well be – taking into consideration that I have it on good word that several fellow cops saw John in uniform going to the OSI Office, and not to just pass the day!

Malcolm Zickler, through his wife's home estate business in Florida, has been contacted many times by email, but declines to answer which is his prerogative – who can blame him. I guess he has a lot to tell! Notable that Munroe Nevels can't recall timeline anomaly, but he sure does remember with the finest details everything else, or so he claims!

Odd that those that make the loudest of noises, squeak like mice and decline to even make any comments; John Hanson emailed Bruce Englund and asked for clarification in 2020/2021 but he has failed to reply. Ok, for arguments sake, let's say that Monroe Nevels did go out into the forest, after being ordered by Ted Conrad, and they chose not to tell me, if ordered by Ted Conrad. So what? This is no big deal! What is a big deal is that only now does there seem to be a concerted effort to attack my character … I smell a rat!

Nick Pope comments

Nick Pope commented on the earlier visit of Monroe Nevels to the Forest. *"Monroe Nevels **told me a while ago that he'd been out in the forest before he went out with Halt.** I believe it may even be covered in my interview with him in the episode of* The Unexplained Files, *titled 'Are Aliens attacking our Nuclear Arsenal?'"*

THE HALT PERSPECTIVE 2

John Hanson: I viewed this film and found there was a reference by the programme host to Monroe having gone **back out again to the landing site with Colonel Halt**, but this was curiously all. I thought Monroe would have been invited to expand on that, but he wasn't asked.

In **October 2015**, I contacted Monroe Nevels with regard to sorting out this ambiguity. He told me that too many lies had been said about his role, and that *"I did go out to the site with Lt. Bruce Englund on the third night, after being directed to do so by Colonel Conrad, and reported my findings to him, before Colonel Halt asked me to go out with him."*

Nick Pope – further clarification on this issue

"The confusion over the earlier visit that Monroe Nevels made to the landing site is interesting, but it would be a shame if he and Charles Halt fell out over this, as it doesn't detract from the importance of the visit they made to the landing site together, as recorded on Halt's audio tape. I believe I asked Monroe about his earlier visit when I interviewed him for the episode of The Unexplained Files, *entitled 'Are Aliens attacking our Nuclear Arsenal?', but if I did, it clearly didn't make the final edit. That's not surprising, as it is standard practice in the TV industry to film much more material than is required. I do clearly recall discussing this with Monroe informally, off camera, and if he says he was out in the forest earlier that day on the instructions of Colonel Conrad, then I accept that assurance absolutely. If anything, the revelation serves only to reinforce how seriously all the senior command personnel took the incident."*

Book: *Rendlesham Enigma*, further criticism about who ordered who?

Discrepancies over the use of micro recorder, used by Colonel Halt in the Forest. Arguments about size of the object, depressions in the ground...Etc...

Page 190/191 (35) – Jim Penniston is of the view that Col. Halt's desire and fascination with UFO's since boyhood drove him out to the forest with SSgt. Nevels in the hope of seeing a UFO. The third night was an opportunity Col. Halt had sought. He said as much at the 2015 Woodbridge Conference regarding a book on UFO's he had read as a teenager.

Authors (Penniston and Osborn) speculate that if Col. Halt did have a real interest in the phenomenon, that perhaps this was the real reason he joined the USAF.

Charles: Crackpot stuff they need to get a grip on reality or check their hieroglyphics for information... crazy have they ever read my story about the early days of my life.

Page 191 (36) – Jim Penniston's view on the possibility of Col. Conrad 'giving in' and allowing Lt. Col. Halt to go along on the third night. Jim Penniston's view on Munroe Nevels thoughts of 'being in charge' on the third night.

Page 191 (36) – Alleged adverse comments from Ted Conrad regarding Col. Halt recounted by Munroe Nevels during a visit to Ted Conrad's home in 2010 with John Burroughs and Linda Moulton Howe. Munroe Nevels seeks confirmation that Col. Conrad never ordered Lt. Col. Halt to investigate on the third night.

Page 192 (36) – Col. Conrad does not go on record in response to the above confirmation sought by Nevels. Nevels observes that Col. Conrad did not object to what he said.

Page 192 (38) – Assertion that Lt. Col. Halt hijacked Munroe Nevels mission.

Page 193 (44) – Suggests that it would appear that literature which relied on Col. Halt's statements simply reflects Col. Halt's attempts to appropriate Lt. Englund into his own timeline of events. (Also emphasises that this is speculation and Penniston and Osborn leave it to the reader to judge).

THE HALT PERSPECTIVE 2

Page 195/196 (53) – Alleged discrepancy in comments concerning the situation with regard to micro cassette recorder spare batteries/tapes taken into the forest by Lt. Col. Halt.

Page 196/197 (58) – Researcher Ronnie Dugdale asserts that Col. Halt stated that Sgt. Bustinza was **not with him during his investigations**.

Page 199 (71) – Asserts that weight is given to the theory that Lt. Col. Halt had much to gain from giving the public the impression that Nevels and Englund were both part of his team.

Page 206 – Assertion that the objective set by Lt. Col. Halt to visit and examine the landing site was odd as the site was not what Col. Halt had said he was sent out to the forest to investigate.

Page 220 (12) – Alleged discrepancy in the description of depressions on the ground, given by Col. Halt. Book asserted that Jim Penniston's estimate of diameter was more accurate.

Page 250 (5) – Gary Heseltine writes that he was told by Col. Halt that the object was the size of a car. This contradicts what Col. Halt had always said regarding the lighted object being a little larger than a basketball but less than a metre in diameter.

Page 250 (6) – Munroe Nevels says that he always knew that the aerial phenomena that he and Lt. Col. Halt had seen on the third night was closer to the craft that Jim Penniston had reported having examined closely.

Page 252 (29) – Alleges Bustinza and others told to surround a yellow mist like object by Lt. Col. Halt.

Page 254 (43) – Cites several interviews by Col. Halt concerning, amongst other things, accounts of speeds of the object crossing the radar screen at the control tower at Bentwaters.

Page 255 (54) – Asserts that Col. Halt said in an interview that the beam of light aimed at the men's feet referred to in his mini audio cassette tape recording lasted 30 seconds, which was quite a long time for SSgt. Nevels to have missed it.

Page 259/260 – Cites alleged differences in information related to interviews with Col. Halt concerning what occurred when he attended the Command Offices on Bentwaters Base the morning immediately after the events of the third night.

Page 270 – Insulting personal comments regarding John Burroughs eating habits.

Page 272 – Refers to Lt. Col Halt being in receipt of a bogus witness statement from Jim Penniston.

Page 275 – States that Lt. Col. Halt told Jim Penniston to treat all discussion about Rendlesham as 'Top Secret'.

Page 281 (13) – Quote from a Larry Warren interview in which he praises Jim Penniston's professionalism and character.

Charles: Yes I originally thought that Bustinza wasn't there but realised that wasn't the case.

You know it's strange up to now; I've not had any criticism from anyone other than Warren and his disciples. All of a sudden every action I've ever taken with regard to those three nights is under the microscope, by the likes of Jim and Nevels…I suppose they are desperate to flag up any perceived discrepancies I've made, in order to camouflage the ridiculous assertions made linking the UFO sighting with nonsensical messages from the future. Additionally I would like to point out that incredibly I've even been accused of falsifying the audio tape …Where does it end…? This attack on my involvement right from when I first learned of what was happening predominates the whole of Jim's book and also a hefty slice of John's book, orchestrated by one man . . . MONROE NEVELS.

Adrian Bustinza

Bustinza himself stated on the 12th of March 2012 from Whitewright in Texas in a posting on *Facebook* the following: "*Oh believe me they were there and it was real. And I was not drugged but threatened yes. Definitely threatened by the same people that we were working for our Government!! And this is the very reason why I will not go forth with interviews, and even try to get involved. Because every time I turn around and read the nonsense about when Larry, Jim or John say, or write something, everybody wants to jump in and analyse everything, and give their version. Well if you went there, I will say stay out or just hear them. They may not agree to disagree. But I will attest for all three of them. I will back them and I am aware as a lot of others are not aware, as they are, that there were actually three different nights that this all evolved in. But don't tell everybody cause you will only be ridiculed, like everybody else is trying to ridicule everyone else! Yea your right the Halt Tape does sound strange, but you know what; I was there and in those tapes.! And they are as real as you are alive.*"

Charles: Not sure what weight a personal endorsement from Larry Warren should carry given his documented history of lying! In actual fact let me give you another example of further story telling by this man.

Book: *Rendlesham Enigma,* queries about tape recording. More pages of Binary

Page 283 (14) – Cites the possibility that Lt Col. Halt had given out photo copies of both statements and sketches made by Burroughs and Penniston to Col. Conrad and other Command officers to view.

Page 283/284 (15) – Questions how Lt. Col. Halt could have played a cassette tape to SSgt. Penniston and Airman Burroughs when Lt. Col. Halt had already given over the mini cassette recorder and recorded tape to Wing Commander Gordon Williams on the morning of December 28th. Suggests that the tape played to Penniston and Burroughs could have been a copy.

Page 284 (16) – Links Lt. Col. Halt and SSgt. Munroe Nevels observance and encounter with a phenomenon or **craft resembling an eye winking** on 28th December with SSgt Penniston writing down a further three pages of binary code including the text '**EYES OF YOUR EYES**'.

Charles: Seems a tenuous link at best; absolute rubbish! So how come all of the other massive number of witnesses that John Hanson has spoken to over the years, documented in around 16 books, over a period of a quarter of a century has never culminated in witnesses having also been downloaded with binary code? Some of these people have also encountered landed objects which possess similarities to what he alleges to have seen.

Page 284 (17) – Refers to inconsistent details relating to John Burroughs returning to work and handing in his statement. (The Authors: Penniston and Osborn comment – that the statement handed in on 'Tuesday' meant that the date, was December 31, 1980, whereas the Tuesday would have been 30, December 1980).

Page 299 – Refers to **Corporal** Sam Morgan becoming Lt. Col. Halt's new boss. (Assume this to be an error and should state 'Colonel Sam Morgan').

Page 304 – Asserts that whilst Jim Penniston was in his new post as NCOIC of Plans and Programs, after monthly briefing meetings he was usually asked by Lt. Col. Halt to clarify certain things or remember more details about the Rendlesham Forest Incident.

Page 308 – (4) Cites no satisfactory explanation given as to why Lt. Col. Halt allowed a week to go by before visiting Don Moreland.

THE HALT PERSPECTIVE 2

Charles:

Page 310 (6) – Questions timescales regarding the writing of the '*Halt Memorandum*'.

Page 310/311 (8) – Refers to incorrect date of 27 December written in the 'Halt Memorandum' for the date of the first incident and the time of 0300L which conflicts the timeline logged in SSgt. Penniston's notebook. Suggests the date of '29 Dec 80' is also incorrect. This was a working Base with a lot of people, some of whom bent the rules and committed crime. Look at the way in which I have been taken to task over the years for making a mistake with the date. If I had been part of the cover up whatever that means, then why did I bother writing a memo?

I made a simple mistake, about the date, which I later corrected through various interviews. I accept that this initially caused confusion, but nothing like the problems which arose from others, whose stories have continually changed over the years. My account has never changed. I can only tell you what I saw as deputy senior officer in charge at the time.

Page 313 (16) – Questions the truth regarding relations between Lt. Col. Halt and Col. Sam Morgan. Colonel Sam Morgan was a 'gung ho' officer who went around boasting he was the world's greatest fighter pilot. He even passed out wine bottles with his own label stating that he was the world's greatest fighter pilot. You may think this is a personal grievance or maybe a clash of personalities – not at all, but it may be important to bear certain facts in mind when looking at the overall big picture here with regard to the way in which this matter was originally handled, not forgetting the quote from Ted Conrad directed at me . . . '*He should be ashamed and embarrassed by his allegation that his country and England both conspired to deceive their citizens over this issue. He knows better*'.

There were other issues, involving allegations of criminal damage on quite a large scale, when over a hundred windows were shot at with an air rifle, which necessitated Police investigation – especially when the target was also the Chief of Police's house on the Base. This of course meant a number of people were subsequently interviewed, following an allegation that the son of Colonel Morgan and another youth were to blame.

The matter was referred to the Chief of Police who asked me for advice, bearing in mind how delicate the matter was. Given Colonel Conrad's position at the Airbase, the situation was embarrassing to say the least. I told the Chief he had to do his job. He then went to Morgan's home to interview Morgan and his son. According to the Investigator, Morgan went off the deep end. He later complained to Colonel Williams, and anybody who would listen, that I had sent an armed police officer with a badge to his house. Needless to say, the investigation didn't go anywhere: were they responsible? I can't say. Following this, Colonel Morgan was most unkind; blaming what had taken place on me personally.

Soon after that, Williams was promoted and moved to a new assignment in Germany.

Colonel (later General) Pascoe replaced him. Morgan was then selected to replace Conrad as the Base Commander. Morgan let it be known that the first thing he was going to do as Base Commander was to fire me. Knowing this was likely to happen, I started looking for a new job. I contacted many friends and found one in Germany that needed a replacement with my skills. He passed my name and credentials up the chain to the 17th AF Commander. He contacted Colonel Pascoe and asked for me by name. Pascoe told him no and called me into his office, confronting me as to why I wanted to leave. I told him about Morgan's comments and he became upset. He told me it wouldn't happen and to relax and do my job. We had a somewhat difficult relationship after that. Morgan found the copy of the tape from Dec 1980 that Conrad had left in the desk and asked about it. I explained what happened. Later I discovered he was playing the tape for friends, including some British UFO investigators. Somehow Harry Harris a solicitor/UFO Investigator from Manchester talked Morgan into giving him a copy of the tape.

Harry then sold the tape to a Japanese TV Producer for a significant sum of money. I was shocked and disappointed. Subsequently, things were of course very difficult between us; on occasion threats were made to me, which I ignored. As you all know Harry and Mike Sacks came to see me – a matter which has been discussed before – but I reject out of hand the quote made by Ronnie Dugdale that in a memo to Harry I admitted on **page 64** of Jims book that "*At one time we surounded a craft and tried to get in it or on it.*" This come after **page 62**, in which Adrian Bustinza tells Georgina Bruni a version of events that mixes truths with BS during the foray into the forest, including allegations made by him that I and my party surrounded a huge UFO that was sat in a small clearing, **NOT** in the Capel Green field near the edge of the forest. Bustinza says that I ordered him and others to join the men surrounding it. People were filming. I ordered him to seize the cameras. All this is on the so called missing hour of my tape! The readers must be psychic because they know the answer to this rubbish.

After Colonel Morgan left the Base, he asked for a high-ranking military decoration for his service time at Bentwaters. I was asked if I would write it. I flatly refused as, in my opinion, he was undeserving. Several years later, while I was serving as Director of Inspections for the Directorate I was in Hawaii, planning to brief the Pacific Commander on a pending inspection, when I ran into Morgan. I was in my dress uniform, walking to the Officers' Club for lunch prior to my briefing, when a bus pulled up to the club entrance. Who should be the first off the bus but Colonel Morgan; I looked him in the eye and said '*Sam Morgan, I should punch you in the nose*'. I looked directly behind him and who should I see but the four stars General he worked for. I made eye contact with the General and saw the puzzled look on his face. I immediately turned and went into the club. They went to a private dining room and I never saw them again. My briefing went well and I returned home and never heard any more. Morgan has long since retired and, according to several friends, has become very radical with his writing.

Page 327 – Jim Penniston notes that all that was transpiring behind the scenes in spring 1983 would come out later through discreet discussions.

Charles: I'm not sure what on earth he is talking about?

Page 328/329 – Jim Penniston asserts that he reminded Colonel Halt of the prohibition regarding talking in public about an event that happened on active duty under AFR 30-30. Penniston also asserts that he walked a 'fine line' with Colonel Halt.

Charles: Well I don't have any memory of being advised by the Technical Sergeant of the dangers of talking to the public. I happened to be busy running the Base at the time. With all due respect, it's none of his business!

Page 349 (9) – Alleges Harry Harris and colleagues had struck a deal with Col. Halt.

Page 351 (12) – Makes an assumption that Col. Halt was negotiating a deal with Keith Beabey (*News of the World*) reporter behind Harry Harris's back.

Page 356 (20) – Questions the direction of the lighted object seen by Lt. Col. Halt and his team.

Page 358 (27) – States that it appears that Col. Halt had thought it reasonable to ask Keith Beabey for a fee of £25,000 for his story.

Charles: This would be Harry and Mike Sacks, not colleagues; you've got it wrong again. If you read the *Halt Perspective* you wouldn't be asking this question. Let me refresh your memory. In August 1983, I did have a meeting with the two men at the Air Base, after Harry Harris, a Manchester solicitor, telephoned General Gordon Williams in the States seeking permission to listen to a copy of the audio tape. Although I would refute any legal arrangement was made with General Gordon Williams. Subsequently this was arranged and they were then allowed onto Base, where I met them. After discussing UFOs generally, we

THE HALT PERSPECTIVE 2

sat around the table and I played the tape. We then signed a contract forbidding us from talking about what had been discussed that day, but they chose to ignore the agreement. I was very disappointed when the gang – Brenda, Dot, Jenny, Harry and Mike sold the story to the *News of the World*. That wasn't supposed to happen and it took years before I trusted Harry and Mike again. A copy of my memo was sent to Dot Street, who passed it on to Harry, who sold it to the *News of the World* for £12,000 – this sum having been negotiated by Mike Sacks, who told John Hanson in 2015 that the amount was then shared equally between the five persons involved. On the 15th of December 1983, following an enquiry from Brenda Butler to the *News of the World,* she was told that the 'story' was sold to them by Jenny Randles, Mike Sacks and Harry Harris, seems unfair, bearing in mind that it was actually Brenda and Dot that started this off. As for the claim that I asked Keith Beabey for £25,000 for the story . . . he contacted me and offered that amount . . . I discussed it with the Base Lawyer, thinking I could maybe support local charity, he advised not to get involved, so I didn't.

Page 359 (28) – Cites phone conversation between Philip Klass (UFO) sceptic and Col. Sam Morgan in which Col. Morgan says the following: "*Halt really had no authority out there in the forest anyhow. So he was a kind of hobbyist on his own lurking around. When I . . . looked into it I concluded it was just a bunch of guys screwing around in the woods.*"

Page 359 (28) – Cites a 2010 email exchange between Peter Brookesmith and Col. Sam Morgan regarding Col. Morgan's take on Col. Halt's story.

Page 377 – States that both Col. Halt and Munroe Nevels deny most strongly that *nothing* military was flying during the 'third night' they were involved.

Page 394 – States that '. . . the only witnesses we can rely on to give us a logical, rational, realistic assessment of what happened on the third night are Col. Halt and Munroe Nevels, with Nevels testimony being the most consistent and trustworthy.

Charles: Should this statement 'deny most strongly that *anything* military was flying'? On the one hand I am judged as being one of the two witnesses that is capable of giving a logical, rational, realistic assessment of what happened on the third night, on the other construed as being biased in favour of Nevels who is the most consistent and trustworthy – not sure where that leaves me!

Page 418 – States that Col. Halt calling Jim Penniston from various Bases would become common practice.

Page 430 – States that in Jim Penniston's experience, John Burroughs was not reliable and he was often referred to as a 'loose cannon', especially by Col. Halt.

Page 430 – Jim Penniston wonders if Col. Halt had been given instructions to minimize his story, as some of it contradicted what he had been told by Col. Heubusch.

Page 433 – Suggests that Jim Penniston believed that Col. Halt knew nothing about the containment story and that he had no knowledge of the fact that he had really being dealing with disinformation that had been put out by 'useful idiots'.

Page 441 – Suggests that Col. Halt was becoming very impatient with the progress of the work undertaken on a book by Salley Rayl.

Page 520 – Jim Penniston asserts – '*If it were not for Halt having told me in the first place that the incident wasn't classified and that we needed to dispel the lies that were being told, he (Penniston) would have got over his desire to go public with the truth and would have been content with staying 'off grid' about the whole thing.*

THE HALT PERSPECTIVE 2

Page 523 – Jim Penniston states – 'Contrary to what people have assumed and said, Halt never held the notebook'.

Page 526 – Jim Penniston comments that Col. Halt on the '*Larry King Show Live*' mentioned that the equivalent of a laser beam had been directed into the weapons storage area – something that he had always denied personally witnessing on the night he was involved.

Page 529 – In referring to Col. Halt's friendship with Richard Hall, Jim Penniston considers that Halt and Hall's mutual view that the beliefs in extraterrestrials often related to UAP/UFOs were connected with the phenomenon witnessed at Rendlesham were completely 'off base'.

Page 539 – Jim Penniston, in referring to Col Halt's knowledge of the whereabouts of John Burroughs, comments that he had had the possibility lingering in his mind, that <u>Col Halt had not made a mistake and that he had been</u> **deliberately lied to for purposes which were only known to Col. Halt**.

Page 590 – Asserts that John Burroughs was unwilling to look at Gary Osborn's work due to laziness mostly.

Page 595 – Jim Penniston cites John Burroughs alleged dishonesty.

Page 597 – Notes that Col. Halt had given the opinion that John Burroughs tends to take a bad situation and make it worse and cites that the comment was the excuse Col. Halt gave when Penniston confronted him as to why it seemed he had always tried to keep him (Penniston) and Burroughs apart.

Page 597 – Jim Penniston further criticising John Burrroughs behaviour, stating that he was always no help to Penniston when he needed him.

Page 622 – Jim Penniston, in discussing meeting with Dr. Kit Green, gives his views on values and integrity and expresses disappointment at John Burroughs.

Page 628 – Cites John Burroughs acting appallingly.

Page 657 – Gary Osborn promotes the theory of time manipulation by a highly advanced intelligence <u>if it can be proven through forensic testing</u> (my emphasis) that the notebook pages on which the binary code had been written by Jim Penniston date to 1980.

Right: A poster advertising Jim and Gary in 2018

Page 658 (2) – Critical of John Burroughs – States John Burroughs had not really understood what Gary Osborn had discovered. Additionally, John Burroughs 'Consideration Notes' were written for him by someone else and Burroughs had given the impression that he had written the Notes himself.

Page 674 (35) – Suggests that further rigorous forensic testing of Jim Penniston's notebook, is cost prohibitive, estimated to between $8000 and $9000. (This statement seems difficult to justify considering that the integrity of the Code and Osborn's supporting theories surely hinge on establishing once and for all that the Code was physically written by Jim Penniston in 1980).

THE HALT PERSPECTIVE 2

Quote: *"Surely this needs to be done at the very least to help provenance his claim of a binary download?"* Jim is willing to have a forensic test of the pages of the notebook, and this will be done ASAP, because until now it was cost prohibitive to do so.

No codes of conduct here!

Charles: No codes of conduct here! I wonder if 'Jims' 'vendetta' against his fellow co author of a few years ago was motivated by lack of support given to him by John Burroughs. As we all know in more recent television interviews Jim Penniston has exhibited a notebook in which he claims he made real-time notes and sketches of a landed craft for about 45 minutes. However, there are serious problems with this claim. For one thing, the date in the notebook is December 27 and the starting time is noted as 12:20 (presumably meaning 00:20). This, as we know, does not accord with the established date and time. John Burroughs, who was within a few yards of him throughout the incident saw no craft. He told Ian Ridpath in March 2006 that *"Penniston was not keeping a notebook as it went down, he did not have time to make any sketches in a note book while this was going on and did not walk around it for 45 min."*

It's difficult to know where to start and finish with this astonishing tirade of personal attacks made against me by Jim in his new book, ably assisted by what appears to be his star witness, Monroe Nevels, with regard to my memory of what happened now 40 years ago. This was completely unexpected and inconsistent with the conduct of a man whom I had once stood shoulder to shoulder on many occasions in front of audiences. There seems little point in addressing every issue raised by them, in an attempt to change the history of what happened, but under these extraordinary circumstances, I will endeavour to set the record straight.

People that live in glass houses!

Let me tell you about Monroe Nevels; matters that I have never brought to the attention of anybody before because, why should I? Personal attacks on each other is pointless and takes us away from the very heart of the matter . . . but needs must…

Monroe Nevels was a real problem child – very technically competent but with no common sense. One never knew what he was going to say or do? On several occasions he drove the Disaster Preparedness truck into restricted areas and was nearly shot. Often during exercises he would do things that caused real issues. One night he drove his car into his neighbor M.Sgt. Buckholtz's home and nearly killed a teen age boy. He painted all the walls in one of his on-Base home's bedroom's flat black, to make a darkroom. This caused untold problems when he moved out. Everyone that worked with him had issues. Colonel Morgan, who replaced Ted Conrad, as Base Commander, called Nevels **"a space cadet'** and way out there. His supervisor Captain Sue Jones constantly covered for him but finally lost patience. He was given a referral performance review (a potential career-ending document) and became very bitter. He phoned me after leaving Bentwaters and asked for my assistance in appealing the report. I had to politely tell him it was deserved.

Which no doubt left him unhappy with me and one of the main reasons why he has gone on the offensive. Many of the things he provided to Jim Penniston for inclusion in his book, concerning the incident, are blatantly not correct. I have been asked on several occasions why I took Nevels with me. It's like the old saying "when's a bad game a good game?" The answer: when it's the only game in town. Nevels was the only person in his field available and I knew he had a good camera. I was confident I could keep him under control. I was successful then but he's loose now!

Basically they query every facet of my involvement in what I reported took place. In other words they are accusing me of lying, accusations that I strongly refute…

THE HALT PERSPECTIVE 2

You know it's odd that I have, in that book, been found guilty without a trial or at least being given the opportunity of defending myself. As I have remarked so many times in this book about those many occasions when this story has been featured by the 'rag' newspapers, with yet another crazy story put forward to explain away what I and the other airmen saw, **without giving me an opportunity to reply before publication**. Well the fact that this has happened here is a surprise, quite sad really, which of course brings me to ask myself why John and Gary didn't contact me personally? They both have my email and telephone number, cowardly action to say the least.

I see little point in having to defend every action made by me now under attack by four men, two of whom weren't even there at the time. I carried out my orders as a LT Colonel who was second in charge at the Airbase. Up to now nobody has brought up their misgivings about the way in which I handled the situation both on the Base and 'out in the field' – now 40 years ago – because most people know what I've said about my role many times over. You either believe me or you don't. As for the claim by Monroe that John Hanson got it wrong, well John interviewed him personally; he never made any accusations then?

Garry Osborn's theories on the Binary Code

John: I wonder to what real extent Gary Osborn's wife has had an input/influence into the book?

This puzzling book is basically two books, written by Jim and Gary Osborn with assistance from his wife, Heather Elisabeth Osborn. Each packed full of information, according to the publicity surrounding its entrance onto the World UFO stage, never seen before in the public domain. The first half relates to what happened or what didn't happen during the end of December 1980, when mysterious lights were seen over Rendlesham Forest, the narrative supplied by Jim Penniston who was there and **prior to the publication** of this book somebody I had great respect for. (Not any more.)

I'm going to include part of this review on the book, which is on *Amazon* as an excellent assessment paralleling mine and Colonel Halts. I'm sure the gentleman would not mind. Here it is…

"Secondly, while I respect SSgt. Penniston and regard him as an honest and sincere person, I found myself becoming increasingly aggravated by the numerous instances in **which he puts down whomever else is part of the events being discussed while simultaneously elevating his own character, intelligence, and/or actions. Frankly, the further I got into the book, the more childish his comments began to sound.** From his constant belittling and frequent beratement of Airman Burroughs, to his seemingly inevitable mistrust of virtually anyone and everyone with whom he came into contact along the way, I found myself having to struggle to separate the "wheat" in his account of what happened in Rendlesham Forest from the "chaff" of his petulant comments about his fellow airmen involved in the incident. By the end of the book, I'd come to the conclusion that if I ever have the opportunity to talk with any of the principals involved in this matter, I would hope it would be **Colonel Halt. Why? Because his seems to be the most reasoned and even-handed account of this extraordinary incident.** The end of the book takes an even more bizarre turn as the co-author, Gary Osborn, inserts an epilogue entitled "A Code Within a Code About an Ancient Code", an enticingly-titled, 44-page "dissertation" of sorts wherein he tries to link what happened in Rendlesham Forest to ancient Egypt by some clever, numerical machinations he's derived in order to posit that the binary code "downloaded" into SSgt. Penniston's sub-conscious memory that night in Rendlesham was a "message" that was to remain hidden until the time was right for all to be revealed (which, coincidentally, just happens to be now). At this point, the book goes off the rails, and careers into conjecture of the wildest magnitude. It then becomes clearly obvious why the sub-title "Book 1: Timeline" is on the front cover; it implies a "Book 2" is forthcoming, and sure enough, Osborn sets this up nicely toward the end of his epilogue. In my view, Osborn has basically used Jim Penniston's encounter and co-opted the Rendlesham Forest incident as a springboard/lead in to catapult his "discoveries" into a mainstream audience fascinated by the UFO phenomenon, and setting the stage for some lucrative future book deals. Will there be a "Book 3"? A "Book 4"? Time will tell."

Looking at their Facebook site, in 2021 Gary and Heather appear a delightful couple, and in different circumstances I have no doubt I would enjoy their company, particularly sharing the fascination of ancient places like *Tintagel, Clovelly, Avebury, Stonehenge* and *Sedona* in the States, which I visited some years ago. Places that I personally find very interesting and thought provoking, taking into consideration the associations between these locations and sightings of inexplicable phenomenon, which I have documented over the last 25 years.

Heather has some impressive qualification, which include: studied EdD Doctorate of education Kutztown university of Pennsylvania, studied MA English literature-(Hons) at Miami University, studied literature BA-(Hons) at Lake Forest College, studied PHD Research in Goddess mythology at Queen Mary University of London. Presenter subject expert for *Discovery and Science* channel shows: President of Swan Centre priestess.

It's clear that as we pointed out before this is in two sections, but as a co-author surely one has to bear some responsibility for the whole of that book rather than reneging responsibility or blaming it on the co-author. In this case we cannot comprehend what on earth spurred **Jim, the book's co-author, to allow Monroe to saturate the manuscript with so much nastiness.** We decided to look at the *Facebook* site of Gary, a professional man, and his wife, Heather Elizabeth – an attractive, home-loving, educated woman – hoping to gain some clue that might throw any light?

On her website dated the 1st of May 2018 is a SCHULZ cartoon showing a small boy saying if it can be destroyed by the truth, it deserves to be destroyed by the truth. 242 likes with 2938 shares, accompanied by the following statement – *"We are both fed up having to deal with those that are psychotic narcissistic scheming liars and their idiocy. It's tragic and pathetic that they are so fascinated with us and inventing their infantile games instead of doing something productive with their lives…"* Followed by *"Gary and I had to laugh when we saw this (a cartoon) because its sums it up perfectly.* **The truth is going to be revealed about several RFI people who deserved to be destroyed by the truth**, *that's for sure. I can't wait for Gary's book to come out."* We have no idea what this is about. Could it have any bearing?

My personal thoughts on Gary Osborn's take on the Code are that he has used the Code as an opportunity to promote his 'mathematical discoveries' and previously published works concerning ancient pyramids into an all-encompassing theory. He states that he is writing a book about mathematical discoveries he has made concerning the Great Pyramid of Giza – an all-too-convenient tie-in between his theories on pyramids/ancient structures and the Rendlesham Code. Tellingly, there does not appear to be any published scientific peer group review information to support his data and theories. I can't help feeling that some of the mathematical coincidences of the type espoused by Osborne, can be found in many things, if enough latitude is given as to how the data is interpreted; the fact remains that coincidences will always occur. Some of his views will no doubt be considered by many to be fictitious, based on pseudoscience and selective interpretation of data.

A step-by-step process of discovery related to the Great Pyramid is promised in Book 2 of the Rendlesham Enigma! Will this contain new scientific revelations or more mathematical obfuscation including references to 'The Fine Structure Constant' and 'The Golden Cut Latitude'? – Only time will tell. A considerable amount of work has apparently gone into the book (680+ pages) and it appears to have been meticulously referenced. The book will perhaps be considered to be a definitive account by some who have only had limited exposure to the large amount of published work and TV material available about the Rendlesham Incident. It is a pity that Jim Penniston has chosen to be critical of major witnesses to the incident whilst supportive of others: namely Munroe Nevels as a paragon of virtue and truthfulness! This can only fragment things and give rise to further controversy which will play into the hands of hardened sceptics.

Jim Penniston now claims the date and time refer to a stream of binary digits he received telepathically and wrote down while at home the following day, but unfortunately that is not what the notebook shows. *"The binary codes were a direct result of contact with a physical craft, a craft of unknown origin. Meaning it was an unidentified craft and where it came from is still unknown. The communication of binary codes was accomplished, when I physically touch the craft's glyphs, which were located on the outside skin of the craft. It activated a technology which is unknown to me, and apparently to everyone else too... The technology then communicated a series of ones and zeros to me. The communication transfer was accomplished within minutes. There was an area of about fifteen feet which surrounded the outside of the craft. This area I will call the bubble. For within the bubble, static electric pulsed upon my clothes, skin, and hair. Also an appearance, of slowing of time. The air seemed dead, not transmitting any sound. The next day, while looking at my note book... The glyphs in particular – I had the codes running through my head since the incident the day before. I had a feeling to write them down... for I did and immediately after finishing them, the codes were gone from my mind. I was finally at rest with them. The notebook was then put away and retired to a box. For a new one for work I had available. My thoughts at the time, although profound, were actually much more simple. I wanted it to go away, and I had no need to talk about it either. For this was not to be the case. For I was methodically, and consistently interviewed and interrogated by my chain-of-command and other agencies. Every time, I was promised that this was the last interview, and it would be absorbed into the classified annuals of data, and I would need not tell or talk about it no more. This was not the case. I went through at least fourteen debriefings and two by non-air force personnel. I gave all information from memory, and at no time was the notebook ever brought up. The de-briefs were all for the last time, I was promised. Tell all, and tell it correctly and it would be the last of questions on Rendlesham. For these were to continue, no matter what I had said. I do believe the command element, were more for obtaining knowledge. But the external interrogation, were for much more, I am afraid."*

Penniston said he didn't get close enough for a detailed look!

Charles: I am aghast at claims made by Jim against not only the character of John Burroughs but his honesty, this is sinking too low, even for Jim; methinks he has been influenced by other parties that wish to confound the reader even more, with their unfounded procrastinations and attempts to throw people into confusion. Strange that John Burroughs questions Jim's version of events, not surprising as he has also been the subject of many slurs against his character, which is disgraceful. Jim's alleged binary download is a one-off account with no corroboration whatsoever. The *Daily Mail* (8.8.2011) published details of an interview, held between researcher Dr. David Clarke and Colonel Ted Conrad, with regard to Penniston and Burroughs' account, when they followed an unidentified light through the trees, which disappeared behind a low rise in the direction of a farmhouse.

Ted Conrad: *"There was no mention of an encounter, or a notebook. Penniston said he didn't get close enough for a detailed look."*

Back into the past . . . unravelling the truths

So let us go back into the past and review how this came to notice. Jim Penniston told John Burroughs in late 2010 that he had no idea what the zeros and ones written in his pocket book, during the making of a TV documentary, meant. Jim's claim of the binary code download was made public for the very first time at the 30th RFI anniversary conference at Woodbridge in Suffolk in December 2010, organised

THE HALT PERSPECTIVE 2

by Linda Moulton-Howe. John Hanson was there and recalls that the audience were frustrated when dynamic new evidence was mentioned but couldn't be disseminated at the time due to contractual obligations. Jim waited 30 years to tell everyone that he had had a download of information. He told the audience he did not know what the zeros and ones meant, yet just days later, he appeared on the *Angela Joiner* radio show and told her he believed they were a message? I also do not understand how he could tell the Woodbridge audience in 2010 that he didn't know what they were when in 1994 he underwent hypnosis and was asked at one point, *'Can you seen the binary code?'* One assumes he must have at some stage picked up a clue when he watched the video afterwards, and heard what he said! Now I'm told he didn't watch it! Seems to make it up as he goes!

In 2010 *Rapport Magazine* quotes Jim with regard to interviews he gave during the mid 1990s. In which, according to them, he talked about being sent to investigate a suspected crashed aircraft in the forest on December 26th or 27th 1980!

He then describes getting to within 10 feet of the object, which he calculated as being *"three metres tall by three metres wide at the base. No landing gear was apparent. It seemed like it was fixed legs. I moved closer and took 36 pictures on my roll of film. I walked around the craft and finally walked right up to it. I noticed the fabric of the shell was more like a smooth opaque black glass. The bluish lights went from black to green to blue. On the smooth exterior shell there was writing of some kind, but I couldn't distinguish it. So I moved up to it. It was three inch lettering rather than symbols that stretched for the length of two feet, maybe a little more. I touched the symbols and I could feel the shapes as if they were inscribed or etched or engraved like a diamond cut on glass."* The object then began to glow brighter. Jim moved away and then, after reaching a height of about 100-200 feet, in the blink of eye was gone. Jim claims that up to 80 people witnessed the craft that night, and that the photos he took could not be developed by the Base lab. However he came up with sketches of the craft. **(Source: Elliot Furniss *East Anglia Daily Times*)**

Interesting that Jim never mentioned about John and also never mentioned the NOTEBOOK!

It's out of this world and seems to fit perfectly into the following poster, I'm sorry to adopt a sense of humour, but boy you need one in this hate-filled morass where so much mud has been slung at me!

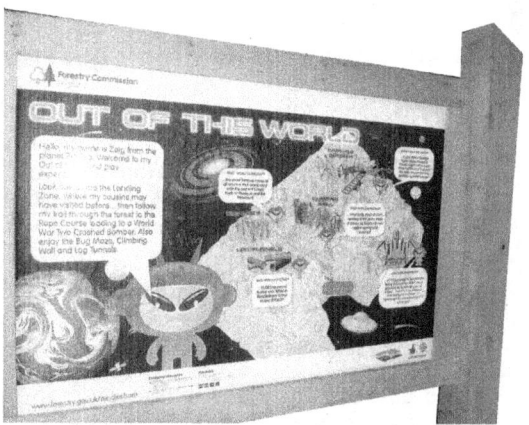

Linda Moulton-Howe

Linda Moulton-Howe certainly knew what binary codes were in 2010 because she had used a part of the transcript of that 1994 hypnosis session in her 1998 book *'Glimpses Of Other Realities'*.

Jim claims that the binary codes have some kind of message for humanity, but appears to be confused as to exactly how many notebook pages contain these transcripts. I've listened to his various podcasts and interviews and note he has given out conflicting statements about the number of pages! He has stated that he would submit the pages from his pocket book to be tested for the date of the ink and the date of the paper used. Was that ever done and if it has been done have the results ever been released? I gather that this would be very expensive, but with all due respects, if he can pick myriads of faults with me, then I have to right to not only rebut but point out my misgivings about this charade!

THE HALT PERSPECTIVE 2

When the code was first disclosed to the public in the *'Ancient Aliens'* episode, first televised on December 30th, 2010, (30 years to the day after it is claimed, by who exactly? . . . That agents in the AFOSI building blocked the download of the code from SSgt. Jim Penniston's memory on Dec 30, 1980) unaware that Jim had already written down the ones and zeros in his notebook! Jim states he didn't know it was binary code at the time, and the reason why he kept quiet was because he thought that writing down ones and zeros into his notebook was due to a momentary lapse of sanity – part of his trauma over the incident. I'm told that it was his intention to get the notebook checked to confirm the age, in order to prove to those who allege it was an up-to-date notebook. But due to the potential cost has changed his mind. Apparently he's very reluctant to now allow anyone to see it. Another source alleges that one of the notebook pages – the last page of ones and zeros – (the ink) was authenticated, but not forensically, by Dr Robert M. Wood in July 2012. It was Bob Wood who worked on the MJ12 documents. He dated the page and the ink upon it back to 1980, and this was confirmed in an email sent to Jim Penniston dated Aug 3, 2012. I wasn't aware of this ... John Hanson has tried to contact Dr Wood but without success so far. With all due respect, I need more than this to prove to my satisfaction this was written during the 1980s. Apart from that, can you date a page specifically in any given year? I doubt that very much! It just gets weirder, as it's claimed that the report was not given to Jim Penniston because its apparently common knowledge that John Burroughs, who had been taking care of the page, intervened and stipulated that Bob Wood sign a non-disclosure form, which Bob Wood was unwilling to do, and an issue arose over this, and so a report was not sent to Jim Penniston personally. However, a copy of the report was given to Ali Dubrow, the producer for a documentary Jim was going to appear in, as it was she and her company who had Bob Wood authenticate the page. Jim then lost track of Ali Dubrow when she left the company.

Landing site – which one?

Penniston's statement and sketch map clearly refer to the "traditional" landing site as shown on the eastern side of the forest, where the supposed landing marks and tree damage were found and which the local police were called to see the following morning. However, on a *Sci Fi Channel* programme Penniston claimed there was a second landing site on the near side of the forest, only a few hundred yards from East Gate, where he approached and examined the craft.

This site is not confirmed by other witnesses and is not referred to in his original statement or sketch map. On the 30th anniversary of the event, in December 2010, Penniston dropped this alternative landing site in favour of one in the southern part of the farmer's field. However, this does not accord with their story of taking a direct route towards the light, nor of seeing a light in line with the farmhouse that turned out to be the Orford Ness lighthouse.

In an email sent to Ian Ridpath in November 2019 I wrote: "*I handled the notebook several times including while filming the 2003 program. No code or missing pages.*" That statement would seem to disqualify most of the claims Penniston has subsequently made about the contents of the notebook.

Ian Ridpath writes on his website 2020: "There are other troubling inconsistencies. In Penniston's undated witness statement made shortly after the event he drew the craft as boxy in shape and apparently on legs. An inset **detail of the craft is accompanied by a question mark, presumably indicating some uncertainty. One is left to wonder why he would query the drawing if he had examined the craft in close-up for 45 minutes**. In another, more detailed sketch, made at some unknown time and dated "27 December", Penniston depicts the craft as triangular, like the landing marks, and shows it from three directions: front, side and top. The impression is sometimes given that this sketch of a triangular craft was part of Penniston's original witness statement, but it was not. Neither does it come from his notebook, because the paper is different. **This sketch seems to have surfaced around 1997 at the same time as an interview he gave with Salley Rayl,** *and was published on the Microsoft Network's UFO forum. Penniston claims to have made these notes and sketches at the time of the incident. When I asked him in 2010 April, via the Rendlesham Forest Incident online forum, to explain the inconsistency in date and time with the known date and time of the incident (i.e. 3 a.m. on December 26), he replied that the figures in his notebook 'are the actual time and date of the event'. Unfortunately, we have independent evidence that they are not. This basic error in date and time is enough to raise serious doubts about whether the notes were made during the encounter as Penniston claims."* Well I suppose I could go on and on expressing my opinion about this awful book which, like so many others, relies on one man's word uncorroborated by others. Thanks go to David Boardman for spending time researching the book!

David Boardman

Another strange false claim brought to my attention!

Charles: Rotherham-based **Bryan Swann,** who is a former fire safety inspector at South Yorkshire fire and rescue and amateur astronomer, claimed in 2019, on *Facebook*: **he was with me when the plaster cast was taken**! John Hanson emailed him asking him if he could elaborate the circumstances in which he was involved on what was such an important matter, he replied "*I was only going to tell you about my friends who were with me in the air force at Finningley and no names are available to you. Charles Halt was having coffee at the time. I know more than you can imagine. Keep watching my profile and see wonders…*" Despite emails sent to him asking to explain further – nothing else was heard – how odd! So much for wonders! Bryan Swan's claims – yet another example of someone's vivid imagination and attempts to secure some attention – who knows what makes these guys tick?! <u>For a start I don't drink coffee</u> and of course Jim Penniston took the plaster casts. Never heard of the guy, Swann, yet another person who makes wild unsubstantiated claims – will it never end? What puzzles me about people like him and others that still keep coming forward is – why they do it? Is it for self attention bearing in mind the media appears to be far more interested in crazy stories about what happened outside the Air Base, rather than the truths? John's post is still on his Facebook web page dated 28th June 2019, along with a list of UFO sightings.

THE HALT PERSPECTIVE 2

BBC transfers HP Lovecraft drama to site of Rendlesham UFO incident

By Nick Rigby *BBC News East* – **28 December 2019,** podcast based on a 1930 American horror story, has been relocated due to fresh inspiration from "rural English mythology" and an alleged UFO sighting. The *BBC Sounds* drama **The Whisperer in Darkness** incorporates reports by US airmen who claimed to have seen a UFO in Rendlesham Forest, Suffolk in 1980. Writer, Julian Simpson, visited locations in Suffolk with actress Jana Carpenter, before penning the series. His version is loosely based on the novella set in Vermont by HP Lovecraft. Lovecraft's story is about strange sightings in the New England area of the USA .

Graphic novel to celebrate East Anglia's demon dog. How home county inspired MR James trials

The new *BBC* drama tells the story of an investigation into witchcraft, the occult and secret government operations – centred on Rendlesham Forest, which was home to the US airbase of RAF Woodbridge when the alleged "**Rendlesham Forest Incident**" occurred in December 1980. Simpson said there were parallels between Lovecraft's story and the UFO incident – which has never been conclusively explained. The Lovecraft tale is about a guy who lives in the woods. "He's being visited by something – a kind of cosmic horror," he said. "You never find out what is watching him, but there is an inference it is somehow otherworldly. Lovecraft was reading people like Arthur Machen and MR James [who set **a number of his ghost stories in East Anglia**] and was taking in a lot of their rural English mythology and turning it into his own thing." Jana Carpenter, who plays one of the main characters called Kennedy Fisher, said: "*Basically we just got in the car and drove around to all these places that we were thinking of using. We went to Woodbridge, Dunwich, Aldeburgh, Orford. You definitely get the sense that you're in a unique environment and it's not surprising that lots of mythologies can build up in this environment. It still feels disconnected, especially when you go to Orford, you have to drive through the forest to get to it.*" **The disappearance of a character in this drama is aligned to Rendlesham Forest and its 'dark' magic.** This article included a photo of Charles Halt then and now.

THE HALT PERSPECTIVE 2

THE HALT PERSPECTIVE 2

PART 15

HANDSHAKE WITH A MARTIAN WHATEVER NEXT?

2020

JOHN: It's never too late to mention the assistance and support from so many people who were to meet Colonel Halt over the years. The photograph opposite was taken by Torbay student of photography Samuel Fradley, who came to my home address in 2019, and photographed many of my UFO files and material in my possession. In June 2018, Samuel was awarded £2000 as part of the *Santander Graduate Entrepreneurial Bursary Scheme* and founded *The South West Collective of Photography Ltd*, a company dedicated to promoting photography and art across the South West of England and further afield.

He was one of the winners of the British Journal of Photography's Portrait of Britain Prize, and in 2020 was the winner of the Exposure Photography Festival Yearbook Award.

Sam searches for stories that are different, unique and often on the fringe of society, as he believes these make for the most interesting stories. His work also explores other genres of photography, while occasionally focusing on current global events or responding to stories closer to home. Samuel was then currently working on several ongoing projects including "*A Handshake With A Martian*" and "*The White

Lady*". Samuel graduated The University of Plymouth in 2018 with distinction. Sam: *"I was very fortunate and delighted to be selected as the winner of the Exposure Photography Festival YEARBOOK 2020 award."*

Amazon Book: *The Rendlesham Forest UFO Conspiracy* – Nick Redfern

A Close Encounter Exposed as a Top Secret Government Experiment

1st May 2020 Reviews: – 5 star 52%, 4 star 30%, 3 star 9%, 2 star/3 star 4%

Amazon Introduction by Dr. Raymond W. Boeche:

I think you have produced the first truly credible examination of the entire event that is both coherent and correspondent in regard to all of the facts. – Founder and former director of the Fortean Research Center, **Dr. Raymond W. Boeche**

"**The object was hovering on legs**" – "**Something being tested in the area**" – "**A world of trouble**" – "**Minds were manipulated** "

Advertising blurb: In the final days of December 1980, strange encounters and bizarre incidents occurred in the heart of Rendlesham Forest, Suffolk, England. Based upon their personal encounters, many of the military personnel who were present at the time believed that something extraterrestrial came down in those dark woods. What if, however, there was another explanation for what happened four decades ago? What if that explanation, if revealed, proved to be even more controversial than the theory that aliens arrived from a faraway world? The ramifications for the field of Ufology would be immense. In his new, sensational book, Nick Redfern reveals that one of the most famous UFO cases of all time was really a series of **top secret experiments using holograms, mind-control programs, deception, disinformation, conspiracies and cover-ups**. The shocking truth of a forty-year-old mystery is now revealed. *End of blurb.*

Nick Redfern is the author of more than 60 books. They include *Flying Saucers from the Kremlin; The Roswell UFO Conspiracy; Women in Black; Men in Black; Nessie; Chupacabra Road Trip; The Black Diary;* and *365 Days of UFOs*. Nick has appeared on many TV shows, including the National Geographic Channel's *Paranatural*; the SyFy Channel's *Proof Positive*; and the Travel Channel's, *In Search of Monsters*.

Founder and former director of the Fortean Research Center

The Reverend Dr. Raymond W. Boeche has been involved in the study of unexplained phenomena since 1965. He has served as Nebraska State Director for the Mutual UFO Network, on the Board of Advisors for Citizens Against UFO Secrecy, and in various capacities with numerous other organizations around the world, involved in the study of unexplained phenomena. Ray Boeche has delivered juried papers at two MUFON International Symposia; was retained by the University of Nebraska as a consultant to organize, host, and presented research papers at two major international conferences on the unexplained in 1982 and 1983. He has had numerous articles published, as well four books: a collection of his writings, "*An Anthology of the Unexplained*"; "The *Collected Annals of the Journal of the Fortean Research Center*"; "*Bloodless Cuts: The Complete Collected Works of Thomas R. Adams*"; and "*A Time to Stand: When Government Turns Its Back on God.*"

Ray is also well-known as one of the primary investigators of the 1980 Bentwaters (UK) UFO incident. He is also recognized for his extensive work in the areas of animal mutilations, out-of-place animal sightings, and Bigfoot reports, the Men-in-Black phenomenon, and occult religions and philosophies. A graphic artist and book designer with the prestigious University of Nebraska Press for nearly twenty years before retiring, Dr. Boeche holds a B.A. from Peru State College, a Th.M. degree from St. Mark's School of Divinity, and a ThD. from St. Paul Theological College. As a theologian and apologist, Dr. Boeche headed an outreach to the academic community and the 'New Age' movement called **Reasonable Defense"** from 1987 through 1994. His concentrations in apologetics and systematic theology are focused principally on biblical responses to cults and occult practices, paranormal events, religious experience, and working to resolve the false dichotomy created between science and theology, both to the public and the academy. As a pastor and Anglican priest (ordained in the Reformed Episcopal Church) who has served Baptist and Anglican congregations, Dr. Boeche served from 2008 through 2018, as pastor for adult education at one of the nation's largest Lutheran Church – Missouri Synod congregations, in Lincoln, Nebraska.

Dr. Ray Boeche

Dr. Boeche concluded his career as the bereavement coordinator for the oldest hospice service in the state of Nebraska. Now engaged in personal research projects concerning the paranormal, the occult, and the theological ramifications of those activities, Dr. Boeche is working to complete several compilations of research on a number of topics.

Speedy wishes for his recovery!

Ray was diagnosed with mantle cell lymphoma in August 2019. Treatment consists of three days of chemotherapy and immunotherapy once a month for six months which began in October 2019. The fatigue from these treatments is relentless. It has weakened his immune system and threatens with infection to take over. He had a heart attack in 1997 and a bronchial carcinoid tumour in 2001 that claimed most of his right lung. In short, Ray is fighting his lymphoma with one lung, but also with the big heart that he has shared with so many of us.

Flying saucers to pies in the sky!

Charles: I'm sorry to hear of Ray's medical trauma, he's very well respected for his commitment to his parishioners and also his interesting views on the UFO/Paranormal subject, a scholar and gentleman. I wish him well and hope that he makes a speedy recovery.

John Hanson and I, have a lot of respect for Nick Redfern, he is well known and was part of the Staffordshire-run UFO group led by Irene Bott and Graham Allen. John tells me that he has lectured there in the past. He's still waiting for his wooden '***flying saucer'*** model which was presented to the speakers 20 years on! The venue was held in Rugeley and always well attended.

THE HALT PERSPECTIVE 2

Reg Presley, Irene Bott and Elsie Oakensen (rear)

Nick appeared recently on *Coast to Coast*, talking about his latest book about Rendlesham. Nick believes what those witnesses saw that night was not an extraterrestrial UFO, but a man-made object, an intentional mind control experiment, created by humans.

Detailing several elements which informed this hypothesis, Nick revealed there exists a decades-long history of *"secret experiments and highly classified facilities all located less than 11 miles of Rendlesham Forest"*. He brings the reader's attention to a now-declassified 1964 experiment that occurred in a different British forest which saw soldiers surreptitiously given LSD in order to gauge their response to the drug under those conditions. He coupled this with insights about projects aimed at developing *"sophisticated holographic technology"* which can produce imagery that looks incredibly real.

Nick: *"Years ago, when I first heard about this case, my first thought was: mind control, government ops, etc. It seemed obvious to me, and I didn't even know about the proximity of installations nearby that played around with such things as mind control and LSD MK ULTRA type experiments. The plot thickens. I've been saying for decades that much of the UFO phenomena, including abductions, missing time and other high weirdness are the scenarios created by humans. But here's the thing: at the same time, those humans know damn well about the reality of others out there, including various ETs and other non-human entities, terrestrial and non. Manipulating and tapping into these energies is what these humans do."*

At the beginning of his book Nick says that several authors have *"cashed in"* by writing books on Rendlesham. I've read most of them, and some – not all – have made sense. Isn't that what Nick's done? Best of luck to him, at least he hasn't attacked me personally!

Where is the evidence?

I have to say though that Nick Redfern and John Burroughs are barking up the wrong tree here! They appear to have taken a number of random thoughts and ideas from other sources/books, and constructed them into what they believe to be highly likely and plausible. What people don't know or

THE HALT PERSPECTIVE 2

have forgotten is that, before I worked my way up the ranks of the Air Force to Colonel, I spent a lot of time as young man studying chemistry, which was going to be my chosen career, including tear gas to nitro-glycerine. Looking back now maybe I should have opted for the quite life, not knowing in my wildest dreams that, a complete U-turn in career would thrust me into the public eye of the media, now over half a century later! Casting my mind back I remember Bob Graham, Executive Vice President of US Steel asking me about my future plans, after I told him I wanted to be a chemist or chemical engineer. He told me their big libriary was in Duquesne, PA and not far from my grandparents' home and asked if I would be interested in being an intern. I immediately accepted the offer. I learned the routine of all the chemists and filled in for them as they took their summer vacations. Additionally, I worked with the Chief Chemist on a research project trying to find a practical way to extract Germanium from iron ore. I quickly realized that being cooped up in a lab for a career and with luck eventually becoming the Chief Chemist was not what I wanted. Thus, I changed my major to business/economics with a minor in chemistry.

Common sense, never mind the parameters of what would have been needed to set up a holographic projection (especially which could also leave physical evidence) and the development of weaponry based on ball lightning referred to, is totally implausible.

If that was the case why, since the use of such advanced technology implemented as an experiment 40 years ago, do the world's armed forces continue to use conventional weaponry? Which leads me to then wonder if that was a viable option – why wasn't this medium of warfare used to save lives rather than the opposite during the many armed conflicts where lives were lost? The Falklands War, Bombing of Libya, Afghanistan, Panama, Syria, Gulf War, etc…

More seriously if the 'Hallucogenic' weapons were tested on the Bentwaters/Woodbridge guys, then this could have had serious repercussions, not only to the nearby communities but to the Base itself taking into consideration, armaments/fuel stored at the Base! Not forgetting this was at the time of an international crisis. Also we should take into account the energy source required to generate the 'wizard' of all weapons – where was this located? In the forest? How many personnel were required, if so, who were they? It doesn't make logistical sense.

So what is he doing exactly that will convince me otherwise? Nick has written over 60 books and no doubt made a good living; best of luck to him . . . Having said that I was taken aback when he says, he **DOES NOT BELIEVE IN UFO's** anymore! This means everything he has written is flawed and can't be taken as read. At least with regard to possible explanations. As for ball lightning being '*possibly the source*' of UFO reports, well then, tell that to the many people whose accounts are contained within this book.

I'm not going to drag this on because there will always be people who suggest I'm biased, I'm covering up the real truth, or I'm still working with the Government. You want to know the real truth? I wish I did! If I did then you would be the first to know!

The Media love it!

By now the reader, especially the folks who know little about the subject and want to learn, will see that there is a vast difference between, not only the way in which this is written up, but the way in which the Media eagerly seize upon all manner of crazy explanations put forward in a never-ending cacophony of stories that, make no mistake about it, which may – **probably like its Roswell counterpart – still be doing the rounds in 50 years!** At least you have heard my side of things. I dont like being called a liar, and can only at least try and put the record straight, which at the end of the day is all we can do. My conscience is clear.

THE HALT PERSPECTIVE 2

Looking at the Tabloids for May 2020, with regard to their coverage of Nick Redfern's new book, it seems odd that when *The Halt Perspective* was published in 2016, there was minimal interest displayed by the British/US newspapers, despite a Press release being prepared and released by us to many newspapers. WHY this is we don't know. But guess it's because it was based on facts not silly stories and crazy theories.

One newspaper *The Sun*, did cover Nick's release of the book – the coverage paled into mere insignificance compared to the media's interest during December 2020, the anniversary of the incident in Suffolk. Anyway here is what *The Sun* had to say:

***The Sun,* 11th May 2020 – BRITAIN'S most famous UFO sighting was a top secret military mind-bending experiment, it has been claimed.**

QUOTE: For the last 40 years the Rendlesham Forest incident has been regarded as the country's very own Roswell. Troops at two US airbases in Suffolk told how they witnessed strange bright lights for three nights on the trot. Officers carried out sorties and one even claimed to have got close enough to touch a triangular spacecraft. But a new book claims to have solved the 1980 mystery once and for all – and suggests a far more disturbing explanation.

British researcher Nick Redfern says he has uncovered evidence which shows it was part of a trial to weaponise hallucinogens on the battlefield. 'STRANGE LIGHTS' Boffins at secret research lab Porton Down in Wiltshire were allegedly behind the project to manipulate the minds of the enemy. US-based Nick, 55, said: "Based upon their personal encounters, many of the military personnel who were present at the time believed that something extraterrestrial came down in those dark woods. What if, however, there was another explanation for what happened four decades ago?" "**What if that explanation, if revealed, proved to be even more controversial than the theory that aliens arrived from a faraway world**? The ramifications for the field of Ufology would be immense. But I'm certain one of the most famous UFO cases of all time was really a series of top secret experiments using holograms, mind-control programs, deception, disinformation, conspiracies and cover-ups. The shocking truth of a forty-year-old mystery can now be revealed."

"The whole situation was nothing but an incredible, disturbing, series of tests to see just how far the human mind could be manipulated – and how such technologies could potentially, one day, play significant roles on the battlefield."

In his controversial new book – *The Rendlesham Forest UFO Conspiracy* – Nick suggests they used hallucinogens to affect some of the men and advanced holograms to create images of UFOs. The incident took place over three nights between **26th and 28th December** outside the twin Suffolk Air Bases of RAF Woodbridge and RAF Bentwaters.

Military personnel, including the Deputy Base Commander, Col Charles Halt, witnessed strange lights in the forest and hovering above the Bases. The incident sparked questions in the Houses of Parliament but defence chiefs at the time said it was "**of no defence significance**." It has even been suggested that it was a prank launched by the SAS in revenge for a brutal interrogation of one of their men days earlier. Nick, who has written over 40 books on unsolved mysteries, added: "***Clearly, exposing military personnel to advanced hologram-based technology in those woods, and late at night, would have been a perfect way of gauging just how successfully the manufactured visions had achieved their goals. Those goals were: the creation of holographic UFOs that could interact with not just the environment, but with those who were in its presence, too. There's also evidence that at least some of the men were affected by hallucinogens.***" End of Quote.

Charles: I'm not going to labour the point here, I am pleased that John Burroughs eventually obtained his pension and backdated monies. I do not believe that John was exposed to anything manmade; far

THE HALT PERSPECTIVE 2

from it . . . the answer lies in a UFO conundrum that has been plaguing mankind for far too many years. We can't prove what it is and where it comes from.

What we **can prove**, from the very nature of this book, is that for far too long people have had to endure the side effects which can arise from encounters with these anomalous objects. John has built up a large number of reports/encounters which detail all manner of maladies. Of course, such things shouldn't exist in our modern society. Problem is – they do! Do we ignore them at our own risk?

Jim Penniston says: *". . . they were from CIA Langley Research Laboratory. I don't know but whoever they were, what they were doing was on British territory?* How does Jim know, when I didn't? Langley was where Dr 'Kit' Green was stationed – is he alluding to him? Kit told me that he learned about what had taken place shortly after my memo was despatched to the States, but denies strenuously any involvement in what occurred in December 1980, other than what he has already told me, which I accept.

In the book *Encounter In Rendlesham Forest* by Nick Pope with John Burroughs and Jim Penniston, on page 44, published in 2014, Jim says: **"I fully support Colonel Halt on his assessment and there was a cover up (containment) initiated from the outset. Halt is right."**

Burroughs: "(John) Alexander is still following the Company line about what he knows. **Halt seems to be opening up with new details on what he has known for years".** Another accolade from Jim on **page 75** of the same book: **"Colonel Halt was respecting our privacy, as he had guaranteed. Also he believed it would never see the light of the day. I think it said enough."**

I know John Alexander, and while not agreeing with all of his views, remain a good friend. I can see that time, money, effort, along with using a vast power house of scientific intelligence, was used to determine the possibility of being able to influence individual personalities, through the use of mind control – commonly referred to **as weaponization.** But did anything come to fruition? Was it viable, and has it been used? Highly unlikely one would have thought, especially at Rendlesham Forest in December 1980.

CONTACT INTERNATIONAL UFO RESEARCH

John: The Former President of this long running organisation was the **8th Lord Clancarty**.

Other Presidents include **Bernard Delair** and **Ruth Rees**. The current Vice President is **Geoff Ambler**. The organisation includes my dear friend **Margaret Fry**, whose account of what she witnessed in **1955** while living in Bexleyheath, Kent, is included. She is the Welsh representative/Honorary Life member. **Fran Copeland,** is in charge of membership/case files. **Mike Soper** is in charge of Press and Media enquiries. **Website www.contactuforsearch.com**

From their website

CIUFOR was founded in 1967 by the 8th Lord Clancarty, Brinsley le Poer Trench, author of several UFO books written in the 1960-70's period. Brinsley had already created a group called the International Sky Scouts in the early 60's from which **Contact** emerged. As a well known face in Ufology, Clancarty became a media consultant whenever the subject of UFOs was discussed and seemed to have cult followings all over the world. Indeed, as a result 30-50 overseas branches were set up in the 1970's and membership overall was claimed to have reached 11,000.

Fran Copeland

THE HALT PERSPECTIVE 2

The group's magazines **Awareness** and **UFO Register** first appeared in 1968 and remained active up to two years ago when it was decided that only the *Awareness* magazine would continue, which to date, it still does. After a vague editorial start, J Bernard Delair (the current President) was editor of *Awareness* for most of the 1970s. Since 1980 Geoffrey E Ambler (current Vice President) is now actively in the role. The magazine contains general articles on Ufology, sightings and other articles of interest by contributors worldwide.

John: In early January 2021, I spoke to Mike Soper, Press and Media spokesman/Lecturer for the above group which still publish a small informative magazine covering all manner of UFO reports, asking for permission to publish their review of the Nick Redfern book. After an illuminating exchange of views and opinions about the whole subject, Mike agreed. They are a small but very professional UFO organization from the Oxfordshire area and have been the source of valuable information over the last 25 years, much of which has been thoroughly investigated by them.

(Contact UK) *Awareness Magazine, Volume 38, Number 2,* December 2020 LATEST NEWS ITEM on page 3 – RENDLESHAM SOLVED – NO WAY

Editorial review

It was mentioned in the last edition 38/1 that prolific writer on UFOs and the paranormal, Nick Redfern, had just issued a new title, *The Rendlesham UFO Conspiracy*, declared as a top secret government experiment. The gist is that a team of experimental scientist and engineers were dispatched from the infamous **Porton Down** Laboratory near Salisbury, where all sorts of research into chemical and biological weaponry takes place on behalf of the UK Government.

The aim according to the author, was to set up a far reaching experiment in Rendlesham Forest Suffolk, where they would create a massive light display using controlled ball lightning and lasers to attract security patrols from the adjacent Bentwaters USAF Base, who would then be subject to holographic images and sprayed with hallucinogens emitted from aerosols which would falsely generate the impression to the victims that an **alien craft had come down in the forest.**

Arrived in secret Christmas Day

Redfern suggests the team arrived in secret on Christmas Day assuming that few people would be out and about, and set up their equipment to activate late on the next day, Boxing Day. He also assumes few people would be roaming in the forest then – a notion *not* borne out by the evidence that loads of family groups tend to go for walks after a time of great indulgence on Christmas Day.

Rendlesham Forest would be the ideal place to clear heads. **There are absolutely no technical details about the devices set up and where they were positioned.**

In fact it was not until **3am on the 26th of December** that the first encounter took place when a strange glowing object was seen in the forest. The Deputy Base Commander, Colonel Halt, then became involved subsequent to the first experience and found increased levels of radiation at certain points where a supposed landing had taken place. He was also a witness to the second experience which he fully documented two nights later on the 28th of December. **So were the Porton Down crews hanging about in the forest for close on four days dressed in full Hazmat protective suits?** Surely they would have been detected by a greater number of patrolmen out on the second occasion, and even spotted in the day time.

Redfern fails to identify any single person working on the project, or how many there were in total. His evidence comes from snippets of information from other authors' books on Rendlesham, particularly the late Georgina Bruni's investigations. Of course all the authors' attempts to communicate with Porton Down were met with stony silence! Applying some sound logic – the Porton Down Group, if they existed, would want to know the effects on the victims of their very regular activity. A handful of USAF patrolmen made close contact, but their identities would be totally unknown to the hidden observers, and there is no evidence that any of these men were contacted subsequent to their experience.

The stories have been well documented by ufologists over the years – but to nobody at Porton Down that we know of. Redferrn does refer to the times in the *1950's 60's, when service personnel were offered incentives such as extra leave if they would take part in a few 'harmless' experiments involving biological/chemical agents, whose corrosive nature was not fully explained to the volunteers, and at least one person is known to have died. **Would the Porton Down authorities then try out some hare brained plan where they would not even know who had been in contact with chemical weapons and the victims were British citizens?**

It may be true that a team arrived from Porton Down, the day after the first incidents, to monitor radiation and find chemical residues, but not that they were responsible for the whole thing in the first place, as Redfern suggests. After about 50 pages the author appears to suffer from 'mission creep' going over dozens of old UFO cases to somehow verify that they might be caused by the use of **hallucinogens, holograms, or controlled ball lightning**. Any connection to Porton Down, however tenuous, is also picked out as important evidence.

Ralph Noyes

In a Court of law most of this would be thrown out as purely circumstantial. Among the many names mentioned in the text are three that worked for the Defence Ministries, or were involved in Government, namely **Nick Pope and Ralph Noyes.**

None of these gentlemen were able to express a definitive answer to the mystery or indicated they knew more. **Should a senior officer such as Halt,**

---

*The Daily Mail in their edition of the 30th of December 2006, **'New Porton Down Scandal looming** – Further covert operation was carried out by Porton Down scientists for the MOD during the period 1957-1964.' Apparently fearing nerve gas attacks from the USSR at the height of the Cold War, special trials were carried out spraying certain areas of England with a fluorescent compound containing **CADMIUM** (Cd) the idea being to track the movement of fine particles across the country, subsequently as a simulation for nerve gas. It has been known for many years that Cadmium is particularly poisonous to the human body and the cause of cancer. None-the-less Porton Down apparently had no qualms about the health of Joe Public in devising these experiments.

THE HALT PERSPECTIVE 2

who got close up on the second night have been subjected to the hallucinogens that the author insist were used, what might have been the consequence to the control of an airbase housing nuclear weapons?

It is well known that the author originally comes from the Midlands, but is now domiciled in Texas, USA. It is therefore somewhat of a surprise that he is **claiming fresh evidence**. The long bibliography, quoting 150 interviews, books or websites, garners a few nuggets of value from each, **but nowhere is the killer document or confession that proves beyond doubt that the Rendlesham was "a close encounter exposed as a secret Government experiment."**

Daily Mail: Porton Down guilty as charged on this occasion!

REVIEW of the book by Geoff Ambler (abbreviated)

On **Page 29** of the same booklet Geoff Ambler also comments on the '*216 page 9 chapters*' book.

He reminds the reader that Nick has now published **60 books** on the UFO/Paranormal subject, which "*probably indicates that he hasn't spent a lifetime on his research into the one subject. **Redfern fails miserably in this task***. *His claim that a team from the UK biological and chemical warfare laboratory at Porton Down devised the whole plan and went down to the Forest on Christmas Day, 1980, to set up some mind-boggling equipment, takes some believing. There is also a suggestion that **fake radar traces had been implemented** to make it appear that UFOs were present on the nights in question? Having said all of this, the book is easy to read, with chapters subdivided into short sections with separate titles, but which may indicate there is nothing of substance, in this jumping from one subject to another, but plenty of confusion. The overview in this book has been concocted to fit into the 40th Anniversary of the Rendlesham Forest UFOs. It does not look like original research.*"

John: I see no point in discussing this any further the 'writing' is on the wall as far as I'm concerned.

Authors: See page 55 for sighting by Frank Redfern & page 133, PC Perks sighting.

Chill Factor Film – '*Codename Rendlesham*'

Another offering into the public domain of interest with regard to celebrating the 40th Anniversary, was a film, titled '**Codename Rendlesham,** advertised as '**The story of an incredible series of events that took place in Rendlesham Forest in Suffolk, England'** which 'retraces the story from its earliest days of local rumours in Suffolk, through to its current day, "*British Roswell*" status and examines the elements that have made this, one of our great modern legends. English HD 1080 Stereo Rent: English SD 480 Stereo – **Cast Dr David Clarke, John Burroughs. Studio-Chill Factor Films** – **Director Adrian Frearson** Available on *Amazon Prime* and Direct

Advertising blurb: The story of an incredible series of events – that took place in Rendlesham Forest in Suffolk, England. The incident involved USAF personnel in a close encounter with unknown craft at the very perimeter of RAF Woodbridge. Being leased to the USAF at the time the twin

THE HALT PERSPECTIVE 2

bases of RAF Woodbridge and RAF Bentwaters were highly sensitive as they (although denied at the time) housed nuclear weapons. In the last few days of 1980, several security personnel investigated lights in the woods at the end of the runway, believing them to be some kind of downed aircraft. What followed over the next few nights has now become part of UFO legend. Little was known of the case by the wider public until 1983 when, through the FOIA the Halt Memo was released by the US government.

The memo consisted of a brief by Lt.Col. Charles Halt to the M.O.D – outlining the events. This was a sensational story for the media and became headline news in the UK. The case was immediately debunked by skeptics, more participants began to emerge and anybody who was anybody in the UFO community began to speculate. **The dates given in the Halt memorandum for the sightings were later found to be incorrect. It's this confusion in part that has led to widespread confusion about the case and subsequent explanations as to the source of the sightings.** Indeed it's the huge amount of conflicting data, counter claims and the incredible mountains of paper trails that have made this, like the Roswell case, a minefield for any researcher. Arguments between the different camps have added to the haze surrounding this now most embarrassing of episodes for the USAF/MOD. What, if this is true, are the security implications of this? According to the MOD the case was considered to be of no defense interest. Could it be that thousands of man hours have been spent by both governments over the years on what is no more than a group of personnel mistaking a lighthouse, soviet satellite or even a tractor as alien visitors? **End of Blurb.**

John: I've had a look at the Film's trailer, which begins showing two or three people with their metal detectors at the ready before setting out into Rendlesham Forest. A trip in the car and shots of **dead animals lying in the forest** presumably associated with comments back in December 1980 of agitated animals seen by the airmen during their foray into the forest! The peace and tranquility shattered by the **scream of jet fighters soaring overhead**. Mysterious lights seen above the trees, followed by screams and the group running through the wrecked gates of East Gate entrance which has fallen foul to alien attack? Then a crescendo of heavy music and flashing lights more in keeping with the soundtrack of *Alien*. Goodness knows what happens next.

Sensational stories sell! FACTS not FICTION!

Charles: Here is a photo taken of my by John at the Robert C. Byrd Green Bank Telescope in Green Bank, West Virginia, US, the world's largest fully steerable radio telescope. A time to reflect on the vastness of space, and something much closer to home, which continually begs an answer.

The lady guide told us that by the time we picked up a signal from distant worlds out in the depths of the universe, those civilisations may have perished thousands of years ago! It puts things in the right perspective.

Also a time to reflect on the unprecedented amount of letters/post sent to me over the years, from ordinary people who expected answers, despite being based at various places and Countries! I always tried my best to answer these as it was the least I could do. As John has seen I have my own files and paperwork stretching back many years.

THE HALT PERSPECTIVE 2

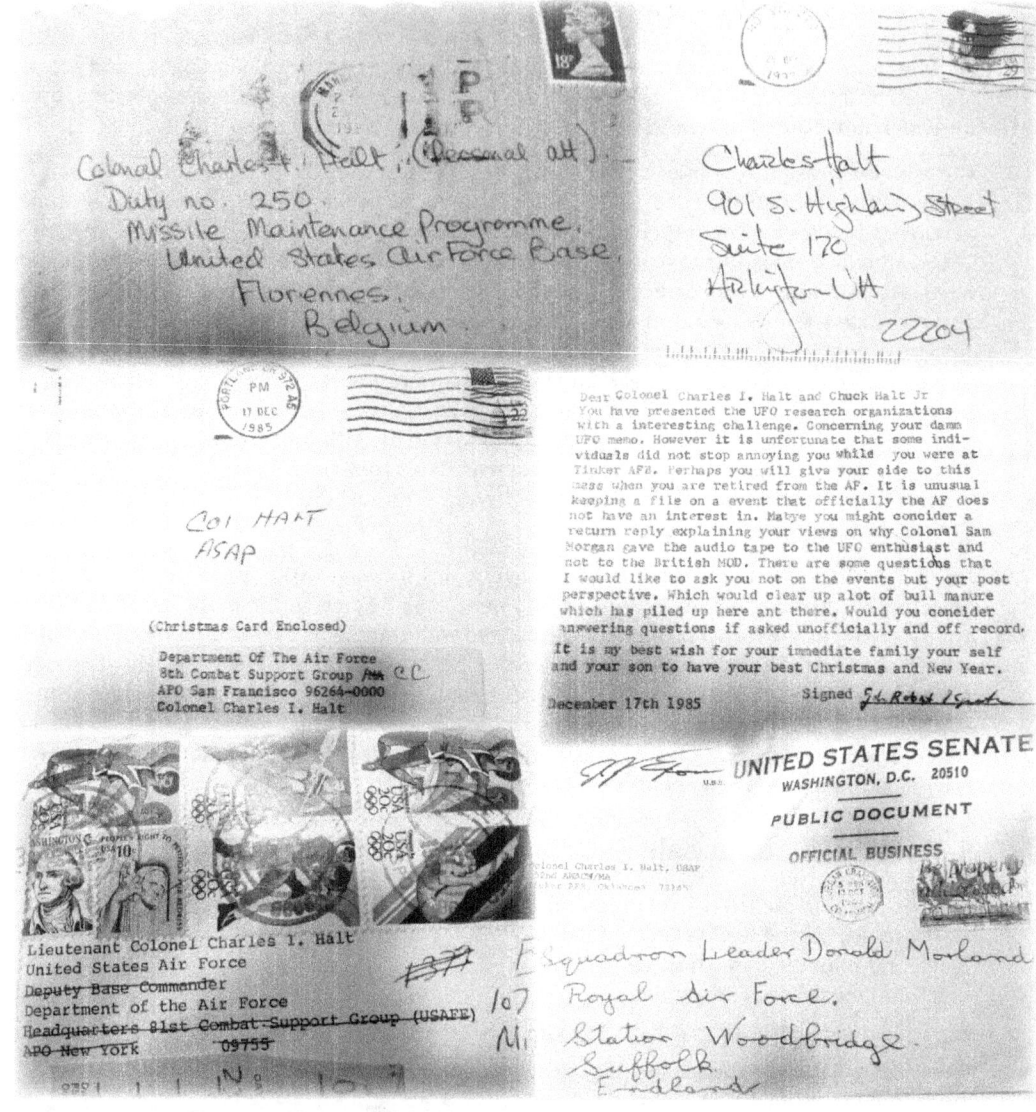

Yes I know that it may be a waste of time trying to correct the gross inaccuracies trotted out time after time by the producers of these films because sensational stories sell. That's life! But each and every offering obfuscates what actually took place and confuses the reader. This will never stop.

Entertainment based on real events is one thing. But when they criticise me well then, their fair game and I have to respond, otherwise people will believe the distortions they publish. I also have a duty to myself and conscience, to ensure that history records, **FACTS rather than FICTION**, otherwise what's the point of this book.

Are we really expected to believe that the **unintentional mistake made by the typist on my memo** was responsible for all of the mayhem that has happened over the last 40 years involving a kaleidoscope of lies and attacks on my character, which has grown in intensity over the last few years? I've never changed what I have said because I'm relying on the truth, rather than, the never ending story of people who were there, and now feel they have to pander to self perceived misconceptions of what they believe the public will want.

The 'blurb' above spouts nonsense – thousands of hours spent by both Governments, over the misidentification of lighthouse, soviet satellite, or tractor! Get real, the public aren't daft they are now realising, that so-called evidence of some of the witnesses is full of loopholes. I've looked at the few reviews on line, and quote: from four people that have watched the film, rather than be accused of being biased!

The only people that know the truth about Rendlesham Forest UFO incident are the people that were there. Documentaries, as a rule, are far too skeptical for my liking – the Lighthouse Theory is so ridiculous and an insult to the intelligence of the witnesses that were there on the night. All the squabbling about who was there, and who was not there and getting the dates mixed up, does not mean a UFO incident didn't happen.

When you get a major UFO incident like Rendlesham all kinds of disinformation will be thrown in to put people off the truth. No wonder **I constantly decline to participate in many documentaries as it's an insult to my intelligence! When they do include for example the object that was seen by Jim, I've seen films where the 'craft' described as being smooth with an absence of exterior imagery, then takes off silently followed by all sorts of telepathic nonsense**. The reality is that over the years many other sightings have happened in this area, as shown!

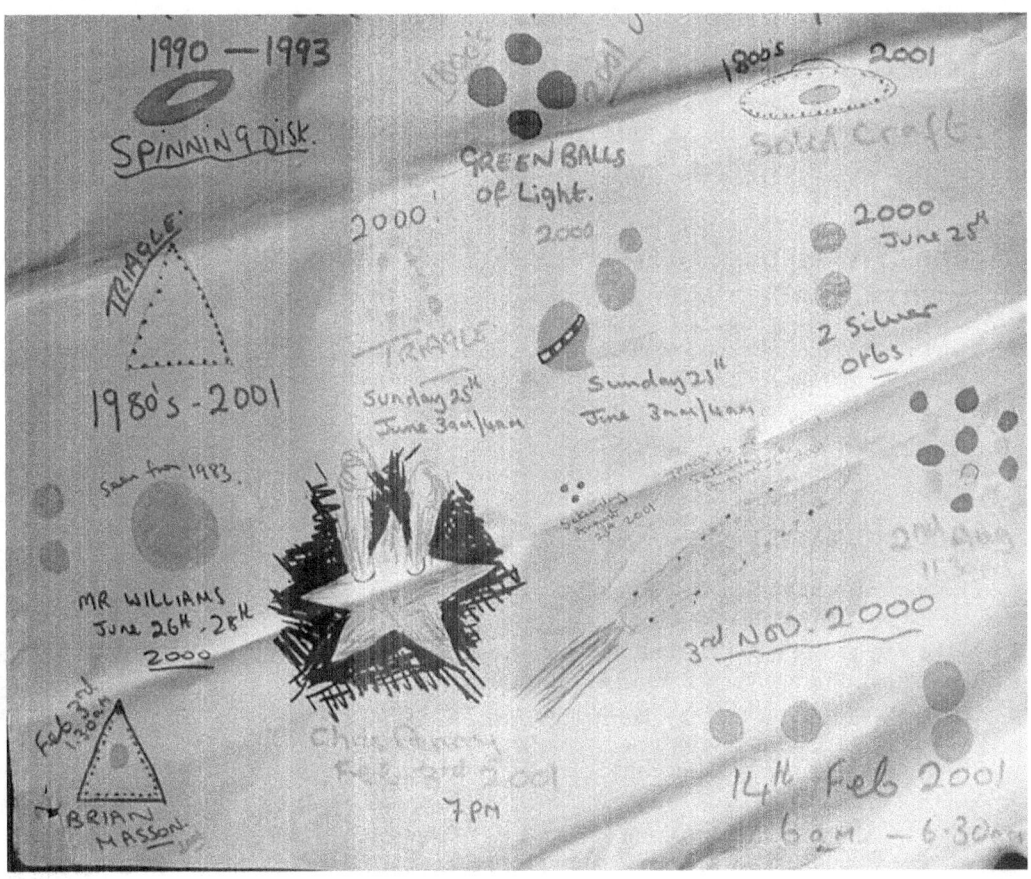

THE HALT PERSPECTIVE 2

As for the John Burroughs' medical issue, which came about through allegations of radiation given off from the UFO, followed by the Government rewarding him with back-dated compensation, best of luck to him. But does it take us any further into identifying the exact nature of what it was that he encountered? Sadly, no.

Now **40 YEARS LATER, in late 2020,** there's been a huge amount of interest, in this incident, culminating in a blitz of books and documentaries, many of which invariably include my tape recorded commentary of what happened on that fateful night, (without even having asked for my permission) used as a backcloth depicting scenarios that had nothing whatsoever to do with what actually happened. Actions orchestrated by a need to excite the imagination of the readers/viewers, anything rather than reality… so many of them this year, just wanting to cash in and make some fast bucks! I've been accused of everything, from associating with the devil to having participated in the second coming of Christ, so you meet some very strange people sometimes in this business, not forgetting the Media's take on all of this – which leaves a lot to be desired. Where do we go from here? I really don't know. I was hoping, maybe, to learn a little more as I have, through the years, prised some more information out of some of the other participants, because they, for very personal reasons, didn't come completely forward on everything; in other words, they were concerned for their career, for their health, for their family – so it's unfortunate things have to be that way – but I think most of you probably understand that.

Did my best to keep what happened from going public!

At the end of the day people should understand that I did my best to keep what happened from going public. It was not career-enhancing and I knew my life would never be the same. Despite my efforts the memo and tape were released. Since then I've been stuck out in the public while my former superiors hid. I've tried to get the real story out, the truth of what occurred, but the Media have made it into a sensational story and misrepresented the facts.

The psychological and physical implications of UFO interaction ignored – why is that?

Looking at the testimonials of those people who have had the misfortune to get too close to a UFO, it appears that on occasion, this *may lead* to something far more serious. Both psychologically and physically, a matter that is, or should be, of great concern to all of us!

Budd Hopkins

I'm not versed in this specialized field of investigation although I knew Budd Hopkins, who was born in Wheeling, West Virginia, well. This is about common sense based on evaluation and analysis of some incredible reports from members of the public who have nothing to gain but great deal to lose by coming forward. Some of the people whom John and I have spoken to over the years who have sighted UFOs particularly at close range would tell of additional strange events of 'high strangeness' that manifested afterwards, but wouldn't realise the possibility of an association with the original UFO incident. This is an opinion corroborated by eminent researchers who maintain the likelihood of a strong association between the paranormal and UFO phenomena.

Whilst we cannot offer any hard evidence that so-called alien beings carry out medical examinations of their human victims, as has been claimed by so many people worldwide, it is clear that this process, which can affect human behavior, is being exerted against the will of the person concerned – by something we have not the faintest clue about! This should concern us all. Often those reports will speak of a forced medical examination of their reproductive system. Abductees sometimes claim to have been warned against environmental abuse and the dangers of nuclear weapons. While many of these experiences are described as terrifying, some have been viewed as pleasurable or transformative. Due to the lack of any substantial physical evidence, most scientists and mental health professionals dismiss the reports of abduction as deception, suggestibility (fantasy-proneness, false-memory syndrome) personality, sleep phenomena, psychopathology, psychodynamics and other environmental factors.

We are not scientists or trained academics in the field of mental health, but we remain curious as to why if this is the answer to allegations of abduction, what part does the UFO sighting take place in all of this, as it is undoubtedly the stimulus required to orchestrate the abduction process? Not forgetting those who do not wish to be regressed but, as time goes by, remember what took place. Often their account is identical to what has been obtained from other witnesses under hypnosis. If UFOs did not exist, then we suppose it would be easier to dismiss such claims. As reported in the *Harvard University Gazette,* in 1992, Dr. John Edward Mack investigated over 800 claimed abductees and spent countless therapeutic hours with these individuals. He declared: *"The majority of abductees do not appear to be deluded, confabulating, lying, self-dramatizing, or suffering from a clear mental illness."*

One cannot ignore the amount of evidence supporting this as fact – enough for John to write three (yet-unpublished) books dedicated to cataloguing all manner of strange effects reported by citizens who have had the misfortune to encounter something that may change their lives forever! If that is not bad enough – sometimes threats are made against UFO witnesses, a fairly common background to a phenomenon which shouldn't exist! There is little doubt that the threats are taken seriously, by those investigating such matters but why aren't these men ever identified…and why aren't the Police involved? I was shocked to read about a farmer whose family was threatened and a message sent to him via his wife to desist interest in UFOs! The majority of people, who report encountering a UFO at fairly close range, don't appear to experience any minor ailments such as tanning of the skin, etc., which appears part and parcel of getting too close to whatever these objects are. Having said that, look at the evidence given by people who have – now, that is worrying – not only to them but ordinary citizens, many of whom don't realise the enormity of what's going on out there. So what the heck is happening and why is nobody, apparently, taking the matter more seriously?

Ted Conrad – Update and Memo

When I talked with Gordon Williams, neither he nor Conrad wanted their name mentioned with the incident. So I was directed to speak to Donald Moreland and see what he wanted as it was to become a 'British affair.' I did so and he asked for a memo. I wrote it and it was typed by Conrad's secretary.

The memo was then shown to Gordon Williams. He or his office, without my knowledge, then gave a copy to the AFOSI/CIA. Actually, it had to be Williams as I kept in touch with his former Executive Officer who had no knowledge of the memo until it went public. **(It was never meant for public dissemination.)**

Williams said he never saw it and would not have let it out– **this is not true!** Obviously, what happened internally is dealt with internally; you all know how my memo was released! But I can assure you I was not disciplined for speaking to the Press during the time I was still serving. At the end of the day, if nothing else, the order shows the concern felt by the authorities who were concerned on the stark fact that we couldn't and can't defend ourselves from something which still puzzles us to this very day.

Conflicting statements

Through the years Conrad has made conflicting statements about the events. First he said he hadn't gone outside to have a look in the sky. He never saw anything! **Apparently he doesn't remember talking to me on the radio about seeing the UFO sending beams of light onto the Base**.

In March, 1983, on page 115, Conrad was interviewed for an article in *OMNI Magazine*, titled *UFO UPDATE*. He describes the first incident and concludes: *"Those lads saw something but I don't know what it was."* Now he's smearing those involved. It's pretty clear there was a very intense confrontation with something in the Forest. **Does Conrad want to talk about how the airmen were then subjected to mind control efforts using drugs and hypnosis by the British and American authorities?**

What happened to me and the other airmen in Rendlesham Forest in 1980 has also been the occasional target of thinly-veiled disbelief by people who haven't a clue about the REALITY of what has occurred over the many years since it happened. Incredibly, even now, I am continually challenged by people who wish to bring various inconsistencies to my attention surrounding the background of this incident, which includes questions of debrief, claims of a structured craft, Bustinza's ever-changing role in the proceedings. It never stops! With all due respect, who out there can remember *exactly* what took place in their lives that length of time ago in a darkened forest? Or what was said during a highly emotional situation involving the presence of something or someone whose identity has never been satisfactorily explained? I recorded what had transpired on a tape recorder and later wrote a memo from memory of the event.

Leslie Kean

At the beginning of this book I mentioned my good friends, Leslie Kean and Budd Hopkins .Not many people know that Leslie Kean is the daughter of environmentalist and philanthropist Hamilton Fish Kean and the granddaughter of Congressman Robert Kean. Leslie has published works relating to UFOs since 2000, and has been a guest on *Coast to Coast AM*. Her book **UFOs: Generals, Pilots and Government Officials Go On The Record,** published by *Penguin* Random House, was a *New York Times* best seller. Three distinguished men wrote first-hand accounts about incidents for Kean's book. They were joined

by Air Force generals and a host of high-level sources – including **Fife Symington III, former governor of Arizona** and Nick Pope.

Her book was translated and published in China, France, Taiwan, Brazil, Germany, Romania, Croatia, Vietnam, Bulgaria, and Serbia. A Spanish edition was released in 2017.

John Podesta, longtime Presidential Counselor and chair of the 2016 Hillary

Clinton Presidential Campaign, wrote in the foreword for Kean's book: "*The time to pull the curtain back on this subject is long overdue.*" Describing himself as *"a curious skeptic"* who understands the difference between fact and fiction, he said the American people "*want to know, and they can handle the truth.*"

Leslie Kean belongs to the UFO organization UFODATA.

In 2016 she wrote she was "privileged to welcome" **Christopher Mellon, the former Deputy Assistant Secretary of Defense for Intelligence in the Clinton and Bush administrations, into the organization.**

On 16 December 2017, the *New York Times* featured an article written by Helene Cooper, Ralph Blumenthal and Kean, which revealed the fact that the **US Department of Defense had spent $22.5M on a secret program titled the Advanced Aerospace Threat Identification Program that investigated UFOs.**

THE HALT PERSPECTIVE 2

A picture paints a thousand words!

PART 16

ROYALTY AND THE UK MEDIA CELEBRATES THE 40TH ANNIVERSARY!

2020

ON November 20th 2020, The *Sun* newspaper printed a story about HRH Prince Philip. Under the headline '***EXCLUSIVE***', accompanied by a ridiculous, illustration showing Prince Philip on the right, a Corgi dog in the middle, flying in the beam of a 'flying saucer', with what looks like the alien out of *ET* to the left, endorsed with the words **'ET Throne Home'** – quote: Prince Philip has library of books on UFOs & aliens.

One can only despair, again and again – so what if he does?! Surely the weight of the evidence presented in this book, covering over 25 years of research into the subject – which forms a tiny part of the colossal number of sightings worldwide – should be taken with seriousness rather than the never-ending way the media present their take on the UFO subject?

It's clear that behind the scenes of official secrecy, and also the Palace, the Air Force views reports of UFOs seriously, never mind the majority of people who now seek an answer to a conundrum that has been with us for a long time!

THE HALT PERSPECTIVE 2

PRINCE Philip is an avid reader of books about UFOs and aliens.

The Duke of Edinburgh, 99, has spent decades building up his collection.

His interest was sparked by his uncle Lord Mountbatten, who wrote an official report about an alien in a silver spaceship landing on his estate.

Philip spent last summer reading The Halt Perspective, revealing the inside story of Britain's Rendlesham Forest incident.

Troops at two US airbases in Suffolk witnessed strange bright lights for three nights running from December 26 1980.

Officers carried out sorties and one even claimed to have got close enough to touch a triangular spacecraft.

The book was co-written by retired US Air Force Col Charles Halt, who was the base deputy commander at the time, and retired West Midlands detective John Hanson. In a letter to

EXCLUSIVE by PAUL SIMS

Mr Hanson, the Duke's private secretary Brigadier Archie Miller-Bakewell wrote: "I am certain it will be read with close interest over the summer."

After receiving another book – Haunted Skies: The Encyclopedia of British UFOs – the Duke's right-hand man replied: "His Royal Highness will add this copy to his collection.

"It will make a most welcome addition to his library."

Last night Mr Hanson said: "Why shouldn't any sensible person have an interest in a phenomena that has baffled mankind for millennia?"

Lord Mountbatten kept his extraterrestrial interests a secret.

But after his death in 1979, a report he filed in 1955 was uncovered.

It told how his bricklayer Fred Briggs had a close encounter on his Broadlands estate in Romsey, Hants.

paul.sims@the-sun.co.uk

Lord Louis Mountbatten of the *Kelly* RIP

Picking up the thread of earlier comments made about Lord Louis Mountbatten, on page 75 and page 82 of this volume, it's of value to refresh the memory of the reader about a sighting which took place in the mid to the late 1950's, involving a matter that was brought to the attention of Prince Philip's maternal uncle, Lord Louis Mountbatten, who was my ex-father-in-law Ted West's friend and Captain aboard HMS Kelly.

This involved an allegation by odd job and repair man NCO Sergeant Briggs, who was employed at Broadlands, the house of Lord Louis, at Romsey, Hampshire. In a statement which was later brought to Lord Louis' attention, Briggs tells of being on his way to work on his bicycle when he saw a large disc-shaped object descending in front of him over a small dell or depression about 100 yards from the house. Although no date was given one presumes that it was winter as snow was on the ground. Sgt Briggs moved towards the object which he described as being 40-60 feet in diameter, now hovering above the dell, some 30-50 feet off the ground. A 'trap door' opened and a portion of the underside of detached itself and floated to the ground.

On this stood a 'man' about 5'6" tall: *"He had fair or silvery hair, wearing blue overalls or a close fitting garment. Seeing me he appeared to change his mind and retreated into the object. I noticed that the 'platform' on which the man had been was suspended from the object by a long metal rod or piston."* At this stage according to Desmond Leslie, who interviewed Mr. Briggs, a green light or 'cow catcher' came on and knocked the witness and his bike to the ground before moving away.

It's odd that Desmond, who published this account in *FSR* Volume 26 No 5, January 1981, didn't include the full name of the witness, and date of the incident? Although he told of an interview being conducted with Mr. Briggs and a copy of the statement handed to him afterwards, which is obviously the one below complete with an illustration of the object.

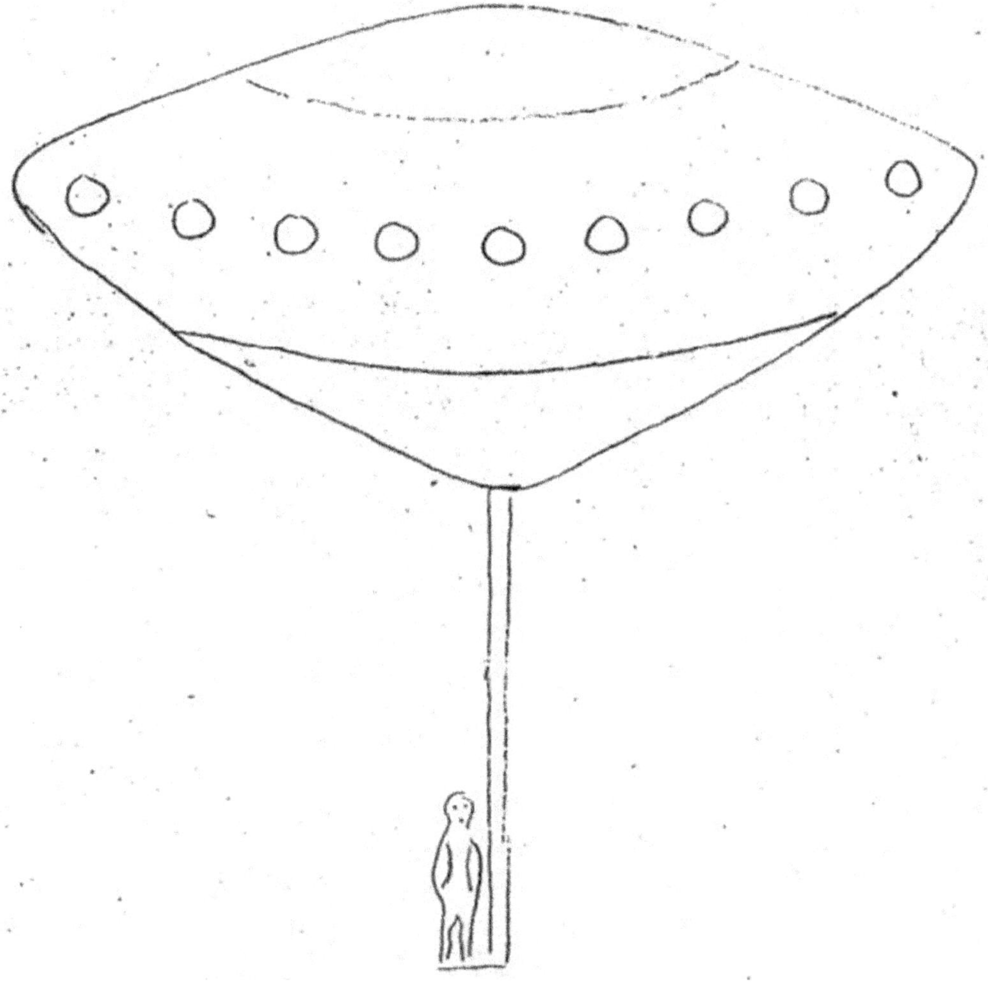

THE HALT PERSPECTIVE 2

The statement from the Broadlands Archive identifies the date as the **23rd of February 1955,** and the witness **Frederick Briggs** of 8 Chamber Avenue. Unfortunately no photographs were taken of the marks in the snow. There is no reason to dispute that Lord Louis showed photographs of UFOs to Mr. Briggs – why not? – He was, after all, irrespective of rank and standing in the community, like the rest of us, wondering what lay behind reports of this nature that still continue to baffle us over 60 years later!

Broadlands was originally named **BRODELANDS** and was the home of Romsey Abbey, founded by the daughter of King Edward the Elder (870-879) – there is little doubt in our opinion that where the incident happened is of importance as many sightings of inexplicable phenomena occur over ancient sites.

Statement by Frederick S. Briggs, 8, Chambers Avenue, Romsey, Hants.

I am at present employed at Broadlands as a bricklayer and was cycling to my work from Romsey on the morning of Wednesday, the 23rd February 1955. When I was about half way between the Palmerston or Romsey Lodge and the house, just by where the drive forks off to the Middlebridge Lodge, I suddenly saw an object hovering stationary over the field between the end of the gardens and Middlebridge drive, and just on the house side of the little stream.

The object was shaped like a child's huge humming-top and half way between 20ft. or 30ft. in diameter.

Its colour was like dull aluminium, rather like a kitchen saucepan. It was shaped like the sketch which I have endeavoured to make, and had portholes all round the middle, rather like a steamer has.

The time was just after 8.30 a.m. with an overcast sky and light snow on the ground.

I turned off the drive at the fork and rode over the grass for rather less than 100 yards. I then dismounted, and holding my bicycle in my right hand, watched.

While I was watching a column, about the thickness of a man, descended from the centre of the Saucer and I suddenly noticed on it, what appeared to be a man, presumably standing on a small platform on the end. He did not appear to be holding on to anything. He seemed to be dressed in a dark suit of overalls, and was wearing a close fitting hat or helmet.

At the time the Saucer was certainly less than 100 yards from me, and not more than 60ft. over the level where I was standing, although the meadow has a steep bank at this point, so that the Saucer would have been about 80ft. over the lower level of the meadow.

As I stood there watching, I suddenly saw a curious light come on in one of the portholes. It was a bluish light, rather like a mercury vapour light. Although it was quite bright, it did not appear to be directed straight at me, nor did it dazzle me, but simultaneously with the light coming on I suddenly seemed to be pushed over, and I fell down in the snow with my bicycle on top of me. What is more, I could not get up again. Although the bicycle only weighs a few lbs. it seemed as though an unseen force was holding me down.

Whilst lying on the ground I could see the tube withdrawn quickly into the Saucer, which then rose vertically, quite as fast as the fastest jet aircraft I have seen, or faster.

There had been no noise whatever until the Saucer started to move, and even then the noise was no louder than that of an ordinary small rocket let off by a child on Guy Fawkes Night.

It disappeared out of sight into the clouds almost instantaneously, and as it went, I found myself able to get up. Although I seemed to be lying a long time on the ground I do not suppose, in reality, it was more than a few seconds.

The attached statement was dictated by Mr. Briggs to Mrs. Travis on the morning of the 23rd February 1955 at my request.

My own electrician, Heath, reported his conversation and I subsequently interviewed Mr. Briggs, with my wife and younger daughter, and as a result of his account, Heath and I accompanied him to the place from which he saw the Flying Saucer.

We followed the marks of his bicycle in the snow very easily, and exactly at the spot which he described the tracks came to an end, and foot marks appeared beside it. Next to the foot marks there were the marks of a body having fallen in the snow, and then the marks of a bicycle having been picked up again, there being a clear gap of 3ft. between where the front wheel marks originally ended and then started again. The rear wheel marks were continuous but blurred. From then on the bicycle tracks led back to the drive.

The bicycle tracks absolutely confirm Mr. Briggs' story, so far as his own movements are concerned.

He, Heath and I searched the area over the spot where the Flying Saucer was estimated to have been, but candidly we could see no unusual signs.

The snow at the bottom of the meadow had melted much more than that at the top, and it would have been difficult to see any marks.

This statement has been dictated in the presence of Heath and Mr. Briggs, and Heath and I have carefully read Mr. Briggs' statement, and we both attest that this is the exact story which he told us.

Mr. Briggs was still dazed when I first saw him, and was worried that no one would believe his story. Indeed, he made a point of saying that he had never believed in Flying Saucer stories before, and had been absolutely amazed at what he had seen.

He did not give me the impression of being the sort of man who would be subject to hallucinations, or would in any way invent such a story. I am sure from the sincere way he gave his account that he, himself, is completely convinced of the truth of his own statement.

He has offered to swear to the truth of this statement on oath on the Bible if needed, but I saw no point in asking him to do this.

Mountbatten of Burma

I confirm that I have read and agree with the above statement.

R K Heath

THE HALT PERSPECTIVE 2

This incident was going to have been published on the front page of the *Sunday Graphic,* but it was cancelled, after a change of mind by the editor (James Gordon McKenzie) who wrote in his letter to Mr. Briggs that *"... it was a marvelous story, what a shame they had to change their minds."* One can only wonder who took the decision not to publish? Could it have been anything to do with Mr. James Gordon McKenzie's interview with the Queen Mother in 1947, as the *Press and Journals* London's Editor? Was pressure put on him?

On a personal footnote I would like to include a photo of Ted's wife, **Winnie,** who is shown with Able Seaman Rocky Wilkins's wife also on the *Kelly* and a great friend of my ex-father-in-law. She is stood next to Lord Louis Mountbatten. This was taken a short time after my father-in-law's death.

Christine Smith who is living in California, the daughter of 'Ted' is shown with Prince Charles in the 1970's at a 'Kelly' reunion in London.

THE HALT PERSPECTIVE 2

H.M.S. KELLY - MALTA - 1941

THE HALT PERSPECTIVE 2

Vanity Fair US magazine covers this incident

This incident was 'resurrected' to the public's attention on the **25th November 2020,** when, the US publication *Vanity Fair*, a monthly magazine covering, culture, fashion and current affairs, told its readers…

Prince Philip is apparently very into reading about aliens

Quote: The royal has reportedly "spent decades collecting a library of books" on the subject of close encounters. By Emily Kirkpatrick. Like all good *X-Files* fans, **Prince Philip** knows that "the truth is out there," which is why the royal has reportedly spent decades preparing himself for a close encounter of the third kind by compiling a library of books on the subject. According to *The Sun*, it was Philip's uncle Lord Mountbatten who first sparked his interest in the subject of extraterrestrials. Mountbatten wrote an official report about a flying saucer landing on his Broadlands estate in Romsey, Hampshire after it was spotted by bricklayer Fred Briggs in February 1955. According to the report, which was kept secret until after his uncle's death in 1979, Briggs claims that he saw a flying saucer hover above the ground and a man dressed in overalls and a helmet emerge before he was knocked off his bike and held to the ground by an "unseen force."

Last summer, the husband of **Queen Elizabeth** also reportedly brushed up on his knowledge of alien sightings by reading *The Halt Perspective* about the Rendlesham Forest Incident which took place over the course of three nights beginning on December 26, 1980 near Suffolk, England. The book chronicles the series of UFO sightings and unexplained lights that took place on two U.S. airbases on those nights, with one officer even claiming he was close enough to touch the spacecraft.

In a letter to one of the co-authors of the book, retired West Midlands detective **John Hanson**, Philip's private secretary *****Brigadier Archie Miller-Bakewell** reportedly wrote, "I am certain it will be read with close interest over the summer." After receiving another book on the topic— *Haunted Skies: The Encyclopedia of British UFOs* – Miller-Bakewell again replied, "His Royal Highness will add this copy to his collection. It will make a most welcome addition to his library." When asked about this recent revelation of the Prince's interest in his book, Hanson told the outlet, **"Why shouldn't any sensible person have an interest in a phenomenon that has baffled mankind for millennia?"** End of quote.

John: Once I naively thought that journalists were like police detectives, eager to establish the truth of what had happened. I now realise that this is not the case, and that their aim is to headline something which is calculated to entice and engage the reader into sharing the content of the article. That's how it works. Stories about UFO encounters, especially involving Royalty captures the imagination. The majority of the population wouldn't realise in their wildest dreams that these are not singular incidents. Should the real truths behind many amazing and quite frightening incidents involving the appearance of unidentified flying objects that cruise our air space with apparent impunity be taken seriously, then there is a problem…

Looking back through the extensive files and checking *Haunted Skies Revised Volume 1* the reader whould be made aware of a multitude of sightings of all manner of strange objects seen by the public and, on occasions, chased by the RAF – frightening in its implications and completely ignored by the media – probably because there is no logical explanation.

---

*One of the longest serving Private Secretary is Brigadier Archie Miller-Bakewell who has worked for the Duke of Edinburgh since 2010, and occasionally represents Prince Philip at events. No photographs are available of this man, which seems odd understanding his illustrious army career. There are Miller-Bakewell entries on face book, but no Archie…. The internet is full of gossip and speculation, about the Princes previous secretary Mike Parker…ex Royal Navy. LT Commander John Michael Avison Parker, CVO, AM, who the media alleges was involved in all manner of salacious activities. Maybe this is the reason why little in fact hardly anything is known about the current secretary? One bitten twice shy?

THE HALT PERSPECTIVE 2

John Lennon summarised the situation nicely: *"If the masses started to accept UFOs it would profoundly affect their attitudes towards life, politics, everything. It would threaten the status quo. Whenever people come to realise that there are larger considerations than their own petty little lives, they are ripe to radical changes on a personal level which would eventually lead to apolitical resolution in society as a whole."*

December 25th 2020 – The *Sun* newspaper lifts the lid!

On the **25th December 2020,** the *Sun* Newspaper (on line) tells us the following: 'TODAY marks the 40th anniversary of the UK's most sensational UFO encounter. Here, a former Ministry of Defence UFO investigator lifts the lid on the case that has been called Britain's Roswell Incident. The article does no such thing, it merely leads us through the original incident, showing pictures of the persons involved with comments by Nick Pope.

December 26th 2020 – *The Star* newspaper

Britain's Roswell' witnesses describe glowing UFO 'like scene from *Star Trek*' 40 years on. EXCLUSIVE: On Boxing Day, 1980, US Air Force servicemen claim they saw a UFO hovering over Rendlesham Forest, next to an American-occupied Base in Suffolk. Investigators say it remains one of the most credible sightings of an other worldly craft.

Reporter, Charles Wade-Palmer**: QUOTE:** A UFO investigator firmly believes an incident dubbed 'Britain's Roswell' represents credible proof of extra-terrestrial life after speaking to those who witnessed the phenomena. This Boxing Day marks 40 years since the scenes, described as being like *"something from Star Trek",* played out in Rendlesham Forest, next to US Air Force base in Suffolk.

Philip Mantle, former Director of Investigations for the British UFO Research Association, has interviewed several witnesses, including US servicemen. He is convinced that what they saw on December 26, 1980, **should be considered as a strong case for proof of aliens travelling to Earth.** Speaking exclusively to *Daily Star*, *Flying Disk Press* publisher Philip said what makes it so credible is the fact it was at an important nuclear base and seen by US Air Force personnel. Philip said: *"On Christmas night, they've all had their dinner they're all full. Lights were seen in the forest, so they sent a security detail of three officers to investigate claims people had seen a UFO land in the forest. Subsequent night, it returned, and this time the deputy base Commander Lieutenant Colonel Charles Holt gathered a small team."* He too went into the forest and also took his little dictaphone and they too encountered a whole host of phenomena, most of which he captured in segments on his dictaphone. Colonel *****Holt** wrote a memo which he sent to the MOD and to his superiors in the Air Force back in the States, and that memo surfaced three years later under the Freedom of Information Act in America – we didn't have one at the time. One or two people had come forward but once the memo was out, the story broke. Since that story, of course, a lot of people who were there have gone on the record with what they saw, as well as the civilians around the base that night that also saw things. Because of what the base was – a nuclear facility – A10 tank busters were there. It was on the frontline against the Soviet Union – in December, 1980, the Soviet military. It wasn't some backwater posting in a little village in Suffolk – it was a sensitive base."

[Charles Halt**: They STILL get my name wrong!]**

Retired USAF Security Police officer Steve Longero told Philip he remembered "reddish fluorescent" lights before they disappeared "like something from Star Trek". Steve said: *"They looked like fluorescent coloured lights, like red and green, glowing lights, just hovering over the treetops, and it was just like an eye that was almost following everybody."* The extraordinary event lasted between 10 and 15 minutes, he recalled. Steve continued: *"It was real kind of quiet and, you know, this thing hovering over the trees, you were like kind of tracking it . . . like: 'What is this?' It was following, like, watching us. That's what it looked like to us. It seemed like something watching us. From what I remember it was aglow. It was really glowing like a reddish, greenish light. It looked like something that was really hot and it was just glowing.*

I remember we had little briefing and everybody was just like...we just could not believe what we were seeing. Your adrenalin was flowing, and I remember people saying, 'What is that?' And then, as people were getting close to this thing, it kind of came nearer to us and then it would go forward and then go back and all of a sudden it just disappeared, like something out of Star Trek.

It was warp speed and we were all, 'What was that?' Then it was gone and that's when they started doing their investigations. After we secured the area they said okay, you're gone, get out of here."

Steve told how he and fellow colleagues could not stop talking about what had just happened until a superior ordered them to quit. He added: *"I think it was something not from this world. Just because the way it hovered and just the way it disappeared. That's what I think – that's what I've always thought."* End of quotes.

Charles: Although I have answered this previously, in view of yet another wrongful claim, may I state that Steve was posted in the Charlie Area and was not, according to other cops, including his supervisor, in the forest the first night. He definitely was not working or in the forest the night I was out (the third night). More nonsense that probably leads back to Warren, and his request made to several cops to put him in the story. Another 'wannabee'. He has the first and third nights wrong. There were no 'lightalls' in the forest the first night, as he claims. He was on duty the first night but according to Jim Penniston (his supervisor) was not in the forest.

Jim Penniston was recently asked to verify this and confirmed Steve was on post on the Base, not in the forest. He was not working the third night so he couldn't have seen me, as he claims.

Warren was in the dorm drinking with others in a makeshift bar the first night, so another "story". Since Steve was Cabansag's roommate he probably picked the story up from him and Warren. It seems every security cop on Base wants to paint himself into the action.

BBC **News – 26th December 2020: Nick Rigby, Rendlesham Forest UFO: 40 years on from the legendary sightings – Forty years ago, a remote forest in Suffolk was the scene of one of the most famous purported UFO sightings in history. So just what did happen, and will we ever know for sure? QUOTE**: Vince Thurkettle was out chopping wood one morning in Rendlesham Forest in late December 1980 when a car drew up. Out stepped two men, aged about 30, dressed in suits. *"Good morning. Do you mind if we ask you some questions?"* asked one, in a well-spoken English accent. Earlier, on 26 and 28 December, United States Air Force (USAF) security personnel stationed at nearby RAF Woodbridge had reported seeing strange lights in the surrounding forest. Forestry worker Mr Thurkettle's unannounced – and unidentified – visitors asked if he had been out the previous night. "I said, 'No,'" he recalls. "They said *'Did you leave the house at all? Did you see anything*?' I said: 'What?'" They said *'Oh, there's a report of some red lights in the forest... We're just checking.'* And the two of them, very politely but firmly, asked me probably about 20 questions. I thought they were journalists. They suddenly said *'Oh well, fair enough. There's probably nothing in it.'* and left. So, I bought the papers every day for the next few days to find out what was going on and, of course, there was nothing. Three years later, however, the sighting made the front page of the *News of the World* after a memo by RAF Woodbridge Deputy Base Commander Lt. Col. Charles Halt, to the Ministry of Defence (MoD), describing an encounter with an apparent UFO in the forest, was released by the US government. Since then, the sighting has been the source of much debate and speculation among UFO enthusiasts and the subject of numerous books, articles and TV programmes.

THE HALT PERSPECTIVE 2

In March, a documentary concluded the sighting **had achieved "legend" status**, like **Loch Ness or King Arthur**. Mr. Thurkettle says the UK authorities have said they did not learn about the incident until Halt's memo. But the memo was not written until two weeks after he received his visit, he says. "So someone must have told them before." Only after the visit did Mr. Thurkettle began to hear rumours of a UFO sighting in the forest. Even has its own official UFO trail, complete with a life-size replica of a flying saucer. He begged his boss to show him the scene, but when he got there, "my heart absolutely plummeted", he says. "It was nothing. It was an absolutely normal glade in the forest with three rabbit scrapes, and they're all carefully marked, that happened to be roughly in a triangle," he says. "I mean, there was a ring of sticks around it, marking it. And I think, fair-do's to the Americans. If they'd been out at night and saw a light and came back in the daytime looking for something, I could totally understand why they... said 'This must be it.'" As a 'countryman born and bred', however, he saw nothing unusual. "It was a completely natural glade. And they've said things like 'But there were broken branches.' Well, the forest is full of broken branches. They saw burn marks on the trees. They said 'Obviously there was heat radiating out from the spacecraft and it burnt these trees.' But it wasn't. It was one of the rangers, Bill Briggs, with an axe." Mr Thurkettle, now 64, was one of the first people to suggest an alternative theory to explain the sighting. It took place, he says, in the only part of the forest where it was possible to see the since-dismantled Orfordness Lighthouse.

"It's weird because you've got a slightly sloping patch of Rendlesham Forest. Then, probably a couple of miles, then Gedgrave Hill. And there was a gap in the trees on Gedgrave Hill, then eight miles or whatever to Orfordness Lighthouse." UFO believers have talked to lighthouse keepers who said 'It never beamed towards the land'. And I think 'Rubbish'. I've stood in the beam of the lighthouse. I've looked at it and the forest." **But who were Mr Thurkettle's *mysterious visitors? He isn't sure, but he gets annoyed when people assume he is claiming to have been visited by the fabled "Men in Black", who, it is said, interrogate and harass UFO eyewitnesses**. "I say 'Oh, that isn't what I'm saying. I'm telling you that the chronology which is part of this story – it's wrong.'"

Journalist and academic Dr David Clarke, whose requests led to the MoD's file on the Rendlesham incident being released, says the most "logical explanation" was that Mr. Thurkettle's visitors were local newspaper reporters, who had possibly learned of the incident from local police.

He says the original sighting by USAF security guards has not been fully explained.

"There is still an element of mystery. What happened to those three guys on the first night I still find baffling. Maybe they did see something that was inexplicable," he says

One of those guards was John Burroughs. He went to investigate the sighting, and says he first saw a beacon in the distance in the forest with green, red, orange and white lights. As he and his colleagues approached, Mr Burroughs says they saw a white light silently explode and then a red, oval, sun-like object in the clearing. It lifted up through the trees and shot back towards the coast. Mr Burroughs, who served in the US armed forces for 27 years, says: "It's been a crazy 40 years [since the encounter]. Just when you think the story is over, another thing happens." This month he has published a new book – *Weaponization of an Unidentified Aerial Phenomenon* – in which he outlines research that, he says, shows the incident was caused by experiments in harnessing an energy field in the forest. "They were studying the energy field for different applications to include military use," he says.

Mr Burroughs claims the lighthouse was "emitting EM (electromagnetic) frequencies towards Rendlesham Forest". He stresses: "I never went on the record to say it was [a spaceship] because I didn't know." What he saw was some sort of energy or "plasma which could be a form of intelligence", he says.

*Authors: These two men were tracked down and identified, they had been sent by Air Marshall Victor Goddard to conduct an investigation into the claims. – all in the *Halt Perspective* book.

THE HALT PERSPECTIVE 2

Writer, **Brenda Butler, of Leiston, Suffolk**, has been amused by some of the UFO tourism that has grown up around the forest. "You realise we've got eight landing sites down here," she says.

"Everybody has got their own take on it. If you go down there with any of the witnesses, they'll take you to somewhere else." Ms Butler, who co-wrote the 1986 book on the case *Sky Crash*, believes the US may have recovered a Russian satellite. "It has got to be something to do with the Americans or the Russians or the Cold War," she says. "There are loads of files still to be released, but there has been such a big cover-up, nobody will ever know what happened. I'd like to get to the bottom of it all but I guess we never will." **End of quotes.**

Daily Mail 2.1 2021

Has the riddle of Britain's true-life X-File finally been solved? A revenge prank by SAS troopers on US soldiers is likely to be behind 'UFO' that landed on nuclear base

The Rendlesham Forest incident began 40 years ago on December 26, 1980

Air Force colonel witnessed something that couldn't possibly be of earthly origin

Lt Colonel Charles Halt was willing to stake his military reputation on that fact

Has the riddle of Britain's true-life X-File finally been solved? A revenge prank by SAS troopers on US soldiers is likely to be behind 'UFO' that landed on nuclear base

[Followed by a lengthy overview of what had taken place. This is a just a short extract]

Halt said: '. . . but I do know whatever we saw was under intelligent control.' For the next 40 years, UFO believers and sceptics would argue furiously about what happened on those two nights. The details did not become public at once, but leaked out slowly. In October 1983, the now-defunct *News Of The World* tabloid obtained a copy of Halt's report and published extracts on its front page under the headline, 'UFO Lands In Suffolk – And That's Official'.

Two years later, a sceptical *Guardian* journalist investigated and concluded that what the airmen had seen must have been the **beam of the Orfordness lighthouse, five miles away.** Seen from one angle, the light appears to track through the trees, winking at just above ground level. The lighthouse also has two red lights mounted on aerials. **According to this theory, the depressions left in the ground by the UFO's tripod feet were in reality rabbit holes, and the scorch marks on trees were left by foresters. The malfunctioning radios were put down to ordinary equipment failure and everything else was delusion caused by fear and over-active imaginations**. There is also the suggestive fact that a post-Christmas celebration was going on in Woody's Bar before the second expedition. **Alcohol might have been a factor** in the sightings and the way they were interpreted.

Other sceptical explanations include collective hallucinations caused by psychotropic drugs which (according to one truly outlandish conspiracy theory) were being administered to personnel at the air bases without their knowledge or consent. More credible is the suggestion that the lights which Colonel Halt interpreted as **'molten metal' falling from the sky were created by a meteor shower.** But none of this explains the radiation readings on the Geiger counter — which have led some amateur investigators to theorise that there could have been an **accident involving a nuclear weapon at the Base**. <u>That would certainly explain the flash of light, though not why all who saw it survived</u>. A more feasible, though still highly speculative, theory was floated by ufologist Nick Redfern last year in a book called *The Rendlesham Forest UFO Conspiracy*. Redfern suggests that the U.S. military was experimenting with ways to **harness ball lightning, a natural phenomenon, as a weapon. End of quote.**

Charles: An insult to intelligence! Why on earth don't these people speak to me before rushing to print stuff that has more in common with flights of imagination? No point in commenting further, other than to say the forest can be a very eerie place, particularly at night time when the mists come sweeping down, as this image shows!

Make of it what you will. I can't give any answers. I stand by what I have said for now over 40 years. I think John and I have made our point probably too many times, but I won't give up telling folks what happened from my personal perspective rather than cajoling what took place with wild stories borne from desperation to attract the Media, who thrive on stories like this. Enough said…

Special feature on GENERAL GORDON WILLIAMS

'The cat being let out the bag'!

The Phenomenon a film by James Fox

Charles: James is the Executive Producer and Director of this film, released in **October 2020** following three critically acclaimed UFO documentaries: **'50 Years Of Denial'**, **'Out Of The Blue'** and **'I Know What I Saw'**.

Out Of The Blue aired on the Sci-Fi channel – and *I Know What I Saw* aired on the History Channel.

All of these documentaries are geared towards sharing eye-witness accounts from individuals with impeccable credentials, breaking the stereotype of the typical UFO witness.

THE HALT PERSPECTIVE 2

While there was nothing on the incident which took place in Rendlesham, as one may have expected there was considerable emphasis on what had taken in the States over the years.

Looking back as we reach the final part of this book, I still find it astonishing that people who I knew all those years back who were under my command, have stooped so low to attack me in print. Unprecedented behaviour in the annals of UFO history – no wonder the public tarnish us all with the same brush.

Okay, nobody is perfect, but you've seen the awards and commendations presented to me by those who served under my command, maybe they were glad to get rid of me! They tell their own story... So why should Monroe, shown on page 478 in the film capture screened in 2011, greeting me with affection, then go on to carry out the vile attack in Jim's book, without at least discussing his grievances with me prior to any publication?

James Fox included an interview with **General Gordon Williams**, who referred to my memo as "*the cat being let out of the bag*". While some may feel this has a hidden meaning, I doubt it, but as you will see towards the end of the book, something odd occurs, surrounding statements brought to my attention by the family of General Gordon Williams which is inexplicable in nature and yet another facet of this incident – which may never be made public. It is claimed that Gordon Williams supported there being a special agency that came to in investigate the incident. Maybe I missed something. I was definitely misquoted. James Fox: "*In my interview regarding an alleged UFO incident at Bentwaters, England (Rendlesham Forest Case), I interviewed the Deputy Base Commander (Colonel Charles Halt) I also interviewed General (Gordon Williams) he informed me that an unknown Government Agency had flown in and sort of sanitised the area, then interviewed witnesses.*"

What exactly does General Gordon Williams mean? Confirmation that the RFI site was sanitised and witnesses interviewed by a Government Agency. I wasn't aware that Gordon Williams had made such a statement before. Could this be part of the information that he passed on to his children prior to his death? You can listen to the interview by searching for **Stripes.com episode eight**. The relevant part starts at around the 20 minute point into the podcast.

What happened at Rendlesham still continues to be the focus of interest now – as it always has been.

General Gordon Edmund Williams passes away

It's only befitting, taking into consideration the role played by USAF General Gordon Williams at RAF Bentwaters, and the confusion surrounding his involvement – if any at all – that we should include details of a much-decorated war hero who dedicated much of his life in serving his country with such distinction, especially as he was a man that I respected both as a friend and superior officer.

Gordon Edmund Williams was a native son of New Hampshire, born in Nashua and resided in the nearby town of Hudson. His parents were Edmund and Doris Williams, hailing from Massachusetts and New Hampshire, respectively. Several years of Gordon's childhood were also spent with his grandparents in Martha's Vineyard. He returned to Hudson to attend Alvirne High School, where he starred on the baseball and basketball teams, played trumpet, and was the president of his class. Continuing his family's commitment to service, his father in the Army Air Corps and his grandfather as a selectman, Gordon did not hesitate at the opportunity to attend the United States Military Academy.

THE HALT PERSPECTIVE 2

THE HALT PERSPECTIVE 2

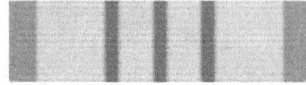

West Point

At West Point he was a member of Company I-2. He continued his athletic pursuits playing pitcher on the corps squad Baseball Team and, in the off-season, being a stalwart on I-2's intramural basketball teams, winning a Brigade Championship and contributing to I-2's two consecutive Banker's Trophies for being the best company in the annual intramural competition. His company mates recognized him as the quintessential nice guy, with a quiet sense of humour and a contagious laugh, always a good listener and an insightful conversationalist. During plebe year they elected him to be the company's hop manager, a position he held for four years. He breezed through academics with no difficulty and was rewarded for his leadership qualities by serving on the battalion staff as a First Classman.

At graduation, Gordon selected Air Force. His USAF career was meteoric. He entered pilot training in August 1957 and received his wings at Laredo AFB, TX in 1958. After an initial assignment with the 510th Tactical Fighter Squadron at Clark Air Base in the Philippines, flying F-100D's, he returned to England AFB in Louisiana. Flying the same aircraft again, he represented the 401st Tactical Fighter Wing at the William Tell worldwide fighter gunnery competition in 1962, during which he was the youngest fighter pilot of all the gunnery teams. He later wrote: *"I finished 5th in the world; not bad by almost any standard, but for a fighter pilot, not very fulfilling."*

Top Gun

This was followed by his selection to attend the prestigious Fighter Weapons School at Nellis AFB, NV, where he received top honours in both academics and flying and was awarded overall Top Gun. In 1964, he was selected for the Navy exchange program, for which he flew an F-4 combat tour in the Gulf of Tonkin aboard the *USS Ranger in 1965-66. He then joined the initial AF contingent in combat evaluation of the A-7, again with Navy aboard the *USS Ranger*. His 322 carrier landings afforded him the **Triple Centurion Patch.**

A note from his commanding officer said this distinction made him **"the only Air Force Triple Centurion in the whole damn world."** He followed his Navy exchange tours with an assignment to Edwards AFB, CA as Air Force project officer for A-7D testing.

Upon returning to California, he married the former Margaret Anne Kropp of Minnesota, where they started their family, eventually having three children.

---

*The seventh *USS Ranger* was the third of four Forrestal-class super carriers built for the United States Navy in the 1950s. Although all four ships of the class were completed with angled decks, Ranger had the distinction of being the first US carrier built from the beginning as an angled-deck ship. Commissioned in 1957, she served extensively in the Pacific, especially the Vietnam War, for which she earned 13 battle stars. Near the end of her career, she also served in the Indian Ocean and Persian Gulf. Ranger was decommissioned in 1993, and was stored at Bremerton, Washington until March 2015. She was then moved to Brownsville for scrapping, which was completed in November 2017.

THE HALT PERSPECTIVE 2

In 1971 he moved to the Pentagon and culminated his tour as Advanced Systems Branch Chief, overseeing a range of new tactical fighters, including the F-15, F-16 and A-10. After attending the National War College, Gordon had joint tours in Izmir, Turkey and Zaragoza, Spain, followed by assignment as Vice Commander, then Commander, of the 81st Tactical Fighter Wing (A-10s) in Bentwaters, England.

RAF Bentwaters

I served under General Gordon Williams at RAF Bentwaters for over a year. I met with him every morning to discuss current activities and from time-to-time as the need arose. He was extremely talented and a pleasure to work for. He gave me great latitude and I always did my best to support him. The night I was in the Forest he overheard all my conversations with the command post concerning the event. When I returned from the Forest I went home, showered, had a bite to eat and because I couldn't sleep, went to the office. I met him on the front steps of the office and he smiled and commented *"that must have been some night"*.

I responded and told him I had a recording of some of the events. He took me into his office and we listened to the tape. He asked for the tape and told me he wanted the tape to play at the 3rd AF Commanders' weekly briefing. This caused me great concern but I had little say. I worriedly waited all week anxious for him to return from the briefing expecting a problem. I met him on the front steps and asked *"Do I still have a job?"*. He laughed and threw me the recorder and smiled. We went into his office and he explained that no one in the General's meeting knew what to do.

The General said *"Since it happened off Base, it's a British affair – case closed"*. **I later learned this was not true as there was a lot of behind-the-scenes activity that I was not privy to.**

However, I didn't learn most of this until years later. I asked Gordon Williams if I needed to do anything and was told to get with the RAF Liaison Officer, Don Moreland. By the way, here are two of the plaques presented to Don, as a token of his colleagues' appreciation.

Moreland was on Christmas holiday, so I waited more than a week to meet with him. He was quite concerned and didn't know what to do. He made several calls and asked me for a memo to talk from. I put together a brief summary and had it typed in the office. My boss, Ted Conrad, the Base Commander, read it and took it to Williams. I was told to give it to Moreland which I did. The intent was for the memo to be used by Moreland as a talking paper not for it to be forwarded to the Ministry of Defence. Several weeks later there was another sighting by the police. I immediately notified Williams and we both rushed to the site only to find the sighted object had vanished. We left disappointed and later learned the object reappeared but having been embarrassed earlier, the police did not report it. All got quiet for several years until someone who was not directly involved started making wild claims. Williams and I moved on in our careers.

THE HALT PERSPECTIVE 2

General taken ill

In 1984 I was assigned to Kunsan AFB in Korea as the Base Commander and I discovered Williams was the 13 AF Commander stationed in the Philippines. Every year a large scale war game called *Team Spirit* was conducted on the Korean Peninsula. It involved all the AF units in the Pacific as well as many stateside Air National Guard and Reserve flying units. All the Commanders met for a briefing at Osan AB. Williams and I were in attendance. We talked about our time together at Bentwaters and he indicated he didn't feel well. Most of the participants were going to spend the afternoon playing golf. Williams was an avid golfer but stated he was going to go rest. Late that afternoon we all got together for a wrap-up session and I discovered that Williams was critically ill and air evacuated with his survival in doubt. I later learned that Williams survived but with serious limitations. After we both retired we exchanged several e-mails and he remembered me and was quite complementary. **By then I had learned that he knew some, if not all, of the behind activities from the 1980 incident. He indicated that he had been sworn to secrecy and would say no more.**

In the late 90's Georgina Bruni was putting together a book called *'You Can't Tell The People'*. She and I had long conversations in which I worked with her to keep her focused on the actual events from the Bentwaters incident. She was a skilled detective and constantly discovering new facts. She explained that she had hosted Williams at her flat and although he wouldn't say too much he did reveal some interesting things.

Georgina Bruni with Peter Parish during her book launch in the UK

THE HALT PERSPECTIVE 2

On his way to England Williams had stopped in a gift shop and bought a ball cap for her that had a small alien on the front with the notation *"The Truth Is Out There"*. He had **Bentwaters 1980** embroidered on the back.

I am convinced he was trying to tell her something. He also indicated to her that there are more things in the universe that we may never know about. He went further to state he believed that there may be a more advanced civilization who had mastered the technology to travel through time!

In 1981 he was promoted to Brigadier General and assigned to Headquarters, USAFE, at Ramstein AFB, Germany. After receiving his second 'star' at Norton AFB, CA, he returned to the locale of his first fighter assignment, Clark AB, to take command of 13th Air Force in 1985.

In 1986, he contracted encephalitis. This event resulted in life-threatening medical challenges, hospitalization, and more than a year's treatment at various civilian medical facilities in the United States. He eventually was able to return to full duty status at the Pentagon. He then moved on to an assignment in Stuttgart, Germany as the J-5 at Headquarters European Command, where he was heavily involved in the intermediate force reductions being negotiated at that time between the United States and the Soviet Union.

At the end of that assignment Gordon retired after 31 years of service

After initially returning to the Washington, DC area, Gordon moved to Tucson, AZ, where in retirement he pursued his lifelong avid interest in the game of golf. It was there also that he met and married **LuAnn Koepke**, a widow and prominent Tucson businesswoman. During his many years in Tucson he served as the president of the West Point Society of Southern Arizona and was active with the Air Force Association, Tucson Chapter. LuAnn predeceased him in death by two years. He was survived by his children: **Arthur, Anne and Susan;** his grandchildren: Christian, Daria, and Samantha; and LuAnn's children and grandchildren. Gordon was a fine officer, an accomplished fighter pilot, a loving father, and a wonderful friend to all those who had the privilege to know him.

In November 2018 General Williams passed away

It appears that prior to his death he decided, after all these years, to reveal what he had kept secret about the RAF Bentwaters incident. According to his son, Art and daughter Susan, on his death bed he detailed his behind-the-scenes involvement. They contacted a UFO researcher in the UK that they thought was working on a film. She verified their relationship and notified me. I located Susan and discovered she was living in the local area. I contacted her and asked if we could meet. However, she kept making excuses but finally after months of pushing agreed to meet at a local bar on March 3, 2019. When I arrived Susan was there with her brother Art. She was extremely nervous and had several drinks. Art did almost all the talking. In so many words he let me know the Williams family was very dysfunctional and they were not talking with their mother and their sister refused to come to the funeral. I politely pressed him for the details his father revealed but he pulled out a five page non-disclosure document and insisted I sign first. I reluctantly signed it and he proceeded to tell me only two

THE HALT PERSPECTIVE 2

words his father said. I could readily tell from the behaviour of both he and Susan that there was more. At that point I decided to back off and give him some room. Not long after, I contacted him trying to get more details – he claimed he knew no more.

Offer of 10,000 dollars to tell all!

Later I was contacted by a Hollywood Screen Writer and was told Art was shopping a book and was willing to tell all that his dad relayed but only for $10,000. This only confirmed my thoughts that there was some real substance to his father's dying comments.

On March 20, 2019 a burial and remembrance service was held for General Williams at Arlington Cemetery followed by a reception at Fort Myer. I attended to show respects and meet former friends from RAF Bentwaters. I was shocked at Art and Susan's comments and especially the way they treated their mother. I spent time talking with their mother, Marge, and family members. My suspicions that Gordon Williams was two people, was confirmed. The one I knew that lived for the Air Force, to fly and play golf and an entirely different one at home. I keep hoping that Art or Susan will realize how important their father's comments are – and talk.

The Super Sabre Society Friday lunchtime meets.

Gordon was also a member of the **Tuscon Arizona Super Sabre Society,** the **Order of Daedalians,** the **Council on Foreign Relations**, and the **Tucson Friday Pilots Group**.

There is also a Super Sabre website, Tucson Arizona, run by retired **Major General Donald William Shepperd**, who presents a short video introducing

THE HALT PERSPECTIVE 2

the men that gathered on Friday lunchtimes to talk and exchange their memories of military exploits. One of them *was* Gordon Williams. He is shown on the front cover on the book halfway down on the left with his now characteristic eye patch.

Gordon Williams on Colonel Halt's tape

General Donald William Shepperd

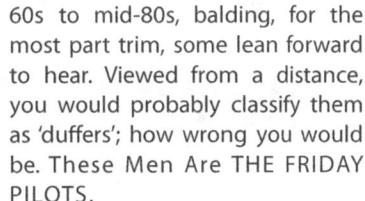

Quote: "Walk into **Hacienda del Sol** on a Friday noon and you will see a table of anywhere between 12 and 20 men. They are older, late 60s to mid-80s, balding, for the most part trim, some lean forward to hear. Viewed from a distance, you would probably classify them as 'duffers'; how wrong you would be. These Men Are THE FRIDAY PILOTS.

The **Friday Pilots** are a group of pilots that flew in the old days, the old airplanes and the early jets! They have been to war, have crashed and burned. They are fighter pilots, bomber pilots, airline pilots, corporate pilots and astronauts.

These men did something almost everyone talks about and few do; they wrote down their memories for their kids, grandkids, families and friends. They are an eyewitness account of the real stories behind the people who keep this great nation free!" **End of quote.**

Welcome to The Friday Pilots

(EXTRACT TAKEN FROM THE SUPER SABRE SOCIETY WEBSITE)

Gordon Williams' claims on Colonel Halt's tape

General Gordon Williams, who was then the Wing Commander of Bentwaters/Woodbridge remembers hearing Halt's tape but he doesn't recall any reports of a craft over the Weapons Storage Area. **Gordon Williams: "I don't recall him ever saying anything about that and certainly I would have known and recognised the significance of that. We're not talking about now things being off-Base in the dark – talking about on-Base and places lit up and that sort of thing, so it doesn't make sense to me that that would have occurred".**

John: I emailed the Super Sabre website apparently set up by Donald W. Shepperd, hoping to learn more of what took place on Friday lunch times at the McMahon Steak House, Tucson, Arizona, when 15-20 men all now retired from the United States military with glowing careers, recanted their wartime and peace,

THE HALT PERSPECTIVE 2

memories. Unfortunately it appears the restaurant went into liquidation and is no more. No reply was received from Donald, who appears to have set the site up and was the author of the book *Friday Pilots*, ensuring from personal interviews made with the men, including Gordon Williams, that those memories were recorded for posterity rather than being lost from history.

On this site there is a lengthy biography spanning half a dozen pages about his life and military career of 'Gordy' who was born in Nashua, State of Hampshire, from a family originally descended from England as did Colonel Halt's.

Gordy: *"The end of my Philippine tour was filled with medical drama. I met a "bad mosquito" and contracted encephalitis, a viral brain infection that can be life-threatening and mine certainly was. I lost my memory and was really down for the count. It was a horrible experience. I was assigned as Deputy for Programs and Resources in the Pentagon but spent most of the*

year in medical rehab at John Hopkins. I am not sure I ever totally recovered. When I returned to duty, I went to Stuttgart, Germany as J-5 for European Command. From there I retired with just over 35 years in the military. Looking back on my career, I am grateful to the Air Force for all the opportunities and challenges they pushed my way. I never had a bad assignment. I met wonderful people, made good friends and held great commands. I got a view of the world few get to see. What a ride!"

Major General Donald William Shepperd

Born in 1940, he is a retired United States Air Force officer and served as the Director of the Air National Guard from 28 January 1994 to 28 January 1998. He holds a Master of Science degree from Troy State University and attended the Air War College at Maxwell Air Force Base. Donald graduated from the United States Air Force Academy in 1962 with distinction.

He also served as the Director, Air National Guard, The Pentagon, and Washington, D.C. As Director, he was responsible for formulating, developing, and coordinating all programs, policies, and plans affecting the almost 117,000 Air Guard members in more than 1,300 units throughout the United States, District of Columbia, Puerto Rico, Guam and the Virgin Islands.

Donald W. "Shep" Shepperd grew up in Colorado and graduated from the fourth class of the United States Air Force Academy in 1962. He flew almost 5,000 hours in fighters (F-100, A-37, A-7, F-106, F-15) throughout his military career in Europe, Asia and the U.S. including 247 combat missions in Vietnam. The retired Major General has also functioned as a military aviation analyst for CNN. His wife is Rose. Donald is an author with five current books on Amazon. His book *Bury Us Upside Down* was published by Random House and has become a Vietnam air war classic.

All book royalties go to the Fisher House charity for military families – the Fisher House provides housing near treatment facilities for military families experiencing severe medical problems.

He performs independent consulting on defense, strategic planning, executive leadership, information technology and visioning and preparation of executive teams for the 21st Century. He was a fighter pilot who flew 247 combat fighter missions in Vietnam. He retired in 1998 from the Pentagon where he served as head of the Air National Guard. He commanded over 110,000 Air National Guard personnel, 1400 aircraft, 88 flying units, and 250 support units spread throughout the 54 states and territories. General Shepperd was a military analyst for CNN.

He is also a writer and provides military commentary for radio in Arizona, Colorado, and the east coast. He serves on several boards and was an ad hoc member of the Air Force Scientific Advisory Board. He lives with his wife in Tucson, Arizona. *Bury Us Upside Down*, is available in bookstores and on-line.

THE HALT PERSPECTIVE 2

THE HALT PERSPECTIVE 2

2021

CHARLES IRWIN HALT OFFERS HIS SYMPATHIES TO THE ROYAL FAMILY

April 2021

BEFORE starting I need, first of all, to offer my deepest sympathies to the Queen and the Royal Family following the passing of **HRH Prince Philip**. John, through his ex-Father-in-law, who served on *HMS Kelly* – which was sunk off Crete in 1941 – met Captain Lord Louis Mountbatten, back in the 1970's.

He was the Uncle of Prince Philip, and both men have received publicity in the British newspapers about their interest in the UFO subject.

John remains perplexed that, for some reason, no acknowledgement was received from the Palace after the Revised Volume 4 of *Haunted Skies* was sent to Prince Philip's secretary and wonders if he had offended him in some way. This is a copy of letter he sent:

> *Dear, Royal Highness Prince Philip,*
>
> *I'd like to thank you for having the 'Haunted Skies' books in your collection, which reflect, now, 25 years of commitment seeking to preserve historically the mysterious events that have taken place in and around our skies going back to the early days of the 2nd World War. Sadly many of the pilots and senior RAF ranking officers are no longer with us but I have been privileged to interview them and on occasion ended up good friends. My ex-Father-in-law, Royal Navy CPO Ted West, served on HMS Kelly under your late Uncle Lord Louis Mountbatten, whom I had the pleasure of meeting many years ago. I am concerned that having sent you Volume 4 'Jubilee' book REVISED covering 1967-197, some months ago through the post – special delivery – I've not received any confirmation (as I have done with all the other books) to say that it has been received. A few weeks ago I wrote to Brigadier Archie Miller Bakewell asking him if he had received it but not received any reply. This is 'Ted' third from the left next to Lord Louis. I hope to hear from you soon and I'm sorry to have bothered you.*
>
> *John Hanson, retired Police Officer.*

Charles: Thanks John. One of the problems with the media is that THEY NEARLY ALWAYS GET IT WRONG. Why don't they contact John and ask him to show the many letters he has had from the Palace?

THE HALT PERSPECTIVE 2

Here is a photo from the many newspapers showing Archie Miller Bakewell although the reference seems a little ambiguous as to which one he is.

ROLE: Brigadier Miller-Bakewell – sixth from left wearing medals – and his colleagues follow the coffin

ROYAL DIVERSION
The Duke of Edinburgh, 99, has spent decades building up a large library on ufology, an interest kindled by his uncle, Lord Mountbatten (who wrote an official report about an alien landing on his estate). The Duke spent last summer reading *The Halt Perspective* (2016), about the Rendlesham Forest incident.

Another example of inaccuracy by the media relates to USAF Major George Filer, whose account of what he witnessed over the Salisbury area, England, can be found on page (81/109) in this book, but how on earth could they get his name wrong?!

Here is the article, which is of interest and of relevance, as it relates to Prince Philip's interest in the UFO subject – now nearly two and half years ago.

Quote:

Royal SHOCK: Prince Philip embroiled in 'close encounter with UFO'

Once again, where do we start with the way that the media have handled these 'revelations'?

In Nov 2018, *quote:* 'Royal SHOCK: Prince Philip embroiled in 'close encounter with UFO'

PRINCE Philip personally congratulated a military pilot who claimed he chased a UFO out of Britain, according to the veteran involved some 40 years ago.

Major George A. **Giller** was an Air Force intelligence officer for the USAF, who claims to have encountered a UFO over England. He says his jet got a call from London Air Traffic Control about an aircraft that had failed to identify itself near Stonehenge, Salisbury. However, when George got there to inspect, the **"floating cruise ship"** darted from the scene. *End of quote.*

We appreciate that this account is over two years old but, bearing in mind that this incident was covered in this book, we remain curious as to why the wrong name was published? In all probability the journalist couldn't be bothered, slapdash and shoddy rather than deliberate, one would have thought.

Another mention of the Halt Perspective Book

RT question more **25th November 2020 – WWW.**

Prince Philip 'obsessed with aliens and UFOs' since Mountbatten revealed details of unexplained encounter. A photo of an alien next to Prince Philip introduces this article. *Quote:* Philip is said to keep a map of UFO sightings on a wall in Buckingham Palace. He also reportedly asked to see top-secret Ministry of Defence reports into "close encounters." The 99-year-old spent last summer reading '***The Halt***

Perspective', a book which examines the inside story of the infamous Rendlesham Forest incident, which is sometimes dubbed *"Britain's Roswell."* The episode saw a series of reported sightings of unexplained lights in December 1980. Two officers from the nearby Woodbridge US Air Force Base even claimed to have encountered an unknown triangular craft displaying *"hieroglyphic symbols,"* which accelerated away at high speed after they touched it. The book was penned by retired US Air Force Colonel Charles Halt, who was deputy commander at the Base, and retired West Midlands detective John Hanson. In a letter to the former detective, Philip's secretary Brigadier Archie Miller-Bakewell wrote: *"I am certain it will be read with close interest over the summer."* Hanson voiced his approval of Philip's curiosity. *"Why shouldn't any sensible person have an interest in a phenomenon that has baffled mankind for millennia?"* he told *The Sun*. After Philip received another book – **'Haunted Skies: The Encyclopaedia of British UFOs'** – Miller-Bakewell said: *"His Royal Highness will add this copy to his collection...It will make a most welcome addition to his library."* **End of quote**

Some further quotes from the Newspapers and Media, in April 2021

Some quotes from the Newspapers and Media, in April 2021 following the death of Prince Philip: ***The Metro* – 12th April 2021.** Complete with a picture of Prince Philip looking up at a flying saucer, which is misleading but no surprises there! Philip spent the summer of 2019 reading **The Halt Perspective,** which tells the story of Rendlesham Forest incident, dubbed 'Britain's Roswell'. On December 26 and 28, US Air Force personnel at RAF Woodbridge, Suffolk, reported seeing strange lights in surrounding woodlands. As they went out to investigate, one serviceman claims they got within touching distance of a 'craft of unknown origin'. The Duke had a number of other books on extraterrestrials in his collection, including **Haunted Skies: The Encyclopaedia of British UFOs**. The title's author, a retired West Midlands detective, says the Duke had 12 of his books. He told them: **"I've got about 12 letters from the Duke's private secretary that say the prince found the subject interesting.** I'm quite proud of Prince Philip, why shouldn't he have been interested in UFOs, because for goodness sake, that is something that we should treat seriously rather than flippantly? It is a phenomenon that has baffled mankind for millennia. Even Prince Charles is interested in it and Prince William." [John's name omitted]

***The Week* – 13th April 2021.** Prince Philip was very interested in UFOs and aliens, royal aides have revealed. The Duke of Edinburgh was a subscriber to *Flying Saucer Review* and gave his former assistant Sir Peter Horsley "carte blanche" to collect stories about UFOs from the RAF. The Duke read a number of books on the topic, including **Haunted Skies: The Encyclopedia of British UFOs** and **The Halt Perspective**, which tells the story of "Britain's Roswell". Pentagon confirms UFO footage. The Duke may have been interested to learn that the Pentagon has confirmed that images and videos showing UFOs buzzing over Navy warships were taken by branch personnel. The 2019 images and footage, caught off the coast of California, show unidentified objects flying above four US destroyers, including the USS Kidd Navy destroyer. They will be shared as evidence in Congress later this year.

13th April 2021 – *Page 6* – WWW. Prince Philip was fascinated with UFOs. In 2019, Philip read "*The Halt Perspective*," written by retired US Air Force **Col. Charles Halt,** a former deputy commander of RAF Bentwaters, who described how he led a patrol to investigate an alleged UFO landing in the Rendlesham Forest in 1980. The incident was dubbed "Britain's Roswell" after the famous 1947 crash of a US Army Air Force's balloon in New Mexico that spawned rumours that the wreckage came from a "flying disc." Among the books about extraterrestrials in Philip's collection was "**Haunted Skies: *The Encyclopaedia of British UFOs***," whose author, retired West Midlands detective John Hanson, said the Duke had a dozen of his works, according to Metro. "I've got about 12 letters from the Duke's private secretary that say the Prince found the subject interesting," Hanson, who co-wrote "***The Halt Perspective,***" told *I News*. "I'm quite proud of Prince Philip, why shouldn't he have been interested in UFOs, because for goodness'

THE HALT PERSPECTIVE 2

sake, that is something that we should treat seriously rather than flippantly? It is a phenomenon that has baffled mankind for millennia," he said.

15th April 2021 – '9' News, Prince Philip was 'fascinated by UFOs', collected books, reports on phenomena. Prince Philip's wide reading about the subject also included the book *The Halt Perspective*, about the Rendlesham Forest incident in southern England, known as 'The UK Roswell'. The sightings began on the early hours of December 26, 1980 when three US military personnel spotted lights above Rendlesham Forest in Suffolk, and described a triangular craft landing. READ MORE: Forty years ago strange lights were spotted hovering over a pine forest; the mystery still haunts Britain's defence force. Prince Philip also had a number of other books on reported alien sightings, including **Haunted Skies: The Encyclopaedia of British UFOs.**

John: Following what turned out to **over 250 articles** published into the media and the WWW with regard to the Duke's interest in the UFO subject; following his demise I was contacted by a female journalist who asked me for further information regarding my late father-in-law and his friendship with Lord Louis. Suffice to say, after supplying various photos, nothing else was heard and emails sent to her were never answered. Thanks go to Christine Smith (nee West) for all of her help.

This is CPO West shown outside Buckingham Palace after being presented with his bravery medal by the King.

Left to right: Grandma West, Christine aged 5, Ted, Wynne West, wife and Auntie Gladys

Apparently the cameraman presented the photo to Ted copyrighted as he hadn't enough money to purchase the souvenir photo!

Another photo from Christine's collection of memorabilia stored in Covina, California where she lives – Lord Louis Mountbatten:

THE HALT PERSPECTIVE 2

Colonel Charles Irwin Halt – First night concerns

Before starting I need to make two things clear. First these are my conclusions and feel free to draw your own. Secondly, unbeknownst to me at the time, following the events in the forest many of the enlisted participants were drugged, hypnotized and given screen memories. Thus, their current claims should be viewed with that in mind. I didn't learn of the highly questionable "debriefing" sessions until years later. If I had known at the time I would have made an issue of it. I'm now convinced that both Col's Gordon Williams and Ted Conrad were aware of this and did nothing to stop it. What was done to these individuals literally ruined their lives. For this I am truly sorry.

Nearly everyone will agree that what was initially presumed witnessed by Airman Burroughs to be a potential downed aircraft was witnessed by his partner Bud Steffens, Jim Penniston, his rider ED Cabansag,

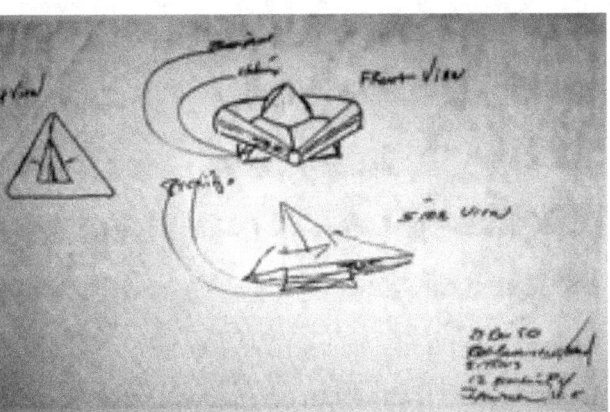

M.Sgt. J. D. Chandler and perhaps others. It's accepted that Penniston, Burroughs and Cabansag left their weapons at the gate and drove into the forest to investigate. They drove down a narrow rutted track as far as they could, then proceeded on foot. From that point forward, accounts are questionable. On returning to the gate Jim's initial claim was that they saw a structured craft with multiple lights and every time they tried to approach it moved. We do know there were radio issues and those at the gate lost contact with them for a period. But made no mention at the time of touching the craft, or seeing a bubble surrounding it or even getting close to it. In radio transmissions to those at the gate it was stated that every time they got close the object moved away. After several such calls they were ordered by M.Sgt. Chandler to return to the Base. Which they did. After turning in their weapons at the armoury the whole security flight boarded the Blue Bird bus and were returned to Bentwaters. Penniston sat next to Richard Bertinino on the bus. Richard says that he asked Penniston to explain the earlier happenings whereupon Jim took out his notebook and drew a sketch of a triangular object and told Richard, "This is what we saw". The only thing in the notebook was the drawing he just made. There were no other drawings or notes visible in the notebook. Jim gave a similar account of a structured craft to his superiors. The C Flight, including Jim, then went on their normal three day break.

I learned of their foray early in the morning of December 26th while collecting the police blotters. I was convinced there was a reasonable explanation for what they claimed had happened. However, after my experience two nights later I realized what had taken place in the forest on both nights was more than unexplainable. I then debriefed and took statements from those involved. At that time there was no mention of the three getting close enough to touch or see symbols on the craft or some kind of bubble surrounding it. After taking statements I took the three individuals to both the Base Commander and the Wing Commander. The witnesses never mentioned a notebook or even getting close to a craft. They all agreed the object avoided them. The comments from Jim about getting close and touching the craft came years later, after he started getting a lot of publicity.

On one occasion while filming for a television documentary program, Jim and I returned to the supposed landing site where I was taken the night I initially went out in 1980. I am confident that was the original site as the initial night I took soil samples from the three circular impressions arranged in a triangle and found them to contain calcium carbonate (residue from Jim taking plaster casts) of the presumed landing gear earlier in the day.

In December 2003 Jim and I returned to the forest to do another TV program which aired as *Invasion At Rendlesham* on the Sci-Fi Channel. The program is available on *YouTube*. We started filming at the Woodbridge East Gate. The producer asked us to walk to the landing site. After going down the East Gate Road about 100 feet Jim said: "The landing site is down here to the right". Everyone became confused but agreed to follow. Jim took us about 2-300 yards parallel to the Base fence and pointed to a grassy area on the left and stated: "This is the landing site". I said in response this is not the landing site that's been repeatedly identified including multiple times by you. In fact it is not the site identified in the original drawing attached to Jim's January 1981 statement. His response was: "There must be two landing sites". Jim further stated that he recognized the spot due to the trees which were there in 1980. Also present for the filming was Vince Thurkettle, the original Forester. Vince commented: "These trees are less than 20 years old, they would have been mere saplings in 1980". To further complicate things a third landing site is referenced in the book *The Rendlesham Enigma*. The program *Invasion At Rendlesham* is available on *YouTube* and you can see it for yourself.

While at that new second site, Jim produced his notebook. It did have many comments and drawings. But no binary code. When asked where the code pages were, he replied: "I took them out and later returned them". If one freeze-frames the notebook on the mentioned *YouTube* program, one will see the date in the notebook as the 27th. Jim's experience was actually early on the morning of the 26th. My now well-known memo mistakenly states that the date of the first event was the 27th. Jim was actually home on break on the 27th. Even more interesting is in September 1983 – Jim phoned Brenda Butler, co-author of *Sky Crash: A Cosmic Conspiracy* and identified himself as James Archer. He wanted to meet her and explain what had really happened. Brenda asked: "How will I know you?" Jim responded he would recognize her and knew her car. That's most interesting. They met on September 10, 1983.

THE HALT PERSPECTIVE 2

I have discussed this with her and have her original notes from the meeting. The notes indicate that Jim and others chased the object but never caught up to it. Jim told Brenda that the event occurred on December 27th at 2:00a.m. Keep in mind that my memo with the incorrect date of December 27th was released in July 1983. Why would Jim use that date unless he took it from my memo trying to reconstruct the event. When I asked him 'why the date of the 27th in the notebook?' he stated: "That date was from a flight exercise". But wait – he was home on break on the 27th. He later changed his story claiming the 27th is when he wrote the code. It looks like the date in the notebook and what he told Brenda came from my memo.

Looking at Jim's claim that notes and drawings were done while he stood next to the landed craft, one might ask how that was done in the dark, as Jim would have been carrying a flashlight, camera, radio and a notebook in addition to his normal police gear. And remember, Richard Bertinino says that Jim drew the craft in the notebook while sitting next to him on the bus. Additionally, his partner John Burroughs claims that he never saw a notebook while they were in the forest. This poses more questions. Intriguing is the fact that the original witness statement by Jim states the craft was triangular but also rectangular. What was the real shape? The fact is that the notebook was never mentioned in multiple earlier TV programs such as *Strange But True* which aired in July 1994. The notebook first popped up in Salley Rayl's 1996 *OMNI Magazine* article in 1996. The code becomes real interesting as Jim first claimed he wrote it on the morning of December 26th at the kitchen table after returning from the forest. He further claimed his then wife Maria observed this. However, when queried, stated she never saw Jim write code. Furthermore Jim's 2011 live-in girlfriend (named in his book as Amie Wilkes) says that she saw him writing code in January 2011 and helped him decode it. She further introduced him to his future co-author Gary Osborn.

There is more, but this information is enough to put the whole code nonsense to question. Does it all come down to his screen memories or perhaps an outright fictional account? You be the judge.

Further . . .

Monroe Nevels was a real problem child. Very technically competent, but with no common sense. One never what he was going to say or do? On several occasions he drove the Disaster Preparedness truck into restricted areas and was nearly shot. Often during exercises he would do things that caused real issues. One night he drove his car into his neighbour M.Sgt. Buckholtz's home and nearly killed a teen age boy. He painted all the walls in one of his on-Base home's bedroom's flat black to make a darkroom. This caused untold problems when he moved out. Everyone that worked with him had issues. Colonel Morgan, who replaced Ted Conrad as Base Commander called Nevels "a space cadet' and way out there. His supervisor Captain Sue Jones constantly covered for him but finally lost patience. He was given a referral performance review (a potential career ending document) and became very bitter. He phoned me after leaving Bentwaters and asked for my assistance in appealing the report. I had to politely tell him it was deserved. Thus, he is most unhappy with me and had said many very unkind and untrue things about me. Many of the things he provided to Jim Penniston for inclusion in his book concerning the incident are blatantly not correct. At least Jim had the sense not to include nasty personal comments Monroe provided. I have been asked on several occasions why I took Nevels with me. It's like the old saying "when's a bad game a good game?" The answer: when it's the only game in town. Nevels was the only person in his field available and I knew he had a good camera. I was confident I could keep him under control. I was successful then but he's loose now!

THE HALT PERSPECTIVE 2

Further on the *UFO Invasion At Rendlesham*!

John: As this book drew to its conclusion, Chuck asked me to include a screen shot from the *UFO Invasion At Rendlesham* film on *YouTube* – produced in 2003 (revived for the anniversary of 2020) – feeling that it would be appropriate to include one scene showing Jim's notebook first page, dated the 27th December. You will remember Chuck referred to this film on page 231, and commented on the suggestion made by Jim that the trees, which are apparently now only 20 years old, were there in 1980! I've watched the film which heralds the following:

'UFO Invasion At Rendlesham Documentary. In late December 1980, in Rendlesham Forest, England, numerous U.S. military personnel witnessed what has come to be regarded as the most significant military-UFO incident in the history of Great Britain. Now *SCI-FI* brings you this shocking exposé, complete with documentation, new physical evidence and firsthand accounts by both military and civilian witnesses – including Penniston and Halt, who have jeopardized their reputations and military pensions in order to seek out the truth. Join host Bryant Gumbel as *SCI-FI* presents its exclusive investigation of one of the most important UFO incidents of the 20th century. Top secret memo releases fire storm!'

Screenshot from 'UFO Invasion At Rendlesham' showing Jim Penniston's notebook entry

While I accept that it was well produced by Kelly McPherson and Jim Milio (who also directed it), hosted by Bryant Gumbel and covering interviews with most of the parties concerned – which included Nick Pope, Adrian Cabansag, Georgina Bruni, The Lord Hill Norton, Nick Redfern, Monroe Nevels, Larry Warren, Peter Robbins, Tim Good and others – it fails to deliver in my opinion!

Charles also asked me to widen the parameters of a comment made on the *Facebook* website by Heather Osborne, found on page 454: " *The truth is going to be revealed about several RFI people who deserved to be destroyed by the truth, that's for sure. I can't wait for Gary's book to come out."*

John: Truth is the property of being in accord with fact or reality. In everyday language, truth is typically ascribed to things that aim to represent reality or otherwise correspond to it, such as beliefs, propositions, and declarative sentences. Truth is usually held to be the opposite of falsehood. In this book we have a liberal dosing of both. I have no idea what Heather, who was very much involved in assisting with the book's preparation, meant. Common sense may dictate that she felt that their definitive book and its perceived explanations with regard to the UFO incidents that took place, now 40 years ago – with regard to the interpretation of the hieroglyphics, as drawn by Jim Penniston on the 26th December 1980 – would crush other viewpoints and opinions? One thing is assured. While so many have chopped, changed and added their stories to suit the ever-changing climate of the media, Colonel Charles Halt has stood firm. His story of what happened has never changed despite assertions to the opposite.

THE HALT PERSPECTIVE 2

Flying saucers do not exist!

Many people wrote to the Ministry of Air wanting to know their views on the question of whether 'flying saucers' existed, taking into consideration reports published in the Press. This was a matter brought to the attention of Parliament. The Under-secretary of State for Air, Nigel Birch, stated that:

*"**Flying saucers do not exist.** Reports of flying saucers, as well as other abnormal objects in the sky, are investigated as they come in, but there has been no formal enquiry. About 90% of the reports have been found to relate to meteors, balloons, flares, and many other objects. The fact that the other objects are unexplained need be attributed to nothing more sinister than lack of data."*

[Some sources give a figure of 15,000 sightings between 1947 and 1954 – only a few of which have survived.]

USAF Secretary of State for Air discounts the existence of UFOs!

In 1955 – after eight years of study by the USAF into reported UFO activity the Secretary of State for the Air Force, Mr Quarles, made public a 316-page booklet based on the investigation of 5000 reported sightings. This showed that all but three per cent (150) proved to be balloons, aircraft, astronomical bodies, birds or mirages.

"In some cases other than the three per cent there has not been enough information to say what gave rise to the reports."

Mr. Quarles disclosed that *". . . the USA in cooperation with Avro Ltd of Canada was building a disc-shaped aircraft with jet engines that will look rather like the public conception of a flying saucer."*

He added that . . . *"There is no evidence that any objects mistaken for flying saucers are of foreign origin. I am sure that even the three per cent of the unexplained objects were in fact conventional phenomena or illusions".*

THE HALT PERSPECTIVE 2

EXCLUSIVE Pilot shocked by close encounter

SUNDAY MIRROR, March 2, 1986 — PAGE 3

CHARLES IN UFO RIDDLE

Dad is a flying saucer believer

By MARTIN BRUNT

PRINCE Charles is at the centre of a bizarre UFO mystery.

The Prince had a close encounter during a flight home from the U.S.A. last week.

The pilot of his RAF VC-10 radioed air traffic control to say he had been startled by a "glowing red object" in the sky.

Incredibly, FOUR other aircraft reported sighting the "UFO" over the same stretch of the Irish Sea.

An immediate investigation was launched—but no trace of the unidentified aircraft has been found.

Other explanations—such as meteors or debris from a satellite—have also been ruled out by experts.

Charles was nearing the end of a 12-hour flight from California when the incident happened.

A source at West Drayton air traffic control near London's Heathrow airport said: "The object was reported by five different aircraft, including the Prince's.

"The pilot described seeing a red glowing object. The light from it lit up his cockpit.

"We just don't know what it was. It's a complete mystery."

A Ministry of Defence spokesman confirmed: "Prince Charles's pilot did report seeing a bright flash, but we are satisfied there was no danger to the Prince's aircraft."

UFO expert Tim Good, an author and lecturer, said last week: "It may not be pure coincidence.

"It is likely that any creature from outer space that is more advanced than us would be aware of the significance of a Royal flight."

PRINCE PHILIP has been a keen UFO follower for the past 30 years.

He is a keen reader of the magazine, Flying Saucer Review.

And he once invited a man who claimed to have seen a UFO landing to come to Buckingham Palace to tell his story to a Royal aide.

Philip's uncle, the late Lord Mountbatten, was also obsessed with alien spacecraft.

Philip—follower

THE HALT PERSPECTIVE 2

INDEX

NOTE to readers: This is a fairly accurate index but we felt we couldn't include everybody and every place because of the amount of information covered. It is not a comprehensive one but will suffice we are sure. For those that constantly ask what else happened during 1980/1981 – which may (or may not) have some bearing on what occurred outside RAF Woodbridge – details can be found on pages 181-205.

A
Abbott, Pauline - 112
Acheson, Tim - 413
Adamski, George - 42, 67
Aerial Phenomena Research Organisation - 41
Air Traffic Control Palmdale airport - 79
Alameda - 35
Albuquerque, New Mexico - 44
Albuquerque Control - 139
Alexander, John - 232
Allan, Brian - 341
Ambler, Geoff - 467
Anderson, Dean - 176
Anderson, Warner - 63
Andover, Hampshire - 35
Andrus, H, Walter - 254
Arnhem - 34
Arnold, Elvis - 169
Arnold, Kenneth - 37
Arnold, Kim - 37
Arnold, Sharon - 169
Austin, Jon - 347

B
Baker, Gary - 260,398
Baker, Oregon - 36
Bakersfield, California - 35
Baron, Michael, Ray, Dibdin, Heseltine - 289
Baroness Symons of Vernham Dean - 264,265,266,311
Barton Power Station - 89
Barton, John - 96
Basford, Dean - 181
Bass Strait, Australia - 34
Bath - 21
BBC Radio Suffolk - 348
BBC transmitter Yorkshire - 45
BBC's Coventry & Warwickshire - 21
Beamsley Beacon Yorkshire - 92
Beccles, Lowestoft - 78
Beer, Lionel - 348

Bender, Charles - 76
Berlin, Germany - 35, 70
Berliner, Don - 24
Bexleyheath, Kent - 79,182
Big Marsh, Poquoson, Virginia - 108
Bill, Stewart - 71
Binchell, Frederick - 45
Bishop, Denise - 280
Blue Book files - 44
Boardman, David - 250,458
Boardman, Julie - 250
Boeche, Ray - 463
Boise, Idaho - 35, 37
Bolsover, Derbyshire - 32
Bolt, Geoffrey - 94
Book: *Encounter in Rendlesham Forest* - 340
Book: *Left At East Gate* - 14
Book: *The Rendlesham Forest UFO Conspiracy* - 462
Bordes, Eileen - 86
Bordes, Frank - 86
Bott, Irene - 464
Box Hill, Surrey - 92
Boyd, Bob - 280
Bridgnorth - 145
Bridport, Dorset,
Briggs, Frederick - 481
British Astronomical Association - 66, 71
Brown, George T - 297
Brown, Rita, Mae - 83
Brown, Sally - 256
Bruni, Georgina - 251,257,262,267,273,312,314,315,316, 319,496
Bryant, David - 168,238,243,348,359
BUFORA: Cleary-Baker, John, Dr - 113
BUFORA: Webb, Paul - 113
Burns, Horace - 114
Bury St Edmunds, Suffolk - 259
Butler, Brenda - 215,236,261,264,288,290,296,307,308,327 348,410
Butley Abbey - 309

THE HALT PERSPECTIVE 2

C
Callaghan, Russell - 243
Capes, Edith - 70
Carey, James - 78
Cayton, David - 97, 99
Chardon Avenue School - 76
Cherry Point Tower - 64
Christie, Sacha - 394,417,435
CIA - Director John McCone - 26
CIA - Gerald K. Haines - 27
CIA - study of UFO's - 26,90
Clacton-on-Sea - 31
Clarke, Chris - 347
Clarke, David, Dr - 16,329,334,489
Claydon, Matthew - 345
Cleary, Walter - 34
Cleethorpes - 92
Close Encounters Conference, Pontefract - 170
Colman, David - 352
Connecticut - 78
Constable, Trevor, James - 22
Contact UK - 467
Copping, Jasper - 330
Coronation Street - 22
Coste, James V - 172
Coverack ,Cornwall - 96
Craig, Montana - 63
Creighton, Gordon - 138,295

D
Daniels, Wilfred - 74
Daniken, Erich Von - 22
Davies, Brian - 65
Davis, Jacqueline - 256
Delair Bernard - 467
Derbyshire, Stephen - 57
Devon & Cornwall Constabulary - 140
Dewey, Oklahoma - 78
Dickinson, J - 141
Don Valley, Brightside, Sheffield - 63
Douglas Cox radio officer - 71
Doulton, Mark - 309
Dover, Kent - 46
Dr. Christopher (Kit) Canfield Green - 232
Dr. Allen Hynek - 44,103
Dr. James E. McDonald - 117
Driver, Betty - 21,177
Driver, Freda - 177
Dugdale, Ronnie - 433
Dunning Brian - 16,321
Duplantier, Gene - 144
DuPont's Chester, Pennsylvania Division - 36
Dutton, Terrence, Roy - 302

E
East Gate - 226
East Troy, Wisconsin - 36
Edge, Stella - 182
Egg Harbor, Wisconsin - 176
Elkton, Maryland - 169

Elmira, New York - 65
Elsinore, California - 66
Emmerson, James - 95
Epping - 112
Erie, Pennsylvania - 32
Evans, Captain Robbie - 294
Evers, Chris - 243,417

F
Farmington, New Mexico - 45
Farnham, Surrey - 70
Federation of American Scientists - 27
Fee, Egerton - 31
Fibich, Rudi - 70
Finlay, Peter - 111
Fishpool Hill, Hereford - 36
Flight International - 70
Flixton, Manchester - 89
Flying Disk Press - 429
Ford, Henry 2nd - 143
Forrestal, James V - 38
Fradley, Samuel - 461
Franklin, Louise - 114
Frostick, Valerie - 66
Fry, Margaret - 79,182
Fulham Palace Road, London - 96
Fund for U.F.O. Research - 27

G
Gagliardo, Patricia - 286
Galena Summit - 35
Gallagher, Tony - Editor *Daily Telegraph* - 334
Gates, Josh - 397
Gatwick Airport - 426
Gibbons, Gavin - 74
Giblin, Henry - 34
Gillette, Mr. L.C - 65
Godbold, Pauline - 294
Godding, Victor - 101
Godfrey, Alan - 274
Godfrey, Arthur Morton - 116
Goldthorpe, Adrian - 181
Gortez , George - 36
Goshen ,Indiana - 45
Gould, Dawn - 66
Grant, Leslie - 83
Green, Allan - 65
Greenfield Massachusetts - 35
Greenwood, Barry - 254,255
Ground Observer Corps observation post - 65
Grusinski, Chester - 107

H
Hailey, Idaho - 35
Hall, Mike - 301
Hall, Richard - 24
Handford, Frank - 36
Hanford Atomic Power Plant - 44
Hanford - 35
Hanger 1: The UFO Files 2010 - 250
Hanger 10 - 343

Hanging Hill Lane, Hutton, Middlesex - 168
Hansard - 55
Harris, Gerry - 239
Harris, Harry - 97, 234, 273
Hawaii - 36
Hazel, James - 348, 419
Heathcote, John - 35
Heathrow Airport - 227
Hellicar, Michael - 18, 19
Hellyer, Paul - 22
Hennesey, Patricia - 72, 73
Heseltine, Gary - 254, 345, 374, 388
Hester, David - 92
Hewins, Leonard - 107
Heywood Dudley - 94
Highway 116 - 103
Highway 60 - 115
Hinton Television Cable Company - 172
Hinton, West Virginia - 172
HMP Hollesley Bay Prison, Suffolk - 238
HMS Caroline - 31
HMS Kelly - 82
Ho, Yong - 17
Holden, Amanda - 346
Holding, Lynn - 169
Holland, Simon - 424
Hollis, Kelli - 395
Holsworthy - 140
Home, Idaho - 44
Hopkins, Budd - 286, 474
Horn, Julian - 263
Hortrop, George - 71
House of Commons - 55, 96
Howard, James - 71
Howe, Moulton, Linda - 456
Howells, Doreen - 420
Hoylake, Wirral, Merseyside - 182
HRH: Prince Charles - 484
Hughes, Howard - 18
Hull Outer Limits Magazine conference - 243
Hulse, Robert - 260
Hunniford, Gloria - 21
Huntingdon, West Virginia - 31
Hyatt Regency Arlington, Virginia - 24

I
Indigo Transmit Films Ltd - 409
Inverness, Scotland - 64
Itkonen, Veikko - 138

J
Jamison, Ben, Professor - 236
Johnson, Dion - 254, 409
Jolly, Brian - 215
Jones, Ben Emlyn - 351, 376
Jones, Isaac - 79
Jones, William - 41

K
Kane, William - 79
Kath Smith, Isle of Wight UFO Society - 31

Kean, Leslie - 474
Kent, William - 36
Kerr, Nigel - 399
Kershaw, 'Liz' - 21
Keyhoe, Donald - 26, 87
Kimber, John - 112
Klass, Philip, Julian - 254
Kobski, Wolfgang - 70
Kollmar, Richard - 80

L
La Paz, Lincoln - 36
Lake Chelan, Washington - 114
Lake Mead, Nevada - 36
Lancashire - 35
Lane, Leona - 78
Leonard H. Stringfield - 86
Lewin Road, Streatham - 137
Liverpool - 21
London Road, Leicester - 92
Long Beach, California - 79
Longcroft, Charles - 92
Lord Peter Hill-Norton - 264, 289, 310
Lord Clancarty - 289, 467
Los Alamos, New Mexico - 44
Los Angeles - 94
Louisiana - 36
Love Diving Company, California - 63
Love, Mr. R.W. - 63
Lowestoft, Suffolk - 31, 70

M
Macpherson, George - 64
Maddison, Gillian - 355
Maddocks, Peter, John - 297
Mae Kilgallen, Dorothy - 80
Magdalena, New Mexico - 35
Mantle, Christine - 417
Mantle, Philip - 170, 322, 417
Market Harborough, Leicestershire - 181
Marrowbone Lake, Tennessee - 45
Marshall, Frank - 96
Martin, Jack - 96
Maryland - 45
Mason, Lloyd - 63
Maury Island, Washington State - 35
Maycroft, Dennis - 45
Mayhew, Tim - 131
McGregor, William - 107
McGruder, Mark - 37
McLennan, Vicky - 289
Meeking, Lloyd - 180
Mera, Steve - 341
Millington, Margaret - 100
Minnis Bay - 44
Miraglia, Mark - 290
Mitchell, Edgar - 22
Mitchell, Peggy - 39
Moore, Harold - 108
Moore, Robert - 317
Mount Hood, Oregon - 44

THE HALT PERSPECTIVE 2

Moyes, David - 238
MP: Ivan Henderson - 304
MP: Charles Orr-Ewing - 106
MP: Frank Beswick - 96
MP: Ieuan Wyn Jones - 304
MP: Major Patrick Wall - 96
MP: Merlyn Rees - 136,140
MP: George Ward - 55
MP: Paddy Ashdown - 304
MP: Prime Minister Tony Blair - 304
MP: Sajid Javid - 19
MP: Sir John Langford-Holt - 136,140
MP: William Hague - 304
MUFON : Linda Zimmer - 266
MUFON: 11, 26
Munciello, Frank - 116
Munday, Arthur - 220
Muroc Army Airfield, California - 36
Murphy, Mark - 353
Murray, Ruth - 78
Muza, Mark - 108
Myers, Adrian - 57
Mysteries of the Skies: UFOs In Perspective - 32

N
National Air War College Alabama - 37
New Mexico - 35,36
Nicholson, Walter - 35
Niemtzow, Dr Richard C - 293
NORAD *Region, Hancock Field, New York* - 175
NORAD *Region, North Bay* - 175
NORAD - 139
North Main Street, Harrisonburg, Virginia - 114
Norwich Astronomical Society - 66
Norwich UFO Group - 308
Norwich - 66
Nottinghamshire - 45
Noyes, Ralph - 467
Nunn, Richard - 251

O
Oakensen, Elsie - 211,464
Ogilvy, David - 111
Olavick, Mr and Mrs - 35
Operation Bulldog - 44
Operation Mainbrace - 53,55
Operation Vigilante - 99
Oregon, Portland - 35
Orford Ness Lighthouse - 15,232
Osborne, Gary - 430
Oval, Kjell - 35

P
Paignton - 94
Palmdale - 79
Parish, Peter - 496
Parry, Emma - 407
Pattison, Rob - 407
Pengilly, Eric - 96
Pennington, Chris - 261
Phenomena Magazine - 341

Philadelphia - 116
Philips, Brian - 96
Philpott, Kerry - 304
Phoenix Arizona - 35, 36
Pickering, Jack - 41
Pike, Andrew - 281,403
Pike, John E. - 27
Pilot First Officer, Lee Boyd - 71
Pilot, Clarence Chiles - 43
Pilot, John Whitted - 43
Pittock, Paul - 301
Platts, Terry - 65
Plunket, Denis - 337
Police Constable: 495 Brett Lyne - 212
Police Constable: Brian Creswell - 251
Police Constable: Clifford Waycott - 140
Police Constable: Colin Perks - 133
Police Constable: David Dawson - 174
Police Constable: Martyn Brophy - 278
Police Constable: Pat Rollason - 293
Police Constable: Roger Willey - 140
Police Inspector: Mike Topliss - 394
Police Lieutenant: Larry Fawcett - 254
Police Maine State - 175
Police Officer: 'Woody' Darnell - 115
Pope, Nick - 17,117,322,340,404,413,444,469
Porcher, Paul - 89
Porterfield, Oliver - 172
Porters Wood, Woodbridge Suffolk - 266
Potter, Mr. F. W. - 66
Potter, Tom - 348,398
Potts, David (pseudonym) - 267
Prentice, Charles - 260
President Jimmy Carter - 261
Presley, Reg - 464
Price, David - 312
Prime Minister David Cameron - 20
Prime Minister Harold Wilson - 140
Prime Minister Winston Churchill - 34,42,80,84
Prime Minister's Question Time - 136
Project 'Moby Dick' - 40
Project Blue Book - 103
Project Condign - 16

R
RAF Intelligence Officers - 96
RAF: Church Lawford - 47
RAF: (Radar) - Frank Redfern - 55
RAF: Air Commodore - Michael Swiney, OBE - 56
RAF: Air Marshal - Lord Dowding - 76
RAF: Air Marshal - Sir Peter Horsley - 57
RAF: Airman - Leonard Burrell - 47
RAF: Alconbury - 295
RAF: Auxiliary Officer - Flight Lt. James Salandin, MBE - 72
RAF: Bawdsey - 75
RAF: Boscombe Down, Wiltshire - 67
RAF: Boulmer - 111
RAF: Brize Norton - 107
RAF: Church Lawford, Rugby - 94
RAF: Coltishall - 211

THE HALT PERSPECTIVE 2

RAF: Farnborough - 45, 70
*RAF: Felixstowe,*Norfolk - 65
RAF: Flight controller - Freddie Wimbledon - 90
RAF: Flight Lieutenant - Harry Goldstone - 92
RAF: Flight Lieutenant - John W. Kilburn - 54
RAF: Flight Lt. - David Crofts - 56
RAF: Flt. Lt. - Cyril George Townsend - Withers - 67
RAF: Flt. Test Pilot - Stanley Hubbard - 45
RAF: GCI Radar type 7 Bawdy - 70
RAF: Ian Fraser - Kerr - 90
RAF: John Brady - 91
RAF: John Cotton SAC 2590718
RAF: Lakenheath - 106
RAF: Little Rissington, Gloucestershire - 56
RAF: Ludham Norfolk - 33
RAF: Manston - 97, 98,111
RAF: Mildenhall - 290
RAF: Ministry of Supply Bombs Trial Unit - 94
RAF: Navigating officer - George Allen - 71
RAF: Neatishead - 36, 55, 90
RAF: Neatishead - 67
RAF: North Weald, Essex, 72
RAF: Odiham, Hampshire - 70,95
RAF: Pilot - Jeremy Lane - 171
RAF: Radar operator - Nigel Kerr - 251
RAF: Radar Station - Dover Kent - 46
RAF: RAF Navigator - Ivan Logan – 90
RAF: Ronald Claridge, DFC, AEA - 33
RAF: Scunthorpe, Lincolnshire - 109
RAF: Serviceman - John Warren - 33
RAF: Serviceman - Sidney Yeakes - 65
RAF: Spitfire Pilot – Desmond Arthur Peter Leslie - 42,480
RAF: Squadron Leader - Derek Coumbe - 250,251
RAF: Squadron Leader - Donald Moreland, - 289,323,399
RAF: Squadron Leader - Ernest Booker - 92
RAF: Test pilot - Derek Dempster M.A - 81, 82
RAF: Watton - 227,264,267
RAF: West Malling, Kent - 92
RAF: Wing Commander - John Arthur Charles Stratton OBE - 55
RAF: Wing Commander - Turner, MBE - 170
RAF: Wing Commander - Whitworth - 95
Ralph, Jeff - 238
Ralston,Greg - 210
Ramshott Arms public house - 239
Randles, Jenny - 267,322,
Ranton, Staffordshire - 73
Rawmarsh, Sheffield, England - 65
Rayl, Sally - 29
Reading, Berkshire - 92
Redfern, Nick - 55,462
Redman, Janet - 92
Redmond, King County,Washington - 108
Rees, Ruth - 467
Revell, 'Pixie' - 181
Reverend Pitt - Kethley - 86
Rey, Eric, Barry - 218
Richardson, Sarah - 269
Ridge, Francis - NICAP - 39

Ridpath, Ian - 16,230
Rivesville, West Virginia - 116
Robbins, Peter - 286,342,353,367,370
Robinson, Malcolm - 346
Rodwell, Mary - 417
Roestenberg, Jessie - 73, 93
Roestenberg, Tony - 73
Rogue River, Oregon - 44
Roundhill Street, Bradford - 84
Royal Navy: Chief Petty Officer, 'Ted West' - 82
Royal: Brigadier Archie Miller - Bakewell - 20
Royal: Buckingham Palace - 20
Royal - HRH: Prince Philip - 20, 57,479
Royal - HRH: Prince William - 110
Royal - Lord Louis Mountbatten - 75, 82,110,480,484
Rush, Eric - 89
Russell, Anthony Rider - 137
Ryder, Mrs. F. - 31

S

Sacks, Mike - 273
Salav, Joe - 103
Samson, Derek - 145
San Antonio, Texas - 66
San Diego - 35
Sandstone Harbour, Portsmouth - 94
Santa Catalina Channel - 79
Santa Rosa, California - 34
Saucedo, Pedro - 103
Schofield, Philip - 346
Sears, Ernie - 106
Sharman, Simon - 334
Sheffield, Louise - 36
Shotbolt, Linda - 297
Shuttlewood Derbyshire - 32
Sinar, Darren - 181
Sinclair, Mary - 417
Sinclair, Paul - 417
Sir Harold Spencer Jones - 76
Sir Patrick Wall - 289
Sirisena, Ananda - 32
Six Miles Mountain - 35
Skyhook balloons - 39
Smith, Louise - 175
Smith, Peter - 107
Sodium pentothal - 15
Solomon, Jack - 308
Sonoma, California - 63
Southampton - 92
Southend - 72
Spencer, Chief Officer V.E.31 -
Spokane, Washington - 46
Stafford, Mona - 175
Stanford, Kentucky - 175
Steamer *St. Andrew* - 31
Steiger, John - 429
Steve Smith - 174
Stewardess Daphne Webster - 71
Strait of Hormuz - 44
Strategic Air Command - 175

THE HALT PERSPECTIVE 2

Street, Richard - 76
Stringfield, Leonard - 42
Stuttgart, Arkansas - 45
Suddards, Ernest - 84
Suddards, Ray - 84
Suisun Air Base, California - 35
Sunday Mail, Glasgow - 21
Swann, Bryan - 458
Swiatek, Rob - 23
Swiatek, Susan - 11

T

Tampa Florida - 36
Tamworth, Staffordshire, England - 36
Taylor, Frederick 'Busty' - 38
Teaticket, Massachusetts - 44
The Halt Perspective - 11,18
The Old Man of Coniston - 57
The Royal Astronomical Society of Canada - 32
The UFO Trilogy - Dramas for The Stage - 429
Thomas, Elaine - 175
Thukarta, Dr - 79
Tibbitts, Bob - 353
Tilley, Mollie - 36
Timmerman, John P - 240
Titicus Reservoir, New York State - 86
Tittl, Melissa - 250
Toronto Canada - 32
Torver - 57
Traylor, John - 266
Tucson Arizona - 35,65
Tyneside UFO group - 114
Tyson, Joyce Mary - 46

U

UFO INVASION AT RENDLESHAM - 231
US: Sgt John T Dressler - 235
US: Marine Corps - Squadron Leader D.R. Higgin - 66
US: Police Officer - Robert Dickerson - 108
US: Aircraft Carrier USS Franklin D. Roosevelt –107
US: Army Private - Robert G Hellman - 35
US: Captain - Thomas F. Mantell - 39
US: Colonel - Robert McNab - 63
US: First Lieutenant - Arrigo Jezzi - 172
US: General Eisenhower - 53
US: Major - Larry Coyne - 172
US: *Mansfield Air Force Base Ohio* - 172
US: *Naval Station Pascoe, Washington* - 35
US: Pilot - Ensign Roland D. Powell - 35
US: Pilot - First Lt Edward Balocco - 64
US: Police - Sheriff Weir Clem - 103
US: Police Burton Ohio Sheriff's Department - 76
US: Police - Pat McCulloch - 103
US: Police - Patrolman Fowler - 103
US: *Portland National Guard* - 108
US: Specialist Robert Yanasek – 172
US: Squadron Leader - Lt Colonel Marion 'Black Mac' Magruder - 37
US: Staff Sergeant - John Healy - 172
USA: First Lady - Hillary Clinton - 22
USA: *Norfolk Naval station* - 64

USA: President - Bill Clinton - 19
USA: President - Jimmy Carter - 19
USA: Senator James Exon - 286

USAF

USAF: Airman - Larry, Warren - 14,230,231,254,267,268,269, 286,287,299,308,314,315,316,332,401,410
USAF: Captain - Lori Rehfeld - 214
USAF: 'Randy' D. Smith - 269
USAF: A.I.C Chris Arnold - 227
USAF: A.I.C. Wagner - 214
USAF: Adrian Bustinza, 254,269
USAF: *Air base Edenton North Carolina* - 64
USAF: Airman - Duffield - 214
USAF: Airman - James C Gouge - 287
USAF: Airman - John Burroughs - 28,30,251,226,229,231 232,244,269,273,340,402,431,489
USAF: Airman - Steve, Longero - 379-386
USAF: Airman - Donald, Montgomery - 220
USAF: Airman - Lindy, Vaughan - 435
USAF: Airman - Michael, Stacy Smith - 252
USAF: Airman - Rick Bobo - 270
USAF: Captain - George, Madden - 63
USAF: Captain - Hector, Quintanilla - 47
USAF: Captain - Kenneth, Scott, Jnr - 70
USAF: Captain - Mike, Verano - 242,251
USAF: Captain - Robert, Salas - 368 - 374
USAF: Captain - Victor, L Warzinski - 290
USAF: *Castle Air Force Base* - 66
USAF: Chief Master Sergeant - Randy Corey - 282
USAF: Colonel - Alan, Brown - 256
USAF: Colonel - Bowden - 256
USAF: Colonel - Gordon Williams - 229,234,244,256,284,291, 333,496,497,498,500,501
USAF: Colonel - Ted Conrad - 229,244,245,251,329,475
USAF: Colonel - Charlie Wicker - 14
USAF: Communications Specialist - Carl Thompson - 246
USAF: Edward Cabansag - 28,226,231
USAF: Flight Chief - Master Sgt. Faile - 214
USAF: General - Charles Alvin Gabriel - 322
USAF: Jeff Weinhertz - 250
USAF: John 'Davey' Engalls - 267,410
USAF: Ken Kern - 214
USAF: *Kirtland Air Force Base* - 103
USAF: *Larson Air Force Base* - 63
USAF: Lieutenant Colonel - Arnold L Persky - 242
USAF: *Lockbourne Air Force Base, Ohio* - 86,116
USAF: *Loring AFB, Maine* - 174
USAF: Lt - Bonnie,Tamplin - 268
USAF: Lt - Bruce Englund - 28,246,251,250,270
USAF: Lt Col - Malcolm Zickler - 244,287
USAF: Lt - David Clarby - 70
USAF: Lt - Frank Briggs - 63
USAF: Lt - Harry Joseph Eckes - 70
USAF: Lt Colonel - Joseph Lee Merkel - 87
USAF: Major - Everett - 236
USAF: Major - Fred G. Padelford - 65
USAF: Major - George A. Filer - 109
USAF: Major - William Guenon - 13
USAF: Master Sergeant - Bobby Ball - 268

USAF: Master Sergeant - Chandler - 226
USAF: Master Sergeant - Ray Gulyas - 251
USAF: MSgt Harrell - 287
USAF: Pilot - Milton Torres - 97
USAF: Pilot - Major Gerald Smith - 171
USAF: *Radar Klamath Falls, Oregon* - 108
USAF: *RAF Lakenheath* - 89
USAF: Sergeant - Monroe Ruby Nevels - 246,250,292
USAF: Sergeant - Wayne Persinger - 233
USAF: Sgt - Bud Steffens - 227
USAF: Sgt - Dennis K Hudson - 287
USAF: Sharpton, Lester - 395
USAF: SMSgt - Farias - 287
USAF: SMSgt - Swain - 287
USAF: SMSgt - Thornton - 287
USAF: Staff Sergeant - 'Crash' McCabe - 226
USAF: Staff Sergeant - Peter Tomaszewksi - 255
USAF: Staff Sergeant - Thomas W. Wharton - 178
USAF: Staff Sgt - Jim Penniston - 28, 29, 226, 229, 231, 241, 250,256,430
USAF: T/Sgt. - George Beyer - 63
USAF: Ypsilanti, Michigan - 95
USN: Commander - J.F. Bodler - 44
Uzunoglu, Dr. Basil - 136

V

Vallee, Jacques - 298
Virginia Beach - 64
Virginia State Police - 115
Virginia - 64

W

Wagstaff, Brenda - 92
Wallasey Coastguard Station, Cheshire - 114
Walters, Valerie - 279
Ward Road, Cambridge - 31
Warminster - 21
Warnock, Richard - 302
Washington DC National Airport - 52
Washington, Elsie - 79

Washington, George - 79
Washington - 11, 36,136
Webb, Olive - 95
Wertz, Laverne - 108
West Freugh, Scotland - 94
West Virginia - 11, 17
West, Ron - 21,296,304,307
Wettstein, Edward - 76
White House - 52
White, Harry - 32
Whiting, Fred - 24
Whiting, John - 94
Whitstable, Kent - 181
Wigg, Mrs - 31
Wikipedia - 15,16
Wilcox, Toyah - 21
Wild, George - 107
Wildman, Ronald - 108
Wilkins, Dr H.P. - 71
Wills, Steve - 348,417
Wilmslow, Cheshire - 133,134
Wilson-Sharp, Kathleen - 55
Wisbech, Cambridgeshire - 96
Wisconsin - 169
Wood, Dave (ASSAP) - 336
Woodbridge Community Hall, Suffolk - 348
Woodhall Catering - 215
Worcester, Massachusetts - 34
Worrow, James - 431
Wright Field, Dayton, Ohio - 37
Wright, Dennis - 111
Wyatt, Cameron - 181
Wyken Estate - 294
Young, Jeff - 420

Z

Zamora, Lonnie - 113
Zeidman, Jennie - 173

www.ingramcontent.com/pod-product-compliance
Lightning Source LLC
Chambersburg PA
CBHW060307240426
43661CB00059B/2686